Macmillan/McGraw-Hill **READING**

McGraw Hill **Macmillan**
McGraw-Hill

Contributors

The Princeton Review, Time Magazine, Accelerated Reader

The Princeton Review is not
affiliated with Princeton
University or ETS.

Students with print disabilities may be eligible to obtain an accessible, audio version
of the pupil edition of this textbook. Please call Recording for the Blind & Dyslexic at
1-800-221-4792 for complete information.

The *McGraw·Hill* Companies

Macmillan
McGraw-Hill

Published by Macmillan/McGraw-Hill, of McGraw-Hill Education, a division of The McGraw-Hill Companies, Inc.,
Two Penn Plaza, New York, New York 10121.

Printed in the United States of America

6 7 8 9 073/043 09 08 07 06 05

Macmillan/McGraw-Hill READING

Authors

James Flood

Jan E. Hasbrouck

James V. Hoffman

Diane Lapp

Donna Lubcker

Angela Shelf Medearis

Scott Paris

Steven Stahl

Josefina Villamil Tinajero

Karen D. Wood

Macmillan
McGraw-Hill

Managing the

Computer Center

Working with Words Station

Writing Station

Reading and Listening Station

Word Box

Classroom

Social Studies Station

TEACHING TIP

MANAGEMENT
Provide children in each group with their own list of centers they will go to. Children can check off each center after finishing their work. Early finishers can read a book from the Reading Center.

Teacher Directed
Small Group Instruction

Sample Management Plan

Group 1	Group 2	Group 3	Group 4
With Teacher	Reading or Writing Workstation	Working with Words Station	Cross-Curricular or Computer Station
Reading or Writing Workstation	**With Teacher**	Cross-Curricular or Computer Station	Working with Words Station
Working with Words Station	Cross-Curricular or Computer Station	**With Teacher**	Reading or Writing Workstation
Cross-Curricular or Computer Station	Working with Words Station	Reading or Writing Workstation	**With Teacher**

Creating WORKSTATIONS

Establishing independent workstations and other independent activities is a key to helping you manage the classroom as you meet with small groups.

Reading

Set up a classroom library including the Leveled Books and other independent reading titles that have been previously read during small-group instruction. See the Theme Bibliography on pages T88–T89 for suggestions. Include titles based on discussions of students' fiction and nonfiction preferences.

- Self-Selected Reading
- Paired Reading
- Student Anthology selection from the Listening Library

Computer

Students can access the Internet to complete the Research and Inquiry activities suggested throughout the unit. Look for Internet connections in the following Research and Inquiry projects:

- Find Out More project at the end of each selection
- Cooperative Theme Project: A Book of Questions and Answers
- Cross-Curricular Activities
- Bringing Groups Together project

Writing

Focus the unit's writing projects on comparative writing. Weekly writing assignments are found at the end of each selection. The unit writing process project, Writing That Compares, can also be the focus of the Writing Station. Equip the Writing Station with the following materials:

- Samples of published comparative writing
- Comparative Writing samples, available in the **Teacher's Writing Resource Handbook**, pages 28–29

Working with Words

Selection Vocabulary
Have students create "What Word Am I?" riddles using the selection vocabulary. They may choose to give hints about the word's part of speech and number of syllables in addition to the word's meaning.

High-Frequency Words
Write these high-frequency words on a chart: *five, been, because, many, name, near.* Have students search for those words in child-appropriate magazines or newspapers, then cut and paste them into a word collage.

Cross-Curricular

STATIONS

Set up a Cross-Curricular Station to help extend selection concepts and ideas. Cross-Curricular activities can be found throughout the unit.

Science

- Cat Breeds, 22
- Tree Planting, 56
- Sharks, 84
- Echolocation, 100

Social Studies

- Where Cats Live, 34
- Map Skills, 58
- The Grand Canyon, 82
- Popular Pets, 104

Math

3 + 2

- Making a Schedule, 36
- Time Travel, 52
- Measurement, 78
- 2001 Dog Bones, 96

Art

- Cats in Art, 26
- Bats, 80

Additional Independent Activities

The following independent activities offer a means to practice and reinforce concepts and skills taught within the unit.

PUPIL EDITION: READER RESPONSE

Story Questions to monitor student comprehension of the selection. The questions are leveled, progressing from literal to critical thinking.

Story Activities related to the selection. Four activities are always provided: one writing activity, two cross-curricular activities, and a research and inquiry activity in the Find Out More project that encourages students to use the Internet for research.

LEVELED PRACTICE

Each week, Reteach, Practice, and Extend pages are offered to address the individual needs of students as they learn and review skills.

McGraw-Hill Reading

Theme Chart

MULTI-AGE Classroom

Using the same global themes at each grade level facilitates the use of materials in multi-age classrooms.

GRADE LEVEL	Experience	Connections
	Experiences can tell us about ourselves and our world.	**Making connections develops new understandings.**
Kindergarten	**My World** We learn a lot from all the things we see and do at home and in school.	**All Kinds of Friends** When we work and play together, we learn more about ourselves.
Subtheme 1	At Home	Working Together
Subtheme 2	School Days	Playing Together
1	**Day by Day** Each day brings new experiences.	**Together Is Better** We like to share ideas and experiences with others.
2	**What's New?** With each day, we learn something new.	**Just Between Us** Family and friends help us see the world in new ways.
3	**Great Adventures** Life is made up of big and small experiences.	**Nature Links** Nature can give us new ideas.
4	**Reflections** Stories let us share the experiences of others.	**Something in Common** Sharing ideas can lead to meaningful cooperation.
5	**Time of My Life** We sometimes find memorable experiences in unexpected places.	**Building Bridges** Knowing what we have in common helps us appreciate our differences.
6	**Pathways** Reflecting on life's experiences can lead to new understandings.	**A Common Thread** A look beneath the surface may uncover hidden connections.

Themes: Kindergarten – Grade 6

Six Units IN EVERY GRADE

Expression	Inquiry	Problem Solving	Making Decisions
There are many styles and forms for expressing ourselves.	By exploring and asking questions, we make discoveries.	Analyzing information can help us solve problems.	Using what we know helps us evaluate situations.
Time to Shine We can use our ideas and our imagination to do many wonderful things.	**I Wonder** We can make discoveries about the wonders of nature in our own backyard.	**Let's Work It Out** Working as part of a team can help me find a way to solve problems.	**Choices** We can make many good choices and decisions every day.
Great Ideas	In My Backyard	Try and Try Again	Good Choices
Let's Pretend	Wonders of Nature	Teamwork	Let's Decide
Stories to Tell Each one of us has a different story to tell.	**Let's Find Out!** Looking for answers is an adventure.	**Think About It!** It takes time to solve problems.	**Many Paths** Each decision opens the door to a new path.
Express Yourself We share our ideas in many ways.	**Look Around** There are surprises all around us.	**Figure It Out** We can solve problems by working together.	**Starting Now** Unexpected events can lead to new decisions.
Be Creative! We can all express ourselves in creative, wonderful ways.	**Tell Me More** Looking and listening closely will help us find out the facts.	**Think It Through** Solutions come in many shapes and sizes.	**Turning Points** We make new judgments based on our experiences.
Our Voices We can each use our talents to communicate ideas.	**Just Curious** We can find answers in surprising places.	**Make a Plan** Often we have to think carefully about a problem in order to solve it.	**Sorting It Out** We make decisions that can lead to new ideas and discoveries.
Imagine That The way we express our thoughts and feelings can take different forms.	**Investigate!** We never know where the search for answers might lead us.	**Bright Ideas** Some problems require unusual approaches.	**Crossroads** Decisions cause changes that can enrich our lives.
With Flying Colors Creative people help us see the world from different perspectives.	**Seek and Discover** To make new discoveries, we must observe and explore.	**Brainstorms** We can meet any challenge with determination and ingenuity.	**All Things Considered** Encountering new places and people can help us make decisions.

Look Around

There are surprises all around us.

Contents

written by **Barbara Abercrombie**
illustrated by **Mark Graham**

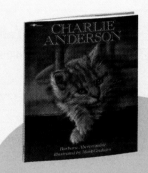

SKILLS			
Phonics	Comprehension	Vocabulary	Study Skill
• **Introduce** /ù/oo	• **Introduce** Draw Conclusions	• **Introduce** Antonyms	• Graphic Aids: Use a Map
• **Review** /ù/oo			

REALISTIC FICTION

written and illustrated by
Douglas Keister

SKILLS			
Phonics	Comprehension	Vocabulary	Study Skill
• **Introduce** Soft *c* and Soft *g*	• **Introduce** Compare and Contrast	• **Review** Antonyms	• Graphic Aids: Read a Chart
• **Review** Soft *c, g;* /ù/oo			

INFORMATIONAL STOR

SKILLS			
Phonics	**Comprehension**	**Vocabulary**	**Study Skill**
• **Introduce** /ô/a, aw, au	• **Review** Draw Conclusions	• **Review** Inflectional Endings	• Graphic Aids: Read a Map
• **Review** /ô/a, aw, au; Soft c, g; /ù/			

INFORMATIONAL STORY

SKILLS			
Phonics	**Comprehension**	**Vocabulary**	**Study Skill**
• **Introduce** Digraphs ph, tch	• **Review** Compare and Contrast	• **Review** Inflectional Endings	• Graphic Aids: Read a Map
• **Review** ph, tch; /ô/; Soft c, g			

NONFICTION

SKILLS			
Phonics	**Comprehension**	**Vocabulary**	**Study Skill**
• **Review** ph, tch; /ô/; Soft c, g; /ù/	• **Review** Compare and Contrast	• **Review** Inflectional Endings	• Graphic Aids: Use a Chart
	• **Review** Draw Conclusions	• **Review** Antonyms	

NONFICTION

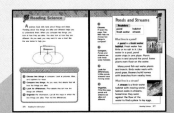

INFORMATIONAL TEXT

Unit Planner

Leveled Books

Week 1
Easy: *How Kittens Grow*
Independent: *The World of Cats*
Challenge: *Freedom Cat*

Week 2
Easy: *John Muir: Making the Mountains Glad*
Independent: *Make a Difference*
Challenge: *Save Our Park Trees*

✓ Tested Skills

Week 1

☑ **Phonics**
Introduce /ù/*oo,* 12G–12H
Review /ù/*oo,* 43E–43F
Review /ù/*oo,* 43G–43H

☑ **Comprehension**
Introduce Draw Conclusions, 43I–43J

☑ **Vocabulary**
Introduce Antonyms, 43K–43L

☑ **Study Skills**
Graphic Aids, 42

Week 2

☑ **Phonics**
Introduce Soft *c* and Soft *g*, 44G–44H
Review Soft *c* and Soft *g*, 67E–67F
Review Soft *c, g;* /ù/*oo,* 67G–67H

☑ **Comprehension**
Introduce Compare and Contrast, 67I–67J

☑ **Vocabulary**
Review Antonyms, 67K–67L

☑ **Study Skills**
Graphic Aids, 66

Minilessons

Week 1
Phonics and Decoding: /ì/*igh,* 21
Inflectional Ending -er, 23
Make Inferences, 25
Summarize, 27

Week 2
Make Inferences, 49
Context Clues, 51
Phonics and Decoding: /ər/*er,* 55
Main Idea, 61

Language Arts

Week 1
Writing: Writing That Compares, 43M
Grammar: Linking Verbs, 43O
Spelling: Words with /ù/*oo,* 43Q

Week 2
Writing: Writing That Compares, 67M
Grammar: Helping Verbs, 67O
Spelling: Words with Soft *c* and Soft *g,* 67Q

Activities

Curriculum Connections

Week 1
Read Aloud: "The Cat Came Back," 12E
Phonics Rhyme: "The Neighborhood Book," 12/13
Science: Cat Breeds, 22
Social Studies: Where Cats Live, 34
Math: Making a Schedule, 36

Week 2
Read Aloud: "Thinking Green," 44E
Phonics Rhyme: "My Gifts," 44/45
Language Arts: Picture Dictionary, 48
Math: Time Travel, 52
Science: Tree Planting, 56
Social Studies: Map Skills, 58

 CULTURAL PERSPECTIVES

Week 1
Purr-fect Pets, 30

Week 2
Breakfast Foods, 50

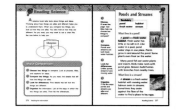

WEEK 3 The Best Vacation Ever	**WEEK 4** Zipping, Zapping, Zooming Bats	**WEEK 5** Going Batty for Bats	**WEEK 6** Review, Writing, Reading Information Assessment

Easy: This Is Your Land
Independent: *The Underground City*
Challenge: *Dear Diary*

Easy: Africa: Animals at Night
Independent: *The Mystery Mess*
Challenge: *Night Animal, Day Animal*

Self-Selected Reading of Leveled Books

Self-Selected Reading

☑ **Phonics**
Introduce /ô/a, aw, au, 68G–68H
Review /ô/a, aw, au, 91E–91F
Review /ô/aw, au, a; Soft c, g; /ù/, 91G–91H

☑ **Comprehension**
Review Draw Conclusions, 91I–91J

☑ **Vocabulary**
Review Inflectional Endings, 91K–91L

☑ **Study Skills**
Graphic Aids, 90

Phonics and Decoding: Long i, 79
Make Inferences, 81
Context Clues, 83
Main Idea, 85

☑ **Phonics**
Introduce Digraphs ph, tch, 92G–92H
Review Digraphs ph, tch, 115E–115F
Review tch; /ô/; Soft c, g, 115G–115H

☑ **Comprehension**
Review Compare and Contrast, 115I–115J

☑ **Vocabulary**
Review Inflectional Endings, 115K–115L

☑ **Study Skills**
Graphic Aids, 114

Phonics and Decoding: Long e: ee, ea, 99
Context Clues, 105
Form Generalizations, 107
Main Idea, 109

☑ **Phonics**
Review ph, tch; /ô/; Soft c, g; /ù/, 116G–116H

☑ **Comprehension**
Review Compare and Contrast, 125E–125F
Review Draw Conclusions, 125G–125H

☑ **Vocabulary**
Review Inflectional Endings, 125I–125J
Review Antonyms, 125K–125L

☑ **Study Skills**
Graphic Aids, 124

☑ **Assess Skills**
/ù/oo
Soft c and Soft g
/ô/a, aw, au
Digraphs ph, tch
Draw Conclusions
Compare and Contrast
Antonyms
Inflectional Endings

☑ **Assess Grammar and Spelling**
Review Verbs, 127K
Review Spelling Patterns, 127L

☑ **Unit Progress Assessment**

☑ **Standardized Test Preparation**

🔍 Reading Science   127A

 Writing: Writing That Compares, 91M
Grammar: Irregular Verbs, 91O
Spelling: Words with /ô/aw, au, augh, 91Q

Writing: Writing That Compares, 115M
Grammar: Irregular Verbs, 115O
Spelling: Words with Digraphs ph, tch, ch, 115Q

Writing: Writing That Compares, 125M
Grammar: Contractions, 125O
Spelling: Words from Science, 125Q

Unit Writing Process: Writing That Compares, 127E

Read Aloud: "Vacation," 68E

Phonics Rhyme: "City Zoo," 68/69

Math: Measurement, 78

Art: Bats, 80

Social Studies: The Grand Canyon, 82

Science: Sharks, 84

Around the World, 76

Read Aloud: "The Day the Sun Hid," 92E

Phonics Rhyme: "Questions About Bats," 92/93

Math: 2001 Dog Bones, 96

Language Arts: Multiple Meanings, 98

Science: Echolocation, 100

Social Studies: Popular Pets, 104

Animal Tales, 102

Read Aloud: "The Bat," 116E

Phonics Rhyme: "Good News About Bats," 116/117

 GROUP **Cooperative Theme Project Research and Inquiry:** A Book of Questions and Answers, 10J

LITERATURE

LEVELED BOOKS

📖 Easy:
- *How Kittens Grow*
- *John Muir: Making the Mountains Glad*
- *This Is Your Land*
- *Africa: Animals at Night*

📖 Independent:
- *The World of Cats*
- *Make a Difference*
- *The Underground City*
- *The Mystery Mess*

📖 Challenge:
- *Freedom Cat*
- *Save Our Park Trees*
- *Dear Diary*
- *Night Animal, Day Animal*

THEME BIG BOOK
Share *Swim for Cover!* to set the unit theme and make content-area connections.

LISTENING LIBRARY Children can listen to an audio recording of the student selections and poetry.

Macmillan/McGraw-Hill

ℹ Intervention ➡
Easy Leveled Books
Skills Intervention Guide
Phonics Intervention Guide

SKILLS

LEVELED PRACTICE

Practice: Student practice for phonics, comprehension, vocabulary and study skills; plus practice for instructional vocabulary and story comprehension. Take-Home Story included for each lesson.

Reteach: Reteaching opportunities for students who need more help with each assessed skill.

Extend: Extension activities for vocabulary, comprehension, story and study skills.

TEACHING CHARTS Instructional charts for modeling vocabulary and tested skills. Also available as **transparencies.**

WORD BUILDING MANIPULATIVE CARDS
Letter and word cards to utilize phonics and build instructional vocabulary.

LANGUAGE SUPPORT BOOK
ESL Parallel lessons and practice for students needing language support.

PHONICS/PHONEMIC AWARENESS PRACTICE BOOK
Additional practice focusing on key phonetic elements.

FLUENCY ASSESSMENT
Evaluation and practice for building reading fluency.

LANGUAGE ARTS

GRAMMAR PRACTICE BOOK
Provides practice for grammar and mechanics lessons.

SPELLING PRACTICE BOOK
Provides practice with the word list and spelling patterns. Includes home involvement activities.

DAILY LANGUAGE ACTIVITIES
Sentence activities that provide brief practice and reinforcement of grammar, mechanics, and usage skills. Available as **blackline masters and transparencies.**

WRITING PROCESS TRANSPARENCIES
Model each stage of the writing process.

HANDWRITING HANDBOOKS
For instruction and practice.

McGraw-Hill School
TECHNOLOGY

Phonics CD-ROM
Provides phonics support.

interNET CONNECTION Extend lesson activities through research and inquiry ideas. Visit **www.mhschool.com/reading.**

Vocabulary PuzzleMaker Provides practice with instructional vocabulary.

Handwriting CD-ROM Provides practice activities.

Mind Jogger Videos Review grammar and writing skills.

Resources for Meeting Individual Needs

	EASY	ON-LEVEL	CHALLENGE	LANGUAGE SUPPORT

UNIT 1

Charlie Anderson

EASY	ON-LEVEL	CHALLENGE	LANGUAGE SUPPORT
Leveled Book: *How Kittens Grow* Reteach, 127–134 **Alternate Teaching Strategies,** T64–T76 **Writing:** Picture and Caption, 43M–43N **Phonics CD-ROM** **Intervention**	**Leveled Book:** *The World of Cats* Practice, 127–134 **Alternate Teaching Strategies,** T64–T76 **Writing:** Diary Entry, 43M–43N **Phonics CD-ROM**	**Leveled Book:** *Freedom Cat* Extend, 127–134 **Writing** Write a Scene, 43M–43N **Phonics CD-ROM**	**Teaching Strategies,** 14A, 14C, 15, 18, 28, 31, 43N Language Support, 136–144 **Alternate Teaching Strategies,** T64–T76 **Writing:** Write a Biography, 43M–43N **Phonics CD-ROM**

Fernando's Gift

EASY	ON-LEVEL	CHALLENGE	LANGUAGE SUPPORT
Leveled Book: *John Muir: Making the Mountains Glad* Reteach, 135–142 **Alternate Teaching Strategies,** T64–T76 **Writing:** Collage, 67M–67N **Phonics CD-ROM** **Intervention**	**Leveled Book:** *Make a Difference* Practice, 135–142 **Alternate Teaching Strategies,** T64–T76 **Writing:** Letter, 67M–67N **Phonics CD-ROM**	**Leveled Book:** *Save Our Park Trees* Extend, 135–142 **Writing:** Journal Entry, 67M–67N **Phonics CD-ROM**	**Teaching Strategies,** 46A, 46C, 47, 55, 59, 67N Language Support, 145–153 **Alternate Teaching Strategies,** T64–T76 **Writing:** Write a Magazine Article, 67M–67N **Phonics CD-ROM**

The Best Vacation Ever

EASY	ON-LEVEL	CHALLENGE	LANGUAGE SUPPORT
Leveled Book: *This Is Your Land* Reteach, 143-150 **Alternate Teaching Strategies,** T64–T76 **Writing:** Traveling Artists, 91M–91N **Phonics CD-ROM** **Intervention**	**Leveled Book:** *The Underground City* Practice, 143–150 **Alternate Teaching Strategies,** T64–T76 **Writing:** Travel Journalists, 91M–91N **Phonics CD-ROM**	**Leveled Book:** *Dear Diary* Extend, 143–150 **Writing:** Travel Plan, 91M–91N **Phonics CD-ROM**	**Teaching Strategies,** 70A, 70C, 71, 73, 79, 81, 91N Language Support, 154–162 **Alternate Teaching Strategies,** T64–T76 **Writing:** Write a Travel Guide, 91M–91N **Phonics CD-ROM**

Zipping, Zapping, Zooming Bats

EASY	ON-LEVEL	CHALLENGE	LANGUAGE SUPPORT
Leveled Book: *Africa: Animals at Night* Reteach, 151–158 **Alternate Teaching Strategies,** T64–T76 **Writing:** Label Pictures, 115M–115N **Phonics CD-ROM** **Intervention**	**Leveled Book:** *The Mystery Mess* Practice, 151–158 **Alternate Teaching Strategies,** T64–T76 **Writing:** Compare Foods, 115M–115N **Phonics CD-ROM**	**Leveled Book:** *Night Animal, Day Animal* Extend, 151–158 **Writing:** Diary Entry, 115M–115N **Phonics CD-ROM**	**Teaching Strategies,** 94A, 94C, 95, 103, 106, 108 Language Support, 163–171 **Alternate Teaching Strategies,** T64–T76 **Writing:** Write a Report, 115M–115N **Phonics CD-ROM**

Going Batty for Bats

EASY	ON-LEVEL	CHALLENGE	LANGUAGE SUPPORT
Review Reteach, 159–166 **Alternate Teaching Strategies,** T64–T76 **Writing:** Word Web, 125M–125N **Phonics CD-ROM** **Intervention**	**Review** Practice, 159–166 **Alternate Teaching Strategies,** T64–T76 **Writing:** Postcard, 125M–125N **Phonics CD-ROM**	**Review** Extend, 159–166 **Writing:** Scrapbook, 125M–125N **Phonics CD-ROM**	**Teaching Strategies,** 118A, 118C, 119, 125N Language Support, 172–180 **Alternate Teaching Strategies,** T64–T76 **Writing:** Write a Speech, 125M–125N **Phonics CD-ROM**

INFORMAL

Informal Assessment

- Phonics, 12H, 39, 43F, 43H; 44H, 63, 67F, 67H; 68H, 87, 91F, 91H; 92H, 111, 115F, 115H; 116H, 120, 121
- Comprehension, 38, 39, 43J; 62, 63, 67J; 86, 87, 91J; 110, 111, 115J; 121, 125F, 125H
- Vocabulary, 43L, 67L, 91L, 115L, 125J, 125L

Performance Assessment

- Scoring Rubrics, 43N, 67N, 91N, 115N, 125N
- Research and Inquiry, 10J, 43D, 67D, 91D, 115D, 125D, 127
- Listening, Speaking, Viewing Activities, 12E, 12/13, 14C, 14–39, 43D, 43M–N; 44E, 44/45, 46C, 46–63, 67D, 67M–N; 68E, 68/69, 70C, 70–87, 91D, 91M–N; 92E, 92/93, 94C, 94–111, 115D, 115M–N; 116E, 116/117, 118C, 118–121, 125D, 125M–N
- Portfolio, 43N, 67N, 91N, 115N, 125N
- Writing, 43M–N, 67M–N, 91M–N, 115M–N, 125M–N, 127A–F
- Fluency, 38, 62, 86, 110, 120

Leveled Practice

Practice, Reteach, Extend

- **Phonics and Decoding**
  /ủ/oo, 127, 131, 132, 140, 148, 159
  Soft c and Soft g, 135, 139, 140, 148, 159
  /ô/a, aw, au, 143, 147, 148, 159
  Digraphs ph, tch, 151, 155, 156, 159
- **Comprehension**
  Draw Conclusions, 133, 149, 164
  Compare and Contrast, 141, 157, 163
- **Vocabulary Strategies**
  Antonyms, 134, 142, 166
  Inflectional Endings, 150, 158, 165
- **Study Skills**
  Graphic Aids, 130, 138, 146, 154, 162

FORMAL

Selection Assessments

- **Skills and Vocabulary Words**
  Charlie Anderson, 61–64
  Fernando's Gift, 65–68
  The Best Vacation Ever, 69–72
  Zipping, Zapping, Zooming Bats, 73–76
  Going Batty for Bats, 77–78

Unit 1 Tests

- **Phonics and Decoding**
  /ủ/oo
  Soft c and Soft g
  /ô/a, aw, au
  Digraphs ph, tch
- **Comprehension**
  Draw Conclusions
  Compare and Contrast
- **Vocabulary Strategies**
  Antonyms
  Inflectional Endings

Grammar and Spelling Assessment

- **Grammar**
  Verbs, 101, 107, 113, 119, 125, 127–128
- **Spelling**
  Unit 1 Assessment, 127–128

Fluency Assessment

- Fluency Passages, 42–45

Diagnostic/Placement Evaluation

- Informal Reading Inventories
- Running Record
- Phonemic Awareness Assessment
- Placement Tests

Test Preparation

- Test Power, 43, 67, 91, 115, 125
- Additional standardized test preparation materials available

Reading Test Generator

- Assessment Software

Assessment Checklist

Student .... **Grade** ....

Teacher ....

	Charlie Anderson	Fernando's Gift	The Best Vacation Ever	Zipping, Zapping, Zooming Bats	Going Batty for Bats	Assessment Summary
LISTENING/SPEAKING						
Participates in oral language experiences						
Listens and speaks to gain knowledge of culture						
Speaks appropriately to audiences for different purposes						
Communicates clearly						
READING						
Uses phonological awareness strategies, including						
• blending, segmenting, deleting, substituting sounds						
Uses a variety of word identification strategies:						
• Phonics and decoding: /u̇/oo						
• Phonics and decoding: soft c and soft g						
• Phonics and decoding: /ô/a, aw, au						
• Phonics and decoding: ph, tch						
• Antonyms						
• Inflectional Endings						
Reads with fluency and understanding						
Reads widely for different purposes in varied sources						
Develops an extensive vocabulary						
Uses a variety of strategies to comprehend selections:						
• Draw Conclusions						
• Compare and Contrast						
Responds to various texts						
Analyzes the characteristics of various types of texts						
Conducts research using various sources:						
• Graphic Aids						
Reads to increase knowledge						
WRITING						
Writes for a variety of audiences and purposes						
Composes original texts using the conventions of written language such as capitalization and penmanship						
Spells proficiently						
Composes texts applying knowledge of grammar and usage						
Uses writing processes						
Evaluates own writing and writing of others						

+ Observed   − Not Observed

Introduce the Theme

Look Around

There are surprises all around us.

DISCUSS THE THEME Write the theme statement on the board. Read it aloud to the children. Explain that there are many different surprises and new things to learn about in the world around us. Encourage children to share a time when they were surprised. Then, ask:

- What do you see when you look around your neighborhood? Are there any surprises?

- Is there anything or any place you are curious about and would like to explore?

- What are some of your favorite places to read about? Why?

SHARE A STORY Use the Big Book *Swim For Cover!* as an introduction to the unit theme. Have children discuss how

the octopus's interactions with the other fish relate to Look Around.

PREVIEW UNIT SELECTIONS Have children preview the unit by reading the selection titles, paging through the stories, and looking at the illustrations. Ask:

- How might these stories relate to the theme Look Around?

- How do these selections seem similar and how do they seem different?

- Which story are you most interested in reading, and why?

Ask children to work together in small groups to brainstorm a list of ways that the stories, poems, and the *Time for Kids* article relate to the theme Look Around. Encourage groups to compare lists and discuss.

THEME CONNECTIONS

Each of the five selections relates to the unit theme Look Around as well as to the global theme Inquiry.

Charlie Anderson A family that thinks a cat belongs to them has a big surprise.

Fernando's Gift Fernando gives a friend a special birthday.

The Best Vacation Ever A girl traveling around the country is delighted and surprised by her experiences.

Zipping, Zapping, Zooming Bats Readers will learn some truths about bats that may surprise them.

Going Batty for Bats This article gives surprising information about bats.

Research *and* Inquiry

 Theme Project: A Book of Questions and Answers Have children work in teams to brainstorm questions about things that happen in nature. They will then choose two questions and conduct research to find the answers to their questions.

Make a Resource Chart Ask children to brainstorm what they already know about their topic and list facts they need to gather to answer their questions. Then have them create a three-column chart.

In the first column instruct them to list their questions. In the second column have them list possible resources. As they conduct research they can record their findings in the third column. Remind children to take detailed notes.

A Surprising Presentation
When their research is complete, each team will decide how to present the information. Encourage children to include visual aids such as charts, diagrams, drawings, photographs, and videotape recordings.

QUESTIONS	POSSIBLE RESOURCES	ANSWERS
• Do apples fall only when they are ripe? • Do apples fall because of gravity? • Do apples fall more often at certain times?	• Science book, Internet	

See **Wrap Up the Theme,** page 126.

Research Strategies

Children will most likely be using science books. Share these tips on using different parts of a book:

• Find out how current your book is. Check the copyright date on the page after the title page.
• Scan the Table of Contents and the index for your topic.

• Check your facts by looking in other science books or by asking your science teacher.

*inter***NET** **CONNECTION** Children can learn more about using parts of a science book by visiting *www.mhschool.com/reading.*

Poetry

Read the Poem

READ ALOUD Read "River Winding" by Charlotte Zolotow aloud to children. Challenge them to answer the questions the poet asks. Afterward, ask:

- What surprises does the poem contain?
- What does the poem explore?
- What do you notice about the last word in each line of the poem?

 **Listening Library** Children can listen to an audio recording of the poem.

CHORAL READING Read the poem, "River Winding" aloud to children, modeling the rhythmic patterns for them. Then have children read the poem aloud. Ask them to reflect on the rhythm and rhyme in the poem.

Learn About Poetry

RHYTHM Review that rhythm in poetry is similar to the beat in music. It creates recognizable patterns by accenting certain words.

- Have children reread "River Winding" aloud. Afterward, ask them which words they accented and why.
- Have children discuss how the punctuation, such as commas, contributes to the rhythm of the poem.

RHYME PATTERN Explain:

- Rhyme pattern is formed by the repetition of certain sounds in certain places of a poem (at the end of a line, within the line, or on a stressed syllable).
- Rhyme pattern contributes to the rhythm of a poem. Have children identify examples of rhyming words in "River Winding." Ask them where the rhyme pattern occurs. Discuss how the rhyme pattern contributes to the overall feeling and flow of the poem.

10

MEET THE POET

ABOUT CHARLOTTE ZOLOTOW Born in 1915 in Norfolk, Virginia, Charlotte Zolotow wrote her first essay when she was in fourth grade. "My teacher, Miss Knox, read the piece aloud to the class and made me feel like a writer."

Author of dozens of books and winner of a Newbery Honor award, Zolotow believes young children have a natural kinship with poets. "Their reactions are so completely open."

Look Around

River Winding

Rain falling, what do you grow?
Snow melting, where do you go?
Wind blowing, what trees do you know?
River winding, where do you flow?

by Charlotte Zolotow

11

Poetry

PATTERNED STRUCTURES Explain that poets often repeat sounds, words, phrases, or punctuation in a poem for dramatic effect.

- Have children identify repeated sounds, words, and punctuation repeated in "River Winding."
- Discuss the patterns formed by these elements and have children identify examples.
- Select a volunteer to explain how the pattern structure affects the impact of the poem.

Write the poem on the chalkboard or chart paper. Have children use a different colored chalk or marker to circle each new pattern they discover.

Oral Response

SMALL-GROUP DISCUSSIONS Have 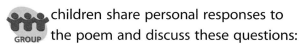 children share personal responses to the poem and discuss these questions:

- What is the writer curious about?
- How does this poem make you feel about nature?
- Does the title "River Winding" fit the poem? Why or why not?
- Look around. What are you curious about? Would you want to write about it?

Discuss how writing can help you explore a new topic of interest.

WRITE A POEM

Write a Poem Encourage children to write a poem about something in nature. They may choose to include patterned structures, as in "River Winding," or you may provide another poem as a model to follow. To begin the activity, take a nature walk with the class. Then have children discuss their observations. Help them map the discussion. Write key descriptive phrases to help them get started.

Make a Poetry Wall Invite children to illustrate their poems and hang them on a bulletin board. You may want to have children pick up items on their nature walk to create an interesting border for their display.

Concept
- Characteristics of Cats

Phonics
- Variant Vowel /u̇/ *oo*

Vocabulary
- chocolate
- clothes
- middle
- offered
- roof
- upstairs

Anthology
Charlie Anderson

Selection Summary Children will read about a cat who lives a double life: He lives with one family at night, and another one during the day.

Barbara Abercrombie
illustrated by Mark Graham

Listening Library

Rhyme applies to phonics

INSTRUCTIONAL pages 14–43

About the Author Barbara Abercrombie says, "When I was little, my favorite pastime was making up stories for my paper dolls. I had whole families of dolls— their clothes, houses, towns, pets, all the details of their lives carefully worked out."

About the Illustrator Mark Graham has illustrated several books for children, including picture books and a biography. He lives in New York with his wife and three sons. Mr. Graham often uses his family and friends as models for his illustrations.

Same Concept, Skills and Vocabulary!

Leveled Books

EASY
Lesson on pages 43A and 43D
DECODABLE

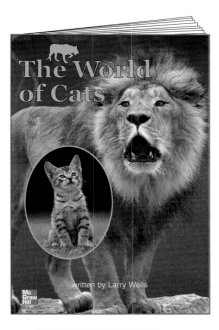

INDEPENDENT
Lesson on pages 43B and 43D

🏠 *Take-Home version available*

CHALLENGE
Lesson on pages 43C and 43D

Leveled Practice

EASY
Reteach, 127–134 Blackline masters with reteaching opportunities for each assessed skill

INDEPENDENT/ON-LEVEL
Practice, 127–134 Workbook with Take-Home stories and practice opportunities for each assessed skill and story comprehension

CHALLENGE
Extend, 127–134 Blackline masters that offer challenge activities for each assessed skill

Quizzes Prepared by **Accelerated Reader®**

WORKSTATION Activities

Social Studies ... Where Cats Live, *34*

Science .... Cat Breeds, *22*

Math .... Making a Schedule, *36*

Art .... Cats in Art, *26*

Language Arts .. Read Aloud, *12E*

Cultural Perspectives ..... Purr-fect Cats, *30*

Writing .... Write a Biography, *40*

Research and Inquiry ...... Find Out More, *41*

 Internet Activities .... www.mhschool.com/reading

Suggested
Lesson Planner

READING AND LANGUAGE ARTS	**DAY 1** Focus on Reading and Skills	**DAY 2** Read the Literature
● **Phonics Daily Routines**	Daily **Phonics** Routine: **Word Building,** 12H **Phonics** CD-ROM	Daily **Phonics** Routine: **Segmenting,** 14A **Phonics** CD-ROM
● **Phonological Awareness** ● **Phonics** /ù/oo ● **Comprehension** ● **Vocabulary** ● **Study Skills** ● **Listening, Speaking, Viewing, Representing**	**Read Aloud: Poem,** 12E "The Cat Came Back" ☑ **Develop Phonological Awareness,** 12F /ù/oo ☑ **Introduce /ù/oo,** 12G–12H **Teaching Chart 106** **Reteach, Practice, Extend,** 127 **Phonics/Phonemic Awareness Practice Book,** 91–94 **Read** **Apply /ù/oo,** 12/13 "The Neighborhood Book" ⓘ Intervention Program	**Build Background,** 14A Develop Oral Language **Vocabulary,** 14B–14C	chocolate	middle	roof	|---|---|---|	clothes	offered	upstairs	**Word Building Manipulative Cards** **Teaching Chart 107** **Reteach, Practice, Extend,** 128 **Read** **Read the Selection,** 14–39 Comprehension ☑ /ù/oo ☑ Draw Conclusions **Genre:** Realistic Fiction, 15 **Cultural Perspectives,** 30 **Writer's Craft:** Mood, 28 ⓘ Intervention Program
● **Curriculum Connections**	**Link** Language Arts, 12E	**Link** Science, 14A
● **Writing**	**Writing Prompt:** Have you ever had to share a pet or a favorite toy?	**Writing Prompt:** Write a story about two pets sharing one owner. How do the pets feel about each other? How does the owner spend time with both? **Journal Writing** Quick-Write, 39
● **Grammar**	**Introduce the Concept: Linking Verbs,** 43O Daily Language Activity: Write the correct form of the linking verb. **Grammar Practice Book,** 97	**Teach the Concept: Linking Verbs,** 43O Daily Language Activity: Write the correct form of the linking verb. **Grammar Practice Book,** 98
● **Spelling** /ù/	**Pretest: Words with /ù/oo,** 43Q **Spelling Practice Book,** 97, 98	**Teach the Pattern: Words with /ù/oo,** 43Q **Spelling Practice Book,** 99

Meeting Individual Needs

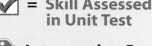 = Skill Assessed in Unit Test

 i Intervention Program Available

 Read EVERY DAY

DAY **3** *Read the Literature*	DAY **4** *Build Skills*	DAY **5** *Build Skills*
Daily **Phonics** Routine: **Letter Substitution,** 41  **Phonics** CD-ROM	Daily **Phonics** Routine: **Fluency,** 43F **Phonics** CD-ROM	Daily **Phonics** Routine: **Writing,** 43H **Phonics** CD-ROM

 **Rereading for Fluency,** 38

Story Questions and Activities, 40–41
Reteach, Practice, Extend, 129

Study Skill, 42
☑ Graphic Aids
Teaching Chart 108
Reteach, Practice, Extend, 130

Test Power, 43

 Read the Leveled Books, 43A–43D
Guided Reading
☑ /ù/ oo
☑ Draw Conclusions
☑ Instructional Vocabulary

i Intervention Program

 **Read the Leveled Books and the Self-Selected Books**

☑ Review /ù/ oo, 43E–43F
Teaching Chart 109
Reteach, Practice, Extend, 131
Language Support, 141
Phonics/Phonemic Awareness
Practice Book, 91–94

☑ Cumulative Review, 43G–43H
Teaching Chart 110
Reteach, Practice, Extend, 132
Language Support, 142
Phonics/Phonemic Awareness
Practice Book, 91–94

Minilessons, 21, 23, 25, 27

i Intervention Program

 Read Self-Selected Books

☑ Introduce Draw Conclusions, 43I–43J
Teaching Chart 111
Reteach, Practice, Extend, 133
Language Support, 143

☑ Introduce Antonyms, 43K–43L
Teaching Chart 112
Reteach, Practice, Extend, 134
Language Support, 144

Listening, Speaking, Viewing, Representing, 43N

Minilessons, 21, 23, 25, 27

i Intervention Program

Activity Science, 22

Activity Art, 26

Activity Social Studies, 34   Math, 36

Writing Prompt: Do you have or know a pet that never goes outside? Describe its day.

Writing That Compares, 43M
Prewrite, Draft

Writing Prompt: Charlie's two families are getting together for a picnic. Write an invitation.

Writing That Compares, 43M
Revise

Meeting Individual Needs for Writing, 43N

Writing Prompt: Imagine you are building a special house for a pet. What would it look like? What would be special about it?

Writing That Compares, 43M
Edit/Proofread, Publish

Review and Practice: Linking Verbs, 43P
Daily Language Activity: Write the correct form of the linking verb.

Grammar Practice Book, 99

Review and Practice: Linking Verbs, 43P
Daily Language Activity: Write the correct form of the linking verb.

Grammar Practice Book, 100

Assess and Reteach: Linking Verbs, 43P
Daily Language Activity: Write the correct form of the linking verb.

Grammar Practice Book, 101, 102

Practice and Extend: Words with /ù/oo, 43R

Spelling Practice Book, 100

Proofread and Write: Words with /ù/oo, 43R

Spelling Practice Book, 101

Assess: Words with /ù/oo, 43R

Spelling Practice Book, 102

Language Arts

Read Aloud

The Cat Came Back
an American folk song arranged by Mary Goetze

Old Farmer Johnson has

troubles all his own.

He had a little cat

that wouldn't leave his home.

He tried and he tried

to give that cat away!

He gave it to a man going far,

far away.

Refrain

But the cat came back

the very next day

The cat came back!

We thought he was a goner,

But the cat came back!

He just wouldn't stay away.

Continued on page T2

Oral Comprehension

LISTENING AND SPEAKING Sing or play a recording of this song about a cat who wouldn't leave. Ask children to think about the sequence of events as they listen. When you have finished, ask, "What were the three ways people tried to get rid of the cat?"

GENRE STUDY: FOLK SONG Discuss the nature of folk songs and some of the techniques used in *The Cat Came Back*:

• Discuss how repetition in plot makes this folk song easy to sing. Encourage children to create new verses and sing them together with the refrain.

• Have children draw a picture of Farmer John's home. Point out that folk songs usually take place in a rural setting.

• Discuss how folk songs tend to use stereotypical characters that are not fully developed. Have children talk about Farmer John from the cat's perspective. Does the cat see the farmer as good or bad?

Activity Encourage children to imagine new ways to get rid of the cat and to illustrate them. Remind children that the joke of the song is that the cat always comes back, which should be part of their illustrations.

▶ **Visual**

Develop Phonological Awareness

Blend Sounds

MATERIALS
- Phonics Picture from *Word Building Cards:* foot

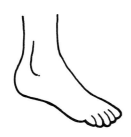

Teach Hold up the Phonics Picture for *foot.* Say the sounds for the word and then blend the sounds to say the word *foot:* /f/-/u̇/-/t/. Invite children to listen as you say some more sounds. Say, /g/-/u̇/-/d/. *If you put the sounds together, what is the word?* (good)

Practice Have children say and then blend the sounds for the following words: *cook, hood, shook, brook, wood, stood, book,* and *nook.*

Segment Sounds

MATERIALS
- Word Building Boxes from *Word Building Cards*
- counters

Teach Display a Word Building Box with four sections. Say: *book . . .* /b/-/u̇/-/k/. The word *book* has three sounds. Place a counter in the first three boxes. Have children say the sounds with you as you point to each box. Then point to the middle box and tell children the /u̇/ sound is the middle sound in the word *book.*

Practice Distribute Word Building Boxes and counters to each child. Then have them segment the following words: *look, stood, cook, wool, crook, hoof,* and *soot.* After each word, have children place a counter in the box that shows either the beginning, middle, or end sound. For example, point to the box that shows the /f/ sound in *hoof.*

Substitute Sounds

MATERIALS
- colored blocks

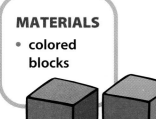

Teach Display a set of red and green colored blocks. Say: *took . . .* /t/-/u̇/-/k/ as you place three green blocks in front of you. Then say, *Now I'll change a sound in the word to make it: book . . .* /b/-/u̇/-/k/. Replace the first green block with a red block.

Practice Give each child a set of red and green blocks. Have them substitute sounds using the colored blocks as you say the following sets of words: *cook/look; lead/head; hood/wood; pick/kick; wet/pet; foot/soot.*

INFORMAL ASSESSMENT Observe children as they blend, segment, and substitute sounds. If children have difficulty, see Alternate Teaching Strategies on p. T64.

OBJECTIVES

Children will:

• identify the /ù/ sound.

• decode and read words with the /ù/ sound.

....

MATERIALS

• letter and variant vowel cards and word building boxes from the **Word Building Manipulative Cards**

• **Teaching Chart 106**

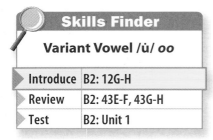

Skills Finder	
Variant Vowel /ù/ _oo_	
▶ Introduce	B2: 12G–H
▶ Review	B2: 43E–F, 43G–H
▶ Test	B2: Unit 1

SPELLING/PHONICS
CONNECTIONS
Words with /ù/: See the 5-Day Spelling Plan, pages 43Q–43R.

TEACHING TIP

PRONUNCIATION Point out that in some words, _oo_ stands for the /ü/ sound as in _boot_, and in other words it stands for the /ù/ sound as in _foot_. Explain that in the word _roof_, _oo_ can stand for /ü/ or /ù/, since this word can be pronounced both ways.

Introduce /ù/ _oo_

> **TEACH**

Identify the /ù/ Sound   Let children know that they will learn to read words in which the letters _oo_ stand for the /ù/ sound. Introduce the letter card for this sound. Display **Teaching Chart 106**.

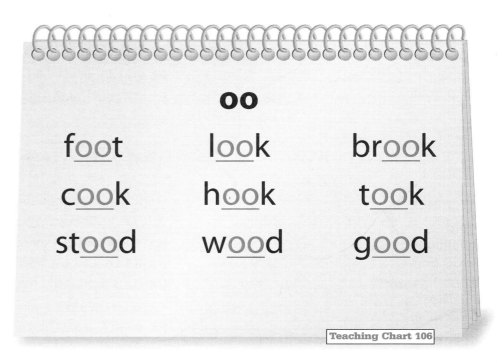

oo

foot	look	brook
cook	hook	took
stood	wood	good

Teaching Chart 106

BLENDING
Model and Guide Practice with /ù/ Words

• Write the letters _oo_ in the first column to make the word _foot_. Read the word aloud. Repeat, asking children to listen to the vowel sound, and to identify it as /ù/.

• Review that the /ù/ sound is represented by the letters _oo_.

• Reread _foot_. Ask children to follow your finger as you blend the sounds. Have them repeat the word with you.

• Write _oo_ on the line between the letters _c_ and _k_ on the chart. Blend the sounds together. Have children repeat _cook_.

• Invite children to add the letters that stand for the /ù/ sound to form the word _stood_. Have them blend the sounds together and read the word _stood_.

Use the Words in Context

• Use the words in sentences to reinforce their meanings. Example: _I stood on one foot._

Repeat the Procedure

• Repeat the procedure to model and guide practice with the rest of the words on the chart.

PRACTICE

LETTER SUBSTITUTION Blend Words with the /ù/ Sound

ONE

Use letter cards to build *cook*. Read it aloud and have children repeat it. Change the word to *look* by replacing *c* with *l*. Read aloud and have children repeat. Next have children build the following words by changing/adding the needed letters: look —> hook —> hood —> good —> stood. ▶ **Linguistic/Visual**

ASSESS/CLOSE

Spell and Write Sentences Using /ù/ Words

To assess children's ability to build and decode words with the /ù/ sound, observe them as they work on the Practice activity. Ask each child to read, spell aloud, and write a word containing the /ù/ sound. Have children then write a sentence using the word.

ADDITIONAL PHONICS RESOURCES

Phonics/Phonemic Awareness Practice Book, pages 91–94

McGraw-Hill School
TECHNOLOGY

Phonics CD-ROM activities for practice with **Decoding and Word Building**

Daily Routines

DAY 1 **Word Building** Draw a foot on the chalkboard surrounded by the letters *g, f, b, k, t,* and *d*. Inside the foot, write *oo*. Have children use the letters to make the words: *good, foot, book.*

DAY 2 **Segmenting** Write *book, took, wood, hood,* and *good* on the chalkboard. Invite volunteers to circle the letters that make the /ù/ sound. Have children read each word aloud.

DAY 3 **Letter Substitution** Using the word building boxes and the word *book* have children replace the first or last letter of the word to make new words.

DAY 4 **Fluency** Write the following words on the chalkboard: *cook, foot, good,* and *look*. Point to each word, asking children to blend the sounds silently. Ask volunteers to read each word aloud.

DAY 5 **Writing** Challenge partners to write sentences about *Charlie Anderson* using as many words with the /ù/ sound as possible.

Meeting Individual Needs for Phonics

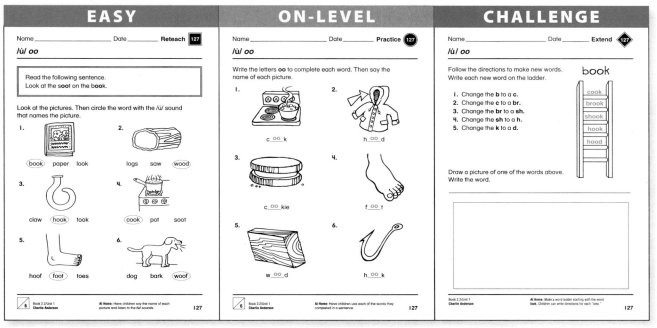

Reteach, 127   Practice, 127   Extend, 127

OBJECTIVES

Children will read and decode words with the /ů/ sound.

Apply /ů/ oo

The Neighborhood Book

I went to a shop
And bought a good book for Marie.
She took the book
And shook my hand and smiled just for me.
When she was finished reading
She took the book to Paul
Who understood and passed it on
When he had read it all.

Anthology pages 12–13

Read and Build Fluency

READ THE POEM Tell children that as you read "The Neighborhood Book" they should listen for the /ů/ sound. Model the smooth pause-and-restart between sentences. Then, for auditory modeling purposes, ask the class to echo your reading style as you reread the poem.

REREAD FOR FLUENCY Pair students of varying reading abilities and have them take turns reading the poem aloud. At the end of thirty seconds, the listener should place a self-stick note after the last word read. Then ask children to count the number of words read. Repeat the activity so each partner has the opportunity to read aloud twice.

Dictate and Spell

DICTATE WORDS Say the /ů/ word *good*. Then segment it into its three individual sounds /g/ /ů/ /d/. Say the word again and use it in a sentence, such as "I had a good time at the party." Have children repeat the word and write the letters for each sound to make the whole word. Ask them if they can find another /ů/ word in the poem to segment. (*book, took, shook, understood*) Then repeat using words other than those in the poem, such as *foot* and *hook*.

Intervention Skills Intervention Guide, for direct instruction and extra practice in /ů/ oo

Build Background

Science

Concept: Characteristics of Cats

Anthology and Leveled Books

Evaluate Prior Knowledge

CONCEPT: CHARACTERISTICS OF CATS Remind children that both people and animals can be characters in stories. Invite children to think about cats they have seen or known, and to recall how those cats behaved.

CREATE A CAT WEB Work with children as a group to record on a web their suggestions about how cats behave.

▶ **Visual/Linguistic**

like to explore places

playful

curious   CATS   independent

rub against your leg

like to chase toys

Graphic Organizer 29

WRITE CAT POEMS Invite children to

ONE   WRITING

write poems about cats. Encourage them to illustrate their poems and share them with the class.

Develop Oral Language

PANTOMIME Use pictures of cats and

ESL pictures of people interacting with cats to start a discussion about how cats behave. Ask children:

- Who knows someone with a cat? What does the cat do? Would you like to be a cat? What would you do if you were a cat?

Have children act out the different qualities they would have as cats, and imitate cat behaviors such as stretching, purring, batting at a toy, or stalking a mouse. Ask:

- How does it feel to stretch like a cat?

- Why do cats purr?

- Is it fun to hunt and chase a mouse?

▶ **Bodily/Kinesthetic**

DAILY Phonics ROUTINES

DAY 2 **Segmenting** Write *book, took, wood, hood,* and *good* on the chalkboard. Invite volunteers to circle the letters that make the /u̇/ sound. Have children read each word aloud.

LANGUAGE SUPPORT

See **Language Support Book,** pages 136–139, for teaching suggestions for Build Background.

upstairs
clothes
middle
roof
offered
chocolate

OBJECTIVES

Children will use context and structural clues to determine the meanings of vocabulary words.

Definitions

upstairs (p. 32) a place you reach after climbing up a set of steps

clothes (p. 21) items that you wear, such as a shirt and pants

middle (p. 20) halfway through a period of time, or between two things

roof (p. 29) the top covering on a house or building

offered (p. 30) gave something to someone; suggested that someone take something

chocolate (p. 30) a food made from toasted cacao beans, usually brown-colored and sweet

Story Words

These words from the selection may be unfamiliar. Before children read, have them check the meanings and pronunciations of the words in the Glossary, beginning on page 390, or in a dictionary.

• stepmother, p. 24
• prowls, p. 34

Vocabulary

Teach Vocabulary in Context

Identify Vocabulary Words

Display **Teaching Chart 107** and read the passage with children. Ask volunteers to circle each vocabulary word, and to underline other words that are clues to its meaning.

Where Is Charlie?

1. Charlie the cat climbed upstairs to Elizabeth's bedroom.
2. Elizabeth liked to dress Charlie up in doll clothes. **3.** In the middle of the night, Elizabeth woke up and listened to Charlie purr. **4.** The next day, rain beat down on the roof, but Charlie was not in the house. **5.** A woman offered Elizabeth some cookies, but she did not take any. **6.** Elizabeth liked chocolate-chip cookies, but she was too worried about Charlie to eat them.

Teaching Chart 107

Discuss Meanings

Ask questions like these to help clarify word meanings:

• What is the opposite of upstairs?

• Describe your favorite clothes.

• If you woke up in the middle of the night, would it be dark outside or light outside?

• What would happen if your house had no roof?

• If someone offered you some cookies, what would you do?

• How does chocolate taste?

Practice

Find the Word  GROUP Read **Teaching Chart 107** to children, substituting a cat sound (meow, purr) for each vocabulary word. Have children hold up the correct vocabulary card to replace the cat sound.

▶ **Linguistic/Auditory**

 **roof**   **middle** **upstairs**

Word Building Manipulative Cards

Write Captions PARTNERS WRITING Have partners draw pictures based on the vocabulary words, and create captions using them. Have children refer to the Glossary as needed. ▶ **Visual/Linguistic**

SPELLING/VOCABULARY CONNECTIONS

See Spelling Challenge Words, pages 43Q–43R.

LANGUAGE SUPPORT

See the **Language Support Book**, pages 136–139, for teaching suggestions for Vocabulary.

Assess Vocabulary

Identify Word Meaning in Context PARTNERS WRITING Ask each child to use one or more vocabulary words in a caption for an imaginary picture. After exchanging captions, have partners draw pictures that match the captions. Ask children to write and draw at least three different captions and pictures.

 **Vocabulary PuzzleMaker**

Provides vocabulary activities.

Meeting Individual Needs for Vocabulary

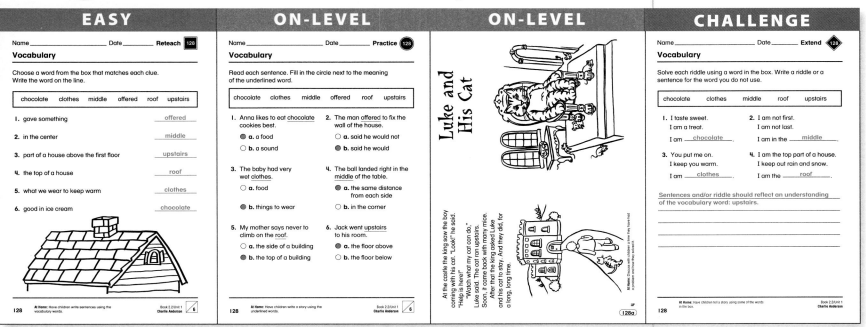

EASY	ON-LEVEL	ON-LEVEL	CHALLENGE
Reteach, 128	Practice, 128	Practice, 128a Take-Home Story	Extend, 128

14C

Comprehension

Prereading Strategies

PREVIEW AND PREDICT Have children read the title and take a **picture walk** through the story's illustrations, stopping at page 30. Discuss how pictures can give clues about characters and setting.

- What clues do the pictures give you about the cat in the story?
- What do you think the story is about?
- Will this be a realistic story or a fantasy? How can you tell? (A realistic story, because the characters and surroundings look real.) *Genre*

Have children record in a chart their predictions about what will happen in the story.

PREDICTIONS	WHAT HAPPENED
The girls have a cat that they love.	
The cat will get lost.	

SET PURPOSES Ask children what they would like to learn as they read the story. For example:

- What happens to the cat in the story?
- What are the girls in the story like?

Charlie Anderson

by Barbara Abercrombie
illustrated by Mark Graham

One cold night a cat walked out of the woods, up the steps, across the deck, and into the house where Elizabeth and Sarah lived.

1

14

Meeting Individual Needs · Grouping Suggestions for Strategic Reading

EASY

Read Together Read the story with children and then have them use the **Listening Library.** Have children use the stick puppets to role-play how the characters feel and act. Comprehension and Intervention prompts offer additional help with decoding and comprehension.

ON-LEVEL

Guided Instruction Preview the story words listed on page 14B. Then choose from the Comprehension questions as you read the story with children. Have them use puppets to monitor any difficulties in reading that they may have. You may wish to have children use the **Listening Library** when they reread the story.

CHALLENGE

Read Independently Have children set purposes before they read. Remind them that making inferences can help them to understand the plot. After reading, have children summarize the story, explaining why the cat's actions did or did not make sense based on what they know about cats.

15

Comprehension

☑ **Phonics** Apply /u̇/

STRATEGIC READING Making inferences means paying attention to how characters feel and act. This can help you to better understand what happens in a story. Let's create stick puppets of the characters (Charlie, Sarah, Elizabeth). We'll use them to act out different scenes in the story.

1 Which characters do you think will be important to the story? (Elizabeth, Sarah, and the cat) *Character, Plot*

Genre

Realistic Fiction

Explain that realistic fiction:

- tells about characters, settings, and events that could be real.
- portrays characters in a believable way.
- can take place in any current setting in the world.

Activity After children read *Charlie Anderson,* ask them to provide examples from the selection showing how the author made the story realistic. Invite volunteers to describe Elizabeth's and Sarah's feelings when Charlie is missing. Ask children how they would have felt if the same thing had happened to them.

LANGUAGE SUPPORT

Blackline masters of the stick puppets are available in the **Language Support Book**.

LANGUAGE SUPPORT 140

15

Comprehension

2 How do you think Elizabeth and Sarah feel about having the cat in their home? How does the story tell you this? (They must like having him there because they allow him to get warm, eat their food, and try out their beds.) *Make Inferences*

2 He curled up next to their fireplace to get warm. He watched the six o'clock news on TV.

16

VIEWING AND REPRESENTING

Invite children to share their thoughts and opinions about the story's illustrations. Point out that the pictures were painted in a soft, fuzzy style. Ask children why this kind of illustration works well with the story. (The pictures are like the cat—soft and furry.)

Guide children to see that illustrators try to use a style that is suited to a story's setting, plot, or ideas. Have volunteers compare and contrast the styles of illustrations in other stories they've read.

He tasted their dinner. He tried out their beds. **3**

17

Comprehension

BLENDING CONSONANTS Let's read page 17 together. What word on this page has the same beginning sounds as the word *trick*? (*tried*)

3 Where does the beginning of this story take place? (in a house in the country near the woods) Could this place exist in real life? (yes) How can you tell this is a real-life setting? *Setting*

MODEL I know this is a realistic setting because the cat and the surroundings look just as they would in real life. The things in the house, such as the fireplace and the TV, are things you find in real houses.

PREVENTION/INTERVENTION

BLENDING CONSONANTS Reread page 17 together with children, emphasizing the *tr* blend in *tried*. Write *tried* on the chalkboard and underline *tr*.

- Say the following words one at a time: *tree, them, tray, drum, trick, time, creek, true, thick,* and *truck.* Have children raise their hands when they hear a word beginning with the *tr* blend, and list those

words on their "Tr Tree."

- Have each child draw a picture of a tree, and title the drawing *Tr Tree.* Tell children to look for words in their reading that begin with the *tr* blend and to list those words on their "Tr Tree." *Graphophonic Cues*

17

Comprehension

4 Does the story give us any clues why Charlie disappears into the woods every morning? (no) Why do you think Charlie disappears into the woods every morning? *Make Predictions*

TEACHING **TIP**

MANAGEMENT While you present the Language Support on page 18, children who are already comfortable with this concept may enjoy writing a brief character sketch of Elizabeth. Encourage them to make up details of Elizabeth's life, such as her hobbies and favorite books, movies, or music.

Fluency

PARTNERS **USE AUDIO RECORDINGS** Model using the audio recording of *Charlie Anderson* as a tool for following the story.

- Play the audio recording of the story. Have children read silently along with the recording.
- Encourage children to focus on how the recorded voice pauses or stops at the appropriate punctuation marks.

4 He decided to stay, and the girls named him Charlie. Every morning Charlie disappeared into the woods again.

18

LANGUAGE SUPPORT

ESL Help children to understand the meaning of the word *disappeared*. Ask one child to leave the room so that she or he cannot be seen. Say, "Jane has *disappeared*. We cannot see her." Provide additional examples of the word *disappear* by having children hide objects around the classroom.

At night when he came home, Elizabeth brushed him clean, fed him dinner, and made a space for him at the foot of her bed.

19

Comprehension

5 Elizabeth does a lot for Charlie—she brushes him, feeds him, and makes a space for him on her bed. What does this tell us about Elizabeth? (She cares a great deal about Charlie: she seems responsible.)
Analyze Character

Let's use our Elizabeth puppet to act out the things she does to care for Charlie.

6 /ù/oo Read the sentence on page 19. Find the word that has the /ù/ sound. Now let's read the last sentence on page 18 and find the word that has the same vowel sound as *foot*. (woods) Let's sound out the word. How is the vowel sound spelled in both words? (oo)
Graphophonic Cues

Comprehension

(7) Although the story doesn't tell me exactly how Charlie feels, I can make a good guess based on what I already know. I know I feel happy and cared for when I have a place to get clean, eat dinner, and get a good night's sleep. What other clue tells us Charlie is probably happy and cared for? (He purrs.)

MODEL I also know Charlie purrs a lot, so I think that he must like living with Elizabeth and Sarah.

Using your Charlie puppet, make the sound of a happy cat. *Role-Play*

PHONICS LONG *e* Ask: Are there any words on page 21 that end with the long *e* sound? (*Baby*) *Graphophonic Cues*

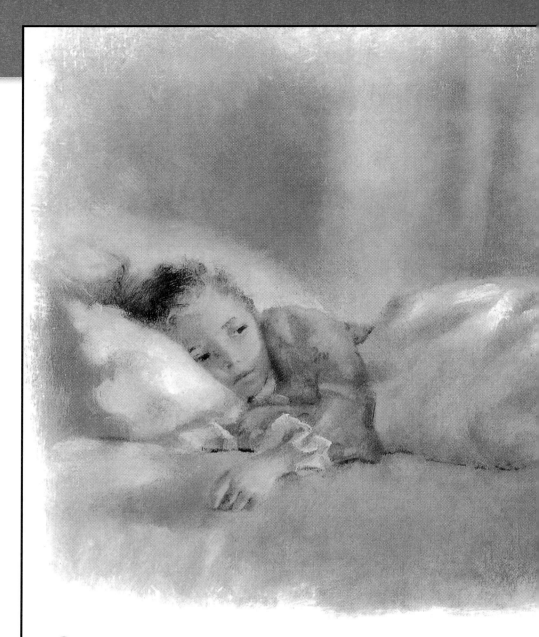

(7)   He liked Elizabeth's bed the best. Sometimes she would wake up in the middle of the night and hear him purring in the dark.

20

PREVENTION/INTERVENTION

PHONICS LONG *e* Write the word *Baby* on the chalkboard. Ask a volunteer to read the word and circle the letter that represents the long *e* sound. (*y*) Ask students to brainstorm other words that end in long *e* spelled *y*. Write the words on the chalkboard and have volunteers circle the letter in each word that represents the long *e* sound. (*y*) *Graphophonic Cues*

Sarah called him Baby and dressed him up in doll clothes.

21

Comprehension

8 Let's compare how Elizabeth acts with Charlie with how Sarah acts with Charlie. How are Sarah and Elizabeth alike? (They both love Charlie.) How are they different? (Elizabeth takes care of Charlie; Sarah plays with him.) *Compare and Contrast*

Comprehension

9 Why does the girls' mother heat Charlie's milk? What kind of a person do you think she is? (She is caring; she likes cats.) **How do you think Charlie feels now? How can you tell?** (Charlie is content. He grows fatter and fatter and purrs louder and louder.) *Make Inferences*

9 When it snowed, Elizabeth and Sarah's mother heated Charlie's milk before he left for the woods.

22

Cross Curricular: Science

CAT BREEDS Explain that there are many kinds, or breeds, of cats. Ask: What kind of cat is Charlie? Have children describe Charlie and write their responses on the chalkboard.

RESEARCH AND INQUIRY Have partners use reference books to prepare a report on some of the different breeds of cats.

• Encourage children to draw a picture of their favorite breed.

▶ **Spatial/Interpersonal**

inter**NET** CONNECTION Children can learn more about cats by visiting **www.mhschool.com/reading.**

A Siamese Cat

He grew fatter and fatter, and every day he purred
louder and louder.

23

Comprehension

10 Some words sound like what they mean (onomatopoeia). For example, the word *moo* means the sound a cow makes, and it is also an imitation of the sound a cow makes. Let's all moo like cows. What does the word *buzz* mean? (It is the sound a bee or a fly makes.) What does the word *purr* mean? (It is the sound a cat makes.) *Literary Element*

Minilesson

REVIEW/MAINTAIN

Inflectional Ending *-er*

Remind children that the comparative ending *-er* means "more than before."

- Reread the sentence on page 23. Write on the board the words *fatter* and *louder*.

- Have volunteers circle the base word in each word (*fat, loud*) and then underline the ending. (*-er*) Discuss how adding *-er* changes the meaning of the base word.

- Remind children that when adding the ending *-er* to a base word, you must often double the final consonant.

Activity Have children brainstorm a list of adjectives and add the ending *-er* to each word. Have them use both a base word and its *-er* form in sentences.

Comprehension

(11) **COMPARE AND CONTRAST** What do you think the girls' mother means when she says: "Charlie's a country cat"? How is a city cat different from a country cat? Let's have two volunteers role-play a conversation between Charlie and a city cat. Tell us how your lives are alike and different. *Compare and Contrast/Role-Play*

SELF-MONITORING STRATEGY

ASK FOR HELP If you don't understand what is happening in a story, ask someone else to describe or retell it for you.

MODEL I don't really understand why the girls go to the city on weekends. I will ask someone who is also reading the story. Talking with someone else about a story helps me to understand it better.

On weekends the girls stayed with their father and stepmother in the city. They wanted to bring Charlie with them, but their mother said he'd miss the woods. "Charlie's a country cat," she told them.

(11)

24

Comprehension

(12) Let's have volunteers role-play Elizabeth and Sarah getting ready to go to the city for the weekend. How do you feel about leaving Charlie? What would you say? *Role-Play*

Minilesson

REVIEW/MAINTAIN
Make Inferences

Remind children that good readers use story clues and what they already know to help them understand a story's characters.

• Have children read page 24 and then study the illustration on page 25. Ask them to describe the characters' body language and facial expressions. Ask: Can you tell how Elizabeth and Sarah feel about leaving Charlie?

Activity Have children look at other pictures of characters in this story or other stories they've read and make inferences about what the characters are feeling.

Comprehension

(13) Why didn't Charlie come home? Where do you think he went? What do you think he will do? *Draw Conclusions/Make Predictions*

MODEL I think Charlie was scared by the storm and is hiding in the woods. Maybe he's hiding in a hollowed-out log or in a hole. Since he spends every night at Sarah and Elizabeth's house, I predict he'll go there when the storm is over.

One stormy night Charlie didn't come home. **(13)** Elizabeth and Sarah stayed out on the deck and called and called his name. But no Charlie.

(14) Where was he? Why wouldn't he come out of the woods? Was he all right?

26

Cross Curricular: Art

CATS IN ART Explain that cats are very popular subjects for paintings, sculptures, and photographs.

- Provide examples of artwork that features cats, or provide books containing artwork that features cats.
- Guide children to see that there are many interpretations of the same subject.

- Invite children to create their own cat art. Provide modeling clay for sculptures, paints for portraits, collage materials, and so on.

▶ **Spatial/Visual**

27

Comprehension

14 Who wants to role-play Elizabeth and Sarah out on the deck? How are you feeling? What would you say? *Character/Role-Play*

Comprehension

 What can you tell about Elizabeth's feelings? Have you ever felt the way Elizabeth feels? What made you feel that way? Show how you would look if your pet were missing in a storm. *Make Inferences/Nonverbal Response*

> ### TEACHING TIP
>
> **CHARACTERIZATION** As students read, point out that one way to understand what a character is feeling is to compare that character's experiences with their own.

Writer's Craft

MOOD

Explain: Mood is the overall feeling a story creates. An author can choose vivid words to create a mood. Some stories have a humorous mood, while some stories have a sad or scary mood. Illustrators also help to create the mood of a story with light and color.

Example: Direct children's attention to anthology pages 28–29. Ask, *Does Elizabeth look worried? How can you tell? How do the pictures and words make you feel? How would you describe the mood of the story?*

PARTNERS Have partners picture walk through other stories. Encourage them to determine the mood of each story as they study the pictures and words.

LANGUAGE SUPPORT

ESL Help children understand the meaning of the word *rattling,* found on page 29. Invite children to shake a jar filled with paper clips. Ask the class to describe what they hear; explain that this is a rattling sound. Have students describe how wind could make a window rattle. Say:

When you shake the jar, it rattles. What would the wind do to make a window rattle? *(shake it)* Ask children to name some other things that make a rattling sound. *(stones in a sand pail, a pencil rolling across the floor)* If possible, demonstrate some of these rattling sounds.

All night long Elizabeth listened to the rain beating
n the roof and the wind rattling the windows. Was he
old? Was he hurt? Where was Charlie?

29

Comprehension

16 Why do you think Elizabeth is awake at night listening to the rain and the wind? (She's worried about Charlie.) What conclusions can you draw from the questions she asks? (She's afraid Charlie is out in the storm and may be hurt or lost.) *Draw Conclusions*

INFLECTIONAL ENDING-*ed*
Have children read the fifth word on page 29. (listened) What ending does the word have? (-ed) What does this ending mean? (It shows that the action happened in the past.)

NFLECTIONAL ENDING-*ed*
Write *listened* on the chalkboard. Cover he ending -*ed* and have children sound out the base word *listen*. Have a volunteer draw a line between the base word and the ending and underline -*ed*. Have children sound out the word *listened*.

• Ask children to describe when the action is taking place. Guide children to see that ending -*ed* indicates "in the past."

• Have children look back through the story for other verbs with the ending -*ed*. Ask them to write the words and underline -*ed*.

• Have children use the words they found in new sentences.
Semantic Cues

Comprehension

17 If you were Sarah or Elizabeth, how might you get others to help you find Charlie? Let's brainstorm things they could do and write them on the chalkboard. (post missing cat posters; ask others if they've seen him.) *Plot*

In the morning Elizabeth and Sarah looked for him. They asked the lady down the road if she'd seen their **17** cat. She said no, and offered them cookies. But they were too worried to eat anything, even her chocolate-chip cookies.

30

CULTURAL PERSPECTIVES

PURR-FECT PETS The earliest records of cats as pets come from ancient Egypt. Early Egyptians treated cats with great respect. Cats were often featured in Egyptian works of art.

RESEARCH AND INQUIRY Have children research the importance of cats in ancient Egypt. Have groups create posters based on their research.
▶ **Visual/Interpersonal**

Cats in Ancient Egypt

- Ancient Egyptians may have been the first people to have cats as pets.

- Cats killed mice and snakes, so they helped farmers.

- People made paintings and statues to honor cats. This statue of a cat was made more than 2,000 years ago.

 They went to the new house on the other side of the woods. "Have you seen our cat?" they asked. "His name is Charlie. He's very fat and has gray striped fur."

31

Comprehension

18 Who would like to be Sarah? What will you ask or say to others in order to get their help in finding Charlie? Think of the important questions you need to ask and facts you need to share. Remember how the girls are feeling. *Character/Role Play*

19 **Phonics** /ů/ Read the last word in the first sentence on page 31. (*woods*) What vowel sound do you hear? Let's read page 30 again and find the words with the same vowel sound as woods. (*looked, cookies*) Who would like to slowly sound out each word? *Graphophonic Cues*

LANGUAGE SUPPORT

ESL Help children understand the meaning of the word *striped,* found on page 31. On the chalkboard, sketch a cat or other animal whose coat could be striped. Ask a volunteer to draw stripes on the animal. Explain that now, the animal is *striped*. Show photographs of other things that are striped, such as candy canes and zebras. Explain to children that stripes are like lines. Have them draw outlines of shapes, such as circles, squares, and triangles. Now tell them to make the shapes striped by adding lines.

Comprehension

20 Without using words, act out how the girls may have reacted when they recognized Charlie coming down the stairs of their neighbors' house. *Character, Plot/Pantomime*

COMPOUND WORDS Read the second word in the last sentence on page 32. (*upstairs*) Slowly sound out the word. What two smaller words make up the word? (*up, stairs*) What is this kind of word called? (compound word)

"We have a cat with gray striped fur," said the man. "But his name's not Charlie, it's Anderson. He's upstairs, asleep on our bed."

32

PREVENTION/INTERVENTION

COMPOUND WORDS Review with children that a compound word is made up of two smaller words. Write the word *upstairs* on the chalkboard. Invite a volunteer to draw a line separating the two small words and to say each word. Explain that knowing the meaning of the smaller words can help them to understand the meaning of the whole word. Repeat this process with the compound words *weekend* and *stepmother*. *Semantic Cues*

They heard a meow, and down the stairs came a very fat cat with gray striped fur. "Charlie!" Sarah and Elizabeth cried.

"No, that's Anderson," said the woman. "We've had him for seven years. Right, Anderson?" **20**

He looked at her and began to purr. **21**

33

Comprehension

21 Are you also surprised to see Charlie? Do you need to draw a different conclusion about why Charlie didn't come back to Elizabeth and Sarah's house? *Critical Thinking: Revise Conclusions*

MODEL I'm surprised to see Charlie because I thought he was lost or hiding in the woods. Now I must conclude that Charlie has another home.

Comprehension

22 How do you think the man and woman felt when Charlie and the girls recognized one another? How would you feel if you had a pet for seven years, and then found out that your pet had another family, too? *Make Inferences*

22 "But it's *Charlie*," Sarah said.

He looked at her and purred louder.

"Is he ever here at night?" Elizabeth asked.

"Anderson is a hunter," said the man. "He prowls the woods at night."

34

Activity

Cross Curricular: Social Studies

WHERE CATS LIVE Display a map of the world and discuss different types of wild cats and where they live. List the names of the cats on the chalkboard.

RESEARCH AND INQUIRY Have partners research three kinds of wild cats and the places they live.

- Have partners draw and label their own world maps to show where the wild cats live.
  ▶**Interpersonal/Spatial**

"Charlie sleeps in my bed at night," Elizabeth said. He leaves for the woods after breakfast."

"Anderson comes home at breakfast time," said the woman. "He leaves right after dinner." They all looked at the cat. He sat at their feet, very happy and very fat. **23**

They call him Charlie Anderson now. **24**

35

Comprehension

23 Was the prediction you made about why Charlie disappeared into the woods every morning correct? *Confirm or Revise Predictions*

24 Why do you think Charlie is so happy and fat? (He has two warm places to stay day and night, and two families who feed him and care for him.) Why do they now call him "Charlie Anderson"? (He belongs to both families.) *Draw Conclusions*

 CONTEXT CLUES Who can tell me what the word *prowls* on page 34 means?

 PREVENTION/INTERVENTION

CONTEXT CLUES Point out to children that when they come across an unfamiliar word in their reading, they can often figure out its meaning by using other words nearby as clues. On the chalkboard, write: "I put galoshes over my shoes before I went out in the rain." Ask children to figure out the meaning of *galoshes* by using nearby words as clues. Ask children to use this strategy to find out the meaning of the word *prowls* on page 34. Explain that they can also use their knowledge of cats to help them. Have children list clues they could use to guess the meaning of the word *prowls*. *Semantic Cues*

Comprehension

25 Charlie purrs when Elizabeth asks him, "Who do you love best, Charlie Anderson?" What do you think Elizabeth believes Charlie is saying? (that he loves her best.) *Character/Make Inferences*

36

Activity

Cross Curricular: Math

MAKING A SCHEDULE Discuss with children the importance of having a schedule.

Discuss how the characters in *Charlie Anderson* have different schedules.

- Help children staple together seven sheets of paper, one sheet of paper for each day of the week.

- Invite children to make a schedule for the upcoming week. Include a list of activities to be accomplished, and the time of day each takes place.

▶ **Logical/Spatial**

• SATURDAY•

8:30 - Eat Breakfast
9:00 - Practice Piano
10:00 - Go to soccer game
12:00 - Eat lunch
12:30 - Help with chores
1:30 - Watch a video

Sometimes, in bed at night, Elizabeth asks him, "Who do you love best, Charlie Anderson?" And she can hear him purring in the dark.

37

Comprehension

 PHONICS /ü/ Ask students to identify the words on page 37 that contain the /ü/ sound. *(who, do) Graphophonic Cues*

PREVENTION/INTERVENTION

PHONICS /ü/ Write *who* and *do* on the chalkboard. Ask students which letter in these words represent the sound /ü/. (*o*) Ask students if any other letter combinations can stand for the sound. (*oo, ue, ew*) Brainstorm with students examples of words with the various spellings of /ü/. Have students call out the letters in each word that represent the /ü/ sound. *Graphophonic Cues*

Comprehension

26 Why is Charlie Anderson a lucky cat?
(He has two families who love him.)
Character, Plot

Retell the Story

Ask volunteers to tell the important events of the story. Children may use their stick puppets to act out the story's events as they retell them. Then have partners write one or two sentences that summarize the story. Have them focus on the main characters, their problem, and how it is solved. *Summarize/Story Props*

STUDENT SELF-ASSESSMENT

Have children ask themselves the following questions to assess how they are reading:

- How does remembering all the events in a story help me to understand it?

- How does understanding the characters and settings help me to understand the plot of the story?

TRANSFERRING THE STRATEGIES

- How can I use these strategies to help me read other stories?

Just like Elizabeth and Sarah, Charlie has two houses, two beds, two families who love him.

He's a lucky cat.

26

38

REREADING FOR *Fluency*

 Have children choose a favorite section of the story to read to a partner. Encourage them to read with feeling and expression.

READING RATE When you evaluate reading rate, have children read aloud from the story for one minute. Place a stick-on note after the last word read. Count words read. To evaluate

children's performance, see the Running Record in the **Fluency Assessment** book.

ℹ Intervention For leveled fluency passages, lessons, and norm charts, see **Skills Intervention Guide**, Part 5, Fluency.

READ TOGETHER

MEET
Barbara Abercrombie

Barbara Abercrombie writes books for children and adults. She has always enjoyed telling stories. She says, "When I was a little girl, my favorite pastime was making up stories for paper dolls." She likes to act, but writing is most important to her. "I like writing for both children and adults. I find that the stories all come from the same place—trying to make sense of life," she says.

MEET
Mark Graham

Mark Graham was born in Salt Lake City, Utah. He went to New York when he was young to study art. Many people across the United States have seen his paintings in art shows. He has also illustrated several books for children. They include picture books and a biography. When he paints, he tries to use light to make his pictures more interesting. He often uses his three sons as models for his pictures.

39

LITERARY RESPONSE

QUICK-WRITE Invite children to use their journals to record their thoughts about the story. They may wish to draw pictures of their favorite scenes.

ORAL RESPONSE Have children discuss these questions:

• Would you ever share a cat with another family?

• Do you think Charlie would want to give up one of his families?

• What would you say to someone who had lost his or her cat?

• What would you like to see happen next in the story?

Comprehension

Return to Predictions and Purposes

Review with children their story predictions and reasons for reading the story. Were their predictions correct? Did they find out what they wanted to know?

PREDICTIONS	WHAT HAPPENED
The girls have a cat that they love.	The girls have a cat that they love, named Charlie.
The cat will get lost.	Charlie also lives with another family.

INFORMAL ASSESSMENT

HOW TO ASSESS

 **Phonics** /u̇/ Ask: What words in the story have the same vowel sound that you hear in the word *woods*? (cookies, roof, foot)

MAKE INFERENCES

• Have children make inferences about Elizabeth, Sarah, and Charlie from their actions.

• Ask how the discovery of Charlie's other family affected the girls.

FOLLOW UP

Phonics /u̇/ Say the following words and have children raise their hands when they hear the /u̇/ sound: *want, shoe, woods, went, raft, good, fat, feet, foot.*

MAKE INFERENCES

Children who are having difficulty making inferences can work with a partner to brainstorm words that describe the characters.

Story Questions

Help children to read the questions on page 40. Have children write or discuss answers.

Answers:

1. He disappears into the woods. *Literal/Plot*

2. He stays with another family during the day. *Literal/Sequence of Events*

3. She is hoping that he loves her best. *Inferential/Make Inferences*

4. Two girls find that their cat has two families, just like they do. *Critical/Summarize*

5. Charlie and Robbie both like people, and both like their families. They are different because Robbie lives in a cage, and Charlie can walk around wherever he wants. Also, Robbie has just one family, while Charlie has two. *Critical/Reading Across Texts*

Write a Biography For a full writing process lesson related to this topic, see the lesson on writing that compares pages 43M–43N.

Story Questions & Activities

READ TOGETHER

1. What does Charlie do every morning?

2. What do the girls find out about Charlie at the end of the story?

3. Why does Elizabeth ask Charlie whom he loves best?

4. What is this story mostly about?

5. Compare Robbie the Rabbit in "Ann's First Day" to Charlie Anderson. How are these two animals alike? How are they different?

Write a Biography

Elizabeth and Sarah's mother says that Charlie is a "country cat" and wouldn't like the city. Write a biography about Charlie Anderson's life. Explain where he stays at night and where he goes during the day.

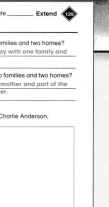

Meeting Individual Needs

EASY	ON-LEVEL	CHALLENGE
Name_____ Date_____ **Reteach** 129	Name_____ Date_____ **Practice** 129	Name_____ Date_____ **Extend** 129
Story Comprehension	**Story Comprehension**	**Story Comprehension**
The following pictures describe events that occurred in "Charlie Anderson." Write a sentence to describe each one. Answers may vary.	Think about the story "Charlie Anderson." Put an **X** next to each sentence that tells about something you found out in this story.	How can Charlie Anderson have two families and two homes? Charlie Anderson spends half the day with one family and half the day with the other family.
1. Charlie sleeps on Elizabeth's bed.	1. X Charlie is a cat.	How can Sarah and Elizabeth have two families and two homes? They live part of the week with their mother and part of the week with their father and stepmother.
2. Charlie goes out each day.	2. X Sarah dresses Charlie in doll clothes.	
	3. ___ Charlie always sleeps in the woods.	Draw a picture of everyone who loves Charlie Anderson.
3. Charlie did not come home.	4. ___ Elizabeth runs away with Charlie.	
	5. X Charlie has two homes.	
	6. X Sarah and Elizabeth are sisters.	
4. The girls find Charlie.	7. ___ The girls take Charlie to visit their father.	
	8. ___ Mother helps the girls look for Charlie.	
	9. X Charlie's other name is Anderson.	
	10. X Charlie is loved by two families.	The picture might include Sarah, Elizabeth, their mother, and the man and woman who live in the new house.
Book 2.2/Unit 1 Charlie Anderson 4 **At Home:** Have children tell about one more event in the story, such as the rain storm. 129	Book 2.2/Unit 1 Charlie Anderson 10 **At Home:** Have children tell about something that happened in "Charlie Anderson." 129	Book 2.2/Unit 1 Charlie Anderson **At Home:** Invite children to draw a picture and write about some people in their neighborhood. 129
Reteach, 129	**Practice, 129**	**Extend, 129**

Time to Share

Charlie's two families decided to share his time. Make a schedule for Charlie. What time will he wake up in the morning? What time will go to his other house? Does he spend the same number of hours at both houses? Tell what he does and where he is each hour of one whole day.

Make a List

Sarah and Elizabeth's mother says that Charlie would miss the woods if he went to the city. Why do you think a cat might like the woods? Make a list of reasons.

Find Out More

Charlie Anderson has two names. Find out what makes your name special. Is it a kind of flower or a month of the year? Were you named after someone in your family? Can you think of a famous person who has the same name as you?

41

Story Activities

Time to Share

Materials: paper, felt-tipped markers

ONE Have children create a schedule for Charlie, including tasks and activities that a cat might have such as: *10:00 A.M.—Catch a mouse. 11:00 A.M.—Play with butterflies.* Invite children to illustrate Charlie's schedule.

Make a List

Materials: paper, felt-tipped markers

GROUP Provide children with pictures of forests and wooded places. Encourage students to think about and list the kinds of things that might appeal to a cat in the woods.

Find Out More

RESEARCH AND INQUIRY Tell students that many names have other meanings: for example, the name *Charlie* means "strong." Ask students to research the meaning of their names.

interNET CONNECTION Go to *www.mhschool.com/reading* for more information on this topic.

FORMAL ASSESSMENT

After page 41, see the Selection Assessment.

DAY 3 **Letter Substitution**
Write the word *book* on the chalkboard. Have children replace the first or last letter of the word with letter cards to make new words.

Study Skills

GRAPHIC AIDS

OBJECTIVES Children will use a map to find routes.

PREPARE Remind children that a map can help them find the way to get somewhere.

TEACH Display **Teaching Chart 108**. Tell children that a map shows a picture of a large area of land. Maps have information that helps you choose your route (a way to get somewhere) such as roads and paths.

PRACTICE Have children use the map to answer questions **1–5**. Review the following answers with them:
1. Charlie's route; **2.** Oak Road; **3.** boat house; **4.** Spring Street; **5.** Answers will vary. Possible answer: Oak Road to Spring Street

ASSESS/CLOSE Have partners write directions for going from the girls' house to the picnic area, without going through the woods.

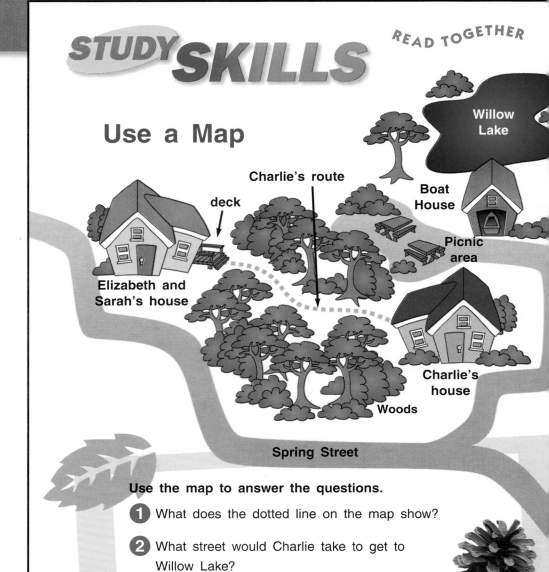

READ TOGETHER

STUDY SKILLS

Use a Map

Willow Lake

Charlie's route

deck

Boat House

Picnic area

Elizabeth and Sarah's house

Charlie's house

Woods

Spring Street

Use the map to answer the questions.

1 What does the dotted line on the map show?

2 What street would Charlie take to get to Willow Lake?

3 What building is next to the picnic area?

4 What street passes by Elizabeth and Sarah's house?

5 What other way could Charlie go to get from his house to Sarah and Elizabeth's?

Meeting Individual Needs

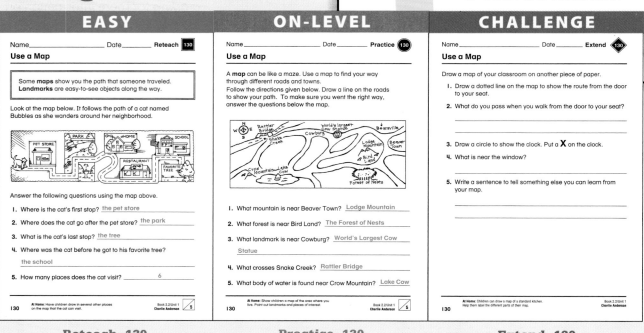

Reteach, 130

Practice, 130

Extend, 130

TEST POWER

Reading the story carefully will make the questions easier to answer.

DIRECTIONS:

Read the story. Then read each question about the story.

SAMPLE

The Cloudy Day

"Look," said Andy. "It's cloudy outside."

Pam came to the window. Andy pointed at the clouds. The clouds came and covered up the sun. Soon, it was dark outside. The wind began to blow.

"I think it's going to rain," said Pam. Andy remembered what his mother told him about rain. She said that it was good for the plants. Plants need water to grow.

"That's fine with me," Andy said. He closed all of the windows and doors in the house. Then, he went to the closet and took out a game.

1 What does Andy do when he thinks it will rain?
- ○ Gets upset
- ○ Takes a nap
- ● Finds something to do inside
- ○ Puts on his raincoat

2 What does Andy remember about the rain?
- ● That plants need water to grow
- ○ That the cellar will get wet
- ○ That it makes the day longer
- ○ That it rained the week before

43

Test Power

THE PRINCETON REVIEW

Read the Page

Explain to children that you will be reading this story as a group. You will read the story, and they will follow along in their books.

Request that children put pens, pencils, and markers away, since they will not be writing in their books.

Discuss the Questions

QUESTION 1: Instruct children to look back to the passage and find some description of what Andy does when it rains. In the last two lines, he closes the windows and takes out a game. The most reasonable inference is that he finds something to do inside.

QUESTION 2: Remind children to reread the lines that discuss what Andy remembers. The answer can be found in the ninth and tenth sentences.

Leveled Books

How Kittens Grow

written by Larry Wells
illustrated by Kristen Goeters

EASY

How Kittens Grow

☑  **Phonics** Variant Vowel /ů/ *oo*

☑ **Instructional Vocabulary**
chocolate, clothes, middle, offered, roof, upstairs

Answers to Story Questions
1. 2 weeks
2. Because they are babies, because they were just born, etc.
3. Kittens grow faster because they try to walk when they are three weeks old, because they eat real food when they are eight weeks old, etc.
4. Kittens change a lot in the first 8 weeks.
5. Answers will vary.

The Story Questions and Activity below appear in the Easy Book.

Story Questions and Writing Activity
1. How old are kittens when their ears stand up?
2. Different kittens in the same litter may be different sizes. But they are all small. Why are they all small?
3. Who do you think grows up faster, children or kittens? Why do you think so?
4. What is the main idea of this book?
5. What do you think Charlie Anderson looked like when he was one week old?

Kitten Calendar
Draw a calendar like the one in the book. Circle three days in a kitten's first eight weeks. Write about what is happening to the kitten on each of those three days.

from How Kittens Grow

Guided Reading

PREVIEW AND PREDICT Talk with children about the illustrations through page 5 of the story. As they take the **picture walk**, have children predict what the story will be about. Chart their ideas.

SET PURPOSES Have children write down why they want to read *How Kittens Grow*. For example: How do I care for a kitten?

READ THE BOOK Use questions like the following to guide children's reading or to ask after they have read the story independently.

Page 3: What are kittens like when they are just born? (cannot see, hear, walk, play, have no teeth) What does this tell you about a kitten's needs? *Draw Conclusions*

Page 4: Find the word *chocolate*. What color is the fur of a kitten whose coat is the color of a chocolate bar? Try to use *chocolate* in a sentence. *Instructional Vocabulary*

Page 11: What kinds of things can kittens do by the time they are three weeks old? Do you think kittens at this age still depend on their mothers? *Draw Conclusions*

Page 14: Find the word *good*. What sound do the letters *oo* make in the word *good*? (/ů/) What other words can you think of that use the letters *oo* to make the /ů/ sound? (*wood, hood, look, book*) *Phonics and Decoding*

RETURN TO PREDICTIONS AND PURPOSES Discuss children's predictions. Ask which were close to the story and why. Have children review their purposes for reading. Did they find out what they wanted to know?

LITERARY RESPONSE Discuss these questions:

- Did this story help you understand what it's like to take care of a baby animal?
- What characteristics do you think young animals share?

Also see the story questions and activity in *How Kittens Grow*.

Phonics **CD-ROM** See the Phonics CD-ROM for practice using words with the /ů/ sound.

Leveled Books

INDEPENDENT

The World of Cats

☑ Variant Vowel /ů/ *oo*

☑ Instructional Vocabulary:
chocolate, clothes, middle, offered, roof, upstairs

Guided Reading

PREVIEW AND PREDICT Discuss each illustration through page 7. As you take the **picture walk**, have children predict what the story will be about. Chart their ideas.

SET PURPOSES Have children write several sentences about why they want to read *The World of Cats*. Children may want to know more about cats in general or may seek information about a specific kind of cat.

READ THE BOOK Use questions like the following to guide children's reading or to ask after they have read the story independently.

Page 6: Find the word *black-footed*. What sound do the letters *oo* make in the word *black-footed*? (ů) Can you think of other words that have the /ů/ spelled *oo*? (*look, took, stood*) *Phonics and Decoding*

Page 6: Do you think sand cats and black-footed cats would make good pets? (No, they are accustomed to living and hunting in the wild.) *Draw Conclusions*

Page 7: Find the word *middle-sized*. Where are you standing if you are in the *middle* of the room? *Instructional Vocabulary*

RETURN TO PREDICTIONS AND PURPOSES Review children's predictions and purposes for reading.

LITERARY RESPONSE Discuss these questions:

- How are wild cats different from house-cats?

- Do you think it's a good idea to put wild animals in zoos? Why or why not?

Also see the story questions and activity in *The World of Cats*.

Phonics CD-ROM See the Phonics CD-Rom for practice using words with the /ů/ sound.

Answers to Story Questions
1. The tiger
2. Because it is too big and it is wild.
3. It lives in the desert, and the desert is covered with sand.
4. There are a lot of different kinds of cats.
5. Answers will vary.

The Story Questions and Activity below appear in the Independent Book.

Story Questions and Writing Activity

1. What is the largest cat in the world?
2. Why would a lion make a bad pet?
3. Reread page 5. How do you think the sand cat got its name?
4. What is the main idea of this book?
5. Does Charlie Anderson remind you of any of the cats you read about in this book? In what way?

Chart the Cats

Look at the chart on page 16. Then make a new chart. Put each group of cats from smallest to biggest.

from The World of Cats

43B

Leveled Books

CHALLENGE

Freedom Cat

☑  **Variant Vowel /ù/ oo**

☑ **Instructional Vocabulary**
chocolate, clothes, middle, offered, roof, upstairs

written by H. H. Cardigan
illustrated by Philip Smith

Guided Reading

PREVIEW AND PREDICT Discuss each illustration up through page 7 of the story. As you take the **picture walk**, have children predict what the story is about. Chart children's ideas.

SET PURPOSES Have children write about why they want to read *Freedom Cat*. For example, children may want to learn more about Thomas Jefferson, the Declaration of Independence, or simply more about Thomas Jefferson's cat.

READ THE BOOK Use questions like the following to guide children's reading or to ask after they have read the story independently.

Page 4: How do you think Thomas Jefferson feels about his cat? How can you tell? *Draw Conclusions*

Page 5: Find the word *upstairs*. Do you have to go upstairs to reach the second floor of a building? (Yes) *Instructional Vocabulary*

Page 10: Find the word *look*. What sound do the letters *oo* make in the word *look*? (/ù/) Can you think of other words that use the letters *oo* to make the /ù/ sound?

(good, cook, foot) Phonics and Decoding

Page 13: What happened after all the men agreed about the letter? (Some had further questions.) What does this tell you about people and their opinions? (People are different with varied opinions.) *Draw Conclusions*

RETURN TO PREDICTIONS AND PURPOSES Review children's predictions and purposes for reading.

LITERARY RESPONSE Discuss these questions:

• Do you think Thomas Jefferson's cat understood what was going on?

• Why do you think some people like to have animals with them when they are working on something hard to do?

Also see the story questions and activity in *Freedom Cat*.

 CD-ROM See the Phonics CD-ROM for practice using words with the /ù/ sound.

Answers to Story Questions

1. July, 1776
2. Because the men signed the letter.
3. The part about the letter to the King.
4. A cat keeps his master, Thomas Jefferson, company while the man writes a letter to the king about freedom.
5. They both enjoy their freedom; neither wants to live in a city.

The Story Questions and Activity below appear in the Challenge Book.

Story Questions and Writing Activity

1. This story happens in a famous month and year. What month and year is it?
2. Why was Mr. Jeff so happy at the end of the story?
3. Some of this story is made up, but most of it is true. What part do you think is real?
4. What is this story mostly about?
5. How are Charlie Anderson and Freedom alike?

Fourth of July

How many years ago was the July 4th in this story? Write about what your family and friends do on the Fourth of July.

from *Freedom Cat*

Bringing Groups Together

Anthology and Leveled Books

 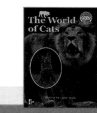 

Connecting Texts

CAT CHARTS
Write the story titles on a chart. Discuss with children the different kinds of cats and their behavior traits highlighted in each book. Call on volunteers from each reading level and write their contributions on the chart.

Use the chart to talk about all kinds of cats.

Charlie Anderson	How Kittens Grow	The World of Cats	Freedom Cat
• He is a domestic cat. • He sometimes hunts at night; sometimes during day.	• They are domestic cats. • They depend on mother when very young. • They learn to play, run, wash themselves, eat with their teeth as they grow.	• There are small house cats that live with people. • There are middle-sized wildcats that hunt. • There are big cats like lions, tigers and leopards that live in the wild.	• He is a domestic cat. • He keeps his companion company. • He looks to his companion for care.

Viewing/Representing

GROUP PRESENTATIONS Divide the class into four groups, one for each of the books read in the lesson. Have each group draw pictures of one or several of the cats featured in the story assigned. Then have each group share its drawings with the class.

AUDIENCE RESPONSE
Ask children to look carefully at the drawings presented by each group and to ask whatever questions they might have.

Research and Inquiry

MORE ABOUT CATS Have children ask themselves what else they might want to learn about cats. Then invite them to:

• look at classroom and library books that provide information about all kinds of cats.

• ask cat owners questions about their pets.

• visit a museum with exhibits of different kinds of wildcats.

 Go to **www.mhschool.com/reading** for more information or activities focusing on cats.

OBJECTIVES

Children will:

• identify /ù/ *oo*.

• decode and read words with /ù/ *oo*.

MATERIALS

• **Teaching Chart 109**

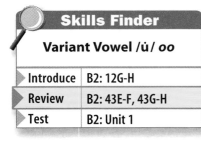

Skills Finder

Variant Vowel /ù/ *oo*

Introduce	B2: 12G-H
Review	B2: 43E-F, 43G-H
Test	B2: Unit 1

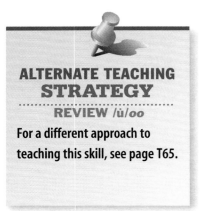

**ALTERNATE TEACHING
STRATEGY**

REVIEW /ù/*oo*

For a different approach to teaching this skill, see page T65.

TEACHING TIP

PRONUNCIATION

Remind children that words with the letters *oo* do not always have the /ù/ sound. In words such as *food* and *pool*, the letters *oo* stand for the /ü/ sound.

Review /ù/ *oo*

PREPARE

Listen for/ù/ Read the following sentence aloud and have children raise their hands whenever they hear a word with the /ù/ sound.

• I am <u>looking</u> for some <u>good</u> <u>cookies</u>.

TEACH

**Review Letters *oo*
as the Symbol
for /ù/**

• Tell children they will review the letters *oo* and the sound they make.

• Write oo on the chalkboard and have children say the /ù/ sound.

Teaching Chart 109

**BLENDING
Model and Guide
Practice with /ù/
Words**

• Display **Teaching Chart 109**. Write the letters *oo* in the first column to make the word *book* and read the word aloud.

• Have children add letters in the next example to create a word with the /ù/ sound.

**Use the Words in
Context**

• Use the words in sentences to reinforce their meanings. Example: *I read a book in the library.*

**Repeat the
Procedure**

• Have children fill in the rest of the blanks to create /ù/ words. Have them read aloud the words they form.

PRACTICE

DISCRIMINATING
Distinguish Between /ů/ and /ü/ Words

Have children brainstorm a list of words in which *oo* stands for the /ů/ sound. Have each child choose a word and read it aloud. Then write the following words on index cards: *pool, hood, good, root, book, cook, moon, took, fool, foot, look, hook, food, cookies, woods, stood*. As you hold the index cards up, have children read the words and sort them into a /ů/ stack and a /ü/ stack. ▶ **Linguistic/Auditory**

ONE

ASSESS/CLOSE

Build, Read, and Spell /ů/ Words

To assess children's ability to blend and read words with /ů/, observe their work during the Practice activity. Ask each child to read aloud and spell a word containing the /ů/ sound. Then have children suggest rhyming words.

ADDITIONAL PHONICS RESOURCES

McGraw-Hill School
TECHNOLOGY

Phonics/Phonemic Awareness
Practice Book,
pages 91–94

Phonics CD-ROM
activities for practice with
Blending and Discriminating

DAILY Phonics ROUTINES

DAY 4

Fluency Write the following words on the chalkboard: *cook, foot, good,* and *look*. Point to each word, asking children to blend the sounds silently. Ask volunteers to read aloud each word.

SPELLING/PHONICS CONNECTIONS

Words with the /ů/*oo* sound: See the 5-Day Spelling Plan, pages 43Q–43R.

i Intervention ▶ Skills Intervention Guide, for direct instruction and extra practice of /ů/ *oo*

Meeting Individual Needs for Phonics

EASY	ON-LEVEL	CHALLENGE	LANGUAGE SUPPORT

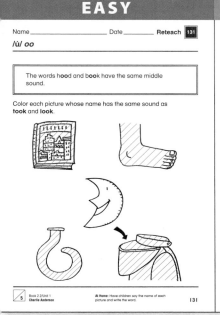

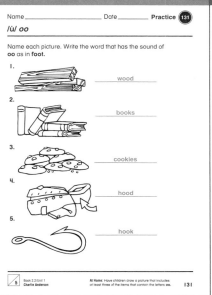

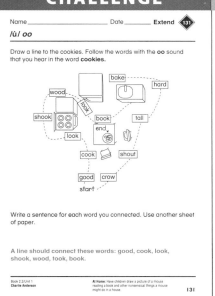

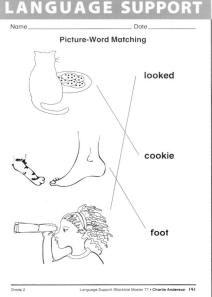

Reteach, 131   **Practice, 131**   **Extend, 131**   Language Support, 141

43F

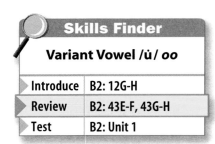OBJECTIVES

Children will:

- review /ù/*oo*.
- read words with /ù/ *oo*.
- discriminate between words with /ù/ *oo* and /ü/ *oo*.

MATERIALS
Teaching Chart 110

Skills Finder	
Variant Vowel /ù/ *oo*	
Introduce	B2: 12G-H
Review	B2: 43E-F, 43G-H
Test	B2: Unit 1

Review /ù/ *oo*

PREPARE

Identify *oo* as the Symbol for /ù/ and /ü/
Remind children that the letters *oo* can stand for two different sounds, /ù/ and /ü/. Write the letters *oo* on the chalkboard, say /ù/ and /ü/, and have children repeat after you.

Discriminate Between /ù/ and /ü/
Say the following words. Have children woof like a dog when they hear words with /ù/, and moo like a cow for words with /ü/. Examples: *cook, hook, spoon, loon, moon, took, cookies, foot, goose, tooth, wood.*

TEACH

BLENDING Model and Guide Practice with /ù/ *oo* and /ü/ *oo*
- Display **Teaching Chart 110**. Read the first two sentences aloud.

1. Look at the goose at the farm!

2. I took off my boots and hung my coat on the hook.

3. I read a good book about a moose in Maine.

4. We camped by a brook where flowers bloomed.

5. I wanted a scoop of ice cream and she wanted cookies.

6. He stuck his foot in the pool to cool off.

Teaching Chart 110

- Have volunteers underline and read the word in the first sentence with /ù/ *oo*.
- Have children circle and read the word in the first sentence with /ü/ *oo*.
- Model blending for any words with which children have difficulty.

Use Words in Context
Reinforce word meanings by having students use them in other sentences. Example: *A goose is a farm animal.*

Repeat the Procedure
Repeat the procedure with the rest of the sentences on the chart.

PRACTICE

WRITING
Write with /ù/ oo and /ü/ oo Words

PARTNERS

Brainstorm with children a list of /ù/oo and /ü/oo words. Then have them work in pairs to write either a poem or the beginning of a short story using three of those words. Tell children that their stories can be as humorous or serious as they wish. Have children share their pieces with the class. ▶ **Linguistic/Interpersonal**

ASSESS/CLOSE

Read a Poem/Story Using /ù/oo and /ü/oo Words

To assess children's ability to identify words with /ù/oo, observe them as they complete the Practice activity. Ask each child to read aloud their poem or story to the class.

ADDITIONAL PHONICS RESOURCES

McGraw-Hill School
TECHNOLOGY

Phonics/Phonemic Awareness Practice Book, pages 91–94

 **CD-ROM**

activities for practice with **Decoding and Discriminating words**

DAY **5** **Writing** Challenge partners to write sentences about *Charlie Anderson* using as many words with the /ù/ sound as possible.

 **CD-ROM**

ALTERNATE TEACHING STRATEGY
/Ù/ oo

For a different approach to teaching this skill, see page T65.

i **Intervention** **Skills**
Intervention Guide, for direct instruction and extra practice of /ù/ oo

Meeting Individual Needs for Phonics

EASY	ON-LEVEL	CHALLENGE	LANGUAGE SUPPORT

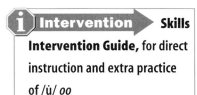

EASY

Name_____ Date_____ Reteach **132**
/ù/ oo

Say the name of the picture. Listen to the sound the letters **oo** stand for in the middle of **book**.
book

Write the name of each picture.

woods	look	hood	hook	cook	foot

1. hood
2. look
3. woods
4. hook
5. cook
6. foot

At Home: Have children write a short story about one of the pictures above.
132
Book 2.2/Unit 1
Charlie Anderson

ON-LEVEL

Name_____ Date_____ Practice **132**
/ù/ oo

Draw a line from each clue to the word it describes.

1. Make some food. — foot
2. Put a shoe on me. — hook
3. Hang up your coat on me. — soot
4. See something. — cook
5. Keep your head warm with me. — hood
6. Sweep a chimney and find me. — look
7. I come from trees. — book
8. You read me. — wood

At Home: Have children read a book to find other words that have the same sound as oo in woods.
132
Book 2.2/Unit 1
Charlie Anderson

CHALLENGE

Name_____ Date_____ Extend **132**
/ù/ oo

shook	brook	cookies	hook	wood

Write words from the box on the lines. Complete the puzzle.

Across
2. I chop some ___wood___ for a fire.
3. We go fishing in the ___brook___.
5. He ___shook___ the milk and ice cream to mix it.

Down
1. I have milk with chocolate chip ___cookies___.
4. Jan hangs her coat on a ___hook___.

Think of a word that rhymes with a word in the crossword puzzle. Use it in a sentence.

At Home: Help children create a crossword puzzle using other words.
132
Book 2.2/Unit 1
Charlie Anderson

LANGUAGE SUPPORT

Name_____ Date_____
Moments with Charlie Anderson

woods	foot	cookies

Charlie sleeps at the ___foot___ of my bed.

We were too worried to eat ___cookies___.

Is Charlie in the ___woods___?

142 Charlie Anderson • Language Support/Blackline Master 78
Grade 2

Reteach, 132   **Practice, 132**   **Extend, 132**   **Language Support, 142**

43H

TESTED OBJECTIVES

Children will draw
conclusions.

Skills Finder

Draw Conclusions

▶ Introduce	B2: 431-J
▶ Review	B2: 91I-J, 125G-H
▶ Test	B2: Unit 1

TEACHING TIP

DRAW CONCLUSIONS

In magazines or books, locate
two to three pictures of people
whose facial expressions
strongly suggest how they feel
(happy, sad, surprised, and so
on). Have children look at the
pictures and describe what
they think the people are feeling. Guide children to see that
they are using facial expressions to draw conclusions
about how the people feel.

SELF-SELECTED
Reading

Children may choose from
the following titles.

ANTHOLOGY

- *Charlie Anderson*

LEVELED BOOKS

- *How Kittens Grow*
- *The World of Cats*
- *Freedom Cat*

Bibliography, pages T88–T89

Introduce Draw Conclusions

PREPARE

**Introduce Draw
Conclusions**

Recount a brief story or a familiar tale to children, but do not tell them
the ending or how the story is resolved. Ask children to tell how they
believe the story ends and to explain their answers.

TEACH

**Draw
Conclusions in
"Maria at the pet
Store"**

Review that a reader can draw a conclusion, even if a story doesn't
provide all the facts. Display **Teaching Chart 111**. Read the chart aloud
together.

Maria at the Pet Store

 Maria loved to visit the pet store. She did the same thing every
time she went. First, she would pet Misty, the owner's cat, who
greeted her as she came through the door. Then she peeked in
at the hamsters spinning away on their wheels. Next, she said
hello to the parrot sitting on its perch. Finally, she would pull up
a small stool in front of the fish tank to watch the fish. There
were so many pretty colors and shapes of fish to see that Maria
would forget to look at the clock. Sometimes she sat on the stool
looking at the fish until it was time for the store to close!

Teaching Chart 111

MODEL The story doesn't come right out and tell me how Maria feels
about animals or if she has a favorite, but there are clues that help
me to figure it out. I can draw the conclusion that Maria really likes
animals because she loves the pet store, and that her favorite animals at the pet store are the fish, because she spends the most
time looking at them.

PRACTICE

Using Clues to Draw Conclusions

GROUP

Have children underline words in **Teaching Chart 111** that provide clues about Maria's feelings about animals and which pets she likes best. ▶**Logical/Interpersonal**

ASSESS/CLOSE

Draw More Conclusions

Tell students the story of *The Three Little Pigs*. Have them draw conclusions about the main characters based on their actions. For example, have them draw conclusions about which pig is the most clever. (the pig that built the brick house)

ALTERNATE TEACHING STRATEGY

DRAW CONCLUSIONS

For a different approach to teaching this skill, see page T67.

 **Intervention** ▶ **Skills Intervention Guide,** for direct instruction and extra practice in drawing conclusions

Meeting Individual Needs for Comprehension

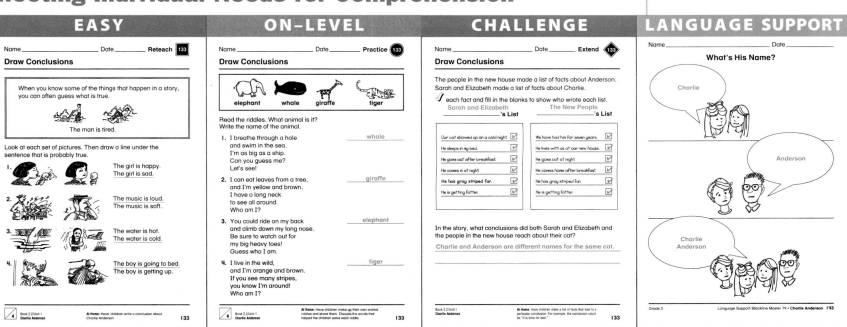

Reteach, 133   Practice, 133   Extend, 133   Language Support, 143

43J

OBJECTIVES

Children will identify antonyms.

MATERIALS
- **Teaching Chart 112**
- **index cards**

Skills Finder

Antonyms

Introduce	B2: 43K-L
Review	B2: 67K-L, 125K-L
Test	B2: Unit 1

TEACHING TIP

ANTONYMS Explain to children that not all words will have an antonym. The most common kinds of words that have antonyms are adjectives and adverbs.

Introduce Antonyms

PREPARE

Role-Play Antonyms
Tell children that an antonym is a word that means the opposite of another word. Have children role-play how it feels to be cold. Then have them role-play the opposite, or the antonym, of this feeling.

TEACH

Read the Passage and Model the Skill
Display **Teaching Chart 112**. Have children read the passage with you, then model the skill using the word *morning*.

A Day at the Pet Store

In the <u>morning</u> Mrs. Chen unlocks the door of the pet store. She turns <u>on</u> the light, says <u>hello</u> to all the animals, and feeds each one. As the customers <u>come</u> and <u>go</u>, Mrs. Chen gives <u>answers</u> to all their <u>questions</u> about the care and feeding of the animals. One boy goes home with a <u>noisy</u> parakeet, another leaves with a <u>silent</u> goldfish.

In the <u>evening</u>, Mrs. Chen says <u>goodbye</u> to the pets, turns <u>off</u> the light, and locks the door.

Teaching Chart 112

MODEL As I read this story, I will look for pairs of words that mean the opposite of each other. I will make a list of any opposites I find as I read. For example, *morning* is the opposite of *evening*.

PRACTICE

Match Antonym Pairs
PARTNERS

Partners can look for more antonyms in **Teaching Chart 112**, such as *hello* and *goodbye*, *on* and *off*, *come* and *go*, *answers* and *questions*, *noisy* and *silent*. Have them write each word on an index card, and use the cards to play a game of concentration: Face all the cards down, and have children flip over two cards at a time in an attempt to "match" antonyms. ▶ **Logical/Interpersonal**

Converse with Antonyms

Have partners make a list of ten words and their antonyms. Then tell them to choose a topic, for example vacations or sports. Have one partner make a sentence about the topic using a word off the list. Then have the other partner use the word's antonym to respond.
▶ **Linguistic/Interpersonal**

ASSESS/CLOSE

Write Antonym Sentences

Have partners brainstorm a list of antonyms and use them to write sentences. Ask children to include at least one pair of antonyms in each sentence. For example: *The pet store is closed at night, but is open during the day.* Invite partners to read their sentences to the rest of the class.

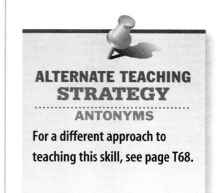

ALTERNATE TEACHING STRATEGY
ANTONYMS

For a different approach to teaching this skill, see page T68.

**Intervention** ▶ **Skills**
Intervention Guide, for direct instruction and extra practice with antonyms

Meeting Individual Needs for Vocabulary

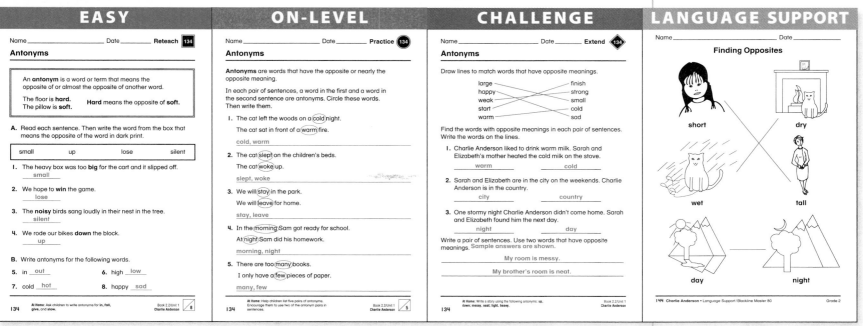

Reteach, 134   **Practice, 134**   **Extend, 134**   Language Support, 144

43L

Writing That Compares

GRAMMAR/SPELLING CONNECTIONS

See the 5-Day Grammar and Usage Plan on pages 430–43P.

See the 5-Day Spelling Plan on words with /ù/.

TEACHING TIP

Technology Use the Internet to find out facts about cats. You can think about how these facts relate to *Charlie Anderson* and use them in your biography.

Transition Words Encourage children to use transition words that compare to describe how two things are alike: *Also, Similarly, In addition to,* and contrast words to help to show differences: *Although, However, On the other hand.* Ask children to describe two pets. As they speak, list the compare/contrast transition words used on the board.

Handwriting CD-ROM

Prewrite

WRITE A BIOGRAPHY Present this writing assignment: Write a biography about Charlie Anderson's life. Explain what Charlie's life is like and use details that will bring Charlie to life.

ASKING QUESTIONS Have children write a list of questions about Charlie's life. For example, they might consider whom he spends time with in each of his homes. How did he find his first home? How are his two homes different?

Strategy: Create a Venn Diagram Have children organize their information in a Venn diagram. Ask them to consider Charlie's life during the day, and during the night.

	DAY			NIGHT
	Different	Alike	Different	

- stays with the man and woman
- is called Anderson

purrs, eats, sleeps, walks through woods

- stays with Elizabeth and Sara
- is called Charlie

Graphic Organizer 14

Draft

USE THE CLUSTER As they write their biographies, children should refer to their diagrams to help them organize information. Remind children to compare Charlie's two lives. Invite them to elaborate their biographies by including "scenes" from Charlie's life, with dialogue between characters.

Revise

SELF-QUESTIONING Ask children to assess their drafts. Have partners exchange work, then discuss their reactions and ask any questions they may have. Have children ask these questions:

- Did I make specific comparisons in my biography?
- Did I tell what Charlie likes about each home?
- Can a reader "see" the characters and settings clearly?

Edit/Proofread

CHECK FOR ERRORS Children should reread their biographies for correct spelling, grammar, and punctuation.

Publish

SHARE THE BIOGRAPHIES Children can read their books aloud to the class. The rest of the class should listen carefully for similarities and differences.

The Biography of Charlie Anderson

Charlie Anderson was born on August 18, 1993. He has two brothers and two sisters, but they don't live with him. At night Charlie lives with two girls named Elizabeth and Sarah. Elizabeth feeds him special tuna-flavored cat food. He likes this a lot! She brushes him with a gray brush that matches his fur. Sarah dresses him up in a pretty, flowered dress and pretends that he is her baby. He doesn't like this very much at all!

During the day, Charlie stays with a man named Frank and a woman named Rita. They feed Charlie chicken-flavored food. Frank's dog Ralph is afraid of Charlie. Charlie chases Ralph all over the house. He loves to chase Ralph!

Presentation Ideas

MAKE A HOME MOVIE Have children make a movie based on their lives. They can draw scenes from Charlie's life on a long roll of paper, and narrate as they unroll each frame. ▶ **Viewing/Representing**

INTERVIEW CHARLIE Two children can role-play an interview with Charlie Anderson. Have the interviewer ask questions about Charlie's life, using another child's biography as a guide. ▶ **Speaking/Listening**

Viewing and Speaking

VIEWING Remind children to
- sit quietly while watching movies.
- pay attention to details.
- take notes and ask questions later.

SPEAKING Have children
- speak clearly and at a volume appropriate for one-on-one interviewing.
- use eye contact during interviews.
- ask clear, direct questions.

Consider students' creative efforts, possibly adding a plus (+) for originality, wit, and imagination.

Scoring Rubric

Excellent	Good	Fair	Unsatisfactory
4: The writer: • presents a well-imagined, well-constructed biography. • makes vivid comparisons between the two story settings. • enhances story facts with interesting details and scenes.	**3:** The writer: • presents a solid comparison of two story settings, in a biography format. • may enhance the comparison with some descriptive detail. • organizes ideas clearly.	**2:** The writer: • attempts to compare two story settings. • may not follow through with biography format or present specific comparisons. • may have trouble organizing facts and ideas.	**1:** The writer: • may not grasp the task to compare, or to use biography format. • may list vague or disconnected story elements and details. • may have severe trouble drafting full sentences, or organizing ideas.

Incomplete   0: The writer leaves the page blank or fails to respond to the writing task. The writer does not address the topic or simply paraphrases the prompt. The response is illegible or incoherent.

LANGUAGE SUPPORT

 Ask ESL students to work with English-fluent partners. Point out that a biography includes details about a person's life. Then have them ask and answer biographical questions about each other.

 Invite children to include their biographies in their portfolios.

Meeting Individual Needs for Writing

EASY

Picture and Caption Have children draw pictures of a place Charlie Anderson might have gone if he had not gone to either of his usual houses. Encourage children to think of places that cats might like. Have them write a caption for the picture.

ON-LEVEL

Diary Entry If children found Charlie Anderson's diary, what would it say? Most of his days would probably be similar. The day that Elizabeth and Sarah discovered his double life was quite a different kind of day. Have children write a diary entry from Charlie's point of view about this special day.

CHALLENGE

Write a Scene Invite children to write about where they would go if they had a secret life like Charlie's. Ask them to include who would be there, when they would go, why they would go there, and whether or not they would go alone. Encourage them to include dialogue, describing a scene from their secret life.

5 Day Grammar and Usage Plan

DAILY LANGUAGE ACTIVITIES

Write the Daily Language Activities on the chalkboard each day or use **Transparency 16.** For each sentence, have children correct the verb orally.

Day 1
1. Charlie am a cat. is
2. I are a child. am
3. The new cats is nice. are

Day 2
1. Charlie were hungry last night. was
2. The girls was his friends. were
3. Soon Charlie were fat. was

Day 3
1. I is happy today. am
2. Cats is animals. are
3. Charlie were lost one night. was

Day 4
1. The man are Charlie's owner now. is
2. The girls was sad before. were
3. Now the sisters is happy. are

Day 5
1. Now Charlie are a lucky cat. is
2. Yesterday I were very busy. was
3. Today I is ready to rest . am

Daily Language Transparency 16

DAY 1 — Introduce the Concept

Oral Warm-Up Write on the board: *The sky is blue.* Ask children if they can find the verb. (is) Explain the that the verb *is* links the sky with the color to describe it.

Introduce Linking Verbs Verbs like *is* do not show action. Present the following:

Linking Verbs

- A **linking verb** is a verb that does not show action.
- The verb *be* is a linking verb.
- The verb *be* has special forms in the present tense (*is, are, am*).

Display these examples: *I am; Pam/he/she/it is; boys/you/we/they are.*

Present the Daily Language Activity. Then have children write three sentences using *am, is,* and *are*. Remind children that these are the present-tense forms of the verb *be.*

 WRITING Assign the daily Writing Prompt on page 12C.

Name _____ Date _____ **Grammar 97**

Linking Verbs

- A **linking verb** is a verb that does not show action.
- The verb *be* is a linking verb.
- The verb *be* has special forms in the present tense.
- I <u>am</u> a student.   John <u>is</u> not tall.   We <u>are</u> friends.

Write *am, is,* or *are* to complete each sentence.
1. Max and Sam __are__ puppies.
2. Max __is__ brown.
3. Sam __is__ older than Max.
4. Max __is__ Sam's friend.
5. Both puppies __are__ sleeping.

5 Book 2.2/Unit 1   **Charlie Anderson**   Extension: Have children tell the location of classroom objects using *is* and *are.*   97

GRAMMAR PRACTICE BOOK, PAGE 97

DAY 2 — Teach the Concept

Review Present-Tense Linking Verbs Write: *The girls are sisters.* Ask children to find the verb. (are) Point out that *are* links the girls to another word that tells more about them.

Introduce Past-Tense Forms of *Be* In the sentence above, change *are* to *were*. Ask children how the sentence is different now. (tells about the past) Discuss:

Display the verbs *was* and *were* with subjects such as the following: *Kim/I/he/she/it was; children/you/we/they were.*

Present the Daily Language Activity. Then have children write three sentences using the past forms of the verb *be.*

 WRITING Assign the daily Writing Prompt on page 12C.

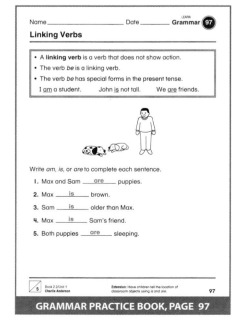

Name _____ Date _____ **Grammar 98**

Linking Verbs

- The verb *be* has special forms in the past tense.

SUBJECT	PRESENT	PAST
I	am	was
singular	is	was
plural and *you*	are	were

I <u>am</u> here now. I <u>was</u> here yesterday.
You <u>are</u> here now. You <u>were</u> here yesterday.
We <u>were</u> both here yesterday.

Choose the correct linking verb. Then write each sentence.
1. Boris and Fred (was, were) good friends.
   Boris and Fred were good friends.
2. Fred (was, were) a Boy Scout.
   Fred was a Boy Scout.
3. Boris (were, was) good at playing ball.
   Boris was good at playing ball.
4. They (was, were) older than I.
   They were older than I.
5. I (was, were) their neighbor.
   I was their neighbor.

98   Extension: Have children write about someone they know using the forms of *be* on the chart.   Book 2.2/Unit 1   **Charlie Anderson** 5

GRAMMAR PRACTICE BOOK, PAGE 98

Linking Verbs

Day 3

Learn from the Literature Review the linking verb *be*. Read the third sentence on page 31 of *Charlie Anderson:*

His name <u>is</u> Charlie.

Have children identify the linking verb in the sentence. Ask them which words it links together. (name, Charlie)

Use the Forms of *Be* Present the Daily Language Activity. Then ask children to write three questions about Charlie, using forms of *be*. For example, *What color was he?* Tell them to put their questions in the past tense. Then have them write the answers to the questions.

 Assign the daily Writing Prompt on page 12D.

Day 4

Review the Linking Verb *Be* Write on the chalkboard the sentences from the Daily Language Activities for Days 1 through 3. Have children tell whether the sentences refer to the present or the past. Then have them tell whether the verb links the subject to a noun or to describing words. Present the Daily Language Activity for Day 4.

Mechanics and Usage Before children do the daily Writing Prompt, review the rules for capitalization. Display and discuss:

Capitalization

* A proper noun begins with a capital letter.
* The name of a day, month, or holiday begins with a capital letter.

 Assign the daily Writing Prompt on page 12D.

Day 5

Assess Use the Daily Language Activity and page 101 of the **Grammar Practice Book** for assessment.

Reteach Have children make a chart showing the present and past tenses of the verb *be*. Use words from the Daily Language Activities to make a list of subjects, a list of the six different forms of the verb be, and a list of nouns and adjectives. Have children copy each on an index card into which they have punched holes. Then have them arrange their cards so that they form sentences, and string them together. Ask them to make sure that the verb agrees with the subject. Display the cards on the bulletin board.

Use page 102 of the **Grammar Practice Book** for additional reteaching.

 Assign the daily Writing Prompt on page 12D.

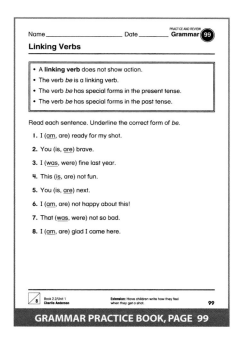

GRAMMAR PRACTICE BOOK, PAGE 99

GRAMMAR PRACTICE BOOK, PAGE 100

GRAMMAR PRACTICE BOOK, PAGE 101

GRAMMAR PRACTICE BOOK, PAGE 102

43P

5 Day Spelling Plan

ESL Place a piece of wood on a book. Say: *The wood is on the book.* Ask children to repeat. Then say the /ù/ sound followed by each spelling word with this sound and have children repeat. For example: /ù/, *stood,* /ù/, *foot,* and so forth.

DICTATION SENTENCES

Spelling Words

1. The wood is by the house.
2. She has a new book.
3. I stood on the mat.
4. My foot is blue.
5. The hat is made of wool.
6. The brook is high.
7. Her hood is red.
8. The pan is on the hook.
9. She shook the rug.
10. I can cook.

Challenge Words

11. The chocolate is good.
12. Her clothes are new.
13. The girl was in the middle.
14. I offered to help.
15. He went upstairs.

DAY 1 Pretest

Assess Prior Knowledge Use the Dictation Sentences at left and **Spelling Practice Book** page 97 for the pretest. Allow students to correct their own papers. If students have trouble, have partners give each other a midweek test on Day 3. Students who require a modified list may be tested on the first five words.

Spelling Words		Challenge Words
1. wood	6. brook	11. **chocolate**
2. book	7. hood	12. **clothes**
3. stood	8. hook	13. **middle**
4. **foot**	9. shook	14. **offered**
5. wool	10. cook	15. **upstairs**

*Note: Words in **dark type** are from the story.*

Word Study On page 98 of the **Spelling Practice Book** are word study steps and an at-home activity.

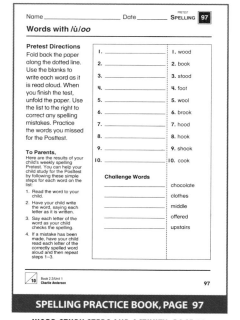

SPELLING PRACTICE BOOK, PAGE 97
WORD STUDY STEPS AND ACTIVITY, PAGE 98

DAY 2 Explore the Pattern

Sort and Spell Words Say *hook* and *cook.* Ask students what vowel sound they hear in each word. Tell students that these words contain the vowel sound /ù/ spelled *oo.*

Ask students to read aloud the ten spelling words before sorting them according to the spelling pattern.

Words ending with			
ook	***ood***	***ool***	***oot***
book	wood	wool	foot
shook	hood		
brook	stood		
cook			
hook			

Word Wall As students enjoy other stories and poems, have them look for new words with the sound /ù/ spelled *oo* and add each word to the classroom word wall, underlining the spelling pattern.

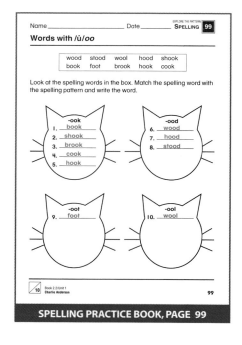

SPELLING PRACTICE BOOK, PAGE 99

Words with /u̇/oo

DAY 3 — Practice and Extend

Word Meaning: Compound Words
Have students find two words from the spelling list that can be combined to form a compound word *(cookbook)*. Then have students try to combine words from the list with other words to form compound words. *(football, notebook, fishhook, cookout)*

Glossary Review the pronunciation key in the Glossary. Have partners:

- write each Challenge Word.
- find the pronunciation of each Challenge Word in the glossary.
- say each Challenge Word aloud and use it in a sentence.

DAY 4 — Proofread and Write

Proofread Sentences Write these sentences on the chalkboard, including the misspelled words. Ask students to proofread, circling incorrect spellings and writing the correct spellings. There are two spelling errors in each sentence.

> The woud is by the bruk. (wood, brook)
> A houd is on the huk. (hood, hook)

Have students create additional sentences with errors for partners to correct.

WRITING Have students use as many spelling words as possible in the daily Writing Prompt on page 12D. Remind students to proofread their writing for errors in spelling, grammar, and punctuation.

DAY 5 — Assess

Assess Students' Knowledge Use page 102 of the **Spelling Practice Book** or the Dictation Sentences on page 43Q for the posttest.

Personal Word List If students have trouble with any words in the lesson, have them create a personal list of troublesome words in their journals. Have students write a context sentence for each word.

Students should refer to their word lists during later writing activities.

Concept
- **Protecting the Environment**

Comprehension
- **Compare and Contrast**

Phonics
- **Soft *c*: /s/ *ce* and soft *g*: /j/ *ge***

Vocabulary
- **diving**
- **explained**
- **harm**
- **noisy**
- **soil**
- **village**

Anthology

Fernando's Gift

Selection Summary   A boy named Fernando learns how important trees are for a beautiful, healthy environment, and so decides to give a special gift of a baby tree to his friend for her birthday.

Rhyme applies to phonics

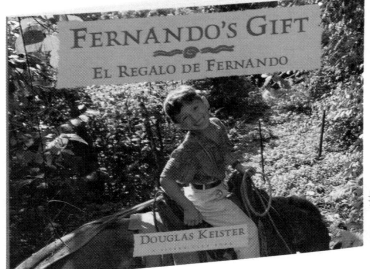

Listening Library

INSTRUCTIONAL pages 46–67

About the Author   Douglas Keister is a photographer and an author. In 1987 he traveled to the rain forest in Central America. He took many photographs of the rain forest and of the people who live there. When he returned home, his friends thought he should use the photographs to write a children's book. *Fernando's Gift* is the result. It is Mr. Keister's first children's book.

Same Concept, Skills and Vocabulary!

Leveled Books

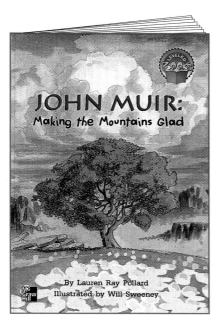

EASY
Lesson on pages 67A and 67D
DECODABLE

INDEPENDENT
Lesson on pages 67B and 67D

🏠 *Take-Home version available*

CHALLENGE
Lesson on pages 67C and 67D

Leveled Practice

EASY
Reteach, 135–142 Blackline masters with reteaching opportunities for each assessed skill

INDEPENDENT/ON-LEVEL
Practice, 135–142 Workbook with Take-Home stories and practice opportunities for each assessed skill and story comprehension

CHALLENGE
Extend, 135–142 Blackline masters that offer challenge activities for each assessed skill

Quizzes Prepared by ⬛ **Accelerated Reader**

WORKSTATION Activities

Social Studies . . . Map Skills, *58*

Science . . . . Tree Planting, *56*

Math . . . . Time Travel, *52*

Language Arts . . Read Aloud, *44E*
Picture Dictionary, *48*

Writing . . . . Write a Magazine Article, *64*

Cultural Perspectives . . . . . Breakfast Foods, *50*

Research and Inquiry . . . . . . Find Out More, *65*

Internet Activities . . . . www.mhschool.com/reading

Suggested
Lesson Planner

READING AND LANGUAGE ARTS	DAY 1 — Focus on Reading and Skills	DAY 2 — Read the Literature
Phonics Daily Routines	Daily **Phonics** Routine: Segmenting, 44H **Phonics** CD-ROM	Daily **Phonics** Routine: Discriminating, 46A **Phonics** CD-ROM
Phonological Awareness **Phonics** *Soft c, g* **Comprehension** **Vocabulary** **Study Skills** **Listening, Speaking, Viewing, Representing**	**Read Aloud: Essay,** 44E "Thinking Green" ☑ **Develop Phonological Awareness,** 44F Soft *c* and Soft *g* ☑ **Introduce Soft *c* and Soft *g*,** 44G–44H **Teaching Chart 113** **Reteach, Practice, Extend,** 135 **Phonics/Phonemic Awareness Practice Book,** 95–98 **Read** **Apply Soft *c* and Soft *g*,** 44/45 "My Gifts" ⓘ **Intervention Program**	**Build Background,** 46A Develop Oral Language **Vocabulary,** 46B–46C *diving harm soil* *explained noisy village* **Word Building Manipulative Cards** **Teaching Chart 114** **Reteach, Practice, Extend,** 136 **Read** **Read the Selection,** 46–63 Comprehension ☑ *Soft c* and Soft *g* ☑ Draw Conclusions **Genre:** Informational Story 47 **Cultural Perspectives,** 50 ⓘ **Intervention Program**
Curriculum Connections	**Link** Science, 44E	**Link** Science, 46A
Writing	✏ **Writing Prompt:** Pretend you are the boy on page 47. Describe what you are doing and where you are going.	✏ **Writing Prompt:** Imagine you are a reporter writing a story about the rainforest. Write about the sights and sounds you see and hear as you walk through the forest. 📓 **Journal Writing** Quick-Write, 63
Grammar	**Introduce the Concept: Helping Verbs,** 67O Daily Language Activity: Write the correct form of the helping verb. **Grammar Practice Book,** 103	**Teach the Concept: Helping Verbs,** 67O Daily Language Activity: Write the correct form of the helping verb. **Grammar Practice Book,** 104
Spelling *Soft c, g*	**Pretest: Words with Soft *c* and Soft *g*,** 67Q **Spelling Practice Book,** 103, 104	**Explore the Pattern: Words with Soft *c* and Soft *g*,** 67Q **Spelling Practice Book,** 105

DAY 3 *Read the Literature*	**DAY 4** *Build Skills*	**DAY 5** *Build Skills*
Daily **Phonics** Routine: **Fluency,** 65 **Phonics** CD-ROM	Daily **Phonics** Routine: **Words in Context,** 67F **Phonics** CD-ROM	Daily **Phonics** Routine: **Writing,** 67H **Phonics** CD-ROM
Rereading for Fluency, 62 **Story Questions and Activities,** 64–65 Reteach, Practice, Extend, 137 **Study Skill,** 66 ☑ Graphic Aids **Teaching Chart 115** Reteach, Practice, Extend, 138 **Test Power,** 67 **Read Read the Leveled Books,** 67A–67D Guided Reading ☑ Soft *c* and Soft *g* ☑ Compare and Contrast ☑ Instructional Vocabulary **Intervention Program**	**Read Read the Leveled Books and the Self-Selected Books** ☑ **Review Soft *c* and Soft *g*,** 67E–67F **Teaching Chart 116** Reteach, Practice, Extend, 139 Language Support, 150 **Phonics/Phonemic Awareness** Practice Book, 95–98 ☑ **Cumulative Review,** 67G–67H **Teaching Chart 117** Reteach, Practice, Extend, 140 Language Support, 151 **Phonics/Phonemic Awareness** Practice Book, 95–98 **Minilessons,** 49, 51, 55, 61 **Intervention Program**	**Read Read Self-Selected Books** ☑ **Introduce Compare and Contrast,** 67I–67J **Teaching Chart 118** Reteach, Practice, Extend, 141 Language Support, 152 ☑ **Review Antonyms,** 67K–67L **Teaching Chart 119** Reteach, Practice, Extend, 142 Language Support, 153 **Listening, Speaking, Viewing, Representing,** 67N Newsletters Talk Show **Minilessons,** 49, 51, 55, 61 **Intervention Program**
Activity Language Arts, 48 Math, 52	**Activity** Science, 56	**Activity** Social Studies, 58
Writing Prompt: Write a letter to Fernando telling him about a day in your life. Write about events as if they were taking place as you write them. **Writing That Compares,** 67M Prewrite, Draft	**Writing Prompt:** Write a conversation between Fernando and Carmina. Talk about how Carmina feels about her gift. **Writing That Compares,** 67M Revise **Meeting Individual Needs for Writing,** 67N	**Writing Prompt:** Look at the picture of Fernando's class on page 54. Describe what you think is happening in the picture. **Writing That Compares,** 67M Edit/Proofread, Publish
Review and Practice: Helping Verbs, 67P Daily Language Activity: Write the correct form of the helping verb. **Grammar Practice Book,** 105	**Review and Practice: Helping Verbs,** 67P Daily Language Activity: Write the correct form of the helping verb. **Grammar Practice Book,** 106	**Assess and Reteach: Helping Verbs,** 67P Daily Language Activity: Write the correct form of the helping verb. **Grammar Practice Book,** 107, 108
Practice and Extend: Words with Soft *c* and Soft *g*, 67R **Spelling Practice Book,** 106	**Practice and Write: Words with Soft *c* and Soft *g*,** 67R **Spelling Practice Book,** 107	**Assess: Words with Soft *c* and Soft *g*,** 67R **Spelling Practice Book,** 108

Read Aloud

Thinking Green

an essay by The Earthworks Group

If you look green, you're probably not feeling very well. But if Earth is green, it's a healthy planet.

A green Earth means that plants are growing. It means that the soil is good, there's plenty of water, the air is clean, animals have places to live and things to eat.

And some wonderful news: Anyone can help keep Earth green. It's so easy. You can plant a seed, give it some water, and watch it grow. You can save paper so that fewer trees will be cut down. You can "adopt" plants that are already growing and help them enjoy life.

Another important thing about plants (especially trees): They help fight the greenhouse effect and give us oxygen, which is the air we need to live.

What a deal!

We need lots of greenery in our world. Let's start planting!

Oral Comprehension

LISTENING AND SPEAKING Read aloud this essay about the environment. When you have finished, ask, *How do trees keep Earth healthy?* Then ask: *What else could people do to help Earth become healthy?* Remind children to look for causes and effects as they read other stories and essays.

GENRE STUDY: ESSAY Discuss the informative nature and techniques used in the essay, *Thinking Green.*

- Have children paraphrase, or retell in their own words, the information that they learned from the essay. Discuss how the information is presented in a logical order.

- Point out that successful essays often use the latest research available. Invite children to look up the greenhouse effect in an encyclopedia and verify whether trees can really help to fight it.

- Have children discuss the main idea in *Thinking Green.* Does it merely provide information? Encourage children to think about how an essay can use information to inspire us to action.

Activity Encourage children to make posters showing how to help planet Earth. Have them use suggestions from the discussion or their own ideas to illustrate their posters. Remind them to write their suggestions on the poster.

▶ **Visual/Linguistic**

Develop Phonological Awareness

Blend Sounds

MATERIALS
- page from a book
- storybook picture of three mice

Teach Tell children you will say the sounds of a word and then put the sounds together to say the word. Hold up the book page, and say: /p/-/ā/-/j/. *When I put the sounds together, I get the word* page. Have children repeat the sounds and the word /p/-/ā/-/j/: *page*. Repeat the activity with the picture of *mice*.

Practice Have children continue blending the sounds to say the following words: /ī/-/s/: *ice*; /r/-/ī/-/s/: *rice*; /ā/-/j/: *age*; /p/-/r/-/ī/-/s/: *price*; /k/-/ā/-/j/: *cage*; /n/-/ī/-/s/: *nice*; /h/-/ū/-/j/: *huge*; and /l/-/ā/-/s/: *lace*.

Segment Sounds

MATERIALS
- Word Building Boxes from *Word Building Cards*
- green paper triangles as counters

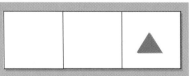

Teach Explain that you will say a word sound by sound. Then you will place a green counter in a word box to show where you hear either the /j/ or /s/ sound. Say: *Cage . . . /k/-/ā/-/j/*. Place a green counter in the third box. Then say: *The /j/ sound is the third sound in cage.* Have children say /j/.

Practice Distribute Word Building Boxes and green counters to each child. Using the following words, have them place a counter in the box where either the /j/ or /s/ sound is heard. Then ask them to repeat the sound: *dice, page, nice, cell, rage, gem,* and *face*.

Substitute Sounds

MATERIALS
- Phonics Picture Posters

Teach Display the Phonics Picture Poster of the cat. Have children say the word *cat* with you. Explain that if you change the ending sound of *cat* to /n/, you make the word *can*. Have children repeat both words with you: *cat/can*. Repeat with words *pig/pit*.

Practice Have children substitute the ending sounds for the following words: *lace/lake; dice/dine; page/pain; face/fake; rage/rate; Mike/mice; price/pride,* and *wage/wake*.

INFORMAL ASSESSMENT Observe children as they blend, segment, and substitute sounds. If children have difficulty, see Alternate Teaching Strategies on p. T69.

OBJECTIVES

Children will:

- **identify words containing the soft *c* sound.**
- **identify words containing the soft *g* sound.**
- **blend and read soft *c* and soft *g* words.**

....

MATERIALS

- **Teaching Chart 113**
- **letter and long vowel cards from the Word Building Manipulative Cards**

Skills Finder

Soft *c* and Soft *g*	
Introduce	B2: 44G-H
Review	B2: 67E-F, 67G-H, 340G-H, 361E-F
Test	B2: Unit 1
Maintain	B2: 221

SPELLING/PHONICS CONNECTIONS

Words with soft *c* and soft *g*: See the 5-Day Spelling Plan, pages 67Q–67R.

LANGUAGE SUPPORT

ESL In many languages, hard *g* is much more familiar than soft *g*. However, in Spanish, *g* followed by *e* or *i* is pronounced somewhat like /h/. You may wish to pair ESL children with English-fluent partners to practice saying *giant* and *large*.

Introduce Soft *c* and Soft *g*

TEACH

Identify the Soft *c* Sound and the Soft *g* Sound

Tell children they will learn to read words with the /s/ sound represented by the letter combination *ce*, and the /j/ sound represented by the letter combination *ge*.

BLENDING
Model and Guide Practice with Soft *c* and Soft *g*

- Display **Teaching Chart 113**. Point to *ce* at the top of the first column. Tell children that this letter combination stands for the /s/ sound.

- Write the letters *ce* on the first blank in column 1 to complete the word. Run your finger under *place*, blending the letters to read the word. Have children repeat after you.

- In the first row below *place,* write the letter combination *ce* in the underlined space to form the word *rice*. Blend the sounds together as you run your finger under the word. Have the children repeat after you.

- Have volunteers suggest letters to help you complete the first column of the chart, making words that end in the /s/ sound. Ask volunteers to blend the sounds together to read the completed words.

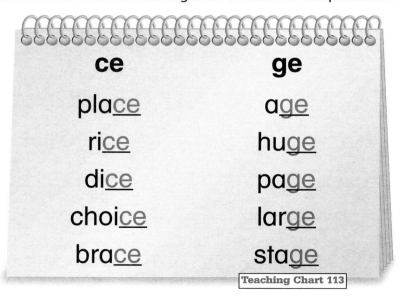

ce	ge
pla<u>ce</u>	a<u>ge</u>
ri<u>ce</u>	hu<u>ge</u>
di<u>ce</u>	pa<u>ge</u>
choi<u>ce</u>	lar<u>ge</u>
bra<u>ce</u>	sta<u>ge</u>

Teaching Chart 113

Use the Words in Context

- Have volunteers use the words in sentences to reinforce their meanings. Example: *The library is a good place to study.*

Repeat the Procedure

- Follow the same procedure to complete Column 2 on the **Teaching Chart**.

PRACTICE

LETTER
SUBSTITUTION
Form Words with
Soft *c* and Soft *g*

ONE

Have children use letter and long vowel cards to build the word *face*.
Then have them replace the *f* card with an *r* to form *race*. Next, have
children replace the long *a* card with a long *i* card to form *rice*. Provide
children with these additional letter cards to create other words with
the /s/ sound: *d, m, l, p.* (*dice, mice, lace, place*) Repeat the process to
form words with the /j/ sound, using the letter and long vowel cards
c, p, h, g, a-e, a-u.

▶ **Spatial/Linguistic**

ASSESS/CLOSE

Identify and Read
With Soft *c* and
Soft *g* Words

To assess children's ability to read words with soft *c* and soft *g*, observe
them as they work on the Practice activity. Have children read the
phonics rhyme on page 45 in their anthologies. Then tell them to identify all of the words with soft *c* and soft *g*.

ADDITIONAL PHONICS RESOURCES

Phonics/Phonemic Awareness
Practice Book,
pages 95–98

McGraw-Hill School
TECHNOLOGY

Phonics **CD-ROM**

activities for practice with
Blending and Segmenting

Meeting Individual Needs for Phonics

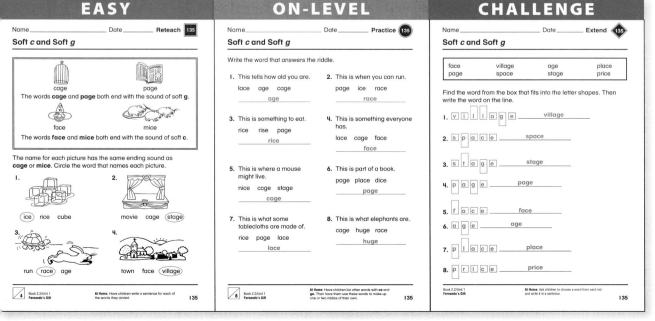

Reteach, 135

Practice, 135

Extend, 135

Daily Routines

DAY 1
Segmenting Write on
the chalkboard a list of
soft *c* and soft *g* words. Invite children to use colored chalk to circle
the letters in each word that stand
for the soft *c* or soft *g* sound.

DAY 2
Discriminating Write
soft *c* and hard *c* words on
the chalkboard. Read the list
aloud, and ask children to hiss like
a snake when they hear a word
with the soft *c* sound.

DAY 3
Fluency Write the following words on the
chalkboard: *race, huge, pace, stage,
brace, page, mice, rice.* Point to each
word, asking children to blend the
sounds silently. Ask a volunteer to
read aloud each word.

DAY 4
Words in Context
Ask children working in
small groups to create a sentence
containing one soft *c* word and one
hard *c* word. Repeat the activity
with soft *g* and hard *g* words.

DAY 5
Writing Have children
write riddles using as
many soft *c* and soft *g* words as
possible. Invite children to read
their riddles aloud.

44H

OBJECTIVES

Children will blend and read soft *c* and soft *g* words.

Apply Soft *c* and Soft *g*

My Gifts

Mom gave me two mice
In two wooden cages.
Dad gave me a notebook
With rice paper pages.
The mice race around
In all places and spaces.
Inside my nice new notebook
I draw little mouse faces.

Anthology pages 44–45

Read and Build Fluency

READ THE POEM Before reading "My Gifts," point out the soft *c* sound in *mice* and the soft *g* sound in *cages*. Then have children follow along in the text as you read with appropriate expression. Invite children to consider how the narrator is feeling in each part of the poem. Tell children to make sure their reading reflects those feelings as they engage in a shared reading with you for auditory modeling purposes.

REREAD FOR FLUENCY Encourage children

PARTNERS to take turns rereading the poem with a partner. Suggest that children picture themselves as the narrator in the poem. Have them ask, "How would I say that?"

Remind children that they can change their voice to show how characters think and feel.

Dictate and Spell

DICTATE WORDS Say the word *cage* aloud and

JOURNAL segment it into its three individual sounds. Use it in a sentence, such as "The cage is made from wood." Do the same for *mice*. Have children write each word. Encourage them to change initial consonant sounds to make new words, such as *page, rage, sage,* and *mice, rice, nice*. Make sure children write the whole word.

> **i** **Intervention** ▸ **Skills Intervention Guide,**
> for direct instruction and extra practice in soft *c* and soft *g*

Build Background

Science

Concept: Protecting the Environment

Evaluate Prior Knowledge

CONCEPT: PROTECTING THE ENVIRONMENT Explain to children that pollution and the overuse of resources cause major damage to the environment every day. Ask children to share ideas about ways people can help the environment, such as buying recycled goods or participating in trash cleanup projects in their community.

CHART THE PROBLEMS Work with children to create a chart showing some of the dangers facing the environment, the causes of these problems, and ways people can reduce these problems. ▶ **Logical/Visual**

PROBLEM	CAUSE	SOLUTION
Overflowing landfills	Overpacking, wasting food	Look for items in the store with less packing. Use food before it spoils. Recycle paper and plastic

MAKE A LIST Encourage children to make a list of five things they can do at home or school to help conserve resources and protect the environment (recycle, reuse grocery bags as trash bags, and so on). Invite them to take the list home and display it as a reminder.

ONE **WRITING**

Develop Oral Language

USE ILLUSTRATIONS Have children **ESL** create pictures of how they might help to clean up the environment. Work with children to develop a list of words they might use in talking about their picture, such as:

* recycle
* reuse
* pollution
* environment

▶ **Spatial/Intrapersonal**

Five Things I Can Do
1. Recycle.
2. Reuse grocery bags for trash.
3. Don't Waste Food.
4. Help keep the school area clean.
5. Don't Waste Water.

DAILY **Phonics** ROUTINES

DAY 2 **Discriminating** Write soft *c* and hard *c* words on the chalkboard. Read the list aloud, and ask children to hiss like a snake when they hear a word with the soft *c* sound.

Phonics CD-ROM

LANGUAGE SUPPORT

See **Language Support Book,** pages 145–148, for teaching suggestions for Build Background.

Children will use context and structural clues to determine the meanings of vocabulary words.

Definitions

village (p. 54) a small group of houses

noisy (p. 53) making much noise

diving (p. 55) going head first into water

explained (p. 58) made something plain or clear

soil (p. 58) earth; dirt

harm (p. 58) hurt or injury

Story Words

These words from the selection may be unfamiliar. Before children read, have them check the meanings and pronunciations of the words in the Glossary, beginning on page 398, or in a dictionary.

- Costa Rica, p. 48
- Fernando, p. 48
- cristobal, p. 57
- waterfall, p. 60

village
noisy
diving
explained
soil
harm

Vocabulary

Teach Vocabulary in Context

Identify Vocabulary Words   Display **Teaching Chart 114** and read the passage with children. Have volunteers circle each vocabulary word and underline other words that are clues to its meaning.

Carmina's News
1. Fernando hurried along the streets of the village where he lived. **2.** It was very noisy because all the children were excited and shouting. **3.** Some of them were cooling off by diving into the river that flowed by the village. **4.** Fernando wondered why everyone was so excited, so Carmina explained to help him understand. **5.** The village will be paid, she told him, to grow new trees and plants in the soil around the village. **6.** The trees will be protected and no one will be able to cut them down or harm them again.

Teaching Chart 114

Discuss Meanings   Ask questions like these to help clarify word meanings:

- How are a village and a city different from one another?
- Where is the noisiest place you've ever been? The quietest?
- What makes diving into water different from jumping into water?
- Tell about a time someone explained something to you. Did you understand?
- What are some things that grow in soil?
- What is the opposite of *harm*?

Practice

Riddle Me This Have partners take turns picking a vocabulary card and making up a riddle for the word. The partner must try to answer the riddle with one guess. ▶ **Kinesthetic/Linguistic**

Word Building Manipulative Cards

Group Sentences Small groups can build a sentence containing a vocabulary word. Without speaking, each person writes a word on paper, then passes it to the next person to continue the sentence. Remember—include the vocabulary word! Have students refer to their Glossary as needed. ▶ **Linguistic/Intrapersonal**

Assess Vocabulary

Identify Word Meaning in Context Invite children to write a context sentence for each vocabulary word, leaving a blank space where the vocabulary word would go. Have them underline any context clues that help show which vocabulary words fit in the sentences. Then have partners trade papers and fill in the missing words.

SPELLING/VOCABULARY CONNECTIONS

See Spelling Challenge Words, page 67Q.

LANGUAGE SUPPORT

See the **Language Support Book**, pages 145–148, for teaching suggestions for Vocabulary.

Vocabulary PuzzleMaker

Provides vocabulary activities.

Meeting Individual Needs for Vocabulary

EASY	ON-LEVEL	ON-LEVEL	CHALLENGE

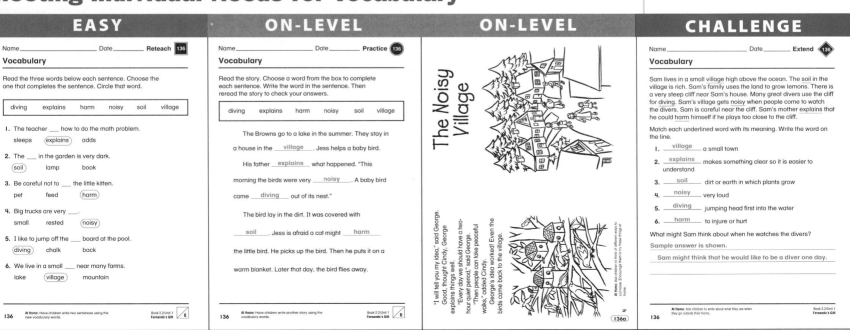

Reteach, 136	Practice, 136	Practice, 136a Take-Home Story	Extend, 136

Comprehension

Prereading Strategies

PREVIEW AND PREDICT Have children read the story title and then take a **picture walk** through the photographs.

- Where do you think this story takes place?
- Will this be a story about real people or is it an animal fable? How can you tell? (real people; it has photographs of people) *Genre*
- What will this story most likely be about?

Have children record their predictions about the story.

PREDICTIONS	WHAT HAPPENED
The story will be about a boy living in the rain forest.	
The story gives information about the rain forest.	

SET PURPOSES Ask children what they would like to find out by reading the story. For example:

- What is it like to live in the rain forest?
- Why is the rain forest important?

READ TOGETHER

NICARAGUA

Lago de Nicaragua

Bluefields

Rivas

Liberia

Puntarenas

San Jose

COSTA RICA

PANAMA

MEET DOUGLAS KEISTER

Douglas Keister is a photographer and an author. In 1987 he traveled to the rain forest in Central America. He took many photographs of the rain forest and of the people who live there. When he returned home, his friends thought he should use the photographs to write a children's book. *Fernando's Gift* is the result. It is Mr. Keister's first children's book.

46

Meeting Individual Needs · Grouping Suggestions for Strategic Reading

EASY

Read Together Read the story with children or have them use the **Listening Library.** Throughout, model the drawing of conclusions, based on information given in the story, as a strategy for better understanding the selection. Comprehension and Intervention prompts offer additional help with decoding, vocabulary, and comprehension.

ON-LEVEL

Guided Instruction Read the selection with children, using the Comprehension prompts. You may wish to have the children read the story first on their own while you monitor any difficulties they have, in order to determine which prompts to emphasize. Afterwards, have children reread the story using the rereading suggestions on page 62.

CHALLENGE

Read Independently Remind children that using details from the story to draw conclusions can help them to better understand the plot. After reading, have children retell the story, explaining what conclusions they drew while reading. Children can also use the questions on page 63 for a group discussion.

FERNANDO'S GIFT
EL REGALO DE FERNANDO

BY DOUGLAS KEISTER ①

47

A blackline master of this chart can be found in the **Language Support Book.**

LANGUAGE SUPPORT, 149

Comprehension

☑ **Phonics** Apply Soft *c* and *g*

☑ **Apply Drawing Conclusions**

STRATEGIC READING Drawing conclusions about the story will help you to understand it better. Let's create a chart that we can use to record our conclusions.

DETAILS	CONCLUSIONS

① What can you tell about the boy in the photo? (He looks happy and excited. He seems to like nature.)

Informational Story

Explain that in an informational story:

• characters and settings are usually realistic.

• information is given in an easy-to-understand way.

• the plot may be very simple.

Activity After children read *Fernando's Gift,* ask them to consider how this informational story compares to the realistic fiction selection, *Charlie Anderson.* Encourage them to use the illustrations to guide the discussion. Have them think about the realistic elements of both plots, and ask them to think about whether the two selections could switch settings and still be effective.

47

Comprehension

2 **DRAW CONCLUSIONS** The author does not tell us whether or not Fernando's grandfather is a good storyteller. What clues in the story suggest he might be a good storyteller?

MODEL The story tells me that some mornings, Fernando's family gathers on the porch to hear his grandfather's stories. I also read that when his grandfather tells stories, even the dogs seem to listen. From these clues I can draw the conclusion that Fernando's grandfather is a good storyteller.

3 **Phonics** **SOFT** *c* *Cecilia* is the name of Fernando's mother. What sound do you hear at the beginning of the name *Cecilia?* (soft *c*) Let's blend the letters together and say the name again.
Blending/Graphophonic Cues

My name is Fernando Vanegas, and I live deep inside the rain forest in Costa Rica. My father, Jubilio, built our house himself. The walls are wood, and the roof is made of tin. At night, the sound of the rain on the roof sings me to sleep.

2 **3** **4** Before breakfast each morning, while my mother, Cecilia, gives my little sister, Evelyn, her bath, the men in my family gather on the porch and talk. Sometimes my grandfather, Raphael Dias, tells us stories. Even our two dogs seem to listen! I hear that in some other places, they give dogs special names, just like people. We call our dogs Brown Dog and Black Dog.

Mi nombre es Fernando Vanegas y vivo en la part más profunda de la selva de Costa Rica. Mi papá, Jubilio, construyó nuestra casa solo. Las paredes son de madera y el techo esta hecho de hojalata. Por la noche, el sonido de la lluv cayendo en el techno me arrulla.

Todas las mañanas antes del desayuno, mientras mi mamá, Cecilia baña a mi hermanita, Evelyn, los hombres de mi familia se reúnen en el portal y conversan. Hay veces que mi abuelo, Rafa Días, nos cuenta historias. ¡Hasta nuestros dos perro parecen escuchar! He oído que en otros lugares, les dan nombres especiales a los perros, igual que a las personas. A nuestros perr les llamamos Perro Café y Perro Negro.

48

Activity

Cross Curricular: Language Arts

PICTURE DICTIONARY Elicit from children that the text of this story appears in both English and Spanish. Point out that the text on the right appears in blue in order to emphasize a foreign language. Discuss how the Spanish text tells the same story as the English text almost word for word.

Invite children to make a picture dictionary of the following Spanish words: *casa* (house), *perro* (dog), *abuelo* (grandfather). Have children illustrate each word and then label it in both Spanish and English. Encourage children to add to their dictionaries as they continue reading the story.

perro dog

casa house

49

Comprehension

4 Do you think this story will be about life in the rain forest? Why or why not?
Make Predictions

Comprehension

5 Fernando describes the different tasks each person in his family does as they prepare for breakfast. What does this tell you about the family? (Everyone helps out; they believe in teamwork.) *Make Inferences*

50

CULTURAL PERSPECTIVES

BREAKFAST FOODS Fernando and his family eat rice and beans for breakfast. Explain to children that in different cultures, different foods are eaten for breakfast.

RESEARCH AND INQUIRY Have children find information about breakfast foods in other cultures. Have them draw a picture of a typical breakfast for someone from a different culture.

▶ **Intrapersonal/Visual**

My father says that he will spend most of the day tending our crop of achiote, a plant that's used to make red dye. Other days, my father spends his time planting trees. He also has a job teaching people about the rain forest.

When it's time for breakfast, my father milks the cow, and my mother and Evelyn chop onions to flavor our meal. This morning we're having rice and beans. If I'm not too full, I might have a banana, too. They grow right outside our house—all I have to do is pick one! **5** **6**

Mi papá dice que se pasará la mayoría del día cuidando nuestra cosecha de achiote, una planta que se usa para hacer tinte rojo. Otros dias, mi papá pasa el tiempo sembrando árboles. Él también trabaja educando a las personas sobre la selva.

A la hora del desayuno, mi papá ordeña la vaca, y mi mamá y Evelyn cortan cebollas para darle sabor a nuestra comida. Esta mañana comeremos arroz y frijoles. Si no estoy muy lleno, puede ser que coma un plátano, también. Ellos crecen afuera de nuestra casa—¡solamente tengo que recoger uno!

51

Comprehension

6 Fernando's father tends his crops, grows trees, and teaches people about the rain forest. What does this tell you about him? (He works very hard. He cares about the rain forest.) *Character*

PHONICS AND DECODING /ch/ Write the word *chop* on the board. Ask children to read the word aloud. Ask them what sound they hear at the beginning of the word. (/ch/)

Minilesson

REVIEW/MAINTAIN

Using Context Clues

Remind children that looking at the pictures or at other words in a sentence or paragraph can often help them understand the meanings of unfamiliar words.

- Point out the word *crop* in the first sentence on this page.
- Have children reread the sentence. Ask them what word might help them figure out what *crop* means. (plant) Then have them look at the photo on page 50 for more clues.

Activity Encourage children to use the same strategy to determine the meaning of the word *tending*. Remind them to use other words and pictures as clues.

 PREVENTION/INTERVENTION

PHONICS AND DECODING /ch/ Write on the board the words *chop, chill,* and *change.* Remind children that the letters *c* and *h* together make the /ch/ sound. Have children silently read the words on the board, and then say each word aloud. Invite children to brainstorm a list of other words that begin with the /ch/ sound.
Graphophonic Cues

Comprehension

7 How do you think Fernando feels about his grandfather? What clues in the story might tell us how he feels? (He seems to respect his knowledge and to enjoy spending time with him.) *Make Inferences*

8 **DRAW CONCLUSIONS** Fernando's grandfather seems to know a lot about the rain forest. What can you conclude from this? (He must care about the rain forest.) Let's begin our charts.

CLUES	CONCLUSIONS
Fernando's grandfather knows a lot about the rain forest.	He must care about the rain forest.

After breakfast, I go to school. It's not very far—only about three miles from our house. Often my grandfather and the dogs walk with me. Grandfather knows everything about the rain forest and what to look for along the way: fruits and nuts, insects and lizards, beautiful flowers, maybe even a bright red parrot. This morning he wants to show

7 me a family of squirrel monkeys. They're not easy to find anymore. Grandfather says

8 that when he was a child, there were many monkeys in the rain forest.

Después del desayuno, me voy a la escuela. No queda muy lejos—solamente unas tres millas de nuestra casa. A menudo mi abuelo y los perros me acompañan. Abuelo sabe todo sobre la selva y lo que se debe buscar en el camino: frutas y nueces, insectos y lagartos, bellas flores, y con suerte un loro rojo brillante. Esta mañana me quiere enseñar una familia de titíes. Ya no son fáciles de encontrar. Abuelo dice que cuando él era niño, había muchos monos en la selva.

52

Activity

Cross Curricular: Math

TIME TRAVEL Fernando lives three miles from school. He walks to school each day. Invite children to share information about the different ways they get to school. Do they walk, take the bus, or ride in a car? Use a street map to help children measure how far they live from school. Invite children to create a chart detailing the distance each of them lives from school. ▶ **Visual/Mathematical**

Name	Distance from school	Method of travel
Angie	½ mile	walk
Brianna	2 blocks	walk
Joey	1½ miles	car

Grandfather spots a squirrel monkey at last. He says it's a full-grown adult, even though it's very tiny. Suddenly we hear howler monkeys barking in the treetops above us. The dogs bark right back. The rain forest can be a noisy place sometimes!

Al fin Abuelo encuentra un tití. Dice que es un adulto maduro, aunque es muy pequeño. De pronto oímos unos monos aulladores ladrando en las copas de los árboles encima de nosotros. Los perros les contestan ladrando. ¡Hay veces que la selva es un lugar de mucho ruido!

53

Comprehension

9 What kinds of things does Fernando see on his way to school? (fruits, nuts, animals, flowers, a squirrel monkey) What do you see on your way to school? How is Fernando's experience the same as yours? How is it different? *Compare and Contrast*

10 Why does Fernando say that the rain forest is noisy? (Because the howler monkeys and the dogs bark.) *Cause and Effect*

Comprehension

11 **Phonics** **SOFT** *g* What word in the first sentence on page 54 contains the /j/ sound? *(village)* Which letters stand for the /j/ sound? *(ge)* **Blending**

12 Fernando says that today is a special day because it is Carmina's birthday. He has not decided what present to give her. What does this tell you about Fernando? (He and Carmina must be good friends. He cares about his friends.) **Character**

P/i **PROPER NOUNS** Can anyone point out the proper nouns on page 54? (Londres, Cordova, Carmina) How do you know that they are proper nouns? (They start with a capital letter and name a place or person.)

SELF-MONITORING **STRATEGY**

REREAD Rereading a paragraph or a few sentences can help a reader to understand a confusing part of a story.

MODEL I'm not sure if Carmina and Fernando are fishing in a big river or a stream. I'm going to look back for clues. Okay, now I see that they are fishing in a small stream, not the big river. It is their two friends who are at the river.

My school is in the village of Londres. Sometimes our teacher, **11** Mr. Cordova, holds classes outside. Today is a special day at school. It's my **12** friend Carmina's eighth birthday. I want to give her a present, but I haven't decided on one yet.

Mi escuela está en el pueblo de Londres. Hay veces que nuestro maestro, el Sr. Córdova, da las clases al aire libre. Hoy es un día especial en la escuela. Mi amiga Carmina cumple ocho años. Le quiero dar un regalo, pero no he escogido uno todavía.

54

P/i **PREVENTION/INTERVENTION**

PROPER NOUNS Point out the proper nouns on page 54. *(Londres, Cordova, Carmina)* Remind children that proper nouns are the names of people, places, or things, and that they are always capitalized. Write on the board a list of proper nouns and common nouns. Invite volunteers to locate the proper nouns, and to circle the clue in each word (initial capital letter) that tells them the word is a proper noun. Use the following examples:

the boy	Mr. Mills
the building	The White House
the city	Houston

Syntactic Cues

After school, Carmina and I go fishing. We have a favorite place—a small stream that flows into the big river, Rio Naranjo. On our way to the stream, we see friends from school |diving| into the cool river waters. We fish for a while, but there are no trout today. We'll have to have something else for supper.

Después de las clases, Carmina y yo vamos a pescar. Tenemos un lugar favorito—un pequeño arroyo que desagua en el río grande, el Río Naranjo. En camino al arroyo, vemos a unos amigos de la escuela saltando al agua fresca del río. Pescamos por un rato, pero hoy no hay truchas. Tendremos que comer otra cosa para la cena.

55

Comprehension

(13) DRAW CONCLUSIONS Why does Fernando say, "We'll have to have something else for supper"? What conclusion can you draw about Carmina and Fernando going fishing? Were they fishing for fun? (No, they were fishing for their supper.)

(14) While they are walking to the stream to fish, what do Carmina and Fernando see their friends doing? (diving into the river) What does this tell you about the place they live? (It has rivers with fish in them. It is hot enough to go swimming.) *Setting*

LANGUAGE SUPPORT

ESL Help children to realize that the word *fish* has two meanings: as a verb, *fish* shows an action; and as a noun, *fish* is a thing. Using pictures of fish and of people fishing, or using props such as a paper cutout of a fish and a "fishing line" made from a pencil and some string, help children to understand the differ-ence between "fish" and "to fish." Then have children reread page 55.

Ask children to compare the English word "fish" with the comparable word in their first language. Are the native-language noun and verb for "fish" the same or different?

Comprehension

15 How do you think Carmina feels when she discovers that her favorite tree is gone? (She feels sad and disappointed.) What clues can you use to make an inference about her feelings? (Look at the picture; use experience to imagine what it feels like to lose something that is your favorite, and so on.) *Make Inferences*

TEACHING TIP

CHARACTERIZATION As children read, point out that one way to understand what a character is feeling is to compare that character's life with their own lives. Like Carmina, have they lost a favorite thing? Like Fernando, have they wanted to think of a special gift to give a friend? How did they feel in these situations?

15

56

Activity

Cross Curricular: Science

TREE PLANTING Explain to children that trees need food and water in order to stay healthy.

RESEARCH AND INQUIRY Have children research what a tree needs in order to grow strong and healthy. Have each child write directions explaining

how to care for a tree. They may illustrate their directions.
▶ **Logical/Linguistic**

*inter*NET **CONNECTION** Children can learn more about trees by visiting **www.mhschool.com/reading**.

1. Needs plenty of sun.
2. Needs lots of water.
3. Needs clean air without too much pollution.

Carmina wants to show me her favorite climbing tree. It's called a cristobal — and it's a very old one. Carmina's grandfather used to play in it, too, when he was our age. But when we get there, we see that someone has cut the tree down. Who would do such a thing? Maybe my grandfather knows the answer.

Carmina me quiere enseñar su árbol favorito para trepar. Se llama un árbol cristóbal y es muy viejo. El abuelo de Carmina jugaba en él también cuando tenía nuestra edad. Pero cuando llegamos, vemos que alguien lo ha cortado. ¿Quién habrá hecho tal cosa? Quizás mi abuelo sepa.

57

Comprehension

 **SOFT** *g* Is there a word on this page that contains the /j/ sound? *(age)* Which letters stand for /j/? *(ge)* **Blending/Graphophonic Cues**

17 What did Fernando and Carmina do after school was over for the day? (They went fishing. Then Carmina tried to show Fernando her favorite tree, but someone had cut it down.) *Sequence of Events*

Comprehension

(18) **DRAW CONCLUSIONS** Grandfather tells the children that people harm the rain forest by cutting down trees. Fernando's father plants trees and teaches people about the rain forest. What can we conclude about Fernando's father's job?
(It is an important job, because he is helping to save the rain forest.)

CLUES	CONCLUSIONS
Fernando's grandfather knows a lot about the rain forest.	He must care about the rain forest.
Fernando's father plants trees and teaches people about the rain forest.	He is helping to save the rain forest.

(19) What do you think Fernando is going to give to Carmina for her birthday?
Make Predictions

(18) Grandfather explains that people have been cutting down trees in the rain forest for many years. Often they don't understand the harm they are doing. He tells us that when trees are cut down, animals no longer have a place to live. Trees also help to keep the soil from washing away. Grandfather says that this is why my father's job planting trees and teaching people about the rain forest is so important. Suddenly **(19)** I know what I will give Carmina for her birthday.

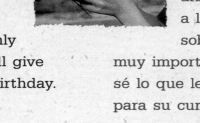

Abuelo nos explica que hace muchos años que la gente corta los árboles en selva. Con frecuencia ellos no comprenden el daño qu hacen. Nos dice que cuand los árboles se cortan, los animales ya no tienen don vivir. Los árboles también ayudan para que l tierra no se desgaste con el agua. Abuelo dice que por eso el trabajo de mi papá, plantando árboles y educand a las personas sobre la selva, es muy importante. De pronto sé lo que le daré a Carmin para su cumpleaños.

58

Activity

Activity Cross Curricular: Social Studies

MAP SKILLS Display a world map. Help children:

- locate the United States, and then the state in which they live.
- locate Central America, and the country of Costa Rica.
- name the oceans that border Costa Rica.
- name the countries that border Costa Rica.

▶ **Spatial/Intrapersonal**

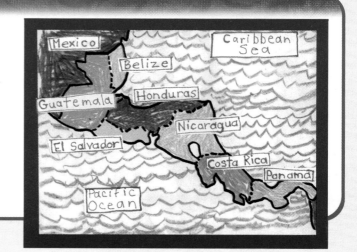

My father has a plant nursery with lots of small cristobal trees in it. If I do some chores for him, he will give me one. That will be Carmina's birthday gift. I decide to let her choose the tree she wants. Then Carmina asks my father if he knows of a place in the rain forest where her tree will be safe.

Mi papá tiene un criadero de plantas con muchos árboles cristóbal. Si hago unas tareas para él, me dará uno. Será el regalo de cumpleaños para Carmina. Decido que ella puede escoger el árbol. Después Carmina le pregunta a mi papá si conoce un lugar en la selva donde estará seguro su árbol.

59

Comprehension

20 **DRAW CONCLUSIONS** What conclusion can you draw about how Fernando's family feels about the rain forest?

MODEL I think Fernando's family cares a lot about the plants and animals in the rain forest. Grandfather explains why trees are needed and why Fernando's father's job is so important. This is the evidence I need to draw the conclusions about how they feel.

21 **Phonics** **SOFT** *c* Let's read the last sentence on page 59. What is the word in this sentence that contains the /s/ sound? *(place)* Blend the sounds together and read the word aloud.
Blending/Graphophonic Cues

Comprehension

 22 What does Fernando mean when he says that Carmina's tree will be safe? What will her tree be safe from? (somebody cutting it down) *Make Inferences*

 COMPOUND WORDS Which two words on page 60 are compound words? *(horseback, waterfall)*

My father and I know a secret spot deep in the rain forest, near a waterfall. It's a long way, even on horseback. No one else seems to know about it. Carmina's tree should be safe there.

Mi papá y yo sabemos de un lugar secreto en la parte más profunda de la selva, cerca de una cascada. Queda muy lejos, hasta a caballo. Nadie más sabe de este lugar. El árbol de Carmina debe estar seguro allí.

22

60

READ WITH EXPRESSION

PARTNERS Have partners take turns reading aloud the paragraphs on these two pages.

Remind children to:

- think about how Fernando is feeling, and read with expression.
- pause briefly at commas.
- pause at the end of sentences.

p/i PREVENTION/INTERVENTION

COMPOUND WORDS Have children read the first two sentences on page 60. Point out the words *horseback* and *waterfall,* and explain that they are compound words, meaning that they are each made up of two smaller words. Ask children to identify the small words in *horseback* and *waterfall.*

Then ask them the meaning of these words. Help children understand that the two smaller words will help them figure out the meaning of the compound word. Have children brainstorm a list of compound words. *Semantic Cues*

After riding for many miles, we reach our secret spot. Carmina and I plant the little tree together. We make a wish that it will be safe and live a long, long time.

 23   **24**

Después de montar a caballo por muchas millas, llegamos a nuestro lugar secreto. Carmina y yo sembramos juntos el arbolito. Deseamos que esté seguro y que viva por mucho, mucho tiempo.

61

Comprehension

23 Are there any volunteers who would like to take on the roles of Carmina and Fernando, and role-play them planting the tree? Show what you would do to plant the tree. Remember to make a wish at the end that the tree will remain safe. *Plot/Kinesthetic/Role-Play*

24 Do you think Carmina's and Fernando's wish will come true? *Make Predictions*

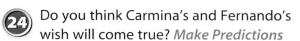

Minilesson

REVIEW/MAINTAIN

Main Idea

Remind children that identifying a story's main idea will help them to understand the story better. A story's main idea is the most important information without too many details. Ask:

- Does this story's main idea have to do with the rain forest in which Fernando lives?
- Guide children to create a main idea statement about the story.

Activity Have children write a sentence expressing the main idea of pages 60 and 61.

Comprehension

(25) DRAW CONCLUSIONS Now that we have finished the story, what can we conclude about how Fernando and Carmina feel about the rain forest? (They planted Carmina's tree and are happy that it is growing. They care a lot about the rain forest.) Let's fill in our charts.

CLUES	CONCLUSIONS
Fernando's grandfather knows a lot about the rain forest.	He must care about the rain forest.
Fernando's father plants trees and teaches people about the rain forest.	He is helping to save the rain forest.
Fernando and Carmina are happy that her tree is growing.	Fernando and Carmina care about the rain forest.

RETELL THE STORY Ask children in groups of three to retell the story. Encourage children to use their chart as an aid in remembering the main ideas of the story. *Summarize*

STUDENT SELF-ASSESSMENT

Have children ask themselves the following questions to assess how they are reading:

• How did drawing conclusions help me to understand the story?

• How did using the chart help me?

TRANSFERRING THE STRATEGY

• How can I use this strategy to help me read other stories?

62

REREADING FOR *Fluency*

PARTNERS Have children choose a favorite section of the story to read to a partner. Encourage children to read with expression.

READING RATE When you evaluate reading rate, have children read aloud from the story for one minute. Place a stick-on note after the last word read. Count words read. To evaluate children's performance, see the Running Record in the **Fluency Assessment** book.

ⓘ Intervention For leveled fluency passages, lessons, and norm charts, see **Skills Intervention Guide**, Part 5, Fluency.

Now, my father and I go to our secret spot whenever we can. Often Carmina comes with us. We may fish or swim or play under the waterfall, but our visits always end with a picnic at Carmina's tree. On our way home, we are happy knowing that it grows tall and strong.

Ahora, mi papá y yo vamos a nuestro lugar secreto cada vez que podemos. Con frecuencia Carmina viene con nosotros. Puede ser que pesquemos, nademos o juguemos debajo de la cascada, pero nuestras visitas siempre terminan con una merienda debajo del árbol de Carmina. En camino a casa, estamos contentos de saber que crece alto y fuerte.

63

Comprehension

Return to Predictions and Purposes

Reread children's predictions about the story. Ask children if the story answered the questions they had before they read.

PREDICTIONS	WHAT HAPPENED
The story will be about a boy living in the rain forest.	The story was about Fernando, a boy who lived in the rain forest.
The story gives information about the rain forest.	Information about the rain forest, and how people are destroying the trees, was part of the story.

INFORMAL ASSESSMENT

HOW TO ASSESS

SOFT *c* AND SOFT *g* Write the words *village* and *place* on the board. Ask children to read them aloud. Have children identify the letters in each word that stand for the /s/ *(ce)* or /j/ *(ge)* sounds.

DRAWING CONCLUSIONS Ask children to share the conclusions that they drew from the story.

FOLLOW UP

SOFT *c* AND SOFT *g* Write on the board lists of words containing the soft *c* and soft *g* sounds. Have children circle the letter combinations that represent those sounds.

DRAWING CONCLUSIONS If children have difficulty drawing conclusions ask them to retell the story. As they tell the story, ask them questions that will require them to draw conclusions. Prompt them by asking them what information from the story they are using to answer your questions.

LITERARY RESPONSE

QUICK-WRITE Invite children to use their journals to record their thoughts about the story and the conclusions they drew about Fernando, his gift, and the rain forest.

ORAL RESPONSE Have children discuss these questions:

• If you could give a gift to Fernando, what would you give him? Why?

• Is Fernando's school similar to or different from your own? How?

• How important is the rain forest to Fernando and his family? Use information from your chart to support your conclusions.

• What is Fernando's father doing to help protect the rain forest?

• What would you like to see happen next in the story?

63

Story Questions

Have children discuss or write answers to the questions on page 64.

Answers:

1. in a small village in the rain forests of Costa Rica *Literal/Setting*

2. so that no one will find it and cut it down *Inferential/Cause and Effect*

3. Answers will vary. Some children might mention that Fernando is helping the forest as well as giving a nice gift to a friend. *Inferential/Drawing Conclusions*

4. life in the rain forest *Critical/Summarize*

5. Luka does not like her gift at first; she does not understand its importance. Carmina at once recognizes the thought behind the gift. *Critical/Reading Across Texts*

Write a Magazine Article For a full lesson related to this writing suggestion, see the lesson on Writing that Compares on pages 67M–67N.

Story Questions & Activities

READ TOGETHER

1 Where does this story take place?

2 Why do Carmina and Fernando plant the tree in a secret place?

3 Why is Fernando's gift important?

4 What is this story mostly about?

5 Fernando and Luka's grandmother each give a gift to someone they care about. How are Carmina's and Luka's reactions different?

Write a Magazine Article

Compare the rain forest to a forest near your home, or one that you've visited or learned about. What kind of plants and animals live in each? What do you like about each of them? Make sure to include words that describe.

Meeting Individual Needs

EASY	ON-LEVEL	CHALLENGE

EASY

Name _____ Date _____ Reteach **137**

Story Comprehension

Color the pictures that describe Fernando's life.

1. 2.
3. 4.
5. 6.

Book 2.2/Unit 1
Fernando's Gift

At Home: Have children draw another picture that describes "Fernando's Gift."

137

ON-LEVEL

Name _____ Date _____ Practice **137**

Story Comprehension

Think about "Fernando's Gift." Write the correct answer to complete each sentence.

1. Fernando lives in
   <u>a rain forest</u> .
   a. a rain forest
   b. a city

2. Fernando's father plants
   <u>trees</u> .
   a. rice
   b. trees

3. The dogs are called
   <u>Brown Dog and Black Dog</u> .
   a. Brown Dog and Black Dog
   b. Fido and Spot

4. Fernando's father also teaches people about the
   <u>rain forest</u> .
   a. dogs
   b. rain forest

5. Carmina takes Fernando to see her favorite <u>climbing tree</u> .
   a. river
   b. climbing tree

6. The tree has <u>been cut down</u> .
   a. been cut down
   b. grown a lot

7. Fernando gives Carmina a new <u>Cristobal tree</u> .
   a. Cristobal tree
   b. toy

8. They plant the tree in
   <u>a secret place</u> .
   a. her yard
   b. a secret place

Book 2.2/Unit 1
Fernando's Gift

At Home: Have children draw a picture of their favorite part of the story. Then ask them to write a sentence about it.

137

CHALLENGE

Name _____ Date _____ Extend **137**

Story Comprehension

Write a letter to Fernando telling him all the things you learned about the rain forest. Tell him why you think his gift of a tree is very special.

Dear Fernando,

I learned _____
trees should be planted to help the animals survive.
_____
_____

I think your gift was very special because _____
it helps people and animals.
_____

Your Friend,
_____

A sample answer is shown.

Book 2.2/Unit 1
Fernando's Gift

At Home: Ask children to read their letter and discuss what else they know about the rain forest. Then have them draw a picture of the rain forest.

137

Reteach, 137   Practice, 137   Extend, 137

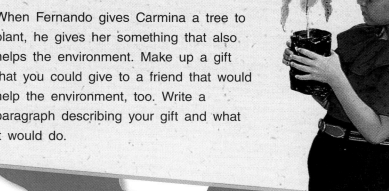

Give a Gift

When Fernando gives Carmina a tree to plant, he gives her something that also helps the environment. Make up a gift that you could give to a friend that would help the environment, too. Write a paragraph describing your gift and what it would do.

Learn About Costa Rica

Costa Rica is a country in Central America. Find Costa Rica on a map. Draw a picture of the country. Write the name of the ocean to the west of Costa Rica.

Find Out More

Fernando and his family live in the rain forest in Costa Rica. What is the rain forest like? Where else are there rain forests? Why are they important to us?

65

Story Activities

Give a Gift

Materials: paper, pencil

ONE Brainstorm with the children a list of the various ways that people can help the environment. Then, consider each idea individually and brainstorm a list of possible related gifts. After brainstorming, encourage children to choose one gift and to draw a picture of what it might look like.

Learn About Costa Rica

Materials: map of Central America, paper, pencil, crayons or paint

ONE Display a map of Central America from an atlas. Invite a volunteer to point to the country of Costa Rica. Invite children to label the names of the countries, cities, and bodies of water in and near Costa Rica on their maps.

Find Out More

RESEARCH AND INQUIRY Have children **GROUP** work in small groups to find additional information on rain forests. Provide encyclopedias and science books. Have children compile their research into a classroom display about the rain forest.

 **inter NET** Have students visit **CONNECTION** *www.mhschool.com/reading* to find more information on rain forests.

FORMAL ASSESSMENT

After page 65, see Selection Assessment.

DAILY  ROUTINES

DAY 3 **Fluency** Write the following words on the chalkboard: *race, huge, pace, stage, brace, page, mice, rice.* Point to each word, asking children to blend the sounds silently. Ask a volunteer to read aloud each word.

Phonics CD-ROM

Study Skills

GRAPHIC AIDS

**OBJECTIVES**

Children will:

- use a chart to find information about a topic.
- identify different items in a chart.

PREPARE Remind children that charts can be useful tools for organizing information. Display **Teaching Chart 115.**

TEACH Explain to children that a chart with columns can make it easy to compare and contrast different pieces of information.

PRACTICE Have children answer questions 1–5. Review the answers with them: **1.** rain forest wildlife **2.** where it lives, what food it eats, and if it is endangered **3.** orangutans, mountain gorillas, and tapirs **4.** orangutans and clouded leopards **5.** They all are homes to endangered animals.

ASSESS/CLOSE Have children research and add other animals to the chart.

STUDY SKILLS READ TOGETHER

Read a Chart

Many animals live in rain forests. This **chart** shows several of them. Some of these animals are **endangered**. This means that soon there might not be any more of them.

Rain Forest Wildlife			
Continent	**Animal**	**Food**	**Endangered**
Asia	Orangutan	fruit, figs	yes
	Clouded leopard	monkeys, deer, wild boar	yes
	Flying dragon	ants, termites	no
Africa	Mountain gorilla	leaves, berries, bark	yes
	Cheetah	hares, birds, gazelle	yes
South America	Amazon River dolphin	fish	yes
	Tapir	leaves, bugs, branches	no

Use the chart to answer the questions.

1. What is the chart about?

2. What does the chart tell about each animal?

3. Which animals eat plants?

4. Which of the animals in Asia are endangered?

5. What do rain forests in the three continents have in common?

Meeting Individual Needs

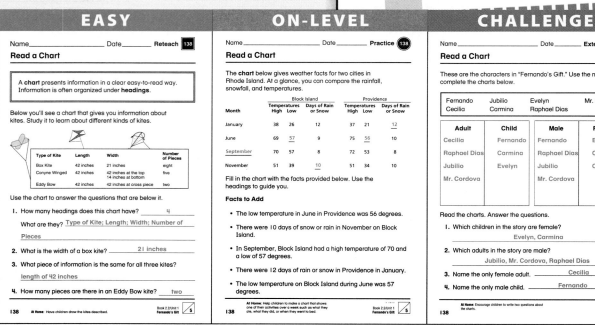

Reteach, 138   Practice, 138   Extend, 138

TEST POWER

Think about how the story's parts fit together.

DIRECTIONS:

Read the story. Then read each question about the story.

EXAMPLE

From the Atlantic to the Pacific

The United States is over three thousand miles wide. The land in the east has small hills. The hills are rounded and are not very tall. There are many beaches good for swimming.

The land in the middle of the country is mostly flat. This is where most of the country's crops are grown.

The land in the west has many mountains. They are mostly tall with rough, pointed peaks. On the coast, there are many cliffs. They drop hundreds of feet down into the Pacific Ocean.

Each part of the United States is different from the others. All are beautiful to visit.

1 Which has higher mountains?
- ○ The east
- ● The west
- ○ The middle of the country
- ○ There are no mountains anywhere.

2 Which conclusion can you draw from this passage?
- ● The United States has many different kinds of land.
- ○ The land in the east is just like the land in the west.
- ○ Most of the crops are grown in the east.
- ○ There are no good beaches in the east.

67

Test Power

THE PRINCETON REVIEW

Read the Page

Explain to children that you will be reading this story as a group. You will read the story, and they will follow along in their books.

Request that children put pens, pencils, and markers away, since they will not be writing.

Discuss the Questions

QUESTION 1: Have children find the lines discussing the mountains. The seventh and eighth sentences state that the west has many tall mountains.

QUESTION 2: Remind children that a conclusion is an idea one gets from the story that is not thoroughly explained. Additional clues can be found in the title and at the end. This story discusses parts of the United States and how each part of the country is different.

Leveled Books

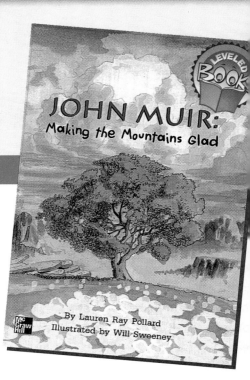

EASY

John Muir: Making the Mountains Glad

☑ Soft *c*: /s/ *ce* and Soft *g*: /j/ *ge*

☑ Compare and Contrast

☑ Instructional Vocabulary: *diving, explained, harm, noisy, soil, village*

By Lauren Ray Pollard
Illustrated by Will Sweeney

Answers to Story Questions

1. Scotland
2. He wanted to travel and learn about nature.
3. Because people liked what he wrote and wanted to talk to him about it. They wanted to learn from him.
4. How a boy who loved the outdoors grew up to be a man who worked to preserve nature.
5. They both care about nature and want to protect it.

The Story Questions and Activity below appear in the Easy Book.

Story Questions and Writing Activity

1. What country did John Muir come from?
2. Why did John Muir leave his job at the factory?
3. Why do you think people came to visit John Muir?
4. What is this story mainly about?
5. In what way is Fernando's father like John Muir?

Write a Postcard

Imagine you are John Muir on one of his trips. Write a postcard telling someone about what you see.

from *John Muir*

Guided Reading

PREVIEW AND PREDICT Discuss each illustration through page 7. As you take the **picture walk**, have children predict what the story is about. Chart their ideas.

SET PURPOSES Have children draw pictures that explain why they want to read the story and share them with the class.

READ THE BOOK Use questions like the following to guide children's reading or after they have read the story independently.

Page 3: Find the word *village*. What sound do the letters *ge* make? /j/ Write the words *age*, *cage*, and *page* on the chalkboard. What sound do the letters *ge* make in each of these words? *Phonics and Decoding*

Page 7: What do you think John Muir saw around him while working in the factory? (machinery, people, tools) How was this different from what he saw as he walked through the woods? *Compare and Contrast*

Page 14: Find the word *harm*. What did John Muir think was harming the mountains? (people cutting trees, cows and sheep eating plants) *Instructional Vocabulary*

Page 16: Do you think our country would have beautiful parks today without the work of John Muir? *Make Predictions*

Page 16: How did John Muir feel when he walked through the woods and fields? How did he feel while working in the factory? What does this tell you about the kind of person John Muir was? *Character and Plot*

RETURN TO PREDICTIONS AND PURPOSES Discuss children's predictions. Ask which were close to the story and why. Have children review their purposes for reading. Did they find out what they wanted to know?

LITERARY RESPONSE Discuss these questions:

- How would you describe John Muir?
- How do you think his work was important?

Also see the story questions and activity in *John Muir: Making the Mountains Glad*.

See the 💿 **Phonics** **CD-ROM** for practice using words with soft *c* and *g*.

Leveled Books

INDEPENDENT

Make a Difference

Make a Difference

Written by J.C. Bates
Illustrated by Felipe Galindo

- ☑ Soft *c*: /s/ *ce* and Soft *g*: /j/ *ge*
- ☑ Compare and Contrast

Instructional Vocabulary:
diving, explained, harm, noisy, soil, village

Guided Reading

PREVIEW AND PREDICT Take a **picture walk** through page 5 of the story. As children enjoy the illustrations, have them predict what the story is about. Chart their ideas.

SET PURPOSES Have students write down five questions they would like to have answered from the story. Have children write sentences describing why they want to read the story. For example: I want to find out how I can help protect our environment.

READ THE BOOK Use questions like the following to guide children's reading or after they have read the story.

Page 3: Find the word *electricity*. What sound does the first *c* make in the word *electricity*? (hard c) What sound does the second *c* make? (soft c, /s/) *Phonics and Decoding*

Page 7: Do you save more water by taking a bath or a shower? (shower) How much water does it take to fill a bathtub? (20 gallons) *Compare and Contrast*

Page 8: Find the word *soil*. What destroys the soil? (coal mines) Try to use the word *soil* in a sentence. *Instructional Vocabulary*

Page 16: Do we use more energy today than long ago? (today) What do we use energy for today? (heating, lighting, transportation, production of products) *Compare and Contrast*

Page 16: What do you think might happen if people do not work together to save our natural resources? *Make Predictions*

RETURN TO PREDICTIONS AND PURPOSES Discuss children's predictions. Ask which were close to the story and why. Have children review their purposes for reading. Did they find out what they wanted to know?

LITERARY RESPONSE Discuss:

- What everyday things can we do to preserve the environment?

Also see the story questions and activity in *Make a Difference*.

See the 🔵 Phonics CD-ROM for practice using words with soft *c* and *g*.

Answers to Story Questions

1. 10 gallons
2. Conserving Water
3. Keeping Cool in the Summer
4. Tips people can use to conserve energy.
5. Answers will vary.

The Story Questions and Activity below appear in the Independent Book.

Story Questions and Writing Activity

1. How many gallons of water do you use each day by brushing your teeth?
2. Which section would you look in to find information about how much water it takes to fill a bathtub?
3. Tell which section the following tip would best fit in: If you turn on the oven, the kitchen will feel much hotter. When the weather permits, try cooking outside, on a grill.
4. What is the main idea of the selection?
5. What if Fernando made up a conservation tip? What would he say?

Taking Action

Choose one of the facts you learned about conserving water and electricity. Draw and caption a picture of what you can do at home to "make a difference."

from Make a Difference

Leveled Books

CHALLENGE

Save Our Park Trees

☑ Soft *c:* /s/ *ce* and Soft *g:* /j/ *ge*
Compare and Contrast

☑ Instructional Vocabulary:
diving, explained, harm, noisy,
soil, village

Written by Barbara Adams
Illustrated by Rick Brown

Guided Reading

PREVIEW AND PREDICT Discuss each illustration through page 5. As you take the **picture walk**, have children predict what the story is about. Chart their ideas.

SET PURPOSES Have children draw pictures that show why they want to read the story. Have children share their drawings with the class.

READ THE BOOK Use questions like the following to guide children's reading or after they have read the story independently.

Page 2: Find the word *city*. What sound does the letter *c* make? (/s/) Look at another word. Write the word *cent* on the chalkboard. What sound does this word begin with? (/s/) *Phonics and Decoding*

Page 5: How do people who want to save the tree feel about the tree? (They think it makes the park a special place.) Why do some people want to cut the tree down? (to make room for a food stand and parking lot) *Compare and Contrast*

Page 13: Find the word *soil*. What does *soil* give trees? (water and food) Use the word *soil* in a sentence. *Instructional Vocabulary*

Page 16: Do you think the tree will be saved or cut down? Why do you think so? *Make Predictions*

Page 16: If someone asked you what the story *Save Our Park Trees* was about, what would you tell them? *Summarize*

RETURN TO PREDICTIONS AND PURPOSES Discuss children's predictions. Ask which were close to the story and why. Have children review their purposes for reading. Did they find out what they wanted to know?

LITERARY RESPONSE Discuss these questions:

• Why do you think people who live in cities might have special feelings about trees?

• Did the story make you think about your local trees in a new way? How?

Also see the story questions and activity for *Save Our Park Trees*.

See the **Phonics** CD-ROM for practice using words with soft *c* and soft *g*.

Activities

Bringing Groups Together

Anthology and Leveled Books

Connecting Texts

CLASS DISCUSSION Write the story titles on the four corners of a chart. Write the words *Protect Our Environment* in the middle of the chart. Have children discuss different ways people can work to protect the environment as featured in each of the stories. List children's contributions under each story title. Draw a line from the words *Protect Our Environment* to each contribution children have made.

ENVIRONMENT CHART Use the chart to talk about different ways of protecting our environment.

Fernando's Gift
Save the rain forest.
Save the trees of the rain forest.

John Muir: Making the Mountains Glad
Keep mountains beautiful by saving trees.
Stop animals from eating all the plants.

Protect Our Environment

Make a Difference
Use less water.
Use less electricity.

Save Our Park Trees
Save trees in danger of being cut down.

Viewing/Representing

GROUP PRESENTATIONS Divide the class into four groups, each group representing one of the four stories in the lesson. Have children in each group work together to make a *Save Our Environment* poster. Have children focus on ways to save our environment that were featured in their stories.

AUDIENCE RESPONSE

Have children look carefully at each of the posters and ask questions.

Research and Inquiry

MORE ABOUT ENVIRONMENTAL PROTECTION
Have children ask themselves what else they might like to know about protecting our environment. Invite them to:

- Look at books about this topic.

- Invite a representative of an environmental protection agency to speak to the class.

- Plan a project that benefits the environment.

interNET CONNECTION Go to **www.mhschool.com/reading** for more information about environmental protection.

 Have children write and draw what they learned about protecting the environment in their journals.

OBJECTIVES

Children will:

- identify words with soft *c* and soft *g*.
- blend and read words with soft *c* and soft *g*.

MATERIALS

- **Teaching Chart 116**
- **index cards**

Skills Finder

Soft *c* and Soft *g*

Introduce	B2: 44G–H
Review	B2: 67E–F, 67G–H, 340G–H, 361E–F
Test	B2: Unit 1
Maintain	B2: 221

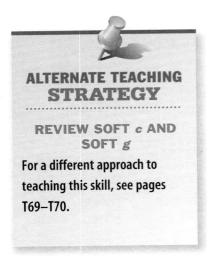

ALTERNATE TEACHING STRATEGY

REVIEW SOFT *c* AND SOFT *g*

For a different approach to teaching this skill, see pages T69–T70.

Review Soft *c* and Soft *g*

PREPARE

Listen for Soft *c* and Soft *g* Words

Read the following sentence aloud. Ask children to clap when they hear the /s/ sound, and to raise their hands when they hear the /j/ sound.

- I know a <u>nice</u> <u>place</u> where <u>huge</u> <u>mice</u> like to hide.

TEACH

BLENDING Model and Guide Practice with Soft *c* and Soft *g*

- Display **Teaching Chart 116.** Run your finger under the word *age,* blending the letters to read the word.
- Remind children that *ge* in *age* stands for the /j/ sound.
- In the second row, add *ge* to make the word *page.*
- Invite a volunteer to circle the letters that stand for /j/.

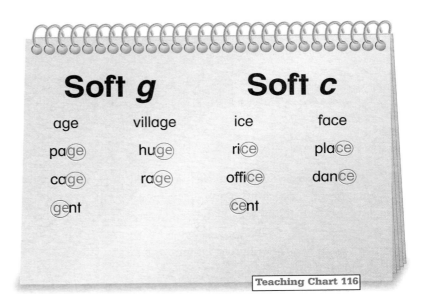

Teaching Chart 116

Use the Word in Context

- Have volunteers use the word in a sentence to reinforce its meaning. Example: *My parrot lives in a cage.*

Repeat the Procedure

- Have volunteers follow the patterns, adding letters to the words in each column and then circling the letters that stand for /j/ and /s/.

PRACTICE

IDENTIFYING
Identify Soft c
and Soft g Words

GROUP

Write words with soft *c* and soft *g* on index cards. Have each child choose a card without looking at the word, and hold the card in front of them so that others in the group can read the word. The other children can take turns dramatizing the word until the child guesses it. As the children guess the words, have them create two piles, one with soft *c* and the other soft *g*. ▶ **Interpersonal/Linguistic/Kinesthetic**

ASSESS/CLOSE

Read and Use
Words with
Soft c and Soft g
in Sentences

To assess children's ability to read soft *c* and *g* words, observe children as they complete the Practice activity. Ask children to save their cards, and to use their words in short sentences.

ADDITIONAL PHONICS RESOURCES

Phonics/Phonemic Awareness
Practice Book,
pages 95–98

McGraw-Hill School
TECHNOLOGY

Phonics CD-ROM

activities for practice with
Blending and Word Building

DAILY Phonics ROUTINES

DAY 4

Words in Context
Ask children working in small groups to create a sentence containing one soft *c* word and one hard *c* word. Repeat the activity with soft *g* and hard *g* words.

Phonics CD-ROM

SPELLING/PHONICS
CONNECTIONS
Words with soft *c* and soft *g*:
See the 5-Day Spelling Plan,
pages 67Q–67R.

i Intervention ▶ Skills
Intervention Guide, for direct
instruction and extra practice
of Soft *c* and Soft *g*

Meeting Individual Needs for Phonics

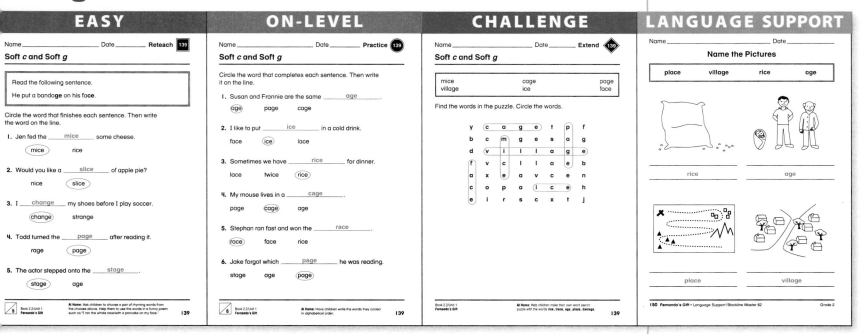

Reteach, 139   **Practice, 139**   **Extend, 139**   **Language Support, 150**

67F

OBJECTIVES

Children will:

- identify soft *c* and soft *g* sounds.
- blend and read words with soft *c* and soft *g*.
- identify words with /ù/*oo*.
- blend and read words with /ù/*oo*.

MATERIALS

- **Teaching Chart 117**

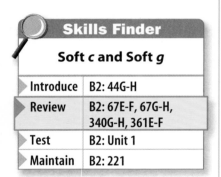

Skills Finder

Soft *c* and Soft *g*

Introduce	B2: 44G-H
Review	B2: 67E-F, 67G-H, 340G-H, 361E-F
Test	B2: Unit 1
Maintain	B2: 221

Review Soft *c*, Soft *g* and /ù/

PREPARE

Identify /s/, /j/, and /ù/ Sounds

Write the following sentences on the chalkboard:

- We put <u>ice</u> on his broken <u>foot</u>.
- To get to the <u>village</u>, go through the <u>woods</u>.

Invite children to underline any words containing /s/, /j/, and /ù/.

TEACH

BLENDING Model and Guide Practice with Words with Soft *c* and *g*, and with /ù/ *oo*

- Display **Teaching Chart 117**. Model blending and read aloud the first pair of words (*peak* and *peace*). Ask children which word contains the soft *c* sound. (*peace*) Underline the word *peace* and say it aloud.

- Invite volunteers to come to the board, blend the sounds in the next pair of words, and underline the word with the soft *c* sound.

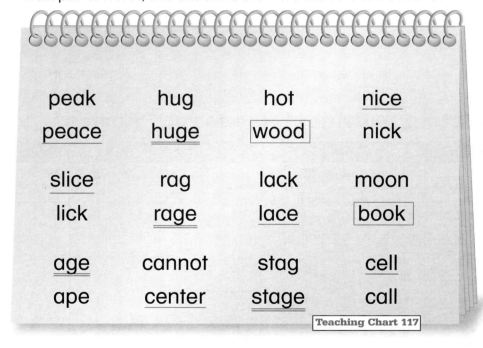

peak	hug	hot	<u>nice</u>
<u>peace</u>	<u>huge</u>		wood		nick
<u>slice</u>	rag	lack	moon
lick	<u>rage</u>	<u>lace</u>		book	
<u>age</u>	cannot	stag	<u>cell</u>
ape	<u>center</u>	<u>stage</u>	call

Teaching Chart 117

Use the Words in Context

- Have volunteers use the words in sentences to reinforce their meanings. Example: *Please have a slice of pie.*

Repeat the Procedure

- Continue for each word pair, having volunteers double-underline words with soft *g* and box words with /ù/ *oo*.

PRACTICE

WRITING
Write a Poem, Song, or Story with Soft c, g, and /ù/oo Words

ONE

Continue to display **Teaching Chart 117**. Invite children to use the words on the chart to write a short poem, song, or story containing as many soft c, soft g, and /ù/oo words as possible. ► **Linguistic/Visual**

ASSESS/CLOSE

Read Text with Soft c, g, and /ù/oo Words

To assess children's ability to blend soft c and soft g words and words with /ù/oo, observe children as they complete the Practice activity. Encourage children to read their poems or sing their songs aloud.

ADDITIONAL PHONICS RESOURCES

McGraw-Hill School
TECHNOLOGY

Phonics/Phonemic Awareness Practice Book, pages 95–98

Phonics CD-ROM

activities for practice with Discriminating and Word Building

DAY 5 **Writing** Have children write riddles using as many soft c and soft g words as possible. Invite children to read their riddles aloud.

Phonics CD-ROM

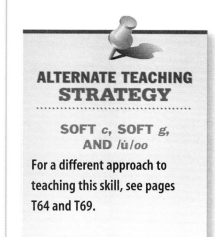

ALTERNATE TEACHING STRATEGY

SOFT c, SOFT g, AND /ù/oo

For a different approach to teaching this skill, see pages T64 and T69.

i **Intervention** ▶ **Skills**
Intervention Guide, for direct instruction and extra practice of soft c, soft g, and /ù/

Meeting Individual Needs for Phonics

EASY	ON-LEVEL	CHALLENGE	LANGUAGE SUPPORT

EASY

Name _____ Date _____ Reteach **140**
Soft c, g; /ù/ oo

I ate some **rice** for dinner.
village space (rice)

Read the sentence. Circle the word that completes the sentence. Then write the word on the line.

1. The dog ran into the ___woods___
   foot (woods) hood

2. My rabbit was in a ___cage___.
   (cage) page age

3. Lake Erie was filled with ___ice___.
   (ice) twice tricycle

4. This is a ___book___ about a cat.
   look cook (book)

5. It was a ___nice___ day outside.
   (nice) mice price

6. I read ten ___pages___ of the book.
   wage stages (pages)

140   At Home: Have children write sentences for two of the words they did not circle.   Book 2.2/Unit 1 Fernando's Gift / 6

ON-LEVEL

Name _____ Date _____ Practice **140**
Soft c, g; /ù/oo

Write a word from the box to complete each sentence.

| book | mice | looked | face | place |
| stage | slice | page | nice | twice |

1. I am reading a ___book___ on cooking.
2. The baby has a smile on her ___face___.
3. I visited the ___place___ where grandma grew up.
4. There are ___mice___ in the field.
5. Actors do shows on a ___stage___.
6. We stopped the car and ___looked___ at the view.
7. We played the game ___twice___.
8. My mother cut me a ___slice___ of cake.
9. A kind person is ___nice___.
10. Turn the ___page___ of the book.

140   At Home: Have children make up a rhyme for the word wood.   Book 2.2/Unit 1 Fernando's Gift / 10

CHALLENGE

Name _____ Date _____ Extend **140**
Soft c, g; /ù/ oo

Jake's Dream

Jake went into the woods to find something to eat. He sat down on a piece of wood near a brook. A weed next to Jake started to grow. Jake watched as it grew straight up into space. Jake climbed the weed. At the top Jake saw a smiling face. It was a huge bear holding a plate of cookies. Jake shook. The bear asked Jake his age. Jake didn't answer. Instead, Jake raced down the weed. Jake woke up. He felt better since it was only a dream.

List each underlined word in one of the boxes below.

ge	oo	ce
huge	woods	space
age	wood	face
	brook	raced
	cookies	since
	shook	

Use some of the words to write your own story on a sheet of paper.

140   At Home: Have children look through advertisements in a newspaper to find words with ce, ge, and oo.   Book 2.2/Unit 1 Fernando's Gift / 9

LANGUAGE SUPPORT

Name _____ Date _____
Name What You See

| path | roof | rice |
| woods | village | age |

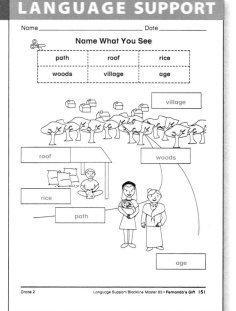

Grade 2   Language Support/Blackline Master 83 • Fernando's Gift   151

Reteach, 140   **Practice, 140**   **Extend, 140**   **Language Support, 151**

OBJECTIVES

Children will compare and contrast elements of a story.

MATERIALS
- **Teaching Chart 118**

Skills Finder

Compare and Contrast

Introduce	B2: 67I-J
Review	B2: 115I-J, 125E-F
Test	B2: Unit 1

TEACHING TIP

COMPARE AND CONTRAST Remind children to use clue words such as *both* and *like* to show a comparison, and clue words such as *unlike, but,* and *however* to show a contrast.

SELF-SELECTED Reading

Children may choose from the following titles.

ANTHOLOGY

- *Fernando's Gift*

LEVELED BOOKS

- *John Muir: Making the Mountains Glad*
- *Make a Difference*
- *Save Our Park Trees*

Bibliography, pages T88–T89

Introduce Compare and Contrast

PREPARE

Introduce the Concept

Write on the board two column headings: *Same* and *Different*. Ask children to call out ways that cats and dogs are similar, and ways that they are different. Record their responses in the appropriate column.

TEACH

Read "Fernando's Village" and Model the Skill

Read **Teaching Chart 118** with children. Ask them to pay attention to how the two settings are different and alike.

Fernando's Village

In Fernando's village, the houses all have <u>tin roofs</u>. It is so <u>quiet</u>, you can hear the wind in the trees. In the city, the houses all have <u>cement roofs</u>. It is so <u>noisy</u>, you can't even hear yourself think! Fernando's village is made up of <u>fifteen houses</u>. In the city, there are more than <u>15,000 houses</u>! But one thing is the same, in the village and the city: (Everybody works very hard.)

Teaching Chart 118

MODEL I see that Fernando's village is being compared with the city. The first difference is the kind of roof on the houses: In the village, there are tin roofs, while in the city, there are cement roofs.

Have volunteers underline the words in the passage that tell how the village and the city are different. Have them circle the words that tell how the village and the city are the same.

GROUP

Create a Compare/Contrast Diagram

Have children create a Venn diagram to show the differences and similarities between the village and the city. Help them get started.

▶ Interpersonal/Visual

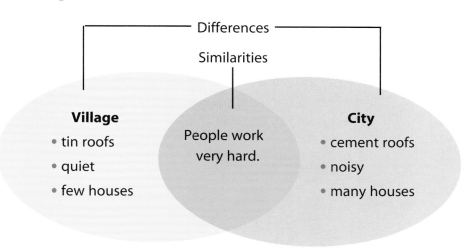

Differences

Similarities

Village
• tin roofs
• quiet
• few houses

People work very hard.

City
• cement roofs
• noisy
• many houses

ASSESS/CLOSE

Compare/Contrast Different Settings

Have children use a Venn diagram to compare and contrast real-life or fictional settings, such as their school, neighborhood, places they visit, or the settings of familiar stories.

ALTERNATE TEACHING STRATEGY

COMPARE AND CONTRAST

For a different approach to teaching this skill, see page T71.

Intervention ▶ **Skills**

Intervention Guide, for direct instruction and extra practice in comparing and contrasting

---

Meeting Individual Needs for Comprehension

EASY	ON-LEVEL	CHALLENGE	LANGUAGE SUPPORT

EASY

Name _____ Date _____ Reteach **141**

Compare and Contrast

Thinking about how story characters are **alike** and **different** can help you understand the story.

Read the story. Then fill in the chart below to show how Tim and Tammy are alike and different. Answers may vary.

Tim and Tammy are best friends. Most of the time they like to do the same things. They play computer games together. They also like to go to the park and play with Tim's dog.
Other times they like to do different things. Tim's favorite sport is baseball. Tammy's favorite sport is soccer. She also likes to swim. Tim would rather go hiking. He enjoys riding his bike, too.

What is the same about Tim and Tammy?
1. like to do the same things 2. play computer games
3. go to the park 4. play with Tim's dog

What is different about Tim and Tammy?

Tim	Tammy
5. likes baseball	6. likes soccer
7. likes hiking	8. likes swimming

Book 2.2/Unit 1 Fernando's Gift 8 **At Home:** Have children compare and contrast their home with their school. 141

ON-LEVEL

Name _____ Date _____ Practice **141**

Compare and Contrast

Imagine that you are a new student. At first you do not have any friends. Soon, you and Pat become good friends.

Write a letter to an old friend. Write about how you felt when you first came to the new school. Then write about how you felt after you got to know Pat.

Dear _____,
I have been at my new school for two weeks.
At first, I felt _____. When we went out to play, I _____.
After I met Pat, I felt _____.
Now when I go out to play, _____.

Your friend,

Book 2.2/Unit 1 Fernando's Gift 6 **At Home:** Have children compare and contrast their feelings about a current event at school, such as the arrival or departure of a class pet. 141

CHALLENGE

Name _____ Date _____ Extend **141**

Compare and Contrast

Compare your day with Fernando's. Complete the charts below.

My Morning	Fernando's Morning

My After School Time	Fernando's After School Time

Write a sentence describing how your day is **similar** to Fernando's.

Write a sentence describing how your day is **different** from Fernando's.

Book 2.2/Unit 1 Fernando's Gift **At Home:** Ask children to compare their day with someone they know. Make a list of the ways they are same and different. 141

LANGUAGE SUPPORT

Name _____ Date _____

Different Worlds

Fernando's home is like this. | How is mine the same?

Fernando's school is like this. | How is mine different?

152 Fernando's Gift • Language Support/Blackline Master 84 Grade 2

Reteach, 141   Practice, 141   Extend, 141   Language Support, 152

67J

OBJECTIVES

Children will recognize words with opposite meanings.

MATERIALS

- **Teaching Chart 119**
- index cards

Skills Finder

Antonyms

Introduce	B2: 43K-L
Review	B2: 67K-L, 125K-L
Test	B2: Unit 1

TEACHING TIP

ANTONYMS Remind children that because some words have more than one meaning, they can also have more than one antonym (*full* and *empty*, or *full* and *hungry*).

Review **Antonyms**

PREPARE

Define Antonyms Write the word *noisy* on the chalkboard. Remind children that an antonym is a word's opposite. Ask children to identify the antonym of *noisy*. *(quiet)*

TEACH

Identify Antonyms With children, read aloud **Teaching Chart 119**.

Late for School

Fernando woke up <u>early</u>, but he was <u>late</u> for school. He could not find his <u>clean</u> shirt. He looked <u>under</u> the bed, and in the closet. He thought he might have to wear a <u>dirty</u> shirt! Fernando felt <u>sad</u> because he thought his shirt was <u>lost</u>. But just then, his mother walked into his room with the shirt <u>over</u> her arm! It had been <u>wrinkled</u>, and she had <u>smoothed</u> it with the iron. Fernando was <u>happy</u> his shirt had been <u>found</u>.

Teaching Chart 119

Help children find and underline two antonyms in the first sentence.

MODEL I know that a word's antonym is another word that has the opposite meaning. In the first sentence, I see the words *early* and *late*. I know that *early* is the opposite of *late*, so I know that these words are an antonym pair.

Have students locate and underline the rest of the antonym pairs in the chart. Explain that the pairs do not always appear in the same sentence.

PRACTICE

Match Antonym Pairs

ONE

Write on index cards the following words: *early, late, clean, dirty, under, over, happy, sad, wrinkled, smooth.* You may wish to add additional antonym pairs so that each child is working with a different word. Have each child choose a card without showing the word written on it to anyone else. Have children walk around the room pantomiming the word on their card, or saying one-word clues (such as *morning* for *early*) until they locate their "antonym partner."

▶ **Interpersonal/Kinesthetic**

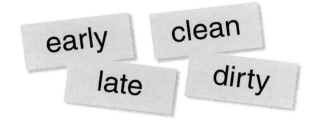

ASSESS/CLOSE

Use Antonyms in a Poem or Song

Observe children as they complete the Practice activity. Then ask children to write a poem or song using the antonyms on their cards.

ALTERNATE TEACHING STRATEGY

ANTONYMS

For a different approach to teaching this skill, see page T68.

ⓘ **Intervention** ▶ **Skills**

Intervention Guide, for direct instruction and extra practice of antonyms

Meeting Individual Needs for Vocabulary

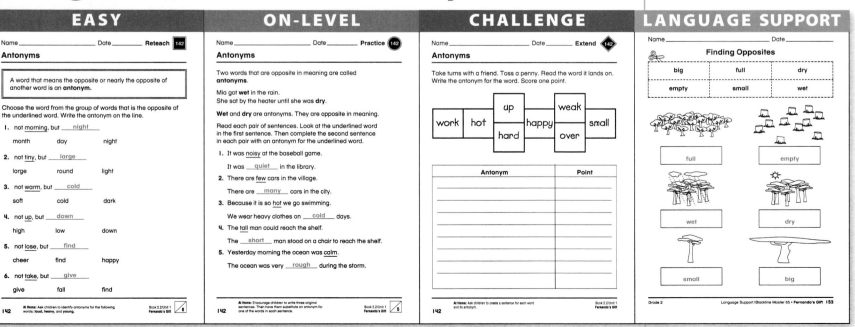

EASY	ON-LEVEL	CHALLENGE	LANGUAGE SUPPORT
Reteach, 142	Practice, 142	Extend, 142	Language Support, 153

67L

TEACHING TIP

Technology Write the title of your magazine article in bold type. Use a bigger size of type for this title. This will make it stand out from the rest of the article.

Handwriting Remind children to print legibly. Ask: *Is your handwriting neat and easy to read? Have you left the correct amount of space between letters and words?* See Handwriting pages T78–T79.

Handwriting
CD-ROM

Writing That Compares

Prewrite

WRITE A MAGAZINE ARTICLE Present this writing assignment: Compare life in the rain forest with life in a city. Show the similarities and differences between the two places, as well as the advantages and disadvantages of each.

BRAINSTORM IDEAS Invite children to brainstorm information about each place. List their resources on the chalkboard.

Strategy: Make a Chart Guide children to create a two-column chart with the headings *Rain Forest* and *City*. Have children write characteristics of each place, under the appropriate heading.

Draft

USE THE CHART Guide children to use their charts to help organize their drafts. Remind children to use word clues that tell the reader they are comparing and contrasting, such as *both, like, unlike, but,* and *however.* Have children elaborate their stories with descriptive words that will help the reader to "see" the similarities and differences between the two places.

Revise

SELF-QUESTIONING Guide children to assess their drafts with the following questions.

• Did I use compare and contrast words like *both* and *but*?

• Did I use vivid words that describe? Can the reader "see" the places that I am writing about?

• Did I give facts about how a city and a rain forest are different and alike?

Edit/Proofread

CHECK FOR ERRORS Children should reread their stories for spelling, grammar, organization of information, and punctuation.

Publish

CIRCULATE THE ARTICLE Make copies of children's articles to share with others in the class, or friends and family. They may also wish to include illustrations of the rain forest and the city.

The Rain Forest and the City

There are many things to see in both the rain forest and the city. However, the things you see in each place are very different. In the rain forest, there are many trees, and often there are wild animals nearby. In the city, there are more buildings than trees, and usually the only animals you see are people's pet dogs and cats.

One thing you might see in both the city and the rain forest is people. People live in both places, work in both places, and go to school in both places. But the ways they get around can be very different. People in the rain forest may travel by riding horses. People in the city ride cars or buses or trains—not horses!

Presentation Ideas

NEWSLETTERS Photocopy children's articles and bind them together to create a newsletter. ▶ **Viewing/Representing**

TALK SHOW Have children imagine that they have been invited onto a talk show to speak about the topic covered in their article. Have children use copies of their article to answer questions from the "audience" and the "host." ▶ **Speaking/Listening**

Consider children's creative efforts, possibly adding a plus (+) for originality, wit, and imagination.

Scoring Rubric

Excellent	Good	Fair	Unsatisfactory
4: The writer	**3:** The writer	**2:** The writer	**1:** The writer
• vividly compares and contrasts the two locales.	• solidly compares and contrasts the two places.	• attempts to compare and contrast the two places.	• may not grasp the concept of comparing.
• elaborates with colorful language.	• adequately organizes the information.	• may present vague or incomplete details.	• may list vague or disconnected facts and details.
• organizes ideas clearly.	• may include some descriptive detail.	• may not use comparison terms.	• may have severe problems with organization or usage.

Incomplete **0:** The writer leaves the page blank or fails to respond to the writing task. The child does not address the topic or simply paraphrases the prompt. The response is illegible or incoherent.

Meeting Individual Needs for Writing

EASY

Collage Have children create one collage of images from the rain forest, and one of images from the city. Then, encourage children to circle in red things that are similar or the same on both collages.

ON-LEVEL

Letter Encourage children to write a letter to Fernando, comparing what life is like where they live to what life is like where he lives.

CHALLENGE

Have children imagine what it might be like to be a tree or animal in a rain forest. Have them write a journal entry about a typical day in their life.

Listening and Viewing

LISTENING Have children

• jot down notes as they listen to each speaker.

• listen for comparison/contrast words.

• use their notes to frame questions.

VIEWING Have children

• look for a common theme in the illustrations.

• discuss details in an illustration they find interesting.

• note the variety of ways that the same message can be communicated.

LANGUAGE SUPPORT

 Ask ESL students to work with English-fluent partners. Have them look through books and magazines together to find pictures of things found in a city and in a rain forest. Have children study the pictures together and make a list of words they might use in their magazine articles.

PORTFOLIO Invite children to include their articles or another writing project in their portfolios.

5 Day Grammar and Usage Plan

LANGUAGE SUPPORT

ESL Write this on the chalkboard: *I have finished the book.* Cover *have* and ask children to name the verb. (finished) Repeat, covering *finished.* Explain that sometimes a verb helps another verb show an action.

DAILY LANGUAGE ACTIVITIES

Write the Daily Language Activities on the chalkboard each day or use **Transparency 17.** Have students correct the sentences orally.

Day 1
1. The men has talked outside. have
2. The boy have called his dog. has
3. It have rained all night. has

Day 2
1. I walking to school. am
2. Cecilia have washed the baby. has
3. My grandfather were telling a story. was

Day 3
1. I is tending the crop. am
2. My father have planted trees. has
3. He were teaching them about the forest. was

Day 4
1. The trees was growing outside. were
2. I has picked one. have
3. They is eating some cereal. are

Day 5
1. The children was fishing. were
2. She are playing in the river. is
3. Fernando were walking with the dogs. was

DAY 1 — Introduce the Concept

Oral Warm-Up Read this sentence aloud. *He has walked to the store.* Ask children what has happened.

Introduce Helping Verbs Explain that *have* and *has* may be used alone or with other verbs. Example: *We have washed the dishes.* Explain that *have* helps show an action in the past.

Helping Verbs

- A **helping verb** helps another verb show an action.
- *Have* and *has* can be helping verbs.

Remind children that *has* is used with singular subjects and *have* is used with plural subjects or *I* or *you.*

Present the Daily Language Activity. Then have children write a sentence using the verb *has* as a helping verb.

 Assign the daily Writing Prompt on page 44C.

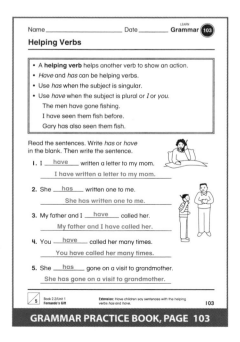

GRAMMAR PRACTICE BOOK, PAGE 103

DAY 2 — Teach the Concept

Review Helping Verbs Ask children what helping verbs do and have them use one in a sentence.

Introduce *Be* as a Helping Verb Tell children that forms of the verb *be* can also be used as a helping verb. Write on the chalkboard: *I am hurrying. It was raining.* Explain that *am* and *was* help another verb show what is or was happening. Point out the *-ing* ending of *hurrying* and *running.* Review the past- and present-tense forms of *be.*

The Verb *Be* as a Helping Verb

Is, are, am, was, and *were* can be helping verbs.

Present the Daily Language Activity. Then have children write three sentences using *is, are,* and *were* as helping verbs.

 Assign the daily Writing Prompt on page 44C.

GRAMMAR PRACTICE BOOK, PAGE 104

Helping Verbs

DAY 3 Review and Practice

Learn from the Literature Review the helping verbs *have* and *be*. Read the sentence on page 56 of *Fernando's Gift:*

> **But when we get there we see that someone has cut down the tree.**

Ask children to identify the helping verb. Guide them to see that the helping verb *has* helps us to understand that the tree was cut down in the past.

Identify Helping Verbs Present the Daily Language Activity. Then write sentences about Fernando on the chalkboard. Some sentences should use *have* and *be* alone and others should use them as helping verbs. Ask children to identify the sentences with the helping verbs.

 Present the daily Writing Prompt on page 44D.

DAY 4 Review and Practice

Review Helping Verbs Write on the chalkboard the corrected sentences from the Daily Language Activities for Day 1 through Day 3. Have children identify the helping verb and the verb it helps in each sentence. Present the Daily Language Activity for Day 4.

Mechanics and Usage Before children do the daily Writing Prompt, review the use of quotation marks. Display and discuss:

Quotation Marks

Use quotation marks at the beginning and end of what a person says.

 Assign the daily Writing Prompt on page 44D.

DAY 5 Assess and Reteach

Assess Use the Daily Language Activity and page 107 of the **Grammar Practice Book** for assessment.

Reteach Have children write the helping verbs *have, has, is, are, am, was,* and *were* on index cards. Then ask them to make the cards for the following: The boys, The girl, The dog, The cats, The man; walking, walked, talking, talked, playing, played, washing, washed. Make three piles of cards: subjects, helping verbs, and other verbs. Then have children take turns making sentences by selecting a card from each pile.

Have children create a word wall with the sentences they have made.

Use page 108 of the **Grammar Practice Book** for additional reteaching.

 Assign the daily Writing Prompt on page 44D.

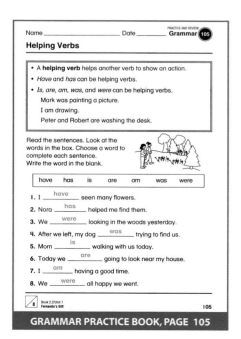

Name _____ Date _____ Grammar **105**

Helping Verbs

- A **helping verb** helps another verb to show an action.
- *Have* and *has* can be helping verbs.
- *Is, are, am, was,* and *were* can be helping verbs.
  Mark was painting a picture.
  I am drawing.
  Peter and Robert are washing the desk.

Read the sentences. Look at the words in the box. Choose a word to complete each sentence. Write the word in the blank.

| have | has | is | are | am | was | were |

1. I _have_ seen many flowers.
2. Nora _has_ helped me find them.
3. We _were_ looking in the woods yesterday.
4. After we left, my dog _was_ trying to find us.
5. Mom _is_ walking with us today.
6. Today we _are_ going to look near my house.
7. I _am_ having a good time.
8. We _were_ all happy we went.

Book 2.2/Unit 1
Fernando's Gift
105

GRAMMAR PRACTICE BOOK, PAGE 105

Name _____ Date _____ Grammar **106**

Quotation Marks

- Use quotation marks at the beginning and end of what a person says.
  "Come here," Dad told the dog.

Read each sentence. Correct it. Write the correct sentence on the line.

1. Let's open the box, Gerry said.
   "Let's open the box," Gerry said.
2. I need a pair of scissors, Lila said.
   "I need a pair of scissors," Lila said.
3. Pull off the tape, Grandpa said.
   "Pull off the tape," Grandpa said.
4. Tear open the end, Gerry said.
   "Tear open the end," Gerry said.

106 **Extensions:** Have students write about a conversation using quotation marks.
Book 2.2/Unit 1
Fernando's Gift 4

GRAMMAR PRACTICE BOOK, PAGE 106

Name _____ Date _____ Grammar **107**

Helping Verbs

Which helping verb best completes the sentence? Mark your answer.

1. Lou _____ found a coin.
   ⓐ have
   ⓑ has
   ⓒ are

2. They _____ asked who lost it.
   ⓐ have
   ⓑ is
   ⓒ has

3. We _____ looking for more coins.
   ⓐ have
   ⓑ am
   ⓒ are

4. Lou and I _____ put them in a safe place.
   ⓐ is
   ⓑ are
   ⓒ have

5. Mom _____ watching them.
   ⓐ is
   ⓑ are
   ⓒ were

Book 2.2/Unit 1
Fernando's Gift
107

GRAMMAR PRACTICE BOOK, PAGE 107

5Day Spelling Plan

Write several words ending in soft *c* on the chalkboard *(rice, space, race).* Then play a game of Simon Says. Tell students to stand up each time you say a word that ends with the soft *c* sound. Repeat with soft *g* words.

DICTATION SENTENCES

Spelling Words

1. I can <u>dance</u>.
2. He can tell her <u>age</u>.
3. The <u>rice</u> is good.
4. Two <u>mice</u> are hidden.
5. Mom can <u>charge</u> the book.
6. She can <u>race</u> the boy.
7. There is <u>space</u> for me.
8. The <u>cage</u> is very small.
9. The cat has a <u>large</u> bone.
10. I can read a <u>page</u>.

Challenge Words

11. He went <u>diving</u>.
12. The girl <u>explains</u> the story.
13. No <u>harm</u> was done.
14. The <u>soil</u> is hard.
15. Her <u>village</u> is far away.

DAY 1 — Pretest

Assess Prior Knowledge Use the Dictation Sentences at left and **Spelling Practice Book** page 103 for the pretest. Allow students to correct their own papers. If students have trouble, have partners give each other a midweek test on Day 3. Students who require a modified list may be tested on the first five words.

Spelling Words		Challenge Words
1. dance	6. race	11. **diving**
2. **age**	7. space	12. **explains**
3. **rice**	8. cage	13. **harm**
4. mice	9. large	14. **soil**
5. charge	10. page	15. **village**

*Note: Words in **dark type** are from the* story.

Word Study On page 104 of the **Spelling Practice Book** are word study steps and an at-home activity.

DAY 2 — Explore the Pattern

Sort and Spell Say *dance* and *charge*. Ask students what sound they hear at the end of each word. Write the words on the chalkboard. Tell students that *dance* ends in soft *c* (/s/) spelled *ce*, and *charge* ends in soft *g* (/j/), spelled *ge*.

Ask students to read aloud the ten spelling words before sorting them as below.

Soft *c* spelled *ce*	Soft *g* spelled *ge*
dance	age
rice	charge
mice	cage
race	large
space	page

Spelling Patterns The letter *e* after the letter *c* or *g* gives it the soft *c* or soft *g* sound. Have students compare spelling words with words ending with *g* or *c*, such as *rag, big* or *music,* and listen for the sound of the letter *c* or *g*. Have them list other words ending with *ce* or *ge*.

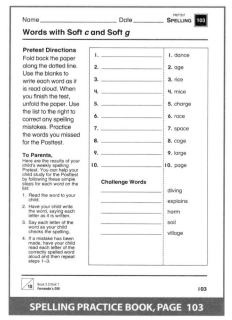

SPELLING PRACTICE BOOK, PAGE 103

WORD STUDY STEPS AND ACTIVITY, PAGE 104

SPELLING PRACTICE BOOK, PAGE 105

Words with Soft *c* and Soft *g*

DAY 3 — Practice and Extend

Word Meaning: Endings Write the sentence *We were hiking up the hill* on the chalkboard. Point out that the ending *-ing* has been added to the verb *hike*. Remind students that words ending in *e* must drop the *e* before an *-ing* can be added. Write the words *race, dance,* and *charge* on the chalkboard. Have students add *-ing* to these words. Then use each of the new words in a sentence.

Glossary Have partners:

- write each Challenge Word.
- look up a synonym for each word in the Glossary.
- write a synonym beside each Challenge Word.

DAY 4 — Proofread and Write

Proofread Sentences Write these sentences on the chalkboard, including the misspelled words. Ask students to proofread, circling incorrect spellings and writing the correct spellings. There are two spelling errors in each sentence.

> The myce are in a cag. (mice, cage)
> It is not a very larje spac. (large, space)

Have students create additional sentences with errors for partners to correct.

WRITING Have students use as many spelling words as possible in the daily Writing Prompt on page 44D. Remind students to proofread their writing for errors in spelling, grammar, and punctuation.

DAY 5 — Assess

Assess Students' Knowledge Use page 108 of the **Spelling Practice Book** or the Dictation Sentences on page 67Q for the posttest.

Personal Word List If students have trouble with any words in the lesson, have them create a personal list of troublesome words in their journals. Have students write a context sentence for each word.

Students should refer to their word lists during later writing activities.

SPELLING PRACTICE BOOK, PAGE 106

Name _____ Date _____ SPELLING 106

Words with Soft *c* and Soft *g*

| dance | rice | charge | space | large |
| age | mice | race | cage | page |

Write a spelling word to complete each sentence.

1. I'd like to see a rocket fly off into _____ space _____ .
2. What _____ age _____ will you be next year?
3. What do you feed those little white _____ mice _____ ?
4. He has very _____ large _____ brown eyes.
5. Mom made red beans and _____ rice _____ for dinner.
6. At the zoo, animals are in a _____ cage _____ .
7. The last _____ page _____ of the book is missing.

Make a new word by dropping **e** and adding **ing** to the spelling words below.

8. charge – e + ing = _____ charging _____
9. race – e + ing = _____ racing _____
10. dance – e + ing = _____ dancing _____

Challenge Extension: Have children write a brief story about helping save a natural resource. Ask them to use at least three of the Challenge Words.

106   Book 2.2/Unit 1 Fernanda's Gift

SPELLING PRACTICE BOOK, PAGE 107

Name _____ Date _____ SPELLING 107

Words with Soft *c* and Soft *g*

Proofreading Activity
There are six spelling mistakes in the paragraph below. Circle each misspelled word. Write the words correctly on the lines below.

Our class has three brown mise. Two are small, so we think they are babies. We are not sure of their agee. Susan brought a caje for them to live in. The biggest mouse seems to be in charje. The others follow what he does. The mice like to danse when we have music. They also like to run. When we put them on the floor, they rase around as fast as they can go.

1. _____ mice _____   2. _____ age _____   3. _____ cage _____
4. _____ charge _____   5. _____ dance _____   6. _____ race _____

Writing Activity
Pets in the classroom are fun. What are some animals that could be a class pet? Write about having a class pet. Use four spelling words. Circle the spelling words you use.

_____
_____
_____
_____

Book 2.2/Unit 1   107

SPELLING PRACTICE BOOK, PAGE 108

Name _____ Date _____ SPELLING 108

Words with Soft *c* and Soft *g*

Look at the words in each set. One word in each set is spelled correctly. Use a pencil to color in the circle in front of that word. Before you begin, look at the sample sets of words. Sample A has been done for you. Do Sample B by yourself. When you are sure you know what to do, you may go on with the rest of the page.

Sample A
- Ⓐ nice
- Ⓑ nic
- Ⓒ nise
- Ⓓ niss

Sample B
- Ⓔ mann
- Ⓕ mahn
- Ⓖ man
- Ⓗ mahne

1. Ⓐ caj Ⓑ cage Ⓒ caaget Ⓓ caje
2. Ⓔ rice Ⓕ risse Ⓖ ris Ⓗ ricce
3. Ⓐ charj Ⓑ charg Ⓒ charje Ⓓ charge
4. Ⓔ danse Ⓕ dans Ⓖ dance Ⓗ danc
5. Ⓐ page Ⓑ paje Ⓒ paag Ⓓ paaj
6. Ⓔ mice Ⓕ mies Ⓖ mics Ⓗ miis
7. Ⓐ larj Ⓑ larg Ⓒ larje Ⓓ large
8. Ⓔ aij Ⓕ aig Ⓖ age Ⓗ aje
9. Ⓐ race Ⓑ raice Ⓒ rase Ⓓ rass
10. Ⓔ spase Ⓕ space Ⓖ spass Ⓗ spac

108   Book 2.2/Unit 1 Fernanda's Gift

Reaching All Learners

Concept

- **Historical Sites and Natural Wonders**

Comprehension

- **Compare and Contrast**

Phonics

- **Variant Vowel /ô/ *aw, au***

Vocabulary

- brave
- guess
- museum
- practice
- vacation
- wonder

Anthology

The Best Vacation Ever

Selection Summary Amanda gets to spend her spring vacation traveling across the United States! Read along as she reports back on all of the exciting places she visits.

Rhyme applies to phonics

Listening Library

INSTRUCTIONAL pages 70–91

About the Author As a little girl in Oregon, Diane Hoyt-Goldsmith loved to read. When she grew up, she went to New York City to study art. Now she lives in California and has written and illustrated many award-winning books about children from different cultures in the United States and around the world.

Same Concept, Skills and Vocabulary!

Leveled Books

EASY
Lesson on pages 91A and 91D
DECODABLE

INDEPENDENT
Lesson on pages 91B and 91D

Take-Home version available

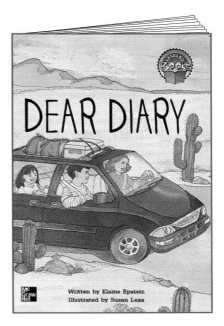

CHALLENGE
Lesson on pages 91C and 91D

Leveled Practice

EASY
Reteach, 143–150 Blackline masters with reteaching opportunities for each assessed skill

INDEPENDENT/ON-LEVEL
Practice, 143–150 Workbook with Take-Home stories and practice opportunities for each assessed skill and story comprehension

CHALLENGE
Extend, 143–150 Blackline masters that offer challenge activities for each assessed skill

Quizzes Prepared by Accelerated Reader®

WORKSTATION Activities

Social Studies . . .	The Grand Canyon, *82*
Science	Sharks, *84*
Math	Measurement, *78*
Art	Bats, *80*
Language Arts . .	Read Aloud, *68E*
Writing	Write a Travel Guide, *88*
Cultural Perspectives	Around the World, *76*
Research and Inquiry	Find Out More, *89*
Internet Activities	www.mhschool.com/reading

The Best Vacation Ever

READING AND LANGUAGE ARTS	DAY 1 — Focus on Reading and Skills	DAY 2 — Read the Literature
Phonics Daily Routines	Daily **Phonics** Routine: **Blending,** 68H  **Phonics** CD-ROM	Daily **Phonics** Routine: **Discriminating,** 70A  **Phonics** CD-ROM
Phonological Awareness **Phonics** /ô/ **Comprehension** **Vocabulary** **Study Skills** **Listening, Speaking, Viewing, Representing**	**Read Aloud: Poem,** 68E "Vacation" ☑ **Develop Phonological Awareness,** 68F /ô/ *a, aw, au* ☑ **Introduce /ô/*a, aw, au,* 68G–68H** **Teaching Chart 120** **Reteach, Practice, Extend,** 143 **Phonics/Phonemic Awareness Practice Book,** 99–102 **Apply /ô/*a, aw, au,* 68/69** "City Zoo" ⓘ Intervention Program	**Build Background,** 70A Develop Oral Language **Vocabulary,** 70B–70C *brave museum vacation* *guess practice wonder* **Word Building Manipulative Cards** **Teaching Chart 121** **Reteach, Practice, Extend,** 144 **Read the Selection,** 70–87 Comprehension ☑ /ô/*a, aw, au* ☑ **Compare and Contrast** **Genre:** Informational Story, 71 **Cultural Perspectives,** 76 ⓘ Intervention Program
Curriculum Connections	**Link** Language Arts, 68E	**Link** Social Studies, 70A
Writing	**Writing Prompt:** What was the best vacation you ever had? Tell what you did.	**Writing Prompt:** What makes a vacation really good? Explain in a short paragraph. **Journal Writing** Quick-Write, 87
Grammar	**Introduce the Concept: Irregular Verbs,** 91O Daily Language Activity: Write the correct form of the irregular verb. **Grammar Practice Book,** 109	**Teach the Concept: Irregular Verbs,** 91O Daily Language Activity: Write the correct form of the irregular verb. **Grammar Practice Book,** 110
Spelling /ô/	**Pretest: Words with /ô/ *a, aw, au, augh,*** 91Q **Spelling Practice Book,** 109, 110	**Explore the Patterns: Words with /ô/ *a, aw, au, augh,*** 91Q **Spelling Practice Book,** 111

 DAY 3   *Read the Literature*

 DAY 4   *Build Skills*

DAY 5   *Build Skills*

DAY 3

Daily  **Routine:**
Segmenting, 89

 **CD-ROM**

Rereading for Fluency, 86

Story Questions and Activities, 88–89
Reteach, Practice, Extend, 145

Study Skill, 90
✓ **Graphic Aids**
Teaching Chart 122
Reteach, Practice, Extend, 146

Test Power, 91

 **Read the Leveled Books,** 91A–91D
Guided Reading
✓ **/ô/a, aw, au**
✓ **Compare and Contrast**
✓ **Instructional Vocabulary**

 **Intervention Program**

 Math, 78   **Art,** 80

Writing Prompt: Pretend you could go anywhere and do anything you wanted. Where would you go? What would you do?

Writing That Compares, 91M
Prewrite, Draft

Review and Practice: Irregular Verbs, 91P
Daily Language Activity: Write the correct form of the irregular verb.
Grammar Practice Book, 111

Practice and Extend: Words with /ô/ a, aw, au, augh, 91R

Spelling Practice Book, 112

DAY 4

Daily  **Routine:**
Fluency, 91F

 **CD-ROM**

 Read the Leveled Books and the Self-Selected Books

✓ **Review /ô/aw, au, a,** 91E–91F
Teaching Chart 123
Reteach, Practice, Extend, 147
Language Support, 159
Phonics/Phonemic Awareness Practice Book, 99–102

✓ **Cumulative Review,** 91G–91H
Teaching Chart 124
Reteach, Practice, Extend, 148
Language Support, 160
Phonics/Phonemic Awareness Practice Book, 99–102

Minilessons, 79, 81, 83, 85

 Intervention Program

 **Social Studies,** 82

Writing Prompt: Write a letter to a friend telling him or her about your pretend vacation.

Writing That Compares, 91M
Revise

Meeting Individual Needs for Writing, 91N

Review and Practice: Irregular Verbs, 91P
Daily Language Activity: Write the correct form of the irregular verb.
Grammar Practice Book, 112

Proofread and Write: Words with /ô/ a, aw, au, augh, 91R

Spelling Practice Book, 113

DAY 5

Daily  **Routine:**
Writing, 91H

 **CD-ROM**

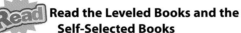 **Read Self-Selected Books**

✓ **Review Draw Conclusions,** 91I–91J
Teaching Chart 125
Reteach, Practice, Extend, 149
Language Support, 161

✓ **Review Inflectional Endings,** 91K–91L
Teaching Chart 126
Reteach, Practice, Extend, 150
Language Support, 162

Listening, Speaking, Viewing, Representing, 91N
Interview Time
Draw Posters

Minilessons, 79, 81, 83, 85

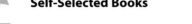 **Intervention Program**

 **Science,** 84

Writing Prompt: You are going on vacation. You can take a real person or someone from a story. Describe the person and tell why you have chosen him or her.

Writing That Compares, 91M
Edit/Proofread, Publish

Assess and Reteach: Irregular Verbs, 91P
Daily Language Activity: Write the correct form of the irregular verb.
Grammar Practice Book, 113, 114

Assess: Words with/ô/ a, aw, au, augh, 91R

Spelling Practice Book, 114

Read Aloud

Vacation
a poem by Mary Ann Hoberman

In my head I hear a humming:

Summer summer summer's coming.

Soon we're going on vacation

But there is a complication:

Day by day the problem's growing—

We don't know yet where we're going!

Mother likes the country best;

That's so she can read and rest.

Dad thinks resting is a bore;

He's for fishing at the shore.

Sailing is my brother's pick;

Sailing makes my sister sick;

She says swimming's much more cool,

Swimming in a swimming pool.

As for me, why, I don't care,

I'd be happy anywhere!

Continued on page T3

Oral Comprehension

LISTENING AND SPEAKING Ask children to think about the problem in this poem as you read it aloud. When you have finished, ask children, "Did the family in the poem solve their problem? Why or why not?" Then ask, "Can you think of a solution for the family?"

GENRE STUDY: POETRY Discuss some of the literary devices and techniques used in "Vacation."

- Help children find the steady rhythm of "Vacation." Lead the class in clapping hands to the beat.

- Have students write down the last word of each sentence and then trace the poem's AABB rhyme scheme.

- Discuss how the poet uses repetition of the word "summer" to present a sense of urgency in the poem.

Activity Ask children to decide where the family will eventually go. Tell them to make a list of rhyming words that describe the place. Encourage children to write their own poems using their list of rhymes. ▶ **Linguistic**

Develop Phonological Awareness

. . . . **Blend Sounds** . . . . **Phonemic Awareness**

MATERIALS
- picture of a ball, or a toy ball

Teach Tell children they are going to put some sounds together to make words. Hold up the picture for *ball*. Say the sounds for the word and have children blend the sounds with you to say the whole word. Say, /b/-/ô/-/l/. *If you put the sounds together what is the word?* (ball) Repeat, using the words *straw* and *cause*.

Practice Have children blend the following sounds to say these words: *saw, call, shawl, hall, claws, law, pause,* and *jaw*.

Segment Sounds . . . . **Phonemic Awareness**

MATERIALS
- Word Building Boxes from *Word Building Cards*
- pink paper squares

Teach Tell children you will count the number of sounds you hear in the word *walk*. Place a counter in a Word Building Box as you say each sound: /w/-/ô/-/k/. Have them say the sounds with you as you point to each box.

Practice Repeat the activity with *draw, shawl, cause, flaw, pause, fawn, tall,* and *launch*. Say each word and have children segment the words. Then have them place a counter in each box as you repeat each sound.

Substitute Sounds . . . . **Phonemic Awareness**

MATERIALS
- Phonics Picture from *Word Building Cards:* fan

Teach Display the Phonics Picture for *fan*. Have children say the word *fan* with you. Then tell children if you change the middle sound of *fan* to /ô/, you make the word *fawn*. If available, show a picture of a *fawn*. Have children repeat both words with you as you point to each picture. Repeat with words *hook/hawk*.

Practice Have children substitute the medial sounds for the following words: *shall/shawl; tale/tall; wake/walk; lean/lawn; hike/hawk; lunch/launch*.

 INFORMAL **ASSESSMENT** Observe children as they blend, segment, and substitute sounds. If children have difficulty, see Alternate Teaching Strategies on p. T72.

OBJECTIVES

Children will:

* identify /ô/*a, aw, au.*
* decode and read words with /ô/*a, aw, au.*

MATERIALS:

* **Teaching Chart 120**
* **Word Building Manipulative Cards**

Skills Finder

/ô/ *a, aw, au*	
Introduce	B2: 68G-H
Review	B2: 91E-F, 91G-H
Test	B2: Unit 1
Maintain	B2: 135

SPELLING/VOCABULARY CONNECTIONS

Words with *a, aw, au*: see the 5-Day Spelling Plan, pages 91Q–91R.

TEACHING TIP

SPELLING Remind children that sometimes the same sound can be spelled in several ways. Write *paw, fault, talk,* and *dog* on the chalkboard. Read aloud and underline the four different spelling patterns that stand for /ô/.

Introduce /ô/ *a, aw, au*

TEACH

Identify *aw, au,* and *a,* as Symbols for /ô/
Tell children they will learn to read words in which the letters *aw, au,* and *a* stand for the sound /ô/.

BLENDING Model and Guide Practice with /ô/*aw, au, a,* Words

* Display **Teaching Chart 120**. Point to *aw* at the top of the first column. Tell children this is a spelling pattern for the sound /ô/.
* Run your finger under the word *saw*, blending the letters to read the word. Ask children to repeat with you.
* In the first word below *saw*, write *aw* in the underlined space to form the word *hawk*. Ask a volunteer to blend the sounds and read the word aloud. Have the class repeat blending and reading *hawk*.

aw	au	a
saw	cause	talk
hawk	astronaut	chalk
draw	caught	walk
shawl	launch	all

Teaching Chart 120

Use the Words in Context
Have volunteers use the words in sentences to reinforce their meanings. Examples: *I saw a hawk flying.*

Repeat the Procedure
Follow the same procedure to complete the remaining examples in the chart. Invite volunteers to write in the missing letters and blend and read the words.

PRACTICE

**BLENDING
Build /ô/ Words
with Letter Cards**

ONE

Use letter and variant vowel cards to build the word *paw*. Blend the sounds together and read the word aloud. Ask children to blend the sounds and read after you. Have children use letter digraph and variant vowel cards to build and read *claw, taught,* and *chalk.* Then have them use the cards to brainstorm more words with /ô/ *a, aw, au.*

▶ **Linguistic/Visual**

t a u g h t

ASSESS/CLOSE

**Read and Write
Sentences Using
/ô/ *aw, au, a*
Words**

To assess children's ability to build and read /ô/ words, observe their work as they build words in the Practice activity. Ask each child to read and spell aloud two words with the /ô/ sound. Then have children read the phonics rhyme on pages 68–69 in their Anthologies. Have children use their words in sentences.

ADDITIONAL PHONICS RESOURCES

McGraw-Hill School
TECHNOLOGY

**Phonics/Phonemic Awareness
Practice Book,
pages 99–102**

Phonics CD-ROM

**activities for practice with
Blending and Word Building**

Meeting Individual Needs for Phonics

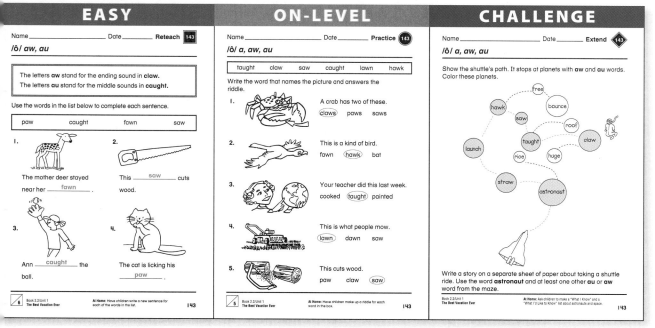

EASY	ON-LEVEL	CHALLENGE
Reteach, 143	Practice, 143	Extend, 143

Daily Routines

DAY 1 **Blending** Write the spelling of each sound in *hawk* as you say it. Have children repeat after you. Ask children to blend the sounds to read the word. Repeat with *caught, walk,* and *talk.*

DAY 2 **Discriminating** Say a list of words, some containing /ô/ (for example: *crawl, fall, boy, eat*). Have children listen for the /ô/ sound and clap their hands each time they hear it.

DAY 3 **Segmenting** Write two words with different spellings for /ô/ on the board (*saw, taught*). Have a volunteer identify and underline the letters in each word that stand for the /ô/ sound.

DAY 4 **Fluency** Write a list of /ô/ words such as *talk, paw, claw, hawk, cause.* Point to each word, asking children to blend the sounds silently. Ask a volunteer to read aloud each word.

DAY 5 **Writing** Have children write a riddle whose answer is a word with the sound /ô/. Have pairs try to answer each other's riddles.

68H

OBJECTIVES

Children will decode and read words with /ô/a, aw, au.

Apply /ô/ *a, aw, au*

City Zoo

At the City Zoo
I saw a paw.
A polar paw on a big white bear.
At the City Zoo
I saw a jaw.
The jaw of a panther sleeping over there.
At the City Zoo
I saw a claw.
The claw of a macaw flying in the air.

68   69

Anthology pages 68–69

Read and Build Fluency

READ THE POEM Have children read the poem, "City Zoo," to themselves. Then read the poem aloud. Request that children listen carefully for the /ô/ sound. Then, as an auditory model, read the poem once more, this time in choral fashion. Remind children to track the print as you read.

REREAD FOR FLUENCY Organize the class into groups of three. Have groups read the poem aloud together, each child reading a stanza. Encourage children to use expressions appropriate to the animal in their stanza. Children who need fluency practice can read the entire poem aloud.

Dictate and Spell

DICTATE WORDS Say the word *paw*. Segment it into its two individual sounds. (/p/ /ô/) Say *paw* again and use it in a sentence, for example, "My cat licked its paw." Encourage children to pronounce the word. Then have them write down the letter or letter patterns for each sound until the word is complete. Repeat the process with other words from the poem: *jaw, claw, macaw*. Then repeat using words other than those in the poem, such as *hawk, draw,* and *shawl*.

Intervention   **Skills Intervention Guide,** for direct instruction and extra practice in /ô/a, aw, au

Build Background

cial Studies

Concept: Historical Sites and Natural Wonders in the United States

Evaluate Prior Knowledge

CONCEPT: HISTORICAL SITES AND NATURAL WONDERS IN THE UNITED STATES Tell children that people often visit historical sites and natural wonders while on vacation. Describe Yellowstone National Park as an example of a natural wonder and the Statue of Liberty as an example of a historical site. Invite children to describe historical sites they have visited, or heard or read about.

MAKE A CHART Work with children to make a chart of historical sites and natural wonders and the states or regions in which they are located. As children brainstorm, ask questions prompting them to mention famous sites in the United States. If they don't know where a famous site is, help them to look it up. ▶ **Logical/Visual/Spatial**

HISTORICAL SITES	LOCATION
White House	Washington, D.C.
Statue of Liberty	New York
Golden Gate Bridge	California

NATURAL WONDERS	LOCATION
Yellowstone National Park	Wyoming, Montana Idaho
Black Hills	South Dakota
Pacific Ocean	West Coast

Graphic Organizer 31

PLAN A TRIP Have children work in small groups to plan a vacation trip. Have each group choose three destinations they would like to visit and write a sentence describing each place.

GROUP **WRITING**

Develop Oral Language

CONNECT WORDS WITH PICTURES

ESL Show children magazines, brochures, or postcards that feature historical and natural sites. Help them to name and describe what they see and what people do there. Then invite volunteers to take turns choosing a picture and giving clues about it while the rest of the group guesses its identity. Clues can be verbal or pantomimed. ▶ **Visual/Kinesthetic**

DAILY Phonics ROUTINES

DAY 2 **Discriminating** Say a list of words, some containing /ô/ (for example: *crawl, fall, boy, eat*). Have children listen for the /ô/ sound and clap their hands each time they hear it.

Phonics **CD-ROM**

LANGUAGE SUPPORT

Use the **Language Support Book**, pages 164–167 to help build background.

OBJECTIVES

Children will use context and structural clues to determine the meanings of vocabulary words.

vacation (p. 72) a time of freedom from school, business, or other activity

museum (p. 74) a building where objects of art, science, or history are shown

wonder (p. 84) to be curious about something

guess (p. 72) to form an opinion without knowing the facts

brave (p. 78) having or showing courage; not afraid

practice (p. 76) to do something over and over to learn how to do it well

Story Words

These words from the selection may be unfamiliar. Before children read, have them check the meanings and pronunciations of the words in the Glossary, beginning on page 390, or in a dictionary.

- Parthenon, p. 77
- Alamo, p. 78
- burrito, p. 78
- binoculars, p. 82
- La Brea, p. 84
- skeletons, p. 84

vacation
museum
wonder
guess
brave
practice

Vocabulary

Teach Vocabulary in Context

Identify Vocabulary Words
Display **Teaching Chart 121** and read the passage with children. Have volunteers circle each vocabulary word and underline other words that are clues to its meaning.

Off to Paris

1. Now that school is out, we are going to Paris for our summer vacation! 2. We will go to museums, where there are art and history exhibits. 3. I wonder what else we will do. I am curious because I have never been to Paris. 4. I guess my parents have things planned, but I suppose they won't tell us until we're there. 5. My brother thinks I am brave because I want to try to speak French when we are there. 6. But I am not afraid because every night I practice saying French words over and over again.

Teaching Chart 121

Discuss Meanings
Ask questions like these to help clarify word meanings:

- When is your next vacation?
- What can you see in an art museum?
- If you're curious about something, do you wonder about it?
- When you guess at something, do you know for sure about it?
- Can you name a brave hero?
- When you practice something, do you do it once or over and over again?

Practice

Picture Clues
Have students work in pairs. Ask one child to pick two vocabulary cards from a pile, then draw a picture or write a clue for each word. The other child matches words and clues.
▶ **Spatial/Interpersonal**

Word Building Manipulative Cards

Write Synonyms
Have pairs of children choose a vocabulary word. Ask each child to write as many words with similar meanings as possible in one minute. Then partners can compare lists, using the Glossary as needed. ▶ **Linguistic/Interpersonal**

Assess Vocabulary

Identify Word Meaning in Context
Encourage children to write a short paragraph about a vacation they would like to take. Ask them to use as many vocabulary words as possible to tell about what they might see on this trip. Children should then exchange papers and check that the vocabulary words are used correctly.

SPELLING/VOCABULARY CONNECTIONS

See Spelling Challenge Words, page 91Q.

LANGUAGE SUPPORT

See the **Language Support Book**, pages 164–167, for teaching suggestions for Vocabulary.

Vocabulary PuzzleMaker

Provides vocabulary activities.

Meeting Individual Needs for Vocabulary

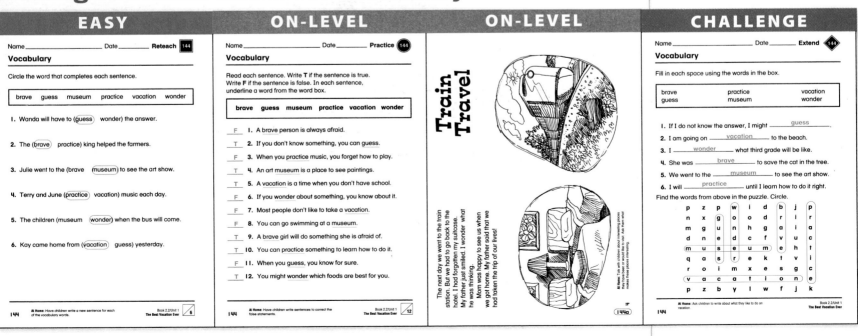

EASY	ON-LEVEL	ON-LEVEL	CHALLENGE
Reteach, 144	Practice, 144	Practice, 144a Take-Home Story	Extend, 144

Comprehension

Prereading Strategies

PREVIEW AND PREDICT Take a **picture walk** through the pages of this selection, discussing illustrations that give clues about the story.

- What clues about the characters and setting do the title and pictures give?
- Are the events in this story happening in one place or many different places?
- Will this story be about real places or imaginary ones? How can you tell? *Genre*
- What do you think this story is about?

Have children record their predictions about the story.

PREDICTIONS	WHAT HAPPENED
A family goes on a vacation in their car.	

SET PURPOSES Ask children what they want to find out by reading the story. For example:

- Why are there letters on some pages?
- Where does the family go?

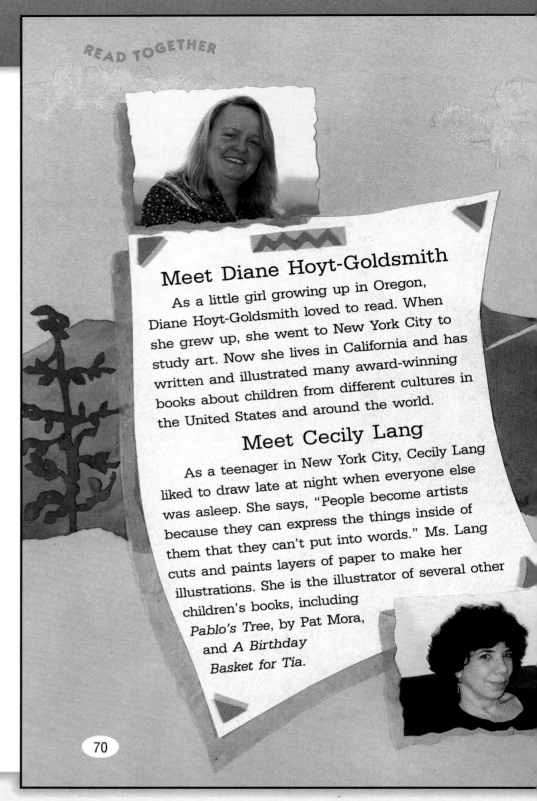

READ TOGETHER

Meet Diane Hoyt-Goldsmith

As a little girl growing up in Oregon, Diane Hoyt-Goldsmith loved to read. When she grew up, she went to New York City to study art. Now she lives in California and has written and illustrated many award-winning books about children from different cultures in the United States and around the world.

Meet Cecily Lang

As a teenager in New York City, Cecily Lang liked to draw late at night when everyone else was asleep. She says, "People become artists because they can express the things inside of them that they can't put into words." Ms. Lang cuts and paints layers of paper to make her illustrations. She is the illustrator of several other children's books, including *Pablo's Tree*, by Pat Mora, and *A Birthday Basket for Tía*.

70

Meeting Individual Needs • Grouping Suggestions for Strategic Reading

EASY	ON-LEVEL	CHALLENGE
Shared Reading Read the story aloud to children, or have them use the **Listening Library.** Have children compare Amanda's and Sammy's feelings about the sites they visited.	**Guided Instruction** Ask children to read the story with you. You may want to have children read the story first on their own. Use the Comprehension prompts to model strategies as you read together. Have children fill in the comparison chart as they read.	**Read Independently** Have children read the story on their own. Encourage children to select two favorite sites from the story and write a short paragraph comparing and contrasting them.

The Best Vacation Ever

by Diane Hoyt-Goldsmith
Illustrated by Cecily Lang

1

71

Comprehension

☑ **Phonics** Apply /ô/ *a, aw, au*

☑ **Apply Compare and Contrast**

STRATEGIC READING Let's keep track of all the places Amanda's family visits. We can make a chart and take notes about Amanda's and Sammy's different reactions to each place. Comparing their reactions will help us understand their interests.

PLACE	AMANDA'S REACTIONS	SAMMY'S REACTIONS

1 Look at the people in this picture. Where are they? How do they look?
(They are standing in front of some mountains. They look happy.) *Setting, Character*

LANGUAGE SUPPORT

A blackline master of the Reaction Chart is available in the **Language Support Book**.

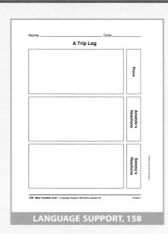
Name _____ Date _____
A Trip Log

Place

Amanda's Reactions

Sammy's Reactions

LANGUAGE SUPPORT, 158

Genre

Informational Story

Explain that an informational story:

- gives information in an easy-to-understand way.
- may include photographs, illustrations, and charts.
- has realistic characters and setting.

Activity After reading *The Best Vacation Ever* have volunteers give examples of facts from the story. Point out the hints that Amanda gives in every P.S. as an example of how the author provides facts and information. Ask them to explain why they think the author included letters, drawings, photographs, and maps in the story.

Comprehension

2 Where is Amanda writing this letter from? (her home in Virginia) **How do you know?** (It says so on the top of the letter.) **Where does Josie live?** (Ohio) **How can you tell?** (Amanda thinks it's a shame they won't be driving through Ohio.) *Setting*

3 How do you think Amanda feels about her family trip? (excited) **How can you tell?** (She uses exclamation points and the word "neat" in her letter to her friend.) *Draw Conclusions*

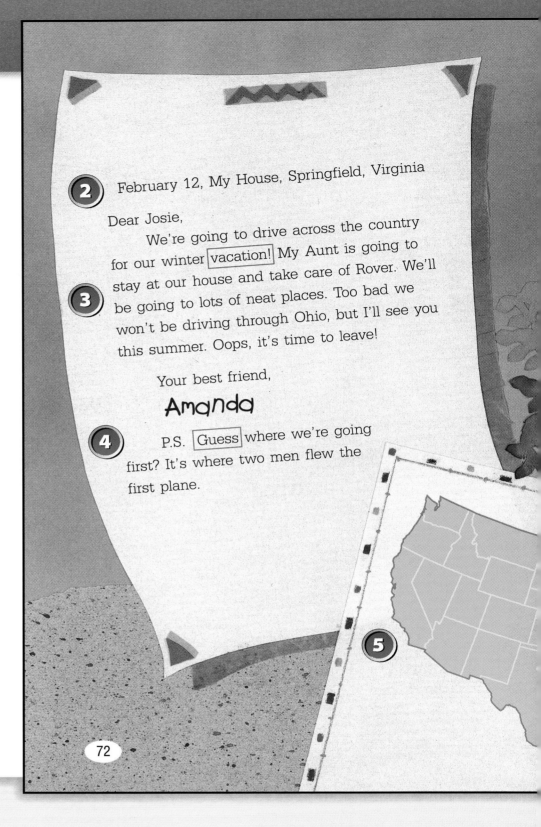

2 February 12, My House, Springfield, Virginia

Dear Josie,
　　We're going to drive across the country for our winter vacation! My Aunt is going to stay at our house and take care of Rover. **3** We'll be going to lots of neat places. Too bad we won't be driving through Ohio, but I'll see you this summer. Oops, it's time to leave!

　　Your best friend,

　　Amanda

4　P.S. Guess where we're going first? It's where two men flew the first plane.

72

Fluency

READ WITH EXPRESSION

Have children point out the punctuation marks on page 72.

Remind children that exclamation points indicate emphasis, and that question marks indicate a question is being asked. Have partners take turns reading Amanda's letter aloud with the expression that Amanda might use if she were excited to be leaving for a trip.

Virginia

73

Comprehension

4 Why do you think Amanda asks a question at the end of her letter? (She likes games; she wants to make the letter more interesting.) *Make Inferences*

5 What do you think is the purpose of the map on pages 72–73? (to show where Amanda and her family live) *Draw Conclusions*

TEACHING TIP

MAP SKILLS Display a large map of the United States with the states labeled. As you read the story with children, track the trip of Amanda's family with self-stick notes or colored push pins.

LANGUAGE SUPPORT

ESL Help children understand the meaning of the word *first*. Tell children that these words can help them know the order events happen in a story. Ask a volunteer to write *1* on the chalkboard. Ask another volunteer to write *2*. Ask a third to write *3*. Ask: *Who came to the board first? Who came to the board second? Who came to the board third?* Tell children in which order to sit down, using the words *first*, *second*, and *third*.

Comprehension

6 **Phonics** /ô/ **WORDS** Let's look at the first sentence of Amanda's letter on page 74. Point to the last word. (*hawk*) Remember that the letters *aw* make one sound. What is it? (/ô/) Now let's read the word together. *Graphophonic Cues*

7 On what date did Amanda's family visit the museum? (February 13) **How did you know?** (The date is at the top of the letter.) When Amanda writes: *Tomorrow we're going to drive to the "home of country music,"* which day is she talking about? (February 14) How long will it take Amanda's family to drive from Springfield, Virginia to Kitty Hawk, North Carolina? (Less than a day) What information helped you to know? (the dates) *Sequence of Events*

8 **COMPARE AND CONTRAST** Now that we've read about the first stop on the trip, let's start filling in our chart.

MODEL Amanda says she likes the sand dunes. I'll add that to the chart. Her brother Sammy bought a model plane. Maybe that's something he's interested in. I'll put that in Sammy's column.

PLACE	AMANDA'S REACTIONS	SAMMY'S REACTIONS
Kitty Hawk	liked the sand dunes	bought a model airplane kit

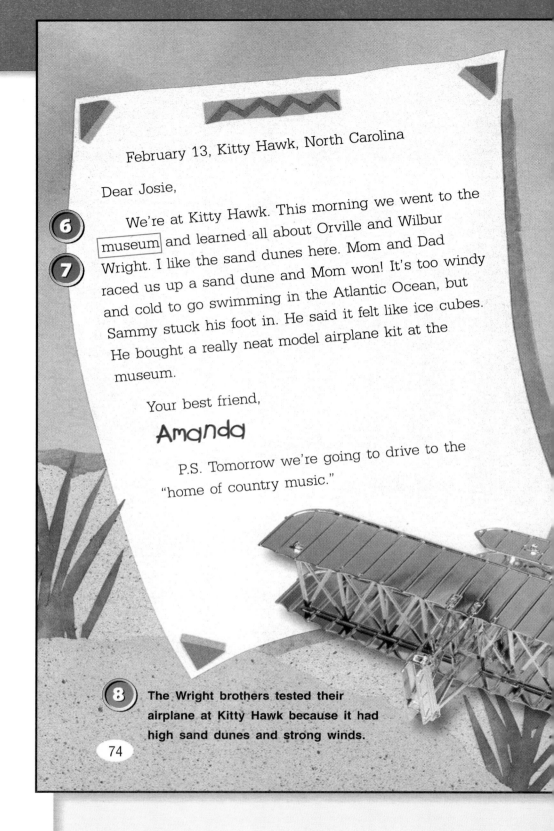

February 13, Kitty Hawk, North Carolina

Dear Josie,

6 **7** We're at Kitty Hawk. This morning we went to the museum and learned all about Orville and Wilbur Wright. I like the sand dunes here. Mom and Dad raced us up a sand dune and Mom won! It's too windy and cold to go swimming in the Atlantic Ocean, but Sammy stuck his foot in. He said it felt like ice cubes. He bought a really neat model airplane kit at the museum.

Your best friend,

Amanda

P.S. Tomorrow we're going to drive to the "home of country music."

8 The Wright brothers tested their airplane at Kitty Hawk because it had high sand dunes and strong winds.

74

The Wright Brothers Memorial in Kitty Hawk, North Carolina

WILBUR WRIGHT ORVILLE WRIGHT

IN COMMEMORATION OF THE CONQUEST OF THE AIR

In 1903, Orville Wright flew the first engine-powered airplane. The plane stayed in the air for just 12 seconds. Even so, the brothers showed that their invention worked.

75

Comprehension

9 A *memorial* helps people remember an important person or event. Sometimes it is a statue or even a whole building. Why do you think there is a Wright Brother's memorial? (Because the Wright Brothers did something important that no one had done before.) *Draw Conclusions*

CONTRACTIONS Can you find the contraction in the first sentence of Amanda's letter? (*we're*) What words does this contraction stand for? (*we are*)

Ⓢelf-Monitoring Strategy

VISUALIZE Picturing in your head events or descriptions from the story can help you understand what you are reading.

MODEL I'm not sure what sand dunes are. I'll try to picture what's happening. Mom and Dad raced Amanda up a sand dune. So a dune must be like a hill of sand. Since Amanda says it's windy at Kitty Hawk, I bet the wind there heaps the sand up into little hills.

P/i PREVENTION/INTERVENTION

CONTRACTIONS Write *we are* and *we're* on the chalkboard. Remind children that a contraction is a shortened form of two words joined together to make a single word. Explain that the apostrophe shows where some letters are left out when the words are joined.

• Which letter is left out of the contraction *we're*? (*a*)
• Can you find another contraction on page 74? (*it's*)
• Which two words does the contraction stand for? (*it is*) *Syntactic Cues*

75

Comprehension

 10 **What do you think the Grand Ole Opry is?** (a place where musicians and singers play) **What clues in the story helped you to know?** ("Nashville has lots of musicians"; ". . . Molly Partridge sings") *Draw Conclusions*

11 **Phonics** /ô/ WORDS Look at the second paragraph in Amanda's letter. Find the last word in the third line. Let's blend the sounds together to read it: a str o n au t astronaut. **What letters make the /ô/ sound?** (*au*) *Blending/Graphophonic Cues*

12 **How does Sammy feel about Amanda's singing?** (He doesn't think she's a good singer.) **How do you know?** (He compares her singing to a dog howling.) *Make Inferences*

13 **What state will Amanda and her family visit after they leave Nashville?** (Texas) *Sequence of Events*

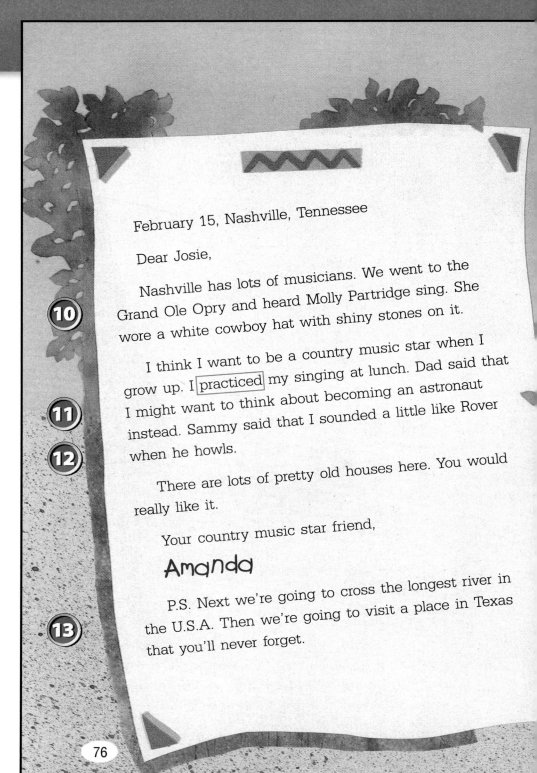

February 15, Nashville, Tennessee

Dear Josie,

10 Nashville has lots of musicians. We went to the Grand Ole Opry and heard Molly Partridge sing. She wore a white cowboy hat with shiny stones on it.

11 I think I want to be a country music star when I grow up. I practiced my singing at lunch. Dad said that I might want to think about becoming an astronaut instead. Sammy said that I sounded a little like Rover **12** when he howls.

There are lots of pretty old houses here. You would really like it.

Your country music star friend,

Amanda

13 P.S. Next we're going to cross the longest river in the U.S.A. Then we're going to visit a place in Texas that you'll never forget.

76

CULTURAL PERSPECTIVES

AROUND THE WORLD Discuss with children the kinds of music that started in the United States (such as country, jazz, Dixieland, bluegrass). Ask children to share other kinds of music they can name from other cultures.

RESEARCH AND INQUIRY Invite children to bring in tapes or CDs of songs from other cultures, and listen to them in class.

▶ **Musical/Kinesthetic**

ne Grand Ole Opry,
famous place to hear
ountry music.

GRAND OLE OPRY

The Cumberland River
flows through Nashville,
the capital of Tennessee.

The Parthenon is in Centennial Park.
It is an exact model in size and detail of
the Parthenon in Athens, Greece, which
was built in the fifth century B.C.

(14)

77

Comprehension

14 What do you think Nashville looks like? (There is a river, lots of old houses, and some tall modern buildings.) **How do you know?** (From Amanda's descriptions and from the photos.) *Setting*

BLENDING WITH LONG *o* Let's look at the caption under the postcard of Nashville. Find the word that describes what the river does and read it aloud. (flows)

TEACHING TIP

MANAGEMENT Read the story with children, or have them read it alone, before you do cultural perspective and cross-curricular activities.

PREVENTION/INTERVENTION

BLENDING WITH LONG *o* Write the word *flows* on the chalkboard. Have a volunteer come up and read the word while running his or her fingers under each letter. Ask children what words on page 76 have blends followed by long *o*. (*stones, grow*) Have volunteers write the words and underline the /ō/ spelling.

Challenge children to find words on page 76 in which the letters *ow* spell a different sound. They should find *cowboy* and *howls*, in which *ow* spell /ou/. *Graphophonic Cues*

Comprehension

15 Amanda bought a book about a woman who lived through the battle at the Alamo. What does this tell you about Amanda? (She is interested in reading and learning about new things.) *Character*

16 Amanda says her Dad ate "the world's biggest burrito." Why does she say this? (She wants Josie to know the burrito was big.) *Figurative Language*

17 What month will it be when Amanda and her family get to the big caves? (March) **How do you know?** (The top of the letter says February 28th. That is the last or second-to-last day of the month. At the bottom of the letter she says they will be there in a few days.) *Sequence of Events*

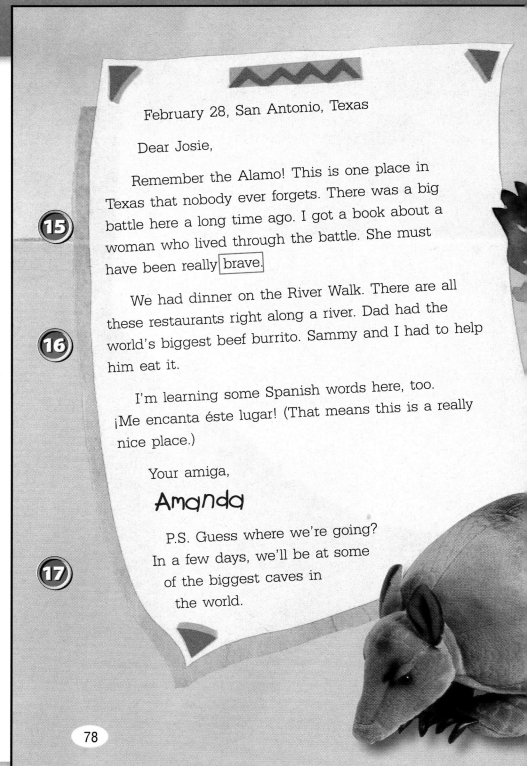

February 28, San Antonio, Texas

Dear Josie,

15 Remember the Alamo! This is one place in Texas that nobody ever forgets. There was a big battle here a long time ago. I got a book about a woman who lived through the battle. She must have been really brave.

16 We had dinner on the River Walk. There are all these restaurants right along a river. Dad had the world's biggest beef burrito. Sammy and I had to help him eat it.

I'm learning some Spanish words here, too. ¡Me encanta éste lugar! (That means this is a really nice place.)

Your amiga,

Amanda

17 P.S. Guess where we're going? In a few days, we'll be at some of the biggest caves in the world.

78

Cross Curricular: Math

MEASUREMENT The River Walk is a long, wide, winding sidewalk along the river, 20 feet below street level.

Have small groups measure out 20 feet on a piece of rope. They can measure distances in the classroom and around the school with the rope as a unit of measurement. Record their measurements; for example, the rope is equal to five teacher desks or the chalkboard equals half of the rope.

▶ **Kinesthetic/Mathematical**

The Alamo is the church in an old Spanish mission. In 1836, there was a war between Texas and Mexico. One of the battles took place at the Alamo. A large Mexican army fought against a small group of Texans. The Texans fought for several weeks, but in the end they lost. After more battles, Texas won its independence from Mexico.

The Paseo del Rio, or River Walk, is a popular place to visit. It is 1.2 miles long and 20 feet below the street. **18**

79

Comprehension

18 **COMPARE AND CONTRAST**
Amanda mentions two places her family visited in the letter on page 78. What are they? (The Alamo; the River Walk) What do these places have in common? (They are both popular places to visit in San Antonio, Texas.) What is different about these places? (The Alamo is an old church where a famous battle took place. The River Walk is a nice place to sit and eat. It's colorful and pretty.)

Minilesson
REVIEW/MAINTAIN

Long *i*

Have children reread page 78. Ask volunteers to find two words containing long *i* spelled *i-e. (time, nice)* Point out that the word *life* has a long *i* sound, but the word *lived* has a short *i* sound. Then have children think of words that rhyme with *time* and *nice*.

Activity Have children find other words with long *i* spelled *i-e* on pages 79–80. *(miles, like)*

LANGUAGE SUPPORT

ESL Ask Spanish-speaking children to help pronounce and explain the Spanish words on this page: *amiga* (girlfriend); *burrito* (flour tortilla rolled with a filling inside); *Me encanta este lugar* (This is a really nice place).

Read the historical note on page 79 to the children. Explain that Texas was once a part of Mexico and had to fight for its freedom. Later it became a part of the United States.

Comprehension

19 With what does Amanda compare the lights in the cave? (diamonds)
Figurative Language

20 **COMPARE AND CONTRAST** Sometimes Amanda and Sammy have different feelings about the places they visit. Is there anything they feel the same about?

MODEL Let's see . . . Sammy was disappointed that he didn't get to see the bats. Amanda says she wants to go to Florida to see the dolphins. It seems like they both like animals. Let's add this information to the chart.

PLACE	AMANDA'S REACTIONS	SAMMY'S REACTIONS
Kitty Hawk	liked the sand dunes	bought a model airplane kit
Carlsbad Caverns	wants to see the dolphins in Florida	is sorry he missed seeing the bats

21 What does a park ranger do? (works in the park to protect it and teach visitors about it) What clues does the story give you? (The ranger explained to Sammy about the bats. The ranger was in the park.) *Draw Conclusions*

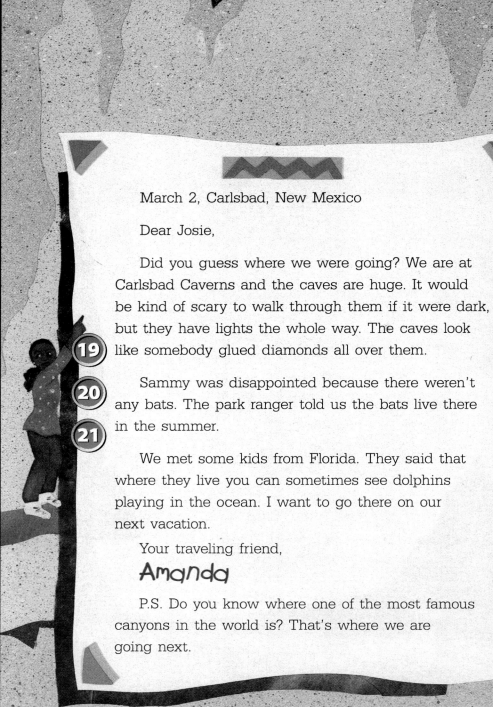

March 2, Carlsbad, New Mexico

Dear Josie,

Did you guess where we were going? We are at Carlsbad Caverns and the caves are huge. It would be kind of scary to walk through them if it were dark, but they have lights the whole way. The caves look **19** like somebody glued diamonds all over them.

20 Sammy was disappointed because there weren't any bats. The park ranger told us the bats live there **21** in the summer.

We met some kids from Florida. They said that where they live you can sometimes see dolphins playing in the ocean. I want to go there on our next vacation.

Your traveling friend,

Amanda

P.S. Do you know where one of the most famous canyons in the world is? That's where we are going next.

80

Activity

Cross Curricular: Art

BATS Tell children that the word's smallest bat is the size of a penny. The world's largest bat has a wing span of six feet! Seven species of bats live in the Carlsbad Caverns.

Have children create bats of wild and wonderful colors and sizes, using pipe cleaners, construction paper, and tissue paper. Suspend finished bats from the ceiling, either flying or hanging upside down by their feet, as bats do.

▶ **Visual/Kinesthetic**

Carlsbad Caverns became a national park in 1930. It is a chain of underground caves. In one of the caves, the ceiling is 285 feet high. That is about half the height of the Washington Monument. An elevator can take visitors down to caves that are 750 and 829 feet underground. **22**

In the summer, millions of bats live in one part of the caverns. When the sun sets, they fly out of the caves in search of insects to eat. **23**

81

Comprehension

22 How would you describe a national park? (a large piece of land owned and protected by the U.S. government) **What might you find in a national park?** (wildlife, forests, campgrounds, monuments, natural wonders) *Form Generalizations*

23 Why do the bats fly out of the caves when the sun sets? (They go out looking for insects to eat.) *Cause and Effect*

Minilesson

REVIEW/MAINTAIN

Make Inferences

Remind children that a character's words and actions help a reader understand the character's thoughts and feelings. Have children reread Amanda's letter on page 80. Ask:

• Do you think Amanda likes dark places? How do you know? (No; she says the caves would be scary without lights.)

Activity Show how Amanda's face might look if she was walking through the caves in the dark.

LANGUAGE SUPPORT

ESL Some children may be unfamiliar with the customary measurement system. Help them understand the dimensions of half the height of the Washington Monument. Display a picture of the Washington Monument with people in the photo for scale reference. Ask children to point to a spot about

halfway up the monument. Remind them that the caption on page 81 says this is about 285 feet. Tell them this equals about 85 meters. Ask children to picture the distance as the ceiling height of an underground cave.

Comprehension

(24) **COMPARE AND CONTRAST** In Amanda's letter, she sounds very excited about being at the Grand Canyon. It seems like Sammy didn't enjoy the mule ride very much. Let's add that information to our chart.

PLACE	AMANDA'S REACTIONS	SAMMY'S REACTIONS
Kitty Hawk	liked the sand dunes	bought a model airplane kit
Carlsbad Caverns	wants to see the dolphins in Florida	is sorry he missed seeing the bats
Grand Canyon	is impressed by the size of the canyon	prefers riding his bicycle to riding a mule

(25) Amanda says she wants to be a park ranger when she grows up. What other job does Amanda say she might have when she grows up? (country singer) Why do you think Amanda changes her mind? (She is excited about learning new things.) *Character*

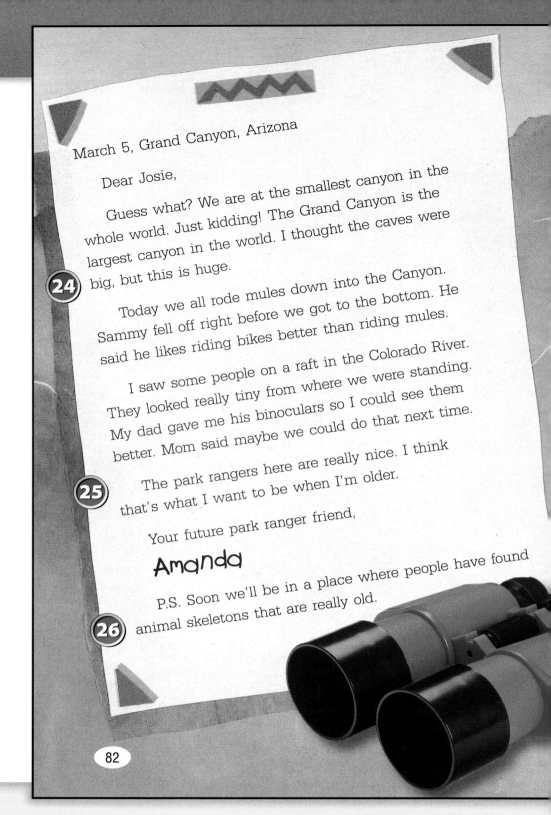

March 5, Grand Canyon, Arizona

Dear Josie,

Guess what? We are at the smallest canyon in the whole world. Just kidding! The Grand Canyon is the largest canyon in the world. I thought the caves were **(24)** big, but this is huge.

Today we all rode mules down into the Canyon. Sammy fell off right before we got to the bottom. He said he likes riding bikes better than riding mules.

I saw some people on a raft in the Colorado River. They looked really tiny from where we were standing. My dad gave me his binoculars so I could see them better. Mom said maybe we could do that next time.

The park rangers here are really nice. I think **(25)** that's what I want to be when I'm older.

Your future park ranger friend,

Amanda

(26) P.S. Soon we'll be in a place where people have found animal skeletons that are really old.

82

Activity

Cross Curricular: Social Studies

PARTNERS **THE GRAND CANYON** Visitors to the Grand Canyon can use many types of transportation in the canyon, from mules to river rafts to helicopters.

RESEARCH AND INQUIRY Children can do research to create travel brochures showing the different ways to travel in or up and down the canyon.

▶ **Linguistic/Visual**

*inter*NET **CONNECTION** Children can learn more about the Grand Canyon by visiting **www.mhschool.com/reading**.

The Grand Canyon is the largest canyon in the world. It is 277 miles long. In some places it is 18 miles wide. It is five miles deep. The Colorado River runs through the canyon.

Visitors can travel down into the canyon by walking along trails or by riding mules. As you go down into the canyon, you can see the many layers of the Earth as it was formed.

83

Comprehension

26 **Phonics** /ô/ SPELLED *a* and *aw*

Let's read the first paragraph of Amanda's letter on page 82. Now point to the word with the /ô/ sound. (*smallest*). What letter or letters spell this sound? (*a*) Find another word on this page that has the /ô/ sound. (*saw*) What letters stand for the sound in this word? (*aw*) *Graphophonic Cues*

Minilesson
REVIEW/MAINTAIN

Context Clues

Remind children that clues to the meaning of an unfamiliar word can be found in both words and pictures.

- Have children find the word *binoculars* on page 82.
- Ask what words helped them understand what binoculars are.
- Ask if a picture also helped them.

Activity Have children write a definition of *canyon*. Have them explain what words and pictures helped them to understand what a canyon is.

Comprehension

27 How did Dad's face look when he fixed the flat tire? Make a face like the one Amanda's dad made. *Character/Pantomime*

28 **COMPARE AND CONTRAST** Let's look back to Amanda's letter from Kitty Hawk on page 74. How can you compare and contrast Los Angeles and Kitty Hawk? (Both places have oceans nearby; Los Angeles is a big city near the Pacific Ocean, Kitty Hawk is a small place near the Atlantic Ocean. The Pacific Ocean is warm and the Atlantic Ocean is cold.)

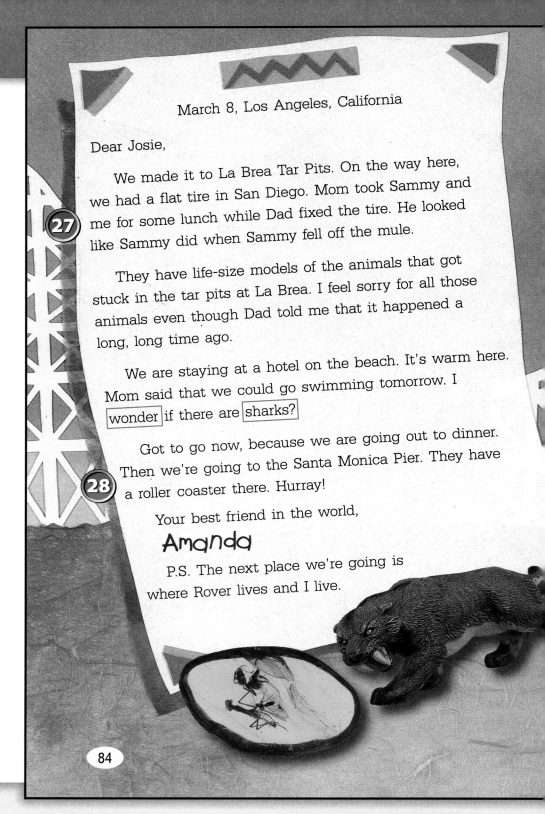

March 8, Los Angeles, California

Dear Josie,

We made it to La Brea Tar Pits. On the way here, we had a flat tire in San Diego. Mom took Sammy and me for some lunch while Dad fixed the tire. He looked like Sammy did when Sammy fell off the mule.

They have life-size models of the animals that got stuck in the tar pits at La Brea. I feel sorry for all those animals even though Dad told me that it happened a long, long time ago.

We are staying at a hotel on the beach. It's warm here. Mom said that we could go swimming tomorrow. I wonder if there are sharks?

Got to go now, because we are going out to dinner. Then we're going to the Santa Monica Pier. They have a roller coaster there. Hurray!

Your best friend in the world,

Amanda

P.S. The next place we're going is where Rover lives and I live.

84

Cross Curricular: Science

SHARKS Tell children that many forms of animal life, including some mammals, live in and near the Pacific Ocean.

RESEARCH AND INQUIRY Have small groups choose an ocean animal to research. Ask each group to write a list of facts about the animal, and to draw a picture of it to share with the class.

▶ **Kinesthetic/Linguistic**

Millions of animal skeletons were found at La Brea Tar Pits. These animals lived during the Ice Age. Skeletons of camels, horses, giant bears, giant ground sloths, giant wolves, and sabre-toothed tigers were found. These animals were trapped in the tar when they came to get water to drink. After the animals died, the layers of sticky tar helped to keep their skeletons in good shape for millions of years.

(29)

85

Comprehension

(29) How do you think layers of sticky tar could help to keep animal skeletons in good shape, or good condition, for millions of years? (probably protected them from water, air, weather, and wind damage) *Draw Conclusions*

 PLURAL NOUNS Point to the word that means more than one wolf. *(wolves)*

Minilesson

REVIEW/MAINTAIN

Main Idea

Remind children that a main idea is the most important idea in a story, paragraph, or sentence. Ask:

• What is the main idea of the paragraph beneath the illustration on page 85?

• What is the main idea of the first paragraph in Amanda's letter on page 84?

Activity Have children go back through the story and choose one page. Ask them to write one sentence for each paragraph that describes its main idea.

PREVENTION/INTERVENTION

PLURAL NOUNS Remind children that *plural* means more than one. Explain that in most words, an *s* is added to a word to form the plural. Example: *book —> books*. Point out, though, that in other words, the last letter *f* is changed to a *v* before adding the letters *–es* to form the plural. Write these sentences on the chalkboard, underlining the last words, and invite volunteers to read them:

I saw one <u>wolf</u>.
Tom saw three <u>wolves</u>.

Ask a volunteer to identify the final consonant in the underlined word in the first sentence. (*f*) Ask children to say what letter replaces the *f* in *wolf* before the *–es* ending is added to form the plural *wolves*. (*v*) Have children form the plural for each of the following words: *calf* (*calves*); *half* (*halves*). *Syntactic Cues*

Comprehension

30 **COMPARE AND CONTRAST** Let's look back through our Reaction Chart to compare Amanda's reactions with Sammy's. Amanda seems to like things in nature—for example, the sand dunes, the caves, the Grand Canyon. Sammy seems to like things that are made or can be built. He buys a model airplane kit, and he prefers riding his bicycle to riding a mule. Both Sammy and Amanda seem to be interested in animals.

RETELL THE STORY Ask children to work in pairs to retell the story. Encourage partners to take turns telling about each destination until they have finished. *Summarize*

STUDENT SELF-ASSESSMENT

Have children ask themselves the following questions to assess how they are reading:

- How did comparing and contrasting Amanda's and Sammy's reactions to the different sites help me to understand their likes and dislikes?
- How did using the chart help me to make comparisons?
- How did using what I know about letters, sounds, and word meanings help me to understand unfamiliar words?

TRANSFERRING THE STRATEGIES

- Can I use these strategies to help me read other stories?

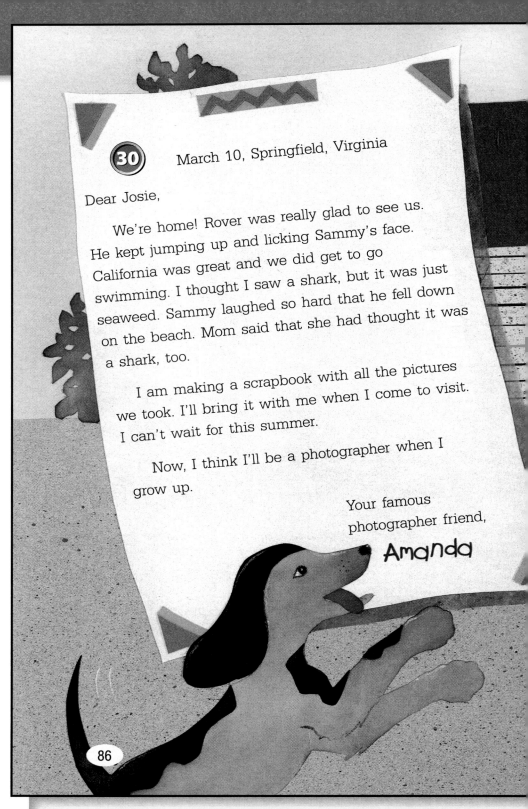

30 March 10, Springfield, Virginia

Dear Josie,

We're home! Rover was really glad to see us. He kept jumping up and licking Sammy's face. California was great and we did get to go swimming. I thought I saw a shark, but it was just seaweed. Sammy laughed so hard that he fell down on the beach. Mom said that she had thought it was a shark, too.

I am making a scrapbook with all the pictures we took. I'll bring it with me when I come to visit. I can't wait for this summer.

Now, I think I'll be a photographer when I grow up.

Your famous photographer friend,

Amanda

86

REREADING FOR *Fluency*

PARTNERS Children who need practice with fluency can read Amanda's letters aloud to a partner.

READING RATE When you evaluate reading rate, have children read aloud from the story for one minute. Place a stick-on note after the last word read. Count words read. To evaluate children's performance, see the Running Record in the **Fluency Assessment** book.

i Intervention For leveled fluency passages, lessons, and norm charts, see **Skills Intervention Guide**, Part 5, Fluency.

Comprehension

Return to Predictions and Purposes

Reread children's predictions about the story. Discuss the predictions, noting which needed to be revised. Then ask children if the story answered the questions they had before they began to read.

PREDICTIONS	WHAT HAPPENED
A family goes on a vacation in their car.	They drive across the United States from Virginia to California and see many places.

INFORMAL ASSESSMENT

HOW TO ASSESS

WORDS WITH /ô/ Have children turn to page 76 and read the last word on the third line in the second paragraph.

COMPARE AND CONTRAST Ask children to compare Amanda's interests with Sammy's. What interests do they share?

FOLLOW UP

WORDS WITH /ô/ Review /ô/ and continue to model *a, aw, au,* blending /ô/ words for children who are having difficulty.

COMPARE AND CONTRAST Suggest that children who are having difficulty comparing and contrasting Sammy's and Amanda's interests go over their charts again to see what things on the lists are similar, and which are different.

LITERARY RESPONSE

QUICK-WRITE Have children choose their favorite of all Amanda's destinations, draw a picture of it in their journals, and write a brief paragraph telling why they liked this place the most.

ORAL RESPONSE Have children discuss these questions:

• Which of the natural wonders that Amanda visited seemed the most beautiful?

• Which of the places from history did you find the most interesting? Why?

• If you went on a trip across the country, would you be more interested in natural places or places that are important parts of history?

Story Questions

Have children discuss or write answers to the questions on page 88.

Answers:

1. Amanda tells her story in letters.
Literal/Genre

2. Answers will vary. Possible answer: They are both near an ocean, but one ocean is cold, the other is warm.
Inferential/Compare and Contrast

3. Possible answer: San Antonio, because she liked the food and learned some Spanish
Inferential/Judgments and Decisions

4. Amanda's vacation and the places she visited *Critical/Summarize*

5. Possible answer: Texas; a quarter with a picture of the Alamo. *Critical/Judgments and Decisions*

Write a Travel Guide For a full writing process lesson related to this suggestion, see the lesson on pages 91M–91N.

READ TOGETHER

Story Questions & Activities

1. How does Amanda tell her story?

2. Amanda visits Kitty Hawk and Los Angeles. How are these places alike? How are they different?

3. Which place was Amanda's favorite? Tell why you think so.

4. What is this story mostly about?

5. Design a new quarter for one of the states Amanda visits. Which state would you choose? What would you put on the coin?

Write a Travel Guide

Choose two of the places Amanda visited. Write a travel guide that tells about both places. Tell what is the same about both places and what is different. Explain why some people would like the first place better, and others would be more interested in the second place.

Meeting Individual Needs

EASY	ON-LEVEL	CHALLENGE
Name_____ Date_____ Reteach **145**	Name_____ Date_____ Practice **145**	Name_____ Date_____ Extend **145**
Story Comprehension	**Story Comprehension**	**Story Comprehension**
Think about "The Best Vacation Ever." Then complete the chart below. Answers may vary.	Read each sentence. Write **T** if the sentence is true. Write **F** if the sentence if false.	On her trip, Amanda imagined what she would be when she grew up. List her ideas.

EASY (Reteach 145):

Characters: Amanda, her family, Josie

Beginning of Story: Amanda and her family are driving across the United States during spring vacation. Amanda sends letters to her friend Josie all along the way.

Middle of Story: They go to many famous places such as Kitty Hawk, Nashville, the Alamo, Carlsbad Caverns, the Grand Canyon, and La Brea Tar Pits.

End of Story: They return home. Rover, their dog, is very glad to see them. Amanda is glad to be home, too!

Book 2.2/Unit 1
The Best Vacation Ever
At Home: Have children draw a picture of a place that they would like to visit. Encourage them to explain their choices.
145

ON-LEVEL (Practice 145):

1. _T_ Amanda drove across the country with her family.
2. _T_ They saw where Orville Wright flew the first plane.
3. _F_ The home of country music is in Kitty Hawk.
4. _T_ The Grand Ole Opry is a place to hear country music.
5. _T_ The Alamo is in Texas.
6. _F_ Amanda said, "Carlsbad Caverns were not very big."
7. _T_ Amanda and her family rode mules in the Grand Canyon.
8. _F_ Sammy liked riding a mule.
9. _F_ After the Grand Canyon, Amanda went home.
10. _T_ There are millions of bones in the La Brea Tarpits.

Book 2.2/Unit 1
The Best Vacation Ever
At Home: Have children tell about one of the places that Amanda visited with her family.
145

CHALLENGE (Extend 145):

Amanda wants to be . . .	1.	Country music star
	2.	Park Ranger
	3.	Photographer

Explain why new experiences can give you new ideas.

Draw a picture of what you want to be when you grow up. Explain the reasons.

Book 2.2/Unit 1
The Best Vacation Ever
At Home: Ask children to imagine they are going to drive across the country like Amanda. Have them make a list of the places they would like to visit.
145

Reteach, 145   Practice, 145   Extend, 145

Make a Travel Poster

Choose one of the places that Amanda and her family visited. Make a travel poster for it. Show the places Amanda visited and the things she and her family did.

Make a Model

Use clay to make your own model of the Grand Canyon or the Carlsbad Caverns. Look at the pictures in the story for a guide.

Find Out More

Amanda tells Josie that she and her family are going to cross the longest river in the United States. What is that river? How long is it? Which states does it flow through?

89

DAILY **Phonics** ROUTINES

DAY 3

Segmenting Write two words with different spellings for /ô/ on the board (*saw*, *taught*). Have a volunteer identify and underline the letters in each word that stand for the /ô/ sound.

 **Phonics CD-ROM**

Story Activities

Make a Travel Poster

Materials: paper or poster board, paint, paintbrushes, markers, crayons

PARTNERS Have partners decide on a destination and research information they want to include on their poster, such as available camping sites or entertainment that can be enjoyed there. The poster should include an illustration and some details comparing the place to other vacation spots.

Make a Model

Materials: clay, photographs of Grand Canyon and Carlsbad Caverns

PARTNERS Have children study photographs of the Grand Canyon and Carlsbad Caverns. Partners can work together to make a clay model of either natural wonder, using flags on toothpicks to label its features.

Find Out More

RESEARCH AND INQUIRY Ask children to **GROUP** list resources they might use to find answers to the questions. (atlas, encyclopedia) Then have them work in small groups to prepare a booklet about the river that includes pictures and captions.

*inter*NET **CONNECTION** For more information on this topic, have children go to **www.mhschool.com/reading.**

FORMAL **ASSESSMENT**

After page 89, see Selection Assessment.

Study Skills

GRAPHIC AIDS

⊘BJECTIVES

Children will:

- identify states, cities, and locations on a map.
- use a map key and a compass rose.

PREPARE Display **Teaching Chart 122**. Preview and discuss the map with children.

TEACH Have a volunteer circle the compass rose, draw a line from San Antonio to Los Angeles, and tell the direction of travel.

PRACTICE Have children answer questions 1–5. Review the answers with them.
1. Tennessee **2.** east **3.** New Mexico **4.** west
5. six

ASSESS/CLOSE Have children plan a trip from their state to a state Amanda visited, identifying the states through which they will travel and in which direction they will go.

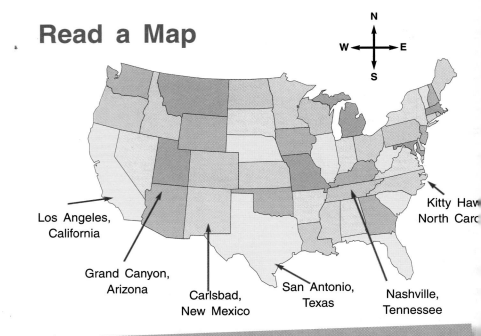

STUDY SKILLS

READ TOGETHER

Read a Map

Los Angeles, California

Grand Canyon, Arizona

Carlsbad, New Mexico

San Antonio, Texas

Nashville, Tennessee

Kitty Hawk, North Carolina

Use the map to answer the questions.

1. In what state is Nashville?

2. Is the Grand Canyon west or east of Los Angeles?

3. What state do you pass through to get from Texas to Arizona?

4. To get from Kitty Hawk to Los Angeles, in what direction would you travel?

5. What is the least number of states you must pass through to get from North Carolina to California?

Meeting Individual Needs

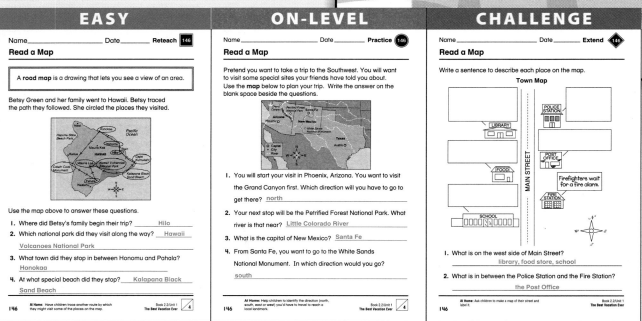

EASY

Name_____ Date_____ Reteach 146
Read a Map

A **road map** is a drawing that lets you see a view of an area.

Betsy Green and her family went to Hawaii. Betsy traced the path they followed. She circled the places they visited.

Use the map above to answer these questions.

1. Where did Betsy's family begin their trip? ___Hilo___
2. Which national park did they visit along the way? ___Hawaii Volcanoes National Park___
3. What town did they stop in between Honomu and Pahala? ___Honokaa___
4. At what special beach did they stop? ___Kalapana Black Sand Beach___

ON-LEVEL

Name_____ Date_____ Practice 146
Read a Map

Pretend you want to take a trip to the Southwest. You will want to visit some special sites your friends have told you about. Use the **map** below to plan your trip. Write the answer on the blank space beside the questions.

1. You will start your visit in Phoenix, Arizona. You want to visit the Grand Canyon first. Which direction will you have to go to get there? ___north___
2. Your next stop will be the Petrified Forest National Park. What river is that near? ___Little Colorado River___
3. What is the capital of New Mexico? ___Santa Fe___
4. From Santa Fe, you want to go to the White Sands National Monument. In which direction would you go? ___south___

CHALLENGE

Name_____ Date_____ Extend 146
Read a Map

Write a sentence to describe each place on the map.

Town Map

1. What is on the west side of Main Street? ___library, food store, school___
2. What is in between the Police Station and the Fire Station? ___the Post Office___

Reteach, 146

Practice, 146

Extend, 146

TEST POWER

Read the story again if the questions seem too hard.

DIRECTIONS:

Read the story. Then read each question about the story.

SAMPLE

Dear Diary

I am so excited! Next week Dad and I are going on a plane ride. I have always wanted to fly in a plane. I don't even have to wait until I turn ten after all.

Dad and I have been invited to Uncle Mike's seventieth birthday party. Dad wants me to meet Uncle Mike because I remind him of Uncle Mike. Dad has been saying that since I was born. I am curious to see if I look like Uncle Mike.

We are flying from Kansas City to Montana on Thursday night. We will be back on Sunday. Dad said that he will buy the tickets tomorrow. I will write more then.

1 How is the author different from Uncle Mike?
- ○ The author likes planes.
- ● The author is not an adult.
- ○ The author likes birthdays.
- ○ Uncle Mike has brown eyes.

2 Which conclusion can you draw from this story?
- ● The author is looking forward to meeting Uncle Mike.
- ○ The author is happy he is missing school.
- ○ The author is buying the airline tickets tomorrow.
- ○ Uncle Mike is a nice man.

91

Test Power

THE PRINCETON REVIEW

Read the Page

Explain to children that you will be reading this story as a group. You will read the story, and they will follow along in their books.

Request that children put pens, pencils, and markers away, since they will not be writing in their books.

Discuss the Questions

QUESTION 1: Have children look for words that describe the author and Uncle Mike. In the fourth sentence, it says that the author is under 10 years old, and in the fifth sentence, it says that Uncle Mike is 70.

QUESTION 2: Remind children that they should eliminate choices they know are wrong. Only the first choice has any support in the passage, since the author says that he is "excited."

Leveled Books

This Is Your Land

written by Anne Lawrence
illustrated by Robert Casilla

EASY

This Is Your Land

☑ **Phonics** Variant Vowel /ô/ *aw, au*

☑ **Compare and Contrast**

☑ **Instructional Vocabulary:** *brave, guess, museum, practice, vacation, wonder*

Guided Reading

PREVIEW AND PREDICT Have children take a **picture walk** through page 5 of the story. As children study the illustrations, ask them to predict what the story is about. Chart children's ideas.

SET PURPOSES Have children write or draw pictures that show why they want to read *This Is Your Land*. Have children share with the class their reasons for reading the story.

READ THE BOOK Use questions like the following to guide children as you read the story together or after they have read the story independently.

Page 4: Can you find the word *guess*? This is one of our new vocabulary words. Have you ever taken a guess? What were you guessing about? Try to use the word *guess* in a sentence. *Vocabulary*

Page 5: Listen to the sound /ô/ in *song*. Find a word on this page with the sound /ô/. *(because)* What letters spell the sound /ô/ in *because*? *(au) Phonics and Decoding*

Page 15: What do you think will happen if the Everglades become polluted? (Animals may die.) How important is it to protect the Everglades? *Draw Conclusions*

Page 16: How are the Everglades like the area where you live? How are they different? *Compare and Contrast*

RETURN TO PREDICTIONS AND PURPOSES Discuss children's predictions. Ask which were close to the story and why. Have children review their purposes for reading. Did they find out what they wanted to know?

LITERARY RESPONSE Discuss these questions:

- What kinds of animals live in the Everglades?

- What do you think should be done to protect the Everglades?

Also see the story questions and activity in *This Is Your Land*.

See the **Phonics** **CD-ROM** for practice using words with the variant vowel /ô/ sound.

Answers to Story Questions

1. A river of grass.
2. The trees are homes for the birds.
3. The canoe—the fast boat rips through grass and scares the animals.
4. Looking at the Everglades from a boat.
5. Answers will vary.

The Story Questions and Activity below appear in the Easy Book.

Story Questions and Writing Activity

1. What is the Everglades called?
2. Why are trees important for the birds?
3. Look at the picture on page 7. Compare the two boats. Which one is better for the Everglades? Why?
4. What is this story mostly about?
5. If Jim got to go with Amanda on her trip across the country, which place do you think he would like best?

Water, Water, Everywhere

Look at the map on page 4. What body of water is to the west of Everglades National Park? Now pretend you live in the Everglades. Draw a picture of something you see every day. Write a sentence about it.

from *This Is Your Land*

Leveled Books

INDEPENDENT

The Underground City

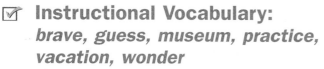

- ☑ **Phonics** Variant Vowel /ô/ *aw, au*
- ☑ **Compare and Contrast**
- ☑ **Instructional Vocabulary:** *brave, guess, museum, practice, vacation, wonder*

The Underground City

Written by Lauren Ray Pollard
Illustrated by Harold Hendrickson

Guided Reading

PREVIEW AND PREDICT Talk with children about the illustrations through page 7. As you take the **picture walk**, have children predict what the story is about. Chart children's ideas.

SET PURPOSES Have children write sentences describing why they want to read *The Underground City*. For example: *I want to find out how a city is built underground.*

READ THE BOOK Use questions like the following to guide children as you read the story together or after they have read the story independently.

Page 3: Look at the word *sawmill*. Which two words make up the word *sawmill*? What sound do the letters *aw* make in the word? (/ô/) *Phonics and Decoding*

Page 8: Why did the people of Seattle decide to build their homes of brick and stone after the fire? (Homes were made of wood before the fire, and these burned too easily.) What else could they do to protect the city? *Draw Conclusions*

Pages 14–15: Find the word *museum*. What will you find in the museum in underground Seattle? (what life was like in Seattle long ago) *Vocabulary*

Page 16: Why do you think the first settlers who came to Seattle were brave? *Draw Conclusions*

Page 16: How would you compare life in Seattle before the fire to life there after the fire? *Compare and Contrast*

RETURN TO PREDICTIONS AND PURPOSES Discuss children's predictions. Ask which were close to the story and why. Have children review their purposes for reading.

LITERARY RESPONSE Discuss these questions:

- What was your favorite part of the story?
- Why do you think so many people come to visit the "Underground City"?

Also see the story questions and activity in *The Underground City*.

See the **Phonics** CD-ROM for practice using words with the variant vowel /ô/ sound.

Answers to Story Questions

1. A pot of glue boiled over and set fire to a wooden floor.
2. Brave means having courage. The people of Seattle had moved to a new part of the country; they stayed in the city after the fire and built their city again.
3. Because wood burns easily and brick and stone don't. Also, brick and stone are stronger than wood.
4. Under Seattle lies the ruins of a city that burned in the 1880s.
5. Answers will vary.

The Story Questions and Activity below appear in the Independent Book.

Story Questions and Writing Activity

1. How did the Great Seattle Fire of 1889 start?
2. What does the word "brave" mean? In what ways were the people of old Seattle brave?
3. Why do you think the people of Seattle rebuilt their city with brick and stone?
4. What is the main idea of the story?
5. Do you think Amanda from *The Best Vacation Ever* would enjoy seeing underground Seattle? What would she write to her friend Josie about Pioneer Square?

Explore an Underground City

Look at the map on page 16. You need to get from the streetcar station in Pioneer Square to the tourist office of the Underground Tour. Use this map to find your way. Write down the directions you use.

from The Underground City

Leveled Books

CHALLENGE

Dear Diary

☑ **Phonics** Variant Vowel /ô/ *aw, au*

☑ **Compare and Contrast**

☑ **Instructional Vocabulary:**
brave, guess, museum, practice, vacation, wonder

Written by Elaine Epstein
Illustrated by Susan Lexa

Guided Reading

Answers to Story Questions

1. They are on vacation.
2. She says "We drive and drive." They are in a different state from where they live.
3. It is different from other places she has been. There is a lot of her family's history there.
4. A girl learns to enjoy her vacation after a visit to cliff houses and a cave at a park in New Mexico.
5. Answers will vary.

The Story Questions and Activity below appear in the Challenge Book.

Story Questions and Writing Activity

1. Why are the girl, her mother, and her father driving in New Mexico?
2. How do you know the girl and her family are far away from home?
3. Why is the girl excited about the park she visits with her parents?
4. What is this story mostly about?
5. In the story, the girl writes in her diary about her experiences. What if she wrote a letter to Amanda or Josie about her vacation? What are some things she might write about?

Bandelier State Park

Pretend you are visiting Bandelier State Park. Write some sentences telling what else you would like to do in this park.

from Dear Diary

PREVIEW AND PREDICT Discuss the illustrations through page 5 of the story. As you take the **picture walk**, have children predict what the story is about. Chart children's ideas.

SET PURPOSES Have children write about why they want to read *Dear Diary*. Invite them to share their reasons.

READ THE BOOK Use questions like the following to guide children as you read the story together or after they have read the story independently.

Page 9: Find the word *saw*. What sound do the letters *aw* make in the word *saw*? (/ô/) Can you think of other words that use the letters *aw* to make the /ô/ sound? *(caw, paw) Phonics and Decoding*

Page 9: How do you think the girl in the story is starting to feel about her vacation? How can you tell? *Draw Conclusions*

Page 10: Find the word *wondered*. *Wondered* is a form of one of our new vocabulary words, *wonder*. What was the girl wondering when she saw the pictures of the cliff dwelling? (She wondered who made the pictures.) *Vocabulary*

Page 16: What did the girl think about her great-grandmother's people? How were they like or unlike people today? *Compare and Contrast*

Page 16: Do you think the girl will want to take another vacation with her parents? Why? Why not? *Draw Conclusions*

RETURN TO PREDICTIONS AND PURPOSES Discuss children's predictions. Ask which were close to the story and why. Have children review their purposes for reading.

LITERARY RESPONSE Discuss these questions:

- Why do you think people made pictures on the walls of their cliff dwellings?

- In what other ways can you record life today for people of the future?

Also see the story questions and activity in *Dear Diary*.

See the **Phonics** CD-ROM for practice using words with the variant vowel /ô/ sound.

Bringing Groups Together

Anthology and Leveled Books

Connecting Texts

U.S.A. CHART
Write the story titles on the four corners of a chart. Write the words *Exploring the U.S.A.* in the middle of the chart. Ask children to discuss the different places featured in each of the stories. Have children list these places, including their special features, under the story titles. Draw a line from the words *Exploring the U.S.A.* to each of their contributions.

Use the chart to discuss interesting places in the United States.

The Best Vacation Ever

Nashville has the Grand Ole Opry.

The Underground City

Seattle has an underground museum.

EXPLORING THE U.S.A.

This Is Your Land

The Everglades has amazing wildlife.

Dear Diary

New Mexico has Bandelier State Park.

Viewing/Representing

GROUP PRESENTATIONS Divide the class into four groups, one group representing each of the four stories in the lesson. Have each group draw pictures of the place featured in their particular story. Have children share their drawings with the group.

AUDIENCE RESPONSE Ask children to look carefully at the drawings of each group. Allow time for questions after each group exhibits its drawings.

Research and Inquiry

MORE ABOUT THE U.S.A. Invite children to learn more about interesting places in the United States. Have them:

- look at classroom and school library books.

- watch a videotape that features national parks or other exciting places in the United States.

*inter*NET **CONNECTION** Have children log on to **www.mhschool.com/reading** for more information and activities on places within the United States.

OBJECTIVES

Children will:

- identify /ô/*aw, au, a.*
- blend and read words with /ô/*aw, au, a.*

....

MATERIALS
- **Teaching Chart 123**

Skills Finder

/ô/ *a, aw, au*

Introduce	B2: 68G–H
Review	B2: 91E–F, 91G–H
Test	B2: Unit 1
Maintain	B2: 135

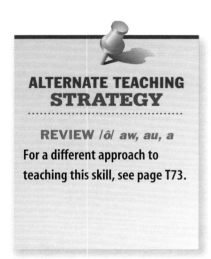

ALTERNATE TEACHING STRATEGY

....

REVIEW /ô/ *aw, au, a*

For a different approach to teaching this skill, see page T73.

Review /ô/ *aw, au, a*

PREPARE

Listen for /ô/ Read the following riddle aloud and have children sqawk like a bird whenever they hear a word with the /ô/ sound: *Why did the hawk walk to the store? Because he didn't want to crawl.*

TEACH

Review *aw, au,* and *a,* as Symbols for /ô/

- Tell children they will review reading words with /ô/ *aw, au,* and *a.*
- Say /ô/. Write *aw, au,* and *a* on the board.

aw	au	a
s<u>aw</u>	bec<u>au</u>se	w<u>a</u>lk
l<u>aw</u>n	t<u>au</u>ght	ch<u>a</u>lk
h<u>aw</u>k	p<u>au</u>se	s<u>a</u>lt
dr<u>aw</u>	v<u>au</u>lt	b<u>a</u>ll

Teaching Chart 123

BLENDING Model and Guide Practice with *aw, au, a*

- Display **Teaching Chart 123**. In the first line of the first column, write *aw* in the underlined spaces to make the word *saw.*
- Run your finger under the letters, blending the sounds aloud.
- Ask a volunteer to write the same letter pair in the underlined spaces in the second row in the column.
- Have students blend the sounds together and read the word aloud as you run a finger under the completed word.

Use the Words in Context Have volunteers use words completed on the chart in sentences to reinforce their meanings. Example: *They were playing ball on the nicely cut lawn.*

Repeat the Procedure Follow the same procedure to complete the remaining columns.

PRACTICE

DISCRIMINATING
Sort Words with
aw, au, a

PARTNERS

Invite children to brainstorm words with /ô/ *aw, au,* and *a*. List their responses on the chalkboard. Help children to classify words into word families. Invite each child to write words with each spelling pattern on cards. Children can work with partners to arrange their words in columns by spelling pattern for the /ô/ sound. ▶ **Interpersonal/Visual**

ASSESS/CLOSE

Read, Spell, and
Write Sentences
Using Words with
aw, au, a

To assess children's ability to build and read words with /ô/ *aw, au,* and *a,* observe their work on the Practice activity. Ask each child to read and spell aloud four of the words he or she wrote. Then tell them to use those words in sentences.

ADDITIONAL PHONICS RESOURCES

Phonics/Phonemic Awareness
Practice Book,
pages 99–102

McGraw-Hill School
TECHNOLOGY
Phonics CD-ROM

activities for practice with
Blending and Word Building

DAILY Phonics ROUTINES

DAY 4
Fluency Write a list of /ô/ words such as *talk, paw, claw, hawk, cause.* Point to each word, asking children to blend the sounds silently. Ask a volunteer to read aloud each word.

Phonics CD-ROM

SPELLING/PHONICS
CONNECTIONS
Words with /ô/ *aw, au, a;* See the 5-Day Spelling Plan, pages 91Q–91R.

i **Intervention** ▶ **Skills**
Intervention Guide, for direct instruction and extra practice of /ô/

Meeting Individual Needs for Phonics

EASY	ON-LEVEL	CHALLENGE	LANGUAGE SUPPORT
Reteach, 147	Practice, 147	Extend, 147	Language Support, 159

EASY — Reteach 147
/ô/ *a, aw, au*

Read the following sentence. Listen to the sounds.
I watered the **lawn** be**cau**se it was dry.

Circle the word with the /ô/ sound that best completes each sentence.

1. The bug is ____ in the web.
   not (caught)
2. Some birds have sharp ____
   (claws) paws
3. Do you like to ____ ?
   (draw) swim
4. Another word for car is ____ .
   out (auto)

Book 2.2/Unit 1
The Best Vacation Ever
At Home: Have the children recite the words they circled.
147

ON-LEVEL — Practice 147
/ô/ *a, aw, au*

A. Circle the word to complete each sentence. Then write it on the line.

1. The crab grabs with its ____ claw .
   hawk (claw) paw
2. I ____ yawn ____ when I get tired.
   lawn paw (yawn)
3. The ____ fawn ____ has many white spots.
   (fawn) draw law

B. Circle the word to complete each sentence. Then write it on the line.

4. We moved to a bigger house ____ because ____ we had a new baby.
   (because) taught caught
5. The teacher ____ taught ____ math yesterday.
   (taught) caught because
6. Billy ____ caught ____ the ball and the game was over.
   taught because (caught)

Book 2.2/Unit 1
The Best Vacation Ever
At Home: Have children write the words they circled in alphabetical order.
147

CHALLENGE — Extend 147
/ô/ *a, aw, au*

Use these words to create a story. Underline the **aw** and **au** words you use.

saw	claw	awful	astronaut
jaw	crawl	straw	daughter
yawn	hawk	fault	launch

Stories will vary but should include some words from the box with *aw* and *au* words underlined.

Trade stories with a friend. Can you find **aw** or **au** words that you did not include?

Book 2.2/Unit 1
The Best Vacation Ever
At Home: Children can draw a picture to illustrate their story.
147

LANGUAGE SUPPORT
Give the Pictures Names

astronaut

hawk

saw

Grade 2
Language Support/Blackline Master 87 • Best Vacation Ever 159

Reteach, 147   **Practice, 147**   **Extend, 147**   Language Support, 159

91F

Review /ô/ aw, au, a Soft c, g; /ŭ/

OBJECTIVES

Children will:

- review /ô/*aw, au, a.*
- review /j/*ge* and /s/*ce.*
- review /ŭ/*oo, u.*
- read words with /ô/*aw, au, a;* soft *c, g;* /ŭ/*oo, u*

MATERIALS

- **Teaching Chart 124**
- **Word Building Manipulative Cards**

Skills Finder

/ô/ *a, aw, au*	
Introduce	B2: 68G-H
Review	B2: 91E-F, 91G-H
Test	B2: Unit 1
Maintain	B2: 135

TEACHING TIP

SOFT C You may want to remind children that they may also see soft *c* in words such as *fancy* and *circus.*

PREPARE

Identify Spelling Patterns for /ŭ/, /ô/, /j/, and /s/

Review that one sound can have several spelling patterns. Write *hawk* and *astronaut* on the board. Underline the letter pairs that stand for /ô/ and read each word. Repeat with *huge* and *jar,* underlining *ge* and *j; face* and *same,* underlining *ce* and *s;* and *put* and *look,* underlining *u* and *oo.*

TEACH

BLENDING Model and Guide Practice with /ô/*aw, au, a;* /ŭ/*oo;* /j/*ge* and /s/*ce* Words

- Display **Teaching Chart 124.** Explain to children that they can make words by choosing a letter pair to write in the blank space.
- Add *aw* and blend the first word on the chart with children. (*hawk*)

h<u>aw</u>k	hu<u>ge</u>	b<u>oo</u>k
aw au	ge ce	au oo

l<u>oo</u>k	partrid<u>ge</u>	astron<u>au</u>t
aw oo	ce ge	au oo

pla<u>ce</u>	practi<u>ce</u>	f<u>a</u>ll
ce ge	ge ce	a aw

Teaching Chart 124

- Ask children to add the other letter pair to the first word. Ask which letter pair creates a real word. (*aw*) Have a volunteer choose a letter pair to write in the space in the second row and read aloud the new word (*lawk* or *look*). Ask children which is a real word. (*look*)

Use the Word in Context

Use the words in context to reinforce their meanings. Example: *A hawk has a sharp beak.*

Repeat the Procedure

Continue with **Teaching Chart 124.** Have children blend the sounds aloud and tell which letter combination makes a real word.

PRACTICE

WORD BUILDING
Build and Write
/ô/aw, au, a;
/ù/oo; /j/ge and
/s/ce Words and
Sentences

GROUP

Have small groups of children use letter cards to build as many words with /ô/aw, au, a as they can. Repeat with letter pairs ge, ce, and/ù/oo. Have each group choose a word for each of the four sounds, write them on an index card, underlining the target sound. Then encourage children to try using as many of those words as they can in one sentence.

▶ **Linguistic/Interpersonal**

ASSESS/CLOSE

Sort and Use
/ô/aw, au, a;
/ù/oo; /j/ge and
/s/ce Words

Observe children's work on the Practice activity to assess their ability to build and write words with /ô/aw, au, a; /ù/oo; /j/ge; and /s/ce. Ask each child to choose one or two words from his or her group's list to spell and read aloud. Have children make a Word Wall of their index cards sorted by sounds.

ADDITIONAL PHONICS RESOURCES

Phonics/Phonemic Awareness
Practice Book,
pages 99–102

McGraw-Hill School
TECHNOLOGY

 CD-ROM

activities for practice with
Word Building and Sorting

DAY 5 Writing Have children write a riddle whose answer is a word with the sound /ô/. Have pairs try to answer each other's riddles.

 CD-ROM

ALTERNATE TEACHING STRATEGY

For a different approach to teaching these skills, see pages T64–T65, T69–T70, T72–T73.

ℹ **Intervention** Skills
Intervention Guide, for direct instruction and extra practice of /ô/, Soft c, Soft g; and /ù/

Meeting Individual Needs for Phonics

| EASY | ON-LEVEL | CHALLENGE | LANGUAGE SUPPORT |

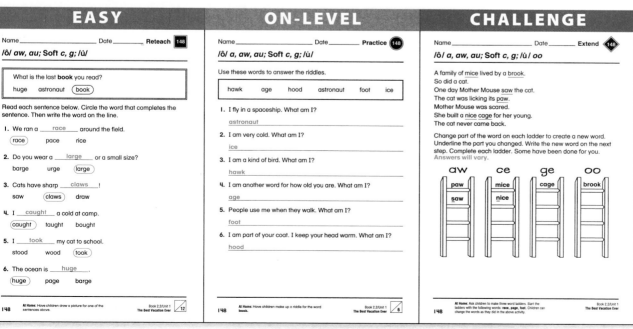

Reteach, 148   Practice, 148   Extend, 148   Language Support, 160

OBJECTIVES

Children will use information to draw conclusions.

MATERIALS

• **Teaching Chart 125**

Skills Finder

Draw Conclusions

Introduce	B2: 43I-J
Review	B2: 91I-J, 125G-H
Test	B2: Unit 1

TEACHING TIP

COMPARE AND CONTRAST Tell children that the Liberty Bell is one of many historical sites in Philadelphia. Distinguish historical sites from natural wonders such as the La Brea Tar Pits or the Grand Canyon.

SELF-SELECTED Reading

Children may choose from the following titles.

ANTHOLOGY

• *The Best Vacation Ever*

LEVELED BOOKS

• *This Is Your Land*
• *The Underground City*
• *Dear Diary*

Bibliography, pages T88–T89

Review Draw Conclusions

PREPARE

Review Drawing Conclusions Remind children that we draw conclusions from two or more ideas or facts in a story.

TEACH

Read "The Liberty Bell" and Model Drawing Conclusions Display **Teaching Chart 125** and read aloud "The Liberty Bell." Ask children to think about conclusions they might draw from what they read about this famous bell and people's reactions to it.

The Liberty Bell

Dear Josie,

　My class took a trip to Philadelphia last fall. We saw the Liberty Bell. It is kept in a special building with a guard watching it. We had to wait in line for an hour just to see it. It is probably the most famous bell in the world. They rang it in July, 1776, to let people know about the Declaration of Independence. It has a crack in it from over a hundred years ago. I wonder why they haven't fixed it yet.

　Love From Your Fellow American,

　Amanda

Teaching Chart 125

MODEL I wonder why the bell didn't get fixed if it broke so long ago. I know it means a lot to Americans. It is kept in a special place with a guard watching it, and lots of people come to see it. Maybe it can't be fixed.

PRACTICE

Use Facts and Details to Draw a Conclusion

Have children use **Teaching Chart 125** and their own background knowledge to draw a conclusion about why the Liberty Bell still has a crack in it. Ask them to underline facts that can help them draw a conclusion. ▶ **Logical/Linguistic**

ASSESS/CLOSE

Draw and Support Conclusions

Ask children whether each of the following is a historical site or a natural wonder. Write their conclusions on the chalkboard. Ask them to support each conclusion with factual information from what they have read and their own background knowledge.

Grand Canyon
Grand Ole Opry
Wright Brothers' Memorial
The Alamo
Mississippi River
Carlsbad Caverns

ALTERNATE TEACHING STRATEGY

DRAW CONCLUSIONS

For a different approach to teaching this skill, see page T67.

 **Intervention** **Skills**

Intervention Guide, for direct instruction and extra practice in drawing conclusions

---

Meeting Individual Needs for Comprehension

EASY	ON-LEVEL	CHALLENGE	LANGUAGE SUPPORT

EASY

Name _____ Date _____ Reteach 149

Draw Conclusions

You can use picture clues and what you know to help you **draw conclusions** about what is happening.

Look at the picture. Read the place names. Circle the place where each person is going. Then tell what clues in the picture helped you.

1. (grocery store)   cleaners   farm
   shopping cart and list

2. restaurant   (school)   zoo
   book and back pack

3. library   pool   (park)
   skates and a helmet

4. museum   (beach)   store
   sunglasses and a towel

Book 2.2/Unit 1
The Best Vacation Ever
At Home: Have children draw conclusions about pictures they see in books or magazines. 149

ON-LEVEL

Name _____ Date _____ Practice 149

Draw Conclusions

Read the story. Write the answer to each question. Use a complete sentence. Answers will vary.

Jamie loves to do magic tricks. She wants to buy the magic kit in Mr. Britt's store. First she has to save enough money from her weekly allowance. Every day Jamie walks by the store to make sure the kit is in the window. Mr. Britt told her he would save one for her. Many weeks later, Jamie finally has enough money. When she gets to the store, the kit is gone from the window!

1. Do you think that the magic kit costs a little bit of money or a lot of money?
   It must cost a lot of money.

2. What makes you think this?
   It took Jamie many weeks to save enough money to buy it.

3. How do you think Jamie felt when she didn't see the magic kit?
   She felt disappointed because she looked for it every day.

4. Do you think Jamie finally got the magic kit? Why?
   Yes, because Mr. Britt said he would save one for her.

Book 2.2/Unit 1
The Best Vacation Ever
At Home: Have children change some of the information in the story. Ask them how this would change the conclusions they first made. 149

CHALLENGE

Name _____ Date _____ Extend 149

Draw Conclusions

What are three conclusions Josie might reach after reading Amanda's letters? Sample answers are shown.

Amanda loves to travel.

Amanda isn't sure what she wants to be when she grows up.

There are many interesting things to see in the U.S.

Write a letter to Amanda telling her why Josie reached one of the conclusions. Make sure you use information from the story to explain your idea.

Dear Amanda,
_____
_____
_____
_____
_____

Your Friend,
_____

Book 2.2/Unit 1
The Best Vacation Ever
At Home: Have children discuss why Josie might have reached the two other conclusions written above. 149

LANGUAGE SUPPORT

Name _____ Date _____

What Does Amanda Want to Be?

Amanda loves country music.

Amanda thinks park rangers are nice.

Amanda makes a photo scrapbook.

Grade 2
Language Support/Blackline Master 89 • Best Vacation Ever 161

Reteach, 149   Practice, 149   Extend, 149   Language Support, 161

Children will read words with inflectional endings -*er* and -*est*.

MATERIALS
• **Teaching Chart 126**

Skills Finder

Inflectional Endings

Introduce	B1: 35K-L
Review	B1: 55K-L, 123K-L; B2: 91K-L, 115K-L
Test	B1: Unit 1
Maintain	B2: 23

TEACHING TIP

INFLECTIONAL ENDINGS Invite volunteers to compare classroom objects using -*er* and -*est* endings.

Review Inflectional Endings

PREPARE

Review -*er*, -*est* Endings

Write the words *big, bigger, biggest,* with the word *big* written large and the other two words in increasing size order. Ask a volunteer to read aloud each word. Discuss word endings -*er* or -*est*. Remind children that these endings are added to words to show comparisons.

TEACH

Identify Root Words

Point to *big, bigger, biggest*. Ask children to identify the root word. Point out that the final consonant of the root word is doubled here before adding the -*er* and -*est* endings. Then read **Teaching Chart 126** with children. Call on children to come to the chart to underline words that have -*er* and -*est* endings. Ask others to identify and circle the three different root words.

Tall, Taller, Tallest!

Dear Josie,

I grew taller while I was away! Before we left, my dad said I was four feet, two inches tall. I thought that was pretty tall. But when we got back, I was an inch taller! Sammy is the youngest, but he is almost as tall as I am. My mom is taller than either of us. My dad is the tallest one in our family. Are you taller or shorter than I am? Who's the youngest one in your family? Who is the tallest?

Love From Your Tall Friend,

Amanda

Teaching Chart 126

MODEL I see that Amanda compares how tall people are by adding the endings -*er* and -*est* to root words. The word *tall* appears many times, and it is part of other words, too. I bet it is a root word. Who is Amanda taller than? She says she is taller than she was before, and she's taller than her brother.

PRACTICE

Use Words with -er and -est

GROUP

Pose a variety of oral questions about who is taller, younger, and older, based on Amanda's letter. Ask volunteers to use the information in the letter to answer your questions. Have each child orally compare two or three objects in the classroom, using -er and/or -est.

▶ **Linguistic**

ASSESS/CLOSE

Complete Sentences

Ask children to write each of the words listed below. Explain that these are all root words. Then have children rewrite each word adding -er and -est to each. Ask them to pretend they are on a fun vacation, and to write sentences on a "postcard" comparing things, using each of the three root words and both endings.

loud   sweet   bright

ALTERNATE TEACHING STRATEGY

ENDINGS -er AND -est

For a different approach to teaching this skill, see page T74.

ⓘ Intervention ▶ **Skills Intervention Guide,** for direct instruction and extra practice of inflectional endings

---

Meeting Individual Needs for Vocabulary

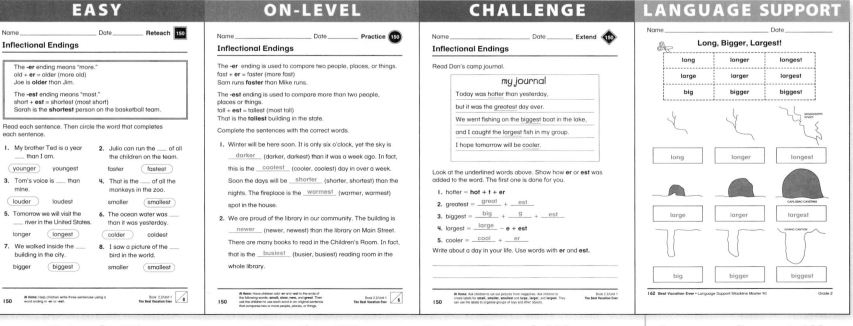

EASY — Reteach, 150

ON-LEVEL — Practice, 150

CHALLENGE — Extend, 150

LANGUAGE SUPPORT — Language Support, 162

GRAMMAR/SPELLING
CONNECTIONS

See the 5-Day Grammar and Usage Plan on irregular verbs, pages 91O–91P.

See the 5-Day Spelling Plan on words with /ô/, pages 91Q–91R.

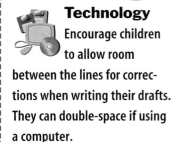

TEACHING TIP

Technology
Encourage children to allow room between the lines for corrections when writing their drafts. They can double-space if using a computer.

Handwriting CD-ROM

Writing That Compares

Prewrite

WRITE A TRAVEL GUIDE Present this writing assignment: Choose two of the places Amanda visited. Write a travel guide that tells about both places. Tell what is the same about the two places and what is different. Explain why some people might be more interested in the first place, and others would like the second place better.

EXPLORE THE TOPIC Ask children to choose the two destinations that most interest them. Have them reread what the selection says about the places they have chosen.

Strategy: Make Lists Have children make two lists and brainstorm as many things as they can think of about each place. Suggest the following:

• facts about the geography and climate
• important people and historical events
• interesting or fun things to do

Draft

USE THE LISTS Guide students to draft their ideas without self-editing. They can consult the lists to keep their ideas in order. Remind them to organize each specific topic area in its own paragraph. Encourage them to enrich their texts with vivid details and with their own observations on the differences between the two places.

Revise

TAKE TIME OUT Suggest that children put their drafts aside for awhile and work on something else. When they are ready, they can look at their drafts with a fresh eye. This might help them see ways to include more interesting details that will show more clearly how the two places are alike and different.

PARTNERS Ask partners to exchange travel guides and discuss whether any details or additional information could be added.

Edit/Proofread

CHECK FOR ERRORS Have children reread their travel guides and correct any errors in spelling, grammar, and punctuation.

Publish

CREATE A TRAVEL MAGAZINE Have children combine their travel guides into a booklet or magazine entitled "See the U.S.A."

Kitty Hawk, North Carolina, is next to the Atlantic Ocean. The air is warm and damp. It's famous because the Wright Brothers flew the first engine-powered airplane there. You can visit a museum that has photographs and models of the Wright Brothers and early airplanes.

San Antonio, Texas, is a very different place. First of all, it's next to a river instead of the ocean. The weather is very warm and dry. It's famous for the battle of the Alamo, where Texan soldiers fought the Mexican army.

If you like airplanes, you will love Kitty Hawk. But if you are interested in famous battles, San Antonio is the place for you!

Presentation Ideas

INTERVIEW TIME Have partners take turns interviewing each other about the places in their travel guides. Tell children that they can pretend to have visited the places featured. ▶ **Speaking/Listening**

DRAW POSTERS Have children draw posters of each place they described. They can show the posters as they are being interviewed. ▶ **Viewing/Representing**

Consider students' creative efforts, possibly adding a plus (+) for originality, wit, and imagination.

Scoring Rubric

Excellent	Good	Fair	Unsatisfactory
4: The writer	**3:** The writer	**2:** The writer	**1:** The writer
• vividly identifies two travel destinations.	• clearly identifies and describes two travel destinations.	• names two destinations but does not provide detailed information.	• may not identify or describe two different places.
• provides richly detailed descriptions of each place and shows how they are similar and different.	• gives major details on how the places are similar and different.	• may not clearly state or compare differences and similarities.	• may present vague or disorganized facts and ideas.
• presents well-organized facts and observations.	• solidly organizes facts and ideas.	• may show problems organizing facts or clearly expressing observations.	• may not grasp the concept of comparison.

Incomplete   0: The writer leaves the page blank or fails to respond to the writing task. The student does not address the topic or simply paraphrases the prompt. The response is illegible or incoherent.

Meeting Individual Needs for Writing

EASY

Traveling Artists Have children draw a picture of a place they would like to visit. Tell them to write a sentence describing why they would like to go there.

ON-LEVEL

Travel Journalists Have children write about an interesting place they have visited, either on a family vacation or during a class trip. They should tell where they went and what they did there.

CHALLENGE

Travel Plan Have children identify a natural wonder or historic site they would like to visit someday. Invite them to write about why they are interested in the place and what they could expect to see and do there.

Listening and Speaking

LISTENING Have children
- listen for details about the place being described.
- take notes while their partners are speaking.
- maintain eye contact with the speaker.

SPEAKING Remind children to
- use comparison/contrast words when describing their posters.
- speak in a clear voice.
- hold up the poster as they are being interviewed.

LANGUAGE SUPPORT

 Remind the class that other countries have their own historic sites and natural wonders. Ask ESL students to talk about a famous place in their own country. Encourage them to compare it to one of the places Amanda visited, telling what is the same and what is different about it.

Invite children to include their travel guides or another writing project in their portfolios.

5 Day Grammar and Usage Plan

ESL Reinforce the concept of present and past tense by eliciting responses to these questions: What do you do in class every Friday? What did you do in class last Friday? Write some responses on the board and point out the present and past tense forms of verbs in their sentences.

DAILY LANGUAGE ACTIVITIES

Write the Daily Language Activities on the chalkboard each day or use **Transparency 18**. Tell Children that the verbs should be in the past tense. Have children orally correct the verbs.

Day 1
1. The girls go away last week. went
2. I go on vacation a year ago. went
3. We do our chores last night. did

Day 2
1. The boys see the Alamo last year. saw
2. They say they liked the place. said
3. I see many places last month. saw

Day 3
1. I see the Grand Ole Opry before. saw
2. Molly do not make the trip last May. did
3. Sammy go to the show last week. went

Day 4
1. Last June, they go to the caves. went
2. Sammy say he did not like them. said
3. Molly see the cave walls last year. saw

Day 5
1. Sammy do not go on a trip last year. did
2. Molly say she went to Texas. said
3. They see many places they liked. saw

Daily Language Transparency 18

DAY 1 Introduce the Concept

Oral Warm-Up Ask children what a verb in the past tense tells about. (something that already happened) Ask how most verbs in the past tense end. (with -ed)

Introduce Irregular Verbs Tell children that some verbs have other ways of forming the past tense.

Irregular Verbs

- Some verbs do not add *-ed* to form the past-tense.
- The verbs *go* and *do* have special forms in the past-tense.

present-tense	past-tense
go	went
do	did

Present the Daily Language Activity. Then have children write sentences using the past tense of the verbs *do* and *go*.

 WRITING Assign the daily Writing Prompt on page 68C.

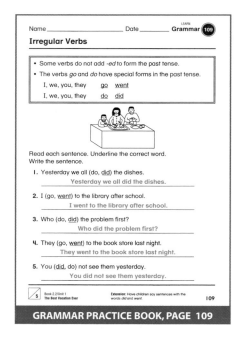

GRAMMAR PRACTICE BOOK, PAGE 109

DAY 2 Teach the Concept

Review Irregular Verbs Write these verbs on the chalkboard: *kick, walk, go, do.* Have children identify which need an *-ed* ending and which change form when used in the past-tense.

Introduce More Irregular Verbs Tell children that there are other verbs besides *go* and *do* that have special past-tense forms. Present:

Irregular Verbs

The verbs *say* and *see* have special forms in the past-tense.

present-tense	past-tense
say	said
see	saw

Present the Daily Language Activity. Then have children write sentences using the verbs *see* and *say* in the past-tense.

 WRITING Assign the daily Writing Prompt on page 68C.

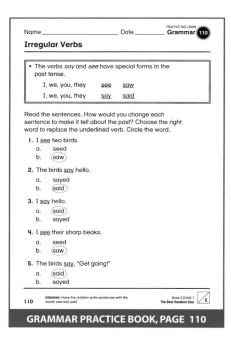

GRAMMAR PRACTICE BOOK, PAGE 110

Irregular Verbs

DAY 3 — Review and Practice

Learn from the Literature Review irregular verbs. Read the sentences on page 76 of *The Best Vacation Ever.*

> **We went to the Grand Ole Opry and heard Molly Partridge sing.**
>
> **Sammy said that I sounded a little like Rover when he howls.**

Have children identify the past tense of the verbs *go* and *say* in the sentences.

Use Irregular Verbs Present the Daily Language Activity. Then have children write sentences about a place they visited. Have them make statements that indicate the visit took place in the past. Be sure children use the verbs *go, do* and *see* in their sentences.

 Assign the daily Writing Prompt on page 68D.

DAY 4 — Review and Practice

Review Irregular Verbs Write four sentences on the chalkboard that use incorrect past-tense forms of *go, do, say,* and *see* (examples: *goed, done, sayed, seed*). Have children orally correct the sentences. Then have children do the Daily Language Activity.

Mechanics and Usage Before children do the daily Writing Prompt on page 68D, display and discuss:

Letter Punctuation
- Begin the greeting and closing in a letter with a capital letter.
- Use a comma after the greeting in a letter.
- Use a comma after the closing in a letter.
- Use a comma between the day and year in a date.
- Use a comma between the names of a city and a state.

 Assign the daily Writing Prompt on page 68D.

DAY 5 — Assess and Reteach

Assess Use the Daily Language Activity and page 113 of the **Grammar Practice Book** for assessment.

Reteach Have children work with a partner to prepare flash cards for irregular verbs. They write the words *go, do, say* and *see* on separate index cards, and then write the past-tense forms on the backs. Have partners test one another on the past-tense forms, using the cards to check answers.

Write sentences using the present tense of the verbs *do, say, see,* and *go* on individual strips of paper and pin them on the bulletin board. Have children change the sentences to past-tense by pinning each flash card so that the past-tense form replaces the appropriate present-tense verb.

 Assign the daily Writing Prompt on page 68D.

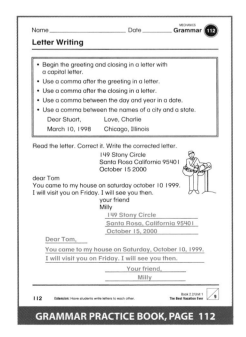

GRAMMAR PRACTICE BOOK, PAGE 111

GRAMMAR PRACTICE BOOK, PAGE 112

GRAMMAR PRACTICE BOOK, PAGE 113

GRAMMAR PRACTICE BOOK, PAGE 114

91P

5Day Spelling Plan

ESL Draw on the board simple pictures illustrating the words in the spelling list. Write the spelling word under each picture. Then, as you point to each picture, say the vowel sound and the word and ask children to repeat. For example, say /ô/, *paw*, /ô/, *caught*, and so forth.

DICTATION SENTENCES

Spelling Words

1. The cat hurt her <u>paw</u>.
2. I <u>caught</u> a fish.
3. She took the bike away <u>because</u> it broke.
4. I can <u>talk</u> to you.
5. The baby has the <u>straw</u>.
6. The <u>hawk</u> can fly.
7. I have more <u>salt</u>.
8. The children played on the <u>lawn</u>.
9. She <u>taught</u> me to cook.
10. It is my <u>fault</u>.

Challenge Words

11. I can take a <u>guess</u>.
12. The boys go to the <u>museum</u>.
13. I <u>practice</u> every day.
14. My <u>vacation</u> is over.
15. I <u>wonder</u> why the sky is blue.

DAY 1 — Pretest

Assess Prior Knowledge Use the Dictation Sentences at left and **Spelling Practice Book** page 109 for the pretest. Allow students to correct their own papers. If students have trouble, have partners give each other a midweek test on Day 3. Students who require a modified list may be tested on the first five words.

Spelling Words		Challenge Words
1. paw	6. **hawk**	11. **guess**
2. caught	7. salt	12. **museum**
3. **because**	8. lawn	13. **practice**
4. talk	9. taught	14. **vacation**
5. straw	10. fault	15. **wonder**

*Note: Words in **dark type** are from the* story.

Word Study On page 110 of the **Spelling Practice Book** are word study steps and an at-home activity.

DAY 2 — Explore the Pattern

Sort and Spell Words Say *hawk, because, taught*. Ask students what vowel sound they hear in each word. These words contain the variant vowel /ô/ spelled *a, aw, au*, and *augh*.

Ask students to say the spelling words before sorting them according to spelling pattern.

/ô/ spelled			
a	*aw*	*au*	*augh*
talk	paw	because	caught
salt	straw	fault	taught
	hawk		
	lawn		

Spelling Patterns Ask students to generalize about which spelling of /ô/ often appears at the end of a word. (*aw*) Which ones usually appear in the middle? (*a, au, augh*) Ask students to list other words ending with *aw*.

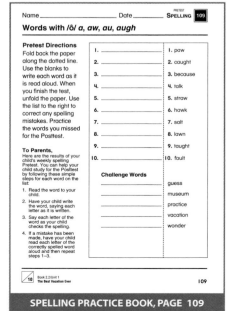

SPELLING PRACTICE BOOK, PAGE 109

WORD STUDY STEPS AND ACTIVITY, PAGE 110

SPELLING PRACTICE BOOK, PAGE 111

Words with /ô/ a, aw, au, augh

DAY 3 Practice and Extend

Word Meaning: Definitions Have students write a definition for each of the spelling words. Then have students work as partners. One partner will read his/her definition as the other will try to guess the spelling word being defined.

Glossary Have students:

- write each Challenge Word.

- look up each Challenge Word in the Glossary to find its part of speech. Some words can be used as two different parts of speech.

- write the part of speech or parts of speech for each Challenge Word.

- write a sentence for each Challenge Word when used as each part of speech.

DAY 4 Proofread and Write

Proofread Sentences Write these sentences on the chalkboard, including the misspelled words. Ask students to proofread, circling incorrect spellings and writing the correct spellings. There are two spelling errors in each sentence.

The hauk cawt the mice. (hawk, caught)

The cat spilled the sault with her pau. (salt, paw)

Have students create additional sentences with errors for partners to correct.

 WRITING Have students use as many spelling words as possible in the daily Writing Prompt on page 68D. Remind students to proofread their writing for errors in spelling, grammar, and punctuation.

DAY 5 Assess

Assess Students' Knowledge Use page 114 of the **Spelling Practice Book** or the Dictation Sentences on page 91Q for the posttest.

Personal Word List If students have trouble with any words in the lesson, have them create a personal list of troublesome words in their journals. Have students write their own riddles, using words from their personal word list.

Students should refer to their word lists during later writing activities.

Page 112

Name _____ Date _____ SPELLING 112

Words with /ô/ a, aw, au, augh

| paw | because | straw | salt | taught |
| caught | talk | hawk | lawn | fault |

Write a spelling word to complete each sentence.

1. The dog gave me its _____paw_____ to shake.

2. She _____caught_____ the ball with one hand.

3. My brother _____taught_____ me how to skate.

4. We made the horse a nice bed of _____straw_____

5. They had a lot to _____talk_____ about _____because_____ they were good friends.

Rhyme Time
Use the picture clues to complete each rhyme.

6. He gave a yawn and lay down on the _____lawn_____

7. It wasn't my _____fault_____ that I spilled the _____salt_____

8. The _____hawk_____ flew high in the big blue sky.

Challenge Extension: Have children write a journal entry about an imaginary vacation they would like to take. Ask them to use at least three Challenge Words.

112   Book 2.2/Unit 1   8
                       The Best Vacation Ever

SPELLING PRACTICE BOOK, PAGE 112

Page 113

Name _____ Date _____ SPELLING 113

Words with /ô/ a, aw, au, augh

Proofreading Activity
There are six spelling mistakes in the paragraph below. Circle each misspelled word. Write the words correctly on the lines below.

People always tawk about how smart dogs are. Jamal taut his dog how to shake hands with his pau. Jamal's dog liked to play in the barn. One day the dog got cawt inside and couldn't get out. It was Jamal's fawlt becaws he had shut the barn door by mistake.

1. _____talk_____   2. _____taught_____   3. _____paw_____

4. _____caught_____   5. _____fault_____   6. _____because_____

Writing Activity
Would you like to visit a farm? Write sentences about a place that you would like to visit. Use four spelling words from the spelling list.

_____
_____
_____
_____

10   Book 2.2/Unit 1
      The Best Vacation Ever   113

SPELLING PRACTICE BOOK, PAGE 113

Page 114

Name _____ Date _____ SPELLING 114

Words with /ô/ a, aw, au, augh

Look at the words in each set. One word in each set is spelled correctly. Use a pencil to color in the circle in front of that word. Before you begin, look at the sample sets of words. Sample A has been done for you. Do Sample B by yourself. When you are sure you know what to do, you may go on with the rest of the page.

Sample A
(A) wawk
(B) waugk
(C) walk
(D) wauk

Sample B
(E) spase
(F) space
(G) spas
(H) spaes

1. (A) hauk
   (B) hawk
   (C) haugk
   (D) hak

2. (E) taught
   (F) tawt
   (G) taugt
   (H) tawght

3. (E) lauun
   (B) laun
   (C) laughn
   (G) lawn

4. (E) sault
   (F) saltt
   (G) salt
   (H) sawlt

5. (A) paw
   (B) paugh
   (C) pau
   (D) paau

6. (E) talk
   (F) taulk
   (G) tawlk
   (H) taughlk

7. (A) becauz
   (B) because
   (C) becawse
   (D) becauze

8. (E) falt
   (F) fawit
   (G) faughlt
   (H) fault

9. (A) caut
   (B) cawt
   (C) caught
   (D) cawht

10. (E) stauw
    (F) straw
    (G) straugh
    (H) staugh

114   Book 2.2/Unit 1   10
       The Best Vacation Ever

SPELLING PRACTICE BOOK, PAGE 114

Reaching All Learners

Concept
- Nocturnal Animals

Comprehension
- Draw Conclusions

Phonics
- Digraphs *ph, tch*

Vocabulary
- disturb
- explore
- fact
- nature
- object
- several

Anthology

Zipping, Zapping, Zooming Bats

Selection Summary Children will read about the exciting nighttime world of bats.

Listening Library

Rhyme applies to phonics

INSTRUCTIONAL pages 94–115

About the Author Bat-watching inspired Ann Earle to write *Zipping, Zapping, Zooming Bats*, which won the Parent's Choice Award and was chosen as a Pick of the Lists by American Booksellers. Ms. Earle has built two bat houses in her backyard in Vermont.

Photographer Henry Cole is a science teacher who studies wildlife in the woods and fields of Virginia. Never afraid to get his feet wet, Mr. Cole searches for his models in swamps and on sandy beaches.

Same Concept, Skills and Vocabulary!

Leveled Books

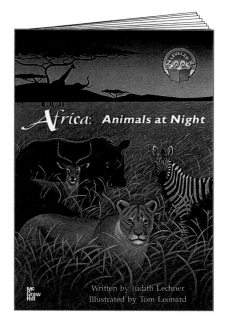

EASY
Lesson on pages 115A and 115D
DECODABLE

INDEPENDENT
Lesson on pages 115B and 115D

🏠 *Take-Home version available*

CHALLENGE
Lesson on pages 115C and 115D

Leveled Practice

EASY
Reteach, 151–158 Blackline masters with reteaching opportunities for each assessed skill

INDEPENDENT/ON-LEVEL
Practice, 151–158 Workbook with Take-Home stories and practice opportunities for each assessed skill and story comprehension

CHALLENGE
Extend, 151–158 Blackline masters that offer challenge activities for each assessed skill

Quizzes Prepared by **Accelerated Reader**®

WORKSTATION Activities

Social Studies ...	Popular Pets, *104*
Science	Echolocation, *100*
Math	2001 Dog Bones, *96*
Language Arts ..	Read Aloud, *92E*
	Multiple Meanings, *98*
Writing	Write a Report, *112*
Cultural Perspectives	Animal Tales, *102*
Research and Inquiry	Find Out More, *113*
Internet Activities	www.mhschool.com/reading

Zipping, Zapping, Zooming BATS
by Ann Earle • illustrated by Henry Cole

Suggested Lesson Planner

READING AND LANGUAGE ARTS

DAY 1 *Focus on Reading and Skills*

DAY 2 *Read the Literature*

● Phonics Daily Routines

Daily **Phonics** Routine:
Segmenting, 92H

 CD-ROM

Daily **Phonics** Routine:
Discriminating, 94A

 CD-ROM

● Phonological Awareness

● Phonics *ph, tch*

● Comprehension

● Vocabulary

● Study Skills

● Listening, Speaking, Viewing, Representing

DAY 1:

Read Aloud: Myth, 92E
"The Day the Sun Hid"

☑ **Develop Phonological Awareness,** 92F
Digraphs *ph, tch*

☑ **Introduce Digraphs *ph, tch*,** 92G–92H
Teaching Chart 127
Reteach, Practice, Extend, 151
Phonics/Phonemic Awareness Practice Book, 103–106

 Apply Digraphs *ph, tch*, 92/93
"Questions About Bats"

DAY 2:

Build Background, 94A
Develop Oral Language

Vocabulary, 94B–94C

| disturb | fact | object |
| explore | nature | several |

Word Building Manipulative Cards
Teaching Chart 128
Reteach, Practice, Extend, 152

 Read the Selection, 94–111
Comprehension
☑ **Digraphs *tch***
☑ **Draw Conclusions**

Genre: Narrative Nonfiction, 95

Cultural Perspectives, 102

Writer's Craft: Synonyms and Antonyms 105

 Intervention Program

 Intervention Program

● Curriculum Connections

Link Language Arts, 92E

Link Science, 94A

● Writing

Writing Prompt: Tell what you know or what you have heard about bats.

Writing Prompt: Write a story about children who formed a "Bats are Terrific" Club. What were the first three things they did?

Journal Writing
Quick-Write, 111

● Grammar

Introduce the Concept: More Irregular Verbs, 115O
Daily Language Activity: Write the correct form of the irregular verb.

Grammar Practice Book, 115

Teach the Concept: More Irregular Verbs, 115O
Daily Language Activity: Write the correct form of the irregular verb.

Grammar Practice Book, 116

● Spelling *ph, tch, ch*

Pretest: Words with Digraphs *ph, tch, ch*, 115Q

Spelling Practice Book, 115, 116

Explore the Pattern: Words with Digraphs *ph, tch, ch*, 115Q

Spelling Practice Book, 117

92C   *Zipping, Zapping, Zooming Bats*    **Intervention Program Available**

Meeting Individual Needs

 = **Skill Assessed in Unit Test**

 Intervention Program Available

 **Read EVERY DAY**

DAY 3 Read the Literature	**DAY 4** Build Skills	**DAY 5** Build Skills

---

Daily Phonics Routine:
Letter Substitution, 113

Phonics CD-ROM

Daily Phonics Routine:
Fluency, 115F

Phonics CD-ROM

Daily Phonics Routine:
Writing, 115H

Phonics CD-ROM

 Rereading for Fluency, 110

Story Questions and Activities,
112–113
  Reteach, Practice, Extend, 153

Study Skill, 114
  ☑ **Graphic Aids**
  Teaching Chart 129
  Reteach, Practice, Extend, 154

Test Power, 115

 Read the Leveled Books,
Guided Reading
  ☑ Digraphs *ph, tch*
  ☑ Draw Conclusions
  ☑ Instructional Vocabulary

 Intervention Program

Read Read the Leveled Books and the Self-Selected Books

  ☑ **Review Digraphs** *ph, tch*, 115E–115F
    Teaching Chart 130
    Reteach, Practice, Extend, 155
    Language Support, 168
    Phonics/Phonemic Awareness
    Practice Book, 103–106

  ☑ **Cumulative Review,** 115G–115H
    Teaching Chart 131
    Reteach, Practice, Extend, 156
    Language Support, 169
    Phonics/Phonemic Awareness
    Practice Book, 103–106

  Minilessons, 99, 105, 107, 109

Intervention Program

Read Read Self-Selected Books

  ☑ **Review Compare and Contrast**
    115I–115J
    Teaching Chart 132
    Reteach, Practice, Extend, 157
    Language Support, 170

  ☑ **Review Inflectional Endings,**
    115K–115L
    Teaching Chart 133
    Reteach, Practice, Extend, 158
    Language Support, 171

  Listening, Speaking, Viewing, Representing, 115N

    Minilessons, 99, 105, 107, 109

Intervention Program

Activity Math, 96, Language Arts, 98

Activity Science, 100

Activity Social Studies, 104

Writing Prompt: Write an article for a newsletter that tells about the first meeting of the B.A.T. Club. Tell where and when it met and what was discussed.

Writing That Compares, 115M
  Prewrite, Draft

Writing Prompt: Write a brief review of *Zipping, Zapping, Zooming Bats.* Make sure to include the title.

Writing That Compares, 115M
  Revise

Meeting Individual Needs for Writing, 115N

Writing Prompt: Has reading about bats changed your mind about them? Do you think people would change their minds if they learned more about bats? Why or why not?

Writing That Compares, 115M
  Edit/Proofread, Publish

Review and Practice: More Irregular Verbs, 115P
  Daily Language Activity: Write the correct form of the irregular verb.

Grammar Practice Book, 117

Review and Practice: More Irregular Verbs, 115P
  Daily Language Activity: Write the correct form of the irregular verb.

Grammar Practice Book, 118

Assess and Reteach: More Irregular Verbs, 115P
  Daily Language Activity: Write the correct form of the irregular verb.

Grammar Practice Book, 119

Practice and Extend: Words with Digraphs *ph, tch, ch,* 115R

Spelling Practice Book, 118

Proofread and Write: Words with Digraphs *ph, tch, ch,* 115R

Spelling Practice Book, 119

Assess: Words with Digraphs *ph, tch, ch,* 115R

Spelling Practice Book, 120

Link

Language Arts

Read Aloud

The Day the Sun Hid

a myth

There was once a beautiful and peaceful country. It was high in the mountains on the roof of the world, and a land of steep, deep green valleys and swift flowing rivers. Every day the sun climbed above the snowy peaks and shone upon the land. People said that if trouble ever *did* come, it would last only as long as the shadow of a flying bird.

One day, however, the bird came, and stayed. Huge and evil, he blotted out the sun and his shadow plunged the country into darkness. Because there was no light, the grass stopped growing, fruit rotted. With no dawn to wake them, animals slept all day. People could not see to work, so they slumbered while the corn withered and died.

At last the evil bird flew off, but the sun had become accustomed to darkness, and wrapped in thick blankets of cloud, he dozed in the high mountains.

A few animals and children, who never sleep for long, decided to find a way to get the sun to shine again.

Continued on pages T3–T4

Oral Comprehension

LISTENING AND SPEAKING As you read, ask children to compare and contrast the ways each character tries to remove the clouds. When you've finished reading, ask:

• What was similar about the way each person or animal tried to remove the clouds?

• What was different about each of their plans?

GENRE STUDY: MYTH Discuss characteristics of the genre and how they apply to "The Day the Sun Hid."

• Explain that most myths reflect the culture and lifestyle of a certain time period. What inferences can children make about the time period of this myth?

• Remind children that myths helped ancient people understand the natural world. Then ask: "What event in nature might this myth be trying to explain? Why do you think that?"

• Children should know that myths often include animals and people with magical abilities. Have children write a list of "magical moments" in "The Day the Sun Hid." Then discuss their lists as a group.

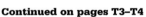 Encourage children to create a mural that shows the animals in this myth. Ask: "What other animal myths have you read or heard?" ▶ **Visual**

Develop Phonological Awareness

Blend Sounds **Phonemic Awareness**

MATERIALS
- Phonics Picture Posters

Teach Tell children they are going to put some sounds together to make words. Hold up the picture for *watch*. Say the sounds for the word and have children blend the sounds with you to say the whole word. Say: /w/-/o/-/ch/: *watch*. Invite children to listen as you say some more sounds. Hold up the picture of the phone. Say: /f/-/ō/-/n/. *If I blend the sounds together, I get the word phone.*

Practice If available, hold up pictures or objects for the words below. Have children blend the sounds to say each word: *graph, match, photo, catch, watch, stitch,* and *pitch.*

Segment Sounds **Phonemic Awareness**

MATERIALS
- colored blocks

Teach Tell children that they will count and say the number of sounds in words. To demonstrate, say the word *batch,* then say the sounds /b/-/a/-/ch/, placing one block in front of you for each sound you say. Then count the blocks and tell children the word *batch* has three sounds.

Practice Distribute five blocks to each child. Have children segment and count the number of sounds in *catch, hatch, sketch, graph, ditch, latch,* and *dutch.*

Substitute Sounds **Phonemic Awareness**

MATERIALS
- Phonics Picture Posters

Teach Display the Phonics Picture Poster of the nest. Tell children that if you change the beginning sound of *nest* to /t/, you make the word *test.* Have children repeat both words with you: *nest/test.* Repeat with words *dog/dot,* changing the ending sound.

Practice Have children substitute the beginning or ending sounds for the following words: *pick/pitch, hatch/match, batch/bat, ditch/hitch, graph/grab, hutch/dutch, cone/phone,* and *watch/wash.*

 **INFORMAL ASSESSMENT** Observe children as they blend, segment, and substitute sounds. If children have difficulty, see Alternate Teaching Strategies on p. T75.

**OBJECTIVES**

Children will:

- review words with /f/*ph*, /ch/*tch*.
- blend and read *ph* and *tch* words.

MATERIALS
- **Teaching Chart 127**
- **Word Building Manipulative Cards**

Skills Finder	
Digraphs *ph, tch*	
Introduce	B2: 92G–H
Review	B2: 115E-F, 116G-H, 250G-H, 281E-F
Test	B2: Unit 2

SPELLING/PHONICS
CONNECTIONS
Words with *ph* and *tch*: See the 5-Day Spelling Plan, pages 115Q–115R.

TEACHING TIP

DIGRAPHS Point out to children that the letters *tch* appear at the end of words, whereas the letters *ph* can appear at the beginning or at the end of words.

Introduce Digraphs *ph, tch*

TEACH

Introduce the Letters *ph* and *tch* as Symbols for /f/ and /ch/ Respectively
Tell children they will read words in which the letter combination *ph* spells the /f/ sound, and words in which the letter combination *tch* spells the /ch/ sound. Display the digraph cards for *ph* and *tch* as you say their sounds.

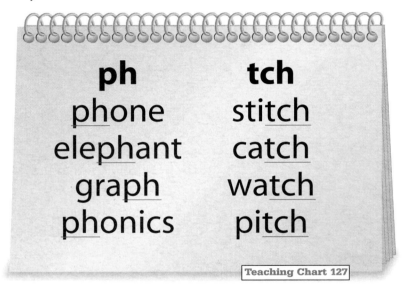

ph
phone
elephant
graph
phonics

tch
stitch
catch
watch
pitch

Teaching Chart 127

BLENDING
Model and Guide Practice with *ph* and *tch* Words
- Display **Teaching Chart 127**.

- Point to the letters *ph* at the top of column 1 and say the sound /f/. Write the letters *ph* in the blank space of the first word. Blend the sounds together and read aloud the word *phone.* Have children repeat after you.

- Review that this letter combination spells the sound /f/. Repeat with the word *elephant.*

- Invite volunteers to add letter combinations that spell the /f/ sound to the words in the rest of the column, and to read aloud the completed words. (*graph* and *phonics*)

Use the Words in Context
- Have volunteers use the words in sentences to reinforce their meanings. Example: *I like to talk on the phone.*

Repeat the Procedure
- Continue the activity with the second column of the chart, blending, building, and reading words with the /ch/ sound.

PRACTICE

LETTER SUBSTITUTION Build /ch/ *tch* and /f/ *ph* Words with Letter Cards

ONE

Have children use letter and digraph cards to build the word *patch*. Replace the *a* card with an *i* to build *pitch*. Now use cards to build the word *phone*. Encourage children to continue to build more words using the cards. Finally, ask children to make a list of *tch* and *ph* words.

▶ Linguistic/Visual/Spatial

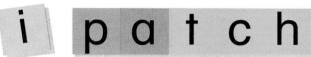
i patch

ASSESS/CLOSE

Read and Write Sentences Using *ph* and *tch* Words

To assess children's ability to blend and read words with *ph* and *tch*, observe their work on the Practice activity. Ask each child to read aloud one *tch* and one *ph* word from his or her list. Ask each child to write a sentence using *ph* words and a sentence using *tch* words.

ADDITIONAL PHONICS RESOURCES

Phonics/Phonemic Awareness Practice Book, pages 103–106

McGraw-Hill School **TECHNOLOGY**

Phonics CD-ROM

activities for practice with Blending and Discriminating

Daily Routines

DAY 1 Segmenting Write *phone, match, graph,* and *pitched* on the chalkboard. Call volunteers to the chalkboard to circle the letters that make the /f/ or /ch/ sounds.

DAY 2 Discriminating Say the following words aloud: *phone, stretch, elephant, match, switch,* and *photo.* Have children raise their hands when they hear a word with the /f/ sound.

DAY 3 Letter Substitution Invite pairs of children to make new *ph* and *tch* words from the words *match* and *phone* by changing one or more letters at a time.

DAY 4 Fluency Write the following words on the chalkboard: *phone, phonics, pitched, itch.* Point to each word, asking children to blend the sounds silently. Ask a volunteer to read aloud each word.

DAY 5 Writing Have pairs of children create silly rhymes with *ph* and *tch* words. (Examples: *Answer the phone, then give the elephant a bone.*)

Meeting Individual Needs for Phonics

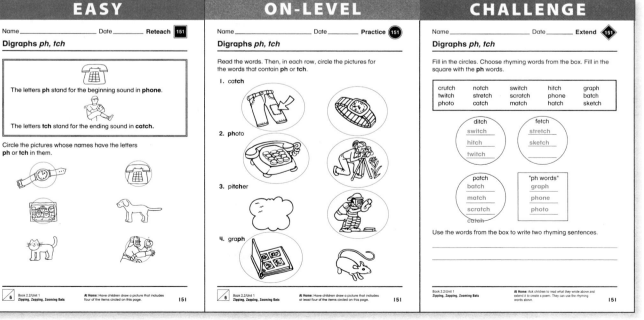

EASY	ON-LEVEL	CHALLENGE
Reteach, 151	Practice, 151	Extend, 151

92H

OBJECTIVES
Children will blend and read *ph* and *tch* words.

Apply Digraphs *ph* and *tch*

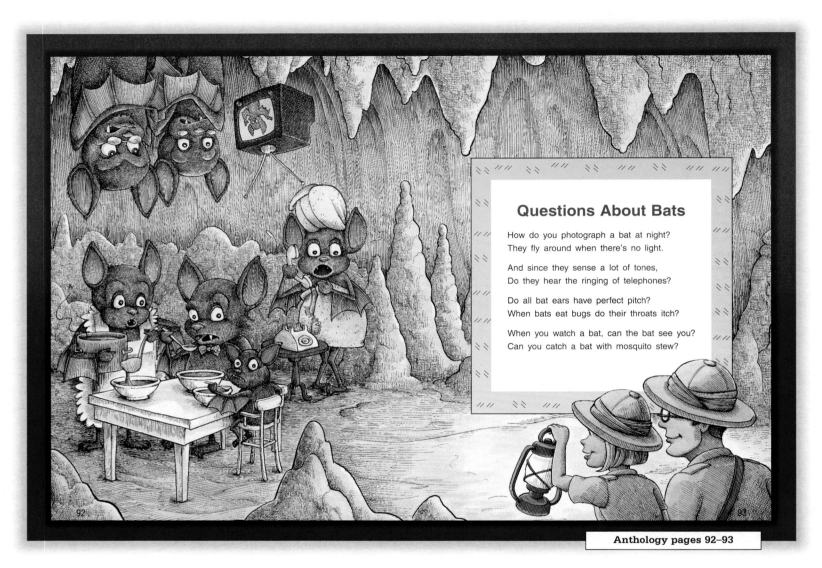

Questions About Bats

How do you photograph a bat at night?
They fly around when there's no light.

And since they sense a lot of tones,
Do they hear the ringing of telephones?

Do all bat ears have perfect pitch?
When bats eat bugs do their throats itch?

When you watch a bat, can the bat see you?
Can you catch a bat with mosquito stew?

Anthology pages 92–93

Read and Build Fluency

READ THE POEM Before reading aloud "Questions About Bats," point out the /f/ sound in *photograph* and the /ch/ sound in *itch*. Model the difference between reading a question and reading a statement as you read and track the text in a deliberate, humorous tone. As an auditory model, have children echo how your voice goes up at the end of a question.

REREAD FOR FLUENCY Have children reread
PARTNERS the poem with a partner. Encourage them to note how their voices change when they read a question.

Dictate and Spell

DICTATE WORDS Say the word *photograph*
JOURNAL aloud. Segment it into its individual parts. (/f/ /ō/ /t/ /ə/ /g/ /r/ /a/ /f/) Use the word in a sentence, such as, "Ray took a photograph." Say the word again. Have children repeat the word and write the letters for each sound to make the whole word. Then repeat these steps with *ph* and *tch* words from the poem. Continue with words not in the poem, such as *graph* and *match*.

> **i Intervention** **Skills Intervention Guide,**
> for direct instruction and extra practice of digraphs *ph* and *tch*

Build Background

Link
Science

Concept: Nocturnal Animals

Evaluate Prior Knowledge

CONCEPT: NOCTURNAL ANIMALS
Display pictures of bats, cats, raccoons, owls and other nocturnal animals. As you present each picture, write a column head with the animal name. Ask children what they know about each animal and write their responses under the appropriate column head for the animal.

As part of the discussion, be sure to ask children what each animal looks like, what it eats, where it lives, and whether it can fly. Ask them what these animals do during the day and during the night, and guide them to understand that all of the animals in the pictures are nocturnal.

MAKE AN ANIMAL FACT CHART List the names of animals down the left side of the chart. Across the top, make headings for What It Eats, Where It Lives, Can It Fly? Fill in children's responses from the previous activity.

Animal	What It Eats	Where It Lives	Can It Fly?
Cat	Cat food	House	No

MAKE A BATMOBILE Encourage children to look at the illustrations in their books before they draw bats for their mobiles. Then, have them draw and cut out shapes from construction paper, and help them to create a hanging mobile. Children may wish to write on the dangling shapes various facts about bats. Encourage them to add realistic details to their drawings.
▶ **Spatial**

Develop Oral Language

COMPARE NOCTURNAL ANIMALS Have Review and summarize the information in the columns on the chalkboard. Then have children, working alone or in pairs, make a Venn diagram in which they compare two of the nocturnal animals discussed. Once children finish the diagrams, ask volunteers to present them to the class.

After each presentation, model ways to ask follow-up questions of the presenters and encourage children to ask any remaining questions they have about the animals.
▶ **Linguistic/Logical**

Bats can fly. — Both come out at night. — Raccoons can't fly.

DAILY Phonics ROUTINES

DAY 2 **Discriminating** Say the following: *phone, stretch, elephant, match, switch,* and *photo.* Have children raise their hands when they hear a word with the /f/ sound.

Phonics CD-ROM

LANGUAGE SUPPORT

ESL For additional help in building background, refer to the **Language Support Book,** pages 163–166.

OBJECTIVES

Children will use context and structural clues to determine the meanings of vocabulary words.

Definitions

explore (p.107) travel to unknown places for the purpose of discovering new things

fact (p. 99) a true or real piece of information

disturb (p.108) make nervous; bother

nature (p.109) the physical universe; all things not made by people

object (p. 100) a thing that can be seen or touched

several (p. 108) a few; more than one, but not many

Story Words

These words from the selection may be unfamiliar. Before children read, have them check the meanings and pronunciations of the words in the Glossary, beginning on page 390, or in a dictionary.

- mosquito, p. 97
- echolocation, p. 101
- membrane, p. 102
- hibernate, p. 106

---

explore
fact
disturb
nature
object
several

Vocabulary

Teach Vocabulary in Context

Identify Vocabulary Words Display **Teaching Chart 128** and read with children. Have volunteers circle each vocabulary word and underline other words that are clues to its meaning.

The Bat Cave

1. Today we are going to (explore) the caves, to see sites we've never seen before. 2. We have already learned (facts) about bats, information about what they eat and how they live. 3. That's how we know to be very quiet; we don't want to (disturb) the bats, and bother them. 4. I've only seen bats at the zoo before, so I'm excited to see them living in (nature) for the first time. 5. Now, we are looking for rocks and other (objects) that are found in caves where bats live. 6. I want to collect (several) rocks, so I will have some things to help me remember our visit.

Teaching Chart 128

Discuss Meanings Ask questions like these to help clarify word meanings:

- Can you show me how you would look if you were exploring a cave?
- Are facts true or made up?
- When you are doing homework or resting, do you like to be disturbed?
- Are cars part of nature? Are trees?
- Can you name three objects in this room?
- If you are sitting with several people, are you sitting with one person or more than two?

Practice

Create Riddles

WRITING
PARTNERS

Have partners choose vocabulary cards from a pile. Invite children to write riddles that can be answered with vocabulary words. Have children exchange and solve each other's riddles.
▶ **Logical/Linguistic**

 disturb   several    explore

Word Building Manipulative Cards

Write Context Sentences

WRITING
PARTNERS

Have partners write context sentences, leaving blanks for the vocabulary words. Invite them to exchange papers and fill in the blanks. ▶ **Linguistic/Oral**

Assess Vocabulary

Identify Word Meaning in Context

WRITING
PARTNERS

Ask each child to write a short paragraph about a favorite animal, using the vocabulary words. Instead of using the actual vocabulary words, however, ask them to write the word *Bats* for each vocabulary word. Then have children exchange paragraphs with partners and write the missing vocabulary word each time they see *Bats*.

SPELLING/VOCABULARY CONNECTIONS

See Spelling Challenge Words, pages 115Q–115R.

LANGUAGE SUPPORT

See the **Language Support Book**, pages 163–166, for teaching suggestions for Vocabulary.

Vocabulary PuzzleMaker

Provides vocabulary activities.

Meeting Individual Needs for Vocabulary

EASY	ON-LEVEL	ON-LEVEL	CHALLENGE

EASY

Name _____ Date _____ Reteach 152
Vocabulary

Choose a word from the box to complete each sentence. Write the word on the line.

disturbs	explore	facts	nature	objects	several

1. Loud noise ___ Henry. _disturbs_
2. I see ___ plants next to the window. _several_
3. Linda and Ed are learning ___ about trees. _facts_
4. On Thursday we took a ___ walk. _nature_
5. Look at the ___ on the bed. _objects_
6. My aunt and uncle like to ___ caves. _explore_

152   At Home: Have children draw a picture about one of the sentences above.   Book 2.2/Unit 1 · 6
Zipping, Zapping, Zooming Bats

Reteach, 152

ON-LEVEL

Name _____ Date _____ Practice 152
Vocabulary

Read the words in the box. Read the clues. Write the correct word on the line next to each clue.

disturb	explore	facts	nature	objects	several

1. This word means more than two.
   several
2. These are things that you know are true.
   facts
3. You can do this to a baby by being noisy.
   disturb
4. These are things that you can see or touch.
   objects
5. You could do this on the moon.
   explore
6. Plants and animals are part of this.
   nature

152   At Home: Have your child make up riddles for some of the words in the box.   Book 2.2/Unit 1 · 6
Zipping, Zapping, Zooming Bats

Practice, 152

ON-LEVEL

Desert Friends

"Welcome," the man said. "Sit down and I will tell you many facts about the desert. This place is a real nature center. See the mountains in the distance? There are great forests on the other side of them."
"I used to live in a forest," said Phil. "Would you like a sandwich?"
"That would be nice," said the old man. And the three became friends.

At Home: Have children write about things they have seen or would like to see on a nature trip.

152a

Practice, 152a
Take-Home Story

CHALLENGE

Name _____ Date _____ Extend 152
Vocabulary

disturb	explore	facts	nature	objects	several

Fill in each space using the words from the box.

1. Things that have happened or are true. _facts_
2. To study or look into something that is unknown to you. _explore_
3. To stop, upset, or bother somebody who is busy. _disturb_
4. More than two, but not many. _several_
5. Things you can see and touch. _objects_
6. Everything in the world that is not made by people, such as plants and animals. _nature_

Imagine you are walking in a forest. Write a story about your experience using the words from the box.

_____
_____
_____
_____
_____

152   At Home: Have children read their story and then draw a picture to illustrate it.   Book 2.2/Unit 1
Zipping, Zapping, Zooming Bats

Extend, 152

Comprehension

Prereading Strategies

PREVIEW AND PREDICT Read aloud the title and then take a **picture walk** through the illustrations. Discuss how illustrations can give clues to what a selection is about.

- What clues do the pictures give you about the selection?
- What will the selection be about?
- Will the selection be a fable about bats or a nonfiction article about bats? *Genre*

Have children record in a chart their predictions about what will happen in the article.

PREDICTIONS	WHAT HAPPENED
This will be an article about bats.	
The article will give facts about what bats eat and how they live.	

SET PURPOSES Ask children what they would like to learn as they read the article. For example:

- Why are there pictures of insects?
- How are bats different from other animals?

Meet Ann Earle

ANN EARLE first became interested in bats when she went on a camping trip out west. Now she often watches them from her backyard in Vermont. She even has two bat houses!

Ms. Earle's book *Zipping, Zapping, Zooming Bats* is a Parent's Choice Award winner.

Meet Henry Cole

HENRY COLE loves to explore the woods and fields around his home in Virginia. There he finds all kinds of bugs and animals to study. Aside from enjoying nature and illustrating children's books, he teaches science. He also likes to spend time sailing his boat at the seashore.

Mr. Cole has illustrated several books for children, including *Four Famished Foxes and Fosdyke* and *Some Smug Slug.*

94

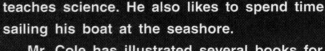

Meeting Individual Needs · Grouping Suggestions for Strategic Reading

EASY

Read Together Read the story aloud, inviting children to join in with you. Model active reading strategies by noting new information and paraphrasing to show comprehension of what you have read. You may wish children to use the **Listening Library** after you have read the story with them.

ON-LEVEL

Guided Instruction Read the selection with children, using the Comprehension prompts. You may wish to have the children read the article first on their own or have them use the **Listening Library.** Remind them to use the Draw Conclusions chart to record meaningful information as they read.

CHALLENGE

Read Independently Have children set purposes before they read. Remind children that drawing conclusions based on information they read will help them to better understand the facts. Have students set up a Draw Conclusions chart as on page 95.

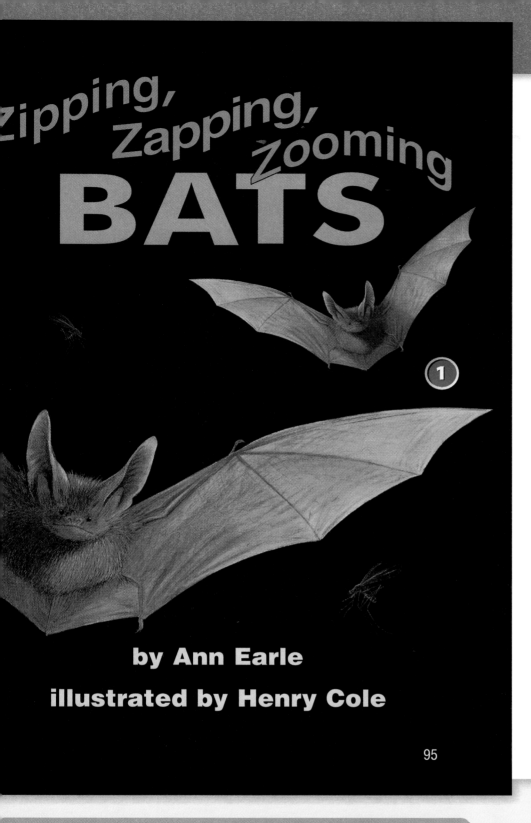

Zipping, Zapping, Zooming BATS

by Ann Earle

illustrated by Henry Cole

95

A blackline master of the Facts/Conclusion Chart can be found in the **Language Support Book**. As children begin their charts, review with them that a fact is something that we know is true.

To help children keep track of the information about bats, have them dictate one-sentence summaries throughout the reading of the selection.

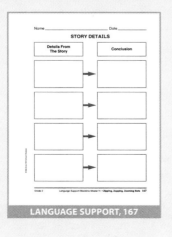

Name _____ Date _____
STORY DETAILS

| Details From The Story | Conclusion |

LANGUAGE SUPPORT, 167

Comprehension

☑ **Phonics** Apply Digraphs *tch*

☑ **Apply Draw Conclusions**

STRATEGIC READING Authors provide facts you can use to figure out something about a person or situation. Drawing conclusions is one way to be sure you've understood what you've read. Let's create a chart of facts we read and the conclusions we draw from those facts.

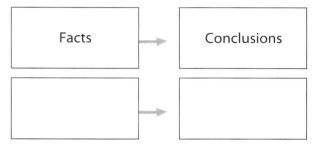

| Facts | | Conclusions |

1 What information does the title give about bats? (Bats can move quickly.)
Make Inferences

Narrative Nonfiction

Explain to children that in narrative nonfiction:

- facts are given in an easy-to-understand way.
- information is presented in the context of a real-life story.
- photographs, illustrations, and other graphics such as charts are used.

Activity As children read *Zipping, Zapping, Zooming Bats,* have them pay attention to how the facts are presented in a way that everyone can understand. Encourage them to take notes as they read the story, jotting down each new fact they learn. Ask them to consider why the author chose to have an illustrator draw the pictures rather than use photographs.

95

Comprehension

2 Why do bats come out to hunt after the sun goes down? (They eat bugs, and bugs come out at night, too!) *Cause and Effect*

3 **DRAW CONCLUSIONS** What facts can we gather from reading and looking at these pages? Let's write them into our charts and see if we can come up with a conclusion.

MODEL This page says bats come out at night to hunt. It also says they eat a lot of insects. The picture shows them flying around. So now I think I have a conclusion: Bats must fly around at night so they can catch insects.

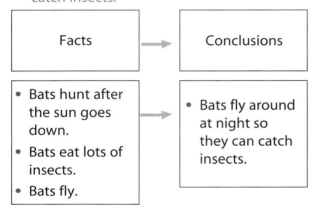

Facts	Conclusions
• Bats hunt after the sun goes down. • Bats eat lots of insects. • Bats fly.	• Bats fly around at night so they can catch insects.

When the sun goes down, bats come out to hunt. You have to look quickly to see a bat before it's gone.

2 Many bats hunt insects. They eat lots of insects. Each night a bat chomps half its own weight in bugs. If you weigh 60 pounds, that's like eating 125 peanut-butter-and-jelly sandwiches every day.

3

96

Activity

Cross Curricular: Math

2001 DOG BONES Have children reread the second paragraph on this page. Tell children to pretend that they have a pet dog or cat that weighs 10 pounds. Ask them to figure out how much food their pet would have to eat each day, in order to eat half its own weight. Invite children to draw pictures of a dog or cat next to the amount of food that is half its weight. Have each child add a caption about weights of items.

▶ **Mathematical/Spatial**

Don't be scared if a bat flies past your head. It won't get into your hair. It's probably catching a juicy mosquito.

4

97

Comprehension

4 **Phonics** **DIGRAPHS** *tch* Do any words on this page contain the /ch/ sound? *(catching)* Run a finger under the word as we blend together the sounds. Which letters stand for the /ch/ sound? *(tch)* *Segmenting/Blending*

P/i **CONTRACTIONS** Can you find any words on this page that contain an apostrophe? There are three. *(don't, won't, it's)* What missing letters does the apostrophe in these words stand for? *(o; o; i)* What kinds of words are these? *(contractions)*

P/i **PREVENTION/INTERVENTION**

CONTRACTIONS As children respond, list on the chalkboard the contractions *don't, won't, it's*. Point out that each of these words is a contraction, a shortened word formed from two other words. For example, *do* and *not* = *don't*. Ask volunteers to circle the apostrophes in each listed word and name the letters that the apostrophe replaces. Prompt children to name the two words that each listed contraction stands for.

don't	do not
won't	will not
it's	it is

Syntactic Cues

Comprehension

5 What does it look like when someone gobbles something? When someone munches something? Show me. *Context Clues/Pantomime*

> **TEACHING TIP**
>
> **MULTIPLE MEANING WORDS** Point out that the word *bat* is a name for a familiar object (a baseball bat) as well as being the name of a kind of animal. Encourage children to think of other animals whose names have more than one meaning. (examples: bear, bug, crane)

5 Bats are terrific hunters. A little brown bat can catch 150 mosquitoes in 15 minutes. The gray bat can gobble 3000 insects in one night.

Bracken Cave in Texas is home to 20 million Mexican free-tailed bats. Together they munch 250 tons of insects every night.

98

Activity

Cross Curricular: Language Arts

MULTIPLE MEANINGS Ask each child to choose a word for a kind of animal that is also a word for something else. On a piece of paper folded in half, have each child illustrate the two meanings of the word. Have them write captions using the word. Ask them to underline the word they have illustrated in each caption. Display children's work on a bulletin board.

▶ **Linguistic/Spatial**

The bat flies in the sky. I play baseball with a bat.

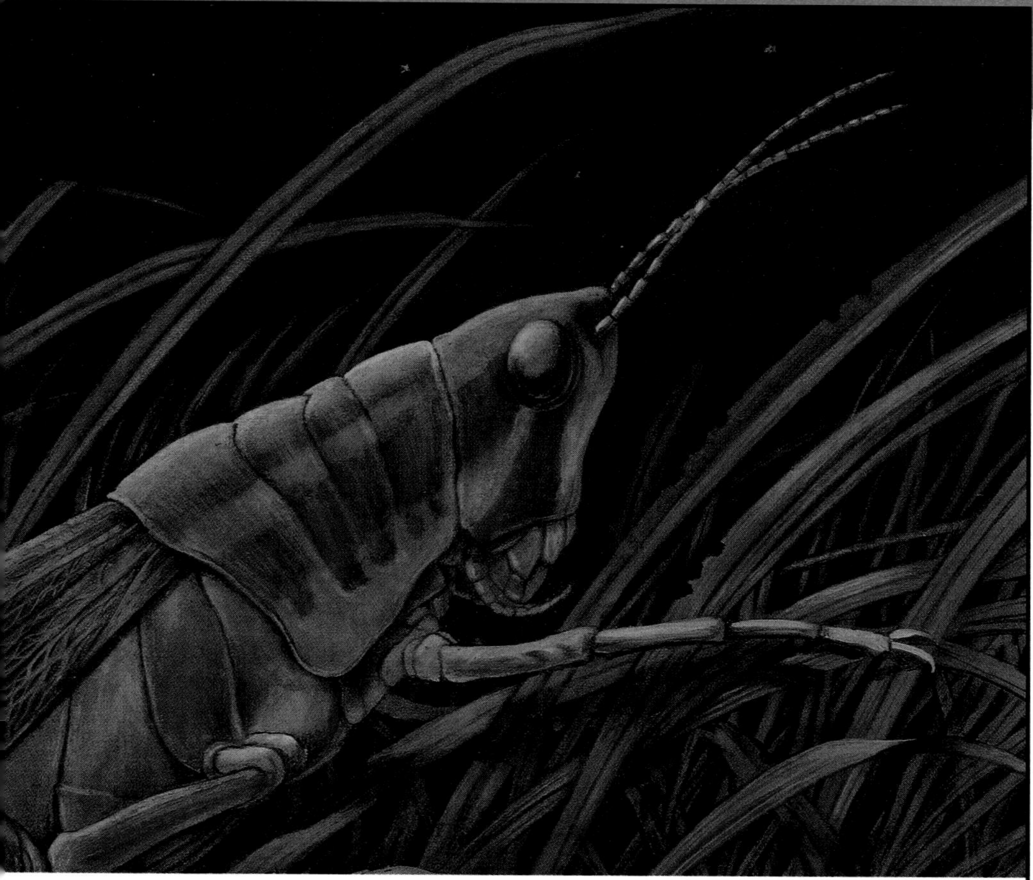

It's a fact that bats help get rid of insects that bite people. Bats also zap moths, beetles, and grasshoppers. These insects eat farmers' crops, the food that you and I need.

6

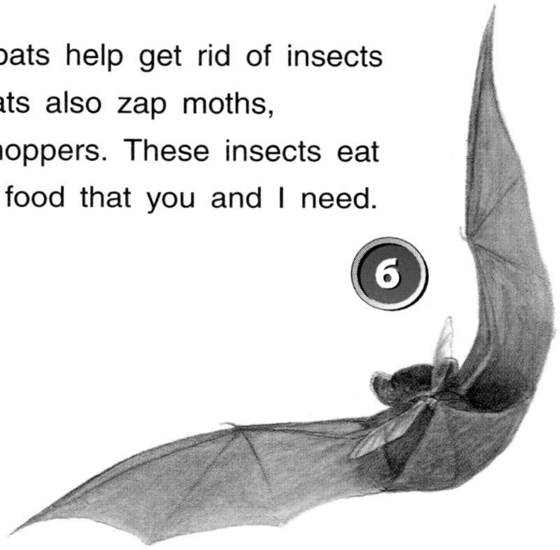

99

Comprehension

6 Imagine you are a farmer. How might bats help your business? (They would eat the insects that eat crops.) What problem might occur if bats didn't zap the beetles, moths, and grasshoppers that eat farmers' crops? (There might not be enough food for people to eat.) ***Cause and Effect***

P/I **COMPOUND WORDS** What two words make up the word *grasshopper*? What do you think a grasshopper is?

P/I PREVENTION/INTERVENTION

COMPOUND WORDS Tell children that *grasshopper* is a compound word—a word made up of two smaller words. Write on the chalkboard the word *grasshopper*. Invite a volunteer to draw circles around each of the smaller words that make up the compound word, and to say each aloud. (*grass, hopper*) Remind children that knowing the meaning of the two smaller words can help them to figure out the meaning of the compound word. (A grasshopper is an insect that lives in the *grass* and moves around by *hopping*.) Ask children for examples of other compound words. (*afternoon, storyteller*) ***Semantic Cues***

Minilesson

REVIEW/MAINTAIN

Long *e: ee, ea*

Ask children to reread the last sentence on this page, and to find two words with the /ē/ sound. As children respond, write on the chalkboard the words *eat* and *need*. With children, blend and read the words aloud. Invite volunteers to identify and underline the letters in each word that represent the long *e* sound. (*ea, ee*)

Activity Ask the class to brainstorm other words with long *e* spelled *ee* and *ea*. Invite volunteers to write words from the list under *eat* or *need,* matching the spelling of the /ē/ sound in the heading.

Comprehension

(7)  **DIGRAPHS** *tch* How many words on pages 100 and 101 contain the /ch/ sound spelled with the *tch* letter combination? (2; *pitched, catch*) Read the words aloud. Can you find a word with the letters *ch* that do not spell the /ch/ sound? (*echoes, echolocation*) What sound does the *ch* letter combination spell in those words? /k/

(8) What is a bat's special way of using sound called? (echolocation) What things does echolocation help bats to do? (hunt and move around quickly in the dark) Imagine you could hear as well as a bat. What kinds of things could you do? How would your daily life be different? (Answers will vary.) *Cause and Effect*

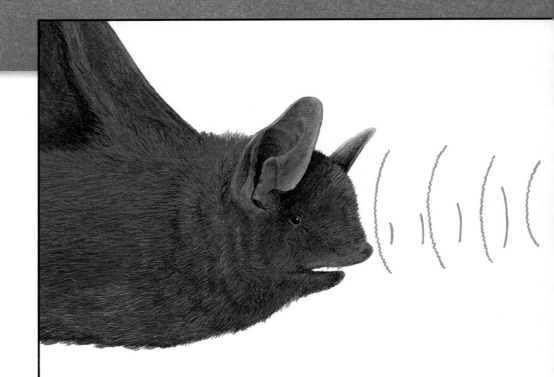

(7) Bats are good hunters because they have a special way of using sound. Bats make high, beeping sounds. These sounds are too high-pitched for our ears, but bat ears can hear things ours can't. The beeps go out from the bat in waves. The sound waves hit objects around the bat. When sound waves hit an object, they bounce back. The bounced sound waves come back to the bat as echoes. The bat can tell by the echoes what kind of insect is near, and exactly where it is. Then the bat can catch it. We call this **(8)** echolocation.

100

Activity

Cross Curricular: Science

ECHOLOCATION Bats' sonar ability allows them to navigate and find food.

Demonstrate echolocation. Use a sponge or sponge ball. Tell children that the sponge stands for the bats' beeps. Bounce the sponge ball off the chalkboard. Catch the ball as it bounces back toward you.

Tell children that when the ball bounced back, you could tell it had hit something.

Have a volunteer throw the sponge into an open space with no obstacles. Ask: *Does the sponge bounce back at me? Why or why not?* (No; because it didn't hit anything.)
▶ **Kinesthetic**

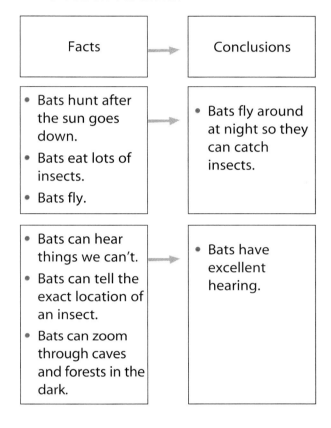

Comprehension

⑨ DRAW CONCLUSIONS Based on the information you've read on pages 100 and 101, can you draw any conclusions about whether bats have good hearing? Let's fill in some facts on our charts.

Facts →	Conclusions
• Bats hunt after the sun goes down. • Bats eat lots of insects. • Bats fly.	• Bats fly around at night so they can catch insects.
• Bats can hear things we can't. • Bats can tell the exact location of an insect. • Bats can zoom through caves and forests in the dark.	• Bats have excellent hearing.

The echoes that bounce off a tree sound different from the echoes that bounce off a bug. Bats use echolocation to "hear" things that are in their way. They can zoom fast through dark forests and black cave tunnels. If a bat gets into your house, open a door or window. The bat will echolocate, and "hear" the opening it can use to fly out. **⑨**

MULTIPLE-MEANING WORDS On page 100, we learn that sounds travel in waves that can hit an object and bounce back. What other meanings does *wave* have? (to wave one's hand, ocean wave)

101

🅟/ᵢ PREVENTION/INTERVENTION

MULTIPLE-MEANING WORDS
Remind children that some words have more than one meaning. Encourage the use of context clues to figure out the intended meaning of a word in a particular sentence. Model this strategy in the first sentence.

• She waves goodbye to her friend.

• I like to ride the waves in the ocean.

• Bats use sound waves to help them hear.

• Have children identify the clues to the meaning of *waves* in the other sentences.

Point out where the word *waves* is a verb and where it is a noun. Then have children write sentences of their own using *wave* as a noun and as a verb. *Semantic Cues*

Comprehension

10 **Phonics** DIGRAPHS *tch* I see a word on this page that contains the /ch/ sound. Can anyone find that word and read it aloud? (*stretches*) Which letter combination spells the /ch/ sound? (*tch*) *Segmenting*

11 How are bats' wings different from birds' wings? How are they the same? Use what you read and what you see on this page to help you find some answers. *Compare and Contrast/Use Illustrations*

TEACHING TIP

DIAGRAMS Encourage children to study the diagrams that accompany the article in order to better understand what is being described. Ask children: How do the illustrations on pages 102–103 help you to understand what a membrane is? How is a bat's wing like a "hand"? Encourage children to look up bats on the Internet to find more bat illustrations.

---

10 **11** Bats are also good hunters because they are expert fliers. Their wings are different from bird wings. Bat wings have long arm bones with extra-long finger bones. A thin skin called a membrane stretches between the bones. The membrane connects the wing bones to the bat's legs and body. It may also join the tail to the legs.

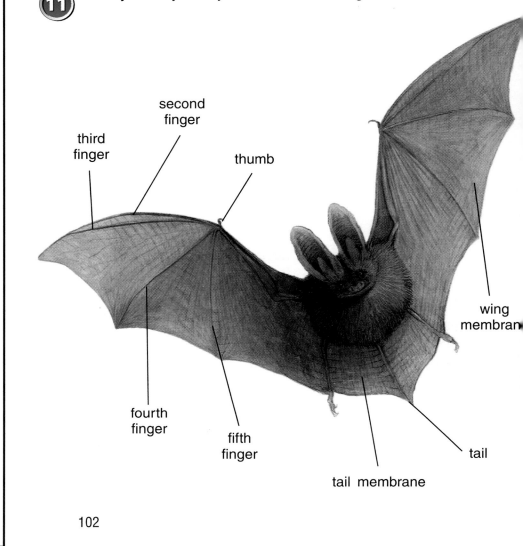

second finger

third finger

thumb

wing membran

fourth finger

fifth finger

tail membrane

tail

102

CULTURAL PERSPECTIVES

ANIMAL TALES Stories about scary and dangerous animals are popular in many cultures. Some of these stories have been told for hundreds of years. People's fears of certain animals come mostly from these stories.

RESEARCH AND INQUIRY Provide children with folktales and stories about scary animals, such as *The Three Little Pigs*. Have them compare the facts they know about the animals with the fantasy of the stories.

The "Big Bad Wolf" isn't bad at all. in fact, wolves

Comprehension

12 What steps do bats complete when they catch the insects they eat? (The bat chases a bug, catches it in its wing, flips it into its tail, and scoops it into its mouth.) *Sequence of Events*

13 **DRAW CONCLUSIONS** After reading pages 102 and 103 what can we conclude about the wings of a bat?

MODEL I know from reading these pages that bats can change the shape of their wings and zigzag after insects. They can even use their wings to catch insects. So I can conclude that a bat's wings help make it a good hunter.

Bat wings are like webbed hands. A flying bat can move its wings much the way you can move your fingers. This means a bat can quickly change the shape of its wings. If a bug dodges away, the bat can zigzag fast and chase it. A bat can catch a flying insect in its wing, flip it into its tail membrane, and then scoop it into its mouth.

103

Comprehension

(14) What is the main idea of the paragraph on page 104? (Bats use their claws for many purposes.) *Main Idea*

(15) This page says bats and cats clean themselves the same way. How do they do it? (by using their claws and their tongues) It also says bats keep themselves as clean as cats. Do cats keep themselves very clean? (yes) Based on this knowledge, and on the information given, can we form any generalizations about animals that use their claws and tongues to clean themselves? (They keep themselves very clean.) *Form Generalizations*

> **TEACHING TIP**
>
> **FORMAL LANGUAGE** Ask children to compare the language in this article to the language in Amanda's letters from *The Best Vacation Ever.* Discuss how writers often use formal language to present facts in an informational article. Invite children to discuss situations in their lives when they use formal and informal language.

Bats have hooked claws on their toes and thumbs. When bats sleep or clean themselves, they hang upside down by their toe claws. They use their claws to move around on their roosts, to comb their fur, and to clean their **(14)** ears. Bats keep themselves as clean as cats, using both their tongues and claws.

(15)

104

Activity

Cross Curricular: Social Studies

POPULAR PETS Tell children that cats are America's most popular pet . . . but most people wouldn't like to live in a house with bats. Do an informal survey of the class to find out what kinds of pets children live with.

RESEARCH AND INQUIRY Have children learn more about what kinds of pets are popular in other cultures. Have each child draw a pet and give a brief oral report on the animal and the place where it is popular.

▶ **Kinesthetic/Interpersonal**

Cats are the most popular pet in our country.

Comprehension

 When people tell stories about vampires, or people that turn into bats, are they telling facts or made-up stories?
Fantasy and Reality

 DRAW CONCLUSIONS Why do you think people are scared of bats? (They hear scary, made-up stories, and don't know the facts.)

SILENT LETTERS Read aloud the last word of the first sentence on page 104. (*thumbs*) What letter in this word is silent? (*b*)

Because bats fly at night, many people are scared of them. Sometimes people tell scary stories about vampires that can change into bats. Dracula and other vampires are not real. Bats fly at night because that's when they can find their favorite meals. Bats are really very gentle.

16

17

105

Minilesson

REVIEW/MAINTAIN

Context Clues

Remind children that they can often figure out the meaning of an unfamiliar word by looking at context clues—pictures and familiar words around the unfamiliar word. Ask:

• Can you use context clues to help you to figure out the meaning of the word *roosts* on page 104?

Activity Have children use context clues to figure out the meaning of the word *supply* on page 107.

 PREVENTION/INTERVENTION

SILENT LETTERS Remind children that in some words the letters *b, l, k, w, g,* and *gh* do not make their sound. Write the following words on the board: *thumb, night, talk, write, sign,* *know.* Ask children to say each word and identify the silent letter in the word. Encourage children to name other words that contain silent letters. *Graphophonic Cues*

Comprehension

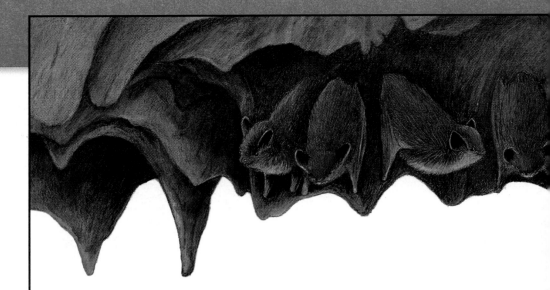

 Why do bats stuff themselves full of food during the last few weeks of warm weather? (to get ready to hibernate; to store the extra food as fat) *Cause and Effect*

SELF-MONITORING STRATEGY

VERIFYING FACTUAL INFORMATION
Knowing and using strategies to discover whether information in a story is true can help you better understand the story. You can check another source, such as a dictionary or an encyclopedia.

- Look up the word *hibernate* in a dictionary. Read the definition and then check how the word is used in the story. Does the story make sense?

- Look up Bats in an encyclopedia. Find additional information about places where bats live to help you better understand the story.

Writer's Craft

ANTONYMS AND SYNONYMS

Explain: Synonyms have almost the same meaning. Antonyms have opposite meanings.

Discuss: Synonyms and antonyms make stories more interesting to read. Synonyms help a writer avoid using the same words over and over, which can be boring to the reader. Antonyms help a writer make comparisons.

WRITING PARTNERS Write this on the board: "Bats get ready for hibernation by stuffing themselves full of food, especially in the last weeks of warm weather." Have partners work together to write the sentence again, using synonyms and/or antonyms for the underlined words.

In winter, many bats hibernate. This means the bats sleep deeply. While bats are hibernating, their breathing slows down and their heart rate drops from 900 to 20 beats a minute. Hibernating bats need less energy to stay alive.

 Bats get ready for hibernation by stuffing themselves full of food, especially in the last weeks of warm weather. Their bodies store the extra food as fat. This fat will be their food through the winter.

106

LANGUAGE SUPPORT

ESL In discussing pages 106 and 107, ask children if they know of other animals that hibernate (bears, squirrels, groundhogs, frogs). For each animal named, ask: Where would this animal go to hibernate? (Bears go to caves, squirrels go to hollow tree trunks, groundhogs go to holes in the ground, frogs go to pond bottoms.)

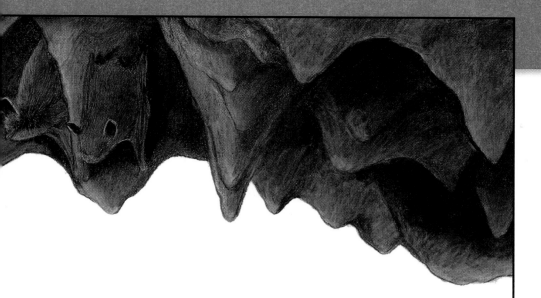

Sometimes when people explore caves, they kill bats by accident. If you went into a cave where bats were hibernating, you would wake them up. Then they would fly to another part of the cave. Each time that happens, the bats use up about a month's supply of fat. If they use up too much stored food, they will starve before spring, when they can hunt again. **19**

107

Comprehension

19 What is the biggest problem facing bats when people explore caves? (If the bats are hibernating and people startle them, they fly away and use up the body fat they need to stay alive.) **What might be a solution to this problem?** (people staying out of caves when bats are hibernating; people being careful and quiet when exploring)
Problem and Solution

Minilesson

REVIEW/MAINTAIN

Form Generalizations

Review that a generalization is a broad statement that applies to many examples. For example, based on the information in the selection about the dangers of disturbing bats while they are hibernating, you might form the generalization: Hibernating animals should not be disturbed.

Activity Invite children to use the information on page 106 to form a generalization about what animals do to get ready to hibernate.

Comprehension

20 Why are several kinds of bats in danger of dying out? (People are destroying their homes.) *Cause and Effect*

21 Read the third sentence in the last paragraph on this page. What does *feast* mean? Do mosquitoes really "feast on us"? Why does the author write that? (The author is using descriptive language to help readers understand that because there are more mosquitoes, we get more mosquito bites!) *Author's Craft*

Fluency

GROUP READING

Model tracking print and rereading to achieve fluency.

- Point to and read aloud the first few words in the first sentence on page 108.
- Run your finger under each word as you read the rest of the sentence without pausing.
- Then have children repeat the process, pointing to each word as they read. Repeat until children achieve fluency.
- To reinforce meaning, have children tell in their own words what they have just read.

If you go into a cave in June or July, be sure to look for baby bats. If you do see pups, never touch or bother them. Leave quickly and quietly.

Bats are mammals. They are the only flying animals that nurse. This means that the mothers' bodies make milk to feed their babies. Bat pups hang together in large groups called nurseries. Each mother returns to feed her pup at least twice a night. The pups need their mothers' milk to survive. If you disturb a nursery cave, the frightened mothers may leave, and the pups will starve.

Besides disturbing their caves, people harm bats by destroying their homes. People close off their attics and tear down old barns. They seal off empty mines and cut down forests, where bats like to live.

20 Several kinds of bats are now in danger of dying out. In some places there aren't enough bats left to keep down the number of insect **21** pests. Farmers lose crops, and mosquitoes feast on us. People could use poisons to kill bugs, but **22** poisons can be dangerous to humans, other animals, and plants.

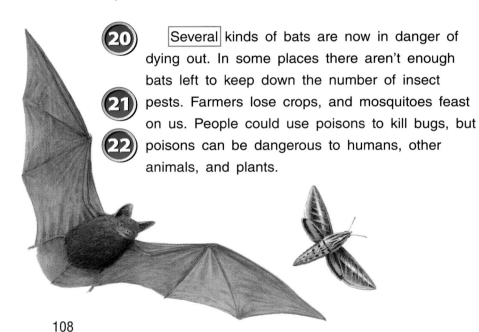

108

Comprehension

22 Why are bats a better way to control bugs than using poison? (Because the poison can be harmful to people and other animals.) *Compare and Contrast*

23 Why is putting a gate over a cave a solution to the problem of bats dying out? (People won't accidentally wander into a cave where bats are hibernating.) *Problem and Solution*

24 Do you think more people are beginning to help bats, instead of being afraid of them? *Make Predictions*

There are many ways people can help bats.

Some people put bat houses in their yards. Public parks and nature centers may have houses for large groups of bats.

Groups who care about wild animals are putting gates on cave entrances. Bats can zip easily through gates, but people can't.

109

Minilesson

REVIEW/MAINTAIN

Main Idea

Remind children that the main idea:

- tells what a book or story is about.
- can be told in one or two sentences.

Work with children to write a sentence or two that tells the main idea of this selection. Have them:

- reread the title.
- think about what they see the bats doing in most of the illustrations.
- look through the selection and note key facts.

Activity Write the main idea of the selection within an outline of a bat. Have children suggest the supporting details. List each detail within the bat's wingspan.

109

Comprehension

(25) DRAW CONCLUSIONS Let's reread our charts. Can you draw conclusions about how the author feels about bats? (The author thinks bats are valuable creatures.)

Facts	→	Conclusions
• Bats hunt after the sun goes down. • Bats eat lots of insects. • Bats fly.	→	• Bats fly around at night so they can catch insects.
• Bats can hear things we can't. • Bats can tell the exact location of an insect. • Bats can zoom through caves and forests in the dark.	→	• Bats have excellent hearing.
• Bats eat insects that bite people. • Many bats are gentle and are scared of people. • Some bats are in danger of dying out.	→	• People should not be scared of bats.

RETELL THE STORY Ask small groups to review the bat facts they have learned. One child should retell the selection as the others in the group act out the facts. *Summarize*

In Midfield, Alabama, elementary school children can join the B.A.T. (Bats Are Terrific) club. Members help spread the word that bats are not scary.

110

STUDENT SELF-ASSESSMENT

REREADING FOR *Fluency*

ONE Children who need fluency practice can read along silently or chime in as the story is read aloud.

READING RATE When you evaluate reading rate, have children read aloud from the story for one minute. Place a stick-on note after the last word read. Count words read. To evaluate children's performance, see the Running Record in the **Fluency Assessment** book.

(i) Intervention ▶ For leveled fluency passages, lessons, and norm charts, see **Skills Intervention Guide**, Part 5, Fluency.

If a bat flies past you in the dark, listen closely. Maybe you can hear the soft, fast flutter of its wings before it's gone. Even if you can't, you can be sure that the bat heard you. **25**

111

Comprehension

Return to Predictions and Purposes

Reread children's predictions about the selection. Discuss predictions, noting which need to be revised. Then ask children if the selection answered the questions they had before they read.

PREDICTIONS	WHAT HAPPENED
This will be an article about bats.	The article was about bats.
The article will give facts about what bats eat and how they live.	The article gave facts about what bats eat, how they live, how they care for their young, and dangers they face from humans.

INFORMAL ASSESSMENT

HOW TO ASSESS

DIGRAPHS *tch* Have child review words from the selection that contain *tch* (*catch, stretches, high-pitched*). Encourage them to write and pronounce each practice word, and to circle the letter combination representing the /ch/ sound.

DRAW CONCLUSIONS Ask children to use the facts they have learned to draw conclusions about bats.

FOLLOW UP

DIGRAPHS *tch* Continue to model the blending of sounds in words that contain /ch/*tch*.

DRAWING CONCLUSIONS Children who are having difficulty can use the pictures from the selection as clues to help them remember facts and draw conclusions about bats.

LITERARY RESPONSE

QUICK-WRITE Invite children to draw a picture of a bat in their journals, and write two interesting facts they learned about bats.

ORAL RESPONSE Have children discuss these questions:

• What fact about bats did you find the most surprising?

• How are bats similar to other animals you know about?

• How are bats different from other animals you know about?

What other stories or books have you read about bats? Were they fact or fiction?

Story Questions

Have children discuss or write answers to the questions on page 112.

Answers:

1. Bats hunt at nighttime. *Literal/Detail*

2. It helps them avoid obstacles, and helps them hunt for insects. *Inferential/Detail*

3. Caves are good places for hibernation, and safe places to leave puppies (baby bats) when the adult bats leave to hunt for food. *Inferential/Drawing Conclusions*

4. Most bats aren't scary or dangerous to people and can even be helpful to people. *Critical/Summarize*

5. Both kinds of animals are feared and/or disliked for the wrong reasons. Both are very special and almost never harm people. *Critical/Reading Across Texts*

Write a Report For a full lesson on writing that compares see pages 115L–115M.

Story Questions & Activities

READ TOGETHER

1. What time of day do bats hunt?

2. Why is echolocation important for bats?

3. Why do bats live in caves?

4. What is the main idea of this selection?

5. Review the article "Sharks." In what way are both bats and sharks misunderstood creatures?

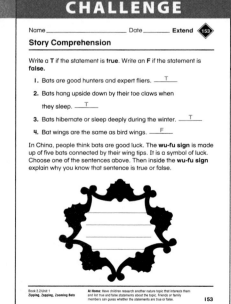

Write a Report

Compare bats with another kind of animal. How does the animal you chose live? How do they communicate? Do they hunt? Do they sleep all winter? What do they eat? Show what is alike about bats and your animal and what is different.

Meeting Individual Needs

EASY	ON-LEVEL	CHALLENGE

Name_____ Date_____ **Reteach** 153

Story Comprehension

Think about "Zipping, Zapping, Zooming Bats." Then complete the chart. *Answers may vary.*

What and When They Hunt
hunt insects; hunt at night

How They Use Sound
make high beeping sounds and use echoes to find food

BATS

Where They Live
in old buildings, trees, and in caves

Why They Are in Danger
People have destroyed bat homes by cutting trees, tearing down buildings, and sealing caves.

Book 2.2/Unit 1
Zipping, Zapping, Zooming Bats

At Home: Have children think of other animals that are endangered and ways to protect these animals.

153

Name_____ Date_____ **Practice** 153

Story Comprehension

Think about "Zipping, Zapping, Zooming Bats." Finish each sentence by underlining the answer.

1. Bats come out to hunt _____.
   a. when the sun goes down
   b. in the daytime

2. Bats eat lots of _____.
   a. peanut butter
   b. insects

3. Bats use _____ to help them hunt.
   a. their eyes
   b. sounds

4. When bats sleep, they _____.
   a. hang upside down
   b. keep their eyes open

5. Bats _____ with their tongues and claws.
   a. clean themselves
   b. hunt in the daytime

6. Many bats _____ during winter.
   a. move
   b. sleep

7. Bats are the only flying _____.
   a. mammals
   b. birds

8. Some kinds of bats are _____.
   a. living at the North Pole
   b. in danger of dying out

Book 2.2/Unit 1
Zipping, Zapping, Zooming Bats

At Home: Have children write about one or two things they learned from the story.

153

Name_____ Date_____ **Extend** 153

Story Comprehension

Write a **T** if the statement is **true**. Write an **F** if the statement is **false**.

1. Bats are good hunters and expert fliers. ___T___

2. Bats hang upside down by their toe claws when they sleep. ___T___

3. Bats hibernate or sleep deeply during the winter. ___T___

4. Bat wings are the same as bird wings. ___F___

In China, people think bats are good luck. The **wu-fu sign** is made up of five bats connected by their wing tips. It is a symbol of luck. Friends or guests can guess whether the statements are true or false. Choose one of the sentences above. Then inside the **wu-fu sign** explain why you know that sentence is true or false.

Book 2.2/Unit 1
Zipping, Zapping, Zooming Bats

At Home: Have children research another nature topic that interests them and list true and false statements about the topic. Friends or family members can guess whether the statements are true or false.

153

Reteach, 153   **Practice, 153**   **Extend, 153**

Make a Bat Flip Book

Use about ten index cards. Draw a bat in the middle of the first card. Continue drawing a bat on each card, making the wings a little bit higher or lower. Staple the cards on one side, making sure to keep them in order. Flip the pages and your bat will appear to zip and zoom!

Bat Math

Some bats eat half their weight in bugs in one night! If a flying fox bat weighed two pounds, how many pounds of bugs would it have to eat to get full?

Find Out More

Bats are animals that are active at night. Find out about another animal that is active at night. Where does it live? What does it eat? How does it find its way in the dark?

113

DAILY **Phonics** ROUTINES

DAY 3 **Letter Substitution**
Invite pairs of children to make new *ph* and *tch* words from the words *match* and *phone*, by changing one or more letters at a time.

Phonics CD-ROM

Story Activities

Make a Bat Flip Book

Materials: 10 index cards per child; pencils, stapler

GROUP Before children draw, use a sample flip book to model flipping through the cards. Then let children see pages individually, so they can understand the idea of drawing incremental motions. Let them know that movies are made of thousands of still pictures much like this—a movie is like a high-technology flip book!

Bat Math

Materials: paper, pencils

ONE Help children to arrive at the answer: one pound of insects. (If a bat weighs two pounds, half its weight would be one pound.) Invite children to create a "dinner party menu" for four bats, each weighing two pounds. (The menu would add up to four total pounds of insects.) Remind children that using paper and pencil can make adding easier.

Find Out More

RESEARCH AND INQUIRY Ask children to work with partners to conduct **PARTNERS** research about bats and other nocturnal animals.

interNET CONNECTION Children can learn more about bats and other nocturnal animals by visiting **www.mhschool.com/reading.**

FORMAL ASSESSMENT

After page 113 see Selection Assessment.

113

Study Skills

GRAPHIC AIDS

OBJECTIVES Children will read information from a map of the world.

PREPARE Ask children to look at the map on page 114. Display **Teaching Chart 129.**

TEACH Remind children that a map is a picture of a region or regions of land. Maps can show the shape of the land, the bodies of water around it or nearby, city names, whether there are roads, and other information, depending on the kind of map it is. Some maps, like this one, tell where certain animals live.

PRACTICE Have children answer questions 1–5, and review the answers with them.
1. where different kinds of bats live **2.** Asia.
3. Hog-nosed bats **4.** California leaf-nosed bats, Mexican free-tailed bat **5.** The map tells where each kind of bat lives.

ASSESS/CLOSE Have children use the world map to locate the name of the continent where flying fox bats live. (Australia)

Study Skills

READ TOGETHER

Read a Map

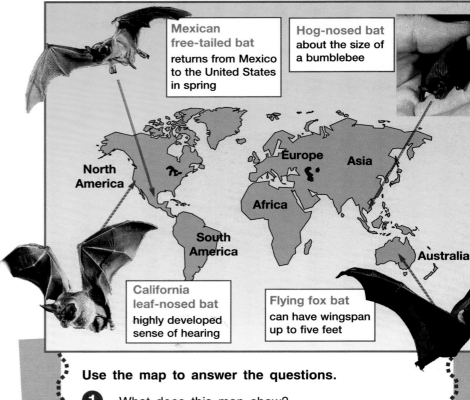

Mexican free-tailed bat returns from Mexico to the United States in spring

Hog-nosed bat about the size of a bumblebee

North America

Europe   Asia

Africa

South America

Australia

California leaf-nosed bat highly developed sense of hearing

Flying fox bat can have wingspan up to five feet

Use the map to answer the questions.

1. What does this map show?

2. Where does the hog-nosed bat live?

3. Which kind of bat is the smallest?

4. Which kinds of bats live in North America?

5. How does the map help you learn about bats?

Meeting Individual Needs

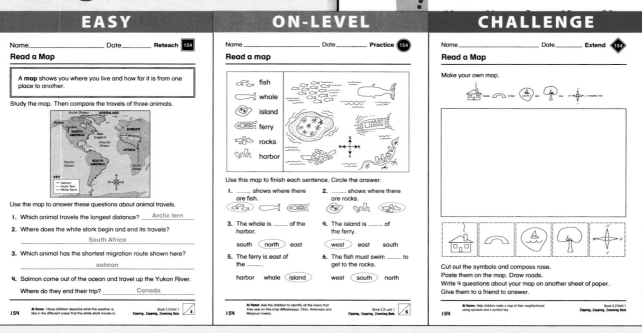

EASY

Name_____ Date_____ Reteach 154
Read a Map

A **map** shows you where you live and how far it is from one place to another.

Study the map. Then compare the travels of three animals.

Use the map to answer these questions about animal travels.

1. Which animal travels the longest distance? ___Arctic tern___

2. Where does the white stork begin and end its travels?
   ___South Africa___

3. Which animal has the shortest migration route shown here?
   ___salmon___

4. Salmon come out of the ocean and travel up the Yukon River. Where do they end their trip? ___Canada___

ON-LEVEL

Name_____ Date_____ Practice 154
Read a map

fish
whale
island
ferry
rocks
harbor

Use this map to finish each sentence. Circle the answer.

1. ___ shows where there are fish.

2. ___ shows where there are rocks.

3. The whale is ___ of the harbor.
   south (north) east

4. The island is ___ of the ferry.
   (west) east south

5. The ferry is east of the ___.
   harbor whale (island)

6. The fish must swim ___ to get to the rocks.
   west (south) north

CHALLENGE

Name_____ Date_____ Extend 154
Read a Map

Make your own map.

Cut out the symbols and compass rose.
Paste them on the map. Draw roads.
Write 4 questions about your map on another sheet of paper.
Give them to a friend to answer.

Reteach, 154   Practice, 154   Extend, 154

TEST POWER

Look back in the story for clues if a question is hard for you.

DIRECTIONS:

Read the story. Then read each question about the story.

SAMPLE

The Dinner Guest

John's family was making dinner. They were expecting John's uncle for dinner.

"John, could you please help me?" his mother asked.

John washed the dishes. Then he set the table. He put the forks, knives, and spoons next to the dishes. John was excited to see his uncle. He lived far away in Japan, and John had not seen him for a long time. But John had good memories of his uncle's visits. He always brought something interesting from Japan for John and his sister.

1 John is—
- happy about his uncle's visit
- ○ confused about how to set the table
- ○ ready to go to school
- ○ hungry for dinner

2 Where did John put the forks, knives, and spoons?
- ○ Back in the drawer
- ○ Into the sink
- ○ Into the dishwasher
- Next to the dishes on the table

Test Power

THE PRINCETON REVIEW

Read the Page

Explain to children that you will be reading this story as a group. You will read the story, and they will follow along in their books.

Request that children put pens, pencils, and markers away, since they will not be writing in their books.

Discuss the Questions

QUESTION 1: Have children look for words that describe feeling or emotion. The seventh sentence says that John was excited to see his uncle.

QUESTION 2: Instruct the children to reread the story and look for mention of utensils. Ask: *What does the story say?*

Leveled Books

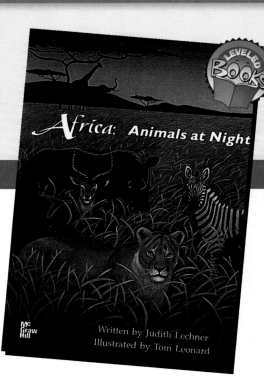

EASY

Africa: Animals at Night

- ☑ **Phonics** Digraphs *ph,tch*
- ☑ **Draw Conclusions**
- ☑ **Instructional Vocabulary:** *disturb, explore, fact, nature, object, several*

Written by Judith Lechner
Illustrated by Tom Leonard

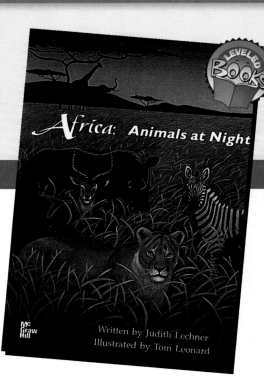

Guided Reading

PREVIEW AND PREDICT Have children look at the illustrations up to page 7. As they take the **picture walk**, have children predict what the animals might be about to do. Write children's responses on the chalkboard.

SET PURPOSES Have children write several sentences describing what they hope to learn about animals, and Africa, as they read *Africa: Animals at Night*.

READ THE BOOK Use questions like the following to guide children's reading or to ask after they have read the story independently:

Pages 2–3: Find the word *facts*. Read the sentence in which you find the word *facts* to see if you can tell what the word means. *Vocabulary*

Pages 5–6: What do hippos, rhinos, and elephants have in common? (all large animals) How are these animals different? (Elephants sleep at night; rhinos and hippos sleep during the day.) *Compare and Contrast*

Page 6: Can you find a name of an animal with the *ph* sound in it? (*elephant*) *Phonics and Decoding*

Pages 12–13: What conclusions can you draw about leopards, lions, and zebras after reading this page? (lions and leopards eat zebras.) *Draw Conclusions*

RETURN TO PREDICTIONS AND PURPOSES Discuss children's predictions. Ask which were close to the story and why.

LITERARY RESPONSE Discuss these questions:

- What was your favorite animal in the story?
- What new facts did you learn?

Also see the story questions and activity in *Africa: Animals at Night*.

See the **Phonics** **CD-ROM** for practice using words with /f/ *ph*, /ch/ *tch*.

Answers to Story Questions

1. Zebras, giraffes, elephants, hippos, and rhinos.
2. He probably got the fruit from the tree and is eating it.
3. Their mother will teach them how to hunt.
4. At night, some animals hunt, some eat grass and plants, and others sleep. Animals must hide well and watch out for danger at night.
5. Answers will vary.

The Story Questions and Activity below appear in the Easy Book.

Story Questions and Writing Activity

1. Name three animals that eat grass.
2. Look at page 7. Where did the bush baby get the fruit? What is he doing with the fruit?
3. What do you think the baby lions will do at night when they get older?
4. What is the main idea of this book?
5. If a bat from *Zipping Zapping Zooming Bats* could talk with one of the night animals in this book, which one do you think it would choose, and why?

An African Animal

Draw a picture of an animal you read about.

Write a sentence telling something you learned about the animal.

from *Africa: Animals at Night*

Leveled Books

INDEPENDENT

The Mystery Mess

- ☑ **Phonics** Digraphs *ph,tch*
- ☑ **Draw Conclusions**
- ☑ **Instructional Vocabulary:** *disturb, explore, fact, nature, object, several*

Guided Reading

PREVIEW AND PREDICT Take a **picture walk** with children through page 7 of the story. Have them pay particular attention to the expressions on the faces of Carlos and Aunt Sara. Have children predict what the story will be about. Chart their ideas.

SET PURPOSES Have children write a few sentences explaining why they want to read *The Mystery Mess*. For example: I want to find out why Carlos looks upset.

READ THE BOOK Use questions like the following to guide children's reading or to ask after they have read the story independently:

Page 4: Find the word *facts* on the page. What are the facts Carlos's aunt is talking about? *Vocabulary*

Page 4: Look at the expressions on the faces of Carlos and Aunt Sara. How are they different? What are their expressions telling us about the way they feel? *Compare and Contrast*

Page 7: Look at the word *phone*. What two letters does the word *phone* begin with?

(ph) What sound do the letters *ph* make when you blend them together? (/f/) *Phonics and Decoding*

Page 12: Why did Carlos tiptoe into the living room? (He wanted to surprise Raphael.) How did he know where to find Raphael? (He heard Raphael's bells jingling.) *Draw Conclusions*

RETURN TO PREDICTIONS AND PURPOSES Discuss children's predictions. Have children review their purposes for reading. Did they meet their goals?

LITERARY RESPONSE Discuss these questions:

- Who was your favorite character in the story, and why?
- How do you think Carlos and Aunt Sara will get along in the future?

Also see the story questions and activity in *The Mystery Mess*.

See the **Phonics** **CD-ROM** for practice using words with /f/ *ph*, /ch/ *tch*.

Answers to Story Questions

1. Raphael.
2. The ringing telephone was noisy, which gave him the idea to get a cat collar with bells.
3. Probably not now that the mystery has been solved. Otherwise the jingling would wake up Carlos and Aunt Sara every night.
4. How Carlos solved the mystery of who was making a mess in his aunt's living room early every morning.
5. Raphael can see well in the dark. Bats use echolocation.

The Story Questions and Activity below appear in the Independent Book.

Story Questions and Writing Activity

1. What is the name of Aunt Sara's cat?
2. How did the telephone ringing help Carlos?
3. Do you think that Raphael will continue to wear the collar with bells?
4. What is story mostly about?
5. How do you think Raphael is able to get around in the dark? How is that different from the way bats are able to find their way?

Big Builder

In *The Mystery Mess*, Carlos enjoys building things with blocks. What is your favorite thing to build or make? Draw a picture of yourself making this item. Then write a sentence telling about what you are making.

from The Mystery Mess

Leveled Books

CHALLENGE

Night Animal, Day Animal

- ☑ **Phonics** Digraphs *ph,tch*
- ☑ **Draw Conclusions**
- ☑ **Instructional Vocabulary:** *disturb, explore, fact, nature, object, several*

Guided Reading

PREVIEW AND PREDICT Discuss the illustrations up to page 5 of the story. As you take the **picture walk**, have children predict the kind of information they will gather from this story. List the information.

SET PURPOSES Have children write what they hope to learn from reading *Night Animal, Day Animal*.

READ THE BOOK Use questions like the following to guide children's reading or to ask after they have read the story independently:

Pages 4–5: Find the word *disturb*. Read the sentence in which the word appears and tell what it means. *Vocabulary*

Page 6: Find the word *catching*. Which letter combination, *ph*, *tch*, or *ch*, is in this word? *(tch)* Pronounce the word. *Phonics and Decoding*

Pages 6–7: How is the behavior of bears and bobcats different? (Bears sleep at night; bobcats hunt at night.) *Compare and Contrast*

Pages 10–11: What do snakes and lizards have in common? (live in desert) How are

they different? (Snake hides from sun; lizard doesn't mind it.) *Compare and Contrast*

Page 15: What animals are wide awake while you are asleep at night? (might include fox, raccoon, bobcat, owl, cat, snake, coyote) *Draw Conclusions*

RETURN TO PREDICTIONS AND PURPOSES Discuss children's predictions about what they expected to learn from the story.

LITERARY RESPONSE Discuss these questions:

- What was the most interesting thing you learned from this story?

- Have you ever seen a wild animal sleeping? Where and when?

Also see the story questions and activity in *Night Animal, Day Animal*.

See the **Phonics** CD-ROM for practice using words with /f/ *ph*, /ch/ *tch*.

Answers to Story Questions

1. Fox, bobcat, owl, raccoon, cat, lizard, coyote.
2. Because he has big eyes for seeing well in the dark and big ears for hearing.
3. No, because raccoons are nocturnal animals and deer are awake during the day.
4. Some animals are up during the day, while others sleep. At night, some animals hunt or eat grass and plants, while others sleep.
5. Answers will vary.

The Story Questions and Activity below appear in the Challenge Book.

Story Questions and Writing Activity

1. Name three animals that hunt at night.
2. Why is the owl such a good night hunter?
3. Do you think raccoons and deer see each other often in the forest?
4. What is the main idea of this book?
5. Which animals in this book are the most like bats? Which are the most different? Explain why.

What Do You Know?

Look at the chart on page 16. Write two sentences about one day animal and one night animal using facts you learned. Draw a picture to illustrate your sentences.

from Night Animal, Day Animal

Bringing Groups Together

Anthology and Leveled Books

Connecting Texts

CHARACTER CHARTS
Write the story titles on a chart. Discuss with children the behavior of the different animals in each book. Call on volunteers from each reading level and write their suggestions on the chart.

Use the chart to discuss animal behavior.

Titles	Animal	Character	Traits
Zipping, Zapping, Zooming Bats	Bats use sound in a special way.	Bats fly at night.	Bats are good hunters.
Africa: Animals at Night	Rhinos sleep most of the day and eat all night.	Giraffes sleep standing up.	Lions are good hunters. They see well in the dark.
The Mystery Mess	Cats sleep during the day.	Cats are active at night.	Cats like to nap in the same place.
Night Animal, Day Animal	Woodpeckers make holes in trees to catch insects.	Bobcats hunt at night. They see well in the dark.	Owls can turn their heads almost all the way around to watch animals.

Viewing/Representing

GROUP PRESENTATIONS Divide the class into groups, one for each of the four books read in the lesson. Have each group work together to pantomime the activity of one or more of the animals in the story chosen.

AUDIENCE RESPONSE Ask children to watch each group's presentation and try to identify the animals being pantomimed. Allow time for questions after each group presentation.

Research and Inquiry

MORE ABOUT ANIMALS AT NIGHT Have children review what they already know about animals at night. Then invite them to learn more about nocturnal animals by:

- Looking for information about nocturnal animals in the school library.

- Working with classmates to make a mural of the nocturnal animals they have learned about.

- Visiting a museum that features animal exhibits.

inter NET CONNECTION Have children log on to **www.mhschool.com/reading** for links to sites about nocturnal animals.

 Children can write and draw what they have learned in their journals.

OBJECTIVES

Children will:

• review words with /f/*ph*, /ch/*tch*.

• blend and read *ph* and *tch* words.

....

MATERIALS

• **Teaching Chart 130**

....

Skills Finder

Digraphs *ph*, *tch*

Introduce	B2: 92G-H
Review	B2: 115E-F, 116G-H, 250G-H, 281E-F
Test	B2: Unit 2

ALTERNATE TEACHING STRATEGY

....

REVIEW DIGRAPHS

ph*, *tch

For a different approach to teaching this skill, see pages T75 and T76.

....

LANGUAGE SUPPORT

ESL Remind children that some letter combinations, like *tch* and *ph*, work together to spell a single sound, rather than representing individual sounds.

Review Digraphs *ph*, *tch*

PREPARE

Review /f/ Spelled *ph* and /ch/ Spelled *tch*

• Tell children they will review the sounds that *ph* and *tch* spell.

• Say *phone* and have children write the letters that spell /f/.

• Say *pitch* and have children write the letters that spell /ch/.

TEACH

Build /f/*ph* and /ch/*tch* Words

• Tell children they will use their knowledge of the /f/ and /ch/ sounds and their symbols to indentify words with *ph* and *tch*.

• Display **Teaching Chart 130**.

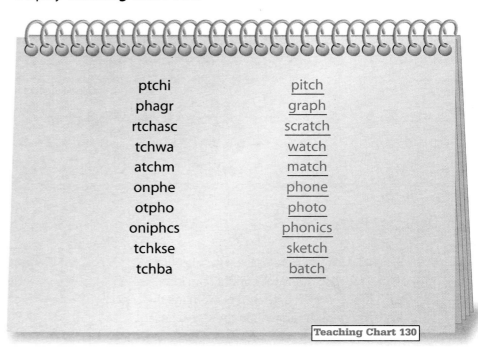

ptchi	pitch
phagr	graph
rtchasc	scratch
tchwa	watch
atchm	match
onphe	phone
otpho	photo
oniphcs	phonics
tchkse	sketch
tchba	batch

Teaching Chart 130

BLENDING Model and Guide Practice with /f/ and /ch/ Words

• Explain to children that the words on the left are all words with the /f/ and /ch/ sound, only the letters have been scrambled. Their knowledge of the symbols for /f/ and /ch/ will help them unscramble the words correctly.

• Work with children to unscramble the first word on the **Teaching Chart** to form the word *pitch*.

Use the Word in Context

• Have volunteers use the unscrambled word in a sentence to reinforce its meaning. Example: *When we camp, we like to pitch our tent.*

Repeat the Procedure

• Follow the same procedure to unscramble the remaining words on the chart.

PRACTICE

IDENTIFYING
Play "I Spy" with
***tch* and *ph* Words**

GROUP

Invite small groups of children to play a game in which they must give clues for words containing *tch* or *ph* letter combinations. For example: *I am thinking of something with a receiver on the end.* (telephone) The other group members will guess what the person is thinking of. Tell children to keep a list of the objects. Help children to classify words into word families. ▶ **Logical/Linguistic/Auditory**

ASSESS/CLOSE

Recognize
Sounds and
Symbols in *ph*
and *tch* Words

To assess children's mastery of blending and reading words that contain *ph* and *tch*, observe them as they complete the Practice activity. Ask children to refer to their lists and point out those letters representing the /ch/ or /f/ sounds. Have them use the words in sentences.

ADDITIONAL PHONICS RESOURCES

McGraw-Hill School
TECHNOLOGY

Phonics/Phonemic Awareness
Practice Book,
pages 103–106

 **CD-ROM**

activities for practice
with Discriminating and
Segmenting words

DAY 4
Fluency Write the following words on the chalkboard: *phone, phonics, pitched, itch*. Point to each word, asking children to blend the sounds silently. Ask a volunteer to read aloud each word.

 CD-ROM

SPELLING/PHONICS
CONNECTIONS
Words with *ph* and *tch*: See the 5-Day Spelling Plan, pages 115Q–115R.

i **Intervention** ▶ **Skills**
Intervention Guide, for direct instruction and extra practice of Digraphs *ph, tch*

Meeting Individual Needs for Phonics

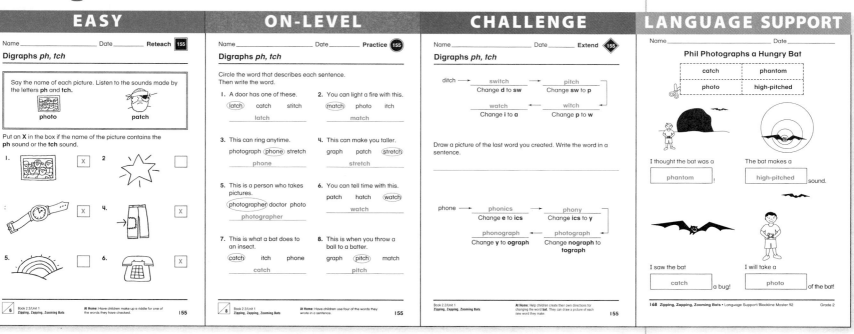

EASY	ON-LEVEL	CHALLENGE	LANGUAGE SUPPORT
Reteach, 155	Practice, 155	Extend, 155	Language Support, 168

OBJECTIVES

Children will:

- read words with /ch/*tch*; /ô/*aw, au, a*; /s/*ce*; /j/*ge*.

MATERIALS

- **Teaching Chart 131**

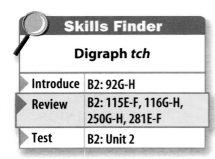

Skills Finder

Digraph *tch*

Introduce	B2: 92G-H
Review	B2: 115E-F, 116G-H, 250G-H, 281E-F
Test	B2: Unit 2

Review *tch*; /ô/; soft *c, g*

PREPARE

Discriminate Sounds

Say aloud, one by one, the following groups of words:

- claws, Austin, <u>care</u> (/ô/)
- catch, stretches, <u>moth</u> (/ch/)
- large, <u>sell</u>, change (/j/)
- <u>cook</u>, places, twice (/s/)

Ask children to identify the sound that two of the words in each group have in common. Then have them identify the word that does not contain this sound.

TEACH

BLENDING
Model and Guide Practice
with /ch/ *tch*, /ô/
***au, aw, a*; /s/ *ce*;**
/j/ *ge*

- Display **Teaching Chart 131**. Invite children to identify which letter combination can be added to create the first word. Write *ge* in the space. With children, blend the letters together and read aloud *large*.

l a r <u>ge</u>	<u>ph</u> one	m a <u>tch</u>
ph ge	ge ph	ge tch
c r <u>aw</u>l	d r <u>aw</u> n	chan <u>ge</u>
au aw	aw au	tch ge
t w i <u>ce</u>*	p a <u>ge</u>	pl a <u>ce</u>
ce tch	ph ge	tch ce

*other possible answer: twitch

Teaching Chart 131

Use Words in Context

- Use the words in context to reinforce their meanings. Example: *An elephant is a large animal.*

Repeat the Procedure

- Repeat the procedure, adding letter combinations to complete and read the remaining words on the chart.

PRACTICE

DISCRIMINATING
Recognize and Write Words

GROUP

Have children draw 4"x4" grids on paper. Explain that the class is going to play Bingo. The first person to complete a row with four /ch/ words, four /ô/ words, four /j/ words, or four /s/ words will win. To win, all words must be spelled correctly. Read aloud a series of about 25 words, including at least five words containing letter combinations representing the winning sounds. ▶ **Linguistic/Logical**

ASSESS/CLOSE

Read and Use Words with /ch/, /ô/, /j/, or /s/ in a Sentence

To ensure that children can comfortably identify and decode /ch/, /ô/, /s/ and /j/ words, have them read aloud words from their completed Bingo sheets. Then have children use all four of their "winning words" in a sentence.

ADDITIONAL PHONICS RESOURCES

Phonics/Phonemic Awareness
Practice Book
pages 103–106

McGraw-Hill School
TECHNOLOGY

 CD-ROM
activities for practice with
Blending and Discriminating
words

DAILY Phonics ROUTINES

DAY 5
Writing Have pairs of children create silly rhymes with *ph* and *tch* words. (Example: *Answer the phone, then give the elephant a bone.*)

 **CD-ROM**

ALTERNATE TEACHING STRATEGY

tch; /ô/; SOFT *c, g*

For a different approach to teaching these skills, see pages T69, T70, T72, T73, and T76.

Intervention ▶ **Skills**
Intervention Guide, for direct instruction and extra practice in *tch, /ô/,* Soft *c,* and Soft *g*

Meeting Individual Needs for Phonics

EASY	ON-LEVEL	CHALLENGE	LANGUAGE SUPPORT

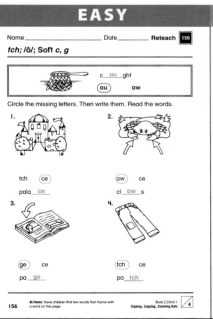

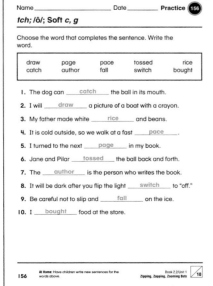

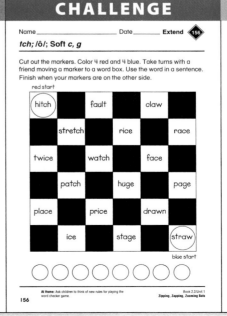

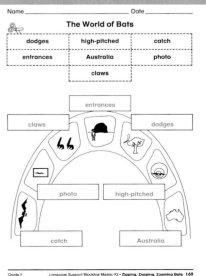

Reteach, 156   Practice, 156   Extend, 156   Language Support, 169

115H

OBJECTIVES

Children will:
- compare and contrast familiar items.
- use a Venn diagram.

Skills Finder

Compare and Contrast

Introduce	B2: 67I-J
Review	B2: 115I-J, 125E-F
Test	B2: Unit 1

TEACHING TIP

COMPARE AND CONTRAST Remind children that "comparing" means looking for similarities, while "contrasting" means looking for differences.

SELF-SELECTED Reading

Children may choose from the following titles.

ANTHOLOGY

- *Zipping, Zapping, Zooming Bats*

LEVELED BOOKS

- *Africa: Animals at Night*
- *The Mystery Mess*
- *Night Animal, Day Animal*

Bibliography, pages T88–T89

Review Compare and Contrast

PREPARE

Review the Concept
Tell children that looking at how two things are alike and different can help them to better understand both things. Explain that children will use a Venn diagram to help them compare and contrast bats and birds.

TEACH

Compare and Contrast Bats and Birds

Bats vs. Birds

Bats and birds seem a lot alike. They both have wings, fly, and live in similar places. But they have big differences. Most strikingly, bats are mammals, like humans, while birds belong to the bird family. Also, while bats are furry, birds have feathers. They even use a branch differently--birds perch upright, while bats hang upside down!

Teaching Chart 132

Display **Teaching Chart 132**. Have children read "*Bats vs. Birds*," then ask them to use facts from this passage and *Zipping, Zapping, Zooming Bats* to compare and contrast the two. Suggest they think of things they would add to a Venn diagram.

MODEL First I'm going to think about what is alike about birds and bats. They both have wings and fly, and they live in similar places. These facts belong in the middle of the Venn diagram. Now I'm going to pay attention to what's different about them. A bat is a mammal, while a bird belongs to the bird family. Birds are feathery, while bats are furry. These are ways bats and birds are different, so they go on the sides of the Venn diagram.

PRACTICE

Use a Venn Diagram

In small groups, invite children to compare and contrast cats and dogs. Encourage children to record differences and similarities in a Venn diagram. ▶ **Logical/Spatial**

GROUP

ASSESS/CLOSE

Compare and Contrast Cats and Dogs

Invite each group to share their Venn diagrams with the class, comparing and contrasting the answers each group recorded about similarities and differences between cats and dogs.

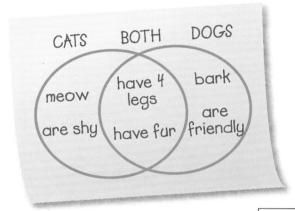

Graphic Organizer 14

ALTERNATE TEACHING STRATEGY

COMPARING AND CONTRASTING

For a different approach to teaching this skill, see page T71.

Intervention ▶ **Skills**

Intervention Guide, for direct instruction and extra practice in comparing and contrasting

Meeting Individual Needs for Comprehension

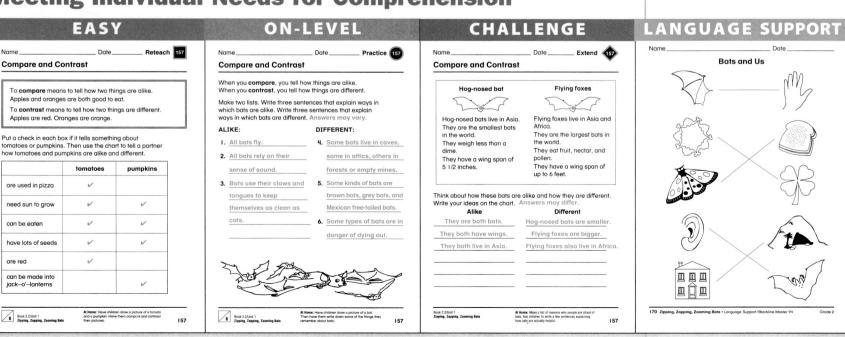

EASY	ON-LEVEL	CHALLENGE	LANGUAGE SUPPORT
Reteach, 157	Practice, 157	Extend, 157	Language Support, 170

115J

OBJECTIVES

Children will:

- read words with inflectional endings *-er* and *-est*.
- identify base words in words with inflectional endings.

MATERIALS
- **Teaching Chart 133**

Skills Finder

Inflectional Endings

Introduce	B1: 35K-L
Review	B1: 55K-L, 123K-L; B2: 91K-L, 115K-L
Test	B1: Unit 1
Maintain	B2: 23

TEACHING TIP

INFLECTIONAL ENDINGS Find three books to compare. Hold up the first book and say *large*. Hold up the second book and say *larger*. Then hold up the third book and say *largest*.

Review Inflectional Endings

PREPARE

Demonstrate Meaning of Inflectional Endings *-er* and *-est*

Write *large*, *larger*, and *largest* on the chalkboard and point to the endings. Explain that the ending *-er* tells the reader that the word compares two things. The ending *-est* says that the word compares three or more things.

TEACH

Identify Base Words

Remind children that base words are words to which prefixes or suffixes have been added to create new words. For example, the base word of *quickly* is *quick*. Explain that finding the base word can help them figure out the meaning of a word ending in *-er* or *-est*.

This dog is smaller.

This dog is smallest.

This dog is the smallest dog of all.

Teaching Chart 133

Display **Teaching Chart 133**.

MODEL I can use what I know about base words to help me read words that end in *-er* and *-est*. The base word of smaller is small. When *-er* is added to a base word, it means the new word compares two things. Compared to the other dog, this dog is smaller.

Ask a volunteer to underline the base word in *smallest*. Invite children to use the strategy above to explain its meaning.

PRACTICE

Draw Word Meanings

PARTNERS

Have each partner fold a piece of paper into four equal boxes. In one box, each child should write three words—a describing word and the two new words formed by adding -er and -est to the word. In each of the other three boxes, have children illustrate one of the words they have written. Then have partners exchange papers and draw arrows from the words to the pictures illustrating them. Help children choose describing words that they can draw. ▶ **Logical/Spatial**

ASSESS/CLOSE

Use Base Words with Inflectional Endings

To assess children's understanding of base words and inflected endings -er and -est, observe their work on the Practice activity.

ALTERNATE TEACHING STRATEGY

INFLECTED ENDINGS -er AND -est

For a different approach to teaching this skill, see page T74.

i) Intervention ▶ Skills

Intervention Guide, for direct instruction and extra practice of inflectional endings

Meeting Individual Needs for Vocabulary

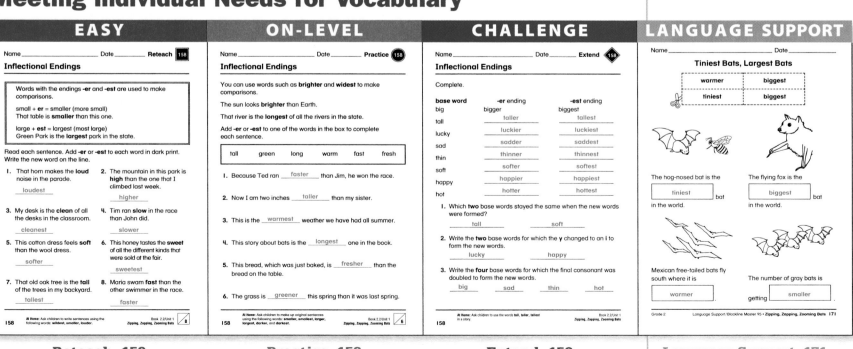

Reteach, 158   Practice, 158   Extend, 158   Language Support, 171

TEACHING TIP

Technology If you want to return to the beginning of the line you are writing, press the **home** key if your computer has one.

Handwriting Children should leave a margin on each side of the paper as they write their final copy. Remind them to look ahead to the end of each line to see if a word will fit. Tell them not to try to fit a word into a space that is too small.

**Handwriting
CD-ROM**

Writing That Compares

Prewrite

WRITE A REPORT Present this writing assignment: Compare bats with another kind of animal. How does the animal you chose live? How does it communicate? Does it hunt? Does it sleep all winter? What does it eat? Show how bats and your animal are alike and how they are different.

BRAINSTORM IDEAS Write these words on the chalkboard: *what, where, when, how, why,* and ask children to use these words to write questions about the animal they are comparing to a bat. Example: What do they eat?

Strategy: Use a Venn Diagram Encourage children to use Venn diagrams. Remind them to:

- Note similarities between the two animals, and write them in the center part of their Venn diagrams.
- Record differences between the two, and write them in the center part of the Venn diagrams.
- Record differences between the two on either side of the Venn diagram.

Draft

FREE WRITE Guide students to draft their ideas without self-editing. Children should use their diagrams to organize their facts. They might first focus on comparing the two animals, then focus on contrasting. Or, they might alternate similarities and differences, and so on. Suggest that children add details and use words that will appeal to the reader's sense of sight, smell, sound, and touch.

Revise

SELF-QUESTIONING Ask children to assess their drafts.

- Did I include similarities between bats and my animal? Did I include differences?
- Did I answer my questions?
- Did I use colorful describing words?

Have children trade reports with classmates for another point of view.

Edit/Proofread

TAKE ANOTHER LOOK Ask children to check spelling, grammar, and punctuation.

Publish

SHARE THE REPORTS Children can illustrate their reports, or read them aloud.

Bats and Owls
By Lucy Falcione

Two animals that sleep in the day and come out at night are bats and owls. They both catch food at night. Bats eat insects, and owls eat mice.

Bats and owls both have wings, and both can fly. The owl is a bird and its wings have feathers. The bat is a *mammal* and its wings have fine hair on them. Owls can hear well and have big eyes that help them see at night. Bats do not need good eyesight. They use echolocation to find their food.

Like most birds, owls live in trees. Many bats live in caves. In fact, they hang upside down in their caves all winter long. When spring comes, they wake up again.

Presentation Ideas

CREATE MODELS Using clay or other art supplies, have children create models of bats and their chosen animals.

▶ *Viewing/Representing*

NATURE SHOW Invite children to pretend they are hosting a nature show, and to tell the audience the differences between bats and another animal. They may use their Venn diagrams or reports.

▶ *Speaking/Listening*

Consider children's creative efforts, possibly adding a plus (+) for originality, wit, and imagination.

Scoring Rubric

Excellent	Good	Fair	Unsatisfactory
4: The writer	**3:** The writer	**2:** The writer	**1:** The writer
• uses supporting details to compare and contrast the animals.	• uses some supporting details to compare and contrast the animals.	• uses only a few supporting details to compare and contrast the animals.	• does not compare or contrast two animals.
• organizes information effectively.	• organizes information coherently.	• does not organize information coherently.	• does not organize information coherently.
• uses vivid, descriptive language.	• uses some descriptive language.	• does not use descriptive language.	• has not written in clear or complete sentences.

Incomplete **0:** The writer leaves the page blank or fails to respond to the writing task. The student does not address the topic or simply paraphrases the prompt. The response is illegible or incoherent.

Meeting Individual Needs for Writing

EASY

Label Pictures Have children draw pictures illustrating a bat and another animal, adding labels that note similarities and differences between the two.

ON-LEVEL

Compare Foods Have children write a short passage comparing and contrasting their favorite food with their least favorite food.

CHALLENGE

Diary Entry Invite children to pretend they are animals, and that they have just been "introduced" to a bat. Encourage them to write a diary entry in which they note their observations on how their new "friend" is different from themselves.

Listening and Speaking

LISTENING Have children

• look for how the models relate to the spoken information.

• listen for comparison/contrast words in the descriptions.

• sit quietly and save questions until the speaker is finished.

SPEAKING Remind children to

• use the voice to emphasize important details.

• use gestures to direct attention to the Venn diagrams.

• maintain eye contact with various areas of the room.

TEACHING TIP

MANAGERIAL Make sure to allot time for children to gather information.

Help children by repeating aloud questions from the writing assignment.

Invite children to include PORTFOLIO their reports or another writing project in their portfolios.

5 Day Grammar and Usage Plan

ESL Pretend you are calling a dog. Say "Come Fido." Ask, "What did I just do?" (You called the dog.) Then ask what Fido did. (He came. He did not come.) Explain that some verbs do not add -ed to form the past tense. Ask children to make up other sentences with verbs that do not use -ed to talk about past events.

DAILY LANGUAGE ACTIVITIES

Write the Daily Language Activities on the chalkboard each day or use **Transparency 19**. Read the sentences with children and have them orally correct each sentence.

Day 1
1. The bat comed out of the cave. came
2. Paul runned when he saw the bat. ran
3. Who comed to see the bat? came

Day 2
1. The bat singed last night. sang
2. Things around the bat gived off sound waves. gave
3. Tom singed a song about bats. sang

Day 3
1. Mark runned away from the bat. ran
2. The bat gived Jill a scare. gave
3. The sound waves comed back to the bat. came

Day 4
1. The bat comed out to hunt. came
2. Karen singed and scared the bats. sang
3. They runned through the caves. ran

Day 5
1. Sally gived me a toy bat. gave
2. What come out of the cave? came
3. The bats runned after the bugs. ran

> Daily Language Transparency 19

DAY 1 — Introduce the Concept

Oral Warm-Up Read these sentences: *Bert came to the door. Carla ran home.* Ask children to identify the verbs. Are they in the past tense or present tense?

Introduce Irregular Verbs Remind children that the past tense shows something that already happened.

Write the following on the chalkboard: *come/came, run/ran.* Explain that *came* and *ran* are the past tense of the verbs *come* and *run.*

More Irregular Verbs
- Some verbs do not add -ed to form the past tense. The verbs *come* and *run* have special forms in the past tense.

Present the Daily Language Activity and have children correct the sentences orally. Then write *came* and *ran* on the chalkboard and have children write a sentence using each verb.

 WRITING Assign the daily Writing Prompt on page 92C.

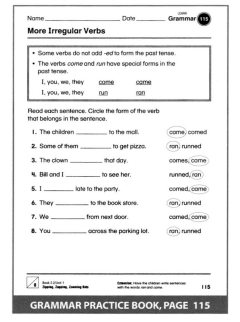

GRAMMAR PRACTICE BOOK, PAGE 115

DAY 2 — Teach the Concept

Review Irregular Verbs Ask children to give the past tense of *come* and *run.*

More Irregular Verbs Write the following on the chalkboard: *give/gave, sing/sang.* Explain that *gave* and *sang* are the past tense of the verbs *give* and *sing.*

More Irregular Verbs
- The verbs *give* and *sing* have special forms in the past tense.

Present the Daily Language Activity. Then have children write sentences using the past tense of the following verbs: *come, run, give, sing.*

 WRITING Assign the daily Writing Prompt on page 92C.

GRAMMAR PRACTICE BOOK, PAGE 116

More Irregular Verbs

Learn from the Literature Review irregular verbs. Read the first sentence on page 96 of *Zipping, Zapping, Zooming Bats*.

> **When the sun goes down, bats come out to hunt.**

Point out the verbs *goes* and *come*. Have children form the past tense of each verb. (*went, came*)

Write Irregular Verbs Present the Daily Language Activity and have children correct the sentences orally.

Write *come, run, give,* and *sing* on index cards, one verb per card. Give one card to each child and have children write a sentence using the verb on their cards.

 Assign the Daily Writing Prompt on page 92D.

Review Irregular Verbs Write the present-tense verbs from the Daily Language Activities for Days 1 through 3 on the chalkboard. Ask children to say the correct past tense of each verb and use it in a sentence.

Mechanics and Usage Before children begin the daily Writing Prompt on page 92D, review the rules for book titles. Display and discuss:

Titles

- Begin the first word and each important word in a title with a capital letter.

- Underline all the words in the title of a book.

 Assign the daily Writing Prompt on page 92D.

Assess Use the Daily Language Activity and page 119 of the **Grammar Practice Book** for assessment.

Reteach Write the following verbs on index cards: *come, run, give, sing, say, see, go,* and *do*. Repeat with *I, you, she, he, we,* and *they*. Have children take turns drawing a card from each pile and making up a sentence. Then ask children to rewrite the sentences in the past tense. For example: She sings well. She sang well.

Children can create a classroom word wall with their sentences.

Use page 120 of the **Grammar Practice Book** for additional reteaching.

 Assign the daily Writing Prompt on page 92D.

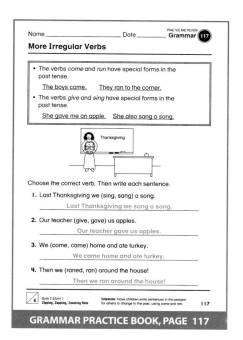

GRAMMAR PRACTICE BOOK, PAGE 117

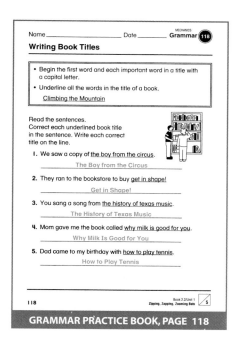

GRAMMAR PRACTICE BOOK, PAGE 118

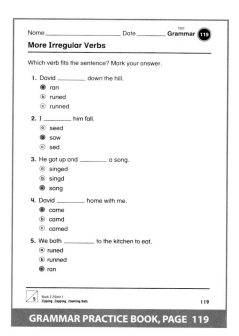

GRAMMAR PRACTICE BOOK, PAGE 119

115P

5 Day Spelling Plan

DICTATION SENTENCES

Spelling Words

1. The <u>phone</u> is blue.
2. He can <u>catch</u> fish.
3. <u>Each</u> coin is new.
4. She has a <u>patch</u> for her eye.
5. The <u>sandwich</u> is good.
6. He can <u>touch</u> the book.
7. Mom can light the <u>match</u>.
8. He made a <u>graph</u>.
9. Do you want to <u>pitch</u> or bat?
10. The <u>beach</u> is hot.

Challenge Words

11. Noise can <u>disturb</u> you.
12. He came to <u>explore</u>.
13. I like <u>nature</u>.
14. What are those <u>objects</u> on the desk?
15. There are <u>several</u> ducks in the pond.

DAY 1 — Pretest

Assess Prior Knowledge Use the Dictation Sentences at left and **Spelling Practice Book** page 115 for the pretest. Allow students to correct their own papers. If students have trouble, have partners give each other a midweek test on Day 3. Students who require a modified list may be tested on the first five words.

Spelling Words		Challenge Words
1. phone	6. **touch**	11. **disturb**
2. **catch**	7. match	12. **explore**
3. **each**	8. graph	13. **nature**
4. patch	9. **pitch**	14. **objects**
5. **sandwich**	10. beach	15. **several**

*Note: Words in **dark type** are from the story.*

Word Study On page 116 of the **Spelling Practice Book** are word study steps and an at-home activity.

DAY 2 — Explore the Pattern

Sort and Spell Words Say *graph, catch, beach.* Ask students to identify the sound they hear at the end of each word. Tell students that these words end with the letters *ph, tch,* and *ch.*

Ask students to read aloud the ten spelling words before sorting them according to vowel sounds.

Words with ph	Words with tch	Words with ch
phone	catch	each
graph	patch	sandwich
	match	touch
	pitch	beach

Word Wall Share with students journals and diaries of famous people (available from most public libraries). Have students look through the journals and diaries for new words with *ph, tch,* and *ch* and add them to the classroom word wall, underlining the spelling pattern in each word.

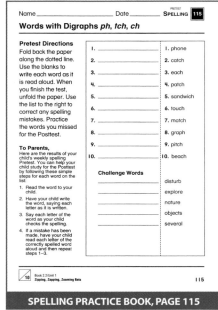

SPELLING PRACTICE BOOK, PAGE 115

WORD STUDY STEPS AND ACTIVITY, PAGE 116

SPELLING PRACTICE BOOK, PAGE 117

Words with Digraphs *ph, tch, ch*

Word Meaning: Plurals Remind students that *-s* is added to most nouns to make them plural, but when a word ends with *ch, -es* must be added. Write the nouns *match, patch, sandwich,* and *beach* from the spelling list. Have students write the plural of each of these nouns and use each plural in a sentence.

Glossary Have students:

write each Challenge Word.

look up the Challenge Words in the Glossary and find which ones have synonyms listed.

write a synonym for each appropriate Challenge Word.

Proofread Sentences Write these sentences on the chalkboard, including the misspelled words. Ask students to proofread, circling incorrect spellings and writing the correct spellings. There are two spelling errors in each sentence.

I can (tuch) the (fone). (touch, phone)

He can (pich), and you can (katch). (pitch, catch)

Have students create additional sentences with errors for partners to correct.

Have students use as many spelling words as possible in the daily Writing Prompt on page 92D. Remind students to proofread their writing for errors in spelling, grammar, and punctuation.

Assess Students' Knowledge Use page 120 of the **Spelling Practice Book** or the Dictation Sentences on page 115Q for the posttest.

Personal Word List If students have trouble with any words in the lesson, have them create a personal list of troublesome words in their journals. Have students write poems, using words from their personal word list.

Students should refer to their word lists during later writing activities.

Name _____ Date _____ PRACTICE AND EXTEND SPELLING 118

Words with Digraphs *ph, tch, ch*

| phone | each | sandwich | match | pitch |
| catch | patch | touch | graph | beach |

Write a spelling word to answer each question.

1. How can you talk to a friend? _phone_

2. What do you sometimes eat for lunch? _sandwich_

3. Where can you swim? _beach_

4. What can you use to fix a rip in your pants? _patch_

5. What can you use to show data? _graph_

6. What do people use to start a fire? _match_

Use the spelling words to complete the sentences.

7. If you _pitch_ the ball to Sam, he will _catch_ it.

8. _Each_ child will be able to _touch_ the bunny.

New Words
Add **es** to each of these words. Write the new word.

9. match + es = _matches_

10. patch + es = _patches_

11. sandwich + es = _sandwiches_

12. beach + es = _beaches_

118

Book 2.2/Unit 1
Zipping, Zapping, Zooming Bats 12

SPELLING PRACTICE BOOK, PAGE 118

Name _____ Date _____ PROOFREAD AND WRITE SPELLING 119

Words with Digraphs *ph, tch, ch*

Proofreading Activity
There are six spelling mistakes in the paragraph below. Circle each misspelled word. Write the words correctly on the lines below.

Every summer my family and I go to the (baech). We take lunch with us. (Eech) of us usually has a peanut butter (sandwich), a glass of lemonade, and some grapes. Then I go to (tutch) the water. If it is not cold, I go swimming. Last summer I couldn't use my inner tube because it needed a (pach). After swimming, we play ball. My father throws and I (katch). A day at the beach is a fun time for my family.

1. _beach_ 2. _Each_ 3. _sandwich_

4. _touch_ 5. _patch_ 6. _catch_

Writing Activity
Write sentences that tell about something that you would like to do next summer. Use four words from the spelling list.

_____

_____

_____

_____

10 Grade 2/Unit 1
Zipping, Zapping Zooming Bats

119

SPELLING PRACTICE BOOK, PAGE 119

Name _____ Date _____ POSTTEST SPELLING 120

Words with Digraphs *ph, tch, ch*

Look at the words in each set. One word in each set is spelled correctly. Use a pencil to color in the circle in front of that word. Before you begin, look at the sample sets of words. Sample A has been done for you. Do Sample B by yourself. When you are sure you know what to do, you may go on with the rest of the page.

Sample A
(A) sutch
(B) soch
(C) such
(D) sech

Sample B
(E) tawk
(F) tauk
(G) talk
(H) tolk

1. (A) pich
   (B) phitch
   (C) pitch
   (D) petch

2. (E) graf
   (F) graph
   (G) grafph
   (H) grph

3. (A) tuch
   (B) toutch
   (C) touch
   (D) tutch

4. (E) tach
   (F) pach
   (G) phatch
   (H) petch

5. (A) beesh
   (B) betch
   (C) beatch
   (D) beach

6. (E) fone
   (F) phone
   (G) fhone
   (H) phon

7. (A) sanwich
   (B) sandwitch
   (C) sanwhich
   (D) sandwich

8. (E) cach
   (F) catch
   (G) chatch
   (H) cetch

9. (A) eech
   (B) each
   (C) eatch
   (D) eetch

10. (E) mach
    (F) maach
    (G) metch
    (H) match

120

Book 2.2/Unit 1
Zipping, Zapping, Zooming Bats 10

SPELLING PRACTICE BOOK, PAGE 120

115R

Cumulative Review with **Expository Text**

Time to Review

Anthology

Going Batty for Bats

Selection Summary Children will learn how important bats are in nature, and why we have less to fear from them than they do from us.

Rhyme applies to phonics

INSTRUCTIONAL pages 118–125

Listening Library

Reread Leveled Books

EASY
Pages 125A and 125D
`DECODABLE`

INDEPENDENT
Pages 125B and 125D
 Take-Home version available

CHALLENGE
Pages 125C and 125D

Leveled Practice

EASY
Reteach, 159–166 Blackline masters with reteaching opportunities for each assessed skill

INDEPENDENT/ON-LEVEL
Practice, 159–166 Workbook with Take-Home stories and practice opportunities for each assessed skill and story comprehension

CHALLENGE
Extend, 159–166 Blackline masters that offer challenge activities for each assessed skill

Quizzes Prepared by Accelerated Reader

WORKSTATION Activities

Science . . . . **Make an Advertisement,** *123*

Make a Mobile of Bats, *123*

Language Arts . . **Read Aloud,** *116E*

Writing . . . . **Write a Speech,** *122*

Research and Inquiry . . . . . . **Find Out More,** *123*

Internet Activities . . . . www.mhschool.com/reading

Suggested Lesson Planner

READING AND LANGUAGE ARTS

	DAY 1 *Focus on Reading and Skills*	**DAY 2** *Read the Literature*

● **Phonics Daily Routines**	Daily  **Routine:** **Discriminating,** 116H
	
	  CD-ROM
		Daily **Routine:** **Blending,** 118A
		
		  CD-ROM

● **Phonological Awareness**
 	
 ● **Phonics** *Review*
 	
 ● **Comprehension**
 	
 ● **Vocabulary**
 	
 ● **Study Skills**
 	
 ● **Listening, Speaking, Viewing, Representing**
	Read Aloud: Poem, 116E
	 "The Bat"
	
	 ☑ **Develop Phonological Awareness,** 116F
	 Review Vowel and Consonant Sounds
	
	 ☑ **Cumulative Review** 116G–116H
	 Teaching Chart 134
	 Reteach, Practice, Extend, 159
	 Phonics/Phonemic Awareness
	 Practice Book, 107–110
	
	  Apply *ph, tch;* **/ô/; soft** *c, g;* **/ù/,** 116/117
	 "Good News About Bats"
	
	 🛈 Intervention Program
		Build Background, 118A
		 Develop Oral Language
		
		 Vocabulary, 118B–118C
		
			breath	crops	scary	
						
							cover	darkness	study	
										
										 Word Building Manipulative Cards
										 Teaching Chart 135
										 Reteach, Practice, Extend, 160
										
										  Read the Selection, 118–121
										 Comprehension
										 ☑ **Phonics Review /ù/** *oo*
										 ☑ **Compare and Contrast**
										
										 Genre: Nonfiction/Science Article, 119
										
										 🛈 Intervention Program

● **Curriculum Connections**	**Link** Language Arts, 116E	**Link** Science, 118A
● **Writing**	✏ **Writing Prompt:** Your best friend is afraid of bats. What would you tell him or her? Write about it.	✏ **Writing Prompt:** Compare bats with another animal, such as a cat, dog, or mouse. Describe things that are alike and things that are different. 📖 **Journal Writing** Quick-Write, 121
● **Grammar**	**Introduce the Concept: Contractions,** 125O Daily Language Activity: Write contractions correctly. **Grammar Practice Book,** 121	**Teach the Concept: Contractions,** 125O Daily Language Activity: Write contractions correctly. **Grammar Practice Book,** 122
● **Spelling** *Words from Science*	**Pretest: Words from Science,** 125Q **Spelling Practice Book,** 121, 122	**Explore the Pattern: Words from Science,** 125Q **Spelling Practice Book,** 123

Meeting Individual Needs

How Kittens Grow

The World of Cats

Freedom CAT

 = Skill Assessed in Unit Test

 Intervention Program Available

Read EVERY DAY

DAY 3 Read the Literature	**DAY 4** Build Skills	**DAY 5** Build Skills
Daily  Routine: **Segmenting,** 123  CD-ROM	Daily **Phonics** Routine: **Fluency,** 125F **Phonics** CD-ROM	Daily **Phonics** Routine: **Writing,** 125H **Phonics** CD-ROM

Rereading for Fluency, 120
 	
Story Questions and Activities,
122–123
    Reteach, Practice, Extend, 161
 	
Study Skill, 124
    ☑ **Graphic Aids**
    Teaching Chart 136
    Reteach, Practice, Extend, 162
 	
Test Power, 125

**Read the Leveled Books,** 125A–125D
    Guided Reading
    ☑ **Phonics Review**
    ☑ **Comprehension Review**
	**Read the Leveled Books and the Self-Selected Books**
	
	☑ **Review Compare and Contrast,**
	125E–125F
	    Teaching Chart 137
	    Reteach, Practice, Extend, 163
	    Language Support, 177
	
	☑ **Review Draw Conclusions,** 125G–125H
	    Teaching Chart 138
	    Reteach, Practice, Extend, 164
	    Language Support, 178
		Read Self-Selected Books
		
		☑ **Review Inflectional Endings,** 125I–125J
		    Teaching Chart 139
		    Reteach, Practice, Extend, 165
		    Language Support, 179
		
		☑ **Review Antonyms,** 125K–125L
		    Teaching Chart 140
		    Reteach, Practice, Extend, 166
		    Language Support, 180
		
		Listening, Speaking, Viewing, Representing, 125N

Intervention Program	Intervention Program	Intervention Program
Activity Art, 123		

Writing Prompt: Would you like to have a pet bat the size of a bumblebee? Why or why not?
 	
Writing That Compares, 125M
    Prewrite, Draft
	Writing Prompt: Would you prefer to have a pet that flies or one that walks? Explain why.
	
	Writing That Compares, 125M
	    Revise
	
	Meeting Individual Needs for Writing, 125N
		Writing Prompt: People are often afraid of animals they don't know much about. What advice would you give them?
		
		Writing That Compares, 125M
		    Edit/Proofread, Publish

Review and Practice: Contractions, 125P
    Daily Language Activity: Write contractions correctly.
 	
Grammar Practice Book, 123
	Review and Practice: Contractions, 125P
	    Daily Language Activity: Write contractions correctly.
	
	Grammar Practice Book, 124
		Assess and Reteach: Contractions, 125P
		    Daily Language Activity: Write contractions correctly.
		
		Grammar Practice Book, 125, 126

Practice and Extend: Words from Science, 125R **Spelling Practice Book,** 124	**Proofread and Write: Words from Science,** 125R **Spelling Practice Book,** 125	**Assess: Words from Science,** 125R **Spelling Practice Book,** 126

Read Aloud

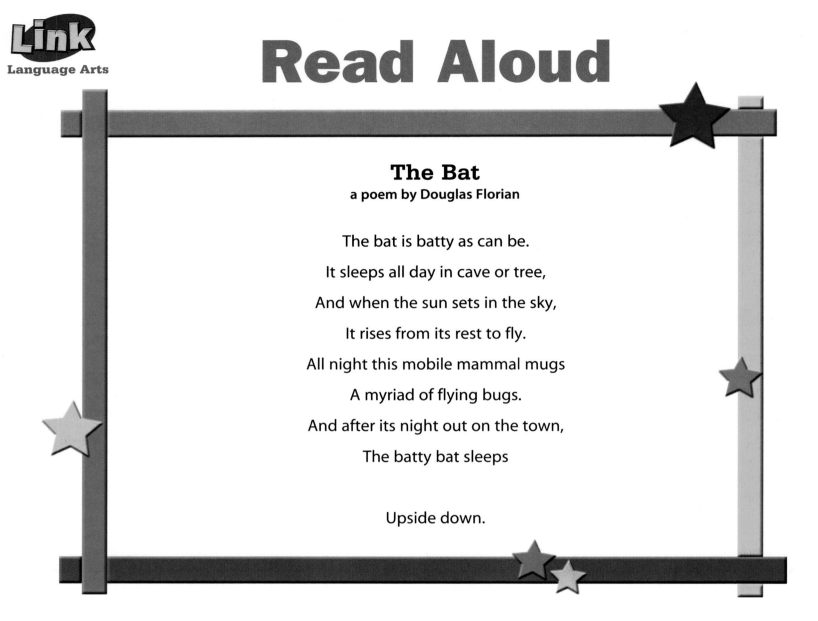

The Bat
a poem by Douglas Florian

The bat is batty as can be.

It sleeps all day in cave or tree,

And when the sun sets in the sky,

It rises from its rest to fly.

All night this mobile mammal mugs

A myriad of flying bugs.

And after its night out on the town,

The batty bat sleeps

Upside down.

Oral Comprehension

LISTENING AND SPEAKING Encourage children to think about the author's purpose as you read aloud this poem about bats. When you have finished, ask, "Do you think the purpose of this poem is to give information or to entertain? Why?" Remind children to look for the author's purpose in other stories and poems they read.

GENRE STUDY: POETRY Discuss some of the literary devices and techniques used in "The Bat."

- Discuss how the poet uses alliteration (the repetition of beginning sounds) in phrases such as "sun sets in the sky" and "mobile mammal."

- Remind children that poets use describing words to help paint a picture of their subject. Have children

draw a picture of a bat based on the information provided in the poem.

- Point out that the last two words of "The Bat" are set apart from the rest of the poem. Ask children why the poet might have chosen to separate these words.

Activity Help children identify the rhythm of "The Bat." Invite them to create a dance based on the rhythm, and have them perform their dances in small groups as you read the poem aloud. Vary your reading tempo to change the pace of the dances. ▶ **Kinesthetic**

Develop Phonological Awareness

Blend Sounds
Phonemic Awareness

MATERIALS
- Phonics Picture Posters

Teach   Tell children they are going to put some sounds together to say words. Display the Phonics Picture Poster for *book*. Say /b/-/ù/-/k/ and have children blend the sounds with you to say the whole word. Invite children to listen as you say some more sounds. Say, /m/-/ī/-/s/. If you put the sounds together what is the word? (mice)

Practice   Use Phonics Picture Posters to have children blend together the sounds of the following words: *fork, fence, baby, stage, phone,* and *watch.*

Segment Sounds
Phonemic Awareness

MATERIALS
- Word Building Boxes from *Word Building Cards*
- counters

Teach   Explain that you will say a word sound by sound. Then you will place a counter in a word box to show where you hear the /ù/ sound. Say: *look . . . /l/-/ù/-/k/.* Place a counter in the second box. Then say: *The /ù/ sound is the second sound in look.*

Practice   Distribute Word Building Boxes and counters to each child. Have them place counters in the box where either the /ù/, /j/, or /s/ sound is heard in these words: *took, wage, gem, nice, lace.* Repeat with /ô/, /ch/, or /f/ words: *claw, match, graph,* and *photo.*

Substitute Sounds
Phonemic Awareness

MATERIALS
- colored blocks

Teach   Demonstrate by saying: *cook . . . /k/-/ù/-/k/* as you place three red blocks in front of you. Then say: *Now I'll change the middle sound /k/-/ā/-/k/ . . . cake.* Replace the middle red block with a yellow block.

Practice   Distribute sets of red and yellow blocks. Have children substitute sounds using the colored blocks as you say these sets of words: *fawn/fan, rice/race, foot/fat, space/spice,* and *loose/lace, mice/mouse, voice/vase.*

INFORMAL ASSESSMENT   Observe children as they as they blend, segment, and substitute sounds. If children have difficulty, see Alternate Teaching Strategies on pages T64, T69, T72, and T75.

OBJECTIVES

Children will:

• review *ph, tch*; /ô/; soft *c, g*; /ù/.

• build, blend, and read words with *ph, tch*; /ô/; soft *c, g*; /ù/.

MATERIALS

• **Teaching Chart 134**
• **Word Building Manipulative Cards**

Skills Finder

Digraphs *ph, tch*

Introduce	B2: 92G–H
Review	B2: 116G–H, 250G–H, 281E–F, 281G–H
Test	B2: Unit 2

Review *ph, tch*; /ô/; soft *c, g*; /ù/

PREPARE

Build and Read Words with *ph; tch*; /ô/; Soft *c, g*; /ù/

Tell children they will review /f/, /ch/, /ô/, /s/ /j/, and /ù/, and letters that work together to spell each sound.

TEACH

BLENDING Model and Guide Practice with /f/*ph*; /ch/*tch*; /ô/*aw, au, a*; Soft *c, g*; /ù/*oo*

• Display **Teaching Chart 134**. Read aloud the word *catch* in the first row. Repeat, asking children to identify the last sound as /ch/.

• Review that the /ch/ sound can be spelled with the letters *tch*.

• Reread *catch*. Ask children to follow your finger to blend the sounds and to repeat the word with you.

• Invite volunteers to add *tch* to the middle and last words in the top row and blend the sounds together. Have children repeat *pitch* and *stretch* and then read aloud the completed row.

• Continue the activity using the *ph, ce, ge, au, oo* spellings.

catch	pitch	stretch
graph	elephant	telephone
race	place	piece
page	large	huge
caught	taught	because
good	book	foot

Teaching Chart 134

Use the Words in Context

• Use the words in sentences to reinforce their meanings.
Example: *If you pitch the ball, I'll catch it.*

PRACTICE

WORD BUILDING
Build *ph, tch;* /ô/;
Soft *c, g;* /u̇/
Words

PARTNERS

Have partners use letter cards to build words with *ph, tch;* /ô/; soft *c,* soft *g,* and /u̇/. Help them get started by building the word *stitch*. Then, have them replace the cards for *s* and *t* with the *p* card, to form *pitch*. Ask partners to take turns changing one or two letters to form other words with /ch/ spelled *tch*. Have each pair keep a list of the /ch/ words they build.

▶ **Visual/Linguistic**

ASSESS/CLOSE

Identify, Read,
and Use
ph, tch; /ô/;
Soft *c, g;* /u̇/
Words in
Context

To assess children's ability to build and read words with *ph, tch;* /ô/; soft *c,* soft *g,* and /u̇/, observe their work on the Practice activity. Have each pair share aloud words they have built, and use them in sentences.

ADDITIONAL PHONICS RESOURCES

**Phonics/Phonemic Awareness
Practice Book,
pages 107–110**

**McGraw-Hill School
TECHNOLOGY**

**Phonics CD-ROM
activities for practice with
Blending and Word Building**

Meeting Individual Needs for Phonics

EASY	ON-LEVEL	CHALLENGE

Reteach, 159   **Practice, 159**   **Extend, 159**

Daily Routines

DAY 1
Discriminating Read aloud these word pairs: *graph/gray, ditch/dash, caught/cat, city/coat, cage/dog, huge/hug, foot/food.* For each pair, ask a child to say the word with the sound /f/, /ch/, /ô/, /s/, /j/, or /u̇/.

DAY 2
Blending Write the spelling of each sound in *catch* as you say it. Have children repeat after you. Ask children to blend the sounds to read the word. Repeat with *rice* and *saw.*

DAY 3
Segmenting Distribute word building boxes. Read aloud these words: *graph, watch, cause, city, gem, foot.* Have children write the spelling of each sound in the appropriate box.

DAY 4
Fluency List on the chalkboard a list of /f/*ph*, /s/*ce*, /j/*ge*, or /u̇/ words. Point to each word, asking children to blend the sounds silently. Ask a child to read each word aloud.

DAY 5
Writing Invite partners to create rhyming couplets using words with *ph, tch,* /ô/, soft *c,* soft *g,* and /u̇/.

116H

OBJECTIVES

Children will review *ph, tch; /ô/; soft c, g; /ů/.*

Apply *ph, tch; /ô/; soft c, g; /ů/*

Good News About Bats

I used to think that bats were awful.
Now I think they're awful nice.
They have been around for ages
And they kind of look like mice.
True, their wings seem sort of phony.
Then again, you must admit:
Bats catch bugs like gnats and beetles,
So they help us quite a bit.

116   117

Anthology pages 116–117

Read and Build Fluency

READ THE POEM Tell children they will listen to a version of the poem, "Good News About Bats," on audio-cassette. Then, as an auditory model, play the tape several times and have children read silently along. Encourage children to focus on how the recorded voice pauses or stops at the appropriate punctuation.

REREAD FOR FLUENCY Have pairs of children take turns listening to the audiocassette reading. One partner may track the print while the other reads the poem. Encourage children to use gestures to simulate the action of the poem while reading.

Dictate and Spell

DICTATE WORDS Write the following list on the chalkboard and underline the phonemic element in each for review as you say the word: phony, catch, nice, ages, awful, look. Ask children to copy the list and circle the important review sound in each word. Say the word *telephone* as you write it on the chalkboard. Ask children to identify the review sound they hear and circle it. (ph) Continue the exercise with the words race, *caught, book, stretch,* and *huge.*

Intervention **Skills Intervention Guide,** for direct instruction and extra practice in *ph, tch; /ô/; soft c, g; /ů/*

Build Background

Science

Concept: Bats Help People

Going BATTY for Bats

Evaluate Prior Knowledge

CONCEPT: BATS HELP PEOPLE Ask children to share facts they know about bats. Prompt children to mention ways that bats help people, by eating insects, for example. Remind them that bats almost never harm people, and prompt discussion about how myths and folktales have created fears about real-life bats.

MAKE A BAT-FACT WORD WEB Work with children to create a word cluster of bat facts. ▶Linguistic

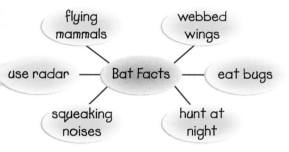

ILLUSTRATE THE WEB Invite children to

draw pictures illustrating
something from the word
cluster. For example, they may draw a picture of a bat eating a fly. Have children write captions for their drawings.

Develop Oral Language

BATS AND CATS Play a game called "Bats

ESL and Cats." Divide children into two teams that take alternating turns. Show them photos of a bat and a cat. The object is to say sentences comparing what the two animals look like. The team gets two points if a player makes an accurate statement, and one point if the player needs a question from you to prompt an answer. For those desiring prompts, ask questions such as:

- Which animal has wings?
- Do either of the animals have claws?
- Which animal has a longer tail?

▶Oral/Interpersonal

LANGUAGE SUPPORT

For additional help in building background, refer to the **Language Support Book,** pages 172–175.

darkness

scary

breath

crops

study

cover

Vocabulary

Teach Vocabulary in Context

OBJECTIVES

Children will use context and structural clues to determine the meanings of vocabulary words.

Definitions

darkness (p. 119) nighttime; a time of no light

scary (p. 119) causing fear, frightening

breath (p. 119) air drawn into the lungs

crops (p. 119) plants grown for food

study (p. 120) look at closely, try to learn about by reading or looking carefully

cover (p. 120) put something over or on

Story Words

These words from the selection may be unfamiliar. Before children read, have them check the meanings and pronunciations of the words in the Glossary, beginning on page 390, or in a dictionary.

• insect, p. 119
• tons, p. 119
• bumblebee, p. 120
• colony, p. 121
• mines, p. 120

Identify Vocabulary Words Display **Teaching Chart 135** and read the passage with children. Have volunteers circle each vocabulary word and underline other words that are clues to its meaning.

Who's Afraid of Bats?

1. When <u>night</u> came, the three friends sat in the ⟨darkness.⟩ **2.** Jill began to tell a ⟨scary⟩ story about bats. Her friends were <u>afraid</u>. **3.** Trudy was so afraid that she <u>put her hands over her nose and mouth</u> and held her ⟨breath⟩. **4.** Sam stopped Jill and said that bats help people by eating insects that kill <u>farmers'</u> ⟨crops⟩ which provide the <u>food</u> we eat. **5.** Then he told his friends about a famous man who likes to ⟨study⟩ bats, so he can <u>learn all about them</u>. **6.** He found out that people ⟨cover⟩ bat caves with <u>gates to keep people out</u>.

Teaching Chart 135

Discuss Meanings Ask questions like these to help clarify word meanings:

• What is the opposite of darkness?

• Do you think horror movies are scary?

• Do you see your breath on cold days?

• What do we study in this class?

• What kinds of crops do farmers grow?

• What will cover your head when it's cold or rainy outside?

Practice

Words in Context

Have children create sentences using vocabulary words, and then copy them onto cards, leaving blanks where the words belong. Have pairs exchange cards and fill in the blanks.

▶ **Kinesthetic/Linguistic**

scary   breath   study

Word Building Manipulative Cards

Write a Story

Have partners write scary stories using vocabulary words. Invite them to read the stories aloud. ▶ **Linguistic/Oral**

Assess Vocabulary

Identify Word Meaning in Context

Invite each child to write questions that use the vocabulary words in context. Then ask them to exchange their questions with a partner. Have partners write answers to each question, using the vocabulary words in their answers whenever possible.

SPELLING/VOCABULARY CONNECTIONS

See Spelling Challenge Words, pages 125Q–125R.

LANGUAGE SUPPORT

See the **Language Support Book**, pages 172–175, for teaching suggestions for Vocabulary.

Vocabulary PuzzleMaker

Provides vocabulary activities.

Meeting Individual Needs for Vocabulary

EASY	ON-LEVEL	ON-LEVEL	CHALLENGE

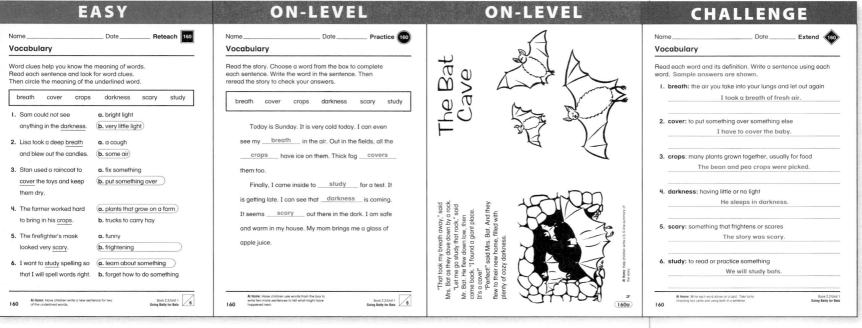

Reteach, 160

Practice, 160

Practice, 160a
Take-Home Story

Extend, 160

Comprehension

Prereading Strategies

PREVIEW AND PREDICT Invite children to read aloud the name of the selection. Then take a **picture walk** through the illustrations, stopping at page 121. Discuss with children how the pictures give clues about what they will read in the selection.

- What will the article most likely be about?
- What clues do the pictures give about bats?
- Are all bats the same?

Will the article be about bat facts, or will it be a fantasy story? How can you tell? *Genre*

SET PURPOSES Ask children what they would like to learn as they read the story. For example:

- How do bats help people?
- Do bats hurt people?
- How big is the biggest bat?

These bats live in Asia.

Going BATTY for Bats

118

Meeting Individual Needs • Grouping Suggestions for Strategic Reading

EASY	ON-LEVEL	CHALLENGE
Read Together Read the article aloud with children. As you read, model the strategy of using the Venn diagram to compare and contrast fears and facts about the bats. Show how this can help them better understand what they read.	**Guided Instruction** Encourage children to share their own ideas about bats before and after reading. Before you read the article with children, you may wish to have them read the article on their own, while you monitor any difficulties they have in order to determine which prompts to emphasize.	**Read Independently** Invite children to set purposes before they read the article. Remind them that comparing and contrasting ideas about bats will help them to understand the article's main idea. Encourage them to share their own ideas about bats before and after reading. Discuss how their ideas change when they learn new facts.

Bats Help People! Really!

Who's afraid of the big black bat?
People who don't know how helpful bats can be.

Night falls. Darkness comes. The wind blows
leaves around your feet. Suddenly a vampire bat
swoops down at you!

Now catch your breath. Scary bat stories have
been around for hundreds of years. In real life,
bats hardly ever hurt people. The flying mammals
are some of nature's biggest helpers.

HOW BATS HELP US

Bats help farmers by
eating insects that kill
crops. The 20 million
Mexican free-tailed bats
that live near San
Antonio, Texas, eat 250
tons of insects every
night! In fact, most bats
can eat up to 600
insects in one hour!

COVER AND RIGHT:MERLIN TUTTLE/PHOTO RESEARCHERS

This heart-nosed bat is about to eat an insect.

119

LANGUAGE SUPPORT

Blackline masters of the Venn diagram can be found in the **Language
Support Book**.

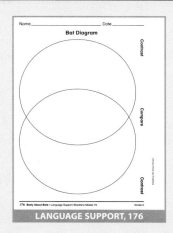

LANGUAGE SUPPORT, 176

Comprehension

☑ **Phonics** Apply /ù/*oo*

☑ **Apply Compare and Contrast**

STRATEGIC READING Comparing and
contrasting can help you to understand what
you read. As we read this article, we'll use a
Venn diagram to compare and contrast our
fears about bats and facts about bats.

1 **COMPARE AND CONTRAST** How
would you feel if a bat flew near you?
Do you have any fears about bats? Before we
read, let's fill in the left circle of the Venn diagram with some of our fears about bats.
(Answers will vary.)

2 Would you be more likely to see a bat if
you went outside at lunchtime or at
bedtime? Why? *Draw Conclusions*

Genre

Nonfiction Science Article

Tell children that nonfiction articles:

- present facts in a logical order.
- give a short description of events, discoveries, or ideas.
- may use headings, captions, diagrams,
  and different typefaces, sidebars and
  other text features.

Activity After children read *Going
Batty for Bats,* have volunteers give examples
of features that make this selection a nonfiction article. Then invite them to compare
this article to the narrative nonfiction,
Zipping, Zapping, Zooming Bats.

119

Comprehension

3 **Phonics** /ù/oo What is the second word in the second paragraph? (*good*) Let's read it aloud together. What is the vowel sound in this word, and what letters spell this sound? (/ù/, *oo*) *Segmenting/Graphophonic Cues*

4 What is the main idea of this article? (Bats are not scary; they are our friends.) What are some details supporting this idea? (Bats do good things like eating insects. Bats should be afraid of us. Bats don't harm people.) *Main Idea and Supporting Details*

5 **COMPARE AND CONTRAST** Have any facts from this article changed your minds about bats? Let's fill in the right circle of our Venn diagrams with facts about bats. Then we'll see if any of our fears stayed the same, and write those in, too. (Answers will vary. Examples:)

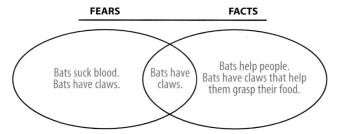

FEARS   FACTS

Bats suck blood. Bats have claws. | Bats have claws. | Bats help people. Bats have claws that help them grasp their food.

ORGANIZE INFORMATION Tell children to organize the information they have learned in the article. Have partners write one or two sentences that summarize facts about bats. *Summarize*

BATS ARE SCARED OF YOU!

Bats should be afraid of people and not the other way around. Today 20 kinds of bats are in danger of dying out. People have burned them out of caves. They have buried them inside mines. "People think every bat is a vampire bat. So they kill all they can find," says Thomas Kunz. He is a scientist who [studies] bats.

3 The good news is that some people are working hard to keep bats safe. A group called Bat Conservation International has built iron gates to [cover] the fronts of some bat caves and mines.

Some people build bat houses in their yards.

RIGHT: MARK HAMLIN/OXFORD SCIENTIFIC FILMS. ABOVE: OXFORD SCIENTIFIC FILMS

DID YOU KNOW?
BAT FACTS

- Bats stand for good luck in Japan and China.
- Bats sleep 20 hours a day.
- Vampire bats will not attack a person unless a person bothers them first.
- There are more than 980 different kinds of bats in the world.
- The hog-nosed bat is the world's smallest mammal. It is the size of a bumblebee, and it weighs less than a dime.
- Baby bats are called pups.

120

REREADING FOR *Fluency*

PARTNERS Children who need fluency practice can pair up and read the article aloud to each other.

READING RATE When you evaluate reading rate, have children read aloud from the story for one minute. Place a stick-on note after the last word read. Count words read. To evaluate

children's performance, see the Running Record in the **Fluency Assessment** book.

 Intervention For leveled fluency passages, lessons, and norm charts, see **Skills Intervention Guide**, Part 5, Fluency.

Many people come to parts of Texas to watch bats fly.

The gates let bats in. But they keep out people who would hurt them. The group is also teaching people about all the good things bats do.

BATS ARE OUR FRIENDS

Some of the bats' best friends live in Austin, Texas. People there are proud of the one million bats that fly out from under the Congress Avenue Bridge when the sun goes down. The bats make up the largest bat colony in any city in the world.

So don't get scared if you happen to see a bat. The scariest things about them **(4)** are the stories people tell. **(5)**

> **FIND OUT MORE**
> Visit our website:
> **www.mhschool.com/reading**
>
> *inter*NET
> **CONNECTION**

Based on an article in *TIME FOR KIDS*.

121

Comprehension

Return to Predictions and Purposes

Reread and discuss children's predictions about the story, noting which ones need to be revised. Then ask children if the article answered the questions they had before they read.

INFORMAL ASSESSMENT

HOW TO ASSESS

Phonics /ů/ *oo* Ask: How do you spell /ů/ as in *good*? Have each child write the letters that make the sound, then add letters to form a new word with /ů/ spelled *oo*.

COMPARE AND CONTRAST Ask: How are bats and birds alike? How are they different? Fill in a Venn diagram with facts and details about bats and birds.

FOLLOW UP

Phonics /ů/ *oo* Continue to model blending words with /ů/ *oo* for children who are having difficulty.

COMPARE AND CONTRAST If children have difficulty comparing and contrasting, remind them that *comparing* means to look for ways things are alike, and *contrasting* means looking for differences. Discuss how a Venn diagram illustrates this.

LITERARY RESPONSE

QUICK-WRITE Invite children to use their journals to record thoughts and feelings about the article.

ORAL RESPONSE Have children discuss the following question:

- Do you think people should be afraid of bats? Why or why not?

RESEARCH AND INQUIRY

*inter*NET **CONNECTION** For more information on this topic go to **www.mhschool.com/reading.**

Story Questions

Going Batty for Bats

Help children discuss or write answers to the questions on page 122.

Answers:

1. Bats help farmers by eating insects that kill crops. *Literal/Summarize*

2. People have killed bats, burned them out of caves, buried them in mines and work sites. *Literal/Summarize*

3. They like bats and want to save 20 kinds that are in danger of dying out. *Inferential/Summarize*

4. Bats help people and should be protected. *Main Idea*

5. (Answers will vary. Accept appropriate facts from both articles.) *Reading Across Texts*

Write a Speech For a full writing-process lesson related to this writing suggestion, see the lesson on Writing That Compares on pages 125M–125N.

Story Questions & Activities

1. How do bats help farmers?

2. Why should bats be afraid of people?

3. Why do you think that Bat Conservation International is teaching people about all the good things bats do?

4. What is the main idea of this selection?

5. Compare "Going Batty for Bats" to "Zipping, Zapping, Zooming Bats." What facts are the same? Which ones are different?

Write a Speech

Write a speech that will help people be less afraid of bats. Give reasons why people are scared of bats. Compare these reasons to facts about bats. Explain how bats help people.

Meeting Individual Needs

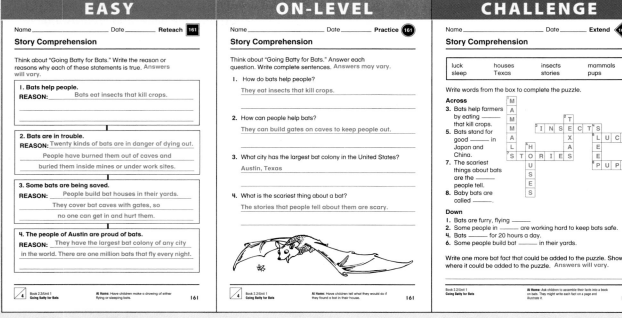

EASY	ON-LEVEL	CHALLENGE
Reteach, 161	Practice, 161	Extend, 161

Make an Advertisement

Think of another animal that seems scary but really isn't. Create an ad for this animal. Give facts about the animal. Explain why people should not be afraid of it. Include a picture of the animal.

Make a Mobile of Bats

Choose three or four different kinds of bats. Draw them on cardboard or heavy paper and cut them out. Thread them with different lengths of thread and hang them from a wire coat hanger.

Find Out More

There are many different kinds of bats. What kind of bats live in your part of the country? If no bats live where you live, find out about another kind of animal in your area that likes the nighttime, such as owls or raccoons.

123

DAILY **Phonics** ROUTINES

DAY 3 **Segmenting** Distribute word building boxes. Read aloud these words: *graph, watch, cause, city, gem, foot.* Have children write the spelling of each sound in the appropriate box.

Phonics CD-ROM

Story Activities

Make An Advertisement

Materials: paper, colored pens

PARTNERS Give children access to animal books and wildlife magazines. Suggest that before creating their ads, they tell their partners what they like about the animals they've chosen, and to use these ideas in their ads. They may also wish to contrast "fears" and "facts" about the animal in their ads.

Make a Mobile of Bats

Materials: hangers, cardboard or heavy paper, thread or yarn, colored pens

GROUP Encourage children to look back at *Going Batty for Bats* and *Zipping, Zapping, Zooming Bats* to make their bat mobiles look real. Suggest that each group member become an "expert" on one kind of bat, and add that bat to the mobile.

Find Out More

PARTNERS **RESEARCH AND INQUIRY** As a class, look at a United States map and ask children to point out the part of the country and the state where they live. Then have partners find out what kinds of bats and other animals live there, too. Suggest that they look for facts in books, magazine articles, and/or on the Internet.

inter NET CONNECTION Children can learn more about bats and where they live by visiting **www.mhschool.com/reading**.

FORMAL ASSESSMENT

After page 123, see the Selection Assessment.

Study Skills

Read a Chart
GRAPHIC AIDS

OBJECTIVES Children will use a chart to compare and contrast.

PREPARE Review what rows and columns are. Ask children to identify them on the chart. Display **Teaching Chart 136.**

TEACH Explain that charts offer facts in an organized way. Discuss with children the subject heading and content of each column, and model using the chart to find facts about certain kinds of bats.

PRACTICE Have children answer questions 1–5. Review answers with them.

1. Central America and South America **2.** 4 inches in wingspan. **3.** flying fox bat, 5 feet **4.** big brown bat and little brown bat **5.** It looks like a fox.

ASSESS/CLOSE Have small groups of children create charts about household pets.

READ TOGETHER

STUDY SKILLS

Use a Chart

Kind of Bat	Wingspan	Where It Lives
big brown bat	12 inches	North America
little brown bat	8 inches	North America
flying fox	5 feet	Australia
common vampire bat	12 inches	Central America and South America

Use the chart to answer the questions.

1 Where does the common vampire bat live?

2 What is the difference in size between the little brown bat and the big brown bat?

3 Which bat has the largest wingspan? How wide is it?

4 Which bats live in North America?

5 How do you think the flying fox got its name?

Meeting Individual Needs

EASY

Name_____ Date_____ Reteach **162**

Use a Chart

Each box in a **chart** contains one kind of information.

The chart below shows different kinds of bats.

Types of Bats

Kind of Bat	Fur Color	Where They Live	Size	Bat Fact
Free-Tailed	dark brown	in caves and in colonies	12 inches	long tail
Hoary	white spotted reddish-brown	alone in trees	16 inches	largest in America
Red	white-tipped red	alone in trees	12 inches	fly south in winter
Silver-Haired	white-frosted brown	in trees, females in groups	13 inches	male is more black than female

Use the facts in the chart above to answer these questions.

1. What does the Red bat do in winter? ___ fly south

2. Which bats live alone in trees? ___ Hoary bats and Red bats

3. Which bat is the largest? ___ Hoary

4. Which bat is white-frosted brown? ___ Silver-haired

At Home: Have children draw a picture of one of the bats described in the chart.

162   Book 2.2/Unit 1 Going Batty for Bats 4

ON-LEVEL

Name_____ Date_____ Practice **162**

Use a Chart

It is often easier to read facts in a **chart** than in a paragraph. Read the paragraph below. Notice how the facts tend to get confusing.

The Kentucky Derby is one of the most famous races in the world. On the first Saturday in May, horses race over one and a quarter miles. The first Kentucky Derby took place in 1875. The winner was a horse called Aristides. It took Aristides two minutes and thirty-seven seconds to finish the course. The jockey was Oliver Lewis. In 1921, a horse called Behave Yourself won the race in two minutes and four seconds. The jockey was Charles Thompson. One of the most famous horses, Whirlaway, was ridden by Eddie Arcaro. In 1941, he won in two minutes, one second. Another famous horse, Seattle Slew, won in 1977, finishing in two minutes and two seconds. The jockey was Jean Cruguet.

Fill in the blanks using the information in the paragraph.

Kentucky Derby Results

Year	Winner	Jockey	Time
1875	Aristides	Oliver Lewis	2 min. 37 sec.
1921	Behave Yourself	Charles Thompson	2 min. 4 sec.
1941	Whirlaway	Eddie Arcaro	2 min. 1 sec.
1977	Seattle Slew	Jean Cruguet	2 min. 2 sec.

At Home: Show children other examples of charts from newspapers and magazines.

162   Book 2.2/Unit 1 Going Batty for Bats 5

CHALLENGE

Name_____ Date_____ Extend **162**

Use a Chart

Use the chart to answer the questions.

Kind of tree	Loses Its leaves?	State tree of
Maple	yes	Rhode Island
Douglas Fir	no	Oregon
Giant Redwood	no	California
Magnolia	yes	Mississippi

1. Which two trees lose their leaves in the fall?
   maple, magnolia

2. What is the difference between the Douglas fir and the giant redwood?
   The Douglas fir is the state tree of Oregon and the giant redwood is the state tree of California.

3. What is the same about the Douglas fir and the giant redwood?
   Neither loses its leaves.

4. What is the state tree of Mississippi?
   magnolia

Write your own question using the information from the chart. Ask a friend to answer it.
   Answers will vary.

At Home: Have children look through newspapers or magazines to find charts.

162   Book 2.2/Unit 1 Going Batty for Bats

Reteach, 162   Practice, 162   Extend, 162

TEST POWER

Tell the story to yourself again, but use your own words.

DIRECTIONS:

Read the story. Then read each question about the story.

SAMPLE

A Trip to the Beach

Leslie and Michelle jumped out of the car. They couldn't wait to see the sand and the water. This was a very special trip for both of them. They had never been to the ocean before.

When they reached the beach, Michelle said, "This is great!" The sand was warm. Leslie's father sat on a towel and read a book. Michelle and Leslie began to build a sand castle right next to the water. The cool water splashed their toes. Leslie's mother watched them from under her beach umbrella.

In a few hours, they all were tired. They walked back up the hill to their car. "Let's come back again soon!" Leslie said.

1 The sand at the beach was—
   ○ colder than ice
   ○ full of rocks
   ○ wetter than before
   ● warmer than the water was

2 Which conclusion can you draw from this story?
   ● The beach is a good place on a hot day.
   ○ The beach is too rough for swimming.
   ○ The beach is full of people.
   ○ There are many rocks in the water at the beach.

125

Test Power

THE PRINCETON REVIEW

Read the Page

Explain to children that you will be reading this story as a group. You will read the story, and they will follow along in their books.

Request that children put pens, pencils, and markers away, since they will not be writing in their books.

Discuss the Questions

QUESTION 1: Have children look for words that describe the sand. The sixth sentence says that the sand was warm.

QUESTION 2: Remind children to eliminate choices that are not supported in the passage. Only the first choice is supported. The second paragraph gives many reasons why the beach is a good place on a hot day.

Self-Selected Reading
Leveled Books

☑

- /ù/ *oo*; /ô/ *au, aw*
- soft *c* and soft *g*
- digraphs *ph, tch*

☑ **Comprehension**

- draw conclusions
- compare and contrast
- Answers will vary. Have children cite examples from the story to support their answers.

EASY

Story Questions for Selected Reading

1. What did you like best in this book?

2. If you could visit one of the places in this book, which would it be? Why?

3. What would be another title for this book? Why?

4. Which illustration did you like best? Why?

5. What questions would you ask the author?

Draw a Picture

Draw a picture of a scene from the book.

EASY

UNIT SKILLS REVIEW

☑

☑ **Comprehension**

Help children self-select an Easy book to read and apply phonics and comprehension skills.

Guided Reading

PREVIEW AND PREDICT Discuss the illustrations in the beginning of the book. As you take the **picture walk**, have children predict what the book will be about. List their ideas.

SET PURPOSES Have children write why they want to read the book. Have them share their purposes.

READ THE BOOK Use items like the following to guide children's reading or to ask after they have read the story independently.

- Model: Listen to the sound /ù/. Do you see any words that contain this sound? Do these words use the letters *oo* to make that sound? *Phonics and Decoding*

- Choose two people, places, or animals in this story. How are they alike? How are they different? *Compare and Contrast*

- What is the author of this book trying to tell you? What makes you think that? *Draw Conclusions*

- Name something that changed in the book. What was it? What was it like before it changed? Afterward? *Compare and Contrast*

RETURN TO PREDICTIONS AND PURPOSES Discuss children's predictions. Ask which were close to the book contents and why. Have children review their purposes for reading. Did they find out what they wanted to know?

LITERARY RESPONSE Have children discuss questions like the following:

- Would you recommend this book to a friend? Why or why not?

- What would you change about this book? Why?

See the **Phonics CD-ROM** for practice with variant vowels /ù/ and /ô/; soft *c* and soft *g*; and digraphs *ph, tch*.

Self-Selected Reading
Leveled Books

INDEPENDENT

UNIT SKILLS REVIEW

☑ **Comprehension**

Help children self-select an Independent book to read and apply comprehension skills.

Guided Reading

PREVIEW AND PREDICT Discuss the illustrations in the beginning of the book. As you take the **picture walk**, have children predict what the book will be about. List their ideas.

SET PURPOSES Have children write why they want to read the book. Have them share their purposes.

READ THE BOOK Use items like the following to guide children's reading or after they have read the story independently:

- Look for words with soft *c* and soft *g* sounds. What are some other words with these sounds? *Phonics and Decoding*

- Think of two persons, places, or animals in this book. How are they alike? How are they different? *Compare and Contrast*

- Name some of the most important facts or events in this book. What do they lead you to believe? *Draw Conclusions*

- Look at the beginning and the end of this book. Is anything different? What? *Compare and Contrast*

RETURN TO PREDICTIONS AND PURPOSES Have children review their predictions. Children can talk about whether their purposes were met, and if they have any questions the story left unanswered.

LITERARY RESPONSE The following questions will help focus children's responses:

- What other things would you like to know about this topic?

- What point was the author trying to make? Do you agree or disagree?

See the  **CD-ROM** for practice with variant vowels /ù/ and /ô/; soft *c* and soft *g*; and digraphs *ph, tch*.

☑ **Phonics**

- /ù/ *oo*; /ô/ *au, aw*

- soft *c* and soft *g*

- digraphs *ph, tch*

☑ **Comprehension**

- draw conclusions

- compare and contrast

Answers will vary. Have children cite examples from the story to support their answers.

INDEPENDENT

Story Questions for Selected Reading

1. What facts did you find most interesting?

2. Did you learn something new from this book? What?

3. What did you learn by looking at the illustrations?

4. What else would you include if you were writing this book?

5. What question would you ask the author?

Make a Chart

Make a chart that shows all the facts you learned from this book.

Self-Selected Reading
Leveled Books

☑ **Phonics**

- /u̇/ *oo*; /ô/ *au, aw*
- soft *c* and soft *g*
- digraphs *ph, tch*

☑ **Comprehension**

- draw conclusions
- compare and contrast
- Answers will vary. Have children cite examples from the story to support their answers.

EXTEND

Have children write and draw a comic book version of this book. Remind them to include all important facts.

CHALLENGE

Story Questions for Selected Reading

1. What was your favorite part of this book? Why?

2. What point was the author trying to make? Do you agree or disagree?

3. How were the illustrations helpful?

4. What would you change if you were the writer of this book?

5. What question would you ask the author?

Write a Review

Write a review of this book. Explain why people should or shouldn't read it.

CHALLENGE

UNIT SKILLS REVIEW

☑ **Comprehension**

Help children self-select a Challenge book to read and apply comprehension skills.

Guided Reading

PREVIEW AND PREDICT Discuss the illustrations in the beginning of the book. As you take the **picture walk**, have children predict what the story will be about. List their ideas.

SET PURPOSES Have children write why they want to read the book. Have them share their purposes.

READ THE BOOK Use items like the following to guide children's reading or to ask after they have read the story independently:

- Look for words with *ph* and *tch*. Can you think of any other words with these sounds? *Phonics and Decoding*

- What was something that changed in the book? How did it change? *Compare and Contrast*

- What are the most important facts or events in this book? What do they lead you to believe? *Draw Conclusions*

- What is something in this book that suprised you? What is different from what you expected? *Compare and Contrast*

RETURN TO PREDICTIONS AND PURPOSES Discuss children's predictions. Ask which were close to the story and why. Have children review their purposes for reading. Did they find out what they wanted to know?

LITERARY RESPONSE Have children discuss questions like the following:

- Was there anyone in this book you would like to meet? Was there a place you'd like to visit? Why?

- What else would you like to know about this topic?

See the 💿 **Phonics CD-ROM** for practice with variant vowels /u̇/ and /ô/; soft *c* and soft *g*; and digraphs *ph, tch*.

Bringing Groups Together

Anthology and Leveled Books

Connecting Texts

LOOK AROUND CHARTS
Choose four stories and write the titles on the four opposite corners of a large square: *Going Batty for Bats, John Muir: Making the Mountains Glad, The Underground City, The World of Cats.* Have children list the main idea under the appropriate story titles. In the middle of the square, have them write what these main ideas have in common.

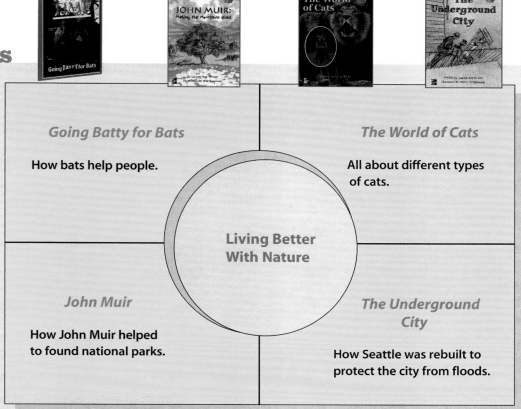

Going Batty for Bats

How bats help people.

The World of Cats

All about different types of cats.

Living Better With Nature

John Muir

How John Muir helped to found national parks.

The Underground City

How Seattle was rebuilt to protect the city from floods.

Viewing/Representing

GROUP PRESENTATIONS Divide the class into groups, in which students have all read some of the same titles. Have students in each group select their favorite story and act out part of the story for the class. It can be a specific event or an activity that the book describes.

AUDIENCE RESPONSE Ask children to pay attention to each group's presentation. Afterwards, the audience can ask questions about how the activity or event relates to the rest of the book.

Research and Inquiry

Have children do a more in-depth investigation of topics that interest them by:

- Searching through classroom and library books for more information on the subject.

- Watching videotapes or listening to audio tapes that offer valuable information.

- Asking questions of adults who may have expertise in these particular fields.

inter NET CONNECTION Have children log on to **www.mhschool.com/reading** for links to Web pages.

 Children can write and draw what they learned in their journals.

JOURNAL

OBJECTIVES

Children will compare and contrast two familiar items.

MATERIALS

• Teaching Chart 137

Skills Finder

Compare and Contrast

Introduce	B2: 67I-J
Review	B2: 115I-J, 125E-F
Test	B2: Unit 1

TEACHING TIP

CULTURAL PERSPECTIVES People from different cultures keep different pets. Have children tell about their pets. Ask them to think of other pets people might have. Encourage children to share what pets are common in their cultures, and invite them to think about the pets they might have if they lived in a different part of the world (for example, in a tropical climate).

ALTERNATE TEACHING STRATEGY

COMPARE AND CONTRAST

For a different approach to teaching this skill, see page T71.

Review Compare and Contrast

PREPARE

Review Compare and Contrast
Remind children that knowing what is alike and different about two topics can help them understand each one more fully.

TEACH

Compare/Contrast Pets with Wild Animals
Display **Teaching Chart 137**. Invite children to read the report on the chart, and then to use a Venn diagram to compare and contrast animals that live as pets and animals that live in the wild.

Pets and Wild Animals

All animals have a home. Most pets live in houses with people. Wild animals live in trees, caves, under water, or almost anywhere else you can think of. Some snakes live under rocks! All animals need to eat. Pets are given food by their keepers, but wild animals eat plants or hunt for food. Pets are friendly and like to live with people. Animals that live in the wild are afraid of people and want to stay away from them. All animals need us to be nice to them and protect them.

Teaching Chart 137

MODEL First I'm going to put headings on my Venn diagram: *Pets* and *Wild Animals*. I'll write *Both* in the middle. I'll add: "Have a home" in the middle, because that is true of all animals. In the *Pets* circle I will write "live with people." In the *Wild Animals* circle I'll put "live in trees, caves, under water, under rocks." Now I'll look for other ways pets and animals in the wild are alike and different.

Ask children to reread the report on **Teaching Chart 137**, and to fill in their Venn diagrams as they find more ways to compare and contrast pets and wild animals.

PRACTICE

Compare/Contrast Classroom Items

GROUP

Ask children to compare and contrast a dictionary and an encyclopedia. As children offer oral responses, add them to a Venn diagram on the chalkboard. Ask: *What is the same about a dictionary and an encyclopedia? What is different?* (*Same:* reference books, information in alphabetical order. *Different:* dictionary tells what words mean, encyclopedia contains longer articles about many different topics.)

▶ **Spatial/Linguistic**

ASSESS/CLOSE

Challenge children to choose two familiar items, and create a Venn diagram comparing and contrasting the two. Have children share and discuss their work with a partner.

DAILY **Phonics** ROUTINES

DAY 4 **Fluency** List on the chalkboard a list of /f/*ph*, /s/*ce*, /j/*ge* or /ü/ words. Point to each word, asking children to blend the sounds silently. Ask a child to read each word aloud.

Phonics CD-ROM

i **Intervention** ▶ **Skills Intervention Guide,** for direct instruction and extra practice in comparing and contrasting

Meeting Individual Needs for Comprehension

EASY	ON-LEVEL	CHALLENGE	LANGUAGE SUPPORT
Name____ Date____ Reteach 163	Name____ Date____ Practice 163	Name____ Date____ Extend 163	Name____ Date____
Compare and Contrast	**Compare and Contrast**	**Compare and Contrast**	**Make Batty Words**

EASY — Reteach, 163

Compare and Contrast

Compare to tell how two things are alike.
Contrast to tell how two things are different.

Read the story. Think about Amy's life before she got the dog. Think about Amy's life after she got the dog. Put an **X** in the correct box to make a comparison.

I am deaf. I can't hear people talk or sing. I can't hear the telephone or the doorbell either. Sometimes I would feel angry because I couldn't hear anything. But last year a very special dog named Annie came to live with me. She is a "hearing" dog. She helps me hear. If the doorbell rings, she bumps my hand and she runs to the door. She lets me know about other sounds, too. She is a good dog.

	Before the Dog	After the Dog
1. Amy did not know when the telephone rang.	X	
2. Amy was angry.	X	
3. Amy knows when someone is at the door.		X
4. Amy is much happier.		X

Book 2.2/Unit 1 **Going Batty for Bats** — **At Home:** Have children compare and contrast their lives during summer vacation with their lives during the school year. — 163

ON-LEVEL — Practice, 163

Compare and Contrast

When you **compare**, you tell how things are alike.
When you **contrast**, you tell how things are different.

Some people are afraid of bats. Help them learn not to be scared. For each statement, write something different that you learned in "Going Batty for Bats." Answers may vary.

1. Bats hurt people.
   Bats hardly ever hurt people.
2. Bats eat farm crops.
   Bats kill insects that eat farm crops.
3. Bats don't eat very much.
   A bat can eat up to 600 insects in one hour.
4. Putting a gate on a cave hurts bats.
   Gates keep people from hurting bats.
5. You should be scared if you see a bat.
   Bats are not scary.

Book 2.2/Unit 1 **Going Batty for Bats** — **At Home:** Have children think of different places that might make a good home for a bat. — 163

CHALLENGE — Extend, 163

Compare and Contrast

Read about mammals.

- All mammals are warm-blooded.
- All mammals have backbones.
- Mammal babies are not hatched from eggs.
- All mammals have hair or fur.

Bats and bears are both mammals. List one way bats and bears are alike and different. Answers will vary.

Bears are similar to bats.	Bears are different from bats.
Both have backbones.	Bats can fly. Bears walk.

List other animals that are mammals. Draw a picture of one in the box.

Book 2.2/Unit 1 **Going Batty for Bats** — **At Home:** Ask children to make a list of animals that are not mammals. — 163

LANGUAGE SUPPORT

Make Batty Words

| fast | est | bigg | est |
| saf | er | small | er |

Grade 2 — Language Support/Blackline Master 97 • Batty About Bats — 177

Reteach, 163   **Practice, 163**   **Extend, 163**   **Language Support, 177**

125F

OBJECTIVES

Children will draw conclusions from facts they hear and read.

......

MATERIALS

• **Teaching Chart 138**

Skills Finder

Draw Conclusions

Introduce	B2: 43I–J
Review	B2: 91I–J, 125G–H
Test	B2: Unit 1

TEACHING TIP

DRAW CONCLUSIONS

Show children pictures from other selections in the anthology and ask them to draw conclusions based on clues they find in the picture, and on what they already know.

ALTERNATE TEACHING STRATEGY

DRAW CONCLUSIONS

For a different approach to teaching this skill, see page T67.

Review Draw Conclusions

PREPARE

Use Facts to Draw Conclusions

Say: Let's pretend that today at my favorite restaurant, they are giving away free food. It's happening right after school. I have nothing else to do then. I'm glad that it's this afternoon, because I only had an apple for lunch. Even though I haven't told you, from the facts I just gave, can you draw a conclusion about what I will do this afternoon?

TEACH

Read "Addie's Day" to Draw Conclusions

Remind children that authors don't always write out all their ideas—sometimes they leave clues so readers have to draw conclusions on their own. Display **Teaching Chart 138.** Before reading it with children, ask them to think about what conclusion can be drawn from the facts in each paragraph.

Addie's Day

1. Last night Addie was reading about bats, and she stayed awake later than she usually does. Now she is yawning. She would like to go to bed.

2. Addie loves to read about bats. She smiles when she talks about them. She finds out about a special cave where bats live.

3. While Addie waits at the bus stop, a boy runs up just as a bus is pulling away. He looks worried. He keeps looking at his watch and looking up the street to see if another bus is coming.

Teaching Chart 138

MODEL The first paragraph doesn't say *Addie is tired*, but it does say she stayed up too late, is yawning, and would like to go to bed. I can draw the conclusion that she is tired.

PRACTICE

Draw Conclusions About Characters

ONE

Invite children to reread the other paragraphs on the chart, and to draw conclusions. Have children write down their ideas. Then discuss their conclusions about each paragraph. ▶ **Logical/Oral**

ASSESS/CLOSE

Play "20 Questions"

To assess children's ability to use information to draw conclusions, invite them to play "20 Questions." Ask them to draw conclusions about classroom objects you have in mind from the clues you give them.

DAILY Phonics ROUTINES

DAY 5 **Writing** Invite partners to create rhyming couplets using words with *ph, tch,* /ô/, soft *c,* soft *g,* and /ů/.

Phonics **CD-ROM**

i Intervention ▶ **Skills Intervention Guide,** for direct instruction and extra practice in drawing conclusions

Meeting Individual Needs for Comprehension

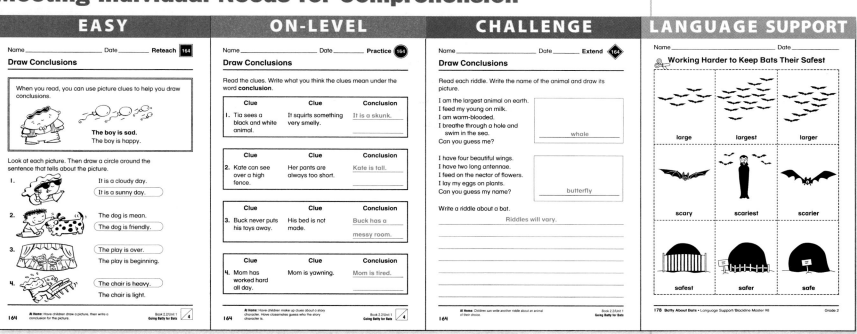

EASY	ON-LEVEL	CHALLENGE	LANGUAGE SUPPORT
Reteach, 164	Practice, 164	Extend, 164	Language Support, 178

OBJECTIVES

Children will:

- read and explain meanings of words with inflectional endings *-er* and *-est*.
- add *-er* and *-est* endings to words.

MATERIALS

- **Teaching Chart 139**

Skills Finder

Inflectional Endings

Introduce	B1: 35K-L
Review	B1: 123K-L, 125I-J; B2: 91K-L, 115K-L
Test	B1: Unit 1
Maintain	B2: 23

LANGUAGE SUPPORT

ESL With your hands, model for children *big, bigger,* and *biggest*. Next ask a child to draw pictures on the board to illustrate the meaning of *a small bat, a smaller bat* and *the smallest bat*. Then have other children point to the picture you describe as you say *small, smaller, smallest*. Repeat the activity with the words *big, bigger, biggest* and *large, larger, largest*, if you wish.

Review Inflectional Endings

PREPARE

Explain Word Meanings
Write on the chalkboard *tall, taller,* and *tallest*. Ask children to imagine that there are three trees growing in the classroom. Ask children to hold out a hand to show you how tall each tree is as you point to each word. Ask children to identify the base word (*tall*), and the added endings. (*-er* and *-est*)

TEACH

Model and Guide Practice with Inflectional Endings *-er* and *-est*
Review that the endings *-er* and *-est* can be added to base words to change their meaning. Prompt children to tell you that *-er* is added to a base word to compare something about two subjects, and *-est* is added to compare more than two things. Display **Teaching Chart 139** and model how to choose the correct ending to the underlined base words.

Small, Smaller, Smallest . . . and Bravest?

1. The little brown bat is only a bit <u>large</u>(r) than a mouse.
2. The little brown bat isn't the <u>small</u>(est) in the world, though.
3. The hog-nosed bat is even <u>small</u>(er) than the little brown bat.
4. In fact, the hog-nosed bat is no <u>large</u>(r) than a bumblebee!
5. I think the <u>small</u>(est) bat in the world must also be the <u>brave</u>(st) bat in the world.
6. Think how much <u>brave</u>(r) you would have to be than you are now if there were other people over a hundred times <u>large</u>(r) than you!

Teaching Chart 139

MODEL The first base word is *large*. I know I should drop the *e* and add the ending *-er* because I want to compare two things, a bat and a mouse. When I add *-er* to large, the sentence makes sense: *The little brown bat is only a bit larger than a mouse.*

Add Inflectional Endings to Words

ONE

Invite children to read the sentences in the rest of **Teaching Chart 139**. Ask them to copy each underlined base word, and to add the endings -er or -est to each to make each sentence make sense. After children have finished working independently, invite volunteers to write in the correct -er and -est endings to the words on the chart. Ask each volunteer to explain how he or she chose the right ending to fit into the sentence, and to state what things the sentence compares.

▶ Linguistic/Oral

ASSESS/CLOSE

Write with Inflectional Endings

Write on the chalkboard the following words: *quick, cute, small*. To assess how well children understand inflectional endings -er and -est, ask each child to write a paragraph comparing some bats, using each word from the chalkboard, along with inflectional endings -er and -est. Invite volunteers to share aloud their paragraphs.

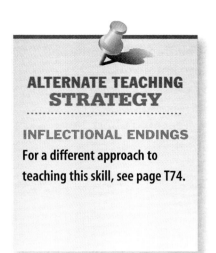

ALTERNATE TEACHING STRATEGY

INFLECTIONAL ENDINGS

For a different approach to teaching this skill, see page T74.

Intervention ▶ **Skills Intervention Guide,** for direct instruction and extra practice of inflectional endings

Meeting Individual Needs for Vocabulary

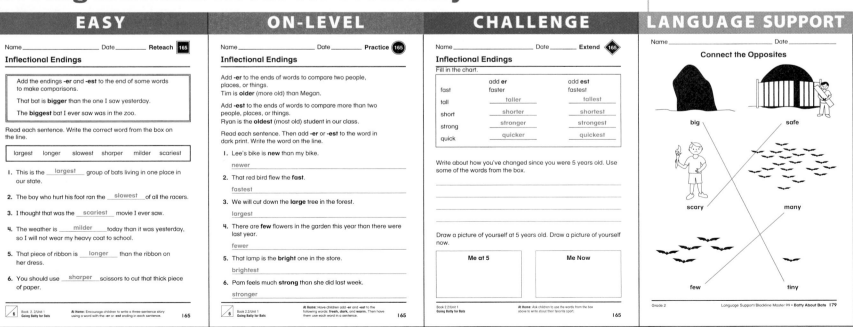

EASY	ON-LEVEL	CHALLENGE	LANGUAGE SUPPORT
Reteach, 165	Practice, 165	Extend, 165	Language Support, 179

125J

Children will identify and use antonyms.

MATERIALS
• **Teaching Chart 140**

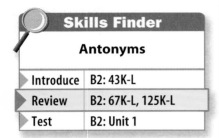

Antonyms	
Introduce	B2: 43K–L
Review	B2: 67K–L, 125K–L
Test	B2: Unit 1

TEACHING TIP

ANTONYMS Point out to children that many words have more than one antonym. Antonyms for *hot,* for example, include *cold, chilly, freezing, icy,* and *frosty.*

Review **Antonyms**

PREPARE

Play an Opposite Game

Explain to children that the object of the game is to say the opposite of what you mean. Example: In the summer, it is very cold. Invite each child to say an "opposite sentence," encouraging the rest of the class to call out what the person really means.

TEACH

Model and Guide Practice with Antonyms

Review with children that antonyms are words that mean the opposite of one another, such as *hot/cold,* and *up/down.* Display **Teaching Chart 140** and model finding antonyms for common words.

Charlie the Bat

One <u>morning</u>, Charlie the bat went hunting with his family. They went to the <u>tiny</u> lake where all the bugs lived. It was so <u>hot</u> out that the lake had frozen. His father caught a <u>little</u> moth for him, but Charlie couldn't eat the whole thing. He wanted to find some <u>dried-up</u> flies. Flies were his favorite meal. They were <u>pretty</u>, but they tasted good. He especially <u>hated</u> horse flies. He would eat as <u>few</u> as he could, as <u>slowly</u> as he could. They tasted <u>terrible</u>!

Teaching Chart 140

MODEL I know that antonyms are words that mean the opposite. In the first sentence I see the word *morning.* The opposite of *morning* is *evening,* so *morning* and *evening* are antonyms.

Invite children to suggest antonyms for the underlined words in the rest of **Teaching Chart 140**. Ask the class if the story makes more sense with the underlined words, or with the antonyms.

PRACTICE

Antonym Songs

GROUP

Invite small groups to create songs or poems that include antonym pairs. (They may wish to rewrite the words of an existing song.) Have groups sing their songs or recite their poems to the class. Ask audience members to raise their hands when they hear antonym pairs in the song. ▶ **Linguistic/Musical**

Conversing With Antonyms

PARTNERS

Make a list of the underlined words from **Teaching Chart 140.** Tell partners to make a three or four sentence story using some of the words from the list. Next, have them tell the "opposite" story by using the antonyms of the words they chose. ▶ **Linguistic/Interpersonal**

ASSESS/CLOSE

Antonym Bee

To ensure that children understand what antonyms are, observe their work on the Practice activity. Divide the class into two teams and hold an "antonym bee," presenting team members with common words such as *wet, tall, cloudy,* or *fast.* A team gets a point for each antonym the player finds for the word you give.

ALTERNATE TEACHING STRATEGY

ANTONYMS

For a different approach to teaching this skill, see page T68.

i Intervention ▶ Skills Intervention Guide, for direct instruction and extra practice of antonyms

Meeting Individual Needs for Vocabulary

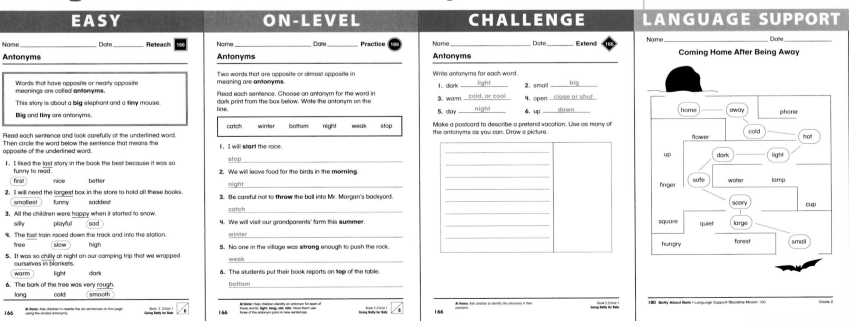

Reteach, 166   Practice, 166   Extend, 166   Language Support, 180

Writing That Compares

Prewrite

WRITE A SPEECH Present this writing assignment: Write a speech that will help people be less afraid of bats. Compare and contrast fears about bats and facts about bats. Talk about how bats help people. Explain how some things people think about bats are not true.

BRAINSTORM IDEAS Have children brainstorm reasons why people shouldn't be afraid of bats and how they can help people. Invite children to reread *Going Batty for Bats* to refresh their memories.

Strategy: Make a List Have children make a list of *Bat Fears* and *Bat Facts*. Have them find supporting facts and details in the article for each category. Suggest the following:

- myths about bats and where the myths came from
- ways bats help people
- facts on bats' eating habits
- why bats need protection from people

Draft

FREEWRITE Encourage children to write freely, using the information from their lists. Tell them to make sure their comparisons are orderly and organized. Suggest first writing all their bat fears and then all their bat facts, or alternating bat fears and bat facts. Remind them to keep their audience in mind when writing their speeches.

Revise

SELF-QUESTIONING Ask children to think about these questions when rereading their drafts.

- Did I include both fears and facts?
- Did I convince people they should be less afraid of bats?
- What might make my speech more effective?

Edit/Proofread

CHECK FOR ERRORS Children should reread their speeches for organization, spelling, grammar and punctuation.

Publish

SHARE THE SPEECHES Children can deliver their speeches to a partner. Have the partners tell each other what was most convincing about their speeches.

> Save the Bats!
> By Kevin Jamison
>
> Fellow 2nd Graders:
>
> I'd like to talk to you about bats. I'm sure most of you have heard scary stories about bats, but bats hardly ever hurt people. In fact, bats are helpful, especially to farmers. They eat insects that kill crops. They also eat flies and mosquitoes. Isn't that a good reason to be nice to them? Bats are in danger of dying out because people are mean to them. So try not to be afraid of bats and remember: the scariest thing about them are the stories people tell.

Presentation Ideas

TOWN MEETING Have children present their speeches at a "town meeting." Encourage the audience to ask questions and to vote on whether to protect bats.
▶ **Speaking/Listening**

PUBLISH A SPEECH Ask children to draw pictures of a bat fact and a bat fear from their speeches. Copy speeches and drawings for a class magazine.
▶ **Viewing/Representing**

BATS ARE GOOD!
BATS ARE GREAT!
THINK OF ALL THE BUGS THEY ATE!

Consider children's creative efforts, possibly adding a plus (+) for originality, wit, and imagination.

Scoring Rubric

Excellent	Good	Fair	Unsatisfactory
4: The writer • presents comparisons and explains them in an orderly, organized manner. • uses vivid language to elaborate supporting details. • shows a keen awareness of audience.	**3:** The writer • presents comparisons in an organized manner. • includes supporting details. • shows some awareness of an audience.	**2:** The writer • presents comparisons, but may lack organization. • uses some supporting details. • shows little awareness of audience.	**1:** The writer • does not make a comparison. • does not include supporting detail. • does not write in speech form.

Incomplete **0:** The writer leaves the page blank or fails to respond to the writing task. The child does not address the topic or simply paraphrases the prompt. The response is illegible or incoherent.

Meeting Individual Needs for Writing

EASY

Word Web Have children create a word web instead of a speech. The word web should include reasons why people should be less afraid of bats, facts about interesting and/or good things that bats do, and how scary stories about bats often aren't true.

ON-LEVEL

Postcard Have children write a postcard to a friend or family member telling about bat facts. Ask children to include what they think is the most amazing or strangest fact they know about bats. If they refer to the story to refresh their memory, remind children to put their ideas in their own words.

CHALLENGE

Scrapbook Have children write out a dialogue about bats. Have them pretend one person believes bats are interesting and helpful to people, and the other person thinks bats are scary and dangerous.

LANGUAGE SUPPORT

LANGUAGE SUPPORT

ESL Present this question and answer pattern: *Is the sky green? No, it isn't.* Explain that *isn't* has the same meaning as the words *is not.* Have pairs make their own questions and answers based on the same pattern.

DAILY LANGUAGE ACTIVITIES

Write the Daily Language Activities on the chalkboard each day or use **Transparency 20.** Have children orally form properly punctuated contractions. Prompt them to spell aloud each contraction, including apostrophes where needed.

Day 1

1. A bat isnt going to hurt you. isn't

2. We arent going into the cave today. aren't

3. Jake hasnt ever seen a bat. hasn't

Day 2

1. The bat didnt seem scary. didn't

2. It doesnt want to hurt us. doesn't

3. Kelli and Roger dont want to see it anyway. don't

Day 3

1. The bat isnt going to fly. isn't

2. It doesnt like to be seen. doesn't

3. Bats havent bitten anyone I know. haven't

Day 4

1. People can not fly like bats can. can't

2. I did not know that. didn't

3. Heather has not read much about bats. hasn't

Day 5

1. Bats do not like to get close to us. don't

2. I have not ever seen so many bats! haven't

3. Mom and Dad are not going to believe it! aren't

Daily Language Transparency 20

DAY 1 Introduce the Concept

Oral Warm-Up Ask this question: *Is the moon square?* Point out the contractions in children's answers.

Introduce Contractions Explain that some pairs of words can be shortened to one word by adding the two words together and leaving out certain letters. Present:

Contractions

- A **contraction** is a short form of two words.

- An **apostrophe** (') takes the place of the letters that are left out.

Display these word pairs and their contractions: *is not/isn't, are not/aren't, has not/hasn't.* Ask children which letter is left out. Point out the apostrophes.

Present the Daily Language Activity. Then have children write two sentences using any of these contractions.

WRITING Assign the daily Writing Prompt on page 116C.

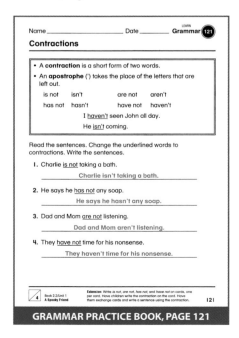

GRAMMAR PRACTICE BOOK, PAGE 121

DAY 2 Teach the Concept

Review *Isn't, Aren't, Hasn't, Haven't*
Ask children what contractions are and what takes the place of the missing letters. Have them identify what contractions can be formed by joining *is, are, has,* and *have* with *not.*

Introduce More Contractions
Display the following word pairs and their contractions: *does not/doesn't, do not/don't, did not/ didn't.* Point out that in *can't* two letters (*n* and *o*) are left out when the contraction is formed.

Present the Daily Language Activity. Then have each child write four sentences using each of the above contractions.

WRITING Assign the daily Writing Prompt on page 116C.

GRAMMAR PRACTICE BOOK, PAGE 122

Contractions

Learn from the Literature Review forming contractions. Read the sentence from page 121 of *Going Batty for Bats*.

> **So don't get scared if you happen to see a bat.**

Ask children to identify the contraction and state what two words are joined in it. (*do* and *not*) Ask a volunteer to identify the letter or letters that were left out and replaced by an apostrophe to form the contraction.

Form contractions Present the Daily Language Activity. Then write on the board the words *is, are, has, have, does, do, can, did*. Ask each child to write two or three sentences about bats, using as many of these words as possible. Then have children trade with partners and rewrite each other's sentences using contractions where appropriate.

 Assign the daily Writing Prompt on page 116D.

Review Contractions Write the incorrect contractions from the Daily Language Activity sentences for Days 1 and 2 on the board. Ask volunteers to spell aloud each contraction, adding the apostrophe where needed. Ask other children what two words each contraction is formed from. Then present the Daily Language Activity for Day 4.

Mechanics and Usage Display and review:

> **Contractions**
>
> An apostrophe takes the place of the letter left out of a contraction.

 Assign the daily Writing Prompt on page 116D. Encourage children to use contractions in their writing.

Assess Use the Daily Language Activity and page 125 of the **Grammar Practice Book** for assessment.

Reteach Have children create a contraction chart. Help them get started by eliciting from them the contractions they have learned this week. Write on the board each contraction and the word pair it was formed from as volunteers spell them aloud. Tell children that these contractions will be easier to remember if they organize them in a chart. Have them fold a paper in half and label the left side "Word Pairs" and the right side "Contractions." Have them write each word pair and its corresponding contraction under the correct label. Display the children's contraction charts.

Use page 126 of the **Grammar Practice Book** for additional reteaching.

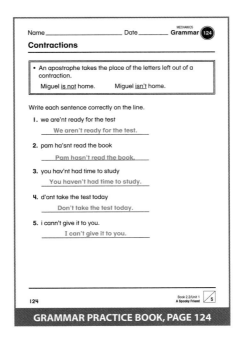 Assign the daily Writing Prompt on page 116D.

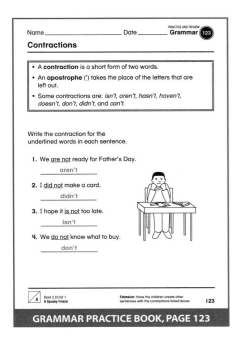

GRAMMAR PRACTICE BOOK, PAGE 123

GRAMMAR PRACTICE BOOK, PAGE 124

GRAMMAR PRACTICE BOOK, PAGE 125

5 Day Spelling Plan

To help students distinguish between long- and short-vowel sounds, present contrasting pairs of words: *sleep, nest; insects, sight;* etc.

DICTATION SENTENCES

Spelling Words

1. I go to <u>sleep</u> at night.
2. The bird has only one <u>wing</u>.
3. The bee can <u>fly</u>.
4. There are four <u>caves</u>.
5. A <u>nest</u> is made of straw.
6. The <u>leaves</u> are green.
7. The <u>insects</u> are gone.
8. Her <u>blood</u> is red.
9. The hills are a pretty <u>sight</u>.
10. The <u>den</u> is for the animals.

Challenge Words

11. He took a <u>breath</u>.
12. What <u>crops</u> does the farmer grow?
13. You can have <u>darkness</u> or light.
14. The book is <u>scary</u>.
15. I <u>study</u> hard.

DAY 1 — Pretest

Assess Prior Knowledge Use the Dictation Sentences at left and **Spelling Practice Book** page 121 for the pretest. Allow students to correct their own papers. If students have trouble, have partners give each other a midweek test on Day 3. Students who require a modified list may be tested on the first five words.

Spelling Words		Challenge Words
1. **sleep**	6. **leaves**	11. **breath**
2. wing	7. **insects**	12. **crops**
3. **fly**	8. blood	13. **darkness**
4. **caves**	9. sight	14. **scary**
5. nest	10. den	15. **study**

*Note: Words in **dark type** are from the story.*

Word Study On page 122 of the **Spelling Practice Book** are word study steps and an at-home activity.

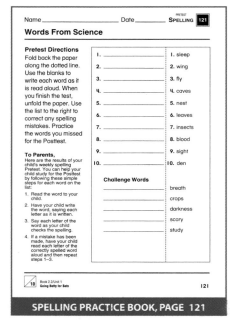

SPELLING PRACTICE BOOK, PAGE 121
WORD STUDY STEPS AND ACTIVITY, PAGE 122

DAY 2 — Explore the Pattern

Sort and Spell Words Say the words *sleep* and *wing*. Ask students which has a long-vowel sound and which has a short-vowel sound. Have them identify the sounds. (long *e* and short *i*) Then have children say each spelling-identifying the short- and long-vowel sounds.

Ask students to read aloud the ten spelling words before sorting them according to the pattern. Point out the unusual spelling of short *u* in *blood*.

Words with short vowel sounds	Words with long vowel sounds
wing	sleep
nest	fly
insects	caves
blood	leaves
den	sight

Word Wall As students read, have them look for new words with long- and short-vowel sounds and add them to the classroom word wall, underlining the spelling of the vowel sounds in each word.

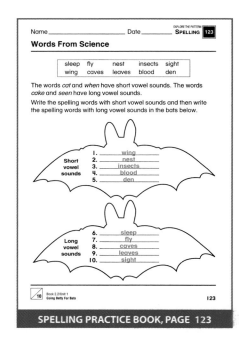

SPELLING PRACTICE BOOK, PAGE 123

Words from Science

DAY 3 — Practice and Extend

Word Meaning: Tell students that each spelling word is science related. See how many of the words students can define in a science context. Then have students use the spelling words to fill in the blanks in sentences such as the following: Birds build _____.

Glossary Have partners:

- write each Challenge Word.

- look up the definition of each Challenge Word in the Glossary.

- write a definition for each Challenge Word.

DAY 4 — Proofread and Write

Proofread Sentences Write these sentences on the chalkboard, including the misspelled words. Ask students to proofread, circling incorrect spellings and writing the correct spellings. There are two spelling errors in each sentence.

> The bird can (fli) to the (nezt.) (fly, nest)
>
> The (caives) are a pretty (sigt.) (caves, sight)

Have students create additional sentences with errors for partners to correct.

 Have students use as many spelling words as possible in the daily Writing Prompt on page 116D. Remind students to proofread their writing for errors in spelling, grammar, and punctuation.

DAY 5 — Assess

Assess Students' Knowledge Use page 126 of the **Spelling Practice Book** or the Dictation Sentences on page 125Q for the posttest.

Personal Word List If students have trouble with any words in the lesson, have them create a personal list of troublesome words in their journals. Have students write poems, using words from their personal word list.

Students should refer to their word lists during later writing activities.

SPELLING PRACTICE BOOK, PAGE 124

Name _____ Date _____ PRACTICE AND EXTEND SPELLING 124

Words From Science

| sleep | fly | nest | insects | sight |
| wing | caves | leaves | blood | den |

Write a spelling word to complete each sentence.

1. Bats sometimes live in _____ caves _____.

2. Bats are not known for their sense of _____ sight _____.

3. In winter a bear stays in its _____ den _____.

4. Bears _____ sleep _____ through the winter.

5. Another name for _____ insects _____ is bugs.

6. Insects like to eat all kinds of _____ leaves _____.

7. In the tree, we found a _____ nest _____.

8. We found a bird with a broken _____ wing _____.

9. We washed the _____ blood _____ from its feathers.

10. We want to help the bird _____ fly _____ again.

124

Book 2.2/Unit 1
Going Batty for Bats 10

SPELLING PRACTICE BOOK, PAGE 125

Name _____ Date _____ PROOFREAD AND WRITE SPELLING 125

Words From Science

Proofreading Activity
There are six spelling mistakes in the story. Circle each misspelled word. Write the words correctly on the lines below.

A bird uses (leafs) and twigs to build its (nesst.) Birds are good parents. They bring worms and (insecs) to their babies. It can be a funny (site) to watch a baby bird learn to (flie.) At first, baby birds are not very good at flying. They flap their (wengs) and nothing happens. They try again and again until they finally take off into the air.

1. _____ leaves _____ 2. _____ nest _____ 3. _____ insects _____

4. _____ sight _____ 5. _____ fly _____ 6. _____ wings _____

Writing Activity
Write a story about nature. Use four spelling words in your story. Circle the spelling words in your story.

_____
_____
_____
_____
_____

10 Book 2.2/Unit 1
Going Batty for Bats

125

SPELLING PRACTICE BOOK, PAGE 126

Name _____ Date _____ POSTTEST SPELLING 126

Words From Science

Look at the words in each set. One word in each set is spelled correctly. Use a pencil to color in the circle in front of that word. Before you begin, look at the sample sets of words. Sample A has been done for you. Do Sample B by yourself. When you are sure you know what to do, you may go on with the rest of the page.

Sample A
- (A) sunn
- (B) sone
- (C) sun ●
- (D) sune

Sample B
- (E) beeche
- (F) baech
- (G) beache
- (H) beach ●

1. (A) leafes
   (B) leaves
   (C) leeves
   (D) leavs

2. (E) weng
   (F) winng
   (G) winge
   (H) wing

3. (A) sihgt
   (B) siight
   (C) sight
   (D) siet

4. (E) nesst
   (F) nest
   (G) neste
   (H) neess

5. (A) caves
   (B) caavs
   (C) cavs
   (D) cavas

6. (E) slepe
   (F) slep
   (G) sleep
   (H) sleepe

7. (A) insectx
   (B) insects
   (C) inseects
   (D) insecks

8. (E) blud
   (F) blod
   (G) bluud
   (H) blood

9. (A) fly
   (B) flly
   (C) fli
   (D) flie

10. (E) dehn
    (F) den
    (G) denn
    (H) denne

126

Book 2.2/Unit 1
Going Batty for Bats 10

Wrap Up the Theme

Look Around

*There are surprises
all around us.*

REVIEW THE THEME Remind children that all the selections in this unit relate to the theme Look Around. Ask them to select a story and tell what happened when the character(s) "looked around." Then invite children to name other stories or movies they know that also fit the theme Look Around.

READ THE POEM Read aloud "Neighbors" by Marchette Chute. After the reading, ask children how the poem connects to the theme Look Around. Guide them to understand that the narrator is observing the small creatures that live in the tall grass.

Reread the poem, having children echo the last word in each line. Encourage children to listen for rhymes.

LISTENING LIBRARY Children can listen to an audio recording of the poem.

MAKE CONNECTIONS Have children work in small groups to brainstorm a list of ways that the stories, poems, and the *Time for Kids* magazine article relate to the theme Look Around. Groups can then compare their lists as they share them with the class.

-126

LOOKING AT GENRE

Have children review *Charlie Anderson* and *Zipping, Zapping, Zooming Bats*. What makes *Charlie Anderson* realistic fiction? What makes *Zipping, Zapping, Zooming Bats* nonfiction?

Help children list the key characteristics of each literary form. Can they name other selections that have the same characteristics?

REALISTIC FICTION *Charlie Anderson*	NON-FICTION *Zipping, Zapping, Zooming Bats*
• Made-up characters and action seem real.	• There are no made up characters.
• There is a plot.	• There is no plot.
• The writer provides entertainment.	• The writer provides information.

Neighbors

If I lie down flat where the tall grass grows
I can watch all the passersby—
The ants, the spiders, and other small things
That creep and that run and that fly.

As long as I stay very quiet and still
They do not mind if I stare.
They like to have me down in the grass
Watching their travels there.

by Marchette Chute

127

LEARNING ABOUT POETRY

Literary Devices: Rhyme Pattern and Rhythm Point out the abcb rhyme scheme of the poem by having children name the rhyming words. Then have them clap to feel the rhythm as they read aloud the poem. Ask children how they feel about this rhyme pattern. Does it make the poem more fun to read?

Poetry Activity Have children write a poem about small creatures, for example: insects, mice, spiders, birds. They can use the same format as "Neighbors," or you may choose to model another poem for them to follow.

WRITING

Activity

Research and Inquiry

GROUP **Complete the Theme Project.** Have children work in teams to complete their group project. Remind children to use drawings, charts, diagrams, and pictures to illustrate their text. Encourage them to share all the tasks so that each member of the team can contribute to the project.

Make a Classroom Presentation
Have teams take turns presenting their projects. They could display and read their questions or answers. Or they might present the information as a dialogue, with one team member asking the question and another answering it. Be sure to include time for questions from the audience. After all the teams have presented their pages, combine them into a class Question and Answer book. Ask a volunteer to make a cover.

Draw Conclusions Have children draw conclusions about what they learned from their research. Was the research chart they made helpful? What other resources, such as the internet, did they use? Finally, ask children if the information they found changed their minds about what they thought was true or not true. What conclusions can they draw from this?

Ask More Questions What other questions about nature would children like to answer? You might encourage them to select another question, research to find the answer(s), and prepare a new presentation.

127

Reading Science

OBJECTIVES Children will:

- compare and contrast ideas and topics to better understand what they read.
- recognize implicit main ideas and details.
- cross-check visual, structural, and meaning cues to figure out unknown words.
- identify **text features** such as subheadings.

BUILD BACKGROUND

- Explain that this lesson comes from a science textbook. However, children might find similar features in nonfiction magazine articles.

FEATURES OF SCIENCE TEXTS

- **scientific terms**
- **glossary**
- **directions**
- **pictures and photographs**
- **labeled diagrams**
- **charts and tables**

- Briefly discuss some of the common features of science texts.
- Encourage children to look through their science textbooks to see if they can find similar features.
- You may want to gather other texts and put them in a designated area for children to examine.
- Tell children that they will learn to use comparisons to read science lessons. Learning how to apply this strategy and then practicing it will help them see the benefits of its use.

TEACHING TIP

Helping Children Read Science

BUILD PRIOR KNOWLEDGE Science texts are often filled with facts, details, and difficult concepts. Teaching children different ways to approach a lesson will help them develop a range of study skills and better prepare them to understand what they read. Provide prereading instruction and as much hands-on experience as possible.

UNDERSTAND NEW VOCABULARY Science lessons often contain new terms, such as *habitat,* along with words that have new meanings, such as *fresh.* Children need to develop strategies for identifying unfamiliar words and to use context to figure out

new definitions for familiar words. Urge them to use the text glossary as a resource.

UNDERSTAND CONCEPTS AND ORGANIZATION In science texts, children may need help understanding the link between concepts. They must also learn how to identify main ideas and important details without being distracted by the unimportant ones.

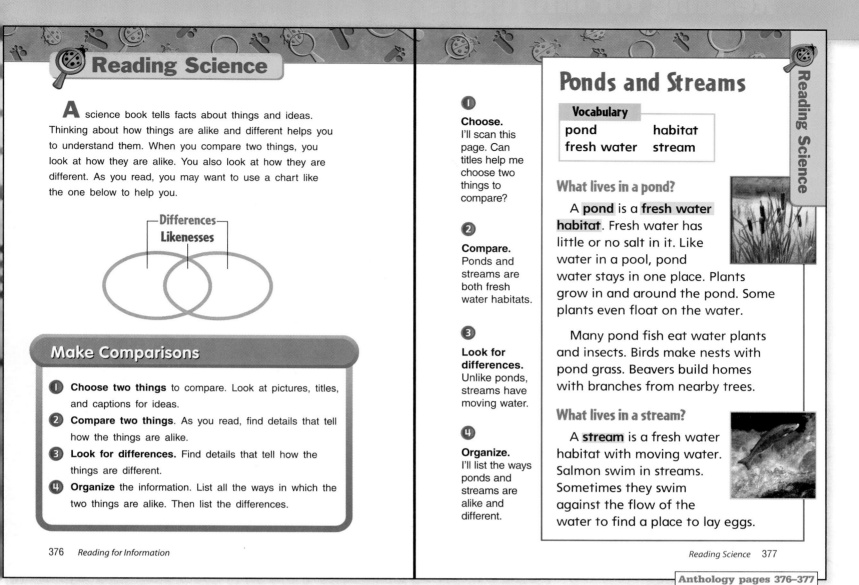

INTRODUCE   Say: Making comparisons is a good way to better understand what you read. You think about how things are alike and how they are different. You are going to use this strategy to better understand information in a science text book. *(Set Purposes)*

Read or have volunteers read the four steps for Making Comparisons. Explain that good readers help themselves understand what they read by

- choosing two things to compare.
- comparing how they are alike.
- exploring how they are different.

PRACTICE   Say: Let's **preview** a page from a science textbook. The numbered sentences on the side of the page show how you can make comparisons to learn more about ponds and streams.

Point out the **text features** such a subheadings and the color-highlighted words. Have children read "Ponds and Streams" to see how they can use the strategy.

- **How can these subheadings help you choose two things to compare and contrast?** (The subheadings name the main ideas in the lesson.)

- **How can looking for ways that two things are the same help you understand what you read?** (You think more about what you read and look for similarities.)

- **How can looking for ways that two things are different help you learn about them?** (You pay attention to details.)

APPLY Have children read page 378 and make comparisons.

MODEL I need to choose something to compare and contrast on this page. I should not choose the mountains and the goat because they are too different from each other. I know! I can choose the mountains and the place where I live. I can compare and contrast these two places in order to understand where the goat lives.

Ask: What can you do if a lesson does not have two similar ideas or things? How can you find two things to compare? (You can compare something from the lesson with something you already know about.)

Discuss: Draw children's attention to the Explore activity on page 379. After they have matched each animal with its habitat, help children apply the strategies by comparing and contrasting two of the "animal" pictures or two of the "habitat" pictures.

Say: Now it's time to read pages 380 and 381. Be sure to make comparisons to learn more about habitats. Then answer the Review Questions on page 381.

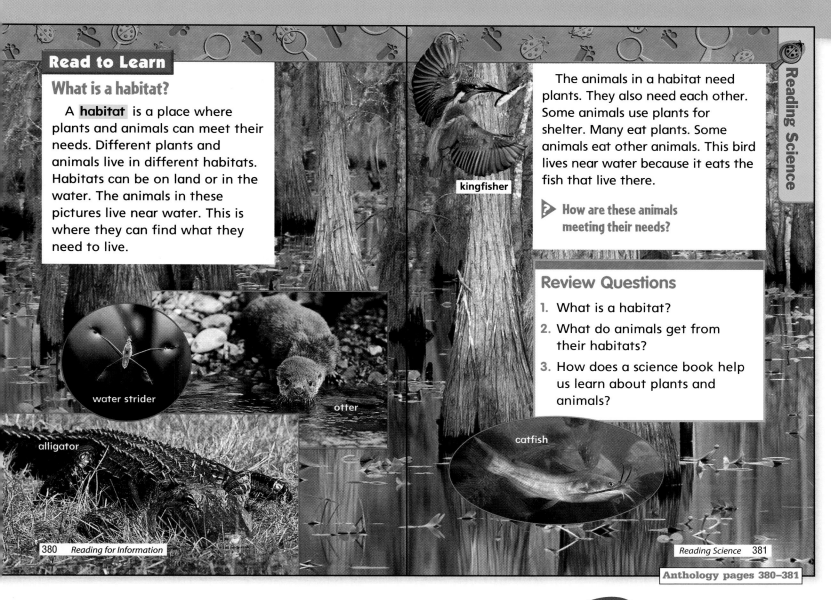

Read to Learn

What is a habitat?

A **habitat** is a place where plants and animals can meet their needs. Different plants and animals live in different habitats. Habitats can be on land or in the water. The animals in these pictures live near water. This is where they can find what they need to live.

water strider

otter

alligator

kingfisher

The animals in a habitat need plants. They also need each other. Some animals use plants for shelter. Many eat plants. Some animals eat other animals. This bird lives near water because it eats the fish that live there.

 How are these animals meeting their needs?

Review Questions

1. What is a habitat?
2. What do animals get from their habitats?
3. How does a science book help us learn about plants and animals?

catfish

380 *Reading for Information*

Reading Science 381

Anthology pages 380–381

ANSWERS TO REVIEW QUESTIONS

1. A habitat is a place where plants and animals can meet their needs for food and shelter.

2. Animals get food and shelter from their habitats.

3. A science book gives facts about plants and animals and explains how they affect one another.

TRANSFER THE STRATEGY

Ask: How did making comparisons help you learn about habitats?

Discuss: Have volunteers mention some other times when making comparisons could help them understand what they read. Mention that they will use the strategy with the following activity.

Activity

Habitats Far and Near

What to do:

1. Choose two animals that live in your state. Select one that lives far from people, in the forest, mountains, or desert. Choose one that lives in or near towns and cities. Draw both animals.

2. Use a Venn diagram to compare how these animals are alike.

3. Use the same Venn diagram to show how they are different.

4. Explain how their different habitats meet their needs for food and shelter.

Children's responses should offer a clear comparison and contrast of two animals from different habitats.

127D

Writing That Compares

Informative/Classificatory

CONNECT TO LITERATURE In a class discussion on *Charlie Anderson*, ask children to compare the things that Charlie does in his two homes. How do they think he spent his days? What did he do at night? Make a chalkboard list of children's ideas.

My mom has a twin sister. They really look alike. They wear their hair the same way and like to wear blue jeans. They are both tall, red-headed, and happy. They have the same smile and even move their hands the same way.

They are very different people, though. My mom loves spicy food. My Aunt Jean can't stand anything hot! On sunny Saturdays, my mom loves to go swimming or bike riding. Aunt Jean stays cool under a big umbrella in her yard. But in the winter Aunt Jean skis and skates, while Mom likes to stay at home and sit by a fire. They really don't like the same things at all, but they still love each other.

Prewrite

PURPOSE AND AUDIENCE Explain to children that they will be writing essays that compare two people that they know. Tell them that the purpose of the essay is to inform through the use of comparison. Ask them to keep their purpose and audience in mind as they write.

STRATEGY: MAKE A VENN DIAGRAM Show children how to chart their characters' similarities and differences on a Venn diagram.

Use **Writing Process Transparency 4A** as a model.

FEATURES OF WRITING THAT COMPARES

- Presents similarities and differences, or advantages and disadvantages, of two people, things, places, or ideas.
- Elaborates on a main idea.
- Organizes information logically, using transition words to connect ideas.
- May state a conclusion based on the facts presented.

TEACHING TIP

ORGANIZATION Help children to list and sort information for their Venn diagrams. First, have them make separate headings for differences and similarities. Under the headings, ask them to list comparative details by categories: appearance, ages, where they live, likes and dislikes, talents, their goals.

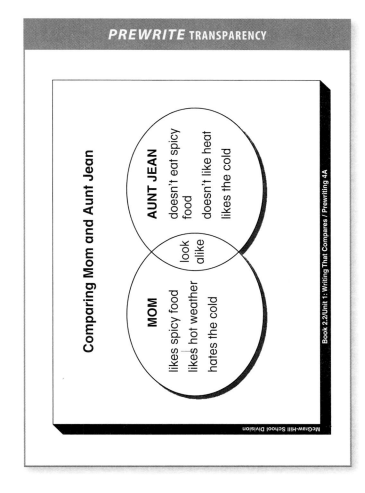

PREWRITE TRANSPARENCY

Comparing Mom and Aunt Jean

AUNT JEAN
doesn't eat spicy food
doesn't like heat
likes the cold

look alike

MOM
likes spicy food
likes hot weather
hates the cold

Book 2.2/Unit 1: Writing That Compares / Prewriting 4A

McGraw-Hill School Division

Writing That Compares

Draft

Some children may work best by choosing two characters from a book. Show them a few story books that your class has read. They can choose a favorite book and then pick two characters from it. Ask them to write a sentence about each character. Work directly with them on structuring the Venn diagram.

STRATEGY: EXPAND ON THE DIAGRAM Guide children to expand their Venn diagrams into first drafts. Remind them to place specific traits, such as characters' goals, into separate paragraphs. Encourage them to use rich, descriptive language to enhance their information.

Use **Writing Process Transparency 4B** to model a first draft.

WORD CHOICE Have children review, compare, and contrast words, such as *different from, same as, alike, like, similar to, unlike, but, as well as, yet, either…or, compared to, although,* and *however.* Suggest that children use these words to write sentences that compare and contrast items from their project diagrams. For example, "Mom and Aunt Jean look alike," or "Mom likes spicy food. However, Aunt Jean does not." Then encourage children to use a variety of compare/contrast transition words as they write their first drafts.

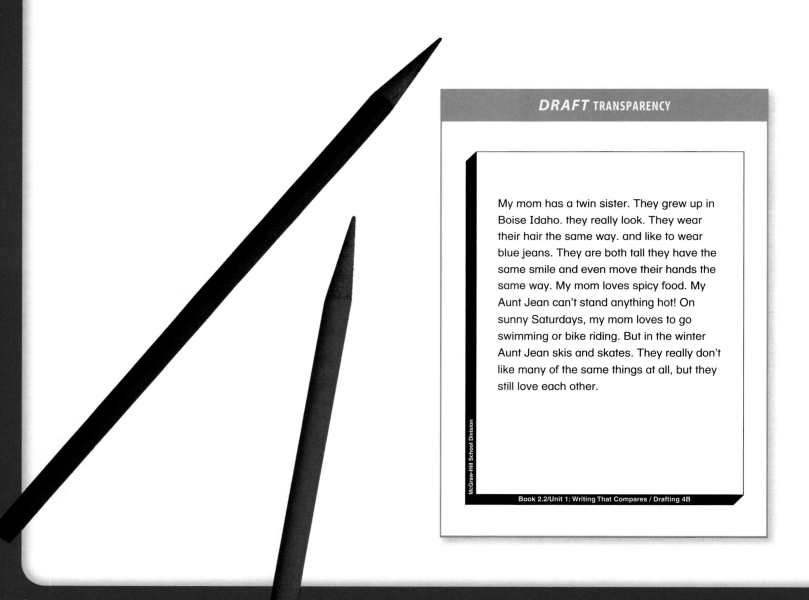

DRAFT TRANSPARENCY

My mom has a twin sister. They grew up in Boise Idaho. they really look. They wear their hair the same way. and like to wear blue jeans. They are both tall they have the same smile and even move their hands the same way. My mom loves spicy food. My Aunt Jean can't stand anything hot! On sunny Saturdays, my mom loves to go swimming or bike riding. But in the winter Aunt Jean skis and skates. They really don't like many of the same things at all, but they still love each other.

McGraw-Hill School Division

Book 2.2/Unit 1: Writing That Compares / Drafting 4B

Revise

Have partners exchange articles. Model how to make creative suggestions that can help them improve their work. Encourage them to tell what they like best about comparisons.

Use **Writing Process Transparency 4C** for classroom discussion on the revision process. Ask children to comment on how revisions may have improved this writing example.

STRATEGY: ELABORATION Have children examine their first drafts for points that may need to be explained in more detail, such as their characters' goals, actions, and feelings. Have them reflect on the following questions:

- Did I show how these characters think alike or differently?

- Have I compared how they look and act?

- Should I write a conclusion about these two characters? What should I say?

TEACHING TIP

TEACHER CONFERENCE

While children are revising, circulate and conference with them individually. You can use these questions to begin a conferencing checklist:

- Does your article have separate paragraphs for each thing you are comparing?

- Does your comparison present information and details clearly?

- Have you included some of your own ideas about the characters?

REVISE TRANSPARENCY

My mom has a twin sister. They grew up in Boise Idaho. they really look alike. They wear their hair the same way. and like to wear blue jeans. They are both tall redheaded, and happy. they have the same smile and even move their hands the same way. My mom loves spicy food. My Aunt Jean can't stand anything hot! On sunny Saturdays, my mom loves to go swimming or bike riding. Aunt Jean stays cool under a big umbrella in her yard. But in the winter Aunt Jean skis and skates, while Mom likes to stay at home and sit by a fire. They really don't like many of the same things at all, but they still love each other.

McGraw-Hill School Division

Book 2.2/Unit 1: Writing That Compares / Revising 4C

Writing That Compares

Edit/Proofread

After children finish revising their articles, have them proofread for final corrections and additions.

GRAMMAR/SPELLING CONNECTIONS

See the 5-Day Grammar and Usage Plans on verbs, pages 430–43P, pages 670–67P, pages 910–91P, pages 1150–115P, pages 1250–125P.

See the 5–Day Spelling Plans, pages 43Q–43R, pages 67Q–67R, pages 91Q–91R, pages 115Q–115R, pages 125Q–125R.

GRAMMAR, MECHANICS, USAGE

- Write complete sentences.
- Use a comma between the names of a city and a state.
- Combine sentences correctly.
- Capitalize proper nouns.

Publish

Children can read their work aloud to the class. You can bind their articles in a class anthology and put a copy in a school library.

Use **Writing Process Transparency 4D** as a proofreading model and **Writing Process Transparency 4E** to discuss presentation ideas for their writing.

PROOFREAD TRANSPARENCY

Two Different Twins

¶ My mom has a twin sister. They grew up in Boise, Idaho. they really look alike. They wear their hair the same way, and like to wear blue jeans. They are both tall, they have the redheaded, and happy. same smile and even move their hands the ¶ They are very different people, though. same way. My mom loves spicy food. My Aunt Jean can't stand anything hot! On sunny Saturdays, my mom loves to go swimming or bike riding. But in the winter Aunt Jean stays cool under a big umbrella in her yard. Aunt Jean skis and skates, They really don't while Mom likes to stay at home and sit by a fire. like many of the same things at all, but they still love each other.

McGraw-Hill School Division

Book 2.2/Unit 1: Writing That Compares / Proofreading 4D

PUBLISH TRANSPARENCY

Two Different Twins

My mom has a twin sister. They grew up in Boise, Idaho. They really look alike. They wear their hair the same way and like to wear blue jeans. They are both tall, redheaded, and happy. They have the same smile and even move their hands the same way.

They are very different people, though. My mom loves spicy food. My Aunt Jean can't stand anything hot! On sunny Saturdays, my mom loves to go swimming or bike riding. Aunt Jean stays cool under a big umbrella in her yard. But in the winter Aunt Jean skis and skates, while Mom likes to stay at home and sit by a fire. They really don't like many of the same things at all, but they still love each other.

McGraw-Hill School Division

Book 2.2/Unit 1: Writing That Compares / Publishing 4E

Presentation Ideas

MAKE A CLASS MAGAZINE Copy children's articles and gather them in a magazine titled "People We Know." Encourage children to comment on the articles. Distribute the magazine to other classes.
▶ **Viewing/Speaking**

MAKE CHARACTER PUPPETS Have children make sock puppets of their characters. They can decorate their puppets with yarn, beads, and buttons. Have them create a short skit for their puppet characters and perform it for the class and invited guests. ▶ **Representing/Speaking**

Assessment

SCORING RUBRIC Consider children's creative efforts, possibly adding a plus (+) for originality, wit, and imagination.

Scoring Rubric: 6-Trait Writing

4 Excellent	**3** Good	**2** Fair	**1** Unsatisfactory
Ideas & Content drafts a careful, focused comparison of two characters; thorough details strengthen the message.	**Ideas & Content** presents a clear, well-thought-out comparison; details show a solid grasp of the topic.	**Ideas & Content** has some control of the comparison task, but some ideas and details are vague or undeveloped.	**Ideas & Content** does not successfully compare two characters; writer seems to have no grasp of a purpose.
Organization shows capable planning; sequences moves the reader smoothly from beginning to end; paragraphs, sentences, and comparisons are tied together.	**Organization** has a careful structure; reader can follow the logic from beginning to end; details fit and build on each other.	**Organization** tries to structure a comparison, but may have trouble keeping facts and observations in order; beginning or ending may be undeveloped.	**Organization** shows extreme lack of organization; text is hard to follow; ideas and details are disconnected, and seem out of order.
Voice has deep involvement with the characters; personal approach enlivens the comparisons, and speaks directly to the reader.	**Voice** shows who is behind the words; personal style helps connect the reader with the characters.	**Voice** communicates the main theme, with a hint of who is behind the words; writer may seem uninvolved with characters and the reader.	**Voice** is not involved in the characters; does not address an audience at all.
Word Choice creates inventive, distinct pictures of each character; vocabulary is striking, but natural.	**Word Choice** uses a variety of clear, specific words to describe character traits; may experiment with new words or use everyday words in a fresh way.	**Word Choice** gets the message across, but experiments with few new words; may not convey a clear picture of each character.	**Word Choice** does not choose words that describe or compare; words do not fit, or are repeated; no new words are attempted.
Sentence Fluency sentences flow naturally, and are easy to read aloud; varying of lengths and patterns add interest to the comparisons.	**Sentence Fluency** crafts sentences that are easy to read and understand; sentence lengths and patterns vary, and fit together well.	**Sentence Fluency** sentences are understandable, but may be choppy, awkward or follow the same pattern; text is hard to follow or read aloud.	**Sentence Fluency** sentences are incomplete or confusing; words and sentences may not fit together; text is hard to read aloud
Conventions skilled in most writing conventions; the paper easy to read and understand; editing is largely unnecessary.	**Conventions** uses a variety of conventions correctly; errors are few and don't interfere with understanding the text; some editing may be needed.	**Conventions** makes noticeable errors that interfere with a smooth reading of the text; extensive need for editing and revision.	**Conventions** has repeated errors in spelling, word choice, punctuation and usage; sentence structures may be confused; reader has a hard time understanding the text.

Incomplete The writer leaves the page blank, or fails to respond to the writing task. The topic is not addressed, or the child simply paraphrases the prompt. The response may be illegible or incoherent.

VOCABULARY

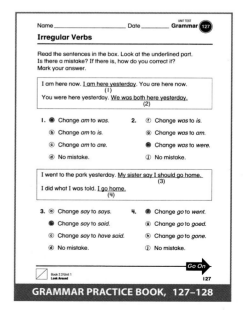

GROUP Assign words from one selection to each team. Using as many of the words as they can, the teams make up two titles for a book and two titles for a movie.

Unit Review

Charlie Anderson

| chocolate | middle | roof |
| clothes | offered | upstairs |

Fernando's Gift

| diving | harm | soil |
| explains | noisy | village |

The Best Vacation Ever

| brave | museum | vacation |
| guess | practice | wonder |

Zipping, Zapping, Zooming Bats

| disturb | facts | objects |
| explore | nature | several |

Going Batty for Bats

| breath | crops | scary |
| cover | darkness | study |

Name _____ Date _____ Practice (167)

Unit 1 Vocabulary Review

A. Use the words in the box to complete the story.

museum   chocolate   explore   vacation   nature   village

I live in a small ___village___ called Hamilton.

We have a library, a ___museum___, and a store that

sells ___chocolate___ - chip cookies. Many people

come to Hamilton for their summer ___vacation___.

They like to ___explore___ the forest. They also go

to the ___nature___ center to learn about plants .

B. Draw a line to the word or words that mean the *opposite*. Then, write this answer on the line.

downstairs	1. upstairs	quiet
help	2. harm	cowardly
light	3. darkness	downstairs
quiet	4. noisy	help
cowardly	5. brave	leave alone
leave alone	6. disturb	light

PRACTICE BOOK, 167–168

GRAMMAR

PARTNERS Each team selects one of the titles it created and writes a plot for a book or movie. Teams can then take turns reading their plots aloud.

Unit Review

Charlie Anderson
Linking Verbs

Fernando's Gift
Helping Verbs

The Best Vacation Ever
Irregular Verbs

Zipping, Zapping, Zooming Bats
More Irregular Verbs

Going Batty for Bats
Contractions

Name _____ Date _____ UNIT TEST Grammar (127)

Irregular Verbs

Read the sentences in the box. Look at the underlined part. Is there a mistake? If there is, how do you correct it? Mark your answer.

I am here now. <u>I am here yesterday.</u> You are here now.
                        (1)
You were here yesterday. <u>We was both here yesterday.</u>
                                      (2)

1. ● Change *am* to *was*.   2. ⓕ Change *was* to *is*.
   ⓑ Change *am* to *is*.   ⓖ Change *was* to *am*.
   ⓒ Change *am* to *are*.   ● Change *was* to *were*.
   ⓓ No mistake.   ⓘ No mistake.

I went to the park yesterday. <u>My sister say I should go home.</u>
                                             (3)
I did what I was told. <u>I go home.</u>
                          (4)

3. ⓐ Change *say* to *says*.   4. ● Change *go* to *went*.
   ● Change *say* to *said*.   ⓖ Change *go* to *goed*.
   ⓒ Change *say* to *have said*. ⓗ Change *go* to *gone*.
   ⓓ No mistake.   ⓘ No mistake.

Go On →

GRAMMAR PRACTICE BOOK, 127–128

SPELLING

GROUP The "caller" holds the list of spelling words and calls one out. The other children look around the room to find something that can be included in a sentence using the word. The first child to find something calls out the word and spells it. If the word is spelled correctly, he or she is the caller for the next word.

Unit Review

/ů/
wood
foot
wool
cook

Digraphs *ph, tch, ch*
patch
sandwich
touch
graph

Soft *c* and Soft *g*
dance
rice
charge
cage

Science Words
wing
caves
nest
leaves

/ô/
paw   because
caught   talk

Name _____ Date _____ UNIT TEST SPELLING **127**

Book 2.2/Unit 1 Review Test

Read each sentence. If an underlined word is spelled wrong, fill in the circle that goes with that word. If no word is spelled wrong, fill in the circle below NONE.
Read Sample A, and do Sample B.

A. I <u>took</u> <u>cheese</u> to the <u>nice</u> lady. A. Ⓐ Ⓑ Ⓒ ●
    A   B   C   NONE

B. <u>Look</u> at him <u>catch</u> the ball and <u>walk</u> away. B. Ⓔ Ⓕ Ⓖ ●
   E   F   G   NONE

1. <u>Because</u> she hurt her <u>foot</u>, she didn't <u>danse</u>. 1. Ⓐ Ⓑ ● Ⓓ
   A   B   C   NONE

2. He wants to <u>talk</u> about the <u>leafes</u> in the <u>caves</u>. 2. Ⓔ ● Ⓖ Ⓗ
   E   F   G   NONE

3. I will <u>cook</u> <u>rice</u> and make a <u>sandwich</u>. 3. Ⓐ Ⓑ Ⓒ ●
   A   B   C   NONE

4. The bird <u>cauwt</u> its <u>wing</u> in the <u>wood</u> door. 4. ● Ⓕ Ⓖ Ⓗ
   E   F   G   NONE

5. Please don't <u>tuch</u> the <u>leaves</u> in the <u>nest</u>. 5. ● Ⓑ Ⓒ Ⓓ
   A   B   C   NONE

6. I won't <u>charge</u> for the <u>wool</u> hat with the <u>pach</u>. 6. Ⓔ Ⓕ ● Ⓗ
   E   F   G   NONE

7. The dog tried to <u>tuch</u> the <u>cage</u> with its <u>paw</u>. 7. ● Ⓑ Ⓒ Ⓓ
   A   B   C   NONE

8. The <u>graph</u> shows the <u>nist</u> with the most <u>leaves</u>. 8. Ⓔ ● Ⓖ Ⓗ
   E   F   G   NONE

9. I will <u>cook</u> <u>rise</u> and put it near the <u>cage</u>. 9. Ⓐ ● Ⓒ Ⓓ
   A   B   C   NONE

→

127

SPELLING PRACTICE BOOK, 127–128

☑ SKILLS & S[KILLS]

Phonics and Decoding
☑ /ů/*oo*
☑ Soft *c* and Soft *g*
☑ /ô/*a, aw, au*
☑ Digraphs *ph, tch, ch*

Comprehension
☑ Draw Conclusions
☑ Compare and Contrast

Vocabulary Strategies
☑ Antonyms
☑ Inflectional Endings

Study Skills
☑ Graphic Aids

Writing
☑ Writing That Compares

MCGRAW-HILL READING

Unit Test

Student Name: _____

Date: _____

Grade 2 · Book 2 · Unit 1

Assessment
Follow-Up

Use the results of the informal and formal assessment opportunities in the unit to help you make decisions about future instruction.

SKILLS AND STRATEGIES	Reteaching Blackline Masters	Alternate Teaching Strategies	Skills Intervention Guide ⓘ
Phonics and Decoding			
/ù/oo	127, 131, 132, 140, 148, 159	T65	✓
Soft c and Soft g	135, 139, 140, 148, 156, 159	T70	✓
/ô/a, aw, au	143, 147, 148, 156, 159	T73	✓
Digraphs ph, tch, ch	151, 155, 156, 159	T76	✓
Comprehension			
Draw Conclusions	133, 149, 164	T67	✓
Compare and Contrast	141, 157, 163	T71	✓
Vocabulary Strategies			
Antonyms	134, 142, 166	T68	✓
Inflectional Endings	150, 158, 165	T74	✓
Study Skills			
Graphic Aids	130, 138, 146, 154, 162	T66	✓

Writing	Alternate Writing Project—Easy	Unit Writing Process Lesson
Writing That Compares	43N, 67N, 91N, 115N, 125N	127E–127J

McGraw-Hill School
TECHNOLOGY

 CD-ROM provides extra phonics support.

*inter***NET**
CONNECTION Research & Inquiry ideas. Visit ***www.mhschool.com/reading.***

Glossary

Introduce children to the Glossary by reading through the introduction and looking over the pages with them. Encourage the class to talk about what they see.

Words in a glossary, like words in a dictionary, are listed in **alphabetical order.** Point out the **guide words** at the top of each page that tell the first and last words appearing on that page.

Point out examples of **entries** and **main entries.** Read through a simple entry with the class, identifying each part. Have children note the order in which information is given: entry word(s), definition(s), example sentence(s), syllable division, pronunciation respelling, part of speech, plural/verb/adjective forms.

Note that if more than one definition is given for a word, the definitions are numbered. Note also the format used for a word that is more than one part of speech.

Review the parts of speech by identifying each in a sentence:

inter.	*adj.*	*n.*	*conj.*	*adj.*	*n.*
Wow!	A	dictionary	and	a	glossary
v.	*adv.*	*pron.*	*prep.*	*n.*	
tell	almost	everything	about	words!	

Explain the use of the **pronunciation key** (either the **short key,** at the bottom of every other page, or the **long key,** at the beginning of the Glossary). Demonstrate the difference between **primary** stress and **secondary** stress by pronouncing a word with both.

Point out an example of the small triangle signaling a homophone. **Homophones** are words with different spellings and meanings but with the same pronunciation. Explain that a pair of words with the superscripts **1** and **2** are **homographs**—words that have the same spelling, but different origins and meanings, and in some cases, different pronunciations.

The **Word History** feature tells what language a word comes from and what changes have occurred in its spelling and/or meaning. Many everyday words have interesting and surprising stories behind them. Note that word histories can help us remember the meanings of difficult words.

Allow time for children to further explore the Glossary and make their own discoveries.

Glossary

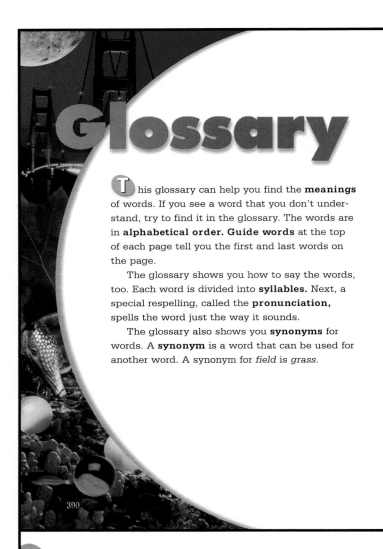

T his glossary can help you find the **meanings** of words. If you see a word that you don't understand, try to find it in the glossary. The words are in **alphabetical order. Guide words** at the top of each page tell you the first and last words on the page.

The glossary shows you how to say the words, too. Each word is divided into **syllables.** Next, a special respelling, called the **pronunciation,** spells the word just the way it sounds.

The glossary also shows you **synonyms** for words. A **synonym** is a word that can be used for another word. A synonym for *field* is *grass.*

Sample Entry

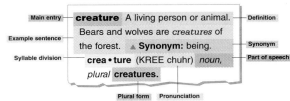

Main entry — **creature** A living person or animal. — Definition
Bears and wolves are *creatures* of
Example sentence — the forest. ▲ **Synonym**: being. — Synonym
Syllable division — **crea • ture** (KREE chuhr) *noun,* — Part of speech
plural **creatures.**

Plural form   Pronunciation

Use the **Pronunciation Key** below to find examples for the sounds you see in the pronunciation spellings.

Phonetic Spelling	Examples	Phonetic Spelling	Examples
a	cat	oh	go, home
ah	father	aw	saw, fall
ay	late, day	or	more, four
air	there, hair	oo	too, do
b	bit, rabbit	oy	toy
ch	chin	ow	out, cow
d	dog	p	pig
e	met	r	run, carry
ee	he, see	s	song, mess
f	fine, off	sh	shout, fish
g	go, bag, bigger	t	ten, better
h	hat	th	thin
hw	wheel	thh	them
ih	sit	u	sun
ī	fine, tiger, my	ů	look, should
ihr	near, deer, here	yoo	music, new
j	jump, page	ur	turn, learn
k	cat, back	v	very, of
l	line, hill	w	we
m	mine, hammer	y	yes
n	nice, funny	z	has, zoo
ng	sing	zh	treasure, division
o	top	uh	about, happen, lemon

Aa

accident Something unlucky that happens without warning. There were many *accidents* the day of the snowstorm.
▲**Synonym:** mishap.
ac•ci•dent (AK sih duhnt) *noun, plural* **accidents.**

afraid Feeling fear; frightened. There is no reason to be *afraid* of bats.
▲**Synonym:** scared.
a•fraid (uh FRAYD) *adjective.*

Alamo (AL uh moh)

alyssum A plant of the mustard family that bears small white or yellow flowers.
a•lys•sum (uh LIHS um) *noun, plural* **alyssum.**

audience A group of people gathered to hear and see something. My family was in the *audience* to watch my school play
▲**Synonyms:** spectators, listeners.
au•di•ence (AW dee uhns) *noun, plural* **audiences.**

auditorium A large room or building where people can gather. The concert will be in the school *auditorium.*
au•di•to•ri•um (aw dih TOR ee uhm) *noun, plural* **auditoriums.**

Bb

binoculars A device that makes distant objects look larger and closer, made up of two small telescopes joined together. We needed *binoculars* to see the ship on the horizon.
bi•noc•u•lars (buh NAHK yoo luhrz) *plural noun.*

borrow To take something to use for a while. Hector let me *borrow* his roller skates.
bor•row (BAHR oh) *verb,* **borrowed, borrowing.**

brachiopod Any of a large group of sea animals having a shell with a top and bottom half. We saw several different *brachiopods* while scuba diving.
bra•chi•o•pod (BRAY kee uh pahd) *noun, plural* **brachiopods.**

brave Having courage. The *brave* lifeguard jumped into the water to save the child.
brave (BRAYV) *adjective,* **braver, bravest.**

bravo Well done! Good! Excellent! The grateful audience clapped and cried *"Bravo!"*
bra•vo (BRAH voh) *interjection, plural* **bravos** or **bravoes.**

breath Air drawn into and forced out of the lungs; respiration. The doctor asked me to take a big *breath.*
breath (BRETH) *noun, plural* **breaths.**

Buenas noches Spanish for "good night." (BWAY nuhs NOH chez)

bulletin board A board for putting up notices, announcements, and pictures. She pinned the advertisement on the *bulletin board*.
> **bul•le•tin board** (BŬL ih tihn bord) *noun, plural* **bulletin boards.**

bumblebee A large bee with a thick, hairy body. Most *bumblebees* have yellow and black stripes.
> **bum•ble•bee** (BUHM buhl bee) *noun, plural* **bumblebees.**

burrito A Mexican food made of a tortilla wrapped around a filling. We had a choice of *burritos* or pizza for dinner.
> **bur•ri•to** (bur EE toh) *noun, plural* **burritos.**

bury To cover up; hide. The letter was *buried* in a pile of papers.
> ▲ **Synonyms:** conceal, hide.
> **bur•y** (BER ee) *verb,* **buried, burying.**

chance 1. A turn to do something. Each child will have a *chance* to ride the pony. **2.** The possibility that something might happen. There is a *chance* that it may snow tomorrow.
> ▲ **Synonym:** opportunity.
> **chance** (CHANS) *noun, plural* **chances.**

change 1. To make or become different. I will *change* the way I sign my name. *Verb.* **2.** The money that is given back when something costs less than the amount paid for it. I gave the ice cream man a dollar and got back twenty cents in *change. Noun.*
> **change** (CHAYNJ) *verb,* **changed, changing;** *noun,* **plural changes.**

cheer The shout you make to give someone hope or courage.
> **cheer** (CHIHR) *noun, plural* **cheers.**

chocolate A food used in making sweet things to eat. Billy unwrapped the bar of *chocolate.*
> **choc•o•late** (CHAWK liht) *noun, plural* **chocolates.**

clear 1. To remove things from. I *cleared* the dishes after supper. *Verb.* **2.** Free from anything that darkens; bright. The sky is *clear* today. *Adjective.*
> **clear** (KLIHR) *verb,* **cleared, clearing;** *adjective,* **clearer, clearest.**

clothes Things worn to cover the body. Coats, dresses, pants, and jackets are kinds of *clothes.*
> ▲ **Synonym:** clothing.
> **clothes** (KLOHZ *or* KLOHTHHZ) *plural noun.*

coach A person who trains athletes. The *coach* made the team practice every day.
> ▲ **Synonym:** trainer.
> **coach** (KOHCH) *noun, plural* **coaches.**

collide To crash against each other. The two players *collided* as they chased the ball.
> **col•lide** (kuh LĪD) *verb,* **collided, colliding.**

colony 1. A group of animals of the same kind that live together. Ants live in *colonies.* **2.** A territory ruled by another country. The British *colonies* became the United States.
> **col•ony** (KOL uh nee) *noun, plural* **colonies.**

coral 1. A hard, stony substance found in tropical seas. We saw huge pieces of *coral* while scuba-diving. *Noun.* **2.** A pinkish red color. Her nail polish matched her *coral* sweater. *Adjective.*
> **cor•al** (KOR uhl) *noun, plural* **corals.**

Costa Rica A country in Central America. (KOH stuh REE kuh)

cousin The child of an aunt or uncle. My *cousin* and I have the same grandfather.
> **cou•sin** (KUZ ihn) *noun, plural* **cousins.**

cover 1. To put something on or over. *Cover* your head with a hat in cold weather. *Verb.* **2.** Something that is put on or over something else. The *cover* will keep the juice from spilling. *Noun.*
> **cov•er** (KUV uhr) *verb,* **covered, covering;** *noun,* **plural covers.**

creature A living person or animal. Bears and wolves are *creatures* of the forest.
> ▲ **Synonym:** being.
> **crea•ture** (KREE chuhr) *noun, plural* **creatures.**

crinoid Any of a group of colorful, flower-shaped saltwater animals. Crinoids are usually found in deep tropical waters. The glass-bottom boat let us see the colorful *crinoids* and coral on the ocean floor.
> **cri•noid** (KRĪ noyd) *noun, plural* **crinoids.**

Cristobal (KRIHS tuh bahl)

crocodile A long animal with short legs, thick, scaly skin, and a long, powerful tail. *Crocodiles* have longer heads than alligators.
> **croc•o•dile** (KROK uh dil) *noun, plural* **crocodiles.**

crop Plants grown to be used as food. I grew my own *crop* of tomatoes in our garden.
> **crop** (KROP) *noun, plural* **crops.**

crowd 1. To put or force too many people or things into too small a space. My cousin *crowded* the shelf with books. *Verb.* **2.** A large group of people in one place. The *crowd* waited for the game to start. *Noun.*
> ▲ **Synonyms:** swarm, flock, assembly.
> **crowd** (KROWD) *verb,* **crowded, crowding;** *noun,* **plural crowds.**

darkness Little or no light. *Darkness* comes earlier in the winter.
> **dark•ness** (DAHRK nihss) *noun.*

daughter The female child of a mother and a father. Claire is the *daughter* of her mother and father. Claire's mother is the *daughter* of Claire's grandmother and grandfather.
> **daugh•ter** (DAW tuhr) *noun, plural* **daughters.**

desert A hot, dry, sandy area of land. It can be hard to find water in the *desert.*
> **des•ert** (DEZ uhrt) *noun, plural* **deserts.**

Glossary

disappear 1. To go out of sight. We watched the moon *disappear* behind the clouds. **2.** To become extinct. The dinosaurs *disappeared* from the earth millions of years ago.
    dis•ap•pear (dihs uh PIHR) *verb,* **disappeared, disappearing.**

disturb To break in on; to interrupt. The telephone call *disturbed* everyone's sleep.
    ▲ **Synonym:** bother.
    dis•turb (dihs TURB) *verb,* **disturbed, disturbing.**

dive To go into the water with your head first. When Maria and Carlos took swimming lessons, they learned how to *dive.*
    ▲ **Synonym:** plunge.
    dive (DĪV) *verb,* **dived** or **dove, dived, diving.**

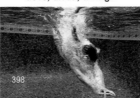

398

dribble To move a ball along by bouncing or kicking it. Players *dribble* the basketball.
    drib•ble (DRIHB uhl) *verb,* **dribbled, dribbling.**

echolocation A method of determining the location of objects by bouncing sound waves off the objects.
    ech•o•lo•ca•tion (EK oh loh KAY shun) *noun.*

eel A long, thin fish that looks like a snake. The *eel* darted swiftly through the water.
    eel (EEL) *noun, plural* **eels.**

endanger To threaten with becoming extinct. Pollution *endangers* many species.
    en•dan•ger (en DAYN juhr) *verb,* **endangered, endangering.**

envy 1. A feeling of disliking or desiring another person's good luck or belongings. I felt *envy* for your new toy. *Noun.*
    ▲ **Synonym:** jealousy.
    2. To feel envy toward. Everyone in our class *envies* you because of your good grades. *Verb.*
    en•vy (EN vee) *noun, plural* **envies;** *verb,* **envied, envying.**

escape To get away from something. People knew a storm was coming and could *escape* before it started.
    es•cape (es KAYP) *verb,* **escaped, escaping.**

evening The time of day when it starts to get dark, between afternoon and night. We eat dinner at 6 o'clock in the *evening.*
    ▲ **Synonyms:** dusk, nightfall, twilight.
    eve•ning (EEV ning) *noun, plural* **evenings.**

explain To give a reason for. *Explain* why you were late.
    ▲ **Synonyms:** make clear, say.
    ex•plain (ek SPLAYN) *verb,* **explained, explaining.**

explore To look around a place and discover new things. Nancy and Robert couldn't wait to *explore* their new neighborhood.
    ▲ **Synonym:** search.
    ex•plore (ek SPLOR) *verb,* **explored, exploring.**

extinct No longer existing. The dodo bird became *extinct* because people hunted it.
    ex•tinct (ek STINGKT) *adjective;* **extinction** *noun.*

fact Something that is real or true. It is a *fact* that there are 50 states in the United States.
    ▲ **Synonym:** truth.
    fact (FAKT) *noun, plural* **facts.**

399

favorite Liked best. I always wear my *favorite* cap.
    ▲ **Synonym:** preferred.
    fa•vor•ite (FAY vuhr iht) *adjective.*

Fernando (fur NAN doh)

field 1. An area of land where some games are played. Football is played on a football *field.* **2.** An area of land that has no trees, used for growing grass or food. We planted corn in this *field.*
    ▲ **Synonym:** grass. **field** (FEELD) *noun, plural* **fields.**

fierce Wild and dangerous. A hungry lion is *fierce.*
    ▲ **Synonyms:** ferocious, savage. **fierce** (FIHRS) *adjective,* **fiercer, fiercest.**

400

forest A large area of land covered by trees and plants. They camped in the *forest.*
    ▲ **Synonym:** woods.
    for•est (FOR ist) *noun, plural* **forests.**

forever 1. For all time; without ever coming to an end. Things cannot stay the same *forever.* **2.** Always; on and on. That grouch is *forever* complaining.
    for•ev•er (for EV uhr) *adverb.*

fossil What is left of an animal or plant that lived a long time ago. Fossils are found in rocks, earth, or clay. The bones and footprints of dinosaurs are *fossils.*
    ▲ **Synonyms:** relic, remains
    fos•sil (FOS uhl) *noun, plural* **fossils.**

fresh Newly made, done, or gathered. We ate *fresh* tomatoes from June's garden.
    ▲ **Synonyms:** sweet, new, unused. **fresh** (FRESH) *adjective,* **fresher, freshest.**

glue 1. A material used for sticking things together. I used *glue* to stick the magazine pictures on the paper. *Noun.* **2.** To stick things together with glue. Please *glue* the pieces of the vase together. *Verb.*
    glue (GLOO) *noun, plural* **glues;** *verb,* **glued, gluing.**

goalie The player who defends the goal in soccer, hockey, and some other games. The *goalie* stopped the puck.
    goal•ie (GOHL ee) *noun, plural* **goalies.**

golden 1. Made of or containing gold. My mother has a pair of *golden* earrings. **2.** Having the color or shine of gold; bright or shining. The field of *golden* wheat swayed in the wind.
    gol•den (GOHL duhn) *adjective.*

guess 1. To form an opinion without sure knowledge. Did you *guess* how much that would cost? *Verb.* **2.** An opinion formed without enough information. My *guess* is that the trip will take four hours. *Noun*
    guess (GES) *verb,* **guessed, guessing;** *noun, plural* **guesses.**

halftime A rest period in the middle of some games. The players had a chance to cool off at *halftime.*
    half•time (HAF tim) *noun, plural* **halftimes.**

401

hammock A swinging bed made from a long piece of canvas or netting. She fell asleep in the *hammock.*
ham•mock (HAM uhk) *noun,* plural **hammocks.**

harm An injury. She put the baby where he would be safe from *harm. Noun.*
▲ **Synonyms:** hurt, wrong, **harm** (HAHRM) *noun,* plural **harms;** *verb,* **harmed, harming.**

heavy Hard to lift or move. The bag of groceries was too *heavy* for Derek to lift.
▲ **Synonyms:** hefty, weighty. **heav•y** (HEV ee) *adjective,* **heavier, heaviest.**

hibernate To spend the winter sleeping. Some bears, woodchucks, frogs, and snakes *hibernate* all winter.
hi•ber•nate (HĪ buhr nayt) *verb,* **hibernated, hibernating;** *noun,* **hibernation.**

hidden Past participle of **hide.** To put yourself or something else in a place where it cannot be seen. My cat likes to stay *hidden* under my bed.
▲ **Synonym:** unseen. **hide** (HĪD) *verb,* **hid, hidden** (HIHD uhn) or **hid, hiding.**

hunt 1. To look hard to find something or someone. I will *hunt* all over my room until I find my watch. *Verb.* 2. A search to try to find something or someone. We went on a *hunt* through all the stores to find the toy he wanted. *Noun.*
hunt (HUNT) *verb,* **hunted, hunting;** *noun,* plural **hunts.**

402

Ii

ichthyosaur Any of an extinct group of porpoise-like marine reptiles. **ich•thy•o•saur** (IHK thee oh sor) *noun.*

iguanodon (ih GWAH nuh don)

insect Any of a large group of small animals without a backbone. Insects have a body divided into three parts, with three pairs of legs and usually two pairs of wings. Flies, ants, grasshoppers, and beetles are *insects.*
in•sect (IN sekt) *noun,* plural **insects.**

intercept To stop or take something on its way from one person or place to another. I tried to pass the ball to a teammate, but a player on the other team *intercepted* it.
in•ter•cept (IHN tuhr sept) *verb,* **intercepted, intercepting.**

Ll

La Brea (lah BRAY uh)

layer One thickness of something. A *layer* of dust covered the table. **lay•er** (LAY uhr) *noun,* plural **layers.**

lily A large flower shaped like a trumpet. **lil•y** (LIHL ee) *noun,* plural **lilies.**

Mm

machine A thing invented to do a particular job. Airplanes are *machines* that fly.
▲ **Synonyms:** device, mechanism. **ma•chine** (muh SHEEN) *noun,* plural **machines.**

403

magazine A printed collection of stories, articles, and pictures usually bound in a paper cover. I read that article about fossils in a nature *magazine.*
mag•a•zine (MAG uh zeen) *noun,* plural **magazines.**

marigold A garden plant that bears yellow, orange, or red flowers in the summer.
mar•i•gold (MAR ih gohld) *noun,* plural **marigolds.**

marvel 1. A wonderful or amazing thing. Space travel is one of the *marvels* of modern science. *Noun.* 2. To feel wonder and astonishment. We *marveled* at the acrobat's skill. *Verb.*
mar•vel (MAHR vuhl) *noun,* plural **marvels;** *verb,* **marveled, marveling.**

medusa A jellyfish.
me•du•sa (muh DOO suh) *noun,* plural **medusas** or **medusae.**

medusa

membrane A thin, flexible layer of skin or tissue that lines parts of the body. The skin that connects a bat's wing bones to its body is called a *membrane.*
mem•brane (MEM brayn) *noun,* plural **membranes.**

middle A place halfway between two points or sides. Noon is in the *middle* of the day.
▲ **Synonym:** center. **mid•dle** (MIHD uhl) *noun,* plural **middles.**

midnight Twelve o'clock at night; the middle of the night. Cinderella's coach turned into a pumpkin at *midnight.*
mid•night (MIHD nit) *noun.*

404

miller A person who owns or operates a mill, especially one for grinding grain. The *miller* sold the wheat to the baker.
mill•er (MIHL uhr) *noun,* plural **millers.**

million 1. One thousand times one thousand; 1,000,000. *Noun.* 2. Having a very large number. It looks like a *million* stars in the sky. *Adjective.*
mil•lion (MIHL yuhn) *noun,* plural **millions;** *adjective.*

mine A large area dug out in or under the ground. Coal and gold are dug out of *mines.*
mine (MĪN) *noun,* plural **mines.**

mosquito A small insect with two wings. The female gives a sting or bite that itches. There were hundreds of *mosquitoes* near the swamp.
mos•qui•to (muh SKEE toh) *noun,* plural **mosquitoes** or **mosquitos.**

museum A building where pieces of art, science displays, or objects from history are kept for people to see. I saw one of George Washington's hats at the history *museum.*
mu•se•um (myoo ZEE uhm) *noun,* plural **museums.**

music A beautiful combination of sounds. When you sing or play an instrument, you are making *music.*
mu•sic (MYOO zihk) *noun.*

musician A person who is skilled in playing a musical instrument, writing music, or singing. The *musician* prepared to play for the audience.
mu•si•cian (myoo ZIHSH uhn) *noun,* plural **musicians.**

405

mussel An animal that looks like a clam. Saltwater *mussels* have bluish-black shells.
▲ Another word that sounds like this is *muscle*. **mus•sel** (MUS uhl) *noun, plural* **mussels.**

Nn

nature All things in the world that are not made by people. Plants, animals, mountains, and oceans are all part of *nature*. **na•ture** (NAY chuhr) *noun.*

nervous 1. Not able to relax. Loud noises make me *nervous*. **2.** Fearful or timid. I am very *nervous* about taking the test.
▲ Synonym: anxious. **nerv•ous** (NUR vuhs) *adjective.*

noisy Making harsh or loud sounds. It is *noisy* at the airport.
▲ Synonym: loud. **nois•y** (NOY zee) *adjective,* **noisier, noisiest.**

Oo

object Anything that can be seen and touched. Is that large, round *object* an orange?
▲ Synonym: thing. **ob•ject** (OB jihkt) *noun, plural* **objects.**

offer To present for someone to take or refuse. Mom *offered* to pick us up if it gets dark before the game ends.
▲ Synonym: volunteer, give. **of•fer** (AHF uhr) *verb,* **offered, offering.**

office A place where people work. The principal's *office* is at the end of the hall.
▲ Synonym: workplace. **of•fice** (AHF ihs) *noun, plural* **offices.**

406

out-of-bounds In sports, outside the area of play allowed. I kicked the ball *out-of-bounds*, so the other team was given the ball. **out•of•bounds** (OWT uv BOWNDZ) *adverb, adjective.*

Pp

package A thing or group of things that are packed in a box, wrapped up, or tied in a bundle. We sent a *package* of treats to my sister at camp.
▲ Synonyms: bundle, parcel. **pack•age** (PAK ihj) *noun, plural* **packages.**

Parthenon (PAHR thuh nahn)

piece A part that has been broken, cut, or torn from something. There are *pieces* of broken glass on the floor. **piece** (PEES) *noun, plural* **pieces.**

practice To do something over and over to gain skill. I *practice* playing guitar every day. **prac•tice** (PRAK tihs) *verb,* **practiced, practicing.**

preserve To keep from being damaged, decayed, or lost; protect. You can *preserve* the wood of the table by waxing it. **pre•serve** (prih ZURV) *verb,* **preserved, preserving.**

princess The daughter of a king or queen; a female member of a royal family other than a queen; the wife of a prince. The people of the kingdom bowed to the *princess*. **prin•cess** (PRIHN sihs *or* PRIHN ses) *noun, plural* **princesses.**

407

principal The person who is the head of a school. The *principal* gave a speech.
▲ Another word that sounds like this is *principle*. **prin•ci•pal** (PRIHN suh puhl) *noun, plural* **principals.**

problem Anything that causes trouble and must be dealt with. A barking dog can be a *problem*. **prob•lem** (PRAHB luhm) *noun, plural* **problems.**

prowl To move or roam quietly or secretly. The tiger *prowled* through the forest. **prowl** (PROWL) *verb,* **prowled, prowling.**

Rr

reptile One of a class of cold-blooded animals with a backbone and dry, scaly skin. Lizards are *reptiles*. **rep•tile** (REP til) *noun, plural* **reptiles.**

restaurant A place where food is prepared and served. We ate at the *restaurant*. **res•tau•rant** (RES tuh ruhnt *or* RES tuh rahnt) *noun, plural* **restaurants.**

roof The top part of a building. There was a leak in the *roof*. **roof** (ROOF *or* RÜF) *noun, plural* **roofs.**

Ss

save 1. To keep from harm; to make safe. The cat *saved* her kittens from the fire. **2.** To set aside for future use. I will *save* some cookies to eat later. **save** (SAYV) *verb,* **saved, saving.**

408

scare To make afraid. Loud noises always *scare* the puppy.
▲ Synonyms: alarm, frighten. **scare** (SKAIR) *verb,* **scared, scaring.**

scary Causing alarm or fear; frightening. Your monster costume is very *scary*. **scar•y** (SKAIR ee) *adjective,* **scarier, scariest.**

score 1. To get a point or points in a game or on a test. The baseball team *scored* five runs in one inning. *Verb.* **2.** The points gotten in a game or on a test. The final *score* was 5 to 4. *Noun.*
▲ Synonym: tally. **score** (SKOR) *verb,* **scored, scoring;** *noun, plural* **scores.**

sea anemone A sea animal shaped like a tube that attaches itself to rocks and to other objects. **sea a•nem•o•ne** (SEE uh NEM uh nee) *noun, plural* **sea anemones.**

seaweed Any plant or plants that grows in the sea, especially certain kinds of algae. **sea•weed** (SEE weed) *noun.*

señor Sir; mister. Spanish form of respectful or polite address for a man. **se•ñor** (sen YOR)

señora Mistress; madam. Spanish form of respectful or polite address for a woman. **se•ño•ra** (sen YOR uh)

servant A person hired to work for the comfort or protection of others. The *servant* brought in their dinner. **serv•ant** (SUR vuhnt) *noun, plural* **servants.**

409

several More than two, but not many. We saw *several* of our friends at the parade.
▲ **Synonym:** various.
sev•er•al (SEV uhr ul *or* SEV ruhl) *adjective; noun.*

shoulder The part on either side of the body from the neck to where the arm joins. I carry the sack over my *shoulder.*
shoul•der (SHOHL duhr) *noun, plural* **shoulders.**

skeleton A framework that supports and protects the body. Birds, fish, and humans have *skeletons* made of bones.
skel•e•ton (SKEL uh tuhn) *noun, plural* **skeletons.**

slip To slide and fall down. Be careful not to *slip* on the wet floor.
▲ **Synonyms:** slide, skid.
slip (SLIHP) *verb,* **slipped, slipping.**

soil The top part of the ground in which plants grow. There is sandy *soil* near the coast.
▲ **Synonyms:** dirt, earth.
soil (SOYL) *noun, plural* **soils.**

station A place of business where something specific is done. We get gas for a car at a gas *station.* Police officers work in a police *station.*
▲ **Synonym:** precinct.
sta•tion (STAY shuhn) *noun, plural* **stations.**

stepmother A woman who has married a person's father after the death or divorce of the natural mother. Dan's *stepmother* came to his school play.
step•moth•er (STEP muthh uhr) *noun, plural* **stepmothers.**

410

storyteller A person who tells or writes stories.
sto•ry•tell•er (STOR ee tel uhr) *noun, plural* **storytellers.**

stretch To spread out to full length. The lazy cat *stretched* and then went back to sleep.
▲ **Synonym:** extend. **stretch** (STRECH) *verb,* **stretched, stretching.**

study To try to learn by reading, thinking about, or looking; examine closely. A detective *studies* clues carefully.
stud•y (STUD ee) *verb,* **studied, studying.**

sway To move back and forth. The tree branches *swayed.*
▲ **Synonyms:** swing, wave, lean.
sway (SWAY) *verb,* **swayed, swaying.**

swift Moving or able to move very quickly. The rider had a *swift* horse.
▲ **Synonyms:** speedy, fast.
swift (SWIHFT) *adjective,* **swifter, swiftest.**

swivel chair A chair with a seat that spins. She spun around on the *swivel chair.*
swi•vel chair (SWIHV uhl chair) *noun, plural* **swivel chairs.**

Tt

teenager A person who is between the ages of thirteen and nineteen.
teen•a•ger (TEEN ay juhr) *noun, plural* **teenagers.**

termite An insect that eats wood, paper, and other materials. The *termites* ate through the floor of the old house.
ter•mite (TUR mit) *noun, plural* **termites.**

411

therapy Treatment for a disability, injury, psychological problem, or illness. He needed physical *therapy* to help heal his broken leg.
ther•a•py (THER uh pee) *noun, plural* **therapies.**

third Next after the second one. We had seats in the *third* row of the theater.
third (THURD) *adjective.*

throne 1. The chair that a king or queen sits on during ceremonies and other special occasions. 2. The power or authority of a king or queen.
throne (THROHN) *noun, plural* **thrones.**

throw To send something through the air. *Throw* the ball to the dog, and she will bring it back to you.
▲ **Synonyms:** toss, fling, pitch.
throw (THROH) *verb,* **threw, thrown, throwing.**

thumbtack A tack with a flat, round head that can be pressed into a wall or board with the thumb. Notices are often pinned to bulletin boards with *thumbtacks.*
thumb•tack (THUM tak) *noun, plural* **thumbtacks.**

ton A measure of weight equal to 2,000 pounds in the United States and Canada, and 2,240 pounds in Great Britain.
ton (tun) *noun, plural* **tons.**

412

tooth One of the hard, white, bony parts in the mouth used for biting and chewing. I got a filling in my front *tooth.*
tooth (TOOTH) *noun, plural* **teeth.**

touch To put your hand on or against something. If you *touch* the stove, you will get burned.
▲ **Synonym:** feel.
touch (TUCH) *verb,* **touched, touching.**

trilobite An extinct sea animal that lived hundreds of millions of years ago.
tri•lo•bite (TRĪ loh bīt) *noun, plural* **trilobites.**

Uu

upstairs 1. On or to a higher floor. My bedroom is *upstairs. Adverb.* 2. On an upper floor. The *upstairs* bathroom was just cleaned. *Adjective.*
up•stairs (UP stairz) *adverb; adjective.*

Vv

vacation A period of rest or freedom. Summer *vacation* begins next week.
va•ca•tion (vay KAY shuhn) *noun, plural* **vacations.**

village A small town. The streets of the *village* were paved with stones.
▲ **Synonym:** community.
vil•lage (VIHL ihj) *noun, plural* **villages.**

voice The sound you make through your mouth. You use your *voice* when you sing.
voice (VOYS) *noun, plural* **voices.**

Ww

warn alert; To tell about something before it happens.
warn (WORN) *verb,* **warned, warning.**

413

Glossary

G7

Glossary

waterfall A natural stream of water falling from a high place. We had a picnic by the *waterfall*. **wa•ter•fall** (WAH tuhr fawl) *noun, plural* **waterfalls.**

wheelchair A chair on wheels that is used by someone who cannot walk to get from one place to another. He needed a *wheelchair* until his leg healed. **wheel•chair** (HWEEL chair *or* WEEL chair) *noun, plural* **wheelchairs.**

whistle 1. To make a sound by pushing air out through your lips or teeth. My dog comes when I *whistle*. *Verb.* **2.** Something you blow into that makes a whistling sound. The police officer blew his *whistle*. *Noun.* **whis•tle** (HWIS uhl *or* WIS uhl) *verb,* **whistled, whistling;** *noun, plural* **whistles.**

wipe To clean or dry by rubbing. ▲ **Synonym:** clean. **wipe** (WĪP) *verb,* **wiped, wiping.**

414

wonder 1. To want to know or learn; be curious about. I *wonder* why the sky is blue. *Verb.* **2.** A surprising or impressive thing. *Noun.* **won•der** (WUN duhr) *verb,* **wondered, wondering;** *noun, plural* **wonders.**

world Place where all things live. **world** (WURLD) *noun, plural* **worlds.**

wrap To cover something by putting something else around it. We will *wrap* the package. **wrap** (RAP) *verb,* **wrapped, wrapping.**

xiphactinus (zee FAK ti nus)

zinnia A garden flower. **zin•ni•a** (ZIHN nee uh) *noun, plural* **zinnias.**

ACKNOWLEDGMENTS

The publisher gratefully acknowledges permission to reprint the following copyrighted material:

"Charlie Anderson" by Barbara Abercrombie, illustrated by Mark Graham. Text copyright © 1990 by Barbara Abercrombie. Illustrations copyright © 1990 by Mark Graham. Reprinted with permission of Margaret K. McElderry Books, Simon & Schuster Children's Publishing Division.

"Fernando's Gift" by Douglas Keister. Copyright © 1995 by Douglas Keister. Reprinted by permission of Sierra Club Books For Children.

"Fossils Tell of Long Ago" by Aliki. Copyright © 1972, 1990 by Aliki Brandenberg. Used by permission of HarperCollins Publishers.

"Neighbors" by Marchette Chute from RHYMES ABOUT US. by Marchette Chute. Published 1974 by E.P. Dutton. Reprinted with permission of Elizabeth Hauser.

"Officer Buckle and Gloria" by Peggy Rathmann. Copyright ©, Peggy Rathmann, 1995. Published by arrangement with Penguin Putnam Books for Young Readers, a division of Penguin Putnam Inc.

"Our Soccer League" from OUR SOCCER LEAGUE by Chuck Solomon. Text copyright © 1988 by Chuck Solomon. Reprinted by arrangement with Random House Children's Books, a division of Random House, Inc.

"Princess Pooh" is the entire text from PRINCESS POOH by Kathleen M. Muldoon with illustrations by Linda Shute. Text copyright © 1989 by Kathleen M. Muldoon. Illustrations copyright © 1989 by Linda Shute. Originally published in hardcover by Albert Whitman & Company. All rights reserved. Used with permission.

"River Winding" from RIVER WINDING by Charlotte Zolotow. Copyright © 1970 by Charlotte Zolotow. Reprinted by permission of Scott Treimel New York.

"Swimmy" from SWIMMY by Leo Lionni. Copyright © 1963 by Leo Lionni. Copyright renewed 1991 by Leo Lionni. Reprinted by arrangement with Random House Children's Books, a division of Random House, Inc.

"To Catch a Fish" by Eloise Greenfield from UNDER THE SUNDAY TREE. Text copyright © 1988 by Eloise Greenfield. Paintings copyright © 1988 by Amos Ferguson. Reprinted by permission of HarperCollins Publishers.

"Tomás and the Library Lady" by Pat Mora. Text copyright © 1977 by Pat Mora. Illustrations copyright © 1997 by Raul Colón. Reprinted by permission of Alfred A. Knopf.

"The Wednesday Surprise" from THE WEDNESDAY SURPRISE by Eve Bunting with illustrations by Donald Carrick. Text copyright © 1989 by Eve Bunting. Illustrations copyright © 1989 by Donald Carrick. Reprinted by permission of Clarion Books, a Houghton Mifflin Co. imprint.

"What Is It?" by Eve Merriam from HIGGLE WIGGLE (MORROW JR BOOKS). Text copyright © 1994 by the Estate of Eve Merriam by Marian Reiner, Literary Executor. Used by permission of Marian Reiner.

"Which?" from CRICKETY CRICKET! THE BEST LOVED POEMS of JAMES S. TIPPETT. Text copyright © 1933, copyright renewed © 1973 by Martha K. Tippett. Illustrations copyright © 1973 by Mary Chalmers. Reprinted by permission of HarperCollins Publishers.

"Zipping, Zapping, Zooming Bats" by Ann Earle. Text copyright © 1995 by Ann Earle. Illustrations copyright © 1995 by Henry Cole. Reprinted by permission of HarperCollins Children's Books, a division of HarperCollins Publishers.

Illustration

Matt Straub, 12–13; Leonor Glynn, 42; Claude Martinot, 43; Kuenhee Lee, 44–45; Myron Grossman, 67; Annette Cable, 68–69; Cecily Lang, 70–87; Claude Martinot, 91; Tim Raglin, 92–93; Claude Martinot, 115; Melinda Levine, 130–131; Mary GrandPre, 132–145; Julia Gorton, 149; Tom Barrett, 150–151; Myron Grossman, 179; Joe Cepeda, 180–181; Leonor Glynn, 210; Julia Gorton, 211; Suling Wang, 212–213; Vilma Ortiz–Dillon, 234; Myron Grossman, 235; Anne Lunsford, 282–283; Myron Grossman, 309; Jerry Smath, 250–251; Julia Gorton, 281; Abby Carter, 310–311;

Claude Martinot, 339; Carol Inouye, 340–341; Claude Martinot, 361; Robert Crawford, 10–11; Taylor Bruce, 126–127; Russ Willms, 128–129; Marina Thompson, 248–249; Sonja Lamut, 372–373; Tom Leonard, 116–117; Myron Grossman, 125, 371; Michael Welch, 236–237; Claude Martinot, 245; Alexandra Wallner, 362–363; John Carozza, 410; Holly Jones, 394, 403; Miles Parnell, 398, 407, 412.

Photography

4: b. Douglas Keister; 5: b. Merline Tuttle/Photo Researchers; 7: b, John Cancalosis/Peter Arnold; 9: b. David Muench/Corbis; 41: r. Renee Lynn/Photo Researchers/l. Renee Lynn/Photo Researchers/ Dough Plummer/Photonica; 42: b.r. Renee Lynn/Photo Researchers; 65: b. Andrea Pistolesi/The Image Bank; 70: b.r. Courtesy of Cecily Lang Studio/t.l. Courtesy of Diane Hoyt–Goldsmith; 75: t. Roy Morsch/The Stock Market/b. Brown Brothers; 77: r. Wernher Kruten/Liaison International/l. Chad Ehlers/Tony Stone Images; 79: Zigy Kalunzy/Tony Stone Images; 81: Merlin D. Tuttle/Bat Conservation International; 83: t. Wesley Hitt/Liaison International/ b. Superstock; 84: Howard Grey/Tony Stone Images; 85: Robert Landau/Westlight; 87: t.r. Hiroyuki Matsumoto/Tony Stone Images/b.r. Marc Biggins/Liaison International/b.l. Tom Bean/ Tony Stone/t.l. Superstock; 89: b. Merlin D. Tuttle/Bat Conservation International/t. Wesley Hitt/Liaison International; 94: t.l. Courtesy of HarperCollins Publishers; 113: b. T. Sawada/Photonica; 114: m.l. Merlin D. Tuttle/Bat Conservation International/t.r. Merlin D. Tuttle/Bat Conservation International/t.l. Merlin D. Tuttle/Bat Conservation International/b.r. Stephen Dalton/Photo Researchers; 122: t. Merlin D. Tuttle/Photo Researchers/m. Joe Mcdonald/Animals Animals/b. Merlin Tuttle/Bat Conservation International; 123 b. PhotoDisc; 132: Courtesy of the artist; 176-177: David Madison/Tony Stone Images; 214: T. Carolina Ambida. 233: b. Jeffrey Sylvester/FPG International; 242: t.l. PhotoDisc/b.r. Howard Grey/Tony Stone Images/m.l. PhotoDisc; 244: l. PhotoDisc/ r. Howard Grey/Tony Stone Images; 252: t. Courtesy of Penguin Putnam Inc.; 279: m.r. Jonathan Nourok/Photo Edit/b. Tom Nebbia/Corbis-Bettman/m.c. David Young-Wolff/Photo Edit/ m.l. Spencer Grant/Photo Edit; 284: t.l. Courtesy Random House/ b.r. Courtesy of Raul Colon/t.l. Courtesy Alfred A. Knopf Inc.; 306-307: Tony Freeman/Photo Edit; 337: b. Jim Cummins/FPG International/m.r. PhotoDisc; 360: t. PhotoDisc/b. PhotoDisc; 368; m. Kit Latham/FPG.

Reading for Information

All photographs are by Macmillan/McGraw-Hill (MMH); Michael Groen for MMH; Ken Karp for MMH; and Chuck Solomon for MMH, except as noted below.

Table of Contents, pp. 374–375

Chess pieces, tl, Wides + Hall/FPG; Earth, mcl, M. Burns/Picture Perfect; CD's, mcl, Michael Simpson/FPG; Newspapers, bl, Craig Orsini/Index Stock/PictureQuest; Clock, tr, Steve McAlister/The Image Bank; Kids circle, bc, Daniel Pangbourne Media/FPG; Pencils, tr, W. Cody/Corbis; Starfish, tc, Darryl Torckler/Stone; Keys, cr, Randy Faris/Corbis; Cells, br, Spike Walker/Stone; Stamps, tr, Michael W. Thomas/Focus Group/PictureQuest; Books, cr, Siede Preis/PhotoDisc; Sunflower, cr, Jeff LePore/Natural Selection; Mouse, br, Andrew Hall/Stone; Apples, tr, Siede Preis/PhotoDisc; Watermelons, br, Neil Beer/PhotoDisc; Butterfly, br, Stockbyte

377: t.r. George Godfrey/Earth Scenes/b.r. Leonard Lee Rue/Stock Boston; 378-379: bkgd. Tom Walker/Stock Boston; 380: m.l. George Bernard/Animals Animals/m.r. M. MC. Chamberlain/DRK Photo/b.l. David Baron/Animals Animals: 380-381 bkgd. William Johnson/ Stock Boston; 381: t.l. Fritz Polking/Dembinsky Photo Assoc./b.l. E. R. Derggingen/Dembinsky Photo Assoc.; 390: l. PhotoDisc; 392: Ron Chapple/FPG International; 393: Jose Azel/Aurora/PNI; 395: David Stockein/The Stock Market; 396: Mark A. Johnson/The Stock Market; 397: Tom Dean/The Stock Market; 398: Wayne Levin/ FPG International; 400: Eric Meola/The Image Bank; 401: David Brooks/The Stock Market; 402: Michel Renaudeau/Liaison; 405: Don Perdue/Liaison; 406: Richard H. Johnston/FPG International; 408: Rick Rusing/Tony Stone Images; 409: Darryl Torchker/Tony Stone Images; 411: Hank de Lespinasse/Image Bank; 412: Adam Woolfitt/Woodfin Camp, Inc.

Art/Illustration

Linda Weller, 44F; Richard Kolding, 180F

Photography

125A: M. Burns, Picture Perfect; Daniel Pagbourne, Media/FPG; 127A: Jeff LaPore/Natural Selection; Stockbyte

---

Cover Illustration: Kenneth Spengler

The publisher gratefully acknowledges permission to reprint the following copyrighted material:

"All Living Things" by W. Jay Cawley. Words and music copyright © 1992 by W. Jay Cawley.

"The Bat" from BEAST FEAST by Douglas Florian. Copyright © 1984 by Douglas Florian. Used by permission of Voyager Books, Harcourt Brace & Company.

"Behind the Museum Door" from GOOD RHYMES, GOOD TIMES by Lee Bennett Hopkins. Copyright © 1973, 1995 by Lee Bennett Hopkins. Used by permission of Curtis Brown Ltd.

"Brothers" from SNIPPETS by Charlotte Zolotow. Copyright © 1993 by Charlotte Zolotow. Illustrations copyright © 1993 by Melissa Sweet. Used by permission of HarperCollins Publishers.

"The Bundle of Sticks" from THE CHILDREN'S AESOP: SELECTED FABLES retold by Stephanie Calmenson. Used by permission of Caroline House, Boyds Mills Press, Inc.

"The Cat Came Back" arranged by Mary Goetze. Copyright © 1984 MMB Music, Inc.

"Covers" from VACATION TIME: POEMS FOR CHILDREN by Nikki Giovanni. Copyright © 1980 by Nikki Giovanni. Used by permission of William Morrow & Company, Inc.

"The Day the Sun Hid" from MICHAEL FOREMAN'S WORLD OF FAIRY TALES. Copyright © 1991 by Pavilion Books Limited. Used by permission of Arcade Publishing, Inc.

"The Dinosaur Who Lived in My Backyard" by B. G. Hennessey. Copyright © 1988 by B. G. Hennessey. Used by permission of Viking Books, a division of Penguin Books USA Inc.

"The Discontented Fish" from Tales from Africa by Kathleen Arnott. Copyright © 1962 by Kathleen Arnott. Used by permission of Oxford University Press.

"The Golden Touch" retold by Margaret H. Lippert from TEACHER'S READ ALOUD ANTHOLOGY. Copyright © 1993 by Macmillan/McGraw-Hill School Publishing Company.

"Gotta Find a Footprint" from BONE POEMS by Jeff Moss. Text copyright © 1997 by Jeff Moss. Illustrations copyright © 1997 by Tom Leigh. Used by permission of Workman Publishing Company, Inc.

"The Great Ball Game: A Muskogee Story" by Joseph Bruchac. Copyright © 1994 by Joseph Bruchac. Used by permission of Dial Books.

"Lemonade Stand" reprinted with the permission of Margaret K. McElderry Books, an imprint of Simon & Schuster Children's Publishing Division from WORLDS I KNOW and Other Poems by Myra Cohn Livingston. Text copyright © 1985 by Myra Cohn Livingston.

Acknowledgments

Acknowledgments

Backmatter Contents

The Cat Came Back
an American folk song
arranged by Mary Goetze

Old Farmer Johnson had troubles all his own.
He had a little cat that wouldn't leave his home.
He tried and he tried to give that cat away!
He gave it to a man going far, far away.

But the cat came back the very next day.
The cat came back!
We thought he was a goner, but the cat came back,
He just wouldn't stay away.

▶But the cat came back!
We thought he was a goner.
The cat came back!
We thought he was a goner.
The cat came back,
He wouldn't stay away.

Du-du-du-doop!
Me-ow!
Du-wa, du-du-du-doop!
Me-ow!
Du-wa!
He just wouldn't stay away.
Du-du-du-doop!
Yeah!

Farmer Johnson's neighbor swore he'd chase him
    out of sight.
He donned his fastest shoes and he ran with all his
    might.
The cat was quick, he ran away and Johnson's
    neighbor fell.
People came from miles away because they heard
    him yell.

He gave it to a man going up in a balloon.
Told him to give it to the man up in the moon.
The balloon came down about ninety miles away.
What happened to the man?
I really couldn't say.

Thinking Green
by The Earthworks Group

If you look green, you're probably not feeling very well. But if the Earth is green, it's a healthy planet.

A green Earth means that plants are growing. It means that the soil is good, there's plenty of water, the air is clean, animals have places to live and things to eat.

And some wonderful news: Anyone can help keep the Earth green. It's so easy. You can plant a seed, give it some water, and watch it grow. You can save paper so that fewer trees will be cut down. You can "adopt" plants that are already growing and help them enjoy life.

Another important thing about plants (especially trees): They help fight the greenhouse effect and give us oxygen, which is the air we need to live.

What a deal!

We need lots of greenery in our world. Let's start planting!

Read Aloud   ▶ Continue reading here.

Vacation

Mary Ann Hoberman

In my head I hear a humming:
Summer summer summer's coming.
Soon we're going on vacation
But there is a complication:
Day by day the problem's growing—
We don't know yet where we're going!

Mother likes the country best;
That's so she can read and rest.
Dad thinks resting is a bore;
He's for fishing at the shore.

Sailing is my brother's pick;
Sailing makes my sister sick;
She says swimming's much more cool,
Swimming in a swimming pool.
As for me, why, I don't care,
I'd be happy anywhere!

In my head I hear a humming:
Summer summer summer's coming.
Soon we're going on vacation
But we have a complication:
Day by day the problem's growing—
Where oh where will we be going?

The Day the Sun Hid

a myth

There was once a beautiful and peaceful country. It was high in the mountains on the roof of the world, and a land of steep deep green valleys and swift flowing rivers. Every day the sun climbed above the snowy peaks and shone upon the land. People said that if trouble ever *did* come, it would last only as long as the shadow of a flying bird.

One day, however, the bird came, and stayed. Huge and evil, he blotted out the sun and his shadow plunged the country into darkness. Because there was no light, the grass stopped growing, fruit rotted. With no dawn to wake them, animals slept all day. People could not see to work, so they slumbered while the corn withered and died.

At last the evil bird flew off, but the sun had become accustomed to darkness, and wrapped in thick blankets of cloud, he dozed in the high mountains.

A few animals and children, who never sleep for long, decided to find a way to get the sun to shine again.

▶ "I will sing to remind the sun of the dawn chorus" said a small red bird, and flew to the top of a dead bamboo. As her voice flew to the sky, more people and animals woke up. It was the first music they had heard since the coming of the darkness. But the sun did not respond and after singing for several days the red bird collapsed, exhausted.

Then a little girl said, "I will build a fire to remind the sun of warmth and light." She took her scythe and began cutting grass and gathering twigs. Other children helped, and soon the pile of kindling was quite high, but because the sun had not shone for many months, the wood was damp and it was difficult to get a good blaze going. But several girls began to fan the smoldering wood with their long striped aprons until the flames flared up and up and lit the sky. But still the sun did not respond, and the fire dwindled and died.

Now the people were getting angry.

"I will shoot the cloud away," said the best archer in the land, and straining every muscle, he fired an arrow straight and true. It flashed into the clouds. But the clouds did not fall, and the sun did not notice.

"One arrow is not enough!" cried a porcupine, and rushing up a hill, did a wild little dance and fired off a whole flight of spines at the clouds. Still the sun did not appear.

Then a gruff old bear got *really* angry. He stormed to the top of the hill and shook both fists at the sky, trying to think of the most threatening thing to shout at the sun. He was so angry and flustered that he could think of nothing terrible enough. All the crowd tried to think of what the bear should shout at the sun, and the bear jumped up and down in his rage.

▶ Continue reading here.

Just then, a bat who had been sleeping soundly throughout the proceedings, woke up. He had missed the red bird's song, the bonfire, the arrows and the porcupine's spines, but he had enjoyed a very lovely dream, and he smiled an enormous beaming smile.

Bats, as you know, sleep upside down, and when the crowd saw the bat's hilarious upside down smile they couldn't help laughing. Even the gruff old bear giggled and then fell to the ground helpless with laughter. The laughter rolled around the valley, and the sun, hearing the noise, parted the clouds slightly and looked down. The thin beam of sunlight fell upon the little bat and his wide upside down smile.

The sun burst out laughing, and his laughter drove away the clouds. The people and animals saw the sun beaming from the mountaintops and then climb once more into the sky.

The Bat
Douglas Florian

The bat is batty as can be.
It sleeps all day in cave or tree,
And when the sun sets in the sky,
It rises from its rest to fly.
All night this mobile mammal mugs
A myriad of flying bugs.
And after its night out on the town,
The batty bat sleeps

Upside down.

Practice 127

Name _____ Date _____ **Practice** 127

/ů/ oo

Write the letters **oo** to complete each word. Then say the name of each picture.

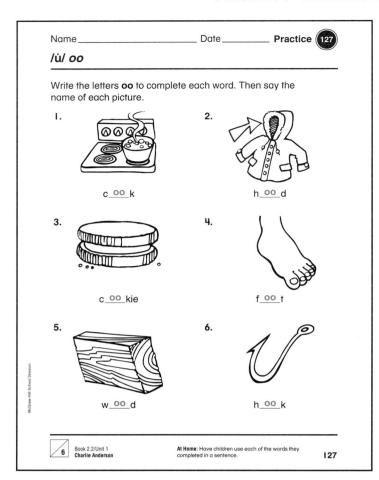

1. c_oo_k
2. h_oo_d
3. c_oo_kie
4. f_oo_t
5. w_oo_d
6. h_oo_k

McGraw-Hill School Division

Book 2.2/Unit 1
Charlie Anderson

6

At Home: Have children use each of the words they completed in a sentence.

127

Practice 128

Name _____ Date _____ **Practice** 128

Vocabulary

Read each sentence. Fill in the circle next to the meaning of the underlined word.

| chocolate | clothes | middle | offered | roof | upstairs |

1. Anna likes to eat <u>chocolate</u> cookies best.
   - ● **a.** a food
   - ○ **b.** a sound

2. The man <u>offered</u> to fix the wall of the house.
   - ○ **a.** said he would not
   - ● **b.** said he would

3. The baby had very wet <u>clothes</u>.
   - ○ **a.** food
   - ● **b.** things to wear

4. The ball landed right in the <u>middle</u> of the table.
   - ● **a.** the same distance from each side
   - ○ **b.** in the corner

5. My mother says never to climb on the <u>roof</u>.
   - ○ **a.** the side of a building
   - ● **b.** the top of a building

6. Jack went <u>upstairs</u> to his room.
   - ● **a.** the floor above
   - ○ **b.** the floor below

128

At Home: Have children write a story using the underlined words.

Book 2.2/Unit 1
Charlie Anderson

6

Luke and His Cat

At the castle the king saw the boy coming with his cat. "Look!" he said.
"Help is here!"
"Watch what my cat can do," Luke said. The cat ran upstairs.
Soon, it came back with many mice. After that the king asked Luke and his cat to stay. And they did, for a long, long time.

At Home: Discuss with children a time they have had a problem and how they solved it.

4

128a

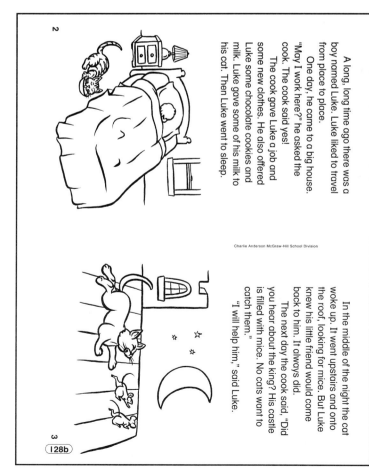

Charlie Anderson McGraw-Hill School Division

2

A long, long time ago there was a boy named Luke. Luke liked to travel from place to place.
One day, he came to a big house.
"May I work here?" he asked the cook. The cook said yes!
The cook gave Luke a job and some new clothes. He also offered Luke some chocolate cookies and milk. Luke gave some of his milk to his cat. Then Luke went to sleep.

In the middle of the night the cat woke up. It went upstairs and onto the roof, looking for mice. But Luke knew his little friend would come back to him. It always did.
The next day the cook said, "Did you hear about the king? His castle is filled with mice. No cats want to catch them."
"I will help him," said Luke.

3

128b

Charlie Anderson • PRACTICE

Story Comprehension

Think about the story "Charlie Anderson." Put an **X** next to each sentence that tells about something you found out in this story.

1. __X__   Charlie is a cat.

2. __X__   Sarah dresses Charlie in doll clothes.

3. _____   Charlie always sleeps in the woods.

4. _____   Elizabeth runs away with Charlie.

5. __X__   Charlie has two homes.

6. __X__   Sarah and Elizabeth are sisters.

7. _____   The girls take Charlie to visit their father.

8. _____   Mother helps the girls look for Charlie.

9. __X__   Charlie's other name is Anderson.

10. __X__   Charlie is loved by two families.

Use a Map

A **map** can be like a maze. Use a map to find your way through different roads and towns.
Follow the directions given below. Draw a line on the roads to show your path. To make sure you went the right way, answer the questions below the map.

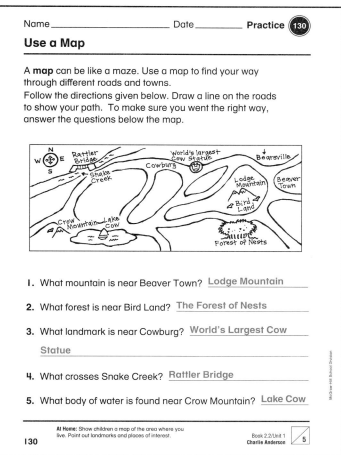

1. What mountain is near Beaver Town? __Lodge Mountain__

2. What forest is near Bird Land? __The Forest of Nests__

3. What landmark is near Cowburg? __World's Largest Cow Statue__

4. What crosses Snake Creek? __Rattler Bridge__

5. What body of water is found near Crow Mountain? __Lake Cow__

/ù/ oo

Name each picture. Write the word that has the sound of **oo** as in **foot**.

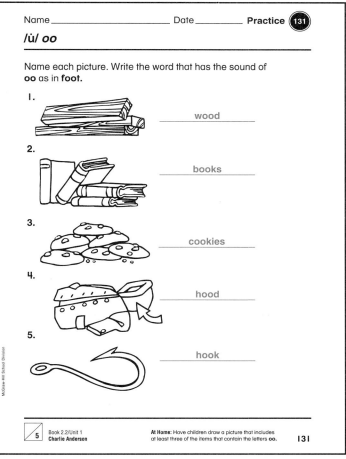

1. __wood__

2. __books__

3. __cookies__

4. __hood__

5. __hook__

/ù/oo

Draw a line from each clue to the word it describes.

1. Make some food.   foot

2. Put a shoe on me.   hook

3. Hang up your coat on me.   soot

4. See something.   cook

5. Keep your head warm with me.   hood

6. Sweep a chimney and find me.   look

7. I come from trees.   book

8. You read me.   wood

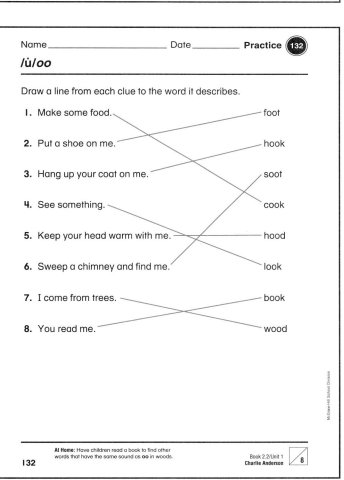

Charlie Anderson • PRACTICE

Draw Conclusions

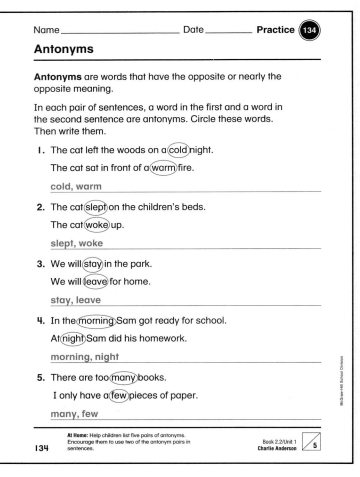

elephant   whale   giraffe   tiger

Read the riddles. What animal is it?
Write the name of the animal.

1. I breathe through a hole
and swim in the sea.
I'm as big as a ship.
Can you guess me?
Let's see!   **whale**

2. I can eat leaves from a tree,
and I'm yellow and brown.
I have a long neck
to see all around.
Who am I?   **giraffe**

3. You could ride on my back
and climb down my long nose.
Be sure to watch out for
my big heavy toes!
Guess who I am.   **elephant**

4. I live in the wild,
and I'm orange and brown.
If you see many stripes,
you know I'm around!
Who am I?   **tiger**

4 Book 2.2/Unit 1
Charlie Anderson

At Home: Have children make up their own animal riddles and share them. Discuss the words that helped the children solve each riddle.

133

Antonyms

Antonyms are words that have the opposite or nearly the opposite meaning.

In each pair of sentences, a word in the first and a word in the second sentence are antonyms. Circle these words. Then write them.

1. The cat left the woods on a (cold) night.

   The cat sat in front of a (warm) fire.

   cold, warm

2. The cat (slept) on the children's beds.

   The cat (woke) up.

   slept, woke

3. We will (stay) in the park.

   We will (leave) for home.

   stay, leave

4. In the (morning) Sam got ready for school.

   At (night) Sam did his homework.

   morning, night

5. There are too (many) books.

   I only have a (few) pieces of paper.

   many, few

At Home: Help children list five pairs of antonyms. Encourage them to use two of the antonym pairs in sentences.

134

Book 2.2/Unit 1
Charlie Anderson 5

Charlie Anderson • RETEACH

Name_____ Date_____ **Reteach** `127`

/ů/ oo

> Read the following sentence.
> Look at the **soo**t on the b**oo**k.

Look at the pictures. Then circle the word with the /ů/ sound that names the picture.

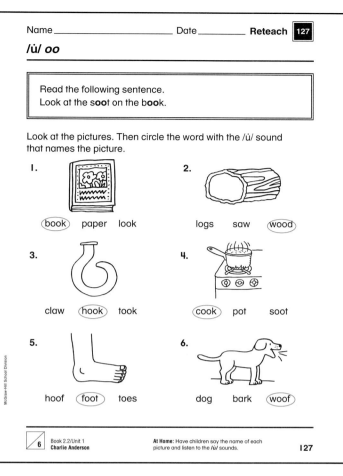

1. (book) paper look
2. logs saw (wood)
3. claw (hook) took
4. (cook) pot soot
5. hoof (foot) toes
6. dog bark (woof)

Name_____ Date_____ **Reteach** `128`

Vocabulary

Choose a word from the box that matches each clue.
Write the word on the line.

| chocolate | clothes | middle | offered | roof | upstairs |

1. gave something — _offered_
2. in the center — _middle_
3. part of a house above the first floor — _upstairs_
4. the top of a house — _roof_
5. what we wear to keep warm — _clothes_
6. good in ice cream — _chocolate_

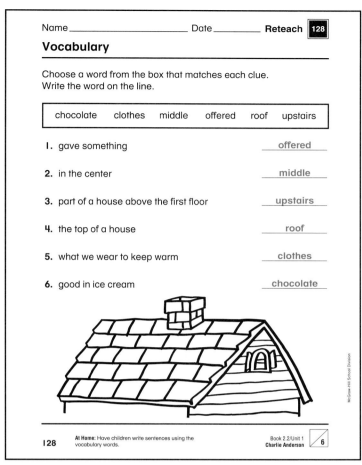

Name_____ Date_____ **Reteach** `129`

Story Comprehension

The following pictures describe events that occurred in "Charlie Anderson." Write a sentence to describe each one. **Answers may vary.**

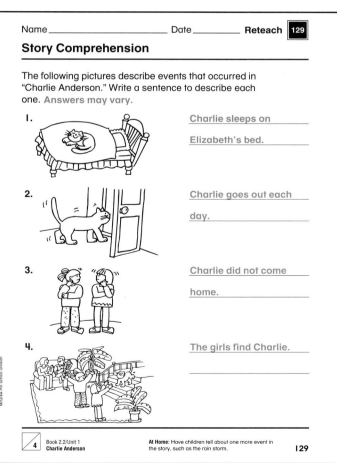

1. _Charlie sleeps on Elizabeth's bed._
2. _Charlie goes out each day._
3. _Charlie did not come home._
4. _The girls find Charlie._

Name_____ Date_____ **Reteach** `130`

Use a Map

> Some **maps** show you the path that someone traveled.
> **Landmarks** are easy-to-see objects along the way.

Look at the map below. It follows the path of a cat named Bubbles as she wanders around her neighborhood.

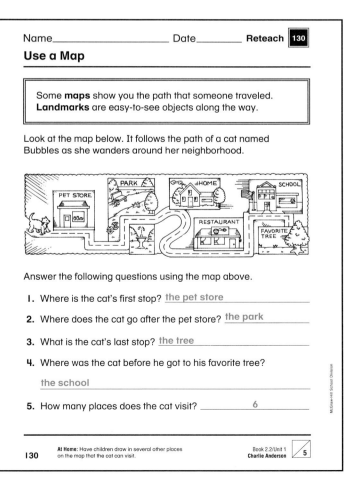

Answer the following questions using the map above.

1. Where is the cat's first stop? _the pet store_
2. Where does the cat go after the pet store? _the park_
3. What is the cat's last stop? _the tree_
4. Where was the cat before he got to his favorite tree?
   the school
5. How many places does the cat visit? _6_

Sheet 131

Name_____ Date_____ **Reteach** 131

/ù/ oo

The words h**oo**d and b**oo**k have the same middle sound.

Color each picture whose name has the same sound as **took** and **look**.

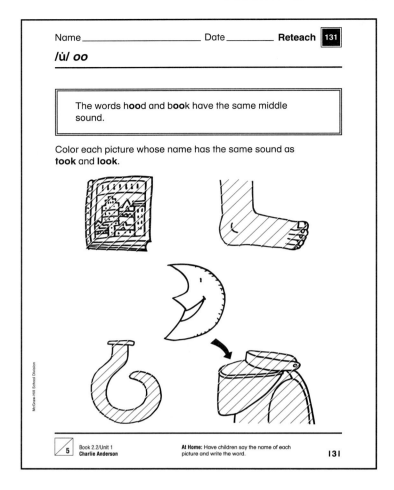

5 Book 2.2/Unit 1
Charlie Anderson

At Home: Have children say the name of each picture and write the word.

131

Sheet 132

Name_____ Date_____ **Reteach** 132

/ù/ oo

Say the name of the picture.
Listen to the sound the letters **oo** stand for in the middle of **book**.

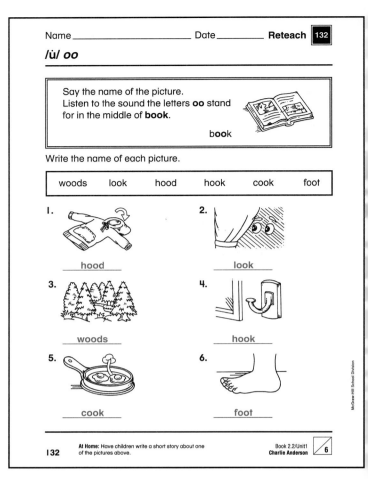

b**oo**k

Write the name of each picture.

| woods | look | hood | hook | cook | foot |

1. ___hood___

2. ___look___

3. ___woods___

4. ___hook___

5. ___cook___

6. ___foot___

132 **At Home:** Have children write a short story about one of the pictures above.

Book 2.2/Unit1
Charlie Anderson 6

Sheet 133

Name_____ Date_____ **Reteach** 133

Draw Conclusions

When you know some of the things that happen in a story, you can often guess what is true.

The man is tired.

Look at each set of pictures. Then draw a line under the sentence that is probably true.

1. The girl is happy.
   The girl is sad.

2. The music is loud.
   The music is soft.

3. The water is hot.
   The water is cold.

4. The boy is going to bed.
   The boy is getting up.

4 Book 2.2/Unit 1
Charlie Anderson

At Home: Have children write a conclusion about Charlie Anderson.

133

Sheet 134

Name_____ Date_____ **Reteach** 134

Antonyms

An **antonym** is a word or term that means the opposite of or almost the opposite of another word.

The floor is **hard.**
The pillow is **soft.** **Hard** means the opposite of **soft.**

A. Read each sentence. Then write the word from the box that means the opposite of the word in dark print.

| small | up | lose | silent |

1. The heavy box was too **big** for the cart and it slipped off.
   ___small___

2. We hope to **win** the game.
   ___lose___

3. The **noisy** birds sang loudly in their nest in the tree.
   ___silent___

4. We rode our bikes **down** the block.
   ___up___

B. Write antonyms for the following words.

5. in ___out___

6. high ___low___

7. cold ___hot___

8. happy ___sad___

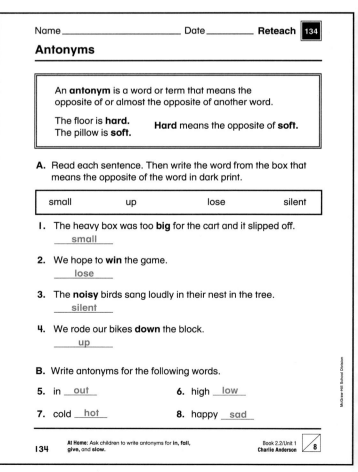

Charlie Anderson • EXTEND

/u̇/ oo

Follow the directions to make new words.
Write each new word on the ladder.

1. Change the **b** to a **c**.
2. Change the **c** to a **br**.
3. Change the **br** to a **sh**.
4. Change the **sh** to a **h**.
5. Change the **k** to a **d**.

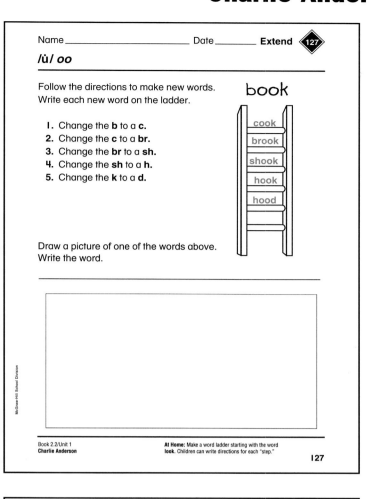

book

cook
brook
shook
hook
hood

Draw a picture of one of the words above.
Write the word.

_____

Book 2.2/Unit 1
Charlie Anderson

At Home: Make a word ladder starting with the word
look. Children can write directions for each "step."

127

Vocabulary

Solve each riddle using a word in the box. Write a riddle or a
sentence for the word you do not use.

chocolate	clothes	middle	roof	upstairs

1. I taste sweet.
   I am a treat.

   I am ____chocolate____.

2. I am not first.
   I am not last.

   I am in the ____middle____.

3. You put me on.
   I keep you warm.

   I am ____clothes____.

4. I am the top part of a house.
   I keep out rain and snow.

   I am the ____roof____.

Sentences and/or riddle should reflect an understanding
of the vocabulary word: upstairs.

_____

_____

_____

128

At Home: Have children tell a story using some of the words
in the box.

Book 2.2/Unit 1
Charlie Anderson

Story Comprehension

How can Charlie Anderson have two families and two homes?

Charlie Anderson spends half the day with one family and
half the day with the other family.

How can Sarah and Elizabeth have two families and two homes?

They live part of the week with their mother and part of the
week with their father and stepmother.

Draw a picture of everyone who loves Charlie Anderson.

The picture might include Sarah, Elizabeth, their mother,
and the man and woman who live in the new house.

Book 2.2/Unit 1
Charlie Anderson

At Home: Invite children to draw a picture and write about
some people in their neighborhood.

129

Use a Map

Draw a map of your classroom on another piece of paper.

1. Draw a dotted line on the map to show the route from the door
   to your seat.

2. What do you pass when you walk from the door to your seat?

   _____

   _____

3. Draw a circle to show the clock. Put a **X** on the clock.

4. What is near the window?

   _____

5. Write a sentence to tell something else you can learn from
   your map.

   _____

   _____

130

At Home: Children can draw a map of a standard kitchen.
Help them label the different parts of their map.

Book 2.2/Unit 1
Charlie Anderson

Page 131

Name _____ Date _____ **Extend** 131

/ù/ oo

Draw a line to the cookies. Follow the words with the **oo** sound that you hear in the word **cookies.**

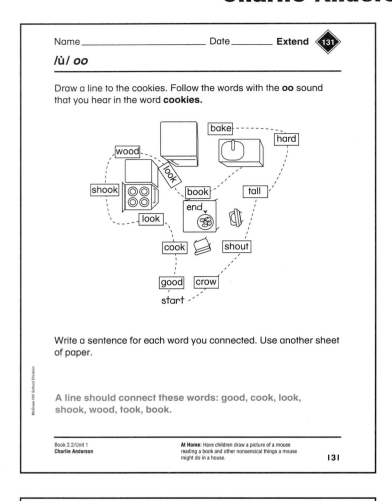

bake

hard

wood

look

shook

book

tall

end

look

cook

shout

good

crow

start

Write a sentence for each word you connected. Use another sheet of paper.

A line should connect these words: good, cook, look, shook, wood, took, book.

Book 2.2/Unit 1
Charlie Anderson

At Home: Have children draw a picture of a mouse reading a book and other nonsensical things a mouse might do in a house.

131

Page 132

Name _____ Date _____ **Extend** 132

/ù/ oo

| shook | brook | cookies | hook | wood |

Write words from the box on the lines. Complete the puzzle.

Across

2. I chop some ___wood___ for a fire.

3. We go fishing in the ___brook___ .

5. He ___shook___ the milk and ice cream to mix it.

Down

1. I have milk with chocolate chip ___cookies___ .

4. Jan hangs her coat on a ___hook___

Crossword puzzle:
Across 2: W O O D
Across 3: B R O O K
Across 5: S H O O K
Down: C O O K I E S, H O O K

Think of a word that rhymes with a word in the crossword puzzle. Use it in a sentence.

_____

_____

_____

At Home: Help children create a crossword puzzle using other words.

132

Book 2.2/Unit 1
Charlie Anderson

Page 133

Name _____ Date _____ **Extend** 133

Draw Conclusions

The people in the new house made a list of facts about Anderson. Sarah and Elizabeth made a list of facts about Charlie.

✓ each fact and fill in the blanks to show who wrote each list.

Sarah and Elizabeth _____'s List

The New People _____'s List

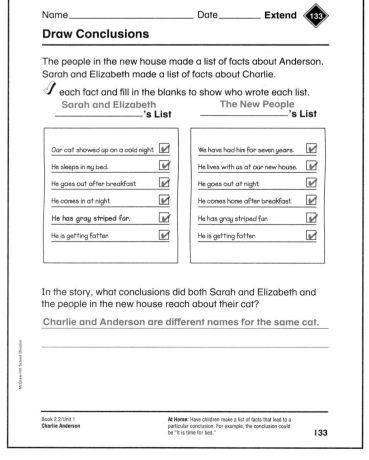

Sarah and Elizabeth's List		The New People's List	
Our cat showed up on a cold night.	✓	We have had him for seven years.	✓
He sleeps in my bed.	✓	He lives with us at our new house.	✓
He goes out after breakfast.	✓	He goes out at night.	✓
He comes in at night.	✓	He comes home after breakfast.	✓
He has gray striped fur.	✓	He has gray striped fur.	✓
He is getting fatter.	✓	He is getting fatter.	✓

In the story, what conclusions did both Sarah and Elizabeth and the people in the new house reach about their cat?

Charlie and Anderson are different names for the same cat.

_____

_____

Book 2.2/Unit 1
Charlie Anderson

At Home: Have children make a list of facts that lead to a particular conclusion. For example, the conclusion could be "It is time for bed."

133

Page 134

Name _____ Date _____ **Extend** 134

Antonyms

Draw lines to match words that have opposite meanings.

large — finish
happy — strong
weak — small
start — cold
warm — sad

Find the words with opposite meanings in each pair of sentences. Write the words on the lines.

1. Charlie Anderson liked to drink warm milk. Sarah and Elizabeth's mother heated the cold milk on the stove.

___warm___   ___cold___

2. Sarah and Elizabeth are in the city on the weekends. Charlie Anderson is in the country.

___city___   ___country___

3. One stormy night Charlie Anderson didn't come home. Sarah and Elizabeth found him the next day.

___night___   ___day___

Write a pair of sentences. Use two words that have opposite meanings. **Sample answers are shown.**

My room is messy.

My brother's room is neat.

At Home: Write a story using the following antonyms: up, down; messy, neat; light, heavy.

134

Book 2.2/Unit 1
Charlie Anderson

Charlie Anderson • GRAMMAR

Linking Verbs

- A **linking verb** is a verb that does not show action.
- The verb *be* is a linking verb.
- The verb *be* has special forms in the present tense.

  I <u>am</u> a student.   John <u>is</u> not tall.   We <u>are</u> friends.

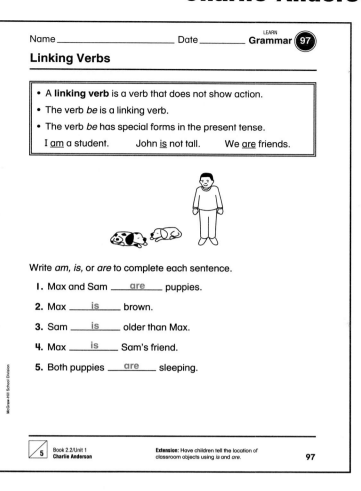

Write *am, is,* or *are* to complete each sentence.

1. Max and Sam ___are___ puppies.

2. Max ___is___ brown.

3. Sam ___is___ older than Max.

4. Max ___is___ Sam's friend.

5. Both puppies ___are___ sleeping.

Linking Verbs

- The verb *be* has special forms in the past tense.

SUBJECT	PRESENT	PAST
I	am	was
singular	is	was
plural and *you*	are	were

  I <u>am</u> here now. I <u>was</u> here yesterday.
  You <u>are</u> here now. You <u>were</u> here yesterday.
  We <u>were</u> both here yesterday.

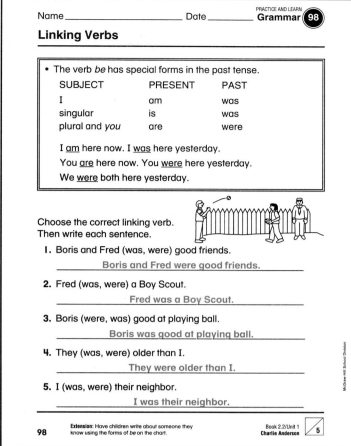

Choose the correct linking verb.
Then write each sentence.

1. Boris and Fred (was, were) good friends.

   _____Boris and Fred were good friends._____

2. Fred (was, were) a Boy Scout.

   _____Fred was a Boy Scout._____

3. Boris (were, was) good at playing ball.

   _____Boris was good at playing ball._____

4. They (was, were) older than I.

   _____They were older than I._____

5. I (was, were) their neighbor.

   _____I was their neighbor._____

Linking Verbs

- A **linking verb** does not show action.
- The verb *be* is a linking verb.
- The verb *be* has special forms in the present tense.
- The verb *be* has special forms in the past tense.

Read each sentence. Underline the correct form of *be*.

1. I (<u>am</u>, are) ready for my shot.

2. You (is, <u>are</u>) brave.

3. I (<u>was</u>, were) fine last year.

4. This (<u>is</u>, are) not fun.

5. You (is, <u>are</u>) next.

6. I (<u>am</u>, are) not happy about this!

7. That (<u>was</u>, were) not so bad.

8. I (<u>am</u>, are) glad I came here.

Proper Nouns

- A **proper noun** begins with a capital letter.
- The name of a day, month, or holiday begins with a capital letter.

  Mike went to camp on Saturday, July 10.

  School will close on New Year's Day.

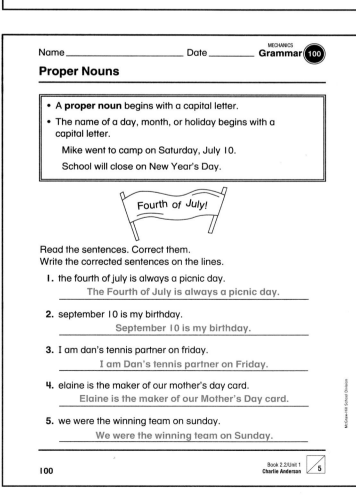

Read the sentences. Correct them.
Write the corrected sentences on the lines.

1. the fourth of july is always a picnic day.

   _____The Fourth of July is always a picnic day._____

2. september 10 is my birthday.

   _____September 10 is my birthday._____

3. I am dan's tennis partner on friday.

   _____I am Dan's tennis partner on Friday._____

4. elaine is the maker of our mother's day card.

   _____Elaine is the maker of our Mother's Day card._____

5. we were the winning team on sunday.

   _____We were the winning team on Sunday._____

Charlie Anderson • GRAMMAR

Linking Verbs

A. Read the sentences. Write the linking verb in each one.

1. I am a member of the swimming team. _____am_____

2. Jim is also a swimmer. _____is_____

3. We were late this morning. _____were_____

4. Lindsey was the first one in the water. _____was_____

B. Read each sentence. Write a linking verb in each one.

| is | are | am | was | were |

5. Now I _____am_____ a good swimmer.

6. Yesterday Jim _____was_____ the winner of the race.

7. Bob and Jim _____were_____ early on Friday.

8. You _____were_____ the best swimmer on Monday.

Linking Verbs

- *Is, are, am, was,* and *were* can be linking verbs.

Write each sentence correctly.
Draw the picture that the sentence tells.

1. The circle (is, are) blue.

   _____The circle is blue._____

2. Two squares (is, are) red.

   _____Two squares are red._____

3. The flag (is, are) red and blue now.

   _____The flag is red and blue now._____

4. It (were, was) black and white yesterday.

   _____It was black and white yesterday._____

Charlie Anderson • SPELLING

Name _____ Date _____

Words with /ù/oo

Pretest Directions

Fold back the paper along the dotted line. Use the blanks to write each word as it is read aloud. When you finish the test, unfold the paper. Use the list to the right to correct any spelling mistakes. Practice the words you missed for the Posttest.

To Parents,

Here are the results of your child's weekly spelling Pretest. You can help your child study for the Posttest by following these simple steps for each word on the list:

1. Read the word to your child.
2. Have your child write the word, saying each letter as it is written.
3. Say each letter of the word as your child checks the spelling.
4. If a mistake has been made, have your child read each letter of the correctly spelled word aloud and then repeat steps 1–3.

1. _____	1. wood
2. _____	2. book
3. _____	3. stood
4. _____	4. foot
5. _____	5. wool
6. _____	6. brook
7. _____	7. hood
8. _____	8. hook
9. _____	9. shook
10. _____	10. cook

Challenge Words

_____	chocolate
_____	clothes
_____	middle
_____	offered
_____	upstairs

Name _____ Date _____

Words with /ù/oo

Using the Word Study Steps

1. LOOK at the word.
2. SAY the word aloud.
3. STUDY the letters in the word.
4. WRITE the word.
5. CHECK the word. Did you spell the word right? If not, go back to step 1.

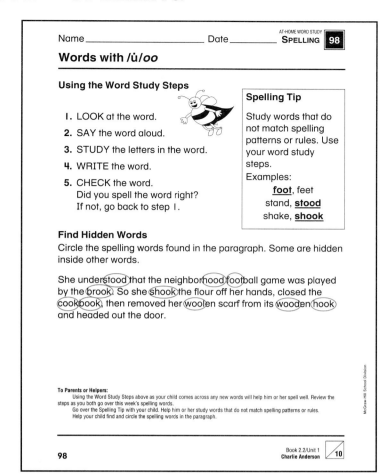

> **Spelling Tip**
>
> Study words that do not match spelling patterns or rules. Use your word study steps.
> Examples:
> **foot**, feet
> stand, **stood**
> shake, **shook**

Find Hidden Words

Circle the spelling words found in the paragraph. Some are hidden inside other words.

She understood that the neighborhood football game was played by the brook. So she shook the flour off her hands, closed the cookbook, then removed her woolen scarf from its wooden hook and headed out the door.

To Parents or Helpers:
Using the Word Study Steps above as your child comes across any new words will help him or her spell well. Review the steps as you both go over this week's spelling words.
Go over the Spelling Tip with your child. Help him or her study words that do not match spelling patterns or rules.
Help your child find and circle the spelling words in the paragraph.

Name _____ Date _____

Words with /ù/oo

wood	stood	wool	hood	shook
book	foot	brook	hook	cook

Look at the spelling words in the box. Match the spelling word with the spelling pattern and write the word.

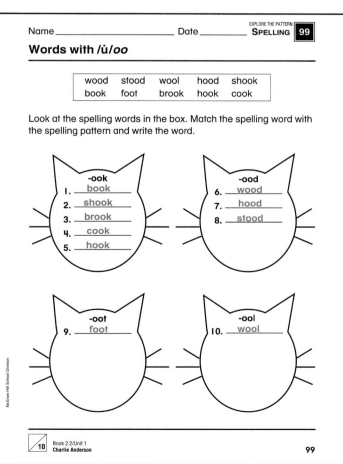

-ook
1. book
2. shook
3. brook
4. cook
5. hook

-ood
6. wood
7. hood
8. stood

-oot
9. foot

-ool
10. wool

Name _____ Date _____

Words with /ù/oo

wood	stood	wool	hood	shook
book	foot	brook	hook	cook

Make a Connection

Write a spelling word to complete each pair of sentences.

1. He poured water.
   He _shook_ salt.

2. The river flows into the sea.
   The _brook_ flows into the river.

3. We keep our hands warm with mittens.
   We keep our head warm with a _hood_.

4. A cat has fur.
   A sheep has _wool_.

5. We sat when the music stopped.
   We _stood_ when the music started.

6. You catch butterflies with a net.
   You catch fish with a _hook_.

New from Two

Make new words by joining two words. Match each spelling word in Column 1 with a word in Column 2. Write the compound words you make in Column 3.

7. cook	land	cookout
8. wood	ball	woodland
9. book	worm	bookworm
10. foot	out	football

Challenge Extension: Have children write a sentence that uses at least two of the challenge words. Have volunteers read their sentences aloud to the class.

Charlie Anderson • SPELLING

Words with /ù/oo

Proofreading Activity

There are six spelling mistakes in the letter below. Circle each misspelled word. Write the words correctly on the lines below.

Dear Sue,

I am having fun at camp. Today, I (stude) by a (bruk) and saw two little frogs jumping. Tonight we are going to (cooke) outside. We found (wud) to make a fire. I am glad my jacket has a (hoode) because it gets cold here at night. I haven't had time yet to read the (buk) you gave me, but I plan to start it soon. I miss you.

Your friend,

May

1. _____stood_____ 2. _____brook_____ 3. _____cook_____
4. _____wood_____ 5. _____hood_____ 6. _____book_____

Writing Activity

Write a letter to May using four spelling words. Tell about something that happened at home.

Circle the spelling words that you use in your letter.

_____

_____

_____

_____

_____

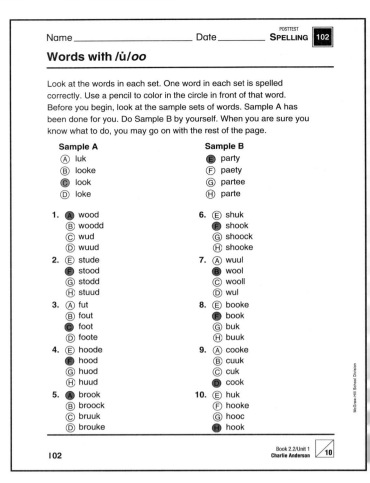

Words with /ù/oo

Look at the words in each set. One word in each set is spelled correctly. Use a pencil to color in the circle in front of that word. Before you begin, look at the sample sets of words. Sample A has been done for you. Do Sample B by yourself. When you are sure you know what to do, you may go on with the rest of the page.

Sample A
- Ⓐ luk
- Ⓑ looke
- ● look
- Ⓓ loke

Sample B
- ● party
- Ⓕ paety
- Ⓖ partee
- Ⓗ parte

1.
- ● wood
- Ⓑ woodd
- Ⓒ wud
- Ⓓ wuud

2.
- Ⓔ stude
- ● stood
- Ⓖ stodd
- Ⓗ stuud

3.
- Ⓐ fut
- Ⓑ fout
- ● foot
- Ⓓ foote

4.
- Ⓔ hoode
- ● hood
- Ⓖ huud
- Ⓗ huud

5.
- ● brook
- Ⓑ broock
- Ⓒ bruuk
- Ⓓ brouke

6.
- Ⓔ shuk
- ● shook
- Ⓖ shoock
- Ⓗ shooke

7.
- Ⓐ wuul
- ● wool
- Ⓒ wooll
- Ⓓ wul

8.
- Ⓔ booke
- ● book
- Ⓖ buk
- Ⓗ buuk

9.
- Ⓐ cooke
- Ⓑ cuuk
- Ⓒ cuk
- ● cook

10.
- Ⓔ huk
- Ⓕ hooke
- Ⓖ hooc
- ● hook

Fernando's Gift • PRACTICE

Soft *c* and Soft *g*

Write the word that answers the riddle.

1. This tells how old you are.

   lace   age   cage

   _____age_____

2. This is when you can run.

   page   ice   race

   _____race_____

3. This is something to eat.

   rice   rise   page

   _____rice_____

4. This is something everyone has.

   lace   cage   face

   _____face_____

5. This is where a mouse might live.

   nice   cage   stage

   _____cage_____

6. This is part of a book.

   page   place   dice

   _____page_____

7. This is what some tablecloths are made of.

   rice   page   lace

   _____lace_____

8. This is what elephants are.

   cage   huge   race

   _____huge_____

At Home: Have children list other words with **ce** and **ge**. Then have them use these words to make up one or two riddles of their own.
135

Vocabulary

Read the story. Choose a word from the box to complete each sentence. Write the word in the sentence. Then reread the story to check your answers.

| diving | explains | harm | noisy | soil | village |

The Browns go to a lake in the summer. They stay in

a house in the ___village___. Jess helps a baby bird.

His father ___explains___ what happened. "This

morning the birds were very ___noisy___. A baby bird

came ___diving___ out of its nest."

The bird lay in the dirt. It was covered with

___soil___. Jess is afraid a cat might ___harm___

the little bird. He picks up the bird. Then he puts it on a

warm blanket. Later that day, the bird flies away.

At Home: Have children write another story using the vocabulary words.
Book 2.2/Unit 1
Fernando's Gift   6

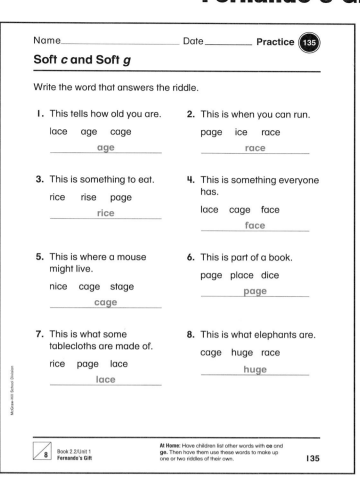

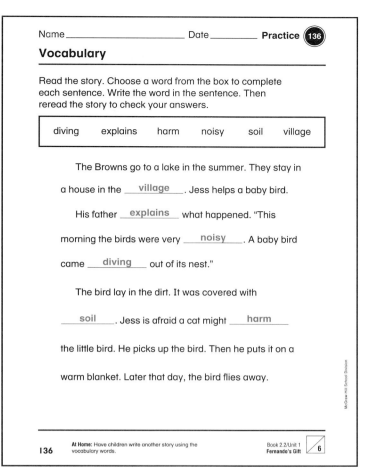

Fernando's Gift • PRACTICE

Name _____ **Date** _____ **Practice** (137)

Story Comprehension

Think about "Fernando's Gift." Write the correct answer to complete each sentence.

1. Fernando lives in <u>a rain forest</u>.
   a. a rain forest
   b. a city

2. Fernando's father plants <u>trees</u>.
   a. rice
   b. trees

3. The dogs are called <u>Brown Dog and Black Dog</u>.
   a. Brown Dog and Black Dog
   b. Fido and Spot

4. Fernando's father also teaches people about the <u>rain forest</u>.
   a. dogs
   b. rain forest

5. Carmina takes Fernando to see her favorite <u>climbing tree</u>.
   a. river
   b. climbing tree

6. The tree has <u>been cut down</u>.
   a. been cut down
   b. grown a lot

7. Fernando gives Carmina a new <u>Cristobal tree</u>.
   a. Cristobal tree
   b. toy

8. They plant the tree in <u>a secret place</u>.
   a. her yard
   b. a secret place

8 Book 2.2/Unit 1
Fernando's Gift

At Home: Have children draw a picture of their favorite part of the story. Then ask them to write a sentence about it.

137

Name _____ **Date** _____ **Practice** (138)

Read a Chart

The **chart** below gives weather facts for two cities in Rhode Island. At a glance, you can compare the rainfall, snowfall, and temperatures.

Month	Block Island			Providence		
	Temperatures High	Low	Days of Rain or Snow	Temperatures High	Low	Days of Rain or Snow
January	38	26	12	37	21	<u>12</u>
June	69	<u>57</u>	9	75	<u>56</u>	10
September	70	57	8	72	53	8
November	51	39	<u>10</u>	51	34	10

Fill in the chart with the facts provided below. Use the headings to guide you.

Facts to Add

- The low temperature in June in Providence was 56 degrees.
- There were 10 days of snow or rain in November on Block Island.
- In September, Block Island had a high temperature of 70 and a low of 57 degrees.
- There were 12 days of rain or snow in Providence in January.
- The low temperature on Block Island during June was 57 degrees.

138

At Home: Help children to make a chart that shows one of their activities over a week such as what they ate, what they did, or when they went to bed.

Book 2.2/Unit 1
Fernando's Gift 5

Name _____ **Date** _____ **Practice** (139)

Soft c and Soft g

Circle the word that completes each sentence. Then write it on the line.

1. Susan and Frannie are the same <u>age</u>.
   (age)   page   cage

2. I like to put <u>ice</u> in a cold drink.
   face   (ice)   lace

3. Sometimes we have <u>rice</u> for dinner.
   lace   twice   (rice)

4. My mouse lives in a <u>cage</u>.
   page   (cage)   age

5. Stephan ran fast and won the <u>race</u>.
   (race)   face   rice

6. Jake forgot which <u>page</u> he was reading.
   stage   age   (page)

6 Book 2.2/Unit 1
Fernando's Gift

At Home: Have children write the words they circled in alphabetical order.

139

Name _____ **Date** _____ **Practice** (140)

Soft c, g; /u̇/oo

Write a word from the box to complete each sentence.

book	mice	looked	face	place
stage	slice	page	nice	twice

1. I am reading a <u>book</u> on cooking.
2. The baby has a smile on her <u>face</u>.
3. I visited the <u>place</u> where grandma grew up.
4. There are <u>mice</u> in the field.
5. Actors do shows on a <u>stage</u>.
6. We stopped the car and <u>looked</u> at the view.
7. We played the game <u>twice</u>.
8. My mother cut me a <u>slice</u> of cake.
9. A kind person is <u>nice</u>.
10. Turn the <u>page</u> of the book.

140 **At Home:** Have children make up a rhyme for the word wood.

Book 2.2/Unit 1
Fernando's Gift 10

T18 *Annotated Workbooks*

Fernando's Gift • PRACTICE

Compare and Contrast

Imagine that you are a new student. At first you do not have any friends. Soon, you and Pat become good friends.

Write a letter to an old friend. Write about how you felt when you first came to the new school. Then write about how you felt after you got to know Pat.

Dear _____,

I have been at my new school for two weeks.

At first, I felt_____. When we went out to

play, I _____.

After I met Pat, I felt _____.

Now when I go out to play, _____.

Your friend,

_____

6 Book 2.2/Unit 1
Fernando's Gift

At Home: Have children compare and contrast their feelings about a current event at school, such as the arrival or departure of a class pet.

141

Antonyms

Two words that are opposite in meaning are called **antonyms**.

Mia got **wet** in the rain.
She sat by the heater until she was **dry**.

Wet and **dry** are antonyms. They are opposite in meaning.

Read each pair of sentences. Look at the underlined word in the first sentence. Then complete the second sentence in each pair with an antonym for the underlined word.

1. It was <u>noisy</u> at the baseball game.

   It was ___quiet___ in the library.

2. There are <u>few</u> cars in the village.

   There are ___many___ cars in the city.

3. Because it is so <u>hot</u> we go swimming.

   We wear heavy clothes on ___cold___ days.

4. The <u>tall</u> man could reach the shelf.

   The ___short___ man stood on a chair to reach the shelf.

5. Yesterday morning the ocean was <u>calm</u>.

   The ocean was very ___rough___ during the storm.

At Home: Encourage children to write three original sentences. Then have them substitute an antonym for one of the words in each sentence.

142

Book 2.2/Unit 1
Fernando's Gift 5

Fernando's Gift • RETEACH

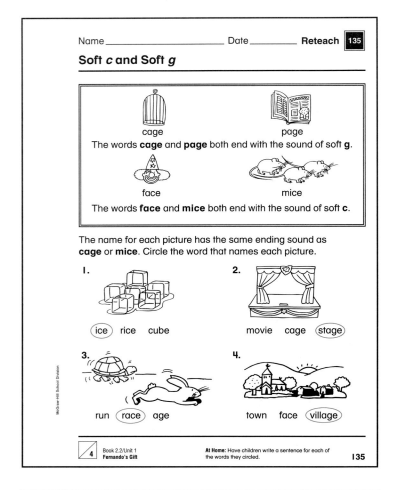

Name _____ Date _____ Reteach **135**

Soft *c* and Soft *g*

cage

page

The words **cage** and **page** both end with the sound of soft **g**.

face

mice

The words **face** and **mice** both end with the sound of soft **c**.

The name for each picture has the same ending sound as **cage** or **mice**. Circle the word that names each picture.

1. (ice)   rice   cube

2. movie   cage   (stage)

3. run   (race)   age

4. town   face   (village)

4   Book 2.2/Unit 1
Fernando's Gift

At Home: Have children write a sentence for each of the words they circled.

135

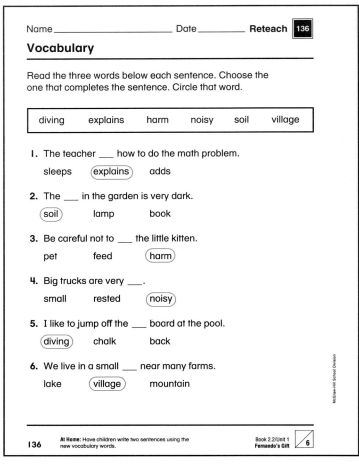

Name _____ Date _____ Reteach **136**

Vocabulary

Read the three words below each sentence. Choose the one that completes the sentence. Circle that word.

| diving | explains | harm | noisy | soil | village |

1. The teacher ___ how to do the math problem.

   sleeps   (explains)   adds

2. The ___ in the garden is very dark.

   (soil)   lamp   book

3. Be careful not to ___ the little kitten.

   pet   feed   (harm)

4. Big trucks are very ___.

   small   rested   (noisy)

5. I like to jump off the ___ board at the pool.

   (diving)   chalk   back

6. We live in a small ___ near many farms.

   lake   (village)   mountain

136   **At Home:** Have children write two sentences using the new vocabulary words.

Book 2.2/Unit 1
Fernando's Gift   6

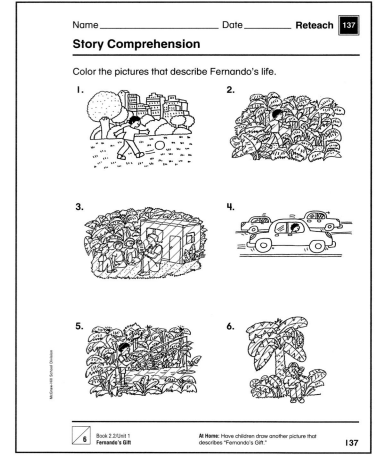

Name _____ Date _____ Reteach **137**

Story Comprehension

Color the pictures that describe Fernando's life.

1.

2.

3.

4.

5.

6.

6   Book 2.2/Unit 1
Fernando's Gift

At Home: Have children draw another picture that describes "Fernando's Gift."

137

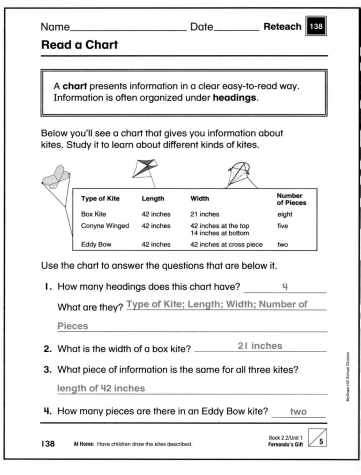

Name _____ Date _____ Reteach **138**

Read a Chart

A **chart** presents information in a clear easy-to-read way. Information is often organized under **headings**.

Below you'll see a chart that gives you information about kites. Study it to learn about different kinds of kites.

Type of Kite	Length	Width	Number of Pieces
Box Kite	42 inches	21 inches	eight
Conyne Winged	42 inches	42 inches at the top 14 inches at bottom	five
Eddy Bow	42 inches	42 inches at cross piece	two

Use the chart to answer the questions that are below it.

1. How many headings does this chart have? ___ 4

   What are they? Type of Kite; Length; Width; Number of Pieces

2. What is the width of a box kite? ___ 21 inches

3. What piece of information is the same for all three kites?

   length of 42 inches

4. How many pieces are there in an Eddy Bow kite? ___ two

Fernando's Gift • RETEACH

Soft *c* and Soft *g*

> Read the following sentence.
>
> He put a banda**ge** on his fa**ce**.

Circle the word that finishes each sentence. Then write the word on the line.

1. Jen fed the _____mice_____ some cheese.

   (mice)   rice

2. Would you like a _____slice_____ of apple pie?

   nice   (slice)

3. I _____change_____ my shoes before I play soccer.

   (change)   strange

4. Todd turned the _____page_____ after reading it.

   rage   (page)

5. The actor stepped onto the _____stage_____.

   (stage)   age

Soft *c*, *g*; /ù/ *oo*

> I ate some **rice** for dinner.
>
> village   space   (rice)

Read the sentence. Circle the word that completes the sentence. Then write the word on the line.

1. The dog ran into the _____woods_____.

   foot   (woods)   hood

2. My rabbit was in a _____cage_____.

   (cage)   page   age

3. Lake Erie was filled with _____ice_____.

   (ice)   twice   tricycle

4. This is a _____book_____ about a cat.

   look   cook   (book)

5. It was a _____nice_____ day outside.

   (nice)   mice   price

6. I read ten _____pages_____ of the book.

   wage   stages   (pages)

Compare and Contrast

> Thinking about how story characters are **alike** and **different** can help you understand the story.

Read the story. Then fill in the chart below to show how Tim and Tammy are alike and different. **Answers may vary.**

   Tim and Tammy are best friends. Most of the time they like to do the same things. They play computer games together. They also like to go to the park and play with Tim's dog.
   Other times they like to do different things. Tim's favorite sport is baseball. Tammy's favorite sport is soccer. She also likes to swim. Tim would rather go hiking. He enjoys riding his bike, too.

What is the same about Tim and Tammy?

1. like to do the same things   2. play computer games

3. go to the park   4. play with Tim's dog

What is different about Tim and Tammy?

Tim	Tammy
5. likes baseball	6. likes soccer
7. likes hiking	8. likes swimming

Antonyms

> A word that means the opposite or nearly the opposite of another word is an **antonym.**

Choose the word from the group of words that is the opposite of the underlined word. Write the antonym on the line.

1. not morning, but _____night_____

   month   day   night

2. not tiny, but _____large_____

   large   round   light

3. not warm, but _____cold_____

   soft   cold   dark

4. not up, but _____down_____

   high   low   down

5. not lose, but _____find_____

   cheer   find   happy

6. not take, but _____give_____

   give   fall   find

Fernando's Gift • EXTEND

Soft c and Soft g

face	village	age	place
page	space	stage	price

Find the word from the box that fits into the letter shapes. Then write the word on the line.

1. v i l l a g e _____ village

2. s p a c e _____ space

3. s t a g e _____ stage

4. p a g e _____ page

5. f a c e _____ face

6. a g e _____ age

7. p l a c e _____ place

8. p r i c e _____ price

Book 2.2/Unit 1
Fernando's Gift

At Home: Ask children to choose a word from each list and write it in a sentence.

135

Vocabulary

Sam lives in a small village high above the ocean. The soil in the village is rich. Sam's family uses the land to grow lemons. There is a very steep cliff near Sam's house. Many great divers use the cliff for diving. Sam's village gets noisy when people come to watch the divers. Sam is careful near the cliff. Sam's mother explains that he could harm himself if he plays too close to the cliff.

Match each underlined word with its meaning. Write the word on the line.

1. ___village___ a small town

2. ___explains___ makes something clear so it is easier to understand

3. ___soil___ dirt or earth in which plants grow

4. ___noisy___ very loud

5. ___diving___ jumping head first into the water

6. ___harm___ to injure or hurt

What might Sam think about when he watches the divers?

Sample answer is shown.

Sam might think that he would like to be a diver one day.

At Home: Ask children to write about what they see when they go outside their home.

136

Book 2.2/Unit 1
Fernando's Gift

Story Comprehension

Write a letter to Fernando telling him all the things you learned about the rain forest. Tell him why you think his gift of a tree is very special.

Dear Fernando,

I learned _____

trees should be planted to help the animals survive.

_____

_____

_____

I think your gift was very special because _____

it helps people and animals.

_____

_____

Your Friend,

_____

A sample answer is shown.

Book 2.2/Unit 1
Fernando's Gift

At Home: Ask children to read their letter and discuss what else they know about the rain forest. Then have them draw a picture of the rain forest.

137

Read a Chart

These are the characters in "Fernando's Gift." Use the names to complete the charts below.

Fernando	Jubilio	Evelyn	Mr. Cordova
Cecilia	Carmina	Raphael Dias	

Adult	**Child**	**Male**	**Female**
Cecilia	Fernando	Fernando	Evelyn
Raphael Dias	Carmina	Raphael Dias	Cecilia
Jubilio	Evelyn	Jubilio	Carmina
Mr. Cordova		Mr. Cordova	

Read the charts. Answer the questions.

1. Which children in the story are female?
   _____ Evelyn, Carmina

2. Which adults in the story are male?
   _____ Jubilio, Mr. Cordova, Raphael Dias

3. Name the only female adult. _____ Cecilia

4. Name the only male child. _____ Fernando

At Home: Encourage children to write two questions about the charts.

138

Book 2.2/Unit 1
Fernando's Gift

Fernando's Gift • EXTEND

Soft *c* and Soft *g*

mice	cage	page
village	ice	face

Find the words in the puzzle. Circle the words.

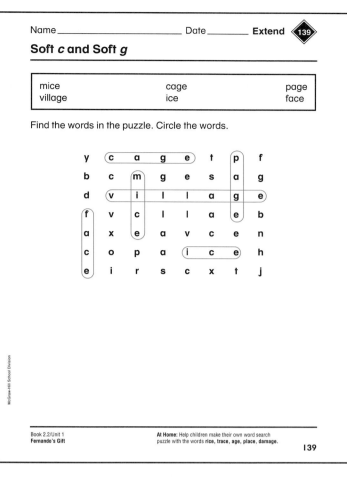

Soft *c, g; /ủ/ oo*

Jake's Dream

Jake went into the woods to find something to eat. He sat down on a piece of wood near a brook. A weed next to Jake started to grow. Jake watched as it grew straight up into space. Jake climbed the weed. At the top Jake saw a smiling face. It was a huge bear holding a plate of cookies. Jake shook. The bear asked Jake his age. Jake didn't answer. Instead, Jake raced down the weed. Jake woke up. He felt better since it was only a dream.

List each underlined word in one of the boxes below.

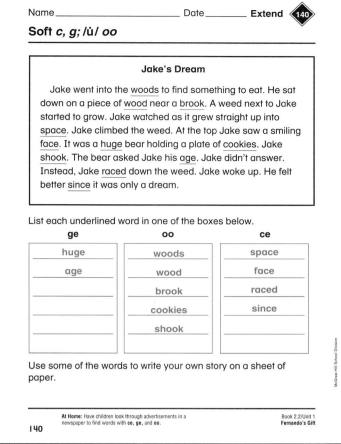

ge	**oo**	**ce**
huge	woods	space
age	wood	face
	brook	raced
	cookies	since
	shook	

Use some of the words to write your own story on a sheet of paper.

Compare and Contrast

Compare your day with Fernando's. Complete the charts below.

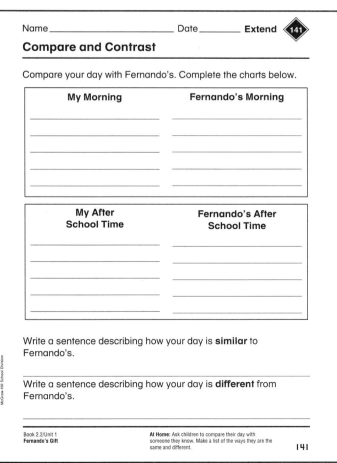

My Morning	**Fernando's Morning**

My After School Time	**Fernando's After School Time**

Write a sentence describing how your day is **similar** to Fernando's.

_____

Write a sentence describing how your day is **different** from Fernando's.

Book 2.2/Unit 1
Fernando's Gift

At Home: Ask children to compare their day with
someone they know. Make a list of the ways they are the
same and different.

141

Antonyms

Take turns with a friend. Toss a penny. Read the word it lands on. Write the antonym for the word. Score one point.

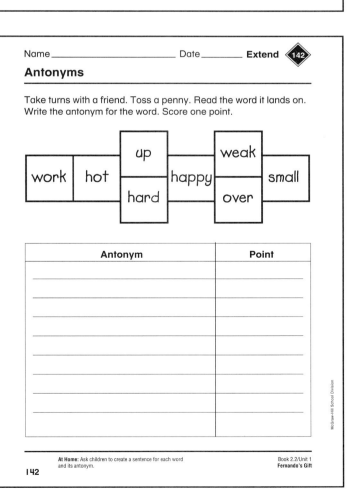

Antonym	Point

142

At Home: Ask children to create a sentence for each word
and its antonym.

Book 2.2/Unit 1
Fernando's Gift

T23

Fernando's Gift • GRAMMAR

Grammar 103 — LEARN

Name _____ Date _____ **Grammar** 103

Helping Verbs

- A **helping verb** helps another verb to show an action.
- *Have* and *has* can be helping verbs.
- Use *has* when the subject is singular.
- Use *have* when the subject is plural or *I* or *you*.
  The men have gone fishing.
  I have seen them fish before.
  Gary has also seen them fish.

Read the sentences. Write *has* or *have* in the blank. Then write the sentence.

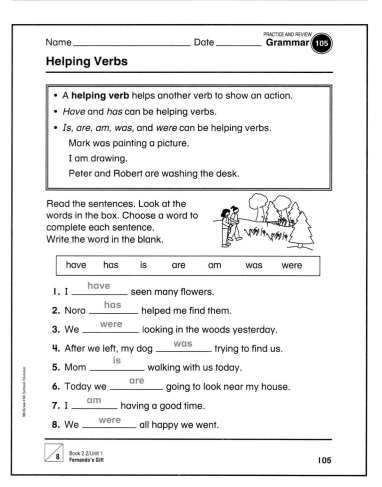

1. I __have__ written a letter to my mom.
   ___I have written a letter to my mom.___

2. She __has__ written one to me.
   ___She has written one to me.___

3. My father and I __have__ called her.
   ___My father and I have called her.___

4. You __have__ called her many times.
   ___You have called her many times.___

5. She __has__ gone on a visit to grandmother.
   ___She has gone on a visit to grandmother.___

5 | Book 2.2/Unit 1
Fernando's Gift
Extension: Have children say sentences with the helping verbs *has* and *have*.
103

Grammar 104 — PRACTICE AND LEARN

Name _____ Date _____ **Grammar** 104

Helping Verbs

- *Is, are, am, was,* and *were* can be helping verbs.
  We <u>were</u> going to the store.
  Sara <u>is</u> coming too.
  Jack <u>was</u> hoping to come.
  <u>Are</u> you going?
  I <u>am</u> going.

Read the sentences. Underline the correct helping verb in each one.

1. I (<u>am</u>, is) having a party.
2. Jack (are, <u>is</u>) coming.
3. Dan (were, <u>was</u>) hoping to come.
4. (Is, <u>Are</u>) you asking Nick and Al?
5. We (was, <u>were</u>) going to call them.
6. They (is, <u>are</u>) taking a trip.
7. I (<u>was</u>, is) having ten people at the party.
8. Now I (<u>am</u>, is) having more.

104 | **Extension:** Have children write sentences using helping verbs *is, are, am, was,* and *were.* | Book 2.2/Unit 1 **Fernando's Gift** | 8

Grammar 105 — PRACTICE AND REVIEW

Name _____ Date _____ **Grammar** 105

Helping Verbs

- A **helping verb** helps another verb to show an action.
- *Have* and *has* can be helping verbs.
- *Is, are, am, was,* and *were* can be helping verbs.
  Mark was painting a picture.
  I am drawing.
  Peter and Robert are washing the desk.

Read the sentences. Look at the words in the box. Choose a word to complete each sentence. Write the word in the blank.

| have | has | is | are | am | was | were |

1. I __have__ seen many flowers.
2. Nora __has__ helped me find them.
3. We __were__ looking in the woods yesterday.
4. After we left, my dog __was__ trying to find us.
5. Mom __is__ walking with us today.
6. Today we __are__ going to look near my house.
7. I __am__ having a good time.
8. We __were__ all happy we went.

8 | Book 2.2/Unit 1
Fernando's Gift
105

Grammar 106 — MECHANICS

Name _____ Date _____ **Grammar** 106

Quotation Marks

- Use quotation marks at the beginning and end of what a person says.
  "Come here," Dad told the dog.

Read each sentence. Correct it. Write the correct sentence on the line.

1. Let's open the box, Gerry said.
   ___"Let's open the box," Gerry said.___

2. I need a pair of scissors, Lila said.
   ___"I need a pair of scissors," Lila said.___

3. Pull off the tape, Grandpa said.
   ___"Pull off the tape," Grandpa said.___

4. Tear open the end, Gerry said.
   ___"Tear open the end," Gerry said.___

106 | **Extensions:** Have students write about a conversation using quotation marks. | Book 2.2/Unit 1 **Fernando's Gift** | 4

Fernando's Gift • GRAMMAR

Helping Verbs

Which helping verb best completes the sentence?
Mark your answer.

1. Lou _____ found a coin.
   - ⓐ have
   - ⓑ has
   - ⓒ are

2. They _____ asked who lost it.
   - ⓐ have
   - ⓑ is
   - ⓒ has

3. We _____ looking for more coins.
   - ⓐ have
   - ⓑ am
   - ⓒ are

4. Lou and I _____ put them in a safe place.
   - ⓐ is
   - ⓑ are
   - ⓒ have

5. Mom _____ watching them.
   - ⓐ is
   - ⓑ are
   - ⓒ were

Linking Verbs

- *Have* and *has* can be linking verbs.
- *Is, are, am, was,* and *were* can be helping verbs.

Read each sentence aloud. Choose the correct word.
Write the sentence.

1. (is, am) Who ___is___ going to the movies?
   Who is going to the movies?

2. (have, has) Nell ___has___ kept the money.
   Nell has kept the money.

3. (is, am) I ___am___ going to the fair.
   I am going to the fair.

4. (have, was) Who ___was___ visiting Uncle Ted?
   Who was visiting Uncle Ted?

5. (was, were) Barbara and Joan ___were___ at his house.
   Barbara and Joan were at his house.

Fernando's Gift • SPELLING

Name _____ Date _____

Words with Soft *c* and Soft *g*

Pretest Directions
Fold back the paper along the dotted line. Use the blanks to write each word as it is read aloud. When you finish the test, unfold the paper. Use the list to the right to correct any spelling mistakes. Practice the words you missed for the Posttest.

1. _____
2. _____
3. _____
4. _____
5. _____
6. _____
7. _____
8. _____
9. _____
10. _____

1. dance
2. age
3. rice
4. mice
5. charge
6. race
7. space
8. cage
9. large
10. page

Challenge Words

_____ diving
_____ explains
_____ harm
_____ soil
_____ village

To Parents,
Here are the results of your child's weekly spelling Pretest. You can help your child study for the Posttest by following these simple steps for each word on the list:

1. Read the word to your child.
2. Have your child write the word, saying each letter as it is written.
3. Say each letter of the word as your child checks the spelling.
4. If a mistake has been made, have your child read each letter of the correctly spelled word aloud and then repeat steps 1–3.

Name _____ Date _____

Words with Soft *c* and Soft *g*

Using the Word Study Steps

1. LOOK at the word.
2. SAY the word aloud.
3. STUDY the letters in the word.
4. WRITE the word.
5. CHECK the word.
   Did you spell the word right?
   If not, go back to step 1.

Spelling Tip

When the /s/ sound is spelled c, c is always followed by **e**, **i**, or **y**.
Examples:
ri**ce**   dan**ce**

When /j/ is spelled g, g is always followed by **e**, **i**, or **y**.
Examples:
ca**ge**   char**ge**

Find and Circle
Where are the spelling words?

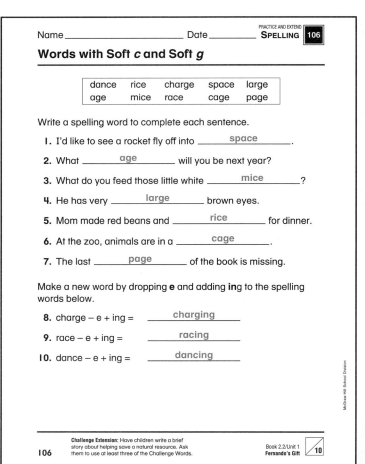

To Parents or Helpers:
Using the Word Study Steps above as your child comes across any new words will help him or her spell well. Review the steps as you both go over this week's spelling words.
Go over the Spelling Tip with your child. Ask if he or she knows other words that rhyme with the spelling words.
Help your child find and circle the spelling words in the puzzle.

Name _____ Date _____

Words with Soft *c* and Soft *g*

dance	rice	charge	space	large
age	mice	race	cage	page

How Nice!
Say each spelling word. Listen to how it ends. Match each word with the spelling pattern. Then, write the word under the correct pattern.

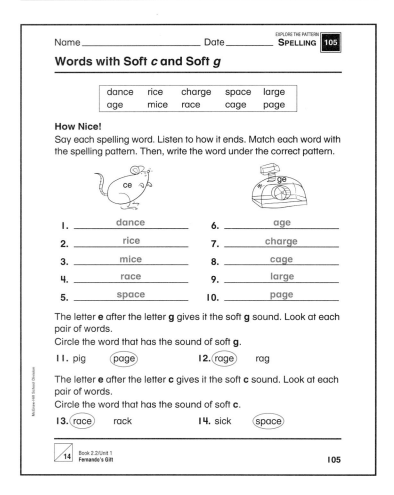

ce

1. dance
2. rice
3. mice
4. race
5. space

ge

6. age
7. charge
8. cage
9. large
10. page

The letter **e** after the letter **g** gives it the soft **g** sound. Look at each pair of words.
Circle the word that has the sound of soft **g**.

11. pig (page)   12. (rage) rag

The letter **e** after the letter **c** gives it the soft **c** sound. Look at each pair of words.
Circle the word that has the sound of soft **c**.

13. (race) rack   14. sick (space)

Name _____ Date _____

Words with Soft *c* and Soft *g*

dance	rice	charge	space	large
age	mice	race	cage	page

Write a spelling word to complete each sentence.

1. I'd like to see a rocket fly off into __space__.
2. What __age__ will you be next year?
3. What do you feed those little white __mice__?
4. He has very __large__ brown eyes.
5. Mom made red beans and __rice__ for dinner.
6. At the zoo, animals are in a __cage__.
7. The last __page__ of the book is missing.

Make a new word by dropping **e** and adding **in**g to the spelling words below.

8. charge – e + ing = __charging__
9. race – e + ing = __racing__
10. dance – e + ing = __dancing__

Challenge Extension: Have children write a brief story about helping save a natural resource. Ask them to use at least three of the Challenge Words.

106 Book 2.2/Unit 1
Fernando's Gift 10

T26 *Annotated Workbooks*

Fernando's Gift • SPELLING

Words with Soft *c* and Soft *g*

Proofreading Activity

There are six spelling mistakes in the paragraph below. Circle each misspelled word. Write the words correctly on the lines below.

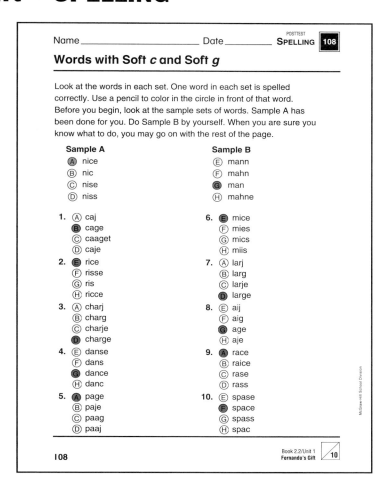

Our class has three brown (mise.) Two are small, so we think they are babies. We are not sure of their (agee.) Susan brought a (caje) for them to live in. The biggest mouse seems to be in (charje.) The others follow what he does. The mice like to (danse) when we have music. They also like to run. When we put them on the floor, they (rase) around as fast as they can go.

1. _____mice_____ 2. _____age_____ 3. _____cage_____

4. _____charge_____ 5. _____dance_____ 6. _____race_____

Writing Activity

Pets in the classroom are fun. What are some animals that could be a class pet? Write about having a class pet. Use four spelling words. Circle the spelling words you use.

_____

_____

_____

_____

Words with Soft *c* and Soft *g*

Look at the words in each set. One word in each set is spelled correctly. Use a pencil to color in the circle in front of that word. Before you begin, look at the sample sets of words. Sample A has been done for you. Do Sample B by yourself. When you are sure you know what to do, you may go on with the rest of the page.

Sample A
- Ⓐ nice
- Ⓑ nic
- Ⓒ nise
- Ⓓ niss

Sample B
- Ⓔ mann
- Ⓕ mahn
- Ⓖ man
- Ⓗ mahne

1. Ⓐ caj
   Ⓑ cage
   Ⓒ caaget
   Ⓓ caje

2. Ⓔ rice
   Ⓕ risse
   Ⓖ ris
   Ⓗ ricce

3. Ⓐ charj
   Ⓑ charg
   Ⓒ charje
   Ⓓ charge

4. Ⓔ danse
   Ⓕ dans
   Ⓖ dance
   Ⓗ danc

5. Ⓐ page
   Ⓑ paje
   Ⓒ paag
   Ⓓ paaj

6. Ⓔ mice
   Ⓕ mies
   Ⓖ mics
   Ⓗ miis

7. Ⓐ larj
   Ⓑ larg
   Ⓒ larje
   Ⓓ large

8. Ⓔ aij
   Ⓕ aig
   Ⓖ age
   Ⓗ aje

9. Ⓐ race
   Ⓑ raice
   Ⓒ rase
   Ⓓ rass

10. Ⓔ spase
    Ⓕ space
    Ⓖ spass
    Ⓗ spac

Practice 143

Name _____ Date _____ **Practice** 143

/ô/ a, aw, au

| taught | claw | saw | caught | lawn | hawk |

Write the word that names the picture and answers the riddle.

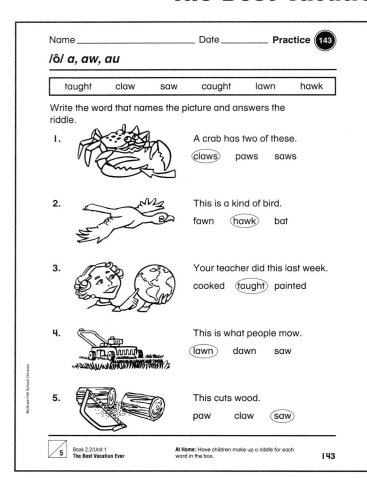

1. A crab has two of these.
   (claws)   paws   saws

2. This is a kind of bird.
   fawn   (hawk)   bat

3. Your teacher did this last week.
   cooked   (taught)   painted

4. This is what people mow.
   (lawn)   dawn   saw

5. This cuts wood.
   paw   claw   (saw)

Book 2.2/Unit 1
The Best Vacation Ever 5

At Home: Have children make up a riddle for each word in the box.

143

Practice 144

Name _____ Date _____ **Practice** 144

Vocabulary

Read each sentence. Write **T** if the sentence is true. Write **F** if the sentence is false. In each sentence, underline a word from the word box.

| brave | guess | museum | practice | vacation | wonder |

F   **1.** A <u>brave</u> person is always afraid.

T   **2.** If you don't know something, you can <u>guess</u>.

F   **3.** When you <u>practice</u> music, you forget how to play.

T   **4.** An art <u>museum</u> is a place to see paintings.

T   **5.** A <u>vacation</u> is a time when you don't have school.

F   **6.** If you <u>wonder</u> about something, you know about it.

F   **7.** Most people don't like to take a <u>vacation</u>.

F   **8.** You can go swimming at a <u>museum</u>.

T   **9.** A <u>brave</u> girl will do something she is afraid of.

T **10.** You can <u>practice</u> something to learn how to do it.

F **11.** When you <u>guess</u>, you know for sure.

T **12.** You might <u>wonder</u> which foods are best for you.

At Home: Have children write sentences to correct the false statements.

Book 2.2/Unit 1
The Best Vacation Ever 12

144

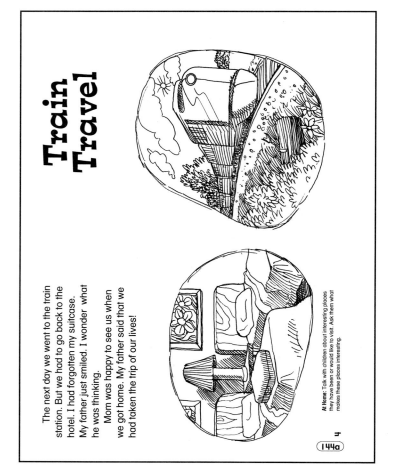

Train Travel

The next day we went to the train station. But we had to go back to the hotel. I had forgotten my suitcase. My father just smiled. I wonder what he was thinking.

Mom was happy to see us when we got home. My father said that we had taken the trip of our lives!

At Home: Talk with children about interesting places they have been or would like to visit. Ask them what makes these places interesting.

144a

4

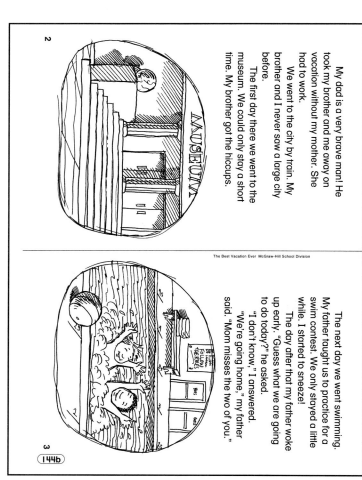

2

My dad is a very brave man! He took my brother and me away on vacation without my mother. She had to work.

We went to the city by train. My brother and I never saw a large city before.

The first day there we went to the museum. We could only stay a short time. My brother got the hiccups.

The Best Vacation Ever McGraw-Hill School Division

The next day we went swimming. My father taught us to practice for a swim contest. We only stayed a little while. I started to sneeze!

The day after that my father woke up early. "Guess what we are going to do today?" he asked.

"I don't know," I answered.

"We're going home," my father said. "Mom misses the two of you."

144b

3

The Best Vacation Ever • PRACTICE

Story Comprehension

Read each sentence. Write **T** if the sentence is true.
Write **F** if the sentence if false.

1. __T__ Amanda drove across the country with her family.

2. __T__ They saw where Orville Wright flew the first plane.

3. __F__ The home of country music is in Kitty Hawk.

4. __T__ The Grand Ole Opry is a place to hear country music.

5. __T__ The Alamo is in Texas.

6. __F__ Amanda said, "Carlsbad Caverns were not very big."

7. __T__ Amanda and her family rode mules in the Grand Canyon.

8. __F__ Sammy liked riding a mule.

9. __F__ After the Grand Canyon, Amanda went home.

10. __T__ There are millions of bones in the La Brea Tarpits.

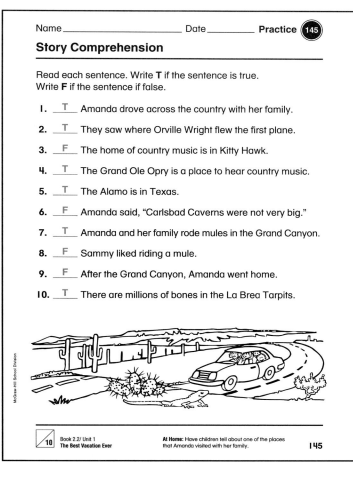

Book 2.2/ Unit 1
The Best Vacation Ever   10

At Home: Have children tell about one of the places
that Amanda visited with her family.   145

Read a Map

Pretend you want to take a trip to the Southwest. You will want
to visit some special sites your friends have told you about.
Use the **map** below to plan your trip. Write the answer on the
blank space beside the questions.

1. You will start your visit in Phoenix, Arizona. You want to visit
   the Grand Canyon first. Which direction will you have to go to
   get there? __north__

2. Your next stop will be the Petrified Forest National Park. What
   river is that near? __Little Colorado River__

3. What is the capital of New Mexico? __Santa Fe__

4. From Santa Fe, you want to go to the White Sands
   National Monument. In which direction would you go?
   __south__

At Home: Help children to identify the direction (north,
south, east or west) you'd have to travel to reach a
local landmark.   146

Book 2.2/Unit 1
The Best Vacation Ever   4

/ô/ a, aw, au

A. Circle the word to complete each sentence. Then write
it on the line.

1. The crab grabs with its _____claw_____.

   hawk   (claw)   paw

2. I _____yawn_____ when I get tired.

   lawn   paw   (yawn)

3. The _____fawn_____ has many white spots.

   (fawn)   draw   law

B. Circle the word to complete each sentence. Then write
it on the line.

4. We moved to a bigger house _____because_____
   we had a new baby.

   (because)   taught   caught

5. The teacher _____taught_____ math yesterday.

   (taught)   caught   because

6. Billy _____caught_____ the ball and the game
   was over.

   taught   because   (caught)

Book 2.2/ Unit 1
The Best Vacation Ever   6

At Home: Have children write the words they circled
in alphabetical order.   147

/ô/ a, aw, au; Soft c, g; /ù/

Use these words to answer the riddles.

hawk	age	hood	astronaut	foot	ice

1. I fly in a spaceship. What am I?

   __astronaut__

2. I am very cold. What am I?

   __ice__

3. I am a kind of bird. What am I?

   __hawk__

4. I am another word for how old you are. What am I?

   __age__

5. People use me when they walk. What am I?

   __foot__

6. I am part of your coat. I keep your head warm. What am I?

   __hood__

At Home: Have children make up a riddle for the word
book.   148

Book 2.2/Unit 1
The Best Vacation Ever   6

The Best Vacation Ever • PRACTICE

Draw Conclusions

Read the story. Write the answer to each question.
Use a complete sentence. Answers will vary.

Jamie loves to do magic tricks. She wants to buy the magic kit in Mr. Britt's store. First she has to save enough money from her weekly allowance. Every day Jamie walks by the store to make sure the kit is in the window. Mr. Britt told her he would save one for her. Many weeks later, Jamie finally has enough money. When she gets to the store, the kit is gone from the window!

1. Do you think that the magic kit costs a little bit of money or a lot of money?

   It must cost a lot of money.

2. What makes you think this?

   It took Jamie many weeks to save enough money to buy it.

3. How do you think Jamie felt when she didn't see the magic kit?

   She felt disappointed because she looked for it every day.

_____

4. Do you think Jamie finally got the magic kit? Why?

   Yes, because Mr. Britt said he would save one for her.

Book 2.2/Unit 1
The Best Vacation Ever
4

At Home: Have children change some of the information in the story. Ask them how this would change the conclusions they first made.

149

Inflectional Endings

The **-er** ending is used to compare two people, places, or things.
fast + er = faster (more fast)
Sam runs **faster** than Mike runs.

The **-est** ending is used to compare more than two people, places or things.
tall + est = tallest (most tall)
That is the **tallest** building in the state.

Complete the sentences with the correct words.

1. Winter will be here soon. It is only six o'clock, yet the sky is

   __darker__ (darker, darkest) than it was a week ago. In fact,

   this is the __coolest__ (cooler, coolest) day in over a week.

   Soon the days will be __shorter__ (shorter, shortest) than the

   nights. The fireplace is the __warmest__ (warmer, warmest)

   spot in the house.

2. We are proud of the library in our community. The building is

   __newer__ (newer, newest) than the library on Main Street.

   There are many books to read in the Children's Room. In fact,

   that is the __busiest__ (busier, busiest) reading room in the

   whole library.

At Home: Have children add -er and -est to the ends of the following words: small, slow, new, and great. Then ask the children to use each word in an original sentence that compares two or more people, places, or things.

150

Book 2.2/Unit 1
The Best Vacation Ever
6

The Best Vacation Ever • RETEACH

/ô/ aw, au

> The letters **aw** stand for the ending sound in **claw**.
>
> The letters **au** stand for the middle sounds in **caught**.

Use the words in the list below to complete each sentence.

paw	caught	fawn	saw

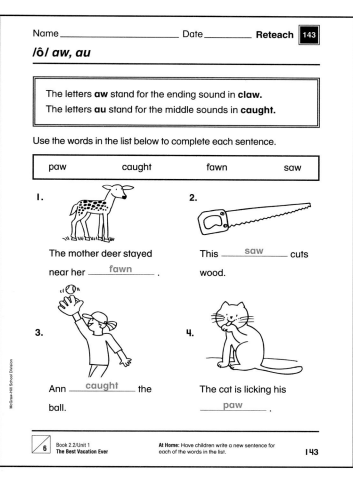

1. The mother deer stayed near her ___fawn___ .

2. This ___saw___ cuts wood.

3. Ann ___caught___ the ball.

4. The cat is licking his ___paw___ .

Vocabulary

Circle the word that completes each sentence.

brave	guess	museum	practice	vacation	wonder

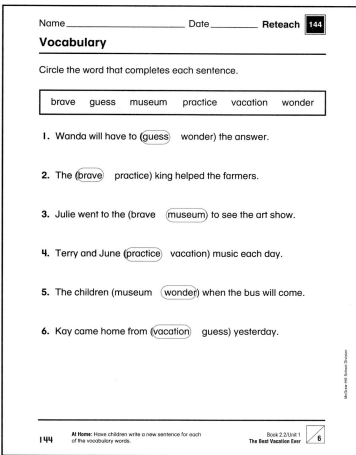

1. Wanda will have to (guess wonder) the answer.

2. The (brave practice) king helped the farmers.

3. Julie went to the (brave museum) to see the art show.

4. Terry and June (practice vacation) music each day.

5. The children (museum wonder) when the bus will come.

6. Kay came home from (vacation guess) yesterday.

Story Comprehension

Think about "The Best Vacation Ever." Then complete the chart below. Answers may vary.

Characters: Amanda, her family, Josie
_____
_____

Beginning of Story: Amanda and her family are driving across the United States during spring vacation. Amanda sends letters to her friend Josie all along the way.

Middle of Story: They go to many famous places such as Kitty Hawk, Nashville, the Alamo, Carlsbad Caverns, the Grand Canyon, and La Brea Tar Pits.

End of Story: They return home. Rover, their dog, is very glad to see them. Amanda is glad to be home, too!
_____

Read a Map

> A **road map** is a drawing that lets you see a view of an area.

Betsy Green and her family went to Hawaii. Betsy traced the path they followed. She circled the places they visited.

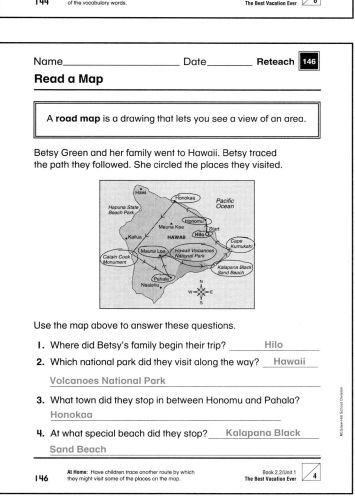

Use the map above to answer these questions.

1. Where did Betsy's family begin their trip? ___Hilo___

2. Which national park did they visit along the way? ___Hawaii Volcanoes National Park___

3. What town did they stop in between Honomu and Pahala? ___Honokaa___

4. At what special beach did they stop? ___Kalapana Black Sand Beach___

The Best Vacation Ever • RETEACH

/ô/ a, aw, au

Read the following sentence. Listen to the sounds.

I **wa**tered the l**aw**n bec**au**se it was dry.

Circle the word with the /**ô**/ sound that best completes each sentence.

1. The bug is _____ in the web.

not (caught)

2. Some birds have sharp _____.

(claws)   paws

3. Do you like to _____ ?

(draw)   swim

4. Another word for car is _____ .

out   (auto)

/ô/ aw, au; Soft c, g; /ù/

What is the last **book** you read?

huge   astronaut   (book)

Read each sentence below. Circle the word that completes the sentence. Then write the word on the line.

1. We ran a _____ race _____ around the field.

(race)   pace   rice

2. Do you wear a _____ large _____ or a small size?

barge   urge   (large)

3. Cats have sharp _____ claws _____ !

saw   (claws)   draw

4. I _____ caught _____ a cold at camp.

(caught)   taught   bought

5. I _____ took _____ my cat to school.

stood   wood   (took)

6. The ocean is _____ huge _____ .

(huge)   page   barge

148   At Home: Have children draw a picture for one of the sentences above.

Book 2.2/Unit 1
The Best Vacation Ever   12

Draw Conclusions

You can use picture clues and what you know to help you **draw conclusions** about what is happening.

Look at the picture. Read the place names. Circle the place where each person is going. Then tell what clues in the picture helped you.

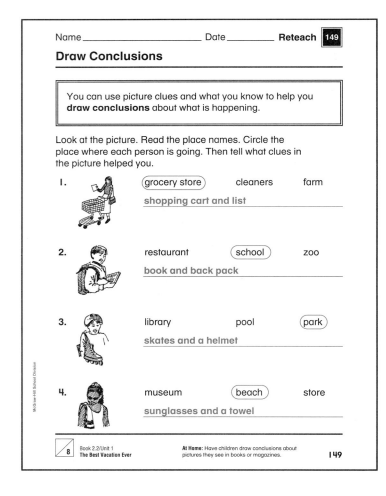

1. (grocery store)   cleaners   farm

shopping cart and list

2. restaurant   (school)   zoo

book and back pack

3. library   pool   (park)

skates and a helmet

4. museum   (beach)   store

sunglasses and a towel

8   Book 2.2/Unit 1
The Best Vacation Ever

At Home: Have children draw conclusions about pictures they see in books or magazines.

149

Inflectional Endings

The **-er** ending means "more."
old + **er** = older (more old)
Joe is **older** than Jim.

The **-est** ending means "most."
short + **est** = shortest (most short)
Sarah is the **shortest** person on the basketball team.

Read each sentence. Then circle the word that completes each sentence.

1. My brother Ted is a year _____ than I am.

(younger)   youngest

2. Julio can run the _____ of all the children on the team.

faster   (fastest)

3. Tom's voice is _____ than mine.

(louder)   loudest

4. That is the _____ of all the monkeys in the zoo.

smaller   (smallest)

5. Tomorrow we will visit the _____ river in the United States.

longer   (longest)

6. The ocean water was _____ than it was yesterday.

(colder)   coldest

7. We walked inside the _____ building in the city.

bigger   (biggest)

8. I saw a picture of the _____ bird in the world.

smaller   (smallest)

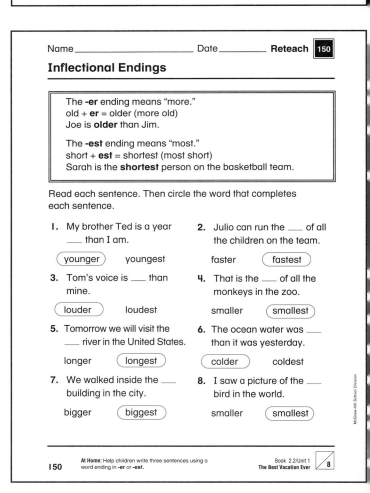

150   At Home: Help children write three sentences using a word ending in -er or -est.

Book 2.2/Unit 1
The Best Vacation Ever   8

The Best Vacation Ever • EXTEND

/ô/ a, aw, au

Show the shuttle's path. It stops at planets with **aw** and **au** words.
Color these planets.

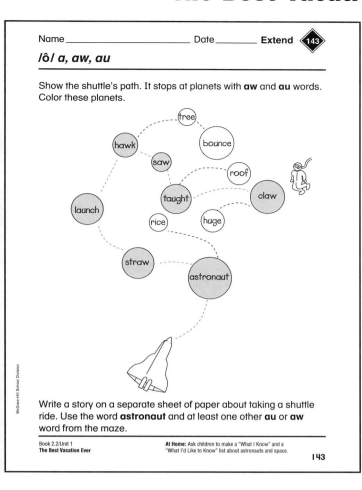

Write a story on a separate sheet of paper about taking a shuttle
ride. Use the word **astronaut** and at least one other **au** or **aw**
word from the maze.

Book 2.2/Unit 1
The Best Vacation Ever

At Home: Ask children to make a "What I Know" and a
"What I'd Like to Know" list about astronauts and space.

143

Vocabulary

Fill in each space using the words in the box.

brave	practice	vacation
guess	museum	wonder

1. If I do not know the answer, I might _____ guess _____.

2. I am going on _____ vacation _____ to the beach.

3. I _____ wonder _____ what third grade will be like.

4. She was _____ brave _____ to save the cat in the tree.

5. We went to the _____ museum _____ to see the art show.

6. I will _____ practice _____ until I learn how to do it right.

Find the words from above in the puzzle. Circle.

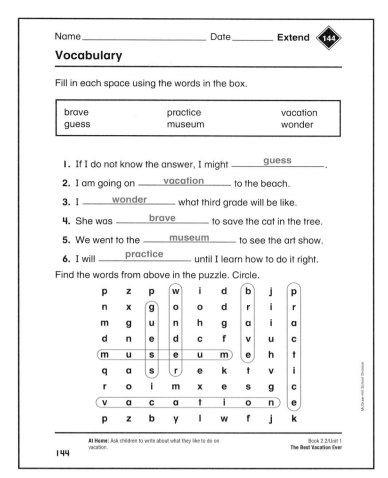

At Home: Ask children to write about what they like to do on
vacation.

Book 2.2/Unit 1
The Best Vacation Ever

144

Story Comprehension

On her trip, Amanda imagined what she would be when she grew
up. List her ideas.

Amanda wants to be . . .	1.	Country music star
	2.	Park Ranger
	3.	Photographer

Explain why new experiences can give you new ideas.

_____

_____

Draw a picture of what you want to be when you grow up. Explain
the reasons.

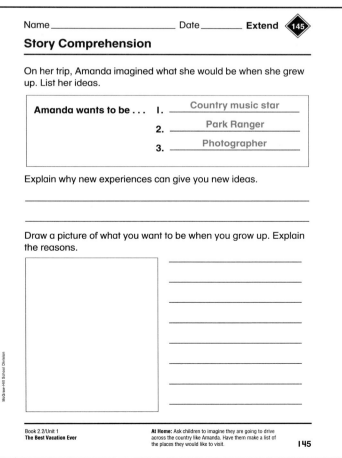

Book 2.2/Unit 1
The Best Vacation Ever

At Home: Ask children to imagine they are going to drive
across the country like Amanda. Have them make a list of
the places they would like to visit.

145

Read a Map

Write a sentence to describe each place on the map.

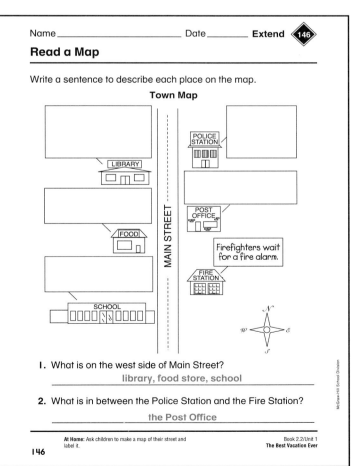

Town Map

1. What is on the west side of Main Street?
   _____ library, food store, school _____

2. What is in between the Police Station and the Fire Station?
   _____ the Post Office _____

At Home: Ask children to make a map of their street and
label it.

Book 2.2/Unit 1
The Best Vacation Ever

146

The Best Vacation Ever • EXTEND

/ô/ a, aw, au

Use these words to create a story. Underline the **aw** and **au** words you use.

saw	claw	awful	astronaut
jaw	crawl	straw	daughter
yawn	hawk	fault	launch

> **Stories will vary but should include some words from the box with *aw* and *au* words underlined.**
>
> _____
> _____
> _____
> _____
> _____
> _____
> _____
> _____
> _____
> _____
> _____

Trade stories with a friend. Can you find **aw** or **au** words that you did not include? _____

Book 2.2/Unit 1
The Best Vacation Ever

At Home: Children can draw a picture to illustrate their story.

147

/ô/ a, aw, au; Soft c, g; /u̇/ oo

A family of <u>mice</u> lived by a <u>brook</u>.
So did a cat.
One day Mother Mouse <u>saw</u> the cat.
The cat was licking its <u>paw</u>.
Mother Mouse was scared.
She built a <u>nice cage</u> for her young.
The cat never came back.

Change part of the word on each ladder to create a new word. Underline the part you changed. Write the new word on the next step. Complete each ladder. Some have been done for you. **Answers will vary.**

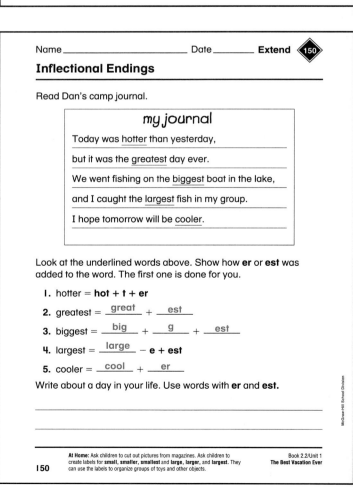

At Home: Ask children to make three word ladders. Start the ladders with the following words: **race, page, foot**. Children can change the words as they did in the above activity.

Book 2.2/Unit 1
The Best Vacation Ever

148

Draw Conclusions

What are three conclusions Josie might reach after reading Amanda's letters? **Sample answers are shown.**

> **Amanda loves to travel.**
>
> **Amanda isn't sure what she wants to be when she grows up.**
>
> **There are many interesting things to see in the U.S.**

Write a letter to Amanda telling her why Josie reached one of the conclusions. Make sure you use information from the story to explain your idea.

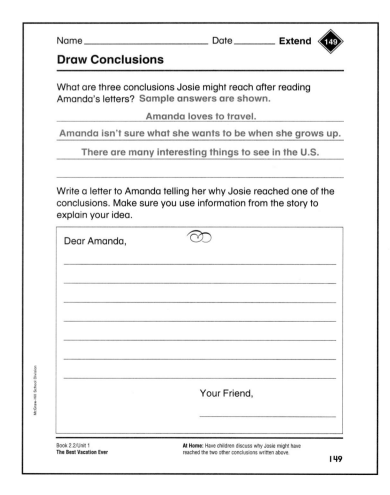

Dear Amanda,

_____
_____
_____
_____
_____
_____
_____

Your Friend,

_____

Book 2.2/Unit 1
The Best Vacation Ever

At Home: Have children discuss why Josie might have reached the two other conclusions written above.

149

Inflectional Endings

Read Dan's camp journal.

> ### my journal
>
> Today was <u>hotter</u> than yesterday,
>
> but it was the <u>greatest</u> day ever.
>
> We went fishing on the <u>biggest</u> boat in the lake,
>
> and I caught the <u>largest</u> fish in my group.
>
> I hope tomorrow will be <u>cooler</u>.

Look at the underlined words above. Show how **er** or **est** was added to the word. The first one is done for you.

1. hotter = **hot + t + er**

2. greatest = __great__ + __est__

3. biggest = __big__ + __g__ + __est__

4. largest = __large__ − **e + est**

5. cooler = __cool__ + __er__

Write about a day in your life. Use words with **er** and **est.**

_____
_____
_____

At Home: Ask children to cut out pictures from magazines. Ask children to create labels for **small, smaller, smallest** and **large, larger,** and **largest.** They can use the labels to organize groups of toys and other objects.

Book 2.2/Unit 1
The Best Vacation Ever

150

The Best Vacation Ever • GRAMMAR

Irregular Verbs

- Some verbs do not add -ed to form the past tense.
- The verbs *go* and *do* have special forms in the past tense.

  I, we, you, they   go   went

  I, we, you, they   do   did

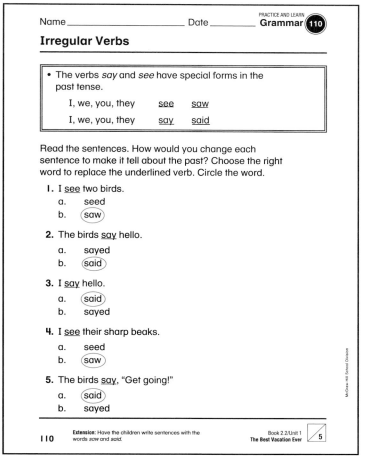

Read each sentence. Underline the correct word.
Write the sentence.

1. Yesterday we all (do, <u>did</u>) the dishes.

   Yesterday we all did the dishes.

2. I (go, <u>went</u>) to the library after school.

   I went to the library after school.

3. Who (do, <u>did</u>) the problem first?

   Who did the problem first?

4. They (go, <u>went</u>) to the book store last night.

   They went to the book store last night.

5. You (<u>did</u>, do) not see them yesterday.

   You did not see them yesterday.

Irregular Verbs

- The verbs *say* and *see* have special forms in the past tense.

  I, we, you, they   see   saw

  I, we, you, they   say   said

Read the sentences. How would you change each
sentence to make it tell about the past? Choose the right
word to replace the underlined verb. Circle the word.

1. I <u>see</u> two birds.
   a. seed
   b. (saw)

2. The birds <u>say</u> hello.
   a. sayed
   b. (said)

3. I <u>say</u> hello.
   a. (said)
   b. sayed

4. I <u>see</u> their sharp beaks.
   a. seed
   b. (saw)

5. The birds <u>say</u>, "Get going!"
   a. (said)
   b. sayed

Irregular Verbs

- Some verbs do not add -ed to form the past tense.
- The verbs *go* and *do* have special forms in the past tense.
- The verbs *say* and *see* have special forms in the past tense.

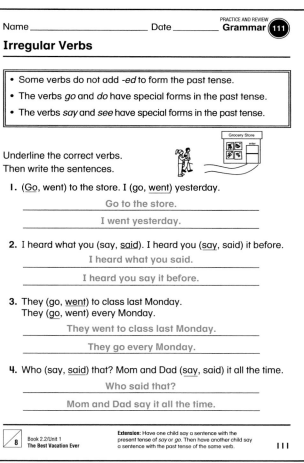

Underline the correct verbs.
Then write the sentences.

1. (<u>Go</u>, went) to the store. I (go, <u>went</u>) yesterday.

   Go to the store.

   I went yesterday.

2. I heard what you (say, <u>said</u>). I heard you (<u>say</u>, said) it before.

   I heard what you said.

   I heard you say it before.

3. They (go, <u>went</u>) to class last Monday.
   They (<u>go</u>, went) every Monday.

   They went to class last Monday.

   They go every Monday.

4. Who (say, <u>said</u>) that? Mom and Dad (<u>say</u>, said) it all the time.

   Who said that?

   Mom and Dad say it all the time.

Letter Writing

- Begin the greeting and closing in a letter with
  a capital letter.
- Use a comma after the greeting in a letter.
- Use a comma after the closing in a letter.
- Use a comma between the day and year in a date.
- Use a comma between the names of a city and a state.

  Dear Stuart,   Love, Charlie

  March 10, 1998   Chicago, Illinois

Read the letter. Correct it. Write the corrected letter.

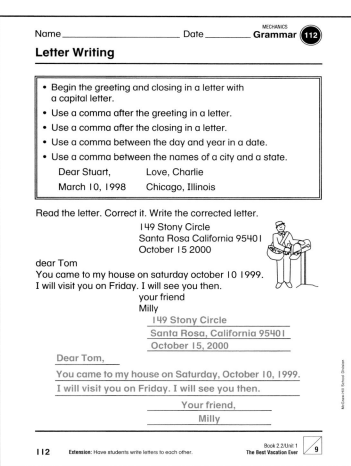

149 Stony Circle
Santa Rosa California 95401
October 15 2000

dear Tom
You came to my house on saturday october 10 1999.
I will visit you on Friday. I will see you then.
     your friend
     Milly

     149 Stony Circle

     Santa Rosa, California 95401

     October 15, 2000

Dear Tom,

You came to my house on Saturday, October 10, 1999.

I will visit you on Friday. I will see you then.

     Your friend,

     Milly

Left Page

Irregular Verbs

A. Read each sentence.
Write the past tense of each verb.

1. go   We ___went___ to the toy store yesterday.

2. do   The store ___did___ not have my toy train.

3. see   I ___saw___ it in another store.

4. say   Mom ___said___ we can buy it there.

B. Read each pair of sentences.
Circle the one in each pair that is correct.

5. I goed to the park.
   (I went to the park.)

6. (My sister said I should go home.)
   My sister sayed I should go home.

7. (I did what I was told.)
   I doed what I was told.

8. I goed home.
   (I went home.)

Right Page

Irregular Verbs

- The verbs *go* and *do* have special forms in the past tense.
- The verbs *say* and *see* have special forms in the past tense.

Look at each picture. Read the words next to it.
Draw a circle around the correct word.

1. The mailman (goed, (went)) to Bob's door.

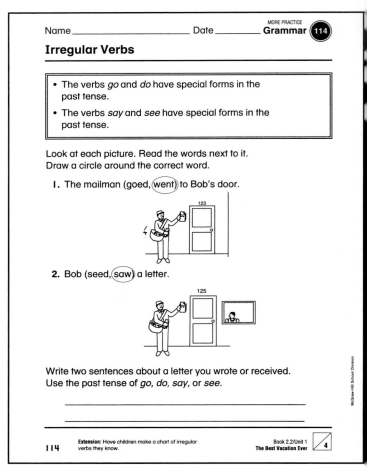

2. Bob (seed, (saw)) a letter.

Write two sentences about a letter you wrote or received.
Use the past tense of *go*, *do*, *say*, or *see*.

_____

_____

114 **Extension:** Have children make a chart of irregular
verbs they know.   Book 2.2/Unit 1
                                          The Best Vacation Ever 4

The Best Vacation Ever • SPELLING

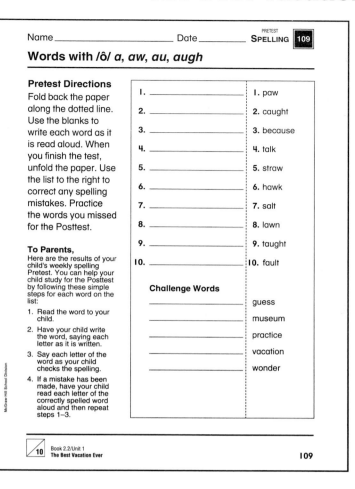

Words with /ô/ a, aw, au, augh

Pretest Directions

Fold back the paper along the dotted line. Use the blanks to write each word as it is read aloud. When you finish the test, unfold the paper. Use the list to the right to correct any spelling mistakes. Practice the words you missed for the Posttest.

To Parents,

Here are the results of your child's weekly spelling Pretest. You can help your child study for the Posttest by following these simple steps for each word on the list:

1. Read the word to your child.

2. Have your child write the word, saying each letter as it is written.

3. Say each letter of the word as your child checks the spelling.

4. If a mistake has been made, have your child read each letter of the correctly spelled word aloud and then repeat steps 1–3.

1. _____
2. _____
3. _____
4. _____
5. _____
6. _____
7. _____
8. _____
9. _____
10. _____

1. paw
2. caught
3. because
4. talk
5. straw
6. hawk
7. salt
8. lawn
9. taught
10. fault

Challenge Words

_____ guess
_____ museum
_____ practice
_____ vacation
_____ wonder

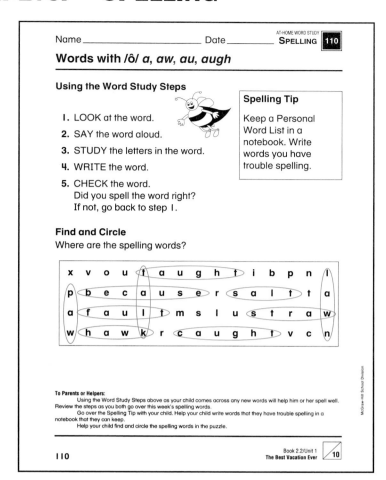

Words with /ô/ a, aw, au, augh

Using the Word Study Steps

1. LOOK at the word.

2. SAY the word aloud.

3. STUDY the letters in the word.

4. WRITE the word.

5. CHECK the word.
   Did you spell the word right?
   If not, go back to step 1.

Spelling Tip

Keep a Personal Word List in a notebook. Write words you have trouble spelling.

Find and Circle

Where are the spelling words?

x	v	o	u	f	a	u	g	h	t	i	b	p	n	l
p	b	e	c	a	u	s	e	r	s	a	l	t	t	a
a	f	a	u	l	t	m	s	l	u	s	t	r	a	w
w	h	a	w	k	r	c	a	u	g	h	t	v	c	n

To Parents or Helpers:

Using the Word Study Steps above as your child comes across any new words will help him or her spell well. Review the steps as you both go over this week's spelling words.

Go over the Spelling Tip with your child. Help your child write words that they have trouble spelling in a notebook that they can keep.

Help your child find and circle the spelling words in the puzzle.

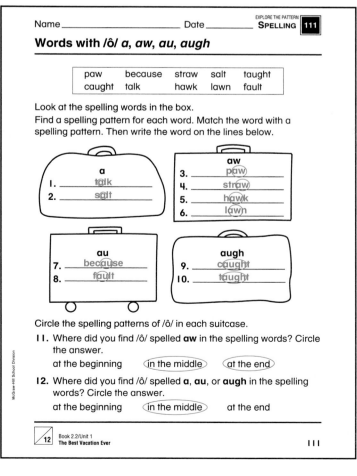

Words with /ô/ a, aw, au, augh

| paw | because | straw | salt | taught |
| caught | talk | hawk | lawn | fault |

Look at the spelling words in the box.
Find a spelling pattern for each word. Match the word with a spelling pattern. Then write the word on the lines below.

a
1. talk
2. salt

aw
3. paw
4. straw
5. hawk
6. lawn

au
7. because
8. fault

augh
9. caught
10. taught

Circle the spelling patterns of /ô/ in each suitcase.

11. Where did you find /ô/ spelled **aw** in the spelling words? Circle the answer.

    at the beginning   (in the middle)   (at the end)

12. Where did you find /ô/ spelled **a**, **au**, or **augh** in the spelling words? Circle the answer.

    at the beginning   (in the middle)   at the end

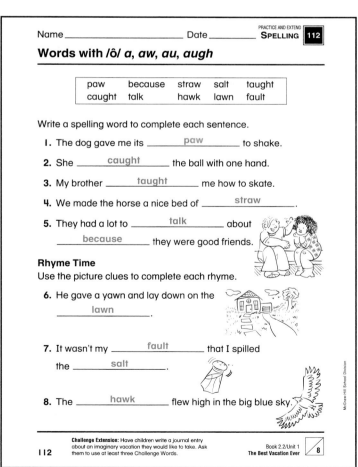

Words with /ô/ a, aw, au, augh

| paw | because | straw | salt | taught |
| caught | talk | hawk | lawn | fault |

Write a spelling word to complete each sentence.

1. The dog gave me its _____ paw _____ to shake.

2. She _____ caught _____ the ball with one hand.

3. My brother _____ taught _____ me how to skate.

4. We made the horse a nice bed of _____ straw _____.

5. They had a lot to _____ talk _____ about _____ because _____ they were good friends.

Rhyme Time

Use the picture clues to complete each rhyme.

6. He gave a yawn and lay down on the _____ lawn _____.

7. It wasn't my _____ fault _____ that I spilled the _____ salt _____.

8. The _____ hawk _____ flew high in the big blue sky.

Challenge Extension: Have children write a journal entry about an imaginary vacation they would like to take. Ask them to use at least three Challenge Words.

T37

The Best Vacation Ever • SPELLING

Words with /ô/ a, aw, au, augh

Proofreading Activity

There are six spelling mistakes in the paragraph below. Circle each misspelled word. Write the words correctly on the lines below.

People always (fawk) about how smart dogs are. Jamal (taut) his dog how to shake hands with his (pau). Jamal's dog liked to play in the barn. One day the dog got (cawt) inside and couldn't get out. It was Jamal's (fawlt) (becaws) he had shut the barn door by mistake.

1. ____talk____
2. ____taught____
3. ____paw____
4. ____caught____
5. ____fault____
6. ____because____

Writing Activity

Would you like to visit a farm? Write sentences about a place that you would like to visit. Use four spelling words from the spelling list.

_____

_____

_____

_____

_____

Words with /ô/ a, aw, au, augh

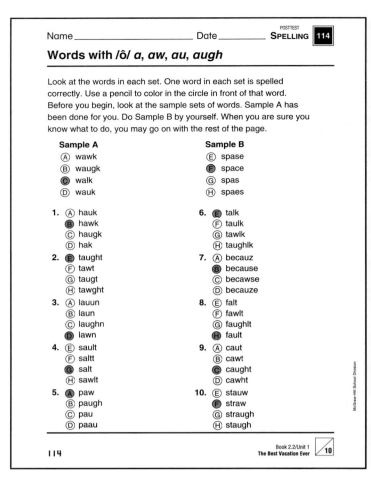

Look at the words in each set. One word in each set is spelled correctly. Use a pencil to color in the circle in front of that word. Before you begin, look at the sample sets of words. Sample A has been done for you. Do Sample B by yourself. When you are sure you know what to do, you may go on with the rest of the page.

Sample A
- Ⓐ wawk
- Ⓑ waugk
- ● walk
- Ⓓ wauk

Sample B
- Ⓔ spase
- ● space
- Ⓖ spas
- Ⓗ spaes

1.
- Ⓐ hauk
- ● hawk
- Ⓒ haugk
- Ⓓ hak

2.
- ● taught
- Ⓕ tawt
- Ⓖ taugt
- Ⓗ tawght

3.
- Ⓐ lauun
- Ⓑ laun
- Ⓒ laughn
- ● lawn

4.
- Ⓔ sault
- Ⓕ saltt
- ● salt
- Ⓗ sawlt

5.
- ● paw
- Ⓑ paugh
- Ⓒ pau
- Ⓓ paau

6.
- ● talk
- Ⓕ taulk
- Ⓖ tawlk
- Ⓗ taughlk

7.
- Ⓐ becauz
- ● because
- Ⓒ becawse
- Ⓓ becauze

8.
- Ⓔ falt
- Ⓕ fawlt
- Ⓖ faughlt
- ● fault

9.
- Ⓐ caut
- Ⓑ cawt
- ● caught
- Ⓓ cawht

10.
- Ⓔ stauw
- ● straw
- Ⓖ straugh
- Ⓗ staugh

Zipping, Zapping, Zooming Bats • PRACTICE

Digraphs *ph, tch*

Read the words. Then, in each row, circle the pictures for the words that contain **ph** or **tch**.

1. ca**tch**

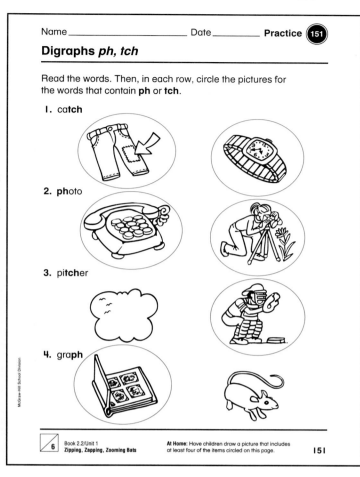

2. **ph**oto

3. pi**tch**er

4. gra**ph**

6
Book 2.2/Unit 1
Zipping, Zapping, Zooming Bats

At Home: Have children draw a picture that includes at least four of the items circled on this page.

151

Vocabulary

Read the words in the box. Read the clues. Write the correct word on the line next to each clue.

disturb explore facts nature objects several

1. This word means more than two.

   several

2. These are things that you know are true.

   facts

3. You can do this to a baby by being noisy.

   disturb

4. These are things that you can see or touch.

   objects

5. You could do this on the moon.

   explore

6. Plants and animals are part of this.

   nature

152
At Home: Have your child make up riddles for some of the words in the box.

Book 2.2/Unit 1
Zipping, Zapping, Zooming Bats
6

Desert Friends

"Welcome," the man said. "Sit down and I will tell you many facts about the desert. This place is a real nature center. See the mountains in the distance? There are great forests on the other side of them."

"I used to live in a forest," said Phil. "Would you like a sandwich?"

"That would be nice," said the old man. And the three became friends.

At Home: Have children write about things they have seen or would like to see on a nature trip.

4

152a

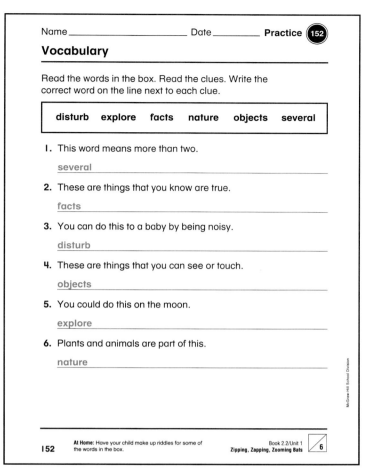

2

One day Phil and his dad left home to explore the desert. They packed water, several sandwiches, and a tent to pitch on their trip.

As they walked, Phil watched many animals and objects he had never seen before. There were plants and rocks. There were birds, lizards, and mice he wanted to photograph.

Zipping, Zapping, Zooming Bats McGraw-Hill School Division

Phil and his dad saw a small house in the distance. As they walked closer they saw a sign on the door that read, "Do Not Disturb!"

"I wonder who lives there?" Phil thought.

Suddenly an old man on crutches stepped out from the house. "Who are you?" he shouted.

"I am Phil. This is my dad. We are exploring the desert."

3

152b

T39

Zipping, Zapping, Zooming Bats • PRACTICE

Name_____ Date_____ **Practice** 153

Story Comprehension

Think about "Zipping, Zapping, Zooming Bats."
Finish each sentence by underlining the answer.

1. Bats come out to hunt
____ .
   a. when the sun goes down
   b. in the daytime

2. Bats eat lots of ____ .
   a. peanut butter
   b. insects

3. Bats use ____ to help them hunt.
   a. their eyes
   b. sounds

4. When bats sleep, they ____.
   a. hang upside down
   b. keep their eyes open

5. Bats ____ with their tongues and claws.
   a. clean themselves
   b. hunt in the daytime

6. Many bats ____ during winter.
   a. move
   b. sleep

7. Bats are the only flying ____ .
   a. mammals
   b. birds

8. Some kinds of bats are ____ .
   a. living at the North Pole
   b. in danger of dying out

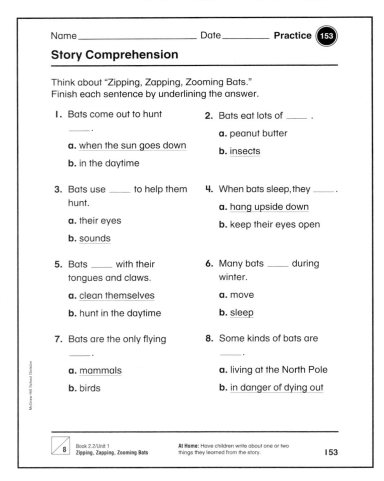

Book 2.2/Unit 1
Zipping, Zapping, Zooming Bats 8

At Home: Have children write about one or two things they learned from the story.

153

Name_____ Date_____ **Practice** 154

Read a map

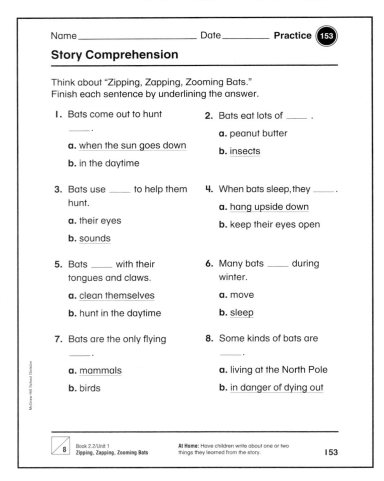

fish
whale
island
ferry
rocks
harbor

Use this map to finish each sentence. Circle the answer.

1. ____ shows where there are fish.

2. ____ shows where there are rocks.

3. The whale is ____ of the harbor.
   south   (north)   east

4. The island is ____ of the ferry.
   (west)   east   south

5. The ferry is east of the ____ .
   harbor   whale   (island)

6. The fish must swim ____ to get to the rocks.
   west   (south)   north

At Home: Ask the children to identify all the rivers that they see on this map (Mississippi, Ohio, Arkansas and Missouri rivers).

154

Book 2.2/ unit 1
Zipping, Zapping, Zooming Bats 6

Name_____ Date_____ **Practice** 155

Digraphs *ph, tch*

Circle the word that describes each sentence.
Then write the word.

1. A door has one of these.
   (latch)   catch   stitch
   _____latch_____

2. You can light a fire with this.
   (match)   photo   itch
   _____match_____

3. This can ring anytime.
   photograph (phone) stretch
   _____phone_____

4. This can make you taller.
   graph   patch   (stretch)
   _____stretch_____

5. This is a person who takes pictures.
   (photographer) doctor photo
   _____photographer_____

6. You can tell time with this.
   patch   hatch   (watch)
   _____watch_____

7. This is what a bat does to an insect.
   (catch)   itch   phone
   _____catch_____

8. This is when you throw a ball to a batter.
   graph   (pitch)   match
   _____pitch_____

Book 2.2/Unit 1
Zipping, Zapping, Zooming Bats 8

At Home: Have children use four of the words they wrote in a sentence.

155

Name_____ Date_____ **Practice** 156

tch; /ô/; Soft *c, g*

Choose the word that completes the sentence. Write the word.

| draw | page | pace | tossed | rice |
| catch | author | fall | switch | bought |

1. The dog can ___catch___ the ball in its mouth.

2. I will ___draw___ a picture of a boat with a crayon.

3. My father made white ___rice___ and beans.

4. It is cold outside, so we walk at a fast ___pace___ .

5. I turned to the next ___page___ in my book.

6. Jane and Pilar ___tossed___ the ball back and forth.

7. The ___author___ is the person who writes the book.

8. It will be dark after you flip the light ___switch___ to "off."

9. Be careful not to slip and ___fall___ on the ice.

10. I ___bought___ food at the store.

At Home: Have children write new sentences for the words above.

156

Book 2.2/Unit 1
Zipping, Zapping, Zooming Bats 10

Zipping, Zapping, Zooming Bats • PRACTICE

Compare and Contrast

When you **compare**, you tell how things are alike.
When you **contrast**, you tell how things are different.

Make two lists. Write three sentences that explain ways in which bats are alike. Write three sentences that explain ways in which bats are different. Answers may vary.

ALIKE:

1. All bats fly.

2. All bats rely on their sense of sound.

3. Bats use their claws and tongues to keep themselves as clean as cats.

DIFFERENT:

4. Some bats live in caves, some in attics, others in forests or empty mines.

5. Some kinds of bats are brown bats, grey bats, and Mexican free-tailed bats.

6. Some types of bats are in danger of dying out.

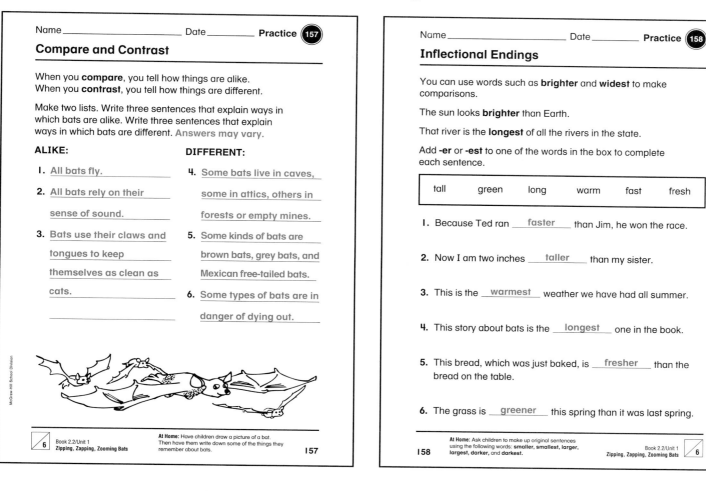

6 Book 2.2/Unit 1
Zipping, Zapping, Zooming Bats

At Home: Have children draw a picture of a bat. Then have them write down some of the things they remember about bats.

157

Inflectional Endings

You can use words such as **brighter** and **widest** to make comparisons.

The sun looks **brighter** than Earth.

That river is the **longest** of all the rivers in the state.

Add **-er** or **-est** to one of the words in the box to complete each sentence.

tall	green	long	warm	fast	fresh

1. Because Ted ran ___faster___ than Jim, he won the race.

2. Now I am two inches ___taller___ than my sister.

3. This is the ___warmest___ weather we have had all summer.

4. This story about bats is the ___longest___ one in the book.

5. This bread, which was just baked, is ___fresher___ than the bread on the table.

6. The grass is ___greener___ this spring than it was last spring.

158

At Home: Ask children to make up original sentences using the following words: **smaller, smallest, larger, largest, darker,** and **darkest.**

Book 2.2/Unit 1
Zipping, Zapping, Zooming Bats 6

Zipping, Zapping, Zooming Bats • RETEACH

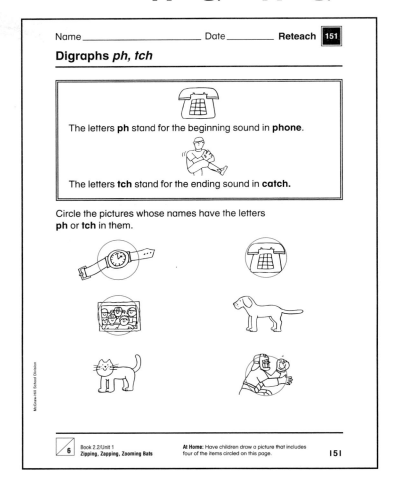

Name _____ Date _____ Reteach **151**

Digraphs *ph, tch*

The letters **ph** stand for the beginning sound in **phone**.

The letters **tch** stand for the ending sound in **catch**.

Circle the pictures whose names have the letters **ph** or **tch** in them.

Book 2.2/Unit 1 — **6**
Zipping, Zapping, Zooming Bats

At Home: Have children draw a picture that includes four of the items circled on this page.

151

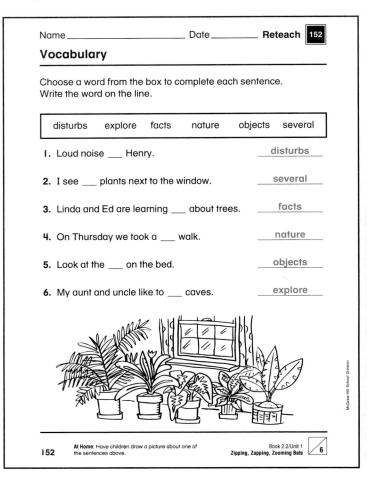

Name _____ Date _____ Reteach **152**

Vocabulary

Choose a word from the box to complete each sentence.
Write the word on the line.

disturbs	explore	facts	nature	objects	several

1. Loud noise ___ Henry. _____disturbs_____

2. I see ___ plants next to the window. _____several_____

3. Linda and Ed are learning ___ about trees. _____facts_____

4. On Thursday we took a ___ walk. _____nature_____

5. Look at the ___ on the bed. _____objects_____

6. My aunt and uncle like to ___ caves. _____explore_____

152

At Home: Have children draw a picture about one of the sentences above.

Book 2.2/Unit 1 — **6**
Zipping, Zapping, Zooming Bats

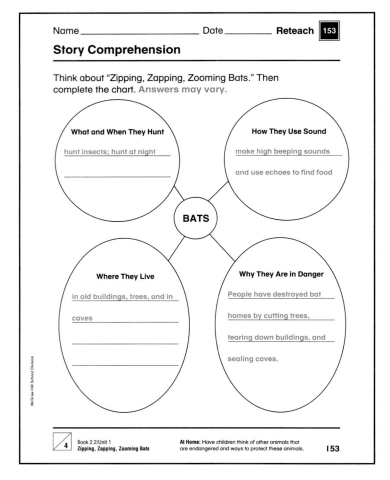

Name _____ Date _____ Reteach **153**

Story Comprehension

Think about "Zipping, Zapping, Zooming Bats." Then complete the chart. **Answers may vary.**

What and When They Hunt
hunt insects; hunt at night

How They Use Sound
make high beeping sounds
and use echoes to find food

BATS

Where They Live
in old buildings, trees, and in
caves

Why They Are in Danger
People have destroyed bat
homes by cutting trees,
tearing down buildings, and
sealing caves.

Book 2.2/Unit 1 — **4**
Zipping, Zapping, Zooming Bats

At Home: Have children think of other animals that are endangered and ways to protect these animals.

153

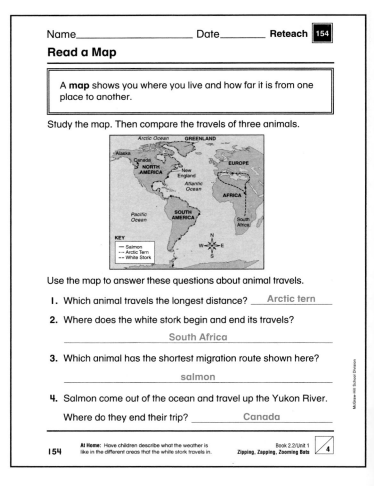

Name _____ Date _____ Reteach **154**

Read a Map

A **map** shows you where you live and how far it is from one place to another.

Study the map. Then compare the travels of three animals.

Use the map to answer these questions about animal travels.

1. Which animal travels the longest distance? _____Arctic tern_____

2. Where does the white stork begin and end its travels?
   _____South Africa_____

3. Which animal has the shortest migration route shown here?
   _____salmon_____

4. Salmon come out of the ocean and travel up the Yukon River.
   Where do they end their trip? _____Canada_____

154

At Home: Have children describe what the weather is like in the different areas that the white stork travels in.

Book 2.2/Unit 1 — **4**
Zipping, Zapping, Zooming Bats

Zipping, Zapping, Zooming Bats • RETEACH

Digraphs *ph*, *tch*

Say the name of each picture. Listen to the sounds made by the letters **ph** and **tch.**

photo   **patch**

Put an **X** in the box if the name of the picture contains the **ph** sound or the **tch** sound.

1. [X]   2. [ ]

[X]   4. [X]

5. [ ]   6. [X]

6 Book 2.2/Unit 1
Zipping, Zapping, Zooming Bats

At Home: Have children make up a riddle for one of the words they have checked.

155

---

tch; /ô/; Soft *c, g*

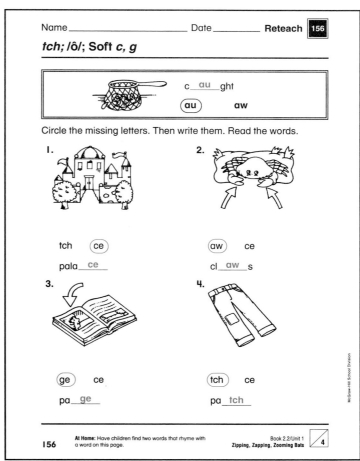

c _au_ ght

(au)   aw

Circle the missing letters. Then write them. Read the words.

1. tch   (ce)
   pala _ce_

2. (aw)   ce
   cl _aw_ s

3. (ge)   ce
   pa _ge_

4. (tch)   ce
   pa _tch_

156   **At Home:** Have children find two words that rhyme with a word on this page.

Book 2.2/Unit 1
Zipping, Zapping, Zooming Bats   4

Compare and Contrast

To **compare** means to tell how two things are alike. Apples and oranges are both good to eat.

To **contrast** means to tell how two things are different. Apples are red. Oranges are orange.

Put a check in each box if it tells something about tomatoes or pumpkins. Then use the chart to tell a partner how tomatoes and pumpkins are alike and different.

	tomatoes	pumpkins
are used in pizza	✔	
need sun to grow	✔	✔
can be eaten	✔	✔
have lots of seeds	✔	✔
are red	✔	
can be made into jack–o'–lanterns		✔

6 Book 2.2/Unit 1
Zipping, Zapping, Zooming Bats

At Home: Have children draw a picture of a tomato and a pumpkin. Have them compare and contrast their pictures.

157

Inflectional Endings

Words with the endings **-er** and **-est** are used to make comparisons.

small + **er** = smaller (more small)
That table is **smaller** than this one.

large + **est** = largest (most large)
Green Park is the **largest** park in the state.

Read each sentence. Add **-er** or **-est** to each word in dark print. Write the new word on the line.

1. That horn makes the **loud** noise in the parade.

   loudest

2. The mountain in this park is **high** than the one that I climbed last week.

   higher

3. My desk is the **clean** of all the desks in the classroom.

   cleanest

4. Tim ran **slow** in the race than John did.

   slower

5. This cotton dress feels **soft** than the wool dress.

   softer

6. This honey tastes the **sweet** of all the different kinds that were sold at the fair.

   sweetest

7. That old oak tree is the **tall** of the trees in my backyard.

   tallest

8. Maria swam **fast** than the other swimmer in the race.

   faster

Zipping, Zapping, Zooming Bats • EXTEND

Page 151

Digraphs *ph, tch*

Fill in the circles. Choose rhyming words from the box. Fill in the square with the **ph** words.

crutch	notch	switch	hitch	graph
twitch	stretch	scratch	phone	batch
photo	catch	match	hatch	sketch

ditch
switch
hitch
twitch

fetch
stretch
sketch

patch
batch
match
scratch
catch

"ph words"
graph
phone
photo

Use the words from the box to write two rhyming sentences.

_____
_____

Page 152

Vocabulary

disturb	explore	facts	nature	objects	several

Fill in each space using the words from the box.

1. Things that have happened or are true. ___facts___

2. To study or look into something that is unknown to you.
   ___explore___

3. To stop, upset, or bother somebody who is busy. ___disturb___

4. More than two, but not many. ___several___

5. Things you can see and touch. ___objects___

6. Everything in the world that is not made by people, such as
   plants and animals. ___nature___

Imagine you are walking in a forest. Write a story about your experience using the words from the box.

_____
_____
_____
_____
_____
_____
_____

Page 153

Story Comprehension

Write a **T** if the statement is **true**. Write an **F** if the statement is **false.**

1. Bats are good hunters and expert fliers. __T__

2. Bats hang upside down by their toe claws when
   they sleep. __T__

3. Bats hibernate or sleep deeply during the winter. __T__

4. Bat wings are the same as bird wings. __F__

In China, people think bats are good luck. The **wu-fu sign** is made up of five bats connected by their wing tips. It is a symbol of luck. Choose one of the sentences above. Then inside the **wu-fu sign** explain why you know that sentence is true or false.

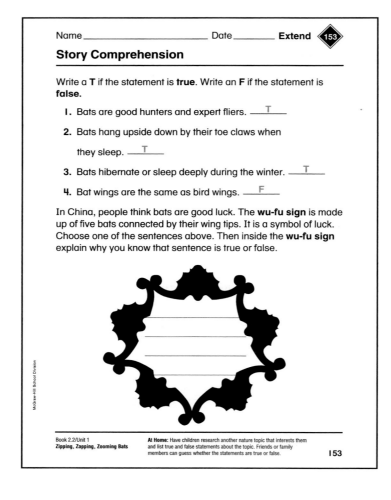

Page 154

Read a Map

Make your own map.

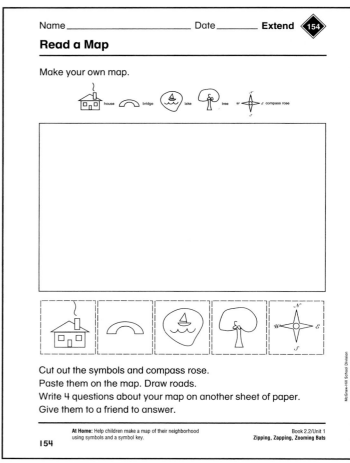

house   bridge   lake   tree   compass rose

Cut out the symbols and compass rose.
Paste them on the map. Draw roads.
Write 4 questions about your map on another sheet of paper.
Give them to a friend to answer.

Zipping, Zapping, Zooming Bats • EXTEND

Digraphs *ph, tch*

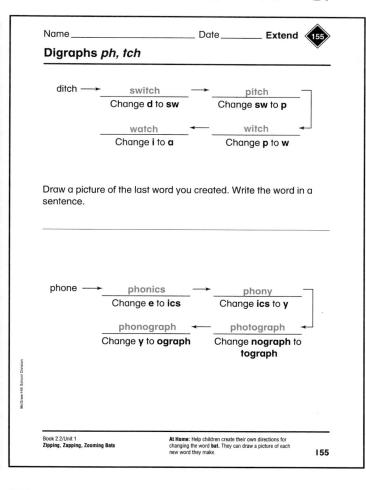

ditch → switch → pitch
Change **d** to **sw**   Change **sw** to **p**

watch ← witch
Change **i** to **a**   Change **p** to **w**

Draw a picture of the last word you created. Write the word in a sentence.

_____

phone → phonics → phony
Change **e** to **ics**   Change **ics** to **y**

phonograph   photograph
Change **y** to **ograph**   Change **nograph** to **tograph**

At Home: Help children create their own directions for changing the word **bat**. They can draw a picture of each new word they make.

---

tch; /ô/; Soft *c, g*

Cut out the markers. Color 4 red and 4 blue. Take turns with a friend moving a marker to a word box. Use the word in a sentence. Finish when your markers are on the other side.

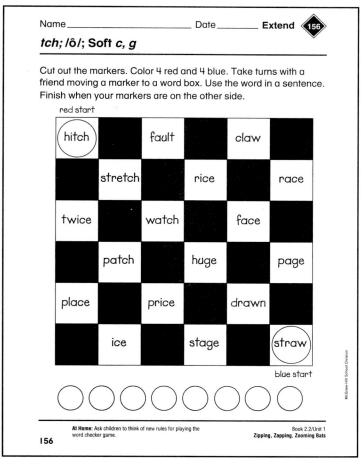

red start

hitch		fault		claw
stretch		rice		race
twice		watch		face
	patch		huge		page
place		price		drawn
	ice		stage		straw

blue start

○ ○ ○ ○ ○ ○ ○ ○

At Home: Ask children to think of new rules for playing the word checker game.

Compare and Contrast

Hog-nosed bat

Hog-nosed bats live in Asia. They are the smallest bats in the world. They weigh less than a dime. They have a wing span of 5 1/2 inches.

Flying foxes

Flying foxes live in Asia and Africa. They are the largest bats in the world. They eat fruit, nectar, and pollen. They have a wing span of up to 6 feet.

Think about how these bats are alike and how they are different. Write your ideas on the chart. Answers may differ.

Alike	**Different**
They are both bats.	Hog-nosed bats are smaller.
They both have wings.	Flying foxes are bigger.
They both live in Asia.	Flying foxes also live in Africa.

At Home: Make a list of reasons why people are afraid of bats. Ask children to write a few sentences explaining how bats are actually helpful.

Inflectional Endings

Complete.

base word	-er ending	-est ending
big	bigger	biggest
tall	taller	tallest
lucky	luckier	luckiest
sad	sadder	saddest
thin	thinner	thinnest
soft	softer	softest
happy	happier	happiest
hot	hotter	hottest

1. Which **two** base words stayed the same when the new words were formed?

   _____ tall _____   _____ soft _____

2. Write the **two** base words for which the **y** changed to an **i** to form the new words.

   _____ lucky _____   _____ happy _____

3. Write the **four** base words for which the final consonant was doubled to form the new words.

   _____ big _____   _____ sad _____   _____ thin _____   _____ hot _____

At Home: Ask children to use the words **tall, taller, tallest** in a story.

Zipping, Zapping, Zooming Bats • GRAMMAR

More Irregular Verbs

> • Some verbs do not add *-ed* to form the past tense.
> • The verbs *come* and *run* have special forms in the past tense.
>
> | I, you, we, they | come | came |
> |---|---|---|
> | I, you, we, they | run | ran |

Read each sentence. Circle the form of the verb that belongs in the sentence.

1. The children _____ to the mall. (came) comed
2. Some of them _____ to get pizza. (ran) runned
3. The clown _____ that day. comes (came)
4. Bill and I _____ to see her. runned (ran)
5. I _____ late to the party. comed (came)
6. They _____ to the book store. (ran) runned
7. We _____ from next door. camed (came)
8. You _____ across the parking lot. (ran) runned

More Irregular Verbs

> • The verbs *give* and *sing* have special forms in the past tense.
>
> | I, we, you, they | give | gave |
> |---|---|---|
> | I, we, you, they | sing | sang |

Read the sentences in the present tense. Change the underlined verbs to the past tense. Write the sentence.

1. I <u>sing</u> funny songs.

   **I sang funny songs.**

2. The boys <u>give</u> money every year.

   **The boys gave money every year.**

3. I <u>sing</u> in a high voice.

   **I sang in a high voice.**

4. The club <u>gives</u> toys to the children.

   **The club gave toys to the children.**

5. They <u>sing</u> in the glee club.

   **They sang in the glee club.**

More Irregular Verbs

> • The verbs *come* and *run* have special forms in the past tense.
>
> <u>The boys came.</u>   <u>They ran to the corner.</u>
>
> • The verbs *give* and *sing* have special forms in the past tense.
>
> <u>She gave me an apple.</u>   <u>She also sang a song.</u>

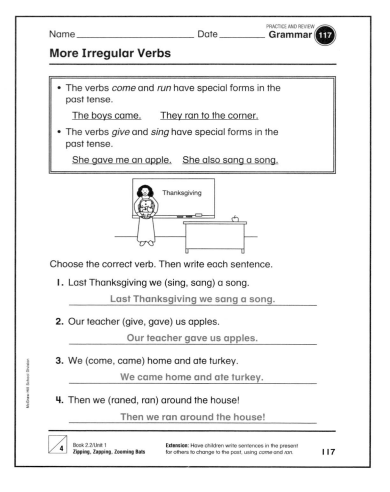

Choose the correct verb. Then write each sentence.

1. Last Thanksgiving we (sing, sang) a song.

   **Last Thanksgiving we sang a song.**

2. Our teacher (give, gave) us apples.

   **Our teacher gave us apples.**

3. We (come, came) home and ate turkey.

   **We came home and ate turkey.**

4. Then we (raned, ran) around the house!

   **Then we ran around the house!**

Writing Book Titles

> • Begin the first word and each important word in a title with a capital letter.
> • Underline all the words in the title of a book.
>
> <u>Climbing the Mountain</u>

Read the sentences.
Correct each underlined book title in the sentence. Write each correct title on the line.

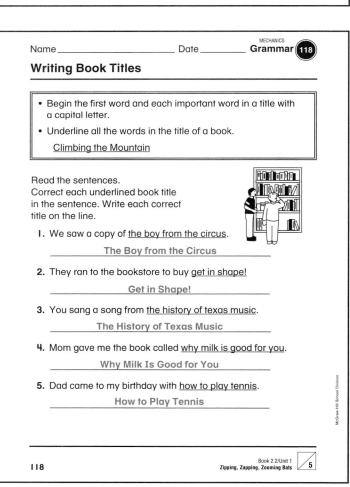

1. We saw a copy of <u>the boy from the circus</u>.

   **The Boy from the Circus**

2. They ran to the bookstore to buy <u>get in shape!</u>

   **Get in Shape!**

3. You sang a song from <u>the history of texas music</u>.

   **The History of Texas Music**

4. Mom gave me the book called <u>why milk is good for you</u>.

   **Why Milk Is Good for You**

5. Dad came to my birthday with <u>how to play tennis</u>.

   **How to Play Tennis**

Zipping, Zapping, Zooming Bats • GRAMMAR

More Irregular Verbs

Which verb fits the sentence? Mark your answer.

1. David _____ down the hill.
   - ⓐ ran ●
   - ⓑ runed
   - ⓒ runned

2. I _____ him fall.
   - ⓐ seed
   - ⓑ saw ●
   - ⓒ sed

3. He got up and _____ a song.
   - ⓐ singed
   - ⓑ singd
   - ⓒ sang ●

4. David _____ home with me.
   - ⓐ came ●
   - ⓑ camd
   - ⓒ camed

5. We both _____ to the kitchen to eat.
   - ⓐ runed
   - ⓑ runned
   - ⓒ ran ●

More Irregular Verbs

- The verbs *come* and *run* have special forms in the past tense.
- The verbs *give* and *sing* have special forms in the past tense.

Read each sentence aloud. Underline the correct form of each verb.

1. Who (gave, give) me the bike?
2. Uncle John (comed, came) to the house.
3. He (gave, gived) it to me.
4. I was so happy I (singed, sang) all day.
5. I (runned, ran) to tell Joy.

T47

Zipping, Zapping, Zooming Bats • SPELLING

Worksheet 115

Name _____ Date _____ PRETEST SPELLING **115**

Words with Digraphs *ph*, *tch*, *ch*

Pretest Directions
Fold back the paper along the dotted line. Use the blanks to write each word as it is read aloud. When you finish the test, unfold the paper. Use the list to the right to correct any spelling mistakes. Practice the words you missed for the Posttest.

1. _____	1. phone
2. _____	2. catch
3. _____	3. each
4. _____	4. patch
5. _____	5. sandwich
6. _____	6. touch
7. _____	7. match
8. _____	8. graph
9. _____	9. pitch
10. _____	10. beach

Challenge Words

_____ disturb

_____ explore

_____ nature

_____ objects

_____ several

To Parents,
Here are the results of your child's weekly spelling Pretest. You can help your child study for the Posttest by following these simple steps for each word on the list:

1. Read the word to your child.
2. Have your child write the word, saying each letter as it is written.
3. Say each letter of the word as your child checks the spelling.
4. If a mistake has been made, have your child read each letter of the correctly spelled word aloud and then repeat steps 1–3.

10 Book 2.2/Unit 1 Zipping, Zapping, Zooming Bats   115

Worksheet 116

Name _____ Date _____ AT-HOME WORD STUDY SPELLING **116**

Words with Digraphs *ph*, *tch*, *ch*

Using the Word Study Steps

1. LOOK at the word.
2. SAY the word aloud.
3. STUDY the letters in the word.
4. WRITE the word.
5. CHECK the word.
   Did you spell the word right?
   If not, go back to step 1.

Spelling Tip
Look for a smaller word in a new word to help you write the new word.

sand + wich = sandwich

Word Scramble
Unscramble each set of letters to make a spelling word. Write the spelling words in the boxes.

1. beach	2. phone	3. match	4. catch	5. touch
6. each	7. graph	8. patch	9. pitch	10. sandwich

1. cheab	2. pohne
3. cmath	4. chatc
5. chout	6. heac
7. rgpha	8. pacht
9. chipt	10. hicwsand

To Parents or Helpers:
Using the Word Study Steps above as your child comes across any new words will help him or her spell well. Review the steps as you both go over this week's spelling words.
Go over the Spelling Tip with your child. Ask if he or she can find other smaller words in new words.
Help your child unscramble the spelling words.

116   Book 2.2/Unit 1 Zipping, Zapping, Zooming Bats 10

Worksheet 117

Name _____ Date _____ EXPLORE THE PATTERN SPELLING **117**

Words with Digraphs *ph*, *tch*, *ch*

phone	each	sandwich	match	pitch
catch	patch	touch	graph	beach

Pattern Power!
Write the spelling words for each of these patterns.

ph
1. phone
2. graph

tch
3. catch
4. patch
5. match
6. pitch

ch
7. each
8. sandwich
9. touch
10. beach

Find Me a Pattern!
Write each word. Circle the letters that are the same.

11. phone   graph

12. patch   pitch

13. beach   sandwich

Rhyme Time
Write the spelling word that rhymes with each of these words.

14. bone _phone_   15. ditch _pitch_

15 Book 2.2/Unit 1 Zipping, Zapping, Zooming Bats   117

Worksheet 118

Name _____ Date _____ PRACTICE AND EXTEND SPELLING **118**

Words with Digraphs *ph*, *tch*, *ch*

phone	each	sandwich	match	pitch
catch	patch	touch	graph	beach

Write a spelling word to answer each question.

1. How can you talk to a friend? _phone_
2. What do you sometimes eat for lunch? _sandwich_
3. Where can you swim? _beach_
4. What can you use to fix a rip in your pants? _patch_
5. What can you use to show data? _graph_
6. What do people use to start a fire? _match_

Use the spelling words to complete the sentences.

7. If you _pitch_ the ball to Sam, he will _catch_ it.
8. _Each_ child will be able to _touch_ the bunny.

New Words
Add **es** to each of these words. Write the new word.

9. match + es = _matches_
10. patch + es = _patches_
11. sandwich + es = _sandwiches_
12. beach + es = _beaches_

118   Book 2.2/Unit 1 Zipping, Zapping, Zooming Bats 12

Zipping, Zapping, Zooming Bats • SPELLING

Words with Digraphs *ph*, *tch*, *ch*

Proofreading Activity

There are six spelling mistakes in the paragraph below. Circle each misspelled word. Write the words correctly on the lines below.

Every summer my family and I go to the (baech). We take lunch with us. (Eech) of us usually has a peanut butter (sandwitch), a glass of lemonade, and some grapes. Then I go to (tutch) the water. If it is not cold, I go swimming. Last summer I couldn't use my inner tube because it needed a (pach). After swimming, we play ball. My father throws and I (katch). A day at the beach is a fun time for my family.

1. _____beach_____   2. _____Each_____   3. _____sandwich_____

4. _____touch_____   5. _____patch_____   6. _____catch_____

Writing Activity

Write sentences that tell about something that you would like to do next summer. Use four words from the spelling list.

_____

_____

_____

_____

_____

Words with Digraphs *ph*, *tch*, *ch*

Look at the words in each set. One word in each set is spelled correctly. Use a pencil to color in the circle in front of that word. Before you begin, look at the sample sets of words. Sample A has been done for you. Do Sample B by yourself. When you are sure you know what to do, you may go on with the rest of the page.

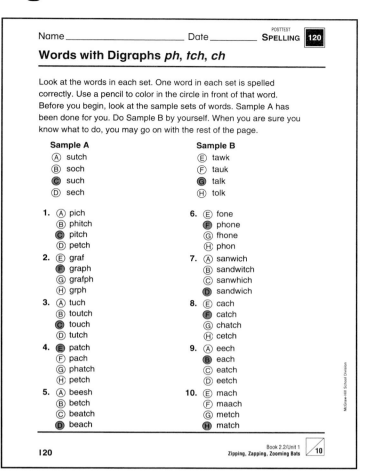

Sample A
- Ⓐ sutch
- Ⓑ soch
- ⬤ such
- Ⓓ sech

Sample B
- Ⓔ tawk
- Ⓕ tauk
- ⬤ talk
- Ⓗ tolk

1. Ⓐ pich
   Ⓑ phitch
   ⬤ pitch
   Ⓓ petch
2. Ⓔ graf
   ⬤ graph
   Ⓖ grafph
   Ⓗ grph
3. Ⓐ tuch
   Ⓑ toutch
   ⬤ touch
   Ⓓ tutch
4. ⬤ patch
   Ⓕ pach
   Ⓖ phatch
   Ⓗ petch
5. Ⓐ beesh
   Ⓑ betch
   Ⓒ beatch
   ⬤ beach

6. Ⓔ fone
   ⬤ phone
   Ⓖ fhone
   Ⓗ phon
7. Ⓐ sanwich
   Ⓑ sandwitch
   Ⓒ sanwhich
   ⬤ sandwich
8. Ⓔ cach
   ⬤ catch
   Ⓖ chatch
   Ⓗ cetch
9. Ⓐ eech
   ⬤ each
   Ⓒ eatch
   Ⓓ eetch
10. Ⓔ mach
    Ⓕ maach
    Ⓖ metch
    ⬤ match

T49

Practice 159

Name_____ Date_____ **Practice** 159

ph, tch; /ô/; Soft *c, g;* /ù/

Circle the word that answers the riddle. Then write the word.

1. This is a very, very big animal.

   mouse (elephant) skunk

   _____elephant_____

2. This is never bad.

   (good)   watch   phone

   _____good_____

3. This is good to drink.

   saw   (juice)   rice

   _____juice_____

4. This could go over a river.

   cage   age   (bridge)

   _____bridge_____

5. This is what my teacher did all year.

   caught   (taught)   laugh

   _____taught_____

6. This is very cold.

   (ice)   face   race

   _____ice_____

7. This will tell you the time.

   stretch   itch   (watch)

   _____watch_____

8. This will cut wood.

   (saw)   paw   aunt

   _____saw_____

McGraw-Hill School Division

8 | Book 2.2/Unit 1
Going Batty for Bats

At Home: Have children make up another riddle for each of the words they circled.

159

Practice 160

Name_____ Date_____ **Practice** 160

Vocabulary

Read the story. Choose a word from the box to complete each sentence. Write the word in the sentence. Then reread the story to check your answers.

| breath | cover | crops | darkness | scary | study |

Today is Sunday. It is very cold today. I can even

see my _____breath_____ in the air. Out in the fields, all the

_____crops_____ have ice on them. Thick fog _____covers_____

them too.

Finally, I came inside to _____study_____ for a test. It

is getting late. I can see that _____darkness_____ is coming.

It seems _____scary_____ out there in the dark. I am safe

and warm in my house. My mom brings me a glass of

apple juice.

160 | **At Home:** Have children use words from the box to write two more sentences to tell what might have happened next.

Book 2.2/Unit 1
Going Batty for Bats | 6

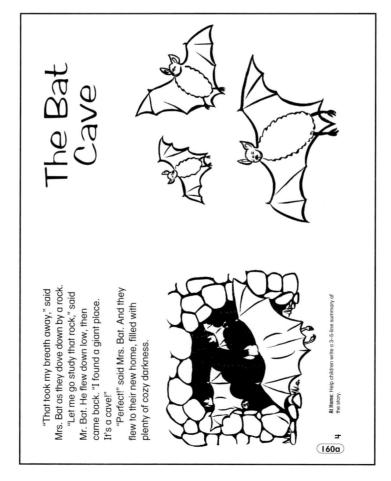

The Bat Cave

"That took my breath away," said Mrs. Bat as they dove down by a rock. "Let me go study that rock," said Mr. Bat. He flew down low, then came back. "I found a giant place. It's a cave!"

"Perfect!" said Mrs. Bat. And they flew to their new home, filled with plenty of cozy darkness.

At Home: Help children write a 3–5-line summary of the story.

160a

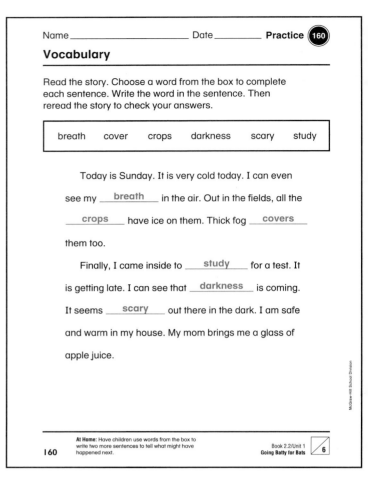

2

"We need a new place to live," said Mrs. Bat.

"Yes," said Mr. Bat. "With Baby Bat we will need more room."

First they looked in a phone booth.

"Too small," said Mrs. Bat.

They flew high over a village.

"Too many people," said Mrs. Bat.

"They are much too scary."

As they flew they watched people working in fields.

"Those are rice crops," said Mr. Bat.

"Fly on," said Mrs. Bat.

Baby Bat was getting tired. He let out a high-pitched yell.

Just then a mean looking hawk flew by.

"Take cover!" said Mr. Bat.

160b

3

Going Batty for Bats McGraw-Hill School Division

Going Batty for Bats • PRACTICE

Story Comprehension

Think about "Going Batty for Bats." Answer each question. Write complete sentences. **Answers may vary.**

1. How do bats help people?

   They eat insects that kill crops.

2. How can people help bats?

   They can build gates on caves to keep people out.

3. What city has the largest bat colony in the United States?

   Austin, Texas

4. What is the scariest thing about a bat?

   The stories that people tell about them are scary.

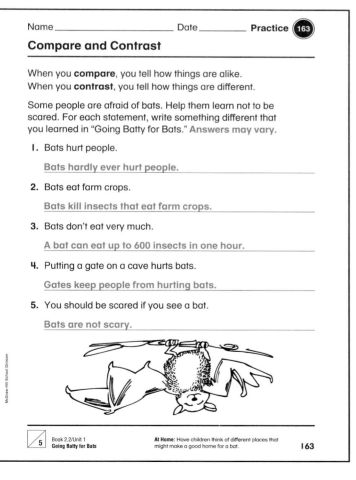

Use a Chart

It is often easier to read facts in a **chart** than in a paragraph. Read the paragraph below. Notice how the facts tend to get confusing.

The Kentucky Derby is one of the most famous races in the world. On the first Saturday in May, horses race over one and a quarter miles. The first Kentucky Derby took place in 1875. The winner was a horse called Aristides. It took Aristides two minutes and thirty-seven seconds to finish the course. The jockey was Oliver Lewis. In 1921, a horse called Behave Yourself won the race in two minutes and four seconds. The jockey was Charles Thompson. One of the most famous horses, Whirlaway, was ridden by Eddie Arcaro. In 1941, he won in two minutes, one second. Another famous horse, Seattle Slew, won in 1977, finishing in two minutes and two seconds. The jockey was Jean Cruguet.

Fill in the blanks using the information in the paragraph.

Kentucky Derby Results			
Year	Winner	Jockey	Time
1875	Aristides	Oliver Lewis	2 min. 37 sec.
1921	Behave Yourself	Charles Thompson	2 min. 4 sec.
1941	Whirlaway	Eddie Arcaro	2 min. 1 sec.
1977	Seattle Slew	Jean Cruguet	2 min. 2 sec.

Compare and Contrast

When you **compare**, you tell how things are alike.
When you **contrast**, you tell how things are different.

Some people are afraid of bats. Help them learn not to be scared. For each statement, write something different that you learned in "Going Batty for Bats." **Answers may vary.**

1. Bats hurt people.

   Bats hardly ever hurt people.

2. Bats eat farm crops.

   Bats kill insects that eat farm crops.

3. Bats don't eat very much.

   A bat can eat up to 600 insects in one hour.

4. Putting a gate on a cave hurts bats.

   Gates keep people from hurting bats.

5. You should be scared if you see a bat.

   Bats are not scary.

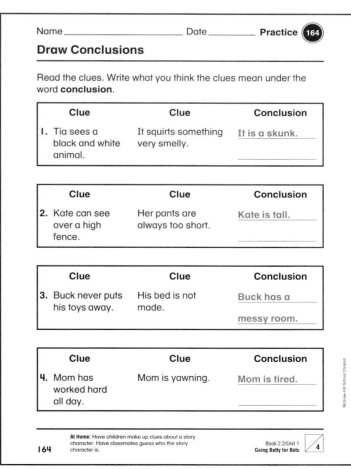

Draw Conclusions

Read the clues. Write what you think the clues mean under the word **conclusion**.

Clue	Clue	Conclusion
1. Tia sees a black and white animal.	It squirts something very smelly.	It is a skunk.

Clue	Clue	Conclusion
2. Kate can see over a high fence.	Her pants are always too short.	Kate is tall.

Clue	Clue	Conclusion
3. Buck never puts his toys away.	His bed is not made.	Buck has a messy room.

Clue	Clue	Conclusion
4. Mom has worked hard all day.	Mom is yawning.	Mom is tired.

Going Batty for Bats • PRACTICE

Name _____ Date _____ Practice **165**

Inflectional Endings

Add **-er** to the ends of words to compare two people, places, or things.
Tim is **older** (more old) than Megan.

Add **-est** to the ends of words to compare more than two people, places, or things.
Ryan is the **oldest** (most old) student in our class.

Read each sentence. Then add **-er** or **-est** to the word in dark print. Write the word on the line.

1. Lee's bike is **new** than my bike.

   newer

2. That red bird flew the **fast**.

   fastest

3. We will cut down the **large** tree in the forest.

   largest

4. There are **few** flowers in the garden this year than there were last year.

   fewer

5. That lamp is the **bright** one in the store.

   brightest

6. Pam feels much **strong** than she did last week.

   stronger

Book 2.2/Unit 1
Going Batty for Bats

At Home: Have children add **-er** and **-est** to the following words: **fresh, dark,** and **warm.** Then have them use each word in a sentence.

165

Name _____ Date _____ Practice **166**

Antonyms

Two words that are opposite or almost opposite in meaning are **antonyms**.

Read each sentence. Choose an antonym for the word in dark print from the box below. Write the antonym on the line.

| catch | winter | bottom | night | weak | stop |

1. I will **start** the race.

   stop

2. We will leave food for the birds in the **morning**.

   night

3. Be careful not to **throw** the ball into Mr. Morgan's backyard.

   catch

4. We will visit our grandparents' farm this **summer**.

   winter

5. No one in the village was **strong** enough to push the rock.

   weak

6. The students put their book reports on **top** of the table.

   bottom

At Home: Help children identify an antonym for each of these words: **light, long, old, late.** Have them use three of the antonym pairs in new sentences.

166

Book 2.2/Unit 1
Going Batty for Bats

Going Batty for Bats • RETEACH

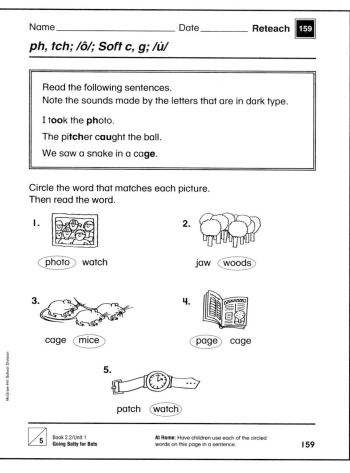

ph, tch; /ô/; Soft c, g; /ù/

> Read the following sentences.
> Note the sounds made by the letters that are in dark type.
>
> I t**oo**k the **ph**oto.
>
> The pi**tch**er c**au**ght the ball.
>
> We saw a snake in a ca**ge**.

Circle the word that matches each picture.
Then read the word.

1. (photo) watch

2. jaw (woods)

3. cage (mice)

4. (page) cage

5. patch (watch)

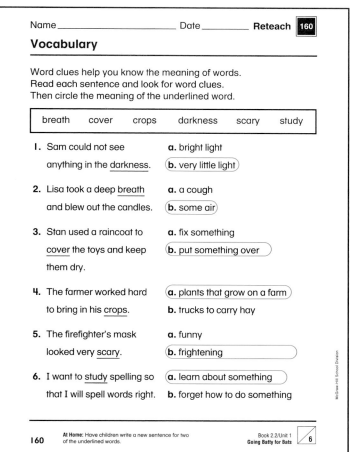

Vocabulary

Word clues help you know the meaning of words.
Read each sentence and look for word clues.
Then circle the meaning of the underlined word.

breath	cover	crops	darkness	scary	study

1. Sam could not see anything in the darkness.
   a. bright light
   (b. very little light)

2. Lisa took a deep breath and blew out the candles.
   a. a cough
   (b. some air)

3. Stan used a raincoat to cover the toys and keep them dry.
   a. fix something
   (b. put something over)

4. The farmer worked hard to bring in his crops.
   (a. plants that grow on a farm)
   b. trucks to carry hay

5. The firefighter's mask looked very scary.
   a. funny
   (b. frightening)

6. I want to study spelling so that I will spell words right.
   (a. learn about something)
   b. forget how to do something

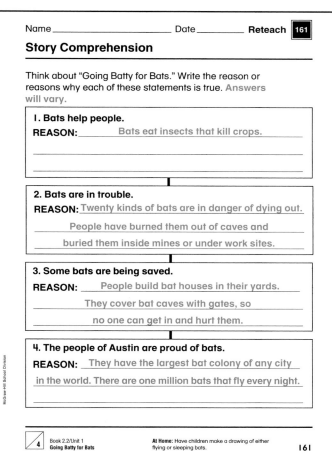

Story Comprehension

Think about "Going Batty for Bats." Write the reason or reasons why each of these statements is true. Answers will vary.

1. Bats help people.
REASON:_____ Bats eat insects that kill crops. _____

2. Bats are in trouble.
REASON: Twenty kinds of bats are in danger of dying out. People have burned them out of caves and buried them inside mines or under work sites.

3. Some bats are being saved.
REASON: People build bat houses in their yards. They cover bat caves with gates, so no one can get in and hurt them.

4. The people of Austin are proud of bats.
REASON: They have the largest bat colony of any city in the world. There are one million bats that fly every night.

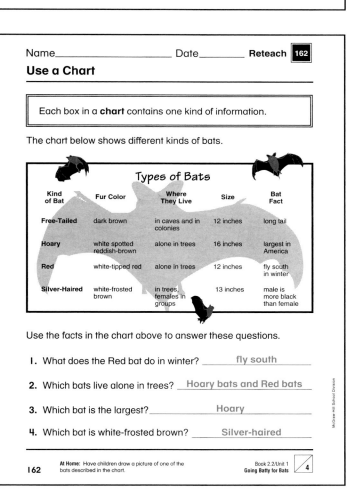

Use a Chart

> Each box in a **chart** contains one kind of information.

The chart below shows different kinds of bats.

Types of Bats

Kind of Bat	Fur Color	Where They Live	Size	Bat Fact
Free-Tailed	dark brown	in caves and in colonies	12 inches	long tail
Hoary	white spotted reddish-brown	alone in trees	16 inches	largest in America
Red	white-tipped red	alone in trees	12 inches	fly south in winter
Silver-Haired	white-frosted brown	in trees, females in groups	13 inches	male is more black than female

Use the facts in the chart above to answer these questions.

1. What does the Red bat do in winter? _____ fly south _____

2. Which bats live alone in trees? _____ Hoary bats and Red bats

3. Which bat is the largest? _____ Hoary _____

4. Which bat is white-frosted brown? _____ Silver-haired

Compare and Contrast

Name_____ Date_____ Reteach **163**

> **Compare** to tell how two things are alike.
> **Contrast** to tell how two things are different.

Read the story. Think about Amy's life before she got the dog. Think about Amy's life after she got the dog. Put an **X** in the correct box to make a comparison.

I am deaf. I can't hear people talk or sing. I can't hear the telephone or the doorbell either. Sometimes I would feel angry because I couldn't hear anything. But last year a very special dog named Annie came to live with me. She is a "hearing" dog. She helps me hear. If the doorbell rings, she bumps my hand and she runs to the door. She lets me know about other sounds, too. She is a good dog.

	Before the Dog	After the Dog
1. Amy did not know when the telephone rang.	X	
2. Amy was angry.	X	
3. Amy knows when someone is at the door.		X
4. Amy is much happier.		X

4 Book 2.2/Unit 1
Going Batty for Bats

At Home: Have children compare and contrast their lives during summer vacation with their lives during the school year.

163

Draw Conclusions

Name_____ Date_____ Reteach **164**

> When you read, you can use picture clues to help you draw conclusions.
>
> **The boy is sad.**
> The boy is happy.

Look at each picture. Then draw a circle around the sentence that tells about the picture.

1. It is a cloudy day.
   (It is a sunny day.)

2. The dog is mean.
   (The dog is friendly.)

3. (The play is over.)
   The play is beginning.

4. (The chair is heavy.)
   The chair is light.

164 **At Home:** Have children draw a picture, then write a conclusion for the picture.

Book 2.2/Unit 1
Going Batty for Bats 4

Inflectional Endings

Name_____ Date_____ Reteach **165**

> Add the endings **-er** and **-est** to the end of some words to make comparisons.
>
> That bat is **bigger** than the one I saw yesterday.
>
> The **biggest** bat I ever saw was in the zoo.

Read each sentence. Write the correct word from the box on the line.

largest	longer	slowest	sharper	milder	scariest

1. This is the ___largest___ group of bats living in one place in our state.

2. The boy who hurt his foot ran the ___slowest___ of all the racers.

3. I thought that was the ___scariest___ movie I ever saw.

4. The weather is ___milder___ today than it was yesterday, so I will not wear my heavy coat to school.

5. That piece of ribbon is ___longer___ than the ribbon on her dress.

6. You should use ___sharper___ scissors to cut that thick piece of paper.

6 Book 2.2/Unit 1
Going Batty for Bats

At Home: Encourage children to write a three-sentence story using a word with the **-er** or **-est** ending in each sentence.

165

Antonyms

Name_____ Date_____ Reteach **166**

> Words that have opposite or nearly opposite meanings are called **antonyms.**
>
> This story is about a **big** elephant and a **tiny** mouse.
>
> **Big** and **tiny** are antonyms.

Read each sentence and look carefully at the underlined word. Then circle the word below the sentence that means the opposite of the underlined word.

1. I liked the last story in the book the best because it was so funny to read.
   (first)   nice   better

2. I will need the largest box in the store to hold all these books.
   (smallest)   funny   saddest

3. All the children were happy when it started to snow.
   silly   playful   (sad)

4. The fast train raced down the track and into the station.
   free   (slow)   high

5. It was so chilly at night on our camping trip that we wrapped ourselves in blankets.
   (warm)   light   dark

6. The bark of the tree was very rough.
   long   cold   (smooth)

166 **At Home:** Ask children to rewrite the six sentences on this page using the circled antonyms.

Book 2.2/Unit 1
Going Batty for Bats 6

Going Batty for Bats • EXTEND

ph, tch; /ô/; Soft c, g; /ů/

Put the words from the box on the chart.

launch	cage	law	book	match	space
graph	astronaut	page	trace	claw	look
catch	stage	face	straw	cook	took

	1	2	3	4
ph	graph			
tch	match	catch		
oo	book	look	cook	took
aw	law	claw	straw	
au	launch	astronaut		
ce	space	trace	face	
ge	cage	page	stage	

1. Write the words from the **aw** row. __law__ __claw__ __straw__

2. How many words are in the **oo** row? __4__

3. Which three rows have 3 words? __aw__ __ce__ __ge__

4. Which two rows have 2 words? __tch__ __au__

5. Write the words from the **tch** row.

   __match__ __catch__

At Home: Look at the chart together. Write another question that children can answer using this chart.

Vocabulary

Read each word and its definition. Write a sentence using each word. **Sample answers are shown.**

1. **breath:** the air you take into your lungs and let out again

   I took a breath of fresh air.
   _____

2. **cover:** to put something over something else

   I have to cover the baby.
   _____

3. **crops:** many plants grown together, usually for food

   The bean and pea crops were picked.
   _____

4. **darkness:** having little or no light

   He sleeps in darkness.
   _____

5. **scary:** something that frightens or scares

   The story was scary.
   _____

6. **study:** to read or practice something

   We will study bats.
   _____

At Home: Write each word above on a card. Take turns choosing two cards and using both in a sentence.

Story Comprehension

| luck | houses | insects | mammals |
| sleep | Texas | stories | pups |

Write words from the box to complete the puzzle.

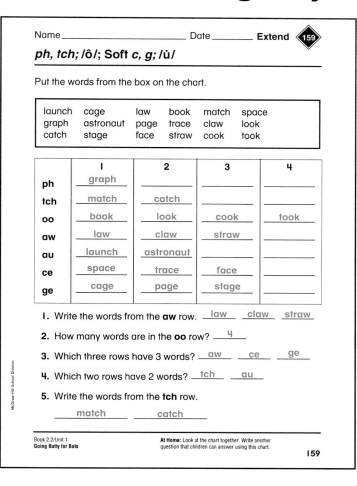

Across
3. Bats help farmers by eating _____ that kill crops.
5. Bats stand for good _____ in Japan and China.
7. The scariest things about bats are the _____ people tell.
8. Baby bats are called _____.

Down
1. Bats are furry, flying _____
2. Some people in _____ are working hard to keep bats safe.
4. Bats _____ for 20 hours a day.
6. Some people build bat _____ in their yards.

Write one more bat fact that could be added to the puzzle. Show where it could be added to the puzzle. **Answers will vary.**

_____

At Home: Ask children to assemble their facts into a book on bats. They might write each fact on a page and illustrate it.

Use a Chart

Use the chart to answer the questions.

Kind of tree	Loses Its leaves?	State tree of
Maple	yes	Rhode Island
Douglas Fir	no	Oregon
Giant Redwood	no	California
Magnolia	yes	Mississippi

1. Which two trees lose their leaves in the fall?

   maple, magnolia

2. What is the difference between the Douglas fir and the giant redwood?

   The Douglas fir is the state tree of Oregon and the giant redwood is the state tree of California.

3. What is the same about the Douglas fir and the giant redwood?

   Neither loses its leaves.

4. What is the state tree of Mississippi?

   magnolia

Write your own question using the information from the chart. Ask a friend to answer it.

   Answers will vary.

At Home: Have children look through newspapers or magazines to find charts.

T55

Going Batty for Bats • EXTEND

Name _____ Date _____ **Extend** 163

Compare and Contrast

Read about mammals.

- All mammals are warm-blooded.
- All mammals have backbones.
- Mammal babies are not hatched from eggs.
- All mammals have hair or fur.

Bats and bears are both mammals. List one way bats and bears are alike and different. **Answers will vary.**

Bears are similar to bats.	**Bears are different from bats.**
Both have backbones.	Bats can fly. Bears walk.

List other animals that are mammals. Draw a picture of one in the box.

_____

_____

_____

_____

_____

Book 2.2/Unit 1
Going Batty for Bats

At Home: Ask children to make a list of animals that are not mammals.

163

Name _____ Date _____ **Extend** 164

Draw Conclusions

Read each riddle. Write the name of the animal and draw its picture.

I am the largest animal on earth.
I feed my young on milk.
I am warm-blooded.
I breathe through a hole and swim in the sea.
Can you guess me?

whale

I have four beautiful wings.
I have two long antennae.
I feed on the nectar of flowers.
I lay my eggs on plants.
Can you guess my name?

butterfly

Write a riddle about a bat.

Riddles will vary.

_____

_____

_____

_____

_____

_____

At Home: Children can write another riddle about an animal of their choice.

164

Book 2.2/Unit 1
Going Batty for Bats

Name _____ Date _____ **Extend** 165

Inflectional Endings

Fill in the chart.

	add **er**	add **est**
fast	faster	fastest
tall	taller	tallest
short	shorter	shortest
strong	stronger	strongest
quick	quicker	quickest

Write about how you've changed since you were 5 years old. Use some of the words from the box.

_____

_____

_____

_____

Draw a picture of yourself at 5 years old. Draw a picture of yourself now.

Me at 5	**Me Now**

Book 2.2/Unit 1
Going Batty for Bats

At Home: Ask children to use the words from the box above to write about their favorite sport.

165

Name _____ Date _____ **Extend** 166

Antonyms

Write antonyms for each word.

1. dark ___ light
2. small ___ big
3. warm ___ cold, or cool
4. open ___ close or shut
5. day ___ night
6. up ___ down

Make a postcard to describe a pretend vacation. Use as many of the antonyms as you can. Draw a picture.

At Home: Ask children to identify the antonyms in their postcard.

166

Book 2.2/Unit 1
Going Batty for Bats

Going Batty for Bats • GRAMMAR

Contractions

- A **contraction** is a short form of two words.
- An **apostrophe** (') takes the place of the letters that are left out.

is not	isn't	are not	aren't
has not	hasn't	have not	haven't

I <u>haven't</u> seen John all day.

He <u>isn't</u> coming.

Read the sentences. Change the underlined words to contractions. Write the sentences.

1. Charlie <u>is not</u> taking a bath.

    Charlie isn't taking a bath.

2. He says he <u>has not</u> any soap.

    He says he hasn't any soap.

3. Dad and Mom <u>are not</u> listening.

    Dad and Mom aren't listening.

4. They <u>have not</u> time for his nonsense.

    They haven't time for his nonsense.

Contractions

- A **contraction** is a short form of two words.
- An **apostrophe** (') takes the place of the letters that are left out.

does not	doesn't
do not	don't
did not	didn't
can not	can't

Sally <u>doesn't</u> have her glasses.

She <u>can't</u> read without them.

Write the contractions for the underlined words. Then write the sentences.

1. <u>Do not</u> go to school without your books.   Don't

    Don't go to school without your books.

2. Bert <u>does not</u> have his lunch.   doesn't

    Bert doesn't have his lunch.

3. Jean <u>did not</u> bring her crayons.   didn't

    Jean didn't bring her crayons.

4. We <u>cannot</u> find our new room.   can't

    We can't find our new room.

Contractions

- A **contraction** is a short form of two words.
- An **apostrophe** (') takes the place of the letters that are left out.
- Some contractions are: *isn't, aren't, hasn't, haven't, doesn't, don't, didn't,* and *can't.*

Write the contraction for the underlined words in each sentence.

1. We <u>are not</u> ready for Father's Day.

    aren't

2. I <u>did not</u> make a card.

    didn't

3. I hope it <u>is not</u> too late.

    isn't

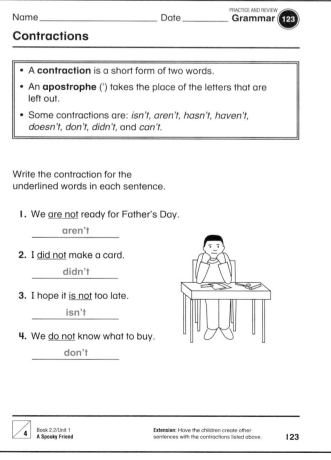

4. We <u>do not</u> know what to buy.

    don't

Contractions

- An apostrophe takes the place of the letters left out of a contraction.

    Miguel <u>is not</u> home.   Miguel <u>isn't</u> home.

Write each sentence correctly on the line.

1. we are'nt ready for the test

    We aren't ready for the test.

2. pam ha'snt read the book

    Pam hasn't read the book.

3. you hav'nt had time to study

    You haven't had time to study.

4. d'ont take the test today

    Don't take the test today.

5. i cann't give it to you.

    I can't give it to you.

Going Batty for Bats • GRAMMAR

Contractions

A. Read each sentence. Write the contraction for the underlined words in each sentence.

1. Our dog Spot <u>is not</u> in the store.

   _____ isn't _____

2. He <u>has not</u> been there all day.

   _____ hasn't _____

3. Mr. and Mrs. Stone <u>have not</u> seen him.

   _____ haven't _____

B. Read each pair of sentences. Circle the correct sentence in each pair.

4. I dont' know where he is.

   ⟨I don't know where he is.⟩

5. Mr. Stone does'nt know either.

   ⟨Mr. Stone doesn't know either.⟩

McGraw-Hill School Division

Contractions

- A **contraction** is a short form of two words.
- An **apostrophe** (') takes the place of the letters that are left out.

Read the sentences about the picture. Put the apostrophe in each contraction where it belongs. Write the new sentence on the line.

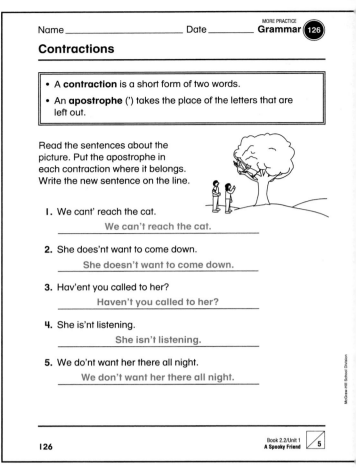

1. We cant' reach the cat.

   _____ We can't reach the cat. _____

2. She does'nt want to come down.

   _____ She doesn't want to come down. _____

3. Hav'ent you called to her?

   _____ Haven't you called to her? _____

4. She is'nt listening.

   _____ She isn't listening. _____

5. We do'nt want her there all night.

   _____ We don't want her there all night. _____

McGraw-Hill School Division

Going Batty for Bats • SPELLING

Words From Science

Pretest Directions

Fold back the paper along the dotted line. Use the blanks to write each word as it is read aloud. When you finish the test, unfold the paper. Use the list to the right to correct any spelling mistakes. Practice the words you missed for the Posttest.

To Parents,

Here are the results of your child's weekly spelling Pretest. You can help your child study for the Posttest by following these simple steps for each word on the list:

1. Read the word to your child.

2. Have your child write the word, saying each letter as it is written.

3. Say each letter of the word as your child checks the spelling.

4. If a mistake has been made, have your child read each letter of the correctly spelled word aloud and then repeat steps 1–3.

1. _____	1. sleep
2. _____	2. wing
3. _____	3. fly
4. _____	4. caves
5. _____	5. nest
6. _____	6. leaves
7. _____	7. insects
8. _____	8. blood
9. _____	9. sight
10. _____	10. den

Challenge Words

_____ breath
_____ crops
_____ darkness
_____ scary
_____ study

McGraw-Hill School Division

10 Book 2.2/Unit 1
Going Batty for Bats   121

Words From Science

Using the Word Study Steps

1. LOOK at the word.

2. SAY the word aloud.

3. STUDY the letters in the word.

4. WRITE the word.

5. CHECK the word.
   Did you spell the word right?
   If not, go back to step 1.

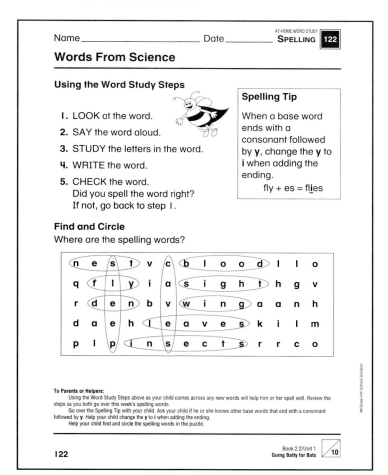

Spelling Tip

When a base word ends with a consonant followed by **y**, change the **y** to **i** when adding the ending.

fly + es = fl**i**es

Find and Circle

Where are the spelling words?

n	e	s	t	v	c	b	l	o	o	d	l	l	o
q	f	l	y	i	a	s	i	g	h	t	h	g	v
r	d	e	n	b	v	w	i	n	g	a	a	n	h
d	a	e	h	l	e	a	v	e	s	k	i	l	m
p	l	p	i	n	s	e	c	t	s	r	r	c	o

To Parents or Helpers:

Using the Word Study Steps above as your child comes across any new words will help him or her spell well. Review the steps as you both go over this week's spelling words.

Go over the Spelling Tip with your child. Ask your child if he or she knows other base words that end with a consonant followed by **y**. Help your child change the **y** to **i** when adding the ending.

Help your child find and circle the spelling words in the puzzle.

McGraw-Hill School Division

122   Book 2.2/Unit 1
Going Batty for Bats 10

Words From Science

sleep	fly	nest	insects	sight
wing	caves	leaves	blood	den

The words *cat* and *when* have short vowel sounds. The words *cake* and *seen* have long vowel sounds.

Write the spelling words with short vowel sounds and then write the spelling words with long vowel sounds in the bats below.

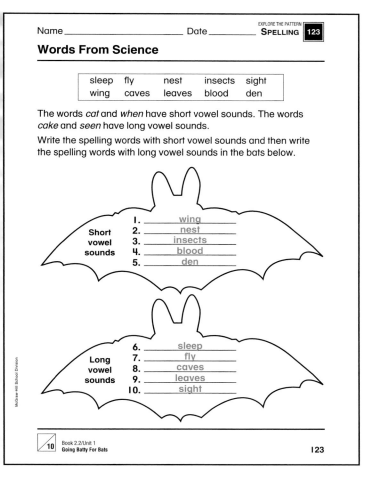

Short vowel sounds
1. wing
2. nest
3. insects
4. blood
5. den

Long vowel sounds
6. sleep
7. fly
8. caves
9. leaves
10. sight

McGraw-Hill School Division

10 Book 2.2/Unit 1
Going Batty For Bats   123

Words From Science

sleep	fly	nest	insects	sight
wing	caves	leaves	blood	den

Write a spelling word to complete each sentence.

1. Bats sometimes live in _____caves_____.

2. Bats are not known for their sense of _____sight_____.

3. In winter a bear stays in its _____den_____.

4. Bears _____sleep_____ through the winter.

5. Another name for _____insects_____ is bugs.

6. Insects like to eat all kinds of _____leaves_____.

7. In the tree, we found a _____nest_____.

8. We found a bird with a broken _____wing_____.

9. We washed the _____blood_____ from its feathers.

10. We want to help the bird _____fly_____ again.

McGraw-Hill School Division

124   Book 2.2/Unit 1
Going Batty for Bats 10

Going Batty for Bats • SPELLING

Words From Science

Proofreading Activity

There are six spelling mistakes in the story. Circle each misspelled word. Write the words correctly on the lines below.

A bird uses leafs and twigs to build its nesst. Birds are good parents. They bring worms and insecs to their babies. It can be a funny site to watch a baby bird learn to flie. At first, baby birds are not very good at flying. They flap their wengs and nothing happens. They try again and again until they finally take off into the air.

1. _____leaves_____   2. _____nest_____   3. _____insects_____

4. _____sight_____   5. _____fly_____   6. _____wings_____

Writing Activity

Write a story about nature. Use four spelling words in your story. Circle the spelling words in your story.

_____

_____

_____

_____

_____

Words From Science

Look at the words in each set. One word in each set is spelled correctly. Use a pencil to color in the circle in front of that word. Before you begin, look at the sample sets of words. Sample A has been done for you. Do Sample B by yourself. When you are sure you know what to do, you may go on with the rest of the page.

Sample A
- Ⓐ sunn
- Ⓑ sone
- ● sun
- Ⓓ sune

Sample B
- Ⓔ beeche
- Ⓕ baech
- Ⓖ beache
- ● beach

1.
- Ⓐ leafes
- ● leaves
- Ⓒ leeves
- Ⓓ leavs

2.
- Ⓔ weng
- Ⓕ winng
- Ⓖ winge
- ● wing

3.
- Ⓐ sihgt
- Ⓑ siight
- ● sight
- Ⓓ siet

4.
- Ⓔ nesst
- ● nest
- Ⓖ neste
- Ⓗ neess

5.
- ● caves
- Ⓑ caavs
- Ⓒ cavs
- Ⓓ cavas

6.
- Ⓔ slepe
- Ⓕ slep
- ● sleep
- Ⓗ sleepe

7.
- Ⓐ insectx
- ● insects
- Ⓒ inseects
- Ⓓ insecks

8.
- Ⓔ blud
- Ⓕ blod
- Ⓖ bluud
- ● blood

9.
- ● fly
- Ⓑ fliy
- Ⓒ fli
- Ⓓ flie

10.
- Ⓔ dehn
- ● den
- Ⓖ denn
- Ⓗ denne

Unit 4 Review • PRACTICE and RETEACH

Practice 167

Name_____ Date_____ **Practice** 167

Unit I Vocabulary Review

A. Use the words in the box to complete the story.

> museum   chocolate   explore   vacation   nature   village

I live in a small ____village____ called Hamilton.

We have a library, a ____museum____, and a store that

sells ____chocolate____ - chip cookies. Many people

come to Hamilton for their summer ____vacation____.

They like to ____explore____ the forest. They also go

to the ____nature____ center to learn about plants .

B. Draw a line to the word or words that mean the *opposite*. Then, write this answer on the line.

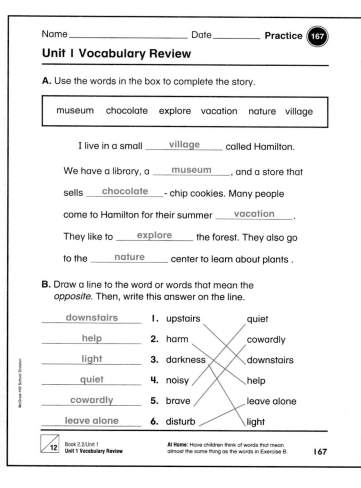

____downstairs____	1. upstairs	quiet
____help____	2. harm	cowardly
____light____	3. darkness	downstairs
____quiet____	4. noisy	help
____cowardly____	5. brave	leave alone
____leave alone____	6. disturb	light

12 | Book 2.2/Unit 1 Unit 1 Vocabulary Review | **At Home:** Have children think of words that mean almost the same thing as the words in Exercise B. | 167

Practice 168

Name_____ Date_____ **Practice** 168

Unit I Vocabulary Review

A. Write a question for each statement below. Use the underlined word in your question. **Answers may vary.**

> I ate some chocolate cake.
> How much chocolate cake did you eat?

1. I bought new clothes. What kinds of clothes did you buy?

2. I study every night. What do you study?

3. She is diving into the pool. Is she good at diving?

4. I tried to guess the right answer. Did you guess the right answer?

5. I practice the piano every day. How long do you practice?

B. Answer **Yes** or **No** to the questions below, and explain your answers. **Answers may vary.**

1. If a friend offered her help building a model airplane, would you take it? Yes, because doing things together is fun.

2. Is a roof the same thing as a floor? No, because a floor is on the bottom and a roof is on the top.

3. Do you ever wear anything to cover your head? Yes; I sometimes wear a hat.

168 | **At Home:** Have children write three questions using vocabulary words from Part A. | Book 2.2/Unit 1 Unit 1 Vocabulary Review | 8

Reteach 167

Name_____ Date_____ **Reteach** 167

Unit I Vocabulary Review

A. Match each sentence below with the word that completes it. Write the letter of the word on the line.

_e._ 1. My teacher ___ math to us.   **a.** scary

_f._ 2. I ___ what that word means.   **b.** study

_d._ 3. I can hold my ___ underwater.   **c.** crops

_c._ 4. My mother is a farmer, and her ___ are doing well.   **d.** breath

_a._ 5. After I read the ___ story, I couldn't sleep.   **e.** explains

_b._ 6. My father will ___ English.   **f.** wonder

B. Circle the word that best answers each question below.

1. What is on top of a house?
   a. vacation   **b.** soil   **(c.)** roof

2. Which of these things can you eat?
   (a.) chocolate   **b.** museum   **c.** breath

3. What do people wear?
   a. village   **b.** soil   **(c.)** clothes

4. What do plants grow in?
   (a.) soil   **b.** roof   **c.** breath

10 | Book 2.2/Unit 1 Unit 1 Vocabulary Review | **At Home:** Have children make up a word search with the words they circled in Exercise B. | 167

Reteach 168

Name_____ Date_____ **Reteach** 168

Unit I Vocabulary Review

A. Underline the word that best fits each definition below.

1. hurt
   a. harm   **b.** dive   **c.** guess

2. loud
   a. scary   **b.** noisy   **c.** brave

3. a small group of houses
   a. clothes   **b.** museum   **c.** village

4. a time of rest
   a. vacation   **b.** practice   **c.** nature

B. Complete the crossword puzzle using the words in the box.

> middle   objects   darkness   diving   several

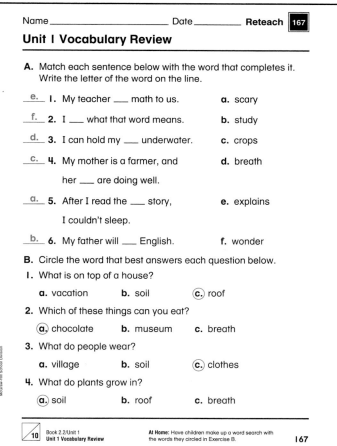

Down

1. not light _____

Across

3. between the beginning and the end _____

4. a way of going into the water _____

5. things _____

6. more than a few _____

168 | **At Home:** Have children make a crossword puzzle using the words they underlined in Exercise A. | Book 2.2/Unit 1 Unit 1 Vocabulary Review | 10

Vocabulary Review

Name _____ Date _____ **Extend** 167

| clothes | brave | chocolate | breath | darkness |

Read the sentence. If it makes sense, put a check. If it is wrong, use a word from the box to correct it.

☐ 1. I need some new **ducks** because I have grown out of my old ones.
_____clothes_____

✔ 2. They were so **noisy** that I had to tell them to stop shouting!
_____

☐ 3. When all the lights went out, I was sitting in the **light**.
_____darkness_____

☐ 4. I took a deep **talk** through my nose.
_____breath_____

☐ 5. I love to eat **soap** cake.
_____chocolate_____

☐ 6. I was so **afraid** that I proudly walked on stage and sang to all the people.
_____brave_____

✔ 7. With a lot of **practice,** I played the piano very well.
_____

Book 2.2/Unit 1
At Home: On one side of a card, write a vocabulary word in a sentence. On the other side, have children illustrate the sentence. Children can have a friend look at the pictures and guess the sentences, then flip the card over to see if the guess was right.
167

Vocabulary Review

Name _____ Date _____ **Extend** 168

Cut out the word cards.

Play with a friend.

Pick a card. Use the word in a sentence to begin a story. Your friend uses the word on the next card in a sentence to add to the story. Take turns until all the cards are used.

chocolate	clothes	middle	offered
roof	upstairs	diving	explains
harm	noisy	soil	village
disturb	explore	facts	nature
objects	several	breath	crops
brave	vacation	scary	wonder

At Home: Ask children to pick two cards and write a silly sentence using both words.   Book 2.2/Unit 1

168

Name _____ Date _____ UNIT TEST **Grammar** 127

Irregular Verbs

Read the sentences in the box. Look at the underlined part. Is there a mistake? If there is, how do you correct it? Mark your answer.

> I am here now. <u>I am here yesterday.</u> You are here now.
> (1)
> You were here yesterday. <u>We was both here yesterday.</u>
> (2)

1. ⓐ Change *am* to *was*.
   ⓑ Change *am* to *is*.
   ⓒ Change *am* to *are*.
   ⓓ No mistake.

2. ⓕ Change *was* to *is*.
   ⓖ Change *was* to *am*.
   ⓗ Change *was* to *were*.
   ⓙ No mistake.

> I went to the park yesterday. <u>My sister say I should go home.</u>
> (3)
> I did what I was told. <u>I go home.</u>
> (4)

3. ⓐ Change *say* to *says*.
   ⓑ Change *say* to *said*.
   ⓒ Change *say* to *have said*.
   ⓓ No mistake.

4. ⓕ Change *go* to *went*.
   ⓖ Change *go* to *goed*.
   ⓗ Change *go* to *gone*.
   ⓙ No mistake.

Book 2.2/Unit 1
Look Around   **Go On** →   **127**

Name _____ Date _____ REVIEW **Grammar** 128

> <u>David run down the hill.</u> I saw him fall. <u>He got up and sing a</u>
> (5)   (6)
> <u>song.</u> David is amazing!

5. ⓐ Change *run* to *ran*.
   ⓑ Change *run* to *runned*.
   ⓒ Change *run* to *runed*.
   ⓓ No mistake.

6. ⓕ Change *sing* to *singed*.
   ⓖ Change *sing* to *sang*.
   ⓗ Change *sing* to *sung*.
   ⓙ No mistake.

> We weren't ready for the test. <u>We don't have time to study.</u>
> (7)
> Pam hadn't read the book. <u>I didn't review my notes.</u>
> (8)

7. ⓐ Change *don't* to *didn't*.
   ⓑ Change *don't* to *hadn't*.
   ⓒ Change *don't* to *can't*.
   ⓓ No mistake.

8. ⓕ Change *didn't* to *don't*.
   ⓖ Change *didn't* to *can't*.
   ⓗ Change *didn't* to *did'nt*.
   ⓙ No mistake.

128   Book 2.2/Unit 1
Look Around 8

Unit 4 Review • SPELLING

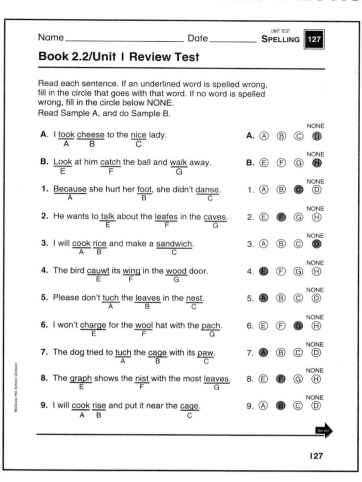

Book 2.2/Unit I Review Test

Read each sentence. If an underlined word is spelled wrong, fill in the circle that goes with that word. If no word is spelled wrong, fill in the circle below NONE.
Read Sample A, and do Sample B.

A. I <u>took</u> <u>cheese</u> to the <u>nice</u> lady.
   A   B   C
   A. Ⓐ Ⓑ Ⓒ ⬤D   *NONE*

B. <u>Look</u> at him <u>catch</u> the ball and <u>walk</u> away.
   E   F   G
   B. Ⓔ Ⓕ Ⓖ ⬤H   *NONE*

1. <u>Because</u> she hurt her <u>foot</u>, she didn't <u>danse</u>.
   A   B   C
   1. Ⓐ Ⓑ ⬤C Ⓓ   *NONE*

2. He wants to <u>talk</u> about the <u>leafes</u> in the <u>caves</u>.
               E   F   G
   2. Ⓔ ⬤F Ⓖ Ⓗ   *NONE*

3. I will <u>cook</u> <u>rice</u> and make a <u>sandwich</u>.
         A   B   C
   3. Ⓐ Ⓑ Ⓒ ⬤D   *NONE*

4. The bird <u>cauwt</u> its <u>wing</u> in the <u>wood</u> door.
              E   F   G
   4. ⬤E Ⓕ Ⓖ Ⓗ   *NONE*

5. Please don't <u>tuch</u> the <u>leaves</u> in the <u>nest</u>.
                 A   B   C
   5. ⬤A Ⓑ Ⓒ Ⓓ   *NONE*

6. I won't <u>charge</u> for the <u>wool</u> hat with the <u>pach</u>.
            E   F   G
   6. Ⓔ Ⓕ ⬤G Ⓗ   *NONE*

7. The dog tried to <u>tuch</u> the <u>cage</u> with its <u>paw</u>.
                    A   B   C
   7. ⬤A Ⓑ Ⓒ Ⓓ   *NONE*

8. The <u>graph</u> shows the <u>nist</u> with the most <u>leaves</u>.
        E   F   G
   8. Ⓔ ⬤F Ⓖ Ⓗ   *NONE*

9. I will <u>cook</u> <u>rise</u> and put it near the <u>cage</u>.
         A   B   C
   9. Ⓐ ⬤B Ⓒ Ⓓ   *NONE*

Go on →

127

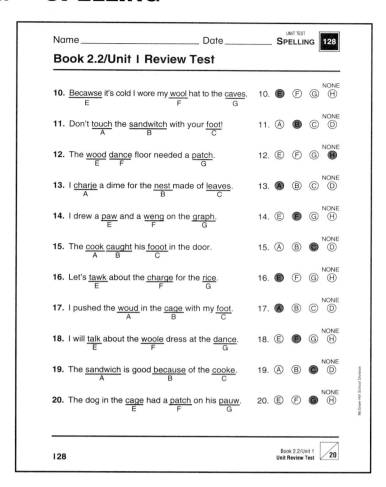

Book 2.2/Unit I Review Test

10. <u>Becawse</u> it's cold I wore my <u>wool</u> hat to the <u>caves</u>.
     E   F   G
   10. ⬤E Ⓕ Ⓖ Ⓗ   *NONE*

11. Don't <u>touch</u> the <u>sandwitch</u> with your <u>foot</u>!
             A   B   C
   11. Ⓐ ⬤B Ⓒ Ⓓ   *NONE*

12. The <u>wood</u> <u>dance</u> floor needed a <u>patch</u>.
         E   F   G
   12. Ⓔ Ⓕ Ⓖ ⬤H   *NONE*

13. I <u>charje</u> a dime for the <u>nest</u> made of <u>leaves</u>.
       A   B   C
   13. ⬤A Ⓑ Ⓒ Ⓓ   *NONE*

14. I drew a <u>paw</u> and a <u>weng</u> on the <u>graph</u>.
                E   F   G
   14. Ⓔ ⬤F Ⓖ Ⓗ   *NONE*

15. The <u>cook</u> <u>caught</u> his <u>fooot</u> in the door.
         A   B   C
   15. Ⓐ Ⓑ ⬤C Ⓓ   *NONE*

16. Let's <u>tawk</u> about the <u>charge</u> for the <u>rice</u>.
            E   F   G
   16. ⬤E Ⓕ Ⓖ Ⓗ   *NONE*

17. I pushed the <u>woud</u> in the <u>cage</u> with my <u>foot</u>.
                  A   B   C
   17. ⬤A Ⓑ Ⓒ Ⓓ   *NONE*

18. I will <u>talk</u> about the <u>woole</u> dress at the <u>dance</u>.
          E   F   G
   18. Ⓔ ⬤F Ⓖ Ⓗ   *NONE*

19. The <u>sandwich</u> is good <u>because</u> of the <u>cooke</u>.
         A   B   C
   19. Ⓐ Ⓑ ⬤C Ⓓ   *NONE*

20. The dog in the <u>cage</u> had a <u>patch</u> on his <u>pauw</u>.
                    E   F   G
   20. Ⓔ Ⓕ ⬤G Ⓗ   *NONE*

128

Book 2.2/Unit 1
Unit Review Test   /20

Phonological Awareness

OBJECTIVES Children will practice blending and segmenting sounds and substituting beginning sounds.

Alternate
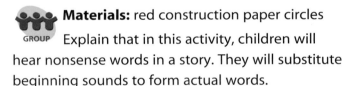

Blend Sounds

NAME THAT WORD

 Use this game to help children practice blending sounds to form words.

- Have children sit in a circle. Tell them they are going to play "Name that Word."

- Invite a volunteer to walk around the circle, saying the sounds of a word until he or she chooses someone to be "it." The child picked must blend the sounds together to guess the word. Then he or she will walk around the circle saying the sounds for another word.

- Suggest children use these words when playing the game: *hood, wood, book, goose, train, lime, skate, dime.*

Segment Sounds

USE THE CLUES

 Tell children that they will use clues to guess secret words. Then they will segment the sounds, tapping their feet as they say each new sound.

- Make up clues for the following words: *wool, brook, loose, bloom, soil.* You may wish to use the following or similar clues: *It's a fabric that comes from the coat of a sheep. It's /w/_____. (wool)/It's like a stream. It's a /b/____. (brook)/ It's the opposite of tight. It's /l/ ___.(loose)/ It's what flowers do in the spring. It's /b/ ___.(bloom)/ It's the earth in which plants grow. It's /s/ ___. (soil)*

- Pause after each word, giving children an opportunity to use the hint to identify the word.

- After they say each word, children divide the word into its sounds and tap their feet once as they say each sound, for example, for the word *wool: /w/ (tap), /ü/ (tap), /l/ (tap).*

Substitute Sounds

WEIRD WORDS

Materials: red construction paper circles

Explain that in this activity, children will hear nonsense words in a story. They will substitute beginning sounds to form actual words.

- Read the following paragraph to children:

Karen and her mom decided to sook (cook) *finner* (dinner). *They decided to troil* (broil) *pork shops* (chops), *mix a green weafy* (leafy) *palad* (salad), *and make grench* (french) *fries. What a wood* (good) *seal* (meal)!

The words in parentheses are the real words that the children will substitute for the nonsense words.

- Reread the paragraph. When children hear a nonsense word, they hold up a red paper circle. Call on a volunteer to say the beginning sound of the nonsense word, say the nonsense word, and then substitute the beginning sound of the real word. Finally, he or she says the real word, for example, */s/ sook, /k/ cook.* Continue until you have read the entire paragraph.

Variant Vowel /u̇/ oo

TESTED ✓**OBJECTIVES** Students will make up chants and mime words with the variant vowel /u̇/, spelled oo.

Alternate

Activities

Visual

BINGO!

GROUP

Materials: bingo cards as described below, bottle caps or other markers

Use the following activity for developing knowledge of the variant vowel /u̇/, spelled oo.

- Create several sets of bingo cards with words students can read. One word in each row or column should contain the variant vowel /u̇/, spelled oo (wood, brook, foot).

- In random order, read words that appear on the cards. Tell students to listen and look for words with the sound /u̇/, spelled oo. Have them cover only these words.

- When students locate and cover a word in each row or column with the variant vowel /u̇/, they call out Bingo! Have students exchange cards before they play again. ▶**Linguistic**

Auditory

OO CHEERS

GROUP

Materials: chart paper, marker

Have students work in small groups to make up cheers using real words and nonsense words with the variant vowel /u̇/ oo.

- Group members can begin by brainstorming real and nonsense words with the oo sound. When students finish planning, group members can write their cheers on chart paper, then make up gestures and motions for the cheers.

- Groups can practice their cheers and present them to the class. ▶**Musical**

Kinesthetic

OO PANTOMIME

GROUP

Materials: small slips of paper

Have students pantomime words with the /u̇/ sound spelled oo.

- On small slips of paper, write words with the variant vowel /u̇/ oo, such as *book, cook, look, took,* and *hook*.

- Have each student in turn pick a slip of paper and act out the word without speaking.

- Members of the class try to guess the oo word. Then a different student takes a turn.

- To make the activity more challenging, you may want to form teams and set a time limit for each team to guess. ▶**Bodily/Kinesthetic**

Phonics CD-ROM

See Reteach 127, 131, 132, 140, 148, 159

Graphic Aids

✓BJECTIVES Students will construct and interpret maps and charts.

Alternate Activities

Kinesthetic

HUMAN BAR GRAPH

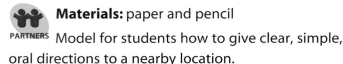

GROUP **Materials:** chalk or paper and markers

Have students brainstorm categories that could be used to create a bar graph on a topic such as birthday months, favorite sports, or favorite colors.

- Write a large label for each category. Tape the labels to a long wall or write them along the chalkboard.

- Have students line up under their category or a category of their choice.

- Tell students in each row to count off. Enter the total number of people for each category under the name of the category.

- Once students are seated again, use the chart data to ask questions such as: *Which color is most popular? Which two months have the same number of birthdays?* ▶**Logical/Mathematical**

Visual

MAKE A MAP

ONE **Materials:** large drawing paper, pencils, thin markers or crayons

Have each student draw a map of the classroom with a legend to indicate objects such as chairs, desks, windows, sink, and door.

- Students can share their maps with others in small groups to compare similarities and differences.

- Provide time for individual students to make corrections or additions to their maps. ▶**Spatial**

Auditory

MENTAL MAPS

PARTNERS **Materials:** paper and pencil

Model for students how to give clear, simple, oral directions to a nearby location.

- Have students work in pairs, giving each other sequential oral directions for getting from one place to another within the school or school grounds. The starting place should be familiar.

- The directions should refer to familiar landmarks and include specific direction words such as *right, left,* and *straight.*

- Tell the listener to draw a map or make notes to record the directions.

- Have the pair try to follow the map or written directions to reach the correct destination. ▶**Spatial**

See Reteach 130, 138, 146, 154, 162

Draw Conclusions

OBJECTIVES Students will draw conclusions based on auditory and visual clues, as well as prior knowledge.

Auditory

TWENTY QUESTIONS

Remind students that we use clues, along with what we already know about a subject, to draw conclusions.

- Give clues for students to use as they draw conclusions about a letter or a number. For example: *It's between 3 and 10. It's an even number. It's the age of many students in this class.* Keep a tally of how many clues it takes before students can identify the answer.

- Help students recognize how they drew conclusions about the numbers and letters. Guide them to summarize how they used what they already knew along with new information. Explain that using new information helps them narrow the choices until they arrive at a conclusion. ▶**Logical/Mathematical**

Visual

FLOOR ME!

Materials: sheet of heavy paper, tinfoil, tape

Provide the following exercise for students to observe and practice drawing conclusions.

- Display a sheet of heavy paper and a piece of tinfoil, both the same size. Ask students to make a guess about which material would make a better floor.

- Place the tinfoil and the paper in separate locations. Tape the paper and foil in place so that they don't slip. Ask a volunteer to walk across each surface.

- Have students describe what they observed, and ask them again which surface would make a better floor. Ask them to explain the conclusions they drew. ▶**Bodily/Kinesthetic**

Kinesthetic

CONSERVATION EXPERIMENT

Materials: two glass or plastic jars of different sizes and shapes, water

Guide students in designing a simple conservation experiment to practice drawing conclusions.

- Have students work in pairs at a water table or by a sink or dishpan to avoid spilling water.

- Give students a pair of empty containers of different sizes and shapes. Ask them to predict which will hold a greater amount of water and why. Challenge students to create an experiment that will help confirm their predictions.

- After the experiments, ask whether students' conclusions were correct. Invite students to share experiment results with classmates. ▶**Interpersonal**

See Reteach 133, 149, 164

Antonyms

 OBJECTIVES Students will practice forming antonym pairs and recognizing words with opposite meanings.

Kinesthetic

OPPOSITE DAY

 Have an opposite day to increase students' awareness of antonyms.

- First, invite students to brainstorm ways they can do "the opposite." For example, they might wear a hat or shirt backward for the day.

- As you remind students today is opposite day, give them instructions such as: *Open your book to the back. The line leader should go to the end of the line.*

- At the end of the day, review some of the antonyms students used during the day.
  ▶**Linguistic**

Visual

ANTONYM CONCENTRATION

 Materials: 12 or more index cards for each partner

Have students write six or more pairs of antonyms, one word on each card.

- Students can use the cards to play *Concentration.* They begin by laying out the cards, face down, on a flat surface.

- Each student picks two cards. If the cards form an antonym pair, the student keeps the cards and takes another turn. If not, the student lays them face down again, and his or her turn is over.

- Students play until all cards have been matched with an antonym. ▶**Logical/Mathematical**

Auditory

ANTONYM AD LIB

 Materials: paper and pencils

Student will replace words in a story with antonyms.

Have each student write a short descriptive story, underlining any word that has an obvious antonym. (*short, big, easy*)

- The student reads only the words from the story that have obvious antonyms. A partner writes a list of the antonyms. (*tall, little, hard*)

- Together, the partners read the story again, this time substituting the antonyms for the underlined words.

- Students may switch stories with another pair and repeat the steps. ▶**Linguistic**

See Reteach 134, 142, 166

Phonological Awareness

OBJECTIVES Children will practice blending and segmenting sounds and substituting ending sounds.

Blend Sounds

CIRCLE TIME

 Tell children that they will blend sounds to form words.

- Have children sit in a circle.

- Tell children to listen carefully to the following words segmented into individual sounds: /r/-/ī/-/s/ (rice), /h/-/ū/-/j/ (huge), /h/-/ü/-/k/ (hook), /b/-/ü/-/t/ (boot), /p/-/l/-/ā/-/s/ (place), /f/-/är/-/m/ (farm), and /h/-/ôr/-/n/ (horn).

- Pause after you say the sounds for each word. Have children blend the sounds into the word. If the word has the /s/ sound, then have children draw a large circle in the air.

Segment Sounds

PLACE THE CENTS

 Materials: Word Building Boxes from *Word Building Kit,* pennies

Tell children that as they pronounce and segment sounds they will place pennies into Word Building Boxes to mark each sound they hear.

- Provide each child with Word Building Boxes and a handful of pennies.

- Have children listen carefully to the following words: *cent, giraffe, spool, ceiling, gym, rice, age,* and *slice.*

- Ask children to segment each word into individual sounds. Have children place one cent in each Word Building Box to represent each sound.

Substitute Sounds

PICK A SOUND

 Materials: Phonics Pictures from *Word Building Kit*

Have children use picture cards to cue ending sound substitutions.

- Display the Phonics Picture of a bib. Ask a volunteer to name the sound they hear at the end of *bib.* (/b/) Ask: *If we change the /b/ ending sound to /g/, what new word do we make? (big)*

- Divide the class into pairs and give each pair three or four Phonics Pictures.

- Tell the pairs to say the name of the picture on the card and then substitute the ending sound with another sound of their choice.

- Encourage children to tell if their new word is a real word or a nonsense word.

Soft *c* and Soft *g*: /s/ce; /j/ge

 OBJECTIVES Students will recognize and decode words with the soft *c* and soft *g* sounds.

Alternate Activities

Auditory

RED OR BLUE?

 Materials: four cards for each student, red and blue markers or crayons

Use the following activity to help students discriminate between hard and soft *c* and *g*.

Have each child write the following letters, one on each index card: a blue *g*, a red *g*, a blue *c*, and a red *c*.

- Explain that for this activity, red letters represent hard sounds and blue letters represent soft sounds.

- Read a list of words, each of which has a hard or soft *c* or *g*. Pause between words for students to display the correct corresponding card.

- You might begin with these words: *go, age, come, place, stage, rage, cab, race, peace, mice, ace, nice, page, card, garden.* ▶Linguistic

Kinesthetic

CIRCLE AROUND

 Materials: masking tape or chalk

- Use chalk or tape to form the letters *c* and *g* inside two large circles on the floor. Make a third circle with no letter inside.

- Tell students you will display words, one by one. Each word may have the soft *c* or soft *g* sound, as in *ace* or *stage*. If they hear one of these sounds, students should hop into the appropriate circle.

- If not, they should stay in the circle with no letter.
  ▶Bodily/Kinesthetic

Visual

PICTURE THAT

 Materials: drawing paper and crayons or markers

Orally review a number of words with the soft *g* and soft *c* sound. Remind students these words are spelled with *ce* or *ge*.

 Give each student two sheets of drawing paper. Have students write *ge* on one page and *ce* on the other.

- Ask students to draw a picture using as many objects as they can whose names have the soft *g* or soft *c* sound.

- Invite volunteers to display their pictures as others try to name all the soft *c* and soft *g* words.

 **CD-ROM**

See Reteach 135, 139, 140, 148, 156, 159

Compare and Contrast

 OBJECTIVES Students will compare and contrast sounds, identify objects by comparisons and contrasts, and respond actively after making comparisons and contrasts.

Alternate Activities

Auditory

NAME THAT SOUND

 GROUP **Materials:** teacher-prepared tape recording, cassette player

Develop students' auditory discrimination and vocabulary as they compare and contrast sounds.

- Record a variety of classroom and outdoor sounds, or call students' attention to these sounds.

- Have students compare and contrast two sounds at a time, using as many descriptive words as they can (e.g., *louder/softer, scratchy/smooth, sweet/annoying*). ▶**Musical**

Visual

I SPY

 PARTNERS Use clues about comparing and contrasting in this version of the classic *I Spy* game.

- Model how to give descriptive clues about an object in the classroom.

- Instead of describing the object directly, use comparative clues, such as: *I spy something that is a brighter red than Andrew's shirt; It is higher than the clock; Or, I spy something that is made of paper, and it's larger than a book.*

- Have students take turns working with partners to choose new objects and give comparative clues as the other person guesses.
▶**Logical/Mathematical**

Kinesthetic

SIMON SAYS

GROUP In this version of *Simon Says*, each direction should include a comparison or contrast.

- Give an oral direction for *Simon Says* that requires students to demonstrate their knowledge of comparison and contrast.

- For example: *Simon says flap your arms like a butterfly. Simon says crawl slower than a turtle. Simon says blink as slowly as you can; now blink fast.*

- Instead of having students who make mistakes sit out, let everyone continue play. Choose a new leader after each batch of commands.
▶**Bodily/Kinesthetic**

See Reteach 141, 157, 163

Phonological Awareness

OBJECTIVES Children will practice blending and segmenting sounds and substituting middle sounds.

Alternate Activities

Blend Sounds

ON MY LAWN

 Materials: green construction paper, crayons or markers

Tell children that they will choose among blended words to identify names of bugs.

- Provide children with green construction paper. Tell them to imagine that this is their lawn. On their lawn, they will have many bugs.

- Tell children to listen carefully to the following list of words divided into individual sounds: /a/-/n/-/t/ (ant), /k/-/l/-/ô/ (claw), /l/-/ā/-/d/-/ē/-/b/-/u/-/g/ (ladybug), /l/-/ô/-/n/ (lawn), /f/-/ô/-/n/ (fawn), /s/-/p/-/ī/ -/d/-/ər/ (spider), /b/-/u/-/t/-/ər/-/f/-/l/-/ī/ (butterfly).

- Pause after each word. If the blended word is a type of bug, then have children draw the bug on their lawn. If the blended word is not a bug, then have a volunteer tell you what the word is.

Segment Sounds

STAND FOR SOUNDS GAME

 Materials: pictures from magazines

Use this game to help children practice segmenting words into individual sounds.

- Display a group of pictures. Organize children in a circle, and tell them that they are going to play a game in which they will say the sounds of words.

- Point to the first picture. Begin going around the room, having each child in turn say a sound in the word.

- The child who says the final sound stands and says the entire word.

- You may want to use pictures of the following objects: a shawl, a saw, a giraffe, a shirt, a school, a house, a stool, a hawk, and a flower.

Substitute Sounds

CHANGE A SOUND

 Have children listen to words and substitute middle sounds to make new words.

- Explain to children that you will give them hints to follow to change the middle sound of words to make new words.

- Say the word *hawk*. Tell children to change the middle sound to make something that fishermen use to catch fish. *(hook)*

- Continue by saying the first word in each of the following pairs and offer a meaning hint for the second word in each pair: *launch/lunch, champ/chimp, tick/tack, gloss/glass, stamp/stump, life/leaf, fawn/fan.*

Variant Vowel /ô/ *a, aw, au*

OBJECTIVES Students will recognize orally, read, and write words with the variant vowel /ô/, spelled *a, aw,* or *au.*

Alternate

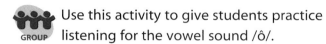

Kinesthetic

/Ô/ BASEBALL

Materials: four large paper squares, marker

GROUP Play a baseball game to draw attention to words with the variant vowel /ô/.

- Prepare three paper "bases," with the letters *a, au,* or *aw* written on each. Label a fourth base *home.* Place the bases in a baseball diamond pattern on the floor.

- Have students form teams. Read a sentence that contains a word with the /ô/ sound, spelled *a, au,* or *aw,* such as: *paw, straw, draw, taught, tall, thaw, awful.*

- If the first student can identify the word with the sound, the student advances one base.

- Students are "out" if they cannot identify the correct word with the /ô/ sound. Repeat with the next player.

- After a correct answer, students advance one base, as players would after a hit in a baseball game. Score a run for any student who rounds the bases. ▶**Bodily/Kinesthetic**

Auditory

SOB STORY

Use this activity to give students practice **GROUP** listening for the vowel sound /ô/.

- Have students make up silly or sad statements, using a word with the vowel sound /ô/, if possible. For example: *Rover hurt his* paw.

- Others listen carefully for a word with the /ô/ sound. If they hear one, they say *aw* after the statement. If no /ô/ words are used, they remain silent. The speaker calls on someone in the group to identify the /ô/ word.

- Continue with another sentence. ▶**Interpersonal**

Visual

BRIGHTLY LETTERED

 Materials: paper, pencil, highlighters

ONE Provide practice for students to recognize visually spellings of the /ô/ sound.

 Have students write words with the /ô/ **WRITING** sound, spelled *a, au,* or *aw.*

- Ask them to highlight the letters that form the vowel sound. ▶**Linguistic**

Phonics CD-ROM

See Reteach 143, 147, 148, 159

Inflectional Endings

✓BJECTIVES Students will recognize and use words with inflectional endings *-er* and *-est*.

Alternate Activities

Kinesthetic

CATCH THAT ENDING?

 Materials: chart, beanbag or soft-filling ball

GROUP Make a large wall chart with the inflectional endings *-er* and *-est* written several times in random order on a grid.

- Have students form two teams. Explain that you will read a sentence that contains a word with an *-er* or *-est* ending. One student from each team should be ready to name the word.

- The first student to tell the word and identify the ending you used gets to toss the beanbag or soft ball at the chart, aiming for the same inflectional ending. You may wish to keep score as students hit the target ending.

- Continue with a new sentence—and the next player on each team. ▶**Bodily/Kinesthetic**

Visual

WORDS AND PICTURES

Materials: drawing paper, crayons or **ONE** markers

Brainstorm with students a number of words to which the inflectional endings *-er* and *-est* may be added, such as *red, bright, young, tall, quick*.

- Have each student choose one of the words.

- Distribute drawing paper, and instruct students to fold it to form three sections.

 They can write the word on the bottom of **WRITING** the left-hand section, write the word with the *-er* ending added in the middle section, and write the word with the *-est* ending added in the right-hand section, leaving room to draw above each word.

- Students illustrate the words they have written in each section.

- Have students share the completed *-er/-est* drawings with classmates. ▶**Spatial**

Auditory

PICK A PAPER

Materials: container, such as a coffee can or **PARTNERS** basket; slips of paper

On slips of paper, write words to which the inflected endings *-er* and *-est* may be added. Place the papers in a container.

- Have pairs of students work together to practice words with the inflected endings *-er* and *-est*.

- One student selects a word from the container and reads it aloud.

- The partner says the words, first adding the inflected ending *-er*— and then the inflected ending *-est*. Then the partner uses the inflected forms in one or two oral sentences.

- The student who picked the word listens to see if the partner uses each word correctly. Then students switch roles. ▶**Interpersonal**

See Reteach 150, 158, 165

Phonological Awareness

OBJECTIVES Children will practice blending and segmenting sounds and substituting beginning and ending sounds.

Alternate **Activities**

Blend Sounds

LINK ARMS

GROUP

Materials: Phonics Picture Cards and Phonics Pictures from *Word Building Kit*

Tell children that they will link arms as they blend sounds into words.

- Display the following picture cards on the chalk ledge or in a pocket chart: apple, fish, monkey, nest, turtle, umbrella, wagon, elephant, mouse, clock, and zebra.

- Choose five volunteers to stand before the class. Assign each child a sound from the word *monkey*:/m/-/u/-/ng/-/k/-/ē/, which they say in the order the sounds appear in the word. The class repeats the sounds.

- After the sounds have been repeated, the five children move together, link arms, and stretch the sounds to form the word *monkey*.

- Continue the activity with different volunteers, using the rest of the picture cards.

Segment Sounds

SOUND MATCH

PARTNERS

Materials: Phonics Pictures from *Word Building Kit*

Use a matching game similar to Concentration to help children practice segmenting words into individual sounds.

- Divide the class into pairs. Give each pair two sets of phonics cards.

- Have pairs mix their cards together and turn them face down on a table.

- When a child finds a match, he or she segments the object's name into individual sounds. Then he or she can try to find another match.

- Children continue until all matches are found.

Substitute Sounds

PICK A TOPIC

GROUP

Materials: Phonics Picture Cards

Tell children that they will change beginning and ending sounds to make new words.

- Ask children to pick a topic in which they can generate lots of words, such as body parts, animals, or numbers.

- Then have a volunteer pick a Phonics Picture Card. Ask children to identify the sound at the beginning of the object's name.

- Tell children to switch that sound with the beginning sounds of other words to create a list for their category. For example, if the *bear* Phonics Picture Card is chosen, children make a list of body parts beginning with the /b/ sound, such as: *band* (hand), *bin* (chin), *beg* (leg), *baist* (waist), *bed* (head), and *beck* (neck).

- Continue the activity by having children substitute sounds at the end of words.

Digraphs *ph, tch*

TESTED OBJECTIVES Students will recognize the sounds of the digraphs *ph* and *tch*.

Alternate Activities

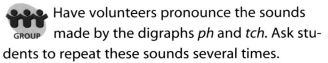

Visual

DIGRAPH LOGOS

 Materials: small sticky notes, pencil or fine marker

Model for students the sounds of the digraphs *ph* and *tch*.

- Have students make up icons that represent the sounds of the digraphs *ph* and *tch*. For example, a telephone receiver might symbolize the *ph* sound, and a small egg might symbolize the *tch* sound, as in *hatch*.

- Tell students to make several copies of their personal icons on small sticky notes. Invite students to attach the icons to objects around the classroom, as well as words they come across in their reading, to help them remember the sound of the digraph. ▶ **Intrapersonal**

Kinesthetic

SAY IT, SEE IT, FEEL IT

 Materials: a bar of soap, a large mirror or individual mirrors

Use soap to write, in large letters, the digraphs *ph* and *tch* on a mirror.

- Have students look in the mirror next to the letters as they watch themselves pronounce words with the digraphs *ph* and *tch*.

- Tell students to observe and describe the positions and feelings of their lips, tongue, and teeth as they form the digraph sounds in words such as *phone, elephant, watch,* and *hatch*. ▶ **Bodily/Kinesthetic**

Auditory

LISTEN FOR THE SOUND

 Have volunteers pronounce the sounds made by the digraphs *ph* and *tch*. Ask students to repeat these sounds several times.

- Read aloud groups of words in which only one word has the digraph *ph*. Have students repeat the digraph sound three times when they hear it in a word.

- Repeat, reading groups of words in which one word has the *tch* digraph. ▶ **Musical**

🔘 **Phonics CD-ROM**

See Reteach 151, 155, 159

A Communication Tool

Although typewriters and computers are readily available, many situations continue to require handwriting. Tasks such as keeping journals, completing forms, taking notes, making shopping or organizational lists, and the ability to read hand-written manuscript or cursive writing are a few examples of practical application of this skill.

BEFORE YOU BEGIN

Before children begin to write, certain fine motor skills need to be developed. Examples of activities that can be used as warm-up activities are:

- **Simon Says** Play a game of Simon Says using just finger positions.
- **Finger Plays and Songs** Sing songs that use Signed English, American Sign Language or finger spelling.
- **Mazes** Mazes are available in a wide range of difficulty. You can also create mazes that allow children to move their writing instruments from left to right.

Determining Handedness

Keys to determining handedness in a child:

- Which hand does the child eat with? This is the hand that is likely to become the dominant hand.
- Does the child start coloring with one hand and then switch to the other? This may be due to fatigue rather than lack of hand preference.
- Does the child cross midline to pick things up or use the closest hand? Place items directly in front of the child to see if one hand is preferred.
- Does the child do better with one hand or the other?

The Mechanics of Writing

DESK AND CHAIR

- Chair height should allow for the feet to rest flat on the floor.
- Desk height should be two inches above the level of the elbows when the child is sitting.
- The chair should be pulled in allowing for an inch of space between the child's abdomen and the desk.
- Children sit erect with the elbows resting on the desk.
- Children should have models of letters on the desk or at eye level, not above their heads.

PAPER POSITION

- **Right-handed children** should turn the paper so that the lower left-hand corner of the paper points to the abdomen.
- **Left-handed children** should turn the paper so that the lower right-hand corner of the paper points to the abdomen.
- The nondominant hand should anchor the paper near the top so that the paper doesn't slide.
- The paper should be moved up as the child nears the bottom of the paper. Many children won't think of this and may let their arms hang off the desk when they reach the bottom of a page.

The Writing Instrument Grasp

For handwriting to be functional, the writing instrument must be held in a way that allows for fluid dynamic movement.

FUNCTIONAL GRASP PATTERNS

- **Tripod Grasp** With open web space, the writing instrument is held with the tip of the thumb and the index finger and rests against the side of the third finger. The thumb and index finger form a circle.
- **Quadrupod Grasp** With open web space, the writing instrument is held with the tip of the thumb and index finger and rests against the fourth finger. The thumb and index finger form a circle.

INCORRECT GRASP PATTERNS

- **Fisted Grasp** The writing instrument is held in a fisted hand.
- **Pronated Grasp** The writing instrument is held diagonally within the hand with the tips of the thumb and index finger on the writing instrument but with no support from other fingers.
- **Five-Finger Grasp** The writing instrument is held with the tips of all five fingers.

TO CORRECT WRITING INSTRUMENT GRASPS

- Have children play counting games with an eye dropper and water.
- Have children pick up small objects with a tweezer.
- Do counting games with children picking up small coins using just the thumb and index finger.

FLEXED OR HOOKED WRIST

- The writing instrument can be held in a variety of grasps with the wrist flexed or bent. This is typically seen with left-handed writers but is also present in some right-handed writers. To correct wrist position, have children check their writing posture and paper placement.

Evaluation Checklist

Functional writing is made up of two elements, legibility and functional speed.

LEGIBILITY

MANUSCRIPT

Formation and Strokes

☑ Does the child begin letters at the top?

☑ Do circles close?

☑ Are the horizontal lines straight?

☑ Do circular shapes and extender and descender lines touch?

☑ Are the heights of all upper-case letters equal?

☑ Are the heights of all lower-case letters equal?

☑ Are the lengths of the extenders and descenders the same for all letters?

Directionality

☑ Are letters and words formed from left to right?

☑ Are letters and words formed from top to bottom?

Spacing

☑ Are the spaces between letters equidistant?

☑ Are the spaces between words equidistant?

☑ Do the letters rest on the line?

☑ Are the top, bottom and side margins even?

CURSIVE

Formation and Strokes

☑ Do circular shapes close?

☑ Are the downstrokes parallel?

☑ Do circular shapes and downstroke lines touch?

☑ Are the heights of all upper-case letters equal?

☑ Are the heights of all lower-case letters equal?

☑ Are the lengths of the extenders and descenders the same for all letters?

☑ Do the letters which finish at the top join the next letter?
(ℓ, o, v, w)

☑ Do the letters which finish at the bottom join the next letter? (a, c, d, h, i, k, l, m, n, r, s, t, u, x)

☑ Do letters with descenders join the next letter? (f, g, j, p, q, y, z)

☑ Do all letters touch the line?

☑ Is the vertical slant of all letters consistent?

Directionality

☑ Are letters and words formed from left to right?

☑ Are letters and words formed from top to bottom?

Spacing

☑ Are the spaces between letters equidistant?

☑ Are the spaces between words equidistant?

☑ Do the letters rest on the line?

☑ Are the top, bottom and side margins even?

SPEED

The prettiest handwriting is not functional for classroom work if it takes the child three times longer than the rest of the class to complete work assignments. After the children have been introduced to writing individual letters, begin to add time limitations to the completion of copying or writing assignments. Then check the child's work for legibility.

Handwriting Models—Manuscript

A B C D E F G H
I J K L M N O P
Q R S T U V W
X Y Z

a b c d e f g h
i j k l m n o p
q r s t u v w
x y z

Handwriting Models—Cursive

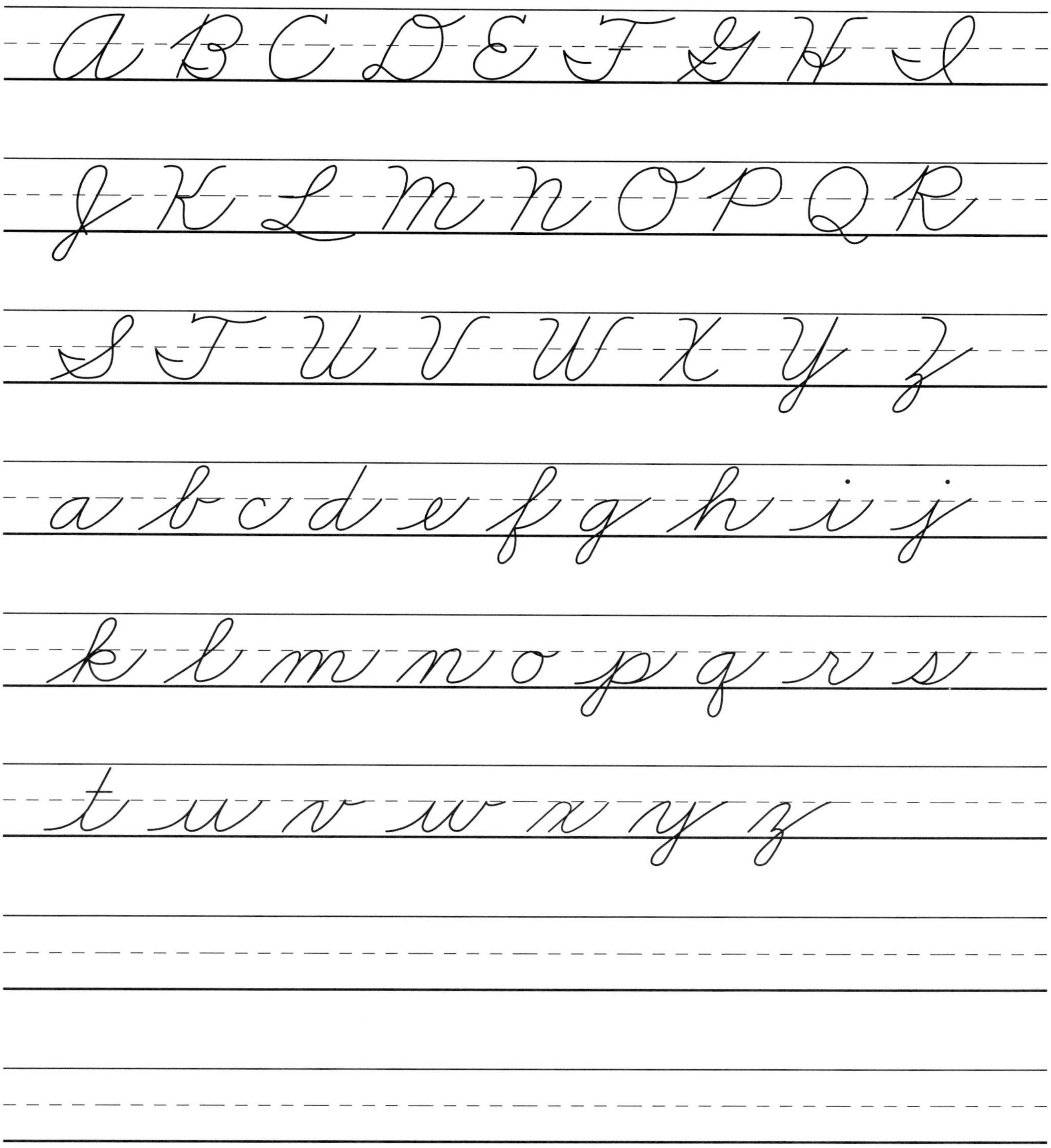

A B C D E F G H I

J K L M N O P Q R

S T U V W X Y Z

a b c d e f g h i j

k l m n o p q r s

t u v w x y z

Handwriting Models—Slant

A B C D E F G H

I J K L M N O P

Q R S T U V W

X Y Z

a b c d e f g h

i j k l m n o p

q r s t u v w

x y z

Handwriting Practice

Selection Titles

Honors, Prizes, and Awards

 HENRY AND MUDGE
Book 1, p.38
by **Cynthia Rylant**
Illustrated by **Suçie Stevenson**

American Book Award Pick of the List (1987)
Author: *Cynthia Rylant,* winner of Caldecott Honor (1983) for *When I Was Young in the Mountains;* ALA Notable (1985) for *Waiting to Waltz: A Childhood: Poems;* ALA Notable, Caldecott Honor (1986), New York Times Best Illustrated (1985) for *The Relatives Came;* ALA Notable (1986) for *Blue-Eyed Daisy;* ALA Notable, Newbery Honor (1987) for *Fine White Dust;* ALA Notable (1988) for *Henry and Mudge Under the Yellow Moon;* ALA Notable (1991) for *Henry and Mudge and the Happy Cat;* ALA Notable (1992), Boston Globe-Horn Book Award (1991) for *Appalachia: The Voices of the Sleeping Birds;* ALA Notable (1993) for *Angel for Solomon Singer;* ALA Notable, Newbery Medal (1993), Boston Globe-Horn Book Award (1992) for *Missing May;* ALA Notable (1996) for *Mr. Putter and Tabby Pick the Pears;* ALA Notable (1996) for *Van Gogh Café*
Illustrator: *Suçie Stevenson,* winner ALA Notable (1988) for *Henry and Mudge Under the Yellow Moon;* ALA Notable (1991) for *Henry and Mudge and the Happy Cat*

 ROUNDUP AT RIO RANCH
Book 1, p.94
by **Angela Shelf Medearis**

Author: *Angela Shelf Medearis,* winner of IRA-Teachers' Choice Award (1995) for *Our People*

 THE MERRY-GO-ROUND
Book 1, p.124
by **Myra Cohn Livingston**

Poet: *Myra Cohn Livingston,* winner of National Council of Teachers of English Award for Excellence in Poetry for Children (1980); ALA Notable (1984) for *Christmas Poems;* ALA Notable (1987) for *Cat Poems;* ALA Notable (1992) for *Poem-Making: Ways to Learn Writing Poetry*

 A LETTER TO AMY
Book 1, p.158
by **Ezra Jack Keats**

Author/Illustrator: *Ezra Jack Keats,* winner of Caldecott Medal (1963) for *The Snowy Day;* Caldecott Honor (1970) for *Goggles;* Boston Globe-Horn Book Award (1970) for *Hi, Cat!*

 THE BEST FRIENDS CLUB
Book 1, p.194
by **Elizabeth Winthrop**
Illustrated by **Martha Weston**

IRA-CBC Children's Choice (1990)
Illustrator: *Martha Weston,* winner of ALA Notable (1989) for *Big Beast Book: Dinosaurs and How They Got That Way*

Selection Titles	Honors, Prizes, and Awards
JAMAICA TAG-ALONG Book 1, p.218 by *Juanita Havill*	**Author: *Juanita Havill,*** winner of Ezra Jack Keats Award (1987)
FOUR GENERATIONS Book 1, p.254 by *Mary Ann Hoberman*	**Poet: *Mary Ann Hoberman,*** winner of American Book Award Paperback Picture Book (1983) for *A House Is a House for Me*
CLOUD DRAGONS Book 1, p.256 by *Pat Mora*	**Author: *Pat Mora,*** winner of National Association for Chicano Studies Creative Writing Award (1983); New America: Woman Artists and Writers of the Southwest Award (1984); Smithsonian Magazine Notable Books for Children (1998) for *Tomás and the Library Lady*
ARTHUR WRITES A STORY Book 1, p.260 by *Marc Brown*	**IRA-CBC Children's Choice (1997)** **Author/Illustrator: *Marc Brown,*** winner of Boston Globe-Horn Book Honor (1980) for *Why the Tides Ebb and Flow;* ALA Notable (1984) for *The Bionic Bunny Show*
BEST WISHES, ED Book 1, p.292 by *James Stevenson*	**Author /Illustrator: *James Stevenson,*** winner of Boston Globe-Horn Book Honor (1998) for *Popcorn: Poems;* Christopher Award (1983) for *We Can't Sleep;* ALA Notable (1984) for *What's Under My Bed;* ALA Notable (1987) for *When I Was Nine;* ALA Notable, Boston Globe-Horn Book Honor (1987) for *Georgia Music;* ALA Notable (1988) for *Grandaddy's Place;* ALA Notable (1991) for *July;* ALA Notable (1993) for *Don't You Know There's a War On?;* ALA Notable (1994) for *Grandaddy and Janetta;* Texas Blue Bonnet Master List (1995), ALA Notable (1996) for *Sweet Corn: Poems;* ALA Notable (1996) for *Grandaddy's Stars*
TIME TO PLAY Book 1, p.380 by *Nikki Grimes*	**Poet: *Nikki Grimes,*** winner of ALA Notable, Coretta Scott King Award (1979) for *Something on My Mind;* ALA Notable (1995) for *Meet Danitra Brown;* ALA Notable (1996) for *Come Sunday*

Selection Titles

Honors, Prizes, and Awards

RIVER WINDING
Book 2, p.10
by *Charlotte Zolotow*

Poet: *Charlotte Zolotow,* winner of Caldecott Honor (1953) for *Storm Book;* Caldecott Honor (1962) for *Mr. Rabbit and the Lovely Present;* Christopher Award (1975) for *My Grandson Leo;* ALA Notable (1996) for *When the Wind Stops*

CHARLIE ANDERSON
Book 2, p.14
by *Barbara Abercrombie*
Illustrated by *Mark Graham*

Redbook Children's Picture Book Award (1990)

ZIPPING, ZAPPING, ZOOMING BATS
Book 2, p.94
by *Anne Earle*
Illustrated by *Henry Cole*

American Book Award Pick of the List (1995)

WHAT IS IT?
Book 2, p.128
by *Eve Merriam*

Poet: *Eve Merriam,* winner of National Council of Teachers of English Award for Excellence in Poetry for Children (1981)

THE WEDNESDAY SURPRISE
Book 2, p.182
by *Eve Bunting*
Illustrated by *Donald Carrick*

ALA Notable Book (1990), IRA-CBC Children's Choice, IRA-Teachers' Choice, School Library Journal Best Book (1989)
Author: *Eve Bunting,* winner of ALA Notable (1990) for *Wall;* ALA Notable (1992) for *Fly Away Home;* Edgar Allen Poe Juvenile Award (1993) for *Coffin on a Case;* ALA Notable, Caldecott Medal (1995) for *Smoky Night;* ALA Notable (1997) for *Train to Somewhere;* National Council for Social Studies Notable Children's Book Award (1998) for *Moonstick,* and *I Am the Mummy Heb-Nefert,* and *On Call Back Mountain*
Illustrator: *Donald Carrick,* winner of ALA Notable (1987) for *What Happened to Patrick's Dinosaurs?*

FOSSILS TELL OF LONG AGO
Book 2, p.214
by *Aliki*

National Science Teachers' Association Outstanding Science Tradebook for Children (1990), Library of Congress Children's Book of 1972

Selection Titles	Honors, Prizes, and Awards
TO CATCH A FISH Book 2, p.246 by **Eloise Greenfield**	**Poet:** *Eloise Greenfield,* winner of Boston Globe-Horn Book Honor (1975) for *She Come Bringing Me That Little Baby Girl;* Jane Addams Book Award (1976) for *Paul Robeson;* Coretta Scott King Award (1978) for *Africa Dream;* Boston Globe-Horn Book Honor (1980) for *Childtimes: A Three Generation Memoir;* ALA Notable (1989) for *Grandpa's Face;* ALA Notable (1989) for *Under the Sunday Tree;* ALA Notable, Coretta Scott King Award (1990) for *Nathaniel Talking;* ALA Notable (1992) for *Night on Neighborhood Street;* National Council of Teachers of English Award for Excellence in Poetry for Children (1997)
OFFICER BUCKLE AND GLORIA Book 2, p.252 by **Peggy Rathmann**	**Caldecott Medal, ALA Notable (1996)** **Author/Illustrator:** *Peggy Rathmann,* winner of ALA Notable (1995) for *Good Night, Gorilla*
TOMÁS AND THE LIBRARY LADY Book 2, p.284 by **Pat Mora** Illustrated by **Raul Colón**	**Smithsonian Magazine Notable Books for Children (1998)** **Author:** *Pat Mora,* winner of National Association for Chicano Studies Creative Writing Award (1983); New America: Woman Artists and Writers of the Southwest Award (1984) **Illustrator:** *Raul Colón,* winner of ALA Notable (1996) for *My Mama Had a Dancing Heart*
SWIMMY Book 2, p.342 by **Leo Lionni**	**Caldecott Honor (1961),** *New York Times* **Best Illustrated (1960)** **Author/Illustrator:** *Leo Lionni,* winner of Caldecott Honor (1961), *New York Times* Best Illustrated (1960) for *Inch by Inch;* Caldecott Honor (1968), *New York Times* Best Illustrated (1967) for *Frederick;* Caldecott Honor (1970) for *Alexander and the Wind-up Mouse*

CHARLIE ANDERSON

FERNANDO'S GIFT

Trade Books

Additional fiction and nonfiction trade books related to each selection can be shared with children throughout the unit.

CHARLIE ANDERSON

My New Kitten
Joanna Cole, photographs by Margaret Miller (Morrow Junior Books, 1995)

A young girl watches her kitten grow from the moment it is born.
Nonfiction

Henry the Sailor Cat
Mary Calhoun, illustrated by Erick Ingraham (Morrow Junior Books, 1994)

Henry the cat sneaks aboard a sail-boat and proves he is seaworthy during a storm.
Fantasy

New Cat
Yangsook Choi (Farrar. 1999)

Mr. Kim owns a tofu factory and has a cat that is his friend and helper. One night the cat saves the factory by preventing the spread of an electrical fire.
Fantasy

FERNANDO'S GIFT

Just a Dream
Chris Van Allsburg (Houghton Mifflin, 1990)

After Walter dreams of an Earth that has become polluted, he has increased awareness of caring for the environment.
Realistic Fiction

Miss Rumphius
Barbara Cooney (Viking, 1982)

As a child, Great-Aunt Alice Rumphius resolves to make the world a more beautiful place when she grows up.
Fiction

Prince William
Gloria Rand, illustrated by Ted Rand (Henry Holt and Company, 1992)

Denny rescues a baby seal from the beach near her home after a huge oil spill in Alaska.
Realistic Fiction

Technology

Multimedia resources can be used to enhance children's understanding of the selections.

Millions of Cats (Weston Woods) Video, 10 min. An old man looks for a cat for his lonely wife and comes home with many cats.

Cats, The World of Pets Series (National Geographic Educational Services) Video or film, 16 min. A look at kittens and cats.

Duncan and Delores (Reading Rainbow/GPN) Video, 30 min. A story about a child's attempts to win a cat's affection.

Alejandro's Gift (AIMS Multimedia) Video, 8 min. Alejandro digs a well to help his desert animal friends survive.

Get Activated, The Green Earth Series (AIMS Multimedia) Video, 15 min. Explores different student projects that promote environmental awareness.

The Air: Pollution and Solutions (United Learning) Video, 15 min. Ways to prevent air pollution and identifying air as a resource. Effects of air pollution are examined, as are ways that young people can help.

BEST VACATION EVER

Henry Hikes to Fitchburg
Donald Johnson (Houghton Mifflin, 2000)

Henry walks to Fitchburg; his friend works all day to earn money and takes the train. Who spent his time more enjoyably?
Realistic Fiction

Stringbean's Trip to the Shining Sea
Vera Williams, illustrated by Vera B. Williams and Jennifer Williams (Greenwillow Books, 1988)

Stringbean describes his trip to the west coast of the United States, in a series of postcards.
Fiction

Ben's Dream
Chris Van Allsburg (Houghton Mifflin, 1982)

Ben dreams that he and his house float past the monuments of the world. *Fantasy*

ZIPPING, ZAPPING, ZOOMING BATS

The Bat in the Boot
Annie Cannon (Orchard Books, 1996)

A family finds a baby bat in their house and takes care of it until its mother returns.
Realistic Fiction

Bats
Gail Gibbons (Holiday House, 1999)

Clear text and well-crafted illustrations create a book filled with fascinating information about these gentle and interesting creatures.
Photo Essay

Bats: Creatures of the Night
Joyce Milton, illustrated by Judith Moffatt (Grosset & Dunlap, 1993)

Learn all about bats and their habits in an easy-to-read format.
Nonfiction

GOING BATTY FOR BATS

A First Look at Bats
Millicent E. Selsam and Joyce Hunt (Walker & Company, 1991)

Learn about the distinctive characteristics of bats of several different species.
Nonfiction

Stellaluna
Janell Cannon (Harcourt Brace Jovanovich, 1993)

After she falls into a bird's nest, a baby bat is raised just like a bird.
Fiction

Bat in the Dining Room
Crescent Dragonwagon, illustrated by S. D. Schindler (Marshall Cavendish, 1997)

A suspenseful story about how a young girl rescues a bat that is flying around in a hotel dining room.
Realistic Fiction

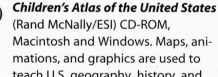

Children's Atlas of the United States (Rand McNally/ESI) CD-ROM, Macintosh and Windows. Maps, animations, and graphics are used to teach U.S. geography, history, and language.

Three Days on a River in a Red Canoe (Reading Rainbow/GPN) Video, 30 min. A camping trip is filled with learning new things.

U.S. History and Geography (Dinosoft Educational Software/ESI) CD-ROM, Macintosh and Windows. An interactive learning adventure that takes students on a historical and geographical tour of the U.S.

Animals (SVE/Churchill) CD-ROM, Macintosh and Windows. This 20-volume reference program provides students with an interactive way to explore the world of animals.

Bats and How They Live (AIMS Multimedia) Video, 19 min. Close-up and slow-motion photography is used to reveal the secrets of bats.

Stellaluna (Reading Rainbow/GPN) Video, 30 min. Based on the story by Janell Cannon. Stellaluna is a young bat who is raised by a family of birds.

Animals That Fly (BFA Educational Media) Video, 11 min. An introduction to insects, birds, and bats.

Mammals: A First Film (BFA Educational Media) Video, 11 min. From flying mammals to mammals of the sea, this is an introduction to the species.

Mammals: A Multimedia Encyclopedia (National Geographic) CD-ROM, Macintosh and Windows. An interactive exploration of the world of mammals.

Publishers Directory

Abdo & Daughters
4940 Viking Drive, Suite 622
Edina, MN 55435
(800) 458-8399 • www.abdopub.com

Aladdin Paperbacks
(Imprint of Simon & Schuster Children's
Publishing)

Atheneum
(Imprint of Simon & Schuster Children's
Publishing)

**Bantam Doubleday Dell Books for
Young Readers**
(Imprint of Random House)

Blackbirch Press
260 Amity Rd.
Woodbridge, CT 06525
(203) 387-7525 • (800) 831-9183
www.blackbirch.com

Blue Sky Press
(Imprint of Scholastic)

Boyds Mills Press
815 Church Street
Honesdale, PA 18431
(570) 253-1164 • Fax (570) 253-0179 •
(877) 512-8366
www.boydsmillspress.com

Bradbury Press
(Imprint of Simon & Schuster Children's
Publishing)

BridgeWater Books
(Distributed by Penguin Putnam)

Candlewick Press
2067 Masssachusetts Avenue
Cambridge, MA 02140
(617) 661-3330 • Fax (617) 661-0565
www.candlewick.com

Carolrhoda Books
(Division of Lerner Publications Co.)

Children's Press (Division of Grolier, Inc.)
P.O. Box 1795
Danbury, CT 06816-1333
(800) 621-1115 • www.grolier.com

Child's World
P.O. Box 326
Chanhassen, MN 55317-0326
(612) 906-3939 • (800) 599-READ •
www.childsworld.com

Chronicle Books
85 Second Street, Sixth Floor
San Francisco, CA 94105
(415) 537-3730 • Fax (415) 537-4460 •
(800) 722-6657 •
www.chroniclebooks.com

Clarion Books
(Imprint of Houghton Mifflin, Inc.)
215 Park Avenue South
New York, NY 10003
(212) 420-5800 • (800) 726-0600 •
www.houghtonmifflinbooks.com/clarion

Crowell (Imprint of HarperCollins)

Crown Publishing Group
(Imprint of Random House)

Dial Books
(Imprint of Penguin Putnam Inc.)

Dorling Kindersley (DK Publishing)
95 Madison Avenue
New York, NY 10016
(212) 213-4800 • Fax (212) 213-5240 •
(888) 342-5357 • www.dk.com

Doubleday (Imprint of Random House)

E. P. Dutton Children's Books
(Imprint of Penguin Putnam Inc.)

Farrar Straus & Giroux
19 Union Square West
New York, NY 10003
(212) 741-6900 • Fax (212) 741-6973 •
(888) 330-8477

Four Winds Press
(Imprint of Macmillan, see Simon &
Schuster Children's Publishing)

Greenwillow Books
(Imprint of William Morrow & Co, Inc.)

Grosset & Dunlap
(Imprint of Penguin Putnam, Inc.)

Harcourt Brace & Co.
6277 Sea Harbor Drive
Orlando, Fl 32887
(407) 345-2000 •
(800) 225-5425 •
www.harcourtbooks.com

Harper & Row (Imprint of HarperCollins)

HarperCollins Children's Books
1350 Avenue of the Americas
New York, NY 10019
(212) 261-6500 • Fax (212) 261-6689 •
(800) 242-7737 •
www.harperchildrens.com

Holiday House
425 Madison Avenue
New York, NY 10017
(212) 688-0085 • Fax (212) 421-6134

Henry Holt and Company
115 West 18th Street
New York, NY 10011
(212) 886-9200 • (212) 633-0748 • (888)
330-8477 • www.henryholt.com/byr/

Houghton Mifflin
222 Berkeley Street
Boston, MA 02116
(617) 351-5000 • Fax (617) 351-1125 •
(800) 225-3362 •
www.houghtonmifflinbooks.com

Hyperion Books
(Division of ABC, Inc.)
77 W. 66th St. 11th floor
New York, NY 10023
(212) 456-0100 • (800) 343-9204 •
www.disney.com

Ideals Children's Books
(Imprint of Hambleton-Hill Publishing, Inc.)
1501 County Hospital Road
Nashville, TN 37218
(615) 254-2451 • (800) 327-5113

Joy Street Books
(Imprint of Little, Brown & Co.)

Just Us Books
356 Glenwood Avenue
E. Orange, NJ 07017
(973) 672-7701 • Fax (973) 677-7570
www.justusbooks.com

Alfred A. Knopf
(Imprint of Random House)

Lee & Low Books
95 Madison Avenue, Room 606
New York, NY 10016
(212) 779-4400 • Fax (212) 683-1894

Lerner Publications Co.
241 First Avenue North
Minneapolis, MN 55401
(612) 332-3344 • Fax (612) 332-7615 •
(800) 328-4929 • www.lernerbooks.com

Little, Brown & Co.
3 Center Plaza
Boston, MA 02108
(617) 227-0730 • Fax (617) 263-2864 •
(800) 759-0190 • www.littlebrown.com

Lothrop Lee & Shepard
(Imprint of William Morrow & Co.)

Macmillan
(Imprint of Simon & Schuster
Children's Publishing)

Marshall Cavendish
99 White Plains Road
Tarrytown, NY 10591
(914) 332-8888 • Fax (914) 332-1888 •
(800) 821-9881 •
www.marshallcavendish.com

William Morrow & Co.
(Imprint of HarperCollins)

Morrow Junior Books
(Imprint of HarperCollins)

Mulberry Books
(Imprint of HarperCollins)

National Geographic Society
1145 17th Street, NW
Washington, DC 20036
(202) 857-7345 • (800) 638-4077 •
www.nationalgeographic.com

Northland Publishing
(Division of Justin Industries)
Box 1389
Flagstaff, AZ 86002
(520) 774-5251 • Fax (800) 744-0592 •
(800) 346-3257 • www.northlandpub.com

North-South Books
1123 Broadway, Suite 800
New York, NY 10010
(212) 463-9736 • Fax (212) 633-1004 •
(800) 722-6657 • www.northsouth.com

Orchard Books (A Grolier Company)
95 Madison Avenue
New York, NY 10016
(212) 951-2600 • Fax (212) 213-6435 •
(800) 433-3411 • www.grolier.com

Owlet (Imprint of Henry Holt & Co.)

Penguin Putnam, Inc.
375 Hudson Street
New York, NY 10014
(212) 366-2000 • Fax (212) 366-2636 •
(800) 631-8571 •
www.penguinputnam.com

Willa Perlman Books
(Imprint of Simon & Schuster
Children's Publishing)

Philomel Books
(Imprint of Putnam Penguin, Inc.)

Puffin Books
(Imprint of Penguin Putnam, Inc.)

G.P. Putnam's Sons Publishing
(Imprint of Penguin Putnam, Inc.)

Random House
1540 Broadway
New York, NY 10036
(212) 782-9000 • (800) 200-3552 •
Fax (212) 782-9452
www.randomhouse.com/kids

Rourke Corporation
P.O. Box 3328
Vero Beach, FL 32964
(561) 234-6001 • (800) 394-7055 •
www.rourkepublishing.com

Scholastic
555 Broadway
New York, NY 10012
(212) 343-7500 • Fax (212) 965-7442 •
(800) SCHOLASTIC • www.scholastic.com

Charles Scribners's Sons
(Imprint of Simon & Schuster Children's
Publishing)

Sierra Club Books for Children
85 Second Street, Second Floor
San Francisco, CA 94105-3441
(415) 977-5500 • Fax (415) 977-5793 •
(800) 935-1056 • www.sierraclub.org

Simon & Schuster Children's Books
1230 Avenue of the Americas
New York, NY 10020
(212) 698-7200 • (800) 223-2336 •
www.simonsays.com/kidzone

Smith & Kraus
177 Lyme Road
Hanover, NH 03755
(603) 643-6431 • Fax (603) 643-1831 •
(800) 895-4331 • www.smithkraus.com

Teacher Ideas Press
(Division of Libraries Unlimited)
P.O. Box 6633
Englewood, CO 80155-6633
(303) 770-1220 • Fax (303) 220-8843 •
(800) 237-6124 • www.lu.com

Ticknor & Fields
(Imprint of Houghton Mifflin, Inc.)

Usborne (Imprint of EDC Publishing)
10302 E. 55th Place, Suite B
Tulsa, OK 74146-6515
(918) 622-4522 • (800) 475-4522 •
www.edcpub.com

Viking Children's Books
(Imprint of Penguin Putnam Inc.)

Watts Publishing
(Imprint of Grolier Publishing;
see Children's Press)

Walker & Co.
435 Hudson Street
New York, NY 10014
(212) 727-8300 • (212) 727-0984 •
(800) AT-WALKER

Whispering Coyote Press
300 Crescent Court, Suite 860
Dallas, TX 75201
(800) 929-6104 • Fax (214) 319-7298

Albert Whitman
6340 Oakton Street
Morton Grove, IL 60053-2723
(847) 581-0033 • Fax (847) 581-0039 •
(800) 255-7675 • www.awhitmanco.com

Workman Publishing Co., Inc.
708 Broadway
New York, NY 10003
(212) 254-5900 • Fax (800) 521-1832 •
(800) 722-7202 • www.workman.com

Multimedia Resources

AGC/United Learning
1560 Sherman Avenue, Suite 100
Evanston, IL 60201
(800) 323-9084 •
Fax (847) 328-6706 •
www.unitedlearning.com

AIMS Multimedia
9710 DeSoto Avenue
Chatsworth, CA 91311-4409
(800) 367-2467 •
www.AIMS-multimedia.com

BFA Educational Media
(see Phoenix Learning Group)

Broderbund
(Parsons Technology;
also see The Learning Company)
500 Redwood Blvd
Novato, CA 94997
(800) 395-0277
www.broderbund.com

Carousel Film and Video
260 Fifth Avenue, Suite 705
New York, NY 10001
(212) 683-1660 • e-mail:
carousel@pipeline.com

Cloud 9 Interactive
(888) 662-5683 • www.cloud9int.com

Computer Plus (see ESI)

Coronet/MTI
(see Phoenix Learning Group)

Davidson (see Knowledge Adventure)

Direct Cinema, Ltd.
P.O. Box 10003
Santa Monica, CA 90410-1003
(310) 636-8200 • Fax (310) 396-3233

Disney Interactive
(800) 900-9234 •
www.disneyinteractive.com

DK Multimedia (Dorling Kindersley)
95 Madison Avenue
New York, NY 10016
(212) 213-4800 • Fax: (800) 774-6733 •
(888) 342-5357 • www.dk.com

Edmark Corp.
P.O. Box 97021
Redmond, WA 98073-9721
(800) 362-2890 • www.edmark.com

Encyclopaedia Britannica Educational Corp.
310 South Michigan Avenue
Chicago, IL 60604
(800) 554-9862 • www.eb.com

ESI/Educational Software Institute
4213 S. 94th Street
Omaha, NE 68127
(800) 955-5570 • Fax (402) 592-2017 •
www.edsoft.com

GPN/Reading Rainbow
University of Nebraska-Lincoln
P.O. Box 80669
Lincoln, NE 68501-0669
(800) 228-4630 • Fax (800) 306-2330 •
www.gpn.unl.edu

Hasbro Interactive
(800) 683-5847 • www.hasbro.com

Humongous
13110 NE 177th Pl., Suite B101, Box 180
Woodenville, WA 98072
(800) 499-8386 • www.humongous.com

IBM Corp.
1133 Westchester Ave.
White Plains, NY 10604
(770) 863-1234 • Fax (770) 863-3030 •
(888) 411-1932 •
www.pc.ibm.com/multimedia/crayola

ICE, Inc.
(Distributed by Arch Publishing)
12B W. Main St.
Elmsford, NY 10523
(914) 347-2464 • (800) 843-9497 •
www.educorp.com

Knowledge Adventure
19840 Pioneer Avenue
Torrence, CA 90503
(800) 542-4240 • (800) 545-7677 •
www.knowledgeadventure.com

The Learning Company
6160 Summit Drive North
Minneapolis, MN 55430
(800) 395-0277 • www.learningco.com

Listening Library
A Subsidary of Random House
One Park Avenue
Greenwich, CT 06870-1727
(800) 243-4504 • www.listeninglib.com

Macmillan/McGraw-Hill
(see SRA/McGraw-Hill)

Maxis
2121 N. California Blvd
Walnut Creek, CA 94596-3572
(925) 933-5630 • Fax (925) 927-3736 •
(800) 245-4525 • www.maxis.com

MECC
(see the Learning Company)

Microsoft
One Microsoft Way
Redmond, WA 98052-6399
(800) 426-9400 • www.microsoft.com/kids

National Geographic Society Educational Services
P.O. Box 10597
Des Moines, IA 50340-0597
(800) 368-2728 • Fax (515) 362-3366
www.nationalgeographic.com/education

National School Products
101 East Broadway
Maryville, TN 37804
(800) 251-9124 • www.ierc.com

PBS Video
1320 Braddock Place
Alexandria, VA 22314
(800) 344-3337 • www.pbs.org

Phoenix Films
(see Phoenix Learning Group)

The Phoenix Learning Group
2348 Chaffee Drive
St. Louis, MO 63146
(800) 221-1274 • e-mail:
phoenixfilms@worldnet.att.net

Pied Piper (see AIMS Multimedia)

Scholastic New Media
555 Broadway
New York, NY 10003
(800) 724-6527 • www.scholastic.com

Simon & Schuster Interactive
(see Knowledge Adventure)

SRA/McGraw-Hill
220 Danieldale Road
De Soto, TX 75115
(800) 843-8855 • Fax (972) 228-1982 •
www.sra4kids.com

SVE/Churchill Media
6677 North Northwest Highway
Chicago, IL 60631
(800) 829-1900 • Fax (800) 624-1678 •
www.svemedia.com

Tom Snyder Productions (also see ESI)
80 Coolidge Hill Rd.
Watertown, MA 02472
(800) 342-0236 • Fax (800) 304-1254 •
www.teachtsp.com

Troll Associates
100 Corporate Drive
Mahwah, NJ 07430
(800) 929-8765 • Fax (800) 979-8765 •
www.troll.com

Voyager (see ESI)

Weston Woods
12 Oakwood Avenue
Norwalk, CT 06850
(800) 243-5020 • Fax (203) 845-0498

Zenger Media
10200 Jefferson Blvd., Room 94,
P.O. Box 802
Culver City, CA 90232-0802
(800) 421-4246 • (800) 944-5432 •
www.Zengermedia.com

BOOK 1, UNIT 1

Vocabulary	**Spelling**

ANN'S FIRST DAY

Vocabulary

carrots
crawls
homework
hurry
lucky
shy

Spelling

Words with short vowels

bat	**desk**	**just**	plant
best	fit	**mom**	**still**
clock	hut		

HENRY AND MUDGE

Vocabulary

different
hundred
parents
searched
weighed
worry

Spelling

Long vowels *a, i, o, u* with silent *e*

alone	fine	mine	take
bike	joke	same	**used**
broke	late		

LUKA'S QUILT

Vocabulary

answered
garden
grandmother
idea
remember
serious

Spelling

Long *a* spelled *ai, ay*
Long *e* spelled *ea, ee, ie*

chief	**green**	mean	seat
clay	**keep**	**plain**	stay
dream	mail		

ROUNDUP AT RIO RANCH

Vocabulary

broken
carefully
cattle
fence
gently
safety

Spelling

Long *o* spelled *oa, oe, ow,* and *o*
Long *i* spelled *i, y,* and *igh*

by	load	row	**slow**
dry	mind	sigh	toe
follow	old		

TIME FOR KIDS: WELCOME TO A NEW MUSEUM

Vocabulary

artist
body
famous
hour
life
visit

Spelling

Words from Social Studies

flags	**place**	tax	trade
law	**slave**	time	vote
peace	speech		

Boldfaced words appear in the selection.

BOOK 1, UNIT 2

Vocabulary   Spelling

LEMONADE FOR SALE

Vocabulary:
- announced
- empty
- melted
- poured
- squeezed
- wrong

Spelling: /ü/ spelled *oo, ue, ew*

blew	few	school	tool
boot	**new**	**too**	true
clue	**room**		

A LETTER TO AMY

Vocabulary:
- candles
- corner
- glanced
- repeated
- special
- wild

Spelling: /ou/ spelled *ou, ow*; /oi/ spelled *oi, oy*

brown	**down**	loud	**out**
coin	**house**	**now**	point
cowboy	joy		

BEST FRIENDS CLUB

Vocabulary:
- allowed
- leaned
- president
- promise
- rule
- whispered

Spelling: /âr/ spelled *are*; /ôr/ spelled *or, ore*; /îr/ spelled *ear*

bare	dear	shore	**tore**
care	**more**	short	year
corn	**porch**		

JAMAICA TAG-ALONG

Vocabulary:
- building
- busy
- edge
- form
- giant
- repair

Spelling: /är/ spelled *ar*; /ûr/ spelled *ir, er, ur*

arm	dirt	hard	herd
birthday	farm	**her**	**turned**
curl	fur		

TIME FOR KIDS: UNDER ATTACK

Vocabulary:
- afraid
- chew
- danger
- lesson
- trouble
- understand

Spelling: Words from Science

animals	**nets**	senses	tide
fin	river	**shark**	wave
head	**seals**		

Boldfaced words appear in the selection.

BOOK 1, UNIT 3

Vocabulary | Spelling

ARTHUR WRITES A STORY

Vocabulary
- decided
- float
- important
- library
- planet
- proud

Spelling — Silent letters *l, b, k, w, gh*

half	knot	right	write
high	**know**	thumb	**wrote**
knee	lamb		

BEST WISHES, ED

Vocabulary
- climbed
- couple
- drifted
- half
- message
- notice

Spelling — /ər/ spelled *er*

corner	father	**other**	**water**
driver	**letter**	**over**	winter
farmer	never		

THE PONY EXPRESS

Vocabulary
- arrive
- early
- finish
- record
- rush
- success

Spelling — Short *e* spelled *ea*

bread	instead	meant	spread
breakfast	**leather**	ready	**weather**
feather	meadow		

NINE-IN-ONE, GRR! GRR!

Vocabulary
- earth
- forget
- lonely
- memory
- mountain
- wonderful

Spelling — Long *e* spelled *y, ey*

baby	key	money	penny
every	lady	party	**tiny**
happy	**many**		

TIME FOR KIDS: CHANGE FOR THE QUARTER

Vocabulary
- collect
- honors
- join
- order
- pocket
- worth

Spelling — Words from Math

buy	dime	nickel	**quarter**
cent	dollar	price	sum
cost	exact		

Boldfaced words appear in the selection.

BOOK 2, UNIT 1

Vocabulary   Spelling

CHARLIE ANDERSON

chocolate
clothes
middle
offered
roof
upstairs

/u̇/ spelled oo

book	**foot**	shook	wood
brook	hood	stood	wool
cook	hook		

FERNANDO'S GIFT

diving
explains
harm
noisy
soil
village

Soft c and soft g

age	dance	page	**rice**
cage	large	race	space
charge	mice		

THE BEST VACATION EVER

brave
guess
museum
practice
vacation
wonder

/ô/ spelled a, aw, au, augh

because	**hawk**	salt	talk
caught	lawn	straw	taught
fault	paw		

ZIPPING, ZAPPING, ZOOMING BATS

disturb
explore
fact
nature
object
several

Words with ph, tch, ch

beach	graph	phone	**sandwich**
catch	match	**pitch**	**touch**
each	patch		

TIME FOR KIDS: GOING BATTY FOR BATS

breath
cover
crops
darkness
scary
study

Words from Science

blood	**fly**	nest	**sleep**
caves	**insects**	sight	wing
den	**leaves**		

Boldfaced words appear in the selection.

BOOK 2, UNIT 2

	Vocabulary	**Spelling**

BREMEN TOWN MUSICIANS

Vocabulary:
- daughter
- music
- scare
- third
- voice
- whistle

Words with *c, k, ck*

act	cover	**luck**	**wake**
bake	kind	sick	**work**
come	**like**		

OUR SOCCER LEAGUE

Vocabulary:
- coaches
- field
- score
- stretches
- throws
- touch

Initial *bl, br, dr, pl,* and *tr*

blow	brass	plan	trap
blue	drag	**play**	**try**
brag	draw		

THE WEDNESDAY SURPRISE

Vocabulary:
- chance
- favorite
- heavy
- nervous
- office
- wrapped

Initial *sl, sm, sp, st, sw*

slide	smooth	**start**	sweet
slip	speak	**story**	swim
smart	spot		

FOSSILS TELL OF LONG AGO

Vocabulary:
- buried
- creatures
- fossil
- fresh
- layers
- millions

Final *nk, nd, ft, st*

bank	**ground**	**past**	soft
chest	**hand**	**sank**	test
end	left		

TIME FOR KIDS: ARE YOU A FOSSIL FAN?

Vocabulary:
- change
- glue
- hunt
- magazine
- piece
- tooth

Words from Social Studies

bone	drill	ocean	**remains**
deep	hill	oil	**stone**
digging	land		

Boldfaced words appear in the selection.

BOOK 2, UNIT 3

Vocabulary   Spelling

OFFICER BUCKLE AND GLORIA

Vocabulary	Spelling
accidents	**Words with *ll, dd, ss, gg***

accidents
audience
cheered
slips
station
wipe

Words with *ll, dd, ss, gg*

add	fill	press	tell
call	**kiss**	sell	**well**
egg	odd		

TOMÁS AND THE LIBRARY LADY

borrow
desert
evenings
midnight
package
shoulder

Words with initial *sh, ch*

chair	cheek	**shared**	**shining**
chase	**children**	shift	shoe
check	shape		

PRINCESS POOH

cousins
crowded
golden
princess
restaurant
world

Words with final *th* and *sh*

bath	dash	**push**	teeth
both	fish	**rush**	**with**
brush	mouth		

SWIMMY

escaped
fierce
hidden
machine
swaying
swift

Words with initial *th* and *wh*

than	**through**	whimper
them	whale	whirl
there	wheel	whisper
thought		

TIME FOR KIDS: THE WORLD'S PLANTS ARE IN DANGER

clear
disappear
forever
problem
save
warn

Words from Science

bloom	**cactus**	root	seed
bud	**flower**	**roses**	stem
bushes	petal		

Boldfaced words appear in the selection.

Listening, Speaking, Viewing, Representing

☑ Tested Skill

Tinted panels show skills, strategies, and other teaching opportunities

LISTENING	K	1	2	3	4	5	6
Learn the vocabulary of school (numbers, shapes, colors, directions, and categories)							
Identify the musical elements of literary language, such as rhymes, repetition, onomatopoeia, alliteration, assonance							
Determine purposes for listening (get information, solve problems, enjoy and appreciate)							
Understand and follow directions							
Listen critically and responsively; recognize barriers to effective listening							
Ask and answer relevant questions (for clarification; to follow up on ideas)							
Listen critically to interpret and evaluate							
Listen responsively to stories and other texts read aloud, including selections from classic and contemporary works							
Connect and compare own experiences, feelings, ideas, and traditions with those of others							
Apply comprehension strategies in listening activities							
Understand the major ideas and supporting evidence in spoken messages							
Participate in listening activities related to reading and writing (such as discussions, group activities, conferences)							
Listen to learn by taking notes, organizing, and summarizing spoken ideas							
Know personal listening preferences							
SPEAKING							
Use repetition, rhyme, and rhythm in oral texts (such as in reciting songs, poems, and stories with repeating patterns)							
Learn the vocabulary of school (numbers, shapes, colors, directions, and categories)							
Use appropriate language, grammar, and vocabulary learned to describe ideas, feelings, and experiences							
Ask and answer relevant questions (for clarification; to follow up on ideas)							
Communicate effectively in everyday situations (such as discussions, group activities, conferences, conversations)							
Demonstrate speaking skills (audience, purpose, occasion, clarity, volume, pitch, intonation, phrasing, rate, fluency)							
Clarify and support spoken messages and ideas with objects, charts, evidence, elaboration, examples							
Use verbal communication in effective ways, when, for example, making announcements, giving directions, or making introductions							
Use nonverbal communication in effective ways, such as eye contact, facial expressions, gestures							
Retell a story or a spoken message by summarizing or clarifying							
Connect and compare own experiences, ideas, and traditions with those of others							
Determine purposes for speaking (inform, entertain, compare, describe, give directions, persuade, express personal feelings and opinions)							
Recognize differences between formal and informal language							
Demonstrate skills of reporting and providing information							
Demonstrate skills of interviewing, requesting, and providing information							
Apply composition strategies in speaking activities							
Monitor own understanding of spoken message and seek clarification as needed							
VIEWING							
Demonstrate viewing skills (focus attention, organize information)							
Understand and use nonverbal cues							
Respond to audiovisual media in a variety of ways							
Participate in viewing activities related to reading and writing							
Apply comprehension strategies in viewing activities, including main idea and details							
Recognize artists' craft and techniques for conveying meaning							
Interpret information from various formats, such as maps, charts, graphics, video segments, technology							
Know various types of mass media (such as film, video, television, billboards, and newspapers)							
Evaluate purposes of various media, including mass media (information, appreciation, entertainment, directions, persuasion)							
Use media, including mass media, to compare ideas, information, and points of view							
REPRESENTING							
Select, organize, or produce visuals to complement or extend meanings							
Produce communication using appropriate media to develop a class paper, multimedia or video reports							
Show how language, medium, and presentation contribute to the message							

Reading: Alphabetic Principle, Sounds/Symbols

☑ Tested Skill

☐ Tinted panels show skills, strategies, and other teaching opportunities

PRINT AWARENESS	K	1	2	3	4	5	6
Know the order of the alphabet							
Recognize that print represents spoken language and conveys meaning							
Understand directionality (tracking print from left to right; return sweep)							
Understand that written words and sentences are separated by spaces							
Know the difference between individual letters and printed words							
Understand that spoken words are represented in written language by specific sequences of letters							
Recognize that there are correct spellings for words							
Know the difference between capital and lowercase letters							
Recognize how readers use capitalization and punctuation to comprehend							
Recognize the distinguishing features of a letter, word, sentence, paragraph							
Understand appropriate book handling							
Recognize that parts of a book (such as cover/title page and table of contents) offer information							

PHONOLOGICAL AWARENESS	K	1	2	3	4	5	6
Listen for environmental sounds							
Identify spoken words and sentences							
Divide spoken sentence into individual words							
Produce rhyming words and distinguish rhyming words from nonrhyming words							
Identify, segment, and combine syllables within spoken words							
Blend and segment onsets and rimes							
Identify and isolate the initial, medial, and final sound of a spoken word							
Add, delete, or substitute sounds to change words (such as *cow* to *how*, *pan* to *fan*)							
Blend sounds to make spoken words							
Segment one-syllable spoken words into individual sounds							

PHONICS AND DECODING	K	1	2	3	4	5	6
Alphabetic principle: Letter/sound correspondence	☑	☑	☑				
Blending CVC words	☑	☑					
Segmenting CVC words	☑						
Blending CVC, CVCe, CCVC, CVCC, CVVC words	☑	☑	☑				
Segmenting CVC, CVCe, CCVC, CVCC, CVVC words and sounds	☑	☑	☑				
Initial and final consonants: /n/n, /d/d, /s/s, /m/m, /t/t, /k/c, /f/f, /r/r, /p/p, /l/l, /k/k, /g/g, /b/b, /h/h, /w/w, /v/v, /ks/x, /kw/qu, /j/j, /y/y, /z/z	☑	☑					
Initial and medial short vowels: *a, i, u, o, e*	☑	☑	☑				
Long vowels: *a-e, i-e, o-e, u-e* (vowel-consonant-e)		☑	☑				
Long vowels, including *ay, ai; e, ee, ie, ea; o, oa, oe, ow; i, y, igh*		☑	☑				
Consonant Digraphs: *sh, th, ch, wh*		☑					
Consonant Blends: continuant/continuant, including *sl, sm, sn, fl, fr, ll, ss, ff*		☑					
Consonant Blends: continuant/stop, including *st, sk, sp, ng, nt, nd, mp, ft*		☑					
Consonant Blends: stop/continuant, including *tr, pr, pl, cr, tw*		☑					
Variant vowels: including /ù/*oo*; /ô/*a, aw, au*; /ü/*ue, ew*		☑	☑				
Diphthongs, including /ou/*ou, ow*; /oi/*oi, oy*		☑	☑				
r-controlled vowels, including /âr/*are*; /ôr/*or, ore*; /îr/*ear*			☑				
Soft *c* and soft *g*			☑				
nk		☑	☑				
Consonant Digraphs: *ck*	☑	☑					
Consonant Digraphs: *ph, tch, ch*			☑				
Short *e: ea*			☑				
Long *e: y, ey*			☑				
/ü/*oo*		☑	☑				
/är/*ar*; /ûr/*ir, ur, er*		☑	☑				
Silent letters: including *l, b, k, w, g, h, gh*			☑				
Schwa: /ər/*er*; /ən/*en*; /əl/*le*;			☑				
Reading/identifying multisyllabic words		☑	☑				
Using graphophonic cues							

Reading: Vocabulary/Word Identification

WORD STRUCTURE	K	1	2	3	4	5	6
Common spelling patterns							
Syllable patterns							
Plurals		☑					
Possessives		☑					
Contractions		☑					
Root, or base, words and inflectional endings (-s, -es, -ed, -ing)		☑	☑	☑		☑	
Compound Words		☑	☑	☑	☑	☑	☑
Prefixes and suffixes (such as un-, re-, dis-, non-; -ly, -y, -ful, -able, -tion)			☑	☑	☑	☑	☑
Root words and derivational endings				☑	☑	☑	☑

WORD MEANING	K	1	2	3	4	5	6
Develop vocabulary through concrete experiences, word walls, other people							
Develop vocabulary through selections read aloud							
Develop vocabulary through reading							
Cueing systems: syntactic, semantic, graphophonic							
Context clues, including semantic clues (word meaning), syntactical clues (word order), and graphophonic clues	☑	☑	☑	☑	☑	☑	☑
High-frequency words (such as the, a, and, said, was, where, is)	☑	☑					
Identify words that name persons, places, things, and actions							
Automatic reading of regular and irregular words							
Use resources and references (dictionary, glossary, thesaurus, synonym finder, technology and software, and context)							
Classify and categorize words							
Synonyms and antonyms			☑	☑	☑	☑	☑
Multiple-meaning words			☑		☑	☑	☑
Figurative language			☑	☑	☑	☑	☑
Decode derivatives (root words, such as like, pay, happy with affixes, such as dis-, pre-, un-)							
Systematic study of words across content areas and in current events							
Locate meanings, pronunciations, and derivations (including dictionaries, glossaries, and other sources)							
Denotation and connotation							☑
Word origins as aid to understanding historical influences on English word meanings							
Homophones, homographs							
Analogies							☑
Idioms							

Reading: Comprehension

PREREADING STRATEGIES	K	1	2	3	4	5	6
Preview and predict							
Use prior knowledge							
Set and adjust purposes for reading							
Build background							

MONITORING STRATEGIES	K	1	2	3	4	5	6
Adjust reading rate							
Reread, search for clues, ask questions, ask for help							
Visualize							
Read a portion aloud, use reference aids							
Use decoding and vocabulary strategies							
Paraphrase							
Create story maps, diagrams, charts, story props to help comprehend, analyze, synthesize and evaluate texts							

(continued on next page)

(Reading: Comprehension continued)

SKILLS AND STRATEGIES	K	1	2	3	4	5	6
Recall story details, including character and setting	☑	☑					
Use illustrations	☑	☑					
Distinguish reality and fantasy	☑	☑	☑				
Classify and categorize	☑						
Make predictions	☑	☑	☑	☑	☑	☑	☑
Recognize sequence of events (tell or act out)	☑	☑	☑	☑	☑	☑	☑
Recognize cause and effect	☑	☑	☑	☑	☑	☑	☑
Compare and contrast	☑	☑	☑	☑	☑	☑	☑
Summarize	☑	☑	☑	☑	☑	☑	☑
Make and explain inferences		☑	☑	☑	☑	☑	☑
Draw conclusions		☑	☑	☑	☑	☑	☑
Distinguish important and unimportant information				☑	☑	☑	☑
Recognize main idea and supporting details	☑	☑	☑	☑	☑	☑	☑
Form conclusions or generalizations and support with evidence from text			☑	☑	☑	☑	☑
Distinguish fact and opinion (including news stories and advertisements)				☑	☑	☑	☑
Recognize problem and solution			☑	☑	☑	☑	☑
Recognize steps in a process		☑	☑	☑	☑	☑	☑
Make judgments and decisions				☑	☑	☑	☑
Distinguish fact and nonfact				☑	☑	☑	☑
Recognize techniques of persuasion and propaganda							☑
Evaluate evidence and sources of information, including checking other sources and asking experts							☑
Identify similarities and differences across texts (including topics, characters, problems, themes, cultural influences, treatment, scope, or organization)							
Practice various questions and tasks (test-like comprehension questions)							
Paraphrase and summarize to recall, inform, and organize							
Answer various types of questions (open-ended, literal, interpretative, test-like such as true-false, multiple choice, short-answer)							
Use study strategies to learn and recall (preview, question, reread, and record)							

LITERARY RESPONSE	K	1	2	3	4	5	6
Listen to stories being read aloud							
React, speculate, join in, read along when predictable and patterned selections are read aloud							
Respond to a variety of stories and poems through talk, movement, music, art, drama, and writing							
Show understanding through writing, illustrating, developing demonstrations, and using technology							
Connect ideas and themes across texts							
Support responses by referring to relevant aspects of text and own experiences							
Offer observations, make connections, speculate, interpret, and raise questions in response to texts							
Interpret text ideas through journal writing, discussion, enactment, and media							

TEXT STRUCTURE/LITERARY CONCEPTS	K	1	2	3	4	5	6
Distinguish forms and functions of texts (lists, newsletters, signs)							
Use text features to aid comprehension							
Understand story structure							
Identify narrative (for entertainment) and expository (for information) text							
Distinguish fiction from nonfiction, including fact and fantasy							
Understand literary forms (stories, poems, plays, and informational books)							
Understand literary terms by distinguishing between roles of author and illustrator							
Understand title, author, and illustrator across a variety of texts							
Analyze character, character's motive, character's point of view, plot, setting, style, tone, mood		☑	☑	☑	☑	☑	☑
Compare communication in different forms							
Understand terms such as *title, author, illustrator, playwright, theater, stage, act, dialogue,* and *scene*							
Recognize stories, poems, songs, myths, legends, folktales, fables, tall tales, limericks, plays, biographies, autobiographies							
Judge internal logic of story text							
Recognize that authors organize information in specific ways							
Recognize author's purpose: to inform, influence, express, or entertain							
Describe how author's point of view affects text				☑	☑	☑	☑
Recognize biography, historical fiction, realistic fiction, modern fantasy, informational texts, and poetry							
Analyze ways authors present ideas (cause/effect, compare/contrast, inductively, deductively, chronologically)							
Recognize literary techniques such as imagery, repetition, flashback, foreshadowing, symbolism							

(continued on next page)

☑ Tested Skill

☐ Tinted panels show skills, strategies, and other teaching opportunities

VARIETY OF TEXT	K	1	2	3	4	5	6
Read a variety of genres and understand their distinguishing features							
Use expository and other informational texts to acquire information							
Read for a variety of purposes							
Select varied sources when reading for information or pleasure							
Know preferences for reading literary and nonfiction texts							
FLUENCY							
Read regularly in independent-level and instructional-level materials							
Read orally with fluency from familiar texts							
Self-select independent-level reading							
Read silently for increasingly longer periods of time							
Demonstrate characteristics of fluent and effective reading							
Adjust reading rate to purpose							
Read aloud in selected texts, showing understanding of text and engaging the listener							
CULTURES							
Connect own experience with culture of others							
Compare experiences of characters across cultures							
Articulate and discuss themes and connections that cross cultures							
CRITICAL THINKING							
Experiences (comprehend, apply, analyze, synthesize, evaluate)							
Making connections (comprehend, apply, analyze, synthesize, evaluate)							
Expression (comprehend, apply, analyze, synthesize, evaluate)							
Inquiry (comprehend, apply, analyze, synthesize, evaluate)							
Problem solving (comprehend, apply, analyze, synthesize, evaluate)							
Making decisions (comprehend, apply, analyze, synthesize, evaluate)							

Study Skills

INQUIRY/RESEARCH AND STUDY STRATEGIES	K	1	2	3	4	5	6
Follow and give directions							
Use alphabetical order							
Use text features and formats to help understand text (such as boldface, italic, or highlighted text; captions; headings and subheadings; numbers or symbols)							
Use study strategies to help read text and to learn and recall information from text (such as preview text, set purposes, and ask questions; use SQRRR; adjust reading rate; skim and scan; use KWL)							
Identify/frame and revise questions for research							
Obtain, organize, and summarize information: classify, take notes, outline, web, diagram							
Evaluate research and raise new questions							
Use technology for research and/or to present information in various formats							
Follow accepted formats for writing research, including documenting sources							
Use test-taking strategies							
Use text organizers (book cover; title page—title, author, illustrator; contents; headings; glossary; index)		☑	☑	☑	☑	☑	☑
Use graphic aids, such as maps, diagrams, charts, graphs, schedules, calendars		☑	☑	☑	☑	☑	☑
Read and interpret varied texts, such as environmental print, signs, lists, encyclopedia, dictionary, glossary, newspaper, advertisement, magazine, calendar, directions, floor plans, online resources		☑	☑	☑	☑	☑	☑
Use print and online reference sources, such as glossary, dictionary, encyclopedia, telephone directory, technology resources, nonfiction books		☑	☑	☑	☑	☑	☑
Recognize Library/Media Center resources, such as computerized references; catalog search—subject, author, title; encyclopedia index		☑	☑	☑	☑	☑	☑

Writing

MODES AND FORMS	K	1	2	3	4	5	6
Interactive writing							
Descriptive writing			☑				
Personal narrative			☑	☑	☑	☑	☑
Writing that compares		☑	☑	☑	☑	☑	☑
Explanatory writing			☑	☑	☑	☑	☑
Persuasive writing				☑	☑	☑	☑
Writing a story		☑	☑	☑	☑	☑	☑
Expository writing; research report	☑	☑	☑	☑	☑	☑	☑
Write using a variety of formats, such as advertisement, autobiography, biography, book report/report, comparison-contrast, critique/review/editorial, description, essay, how-to, interview, invitation, journal/log/notes, message/list, paragraph/multi-paragraph composition, picture book, play (scene), poem/rhyme, story, summary, note, letter							

PURPOSES/AUDIENCES							
Dictate sentences and messages, such as news and stories, for others to write							
Write labels, notes, and captions for illustrations, possessions, charts, and centers							
Write to record, to discover and develop ideas, to inform, to influence, to entertain							
Exhibit an identifiable voice							
Use literary devices (suspense, dialogue, and figurative language)							
Produce written texts by organizing ideas, using effective transitions, and choosing precise wording							

PROCESSES							
Generate ideas for self-selected and assigned topics using prewriting strategies							
Develop drafts							
Revise drafts for varied purposes, elaborate ideas							
Edit for appropriate grammar, spelling, punctuation, and features of published writings							
Proofread own writing and that of others							
Bring pieces to final form and "publish" them for audiences							
Use technology to compose, revise, and present text							
Select and use reference materials and resources for writing, revising, and editing final drafts							

SPELLING							
Spell own name and write high-frequency words							
Words with short vowels (including CVC and one-syllable words with blends CCVC, CVCC, CCVCC)							
Words with long vowels (including CVCe)							
Words with digraphs, blends, consonant clusters, double consonants							
Words with diphthongs							
Words with variant vowels							
Words with r-controlled vowels							
Words with /ər/, /əl/, and /ən/							
Words with silent letters							
Words with soft c and soft g							
Inflectional endings (including plurals and past tense and words that drop the final e and double a consonant when adding -ing, -ed)							
Compound words							
Contractions							
Homonyms							
Suffixes such as -able, -ly, -ful, or -less, and prefixes such as dis-, re-, pre-, or un-							
Spell words ending in -tion and -sion, such as station and procession							
Accurate spelling of root or base words							
Orthographic patterns and rules such as keep/can; sack/book; out/now; oil/toy; match/speech; ledge/cage; consonant doubling, dropping e, changing y to i							
Multisyllabic words using regularly spelled phonogram patterns							
Syllable patterns (including closed, open, syllable boundary patterns)							
Synonyms and antonyms							
Words from Social Studies, Science, Math, and Physical Education							
Words derived from other languages and cultures							
Use resources to find correct spellings, synonyms, and replacement words							
Use conventional spelling of familiar words in writing assignments							
Spell accurately in final drafts							

(continued on next page)

☑ Tested Skill

Tinted panels show skills, strategies, and other teaching opportunities

GRAMMAR AND USAGE	K	1	2	3	4	5	6
Understand sentence concepts (word order, statements, questions, exclamations, commands)							
Recognize complete and incomplete sentences							
Nouns (common, proper, singular, plural, irregular plural, possessive)							
Verbs (action, helping, linking, irregular)							
Verb tense (present, past, future, perfect, and progressive)							
Pronouns (possessive, subject and object, pronoun-verb agreement)							
Use objective case pronouns accurately							
Adjectives							
Adverbs that tell how, when, where							
Subjects, predicates							
Subject-verb agreement							
Sentence combining							
Recognize sentence structure (simple, compound, complex)							
Synonyms and antonyms							
Contractions							
Conjunctions							
Prepositions and prepositional phrases							

PENMANSHIP	K	1	2	3	4	5	6
Write each letter of alphabet (capital and lowercase) using correct formation, appropriate size and spacing							
Write own name and other important words							
Use phonological knowledge to map sounds to letters in order to write messages							
Write messages that move left to right, top to bottom							
Gain increasing control of penmanship, pencil grip, paper position, beginning stroke							
Use word and letter spacing and margins to make messages readable							
Write legibly by selecting cursive or manuscript, as appropriate							

MECHANICS	K	1	2	3	4	5	6
Use capitalization in sentences, proper nouns, titles, abbreviations and the pronoun *I*							
Use end marks correctly (period, question mark, exclamation point)							
Use commas (in dates, in addresses, in a series, in letters, in direct address)							
Use apostrophes in contractions and possessives							
Use quotation marks							
Use hyphens, semicolons, colons							

EVALUATION	K	1	2	3	4	5	6
Identify the most effective features of a piece of writing using class/teacher-generated criteria							
Respond constructively to others' writing							
Determine how his/her own writing achieves its purpose							
Use published pieces as models for writing							
Review own written work to monitor growth as a writer							

Scoring Chart

The Scoring Chart is provided for your convenience in grading your students' work.

- Find the column that shows the total number of items.
- Find the row that matches the number of items answered correctly.
- The intersection of the two rows provides the percentage score.

TOTAL NUMBER OF ITEMS

NUMBER CORRECT	1	2	3	4	5	6	7	8	9	10	11	12	13	14	15	16	17	18	19	20	21	22	23	24	25	26	27	28	29	30
1	100	50	33	25	20	17	14	13	11	10	9	8	8	7	7	6	6	6	5	5	5	5	4	4	4	4	4	4	3	3
2		100	66	50	40	33	29	25	22	20	18	17	15	14	13	13	12	11	11	10	10	9	9	8	8	8	7	7	7	7
3			100	75	60	50	43	38	33	30	27	25	23	21	20	19	18	17	16	15	14	14	13	13	12	12	11	11	10	10
4				100	80	67	57	50	44	40	36	33	31	29	27	25	24	22	21	20	19	18	17	17	16	15	15	14	14	13
5					100	83	71	63	56	50	45	42	38	36	33	31	29	28	26	25	24	23	22	21	20	19	19	18	17	17
6						100	86	75	67	60	55	50	46	43	40	38	35	33	32	30	29	27	26	25	24	23	22	21	21	20
7							100	88	78	70	64	58	54	50	47	44	41	39	37	35	33	32	30	29	28	27	26	25	24	23
8								100	89	80	73	67	62	57	53	50	47	44	42	40	38	36	35	33	32	31	30	29	28	27
9									100	90	82	75	69	64	60	56	53	50	47	45	43	41	39	38	36	35	33	32	31	30
10										100	91	83	77	71	67	63	59	56	53	50	48	45	43	42	40	38	37	36	34	33
11											100	92	85	79	73	69	65	61	58	55	52	50	48	46	44	42	41	39	38	37
12												100	92	86	80	75	71	67	63	60	57	55	52	50	48	46	44	43	41	40
13													100	93	87	81	76	72	68	65	62	59	57	54	52	50	48	46	45	43
14														100	93	88	82	78	74	70	67	64	61	58	56	54	52	50	48	47
15															100	94	88	83	79	75	71	68	65	63	60	58	56	54	52	50
16																100	94	89	84	80	76	73	70	67	64	62	59	57	55	53
17																	100	94	89	85	81	77	74	71	68	65	63	61	59	57
18																		100	95	90	86	82	78	75	72	69	67	64	62	60
19																			100	95	90	86	83	79	76	73	70	68	66	63
20																				100	95	91	87	83	80	77	74	71	69	67
21																					100	95	91	88	84	81	78	75	72	70
22																						100	96	92	88	85	81	79	76	73
23																							100	96	92	88	85	82	79	77
24																								100	96	92	89	86	83	80
25																									100	96	93	89	86	83
26																										100	96	93	90	87
27																											100	96	93	90
28																												100	97	93
29																													100	97
30																														100

Writing That Compares: Comparing Two People

6-Point Writing Rubric

Exceptional	Excellent	Good	Fair	Poor	Unsatisfactory
6: The writer	**5:** The writer	**4:** The writer	**3:** The writer	**2:** The writer	**1:** The writer
• presents an exceptionally well-thought-out comparison of two people.	• presents a well-thought-out comparison of two characters.	• presents a successful comparison of two characters.	• makes a minimally successful attempt to compare two characters.	• makes a largely unsuccessful attempt to compare two characters.	• makes no attempt to compare two characters.
• develops distinct character categories, organized in paragraphs.	• uses paragraphs and transition words to organize material into categories.	• attempts to organize comparisons logically but may not use distinct paragraphs or transition words.	• may not present distinct comparison categories.	• does not use comparison terms or may not state a main topic idea.	• does not indicate a main topic idea.
• presents interesting facts and details and apt, carefully considered comments within each comparison category.	• presents facts, details, and thoughtful comments within each comparison category.	• shows an adequate command of comparison language.	• may exhibit some organizational difficulty, such as disconnected information with no comparisons or transitions.	• may present disorganized facts or observations.	• presents extremely disorganized facts and observations.
• crafts an intriguing introduction to the comparison.	• presents a clearly stated introduction.	• presents pertinent facts, with some elaborating detail.	• may exhibit difficulty with writing conventions.	• exhibits serious problems with writing conventions and overall command of language mechanics.	• presents such a severe inability to employ writing conventions and handle language mechanics that the text is all or partially unreadable.
• displays mastery of the technique of using transition words to link ideas within a logical sequence.	• has followed through with a logical sequence, linked by transition words.	• may present a conclusion about the two characters.	• does not elaborate on the topic with descriptive details or observations.		
• presents a compelling conclusion based on her/his comparison facts.	• may present a conclusion based on her/his comparison facts.		• may exhibit a limited grasp of grammar, usage, and language conventions.		

Incomplete 0: The writer may have left the paper blank or have failed in other ways to respond to the task. The writer may not have addressed the topic or have simply repeated or paraphrased the prompt. Or the writer may have produced an illegible or incoherent response.

Writing That Compares: Comparing Two People

8-Point Writing Rubric

8	7	6	5	4	3	2	1
The writer • presents an extremely well-constructed, well-elaborated comparison of two people. • develops distinct topic categories, organized in fluent, smoothly-connected paragraphs. • presents accurate, precisely-detailed facts in unusually sophisticated language. • makes original, relevant observations. • presents a keen, logical conclusion based on the facts.	The writer • presents a well-constructed, well-elaborated comparison of two people. • develops distinct topic categories, organized in fluent, smoothly-connected paragraphs. • may present accurate, effectively-detailed facts in sophisticated language. • may make original, relevant observations. • may present a thoughtful, logical conclusion based on the facts.	The writer • presents a solidly-researched comparison paper. • develops topic categories, but may not place them in distinct paragraphs. • organizes comparisons logically, but may not cover all the available research. • shows an adequate command of comparison language. • presents pertinent facts, but may not elaborate effectively. • presents a conclusion, but may not directly connect it to the facts.	The writer • attempts to compare two people. • may not present distinct comparison categories. • may exhibit organizational difficulty, such as disconnected facts with few comparisons or transitions. • may exhibit difficulty with conventions. • does not elaborate on the topic with descriptive details or observations. • may not offer a logical conclusion.	The writer • has made an adequate attempt at comparing two people, but may not introduce a clear topic. • may not consistently use comparison terms, or offer adequate detail. • may have trouble organizing facts in distinct categories. • exhibits recurring problems with conventions. • may not offer a relevant conclusion.	The writer • may attempt to compare two things, but may not introduce a topic. • may not present distinct differences or similarities, or offer details. • may not organize facts in clear categories. • exhibits problems with organization and conventions. • may not offer a conclusion.	The writer • makes a largely unsuccessful attempt to compare two people. • does not present distinct differences or similarities. • exhibits serious problems with organization, word choice, and conventions. • does not offer a conclusion.	The writer • does not grasp the task to compare. • may not be easily understood by a reader. • exhibits serious problems with comprehension, word choice, and conventions.

0: This piece is either blank, or fails in other ways to respond to the writing task. The topic may not be addressed, or the child has simply repeated or paraphrased the prompt. The response may be illegible or incoherent.

Notes

Notes

Notes

Notes

Notes

Notes

Guided Reading Support

Macmillan/McGraw-Hill Leveled Books

TITLE	READING LEVEL
How Kittens Grow	I
Africa: Animals at Night	K
This Is Your Land	K
Dear Diary	M
Freedom Cat	M
John Muir: Making the Mountains Glad	M
The Mystery Mess	M
Night Animal, Day Animal	M
Save Our Park Trees	M
The Underground City	M
Make a Difference	N
The World of Cats	N

Additional Leveled Books from The Wright Group

TITLE	READING LEVEL
Meet Me at the Water Hole	H
Shapes in the City	H
The Amazing Maze	I
Dinosaur Detective	I
Good Luck Elephant	I
Hiding Places	I
Just Hanging Around	I
Mrs. Barnett's Birthday	I
My Sloppy Tiger Goes to School	I
Space Race	I

To order these titles or other Wright Group Leveled Book titles, call 1-800-648-2970.

Guided Reading Lesson Plan

Story Introduction

(Each child has a copy of the book.)

- Discuss the cover illustrations, and ask children to speculate about the book's contents.
- Involve children in figuring out the title.
- Provide positive feedback for responses. (Example: I like the way you used the _____ in the cover illustration to figure out that the book might be about_____.)

Picture Walk

(The teacher has the only copy of the book.)

- Show children as many pictures as you can without giving away any surprise endings.
- As you discuss the pictures together, highlight key concepts in the book. Again, try to bring in language from the book, especially unknown words or unusual language patterns, to give children some experience with these words and patterns. Have children say them aloud.
- Encourage children to make predictions about the book's content, using the title, cover art, and pictures.
- Remind children of key book concepts. Close the book, and elicit what children know about these concepts. Record their ideas in a web on the board or on chart paper, making additions or corrections as necessary.

First Reading

- Guide children to use a variety of word-attack strategies when reading. The focus should be on mastery of these strategies.
- Break the book into sections, and for each section, ask questions that encourage predictions. Focus on literary elements such as character development and plot line. (Examples: What do you think _____ will do? What do you think will happen next?)
- Guide children to silently read a section to confirm or revise their predictions.
- When children finish a section, have them orally respond to your questions, locating the text that supports their answers.
- Continue through the story, using this format.
- Option: Have children read the story again independently at their seats and/or respond in literature response journals.

Discussion

- Discuss the literary elements (character, setting, plot) found in the story.
- Relate the story to children's lives whenever possible.
- Give children the opportunity to retell or react to the story. If response journals have been used, encourage children to refer to them.
- Model sharing observations and opinions about the story, and encourage further sharing.
- Invite children to share their response journals.

Minilesson

- A minilesson can take place at any point in the Guided Reading process—wherever it is applicable and as needed by your children.

- Possible focuses for the lesson might be word-attack strategy development, vocabulary, literary elements, or language structures.

Follow-Up Activity

- Have children respond to the reading by writing journal entries and/or engaging in other literature-related activities.

WORD-ATTACK STRATEGY PROMPTS

Focus on meaning cues.

- Did that make sense?
- Look at the pictures.
- What happened in the story when ___?
- What do you think it might be?
- How do you know?
- Provide positive feedback. (Example: I like the way you figured out the word by thinking about what was happening in the story.)

Focus on structure cues.

- Did that sound right?
- Can you reread that?
- Can you say that another way?
- What is another word that might fit here?

Focus on visual cues.

- Does that look right?
- What letter/sound does it start/end with?
- What would you expect to see at the beginning/in the middle/at the end?
- Do you know another word that might start/end with those letters?
- Can you get your mouth ready to say that word/sound?

Focus on self-correcting.

- There is a difficult (or tricky) part here. Can you find it?
- Are you right? Could that be ___?
- Take a closer look at ___.
- How did you know that this word was ___?

Focus on cross-checking.

- How did you know that was ___?
- Is there another way to tell?
- It could be ___, but look at ___.
- Provide positive feedback. (Example: I like the way you checked your answer by looking at the beginning letter again.)

Focus on self-monitoring.

- Try that again.
- You stopped. What did you notice?
- Were you right?
- How did you know?

Additional Theme Resources

Contents

One Stormy Night

Written by Anne W. Phillips
Illustrated by Michael Grejniec

Max the cat is scared of the thunderstorm. No one in the family has time to comfort him until all the lights in their house go out.

Before They Read

BUILDING BACKGROUND Invite volunteers to tell about an experience during a rainstorm. What did they see? What noises did they hear? Build a web for *rainstorm* on the board, using words such as *heavy rain, wind, thunder, crash, lightning, flash,* and *lights go out.* Children might wish to copy and illustrate the web.

INTRODUCING VOCABULARY Display these words on cards and read them with children. Invite volunteers to use the words in sentences.

stormy	beat	rattle	space
brush	decided	middle	purred

Provide children with clues to each vocabulary word and have them write the appropriate word. Use clues such as the following: *This describes a day that is rainy and windy.* (stormy) *This is an area with nothing in it.* (space) *This is between the beginning and the end.* (middle)

STUDENTS ACQUIRING ENGLISH

Encourage children to use the illustrations on pages 10, 14, and 16 to help them understand any unfamiliar words.

SETTING A PURPOSE Show the cover of the book and read aloud the title. Ask children to describe what they see. Also show and discuss the illustration on the title page. Ask children what they think the book is about.

While They Read

READING THE STORY

- Have children make a list of the vocabulary words. As they read the story, ask them to look for the vocabulary words. When they find one, have them circle the appropriate word on their list.

- Show the illustrations so that children can talk about where the story takes place and what the characters are doing. Ask children to pause after page 9 and predict what the characters will do now that the lights have gone out.

- Revisit the story by helping children to analyze the plot and characters. Ask, *How was Max feeling at the beginning of the story? What gave you clues? How did the other characters react to Max? How did things change at the end of the story? What happened to cause this change?*

After They Read

EXTENDING THE STORY Choose from the following activities to provide additional support for vocabulary and comprehension strategies for the different modality needs of your students.

- **Missing Words.** Have children copy each vocabulary word onto separate pieces of paper. Reread the story aloud, saying *blank* instead of a vocabulary word. Ask children to hold up the missing word. *(Verbal/Linguistic)*

- **The Character of Max.** Have children fold a sheet of paper into three sections. In the first section, have them draw Max at the beginning of the story. In the third section, have them draw Max at the end of the story. In the middle section, have them draw what happened to cause the change. *(Visual/Spatial)*

MORE BOOKS TO READ Suggest to children that they read these other books about cats.

- *The Cat Who Wore a Pot on Her Head* by Jan Slepian and Ann Seidler
- *Millions of Cats* by Wanda Gag
- *Have You Seen My Cat?* by Eric Carle

Theme Book

SKILLS AND OBJECTIVES ▶ Character | Identify character traits
Phonograms *-ound* | Identify words with the *-ound* phonogram

River Home

Written by Susan Blackaby
Illustrated by Stephanie Roth

Rudy and her uncle watch the salmon swim upstream to spawn. Uncle George explains that fewer salmon come back now, but that people are working to save the salmon.

Before They Read

BUILDING BACKGROUND Ask students, *Have you ever watched the water in a river and wondered where the river ends?* As they discuss rivers, help children understand that they run to the sea, or ocean, where their water mixes with the salty ocean water. Ask, *Do you think fish that swim in the ocean ever go up into the rivers?*

INTRODUCING VOCABULARY Write each word on a card and ask children to sound it out. Point out the silent *L* in *salmon,* and the *-ound* phonogram in *mound* to help children with their decoding. Explain that they will find more words with *-ound* in the story.

porch	mound	salmon	worn
gravel	rippled	snags	dodged

STUDENTS ACQUIRING ENGLISH

To help children learn the /ou/ sound of the *-ound* phonogram, have them find words with that sound in this and other stories.

SETTING A PURPOSE Show children the cover of the book and read the title. Say, *I wonder why the salmon swims from the ocean into the river. Let's read the story and find out!*

While They Read
READING THE STORY

- As children read the story aloud, stop every few pages and ask volunteers to restate in their own words what the text said.

- Have children reread the story and write down every word that has the *-ound* phonogram that they find. *(mound, round, around, found, pounds, sound)*

- After rereading the story, ask children what words and phrases they would use to describe Rudy. Write them on the board as youngsters dictate them. Lead them to make choices such as *girl, happy, friendly, curious, likes fish, goes for walks, imaginative, helpful,* and *rakes leaves.*

- After finishing the story, review with children the journey the salmon make from the sea back to where they were born.

After They Read

EXTENDING THE STORY Choose from the following activities to provide additional literacy support for the different modality needs of your students.

- **Cite Characteristics.** Have children make a character web about Rudy by writing *Rudy* in a circle and words to describe her in four smaller circles surrounding it. Have children share their webs. Did everyone list the same traits? *(Logical/Mathematical)*

- **Write Rhymes.** Encourage pairs of children to write silly sentences using words with the *-ound* phonogram. For example, *On the* ground *I* found *a 40-*pound hound *and* heard sounds *all* around. Have pairs read their rhymes to the class and clap along. *(Verbal/Linguistic)*

MORE BOOKS TO READ Suggest to children that they read these other books about salmon.
- *Discovering Salmon* by Nancy Field and Sally Machlis
- *The Salmon* by Paula Z. Hogan
- *Red Tag Comes Back* by Frederick B. Phleger

Theme Book

SKILLS AND OBJECTIVES ▶ Compare and Contrast   Compare and contrast illustrations
Consonant Blends *st*   Identify words with the consonant blend *st*

Sunset Surprise

Written by Gail Tuchman
Illustrated by Monica Ann Cohen

A mother takes her little girl to the beach to watch the setting sun. The beautiful sunset is followed by a surprise ... the moon rising!

Before They Read

BUILDING BACKGROUND Ask, *Have you ever watched a sunset? What did you see? After the sun sets, what do you see in the sky?* As children discuss the question, help them understand that the moon and the stars are in the sky in the daytime. But the sun is so big and bright that it is hard to see them.

INTRODUCING VOCABULARY Write these words and phrase on cards. As children help you sound them out, stress words with the initial consonant blend *st*. Define each word or phrase and let children use it in a sentence.

stuffed	tucked	traced
canvas	mosquito	paler
beach	stretched out	

STUDENTS ACQUIRING ENGLISH

Encourage children to use the illustrations on pages 3–5 to help them understand any unfamiliar words.

SETTING A PURPOSE Display the book's cover and read the title. Ask, *What do you see in the picture? Do you think the story will tell us who the people are and why they're on the beach? Let's read to find out.*

While They Read
READING THE STORY

- Have children read the story. Pause after reading pages 6–7 and ask children to describe what is happening in the pictures. Ask, *Is it still daylight?* After reading through page 14, ask children to compare the pictures of the sun (pages 8–9) and moon (pages 13–14). *How are they alike? How are they different?* You may wish to list children's responses on the board in the form of a chart.

- Turn to page 11 and invite a volunteer to read and point out words that start with the /st/ sound: *started* and *straw*. Then have children reread the story and find other *st* words: *stuffed, stretched,* and *stars*.

- Check comprehension by asking children to retell the story in their own words.

After They Read

EXTENDING THE STORY Choose from the following activities to provide additional literacy support for the different modality needs of your students.

- **Sunset Sentences.** Challenge children to write a few sentences about the difference between the sunset and the night sky. Have children illustrate their sentences, then read them aloud. Ask each child to point out any vocabulary words he or she used. *(Verbal/Linguistic)*

- **Rhythm and Rhyme.** Invite the class to make silly *st* rhymes, then clap out the rhythm. For example: *I'm a scarecrow* stuffed *with* straw, *I* stop *crows that* start *to CAW, CAW, CAW! (Musical/Rythmic)*

MORE BOOKS TO READ Suggest to children that they read these other books about the sun and moon.
- *Sun Up, Sun Down* by Gail Gibbons
- *The Sun* by Denny Robson
- *Why Does the Moon Change Its Shape?* by Isaac Asimov

Theme Book

SKILLS AND OBJECTIVES > Diphthongs /ou/ | Identify the diphthong /ou/
Phonograms *-ound, -own* | Build rhymes with *-ound, -own*

Animals of the Desert

Written by Maggie Palmer
Illustrated by James Needham

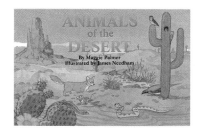

The desert is home to cold-blooded animals, such as snakes and lizards, as well as to nocturnal animals, like kangaroo rats. Desert foxes and different kinds of birds have adapted to desert life, too.

Before They Read

BUILDING BACKGROUND Write the word *desert* and ask, *What do you think of when you think about the desert?* Tell children that they will find out about the kinds of animals that can survive in the desert.

INTRODUCING VOCABULARY Tell children to listen to the following words and hold up a brown crayon every time they hear a word with the /ou/ sound as in *town: door, down, dough, cow, dare, few, ground, fool, found, how, town,* and *draw*. Then review the following words from the story.

down	bound	around	mounds
surroundings	ground	underground	

STUDENTS ACQUIRING ENGLISH

To help children stay focused on the phonograms *-ound, -ow,* and *-own,* ask them to raise their hands each time you say a word with that sound.

SETTING A PURPOSE Ask, *Is there plant life in the desert? Is there animal life? What kind of animals do you think can stay alive in the desert?* Hold up the cover of *Animals of the Desert,* read the title aloud, and invite children to discuss the cover art.

While They Read

READING THE STORY

- As you read the story aloud, ask children to clap when they hear a word with *-ound* or *-own.*

- Read pages 8–10 and have children tell in their own words how snakes and lizards stay alive in the desert. After reading pages 12–15, ask, *How do kangaroo rats survive in the desert? How do desert foxes and desert birds survive?*

- At the end, have children look back through the pages for examples of words with the phonograms *-ound* and *-own.*

After They Read

EXTENDING THE STORY Choose from the following activities to provide additional support for phonics and decoding skills for the different modality needs of your students.

- **Trail Blazers.** Have children draw desert scenes with trails running through them. Along the trails have them write at least six words with the diphthong /ou/ using *-ound* and *-own* phonograms. Children may exchange papers and read the words along different trails. *(Visual/Spatial)*

- **All Around Town.** Have children draw the main street of a busy town. Ask them to title it, "What We Found Around Town." Encourage children to label their pictures, using words with the phonograms *-ound,* and *-own* to tell about things they could find around town. For example: a *hound* dog, a funny *clown,* an upside-*down* sign. *(Verbal/Linguistic)*

MORE BOOKS TO READ Suggest to children that they read these other books about deserts and desert creatures.
- *Desert Voices* by Byrd Baylor
- *Deserts* by Seymour Simon
- *Cactus Hotel* by Brenda Z. Guiberson

Trade Book

SKILLS AND OBJECTIVES ▷ Draw Conclusions   Use information from text to draw conclusions
Compare and Contrast   Make comparisons

Water, Water Everywhere

Written by Mark J. Rauzon and Cynthia Overbeck Bix

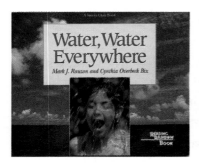

The importance of water is explored in this clear and comprehensive book that examines the water cycle, the effects of water on the land, and the need for clean water to support life on our planet.

Before They Read

BUILDING BACKGROUND Discuss the importance of water in children's everyday lives. Ask, *How do you use water every day?* Children might say that they drink it, bathe in it, brush their teeth with it, play and swim in it, and that their clothes and dishes are washed in it. Then ask, *What other living things need water?* (plants and animals)

Display a globe or a map of the world and point out the oceans. Explain that the water in the oceans is saltwater that we cannot drink. Have children speculate on or explain where fresh water can be found on earth. (lakes, rivers and streams, ponds, rain water)

INTRODUCING VOCABULARY Write these words on the board and pronounce them. Discuss their meanings with children. Have volunteers use *chemicals* and *pollute* in a sentence. Then have children sort the remaining words into two categories: *Things Made of Rock* (canyons, boulders) and *Things Made of Water* (steam, iceberg, vapor, hail, sleet, glaciers).

steam	vapor	sleet	glaciers
chemicals	iceberg	hail	canyons
boulders	pollute		

SETTING A PURPOSE Look at the cover of the book with children and read the title aloud. Have children point to the water they see in the picture. Then begin a K-W-L chart and use the first two columns to record what children already know about water and what they want to find out. Children can complete the chart when they have finished reading the book.

See Graphic Organizers Transparency 27.

STUDENTS ACQUIRING ENGLISH

Use details in the photographs to help clarify difficult concepts for children and to guide them in determining the meaning of any word that is unfamiliar.

If children have difficulty drawing conclusions, give them appropriate clues from the text or from common knowledge, and have them state a conclusion based upon those clues.

While They Read
READING THE STORY

Beginning Ask children to read the beginning of the book. Have them stop after reading page 14 and viewing the picture on page 15.

- Remind children that the bodies of humans and animals are made mostly of water. Then ask, *What other living things have parts made mostly of water?* (The stems and leaves of plants are made mostly of water.) *How is the need for water the same in all living things?* (Humans, animals, and plants all need water to live and grow.)

- Have children draw conclusions about the form in which water droplets fall to earth from clouds. Ask, *If it is a warm summer day, what form will water droplets take as they fall to earth?* (rain) *If it is a very cold day, what form will they take?* (snow) *What might the temperature be if the droplets fall as sleet?* (The temperature might be near freezing, but not cold enough for snow to form.)

Middle Ask children to continue reading the book, stopping after reading page 25.

- Ask, *What are some ways that moving water shapes the earth?* (Rivers wear away the earth and make canyons. Glaciers pick up rocks and boulders and gouge out valleys. Oceans batter the shore and grind cliffs into sand.)

- Help children draw a conclusion by asking, *Why do you think many cities are built along the water?* (Water is a "highway" that brings the goods and people that a city needs to develop and grow.)

- Work with children to complete a Venn diagram comparing saltwater and fresh water. Help children recognize that both types of water are part of the water cycle and are limited on earth. There is more saltwater than fresh. Saltwater is found in oceans, while fresh water is found in lakes, rivers, and glaciers. We drink fresh water, but not saltwater.

  See Graphic Organizers Transparency 14.

End Ask children to finish reading the end of the book.

- Have children compare a clean environment to one that is polluted. Ask, *How is a polluted environment different from a clean one?* (A polluted environment has things that hurt us, such as smoke, fumes, acid rain, chemicals, and litter. A clean environment is a healthy place for all living things.)

- Have children draw a conclusion. Ask, *What might happen if we don't work to stop pollution?* (The earth will become very dirty, and all living things will suffer.)

Summarize Have children summarize what they learned about water in this book by completing the last column in the K-W-L chart.

See Graphic Organizers Transparency 27.

After They Read

EXTENDING THE STORY Choose from the following activities to provide additional support for comprehension strategies for the different modality needs of your students.

- **Draw a Weather Picture.** Review with children that water can fall from the sky as rain, sleet, hail, or snow. Then have children draw a picture of what they like to do on a rainy day or a snowy day. Tell them to label their picture "Rainy Day Fun" or "Snowy Day Fun." Display the pictures on a bulletin board in the classroom. You may wish to post the rainy day pictures on one side of the bulletin board and the snowy day pictures on the other. *(Visual/Spatial)*

- **Make a Water Chart.** Have children make a chart on which they keep track of the different ways that water is used in their household over a one- or two-day period. Children can write about or draw each way that water is used in their household and use tally marks to indicate frequency. Have children work in small groups to compare and contrast their findings. *(Logical/Mathematical, Interpersonal)*

- **Write a Poem.** Invite children to write a poem about a body of water, such as a river, a lake, or an ocean. Children can begin by completing a sense star to describe how the body of water looks, sounds, feels, smells, and tastes. Encourage children to write their poem in rhyming verse if possible. Invite volunteers to read aloud their poems in class. *(Verbal/Linguistic, Intrapersonal)*

  See Graphic Organizers Transparency 35.

- **Write a Persuasive Paragraph.** Have groups discuss why it is important to keep earth's water clean. Then have each child write a short paragraph persuading others not to pollute the water. Children can give examples of what pollutes our water supply and why polluting the water should be avoided. Invite volunteers to share their ideas with the class by reading their paragraph aloud. *(Verbal/Linguistic, Interpersonal)*